Media Law for Canadian Journalists

Detailed Contents

PART ONE
Open Justice

CHAPTER 3

PART TWO
Journalists and the Law

CHAPTER 4

Preface

One day in April 1983 the editor of the Halifax *Daily News* assigned me to cover a trial. Not just any trial—this was an explosive influence-peddling case that would expose an elaborate system of kickbacks on government contracts. The allegations were complex, the case would attract national attention, and one of the former party fundraisers on trial was a senator. I was an unlikely candidate to cover such an important and sensitive case. I had been with the paper for about a month, had no previous experience as a reporter, and knew little about the law. And I had never set foot in a courtroom.

Many journalists can tell similar stories. Editors have long regarded covering the court beat as a rite of passage for a rookie reporter. It's an attitude that persists even though court cases are more like minefields than testing grounds. Journalists face an intimidating array of laws and restrictions—bans on the publication of evidence, orders excluding the public from hearings, the ever-present risk of writing or broadcasting information that might prejudice the defendant's right to a fair trial. This book was written in the belief that journalists need a thorough understanding of their rights and the legal restrictions on their work *before* they head for the courthouse, as well as a reliable reference guide to consult as legal problems crop up. Reporters and editors must know when a publication ban is likely to be imposed, how long it remains in place, and the information that can be reported without violating its terms. They must understand which details about a person facing criminal charges could be considered prejudicial if publicized. They must know when judges have the power to hold a hearing behind closed doors or to seal documents. And they must recognize when the right to freedom of expression and freedom of the press, as guaranteed in the *Canadian Charter of Rights and Freedoms*, can be used to challenge such restrictions.

But knowing the limits on media coverage of the courts is not enough. Journalists need a working knowledge of basic legal rights and principles. They must grasp concepts that lie at the heart of our system of justice—the presumption of innocence, proof beyond a reasonable doubt, the right to silence, judicial independence. The distinctions between criminal prosecutions and civil disputes must be understood, as well as the procedures followed and hearings convened as cases advance through the court system. Each player in the justice system—judges, jurors, prosecutors, defence lawyers—has well-defined responsibilities, and these, too, must be appreciated.

There are other legal limits on how journalists do their jobs. If journalists recklessly malign the reputations of the people and companies they write about, they and their bosses can be sued for defamation. But the law of defamation—or libel, as it is better known—protects media reports that are true, balanced, or based on statements made in a courtroom or other protected forum, no matter how damning the allegation. Defamation law protects good journalism, and this book shows writers and editors how to libel-proof stories and how to recognize potentially libellous statements before they are published or broadcast. As well, journalists must respect copyright and understand how copyright protects their own work. And they have no right to trespass on private property or to violate the personal privacy of the people they cover. Other issues may not be so clear-cut. Must a camera operator obey a police officer's order to leave a crime scene? Is an editor obliged to turn over notes or tapes in response to a search warrant? When is it proper to use unnamed sources? And if a reporter has agreed not to reveal the identity of a source, does a judge have the power to demand that the promise be broken?

This book explores these issues and many more, including how to unlock government secrets using freedom-of-information laws and the ethical dilemmas that journalists face every day. It is a comprehensive guide, for students and working journalists alike, to the media's rights and obligations. It examines how the courts have interpreted restrictions on media coverage, so that reporters and editors will know what to publish or broadcast and what to withhold. It draws on news stories and case studies to show how the law is changing as journalists challenge the limits imposed on their work. This revised and updated edition incorporates the latest legal developments—including landmark Supreme Court of Canada precedents on confidential sources and defamation law—and features new sections exploring the clash between free speech and human rights, the role of press councils, live-blogging from the courtroom, and many other emerging media law issues.

When I walked into a courtroom for the first time in 1983, the Charter had been in force for barely a year. Its guarantee of freedom of the press promised to ease restrictions on media coverage, and that promise has been fulfilled on many fronts. News reports and editorial comment about court cases that would have been cited for contempt two decades ago now appear without causing a ripple. The Internet's global reach and the popularity of social media networks have forced judges to rethink some of the traditional restrictions on media coverage. This book explores these developments and what they mean for journalists.

Acknowledgments

Many people have helped make this book a reality. The publisher and I would like to thank the following people for providing their comments and suggestions during the development of this second edition: Daniel W. Burnett (UBC/Owen Bird Law Corporation), Ted Fairhurst (Centennial College), Elizabeth Rains (Langara College), Alan Shanoff (Humber College), and Ivor Shapiro (Ryerson University).

The original edition of this book benefited greatly from feedback and suggestions from Jim Rossiter and Patrick Duncan. Tim Roberts authored the glossary. The assistance of Kirk Makin, Kevin Cox, and Bryan Cantley was also greatly appreciated. I would also like to thank Tom Claridge, the former editor of *The Lawyers Weekly*, his successor, Tim Wilbur, and David McKie, editor of the Canadian Association of Journalists' magazine, *Media*, for encouraging me to explore media law issues for their publications.

I am grateful for the guidance and insights of media counsel I have worked with over the years, in particular Doug Lutz, Robert Grant, Nancy Rubin, Virve Sandstrom, Geoff Machum, Rob Aske, Will Moreira, and the late Arthur Moreira. Jane Purves, the former managing editor of the *Chronicle-Herald*, encouraged her reporters to dig deeper and I thank her for supporting our efforts to challenge restrictions on news coverage. Thanks as well to the colleagues I have worked with on the court beat over the years—Merle MacIsaac, Cathy Nicoll, Anne Emery, Donna-Marie Sonnichsen, Sherri Borden Colley, Amy Pugsley Fraser, Brian Hayes, Frank Armstrong, and Lisa Taylor. Our debates over what information could be reported, and when, were always helpful.

I had the good fortune to complete the Short Course in the Law for Journalists when it was still offered at the University of Western Ontario, and I thank Robert Martin and his fellow instruct ors for their guidance. I would also like to express my appreciation to media law experts Michael Crawford, G. Stuart Adam, and Stuart Robertson for sharing their insights and advice, both in person and through their writings. Others who encouraged my efforts to improve journalists' understanding of their legal rights include retired Nova Scotia Chief Justice Lorne Clarke, Gail Salsbury,

Dene Rossouw, Jeannie Thomas, David Orchard, Stephen Bindman, Justice William Kelly, Justice Tom Cromwell, Justice Gerald Freeman, and Justice Jamie Saunders.

I would like to thank my colleagues in the School of Journalism at the University of King's College—Kim Kierans, Stephen Kimber, Kelly Toughill, Susan Newhook, Tim Currie, Fred Vallance-Jones, Doug Kirkaldy, and David Swick—for their support, advice, and insights. Former King's colleague Michael Cobden understood that legal training is a vital part of a journalist's education, and I thank him for allowing me to develop the News Media and the Courts in Canada course at King's. The Nova Scotia Law Foundation provided seed money to establish the course, and I am grateful for this support. I would also like to thank the hundreds of students who have taken the course over the years—their questions and insights have made this a better book.

I appreciate the input and encouragement I received from the people at Emond Montgomery Publications—Mike Thompson, David Handelsman, Jim Lyons, Andrew Gordon, Tara Wells, and Shani Sohn.

Two people deserve special thanks. The late Michael Fitz-James, the former executive editor of *Canadian Lawyer* magazine, put me in touch with Emond Montgomery and got the ball rolling for the first edition. And, as always, I am indebted to Kerry Oliver for her unwavering support of this project and all my work.

Dean Jobb
Halifax, Nova Scotia
November 2010

Website

The website accompanying this book offers further commentary, links, and summaries of recent high-profile media law cases (and will be added to in the coming years as relevant decisions are announced): **www.emp.ca/medialaw**.

Readers are also encouraged to read Dean Jobb's regular contributions to **www.J-Source.ca**, under the heading "Rights & Wrongs" (Law).

PART ONE
Open Justice

CHAPTER 1

Justice System 101

Introduction

Ignoring demands to throw the book at a man convicted of manslaughter in the death of a child, a judge imposes a four-year prison term that sparks public outrage. When the Crown attorney closes her case against a group of teenagers charged in a violent swarming, not one of them takes the witness stand to explain their actions. A jury acquits a man of armed robbery despite strong evidence he was the masked gunman who held up a 24-hour gas bar. A woman accused of murder is set free on bail while she awaits trial, despite the seriousness of her alleged crime. A defence lawyer agrees to represent a convicted pedophile who has been accused of molesting yet another child.

Scenarios such as these can be clipped from the pages of any daily newspaper, and each one raises questions about the Canadian justice system and how it works. How can someone accused of killing another person be released from custody until a trial is held? Why would a judge impose a sentence that flies in the face of popular sentiment? How could a jury permit someone who likely committed a crime to get off scot-free? Instead of forcing those accused of crimes to explain themselves, why do the courts permit them to remain silent? And how can any lawyer justify a decision to help a convicted criminal evade punishment?

To answer these questions, it is necessary to explore the principles and legal rights that form the foundation of our justice system. The law has a rationale all its own, honed over centuries in a quest to promote fairness and to protect society. Society must punish those convicted of killing or stealing, and citizens must be able to seek redress if they are hurt in an accident or taken advantage of in a business deal. To determine who's right and who's wrong, we have created a labyrinth of courts and tribunals to weigh evidence and dispense justice. And in the courtroom, judges, juries, and lawyers have well-defined duties and roles to play in the search for truth.

The Rule of Law

In Shakespeare's play *Henry VI, Part II*, a character utters a line to warm the hearts of lawyer-haters everywhere. "The first thing we do," cries Dick the Butcher, "let's kill all the lawyers."[1] Although this may sound like Dick is lawyer-bashing, his intention was to create anarchy, and the scene was emphasizing the pivotal role that the law plays in maintaining social order. Get rid of lawyers and their pesky laws, and the social order is sure to crumble.

Laws are the ground rules for any civilized society. Laws place limits on the conduct of individuals in order to protect the greater good. One scholar has described the law as "the knife-edge on which the delicate balance is maintained between the individual on one hand and the society on the other."[2] There are laws to maintain public order, to regulate commerce, to prevent the theft of property, and to protect the safety of citizens. They reflect our most basic moral values—the Biblical commandment of "Thou shalt not kill" is given the weight of law as the crime of murder. "A society crafts laws, especially laws about crime, to protect its most basic and essential norms and values," Ottawa law professor David Paciocco has noted. "Our law is the collected wisdom of generations of people working to find a way to protect the inherent dignity of human beings."[3]

General application and enforcement of legal rules through the courts are integral facets of the law. They set it apart from rules governing the members of a private club or local customs that can be breached without official punishment. "Law," one British writer has observed, "cannot be more accurately defined than as the sum of rules of human conduct which the courts will enforce."[4] The courts provide an independent, dispassionate forum for adjudicating rights. They determine whether the law has been broken and, if it has, the consequences for those responsible. Our conduct is said to be governed by the rule of law, not by the force of popular opinion or the whim of bureaucrats. The rule of law denotes "an ideal of rationality in the ordering of society, as opposed to the arbitrary making of decisions," in the words of law professor Stephen Waddams. "We will be governed not necessarily by decisions that we would like, but by decisions made by impartial persons applying settled, consistent and rationally defensible general principles."[5] Justice must be administered with fairness and predictability, based on the law and provable evidence rather than on favouritism, spite, or mere suspicion. The symbol of justice as a blindfolded figure, balancing a set of scales, serves as a reminder that justice is best achieved by weighing evidence free from outside influences.

The Two Branches of Law

There are two branches of law, criminal and civil. Each is distinguished by the parties involved, the issues in dispute, the strength of the evidence needed to prove a case, and the redress available from the courts.

Criminal Law

A **crime** is a deliberate or reckless act or omission that injures a person, damages property or takes it away from its owner, or breaches society's moral standards. A teenager steals a car and goes joyriding; a mother fails to seek medical treatment for her sick baby, who subsequently dies; a burglar breaks into a home in search of valuables; a man uses the Internet to disseminate child pornography; two men get into a fight outside a tavern, leaving one bruised and bloodied; someone in the wrong place at the wrong time is killed in a violent robbery. The criminal law is designed to protect citizens and their property from such acts and to punish those who have committed the offence.

Canada's criminal law is set out in the *Criminal Code*, which identifies acts that cross the line between proper and improper conduct, stipulates the possible punishment for each offence, and prescribes the procedure for dealing with prosecutions and trials.[6] The Code was first compiled in 1892 and, although updated and greatly expanded over the years, it still reflects its Victorian roots. Provisions outlawing duelling, feigning marriage, and alarming Her Majesty remain on the books, even if the conduct they seek to prevent is unlikely to occur today.[7] The Code remains a work in progress, as Parliament creates new categories of crime to protect society from computer hackers, biker gangs, and money launderers.[8]

While a criminal offence has a victim, crimes are an offence against us all. Accordingly, in virtually every case, the state—known in Canada as the Crown—is responsible for proceeding against a person charged with committing a crime. (Citizens have the right to pursue criminal charges in the courts as a private prosecution, but these are rare.) Criminals are prosecuted in the name of the sovereign, Canada's head of state, so cases are referred to as *The Queen versus John Doe* or *Regina versus John Doe* (which becomes *The King versus* or *Rex versus* when a king is on the throne). The name of a criminal case is usually abbreviated as *R v. Doe*.

The Crown must prove that the person accused of a crime is guilty; it is considered unfair and unjust to expect defendants to establish their innocence. Guilt must be proven *beyond a reasonable doubt*. This is known as the **standard of proof** and it means that judges or jurors cannot convict someone they believe is probably guilty, or even likely guilty, of a crime. But the Supreme Court of Canada has said the Crown is not expected to prove a person's guilt with absolute certainty; if a judge or jury is "sure" the accused committed the offence, the person should be convicted.[9] The bar is deliberately set high, and the Crown's failure to produce enough evidence to prove guilt beyond a reasonable doubt ensures that some guilty persons will escape punishment. This is a price our justice system is willing to pay in order to guard against the injustice of sending innocent people to prison. William Blackstone, a British jurist of the 18th century, put it best: "It is better that ten guilty persons escape than one innocent suffer."[10] The ordeals of Donald Marshall Jr., David Milgaard, Guy Paul Morin, Steven Truscott, and many others who were wrongfully convicted of murder, only to be exonerated years later, underscore the importance of ensuring that the justice system protects citizens from such a fate.

When a person is convicted of a crime, the judge must choose an appropriate punishment. The penalties a judge can mete out include fines that can run into the thousands of dollars, terms of probation or community service, and prison terms ranging from a few months to life behind bars. The severity of the crime determines the severity of the sentence. In a free society like ours, the loss of liberty is viewed as the ultimate punishment. But even a non-custodial sentence, such as community service, has serious consequences. The stigma of a criminal record alone can make it difficult for the person to find employment or to travel outside Canada.

Civil Law

The civil law is concerned with legal disputes that arise between individuals, corporations, or governments and government actors. Two neighbours squabble over the location of a fence separating their properties; a couple splits and files for divorce; one company claims that another has breached a contract to supply materials; a salesman fired from his job accuses his former employer of wrongful dismissal. If such disputes cannot be settled by negotiation, the person with a grievance has the right to file a civil action asking a court to make a ruling. Civil law is private law—the government only becomes involved in civil cases if it is sued or if it files a lawsuit against a person or company—yet civil cases are fought in a public forum, the nation's courtrooms.

The burden of proving a civil claim lies on the **plaintiff**, the party pressing the claim. Because the liberty of the defendant is not at stake, the standard of proof needed to establish a civil claim is not as high as the standard in criminal cases. A judge or jury need only be satisfied on a *balance of probabilities* that the injury or loss has occurred and that the defendant is responsible. The court must be convinced that the claim is probably true, a measure sometimes defined as better than 50–50, or in legal terms as a preponderance of evidence. The contrast between the standard of proof in criminal cases and civil ones is illustrated by the case of former football star O.J. Simpson, who was acquitted of a double murder by a California jury but later found liable in the civil courts for causing the deaths.

If an action succeeds, the outcome is usually an award of **damages**—money the defendant must pay to compensate the afflicted party, whether for lost income, pain and suffering from physical injuries, or failure to honour an agreement. In some cases a judge may order defendants to follow through on their obligations under a contract. In others, the judge may grant the plaintiff an **injunction** to prevent the defendant from doing something that would harm the plaintiff's interests. For example, a plaintiff might seek an order preventing strikers from picketing stores not directly involved in a labour dispute. The civil courts also hear challenges that seek to strike down a law or a government action as unconstitutional or unjust.

Sources of Canadian Law

The Constitution and the Charter of Rights and Freedoms

The basis for the Canadian state is the *Constitution Act, 1982*.[11] It incorporates the *British North America Act*, the British statute that united the colonies of Nova Scotia, New Brunswick, Ontario, and Quebec upon Confederation in 1867, and established the basis for a federal state that now consists of 10 provinces and three territories.

The *Constitution Act, 1867* sets out the legislative responsibilities of each level of government. The federal government regulates matters of national scope and importance, including defence, foreign policy, transportation, trade between provinces, banking, and the criminal law. Provinces and territories control matters of local and regional concern—public education, land ownership, hospitals, and the development of timber, minerals, and other natural resources. Cities, towns, and other municipal governments, in turn, receive their powers from legislation passed by provincial and territorial governments.

In the field of justice, the division of responsibility between Ottawa and the provinces and territories sometimes creates confusion. Parliament formulates the criminal law as well as laws that govern divorces and control illicit drugs, ensuring that the law on these important matters is the same in all parts of the country. The legislatures of the provinces and territories, however, are responsible for administering the civil law and operate the court system that puts the criminal law into action.

Since Confederation the courts have often been called upon to settle disputes when one level of government is accused of intruding on the jurisdiction of another. If a government is found to have the constitutional power to enact a law, it is said to be *intra vires* or within the scope of its powers. A court will strike down a law found to be outside the scope of a government's powers as *ultra vires*. A provincial legislature, for example, might respond to public demands to curb prostitution by passing a law that enables police to seize the vehicle of a person communicating with a prostitute. The courts may well strike down the law as an infringement on the federal power over the criminal law, because the *Criminal Code* already makes it an offence to communicate with a prostitute.[12]

The constitution also incorporates **conventions**—unwritten rules that carry the full weight of law. Canada has inherited many of these conventions from Britain, which operates without a written constitution. They include such basic facets of our system as the structure of cabinet government and the concept of ministerial responsibility.

The *Constitution Act, 1982* includes a declaration of every citizen's legal, social, and political rights—the *Canadian Charter of Rights and Freedoms*.[13] The Charter protects an array of rights, shielding citizens from unfair laws, discriminatory government policies, and arbitrary police actions.

Rights Protected Under the Charter

- Practising religion and associating with others are fundamental freedoms enjoyed by all Canadians. Another is "freedom of thought, belief, opinion and expression, including freedom of the press and other media of communication."

- Democratic rights include the right to vote in federal and provincial elections and to run as a candidate. The Charter requires governments to face an election at least once every five years, formalizing a constitutional convention inherited from Britain. A government may seek to extend its mandate in a time of national emergency such as war, but must have the support of two-thirds of the members of Parliament or a legislature.

- Mobility rights enable Canadians to enter, leave, or stay in the country as they choose. Citizens and permanent residents have the right to seek work anywhere in Canada, and provinces cannot prevent qualified newcomers from other provinces and territories from pursuing their occupations or professions.

- Legal rights enshrined in the Charter protect those accused of crimes and embody legal rights that the courts have recognized for centuries, such as the right to bring a *habeas corpus* application to seek release from custody and to be presumed innocent until proven guilty. The Charter imposes limits on police powers, shielding citizens from arbitrary detention or arrest as well as searches and seizures of property that are unreasonable.

Once a person is arrested for an offence, she has the right to be told the reason for the arrest, to consult a lawyer without delay, and to appear promptly before a court to apply for release. Persons charged with crimes have the right to stand trial within a reasonable time, cannot be compelled to testify, and are presumed innocent until proven guilty in a trial that is fair, open to the public, and held before an independent and impartial court. Accused persons seeking release while awaiting trial have a right to expect that bail conditions will be reasonable, and they can demand a jury trial if the charges they face are serious. Witnesses who incriminate themselves while testifying in court are assured that the evidence will not become the basis for a prosecution. No one can be tried or punished twice for the same offence, and those convicted of crimes are protected from being subjected to cruel and unusual punishment.

The Charter provides a general guarantee that all Canadians have the right to "life, liberty and security of the person and the right not to be deprived thereof except in accordance with the principles of fundamental justice."

- Equality rights protect Canadians from laws that discriminate on the basis of race, religion, ethnic origin, gender, age, or physical or mental disability. Governments remain free to establish programs to help visible minorities, people with disabilities, and other disadvantaged groups.

- Language rights include the recognition of English and French as Canada's official languages. Both can be used in Parliament and in federal courts, and federal laws and services are available in English and French.

- Aboriginal and treaty rights in existence before the Charter are recognized and afforded constitutional protection.

Legislation

Both the federal and provincial levels of government have the power to create and impose laws, known as **statutes**, to govern matters within their jurisdictions. New laws and amendments to existing ones are introduced in Parliament or a provincial legislature as **bills**. They become law—and are transformed into **acts**—after they are passed by the majority vote of elected representatives, given royal assent, and proclaimed by the government to be in force. The requirement for assent from the Queen's representative—the governor general at the federal level, the lieutenant governor at the provincial level—is a formality, because it is a constitutional convention that the monarch invariably follows the government's advice.

Regulations, another form of legislation, are created under the authority of a statute. Statutes set out the broad principles underlying the law and how it should apply; regulations fill in the details of how these provisions will be implemented and enforced. Cabinet has the power to pass **orders in council** to create and amend regulations, giving the government flexibility to make minor changes to the law without going through the time-consuming process of seeking parliamentary or legislative approval. For instance, a provincial legislature might pass a statute establishing when the season for sportfishing will begin and end, but the fee to obtain a fishing licence would likely be stipulated in a regulation that could be changed to keep pace with inflation. Cabinets also issue orders in council to implement day-to-day decisions authorized by statute, such as appointments to public office or the approval of loans and grants to businesses.

Municipal governments also have law-making powers. Local governments create and enforce legislation, known as **bylaws** or **ordinances**, to deal with matters such as land-use and building permits, parking, garbage disposal, and dog control.

Judge-Made Law

The Common Law

A vast body of Canadian law, including many of our most hallowed legal principles, is derived from the **common law** that originated in Britain. Sometimes referred to as case law or judge-made law, the common law is the sum of countless rulings made by judges, who have interpreted statutes and applied legal principles to disputes that ended up before the courts. Judges draw on the lessons of past cases to help them craft a just decision. In the words of a British judge, Lord Reid, the common law "has been built by the rational expansion of what already exists in order to do justice to particular cases."[14]

Resolving a legal dispute is an exercise in finding the law, as judges and lawyers comb through previously decided cases—known as **precedents**—and legal textbooks for guidance. The search begins with Canadian materials, but can expand to the rulings of courts in Britain, the United States, and other common law jurisdictions if there are few homegrown decisions to offer guidance on a particular legal issue. The common law is also the source of many of the rules that govern how cases proceed through the courts and the admissibility of evidence. In some areas of law, legislators have enacted statutes to formalize and build upon common law rules.

The common law brings a crucial element of certainty and stability to the law. Under a principle known as ***stare decisis***—roughly translated as "standing by former decisions"—judges must follow precedents established by higher courts within their jurisdiction. A lawyer need only scour the law books and online databases for existing rulings on an issue in order to advise a client on the likelihood that a case will be won or lost.

An obvious drawback to this system is that the common law tends to encourage inflexibility; judges may become slaves to precedent, perpetuating concepts and practices long after they have become outdated. As British Judge Lord Simon has warned, "Not all precedents are good precedents."[15] Fortunately, the common law also offers the flexibility that judges need to refine and update the law as times and attitudes change. Because the facts underlying two cases are never the same, judges may have grounds to **distinguish**—and disregard—a particular precedent that appears to stand in the path of doing justice. A much respected British jurist, Lord Denning, advised his fellow judges to follow precedent as they would follow a path through the woods:

You must follow it certainly so as to reach your end. But you must not let the path become too overgrown. You must cut out the dead wood and trim off the side branches, else you will find yourself lost in thickets and brambles. My plea is simply to keep the path to justice clear of obstructions which would impede it.[16]

Principles of Equity

The common law's emphasis on adherence to precedent has the potential to force judges to make rulings that are unfair or unjust. A set of rules known as the **principles of equity**, which developed in tandem with the common law, are intended to reduce the chances that a litigant with a worthy cause will fall through the cracks of the justice system. One equitable principle holds that there must be a legal remedy for every wrong. Another demands that litigants come to court with clean hands with respect to the defendant; the courts will not readily side with a plaintiff who has failed to act honourably or who has tried to take advantage of the defendant. The concept of a trust is a creature of the law of equity. For example, in most provinces unmarried couples do not have the right to seek an equal division of assets if the relationship ends, as married couples do. A court faced with evidence that each partner contributed to the accumulation of assets, however, can invoke the equitable principle of constructive trust. The court can order that assets be split evenly, preventing one person from profiting at the expense of the other.[17]

Quebec's Civil Code

The common law and the principle of *stare decisis* are followed in nine provinces and the territories. Quebec courts, however, adhere to a European-style civil code system. Quebec's *Civil Code*, first enacted in 1866, sets out comprehensive written rules, framed as broad general principles, intended to deal with legal issues and disputes as cases come before the courts.[18] Quebec judges look to the Code for guidance on how the law should apply in each case, then examine rulings made in previous cases. They are not bound to follow such precedents, but often do in the interest of consistency. When dealing with criminal cases, however, Quebec judges operate under the *Criminal Code* and apply common law principles like judges in the rest of the country.

The Courts and the Charter of Rights and Freedoms

In a common law jurisdiction like Canada, the courts have long been in the business of reworking and refining the law. Judges are constantly called upon to pass judgment on the meaning and scope of statutes, sometimes producing rulings that render such laws unenforceable or blunt their impact. As well, courts have long had the power to strike down legislation that exceeds the jurisdiction of the federal government or a province. But the *Charter of Rights and Freedoms* has radically altered the relationship between our elected representatives and the courts. Parliament has declared the constitution, which contains the Charter, to be "the supreme law of Canada, and any law that is inconsistent with the provisions of the Constitution is, to the extent of the inconsistency, of no force and effect."[19]

Although Parliament and the provincial legislatures retain their law-making roles, the courts now have the duty to assess whether laws are consistent with the freedoms all Canadians enjoy and to take action if they are not. Section 24(1) of the Charter enables anyone who claims that his rights have been violated to apply to the courts for a remedy. A court that finds that a right has been violated can make any order it considers "appropriate and just" in the circumstances; judges can declare that a law or government policy is invalid or impose a stay of proceedings to halt an unfair prosecution that is an abuse of the court process. In criminal cases, section 24(2) of the Charter empowers judges to exclude any Crown evidence that was obtained in violation of Charter rights, if introducing the evidence would "bring the administration of justice into disrepute."

Examples of the courts enforcing Charter rights are not hard to find. When an Ontario judge ruled in June 2003 that a 70-month delay in bringing a Toronto couple to trial on a charge of murdering their baby daughter violated their Charter right to stand trial within a reasonable time, the court stayed the charges, ending the prosecution.[20] The same month, the Supreme Court of Canada ruled that police in Manitoba violated the Charter's protection against unreasonable search and seizure when they failed to obtain a search warrant before seizing marijuana from a locker at a bus station. With the drugs excluded as evidence under section 24(2), the Crown's case collapsed and the man who rented the locker was acquitted of possessing a narcotic for the purpose of trafficking.[21]

But the Charter does not give judges the final say on our laws. As constitutional law expert Kent Roach points out, the Charter strikes a compromise, "avoiding the dangers of both judicial supremacy, which gives unelected judges the last word, and legislative supremacy, which gives elected politicians the last word."[22] Section 1 of the Charter allows Parliament and the provincial legislatures to impose limits on rights, provided that these limits are reasonable, prescribed by law, and justifiable in a free and democratic society. This mechanism enables the courts to balance the interests of society against the interests of individuals, and in many cases the courts have ruled that a law infringes on a Charter right but must stand as a reasonable limit under section 1. For example, in 1990 the Supreme Court of Canada found that the *Criminal Code* provision making it an offence to communicate with another person for the purpose of prostitution violated the Charter's guarantee of freedom of expression, but ruled that the infringement was a reasonable limit on that right.[23] As well, the so-called notwithstanding clause in section 33 gives Parliament and the provinces the power to enact laws that violate the Charter's fundamental freedoms and legal rights. However, legislation passed under the notwithstanding clause, to remain in effect, must be reviewed and re-enacted every five years. The clause has been rarely invoked, because few governments seem willing to risk the possible political fallout from a decision to ride roughshod over rights that have been upheld by the courts.

The Charter has created a wave of constitutional challenges from citizens, interest groups, and persons accused of crimes, leading an anonymous wag to dub it "the charter of full employment for lawyers." Charter rulings have tempered the criminal law, improved the legal safeguards for persons accused of crimes, and expanded the rights of gays and lesbians, aboriginal peoples, and other minorities.[24] Even though the Supreme Court of Canada rejects two-thirds of all Charter claims it hears,[25] its power to reshape laws and public policy has generated controversy and prompted some politicians to complain about **judicial activism**. Observers should bear in mind, however, that judges did not usurp this wider role in reviewing legislation; it is a responsibility that our elected representatives thrust upon the courts when the Charter was embedded in the constitution.

The Charter is intended to protect individuals and minority groups from laws and government actions that violate their constitutional rights. It does not apply to civil actions where there is no state involvement. The Supreme Court of Canada, however, has ruled that common law principles should be altered to conform with the values of fairness and justice enshrined in the Charter.[26]

Structure of the Courts

The constitution gives Ottawa and provincial and territorial governments the power to create courts, each with distinct powers and jurisdiction over specific types of cases. The federal government is responsible for *courts of superior jurisdiction*, the highest echelons of Canada's courts. These are the Supreme Court of Canada, the nation's highest court, as well as the court of appeal and the top level of trial court in each province. The federal government appoints and pays the judges who serve on these benches.

The provinces and territories are responsible for *inferior courts*. These courts have limited powers and jurisdiction and, as the name suggests, occupy the lower rungs of the court hierarchy. Inferior courts generally deal with less serious crimes, civil actions to recover modest sums of money, and enforcement of provincial statutes. Inferior court judges are appointed and paid by the provincial or territorial government. Under the constitution, the provinces are responsible for operating the justice system, providing court facilities and support staff, and maintaining court registries and files. As a result, superior and inferior courts often share courthouses and often use the same courtrooms.

Distinctions Between Trials and Appeals

There are important differences between the role of a trial court and an appeal court. At trial, judges and juries sift through the evidence to determine what happened, then apply the law to reach a verdict. In contrast, the Supreme Court of Canada and other courts of appeal review the trial judge's rulings and the transcripts of proceedings in the lower court. The appeal court's job is to determine whether the trial judge understood the evidence presented and properly interpreted the law that applies to the case; in jury trials, the appeal court must be satisfied that the judge correctly explained the law to the jurors.

If there has been an error, the appeal court has the power to overturn the verdict and may order a new trial. An appeal is not a second trial, and appeal courts hear additional evidence only if the information could affect the outcome of the case and was not discovered until after the trial was held. The party pursuing an appeal is known as the **appellant**, while the party arguing against the appeal is referred to as the **respondent**.

The Supreme Court of Canada

The Supreme Court of Canada is the final court of appeal from all other courts. It has jurisdiction to hear cases arising from any area of the law—criminal, civil, constitutional, or administrative. It hears challenges to the rulings of provincial and territorial appeal courts and reviews cases that have been appealed through the Federal Court of Canada and the military justice system.

Based in Ottawa, the court consists of a chief justice and eight other judges. The *Supreme Court Act* requires that at least three judges come from Quebec. The six remaining judges are chosen to ensure regional balance.[27] By tradition, three come from Ontario, two from Western Canada, and one from the Atlantic provinces. Candidates for the Supreme Court tend to be judges promoted from a provincial court of appeal.

The Supreme Court only hears cases that have exhausted all other avenues of appeal in the lower courts. The court is extremely selective, receiving more than 500 applications for leave to appeal each year but hearing only about 80 cases.[28] Most have national implications or deal with issues where the law is novel or unclear. An appellant must file a written application seeking *leave*, or permission, to bring an appeal before the court. Three judges review the application and make a terse announcement that leave has been granted or denied; the court never reveals its reasons for deciding to hear some cases and not others. Leave to appeal is not required in criminal cases where the judgment of the court of appeal has not been unanimous. As well, the federal government may ask the court to rule on the interpretation of the constitution or the validity of legislation, a procedure known as a *reference*.

Provincial/Territorial Superior Courts

Each province and territory has two levels of superior court, one to hear trials and another to hear appeals (with the exception of the territory of Nunavut, where appeals go before the Alberta Court of Appeal). The court of appeal, sometimes known as the appeal division, is the highest court within the jurisdiction. Three judges hear most cases but a panel of five may be convened to decide a significant issue. If there is a difference of opinion, the odd number of judges ensures that there will not be a deadlock. Judges of a court of appeal or the Supreme Court of Canada who disagree with their colleagues are free to write their own ruling, known as a *dissent*, but the majority rules.

One tier below is the trial court of superior jurisdiction, which has various names depending on the province or territory. It is known as the Supreme Court in Nova Scotia, Prince Edward Island, Newfoundland and Labrador, British Columbia, the Northwest Territories, and the Yukon; as the Court of Queen's Bench in New Brunswick, Manitoba, Alberta, and Saskatchewan; as the Superior Court in Quebec; as the Superior Court of Justice in Ontario; and as the Court of Justice in Nunavut. Nunavut has a unified court, with jurisdiction over trials at the superior and inferior court level, so one judge can travel to isolated communities and hear all cases on the docket.

Superior courts have **inherent jurisdiction**, meaning they have the right to deal with any case not specifically assigned to a lower court. Most serious criminal offences, including many crimes of violence, are heard by superior courts. They also hear civil cases and constitutional challenges to provincial laws or policies. Most provinces have created a specialized division of the superior court, known as a unified family court, to deal exclusively with divorce and other family law matters. Trial judges of the superior court also hear appeals from some decisions of lower courts and administrative tribunals.

Inferior Courts

The provinces and territories are responsible for an array of inferior courts at the entry level of the justice system. These courts tend to deal exclusively with provincial and territorial laws, but some have jurisdiction over cases involving federal laws—most notably *Criminal Code* offences. The provincial court, the inferior court that attracts the most public attention, is also the busiest; its judges deal with all pre-trial proceedings in criminal cases and can adjudicate all but the most serious crimes. The provincial court also hears narcotics offences and charges laid under the full slate of federal and provincial laws. Trespassers, fishermen charged with exceeding quotas, polluters, companies accused of false advertising—all are tried in the provincial court. Juries do not hear trials at the provincial court level.[29]

Other examples of inferior courts are small claims courts, which hear civil cases involving the recovery of minor amounts of money, and probate courts, which verify wills and hear disputes over inheritances. Youth courts deal with minors charged with crimes under the provisions of the *Youth Criminal Justice Act*.[30] There are also courts that deal with traffic offences and courts that administer bankruptcies. In provinces that have not established a unified family court, there is a court to hear family law disputes other than divorce, such as child custody and access disputes. Known as family courts, they also hear government applications to have children at risk put into foster care.

Federal Courts

The Federal Court and the Federal Court of Appeal deal exclusively with issues that arise under federal laws. Although these courts are based in Ottawa, their judges hold trials and hearings across the country. The Federal Court's jurisdiction includes disputes between provinces or between Ottawa and a province, citizenship appeals, violations of copyright and patent laws, and cases involving Crown corporations or departments of the government of Canada. It shares jurisdiction over maritime law issues with provincial superior courts, and is the usual forum for hearing legal disputes involving commercial shipping and salvage claims. The court also reviews the decisions of federal boards, commissions, and tribunals.

Military Courts

Military courts preside over the trials of persons charged under the military's *Code of Service Discipline*.[31] The Code applies to all members of the Canadian Armed Forces as well as civilians who accompany the forces on missions. Although it incorporates *Criminal Code* offences, Armed Forces members face trial in the civilian courts if they are accused of a serious offence such as murder, manslaughter, or sexual assault that has been committed in Canada.

There are two types of trials. Most disciplinary infractions are dealt with at a summary trial before a superior or commanding officer, with possible punishments rang-

Figure 1.1   Outline of Canada's Court System

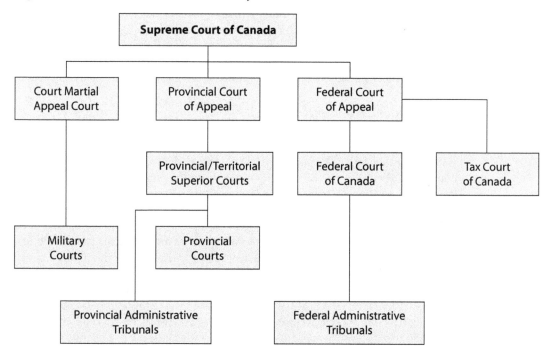

ing from detention or reduction of rank to loss of leave or confinement to barracks. Members of the military accused of serious disciplinary offences and crimes have the right to request a court martial before a military judge or a panel of officers who act as a jury. The Court Martial Appeal Court, which hears appeals from the decisions of military courts, is made up of judges chosen from the Federal Court of Canada and other superior courts.

Administrative Tribunals and Self-Governing Professions

Ottawa, the provinces, and the territories have created a system of administrative tribunals that complements the work of the courts. Tribunals are known as quasi-judicial bodies and operate like courts; they convene hearings, review evidence, and make rulings, but their proceedings tend to be less formal. Federal tribunals may be called upon to settle disputes over entitlement to employment insurance, disability benefits, refugee status, or allegations of human rights violations. Tribunals at the provincial and territorial level deal with matters such as workplace standards, claims for workers' compensation, power rate increases, and police actions. Lawyers, doctors, engineers, and many other professionals belong to self-governing societies that have internal disciplinary committees with the power to investigate and sanction members accused of misconduct.

Most decisions of provincial and territorial tribunals and self-governing societies can be appealed to the superior courts. Rulings of federally appointed tribunals such as the Canadian Human Rights Commission and the National Parole Board are appealed to the Federal Court of Canada. Judges tend to defer to tribunal decisions, recognizing that their members have specialized knowledge of issues like labour standards and welfare entitlements, which rarely come before the courts. Nevertheless, the courts have the power to overturn a tribunal or disciplinary ruling and order a re-hearing if proper procedures were not followed or a decision is clearly unreasonable.

Precedents and the Level of Court

A court ruling's value as a precedent under the common law depends on the level of court that has issued the judgment. Judges at every level of court must follow rulings of the Supreme Court of Canada. As the last stop on the road to justice, the Supreme Court is not bound by its own decisions; at times the court has revisited and even reversed its position on legal issues when faced with compelling arguments that its earlier decision should not stand.[32]

If the Supreme Court has not ruled on a particular issue, judges must take their cue from the decisions of higher courts within their province or territory. So judges of inferior courts must follow any precedent set at the trial level of the superior court, and judges at both the inferior and superior court level must follow the lead of their court of appeal. They are not bound to follow precedents set in another province or territory, even rulings made at the court of appeal level. Although judges often look to rulings from other provinces for guidance, they are free to reach a different conclusion. Rulings may even be at odds with those of other judges on the same court. The media sometimes mistakenly report that a judge at the provincial court level has made a "precedent-setting" decision. The decision may well turn out to set a precedent but, until a higher court tackles the issue on appeal, the ruling is binding on no one, not even on other provincial court judges.

In the Courtroom

Judges and Judicial Independence

In the words of Socrates, "Four things belong to a judge: to hear courteously, to answer wisely, to consider soberly, and to decide impartially."[33] The judge is the central figure in the courtroom and plays the role of an umpire, resolving any disputes that arise over the law and the procedure to be followed. The judge decides whether evidence is relevant and admissible and determines whether Charter provisions have been breached. The judge oversees the proceedings, keeping order in the courtroom and ensuring that the case runs smoothly. To maintain the appearance of impartiality, judges rarely question witnesses and avoid commenting on testimony or the strength of a litigant's case until all the evidence has been heard. In cases without juries, the judge is the trier of fact, assessing the evidence and handing down a verdict. When a person is convicted of a crime, it is the judge's duty to impose punishment.

The Charter enshrines the right of persons accused of crimes to have their cases heard "by an independent and impartial tribunal."[34] Accordingly, judges must reach their own conclusions about whether a person is guilty of a crime or whether a plaintiff in a civil case is entitled to damages. For justice to be done, judges must have the freedom and security they need to make rulings that are sound in law but that may offend the government or outrage the public. Without an independent judiciary, the right to a fair trial would be meaningless and citizens would have little faith that justice would be done. "The rule of law, interpreted and applied by impartial judges, is the guarantee of everyone's rights and freedoms," Antonio Lamer, former chief justice of the Supreme Court of Canada, has declared. "Judicial independence is, at its root, concerned with impartiality, in appearance and in fact. ... Independence is not a perk of judicial office. It is a guarantee of the institutional conditions of impartiality."[35] Judges are appointed and paid by government, but they are not government employees. The government prosecutes crimes and often appears as a litigant in the civil courts; if judges were beholden to the state for their paycheques and jobs, any appearance of impartiality would vanish. Governments do not have direct control over judges' salaries or pensions or the length of time they will serve on the bench. Salaries and benefits are established by independent commissions, although Parliament ultimately must pass legislation to implement raises.[36] Legislation also determines the mandatory retirement age for judges, which is 70 for some courts and 75 for others. One scholar has discussed the three elements of judicial independence and why each is vital:

> If judges do not have security of tenure, then there is a danger that they will tailor their rulings to please the person who can terminate their position. If judges do not have financial security, then they may be tempted to accept favours or the promise of future favours from those who have an interest in the litigation. And if judges do not have a measure of institutional independence over at least the exercise of the judicial function, then the government can, for example, control which judges will hear which cases.[37]

Security of tenure also means that judges are free to make rulings and impose sentences that are unpopular with the public. Justice is not a popularity contest; if it were, convicted criminals—arguably the most unpopular members of any society—would undoubtedly suffer fates far beyond what is reasonable to punish them for their wrongdoing. A Prince Edward Island judge has echoed this sentiment. When faced with picketers marching outside his courthouse, demanding the maximum sentence of life in prison for a man convicted of manslaughter, he observed: "Judges and courts cannot respond to the public perception of what should be justice when the law clearly sets forth the road that the judge or court must follow. ... We are not living in a country where an 'eye for an eye' theory of justice is carried out."[38]

Governments make appointments to the bench after consultation with the courts and the legal community. Lawyers apply for judgeships, and screening committees of judges and lawyers, some with public input, recommend qualified candidates. Despite this process, critics complain that too many appointees are former politicians or have ties to the government that makes the final selection.[39] Since 2006 a parliamentary committee has questioned nominees to the Supreme Court of Canada.[40] Another model for selecting judges, followed in some American jurisdictions, is to allow citizens to vote for judges, electing them to fixed terms in the same way politicians are chosen. But under this system, elected judges and candidates for judicial office must curry favour with voters, perhaps appealing for support with a tough law-and-order platform. Worse, judges and candidates are forced to solicit donations from law firms and corporations to finance their campaigns, further undermining their ability to dispense justice in an independent and impartial fashion.[41]

Despite their independent status, judges remain accountable for their actions. Court proceedings, with few exceptions, are open to the public, enabling citizens and the media to debate and criticize a judge's decisions. Rulings can be challenged in a higher court and will be reversed if found to be wrong in law. As well, litigants and members of the public have the right to lodge formal complaints about a judge's conduct or comments in the courtroom. The Canadian Judicial Council, created in 1971 and made up of the chief justices and associate chief justices of each superior court, investigates complaints about federally appointed judges. Most complaints arise from divorces and other family law cases, where emotions run high. Judges also have been investigated for remarks from the bench that were seen as racist, sexist, or biased. The council has the power to counsel or reprimand a judge and, in extreme cases, can recommend that the federal government take steps to remove a judge from office. In 2008 the council recommended the removal of a judge of the Ontario Superior Court after an inquiry determined he had shown bias and abused his judicial powers during a major trial. The judge resigned before further action was taken.[42] Only Parliament has the power to remove a superior court judge from office; a joint motion of the House of Commons and the Senate is required, but the procedure has not been used since Confederation. Under the *Judges Act*, federally appointed judges can be removed from office on the grounds of misconduct, advanced age or infirmity, or failing to properly exercise the powers of judicial office.[43] Judicial councils have been created at the provincial level to field complaints about inferior court judges, with provincial cabinets or legislatures having the power to remove a judge for misconduct.[44]

In a ruling issued in 2001, the Supreme Court of Canada called the judge "the pillar of our entire justice system" and said the public has a right to demand "virtually irreproachable conduct from anyone performing a judicial function."[45] It is a demanding role. Author Jack Batten, in a book profiling Canadian jurists, noted that a judge "doesn't have to be perfect but he or she had better come awfully close."[46]

The Jury

The Charter guarantees the right to a jury trial to every person charged with a crime punishable by a sentence of five years or more in prison.[47] As well, those accused of many less serious crimes have the right to choose to be tried by a jury. Jurors assume the role of **trier of fact**. The judge oversees the trial and instructs them on the law to be applied when they review the facts in order to reach a verdict. Juries provide an important check on the power of judges and the state, and may acquit defendants in situations where applying the strict letter of the law justifies a conviction. For example, a sympathetic jury may well acquit a doctor charged with murder for administering a lethal dose of medicine to a patient who was dying in extreme agony. The jury system also gives citizens an opportunity to take an active role in the justice system and promotes better public understanding of the trial process.

Criminal cases are heard by juries of 12 persons selected from a pool of citizens summoned for jury duty from names drawn at random, usually from voters' lists. At the outset of a trial, the Crown attorney and defence lawyer choose who will serve. Each side can reject a particular candidate without providing a reason. If the case is sensational or has received extensive media coverage, potential jurors may be questioned about their opinions or their knowledge of the case before the court.

Jurors must be Canadian citizens and at least 18 years of age. Some persons are ineligible to serve on a jury—lawyers and law students, police officers and other justice officials, federal and provincial politicians, members of the Armed Forces, and anyone who has served more than two years in prison for a crime. Judges often exempt other people from service if they have health problems or family commitments. Friends and relatives of a witness, of the accused, or of anyone else involved in a case are asked to declare such conflicts and will not be allowed to serve. Jurors may be excused because of illness or other reasons during the trial. If the number of jurors drops below 10, the judge must declare a mistrial and a new jury will be chosen to re-hear the case.

Jurors swear an oath to be impartial and to base their verdict solely on the evidence presented in the courtroom. They are asked to assess all of the facts in order to determine what happened. The verdict must be unanimous and jurors are not permitted to explain the basis for a decision to convict or acquit. Failure to agree on a verdict will result in a hung jury and the accused will likely stand trial a second time. Jurors only play a role in sentencing if the defendant is convicted of second-degree murder, when the judge will ask them to recommend when the offender—who faces an automatic penalty of life in prison—should be eligible to apply for release on parole. Although the jury can recommend a waiting period ranging from 10 to 25 years, the judge makes the final decision.

Juries also hear a limited number of civil actions, including lawsuits alleging defamation and malicious prosecution, but many provinces are considering the abolition of civil jury trials.[48] Civil juries make findings of fact and are asked to decide how much money should be awarded as damages to a successful party. Civil juries vary in size from province to province—Nova Scotia, for example, sets the number at seven, while British Columbia empanels eight-member juries. The verdict need not be unanimous and typically can be based on a majority vote after the jury has deliberated for a certain number of hours.

The Adversarial System of Justice

The notion of trials as contests between opposing sides is a fundamental feature of Canada's justice system. In the words of the Supreme Court of Canada, an adversarial approach "helps guarantee that issues are well and fully argued by parties who have a stake in the outcome."[49] This approach is taken in both criminal and civil cases, in the belief that the surest route to uncovering the truth is through an independent examination of evidence presented by each side involved in a legal dispute.

The Crown Attorney

Lawyers who prosecute criminal cases and federal and provincial offences are known as **Crown attorneys** or Crown prosecutors, or simply as Crowns. Governments employ staff lawyers or hire lawyers on a *per diem* (day-to-day) basis to pursue cases in the courts on the Crown's behalf.

There are distinct Crown agencies to prosecute offences for each level of government. Lawyers acting for Justice Canada, the federal justice department, are agents of the attorney general of Canada (an office held by the federal minister of justice). These Crowns prosecute narcotics offences under the *Controlled Drugs and Substances Act*[50] as well as violations of federal statutes other than the *Criminal Code*. At the provincial and territorial level, attorneys general (known as ministers of justice in some jurisdictions) are responsible for prosecuting *Criminal Code* offences and violations of provincial laws. This duty is delegated to staff lawyers who work for their department's prosecution service or branch. One province, Nova Scotia, has a prosecution service that reports to the justice minister but operates independently of the government.

The Crown's role carries an enormous discretionary power. Prosecutors provide legal advice to the police before charges are laid, identifying possible violations of the law and whether further investigation is needed. In British Columbia, Quebec, and New Brunswick, prosecutors also have the final say on whether charges will be laid. In the remaining provinces and territories and at the federal level, police forces decide whether charges will be filed. If they are, prosecutors in those jurisdictions assume control of the case and decide whether to pursue the charges in court.[51] Under both charging systems, Crown attorneys have a duty to forgo charges, or withdraw those filed by police, if they believe that it is not in the public interest to prosecute or it is unlikely there is enough evidence to secure a conviction.

Crown attorneys act for the state. They do not appear in court to represent or defend the police, nor do they act on behalf of victims of crime. Most importantly, despite the competitive nature of the adversarial system of justice, it is not their job to secure a conviction at all costs. "The role of prosecutor excludes any notion of winning or losing," the Supreme Court of Canada has said.[52] Crowns have a duty to pursue charges with vigour and to put all available evidence before the court, but they must act with fairness and integrity to ensure that justice is done, whatever the verdict.

Lawyers

Lawyers acting for the plaintiff or defendant in a civil action, or for a person accused of a crime, have a duty to present their client's case fully and forcefully. In the words of a British court, a lawyer has a duty to "fearlessly raise every issue, advance every argument, and ask every question, however distasteful, which he thinks will help his client's case."[53] But lawyers cannot break the law to help their clients, and the self-governing societies that oversee the legal profession can discipline lawyers who breach their ethical duty to act fairly and honourably. Although a lawyer's primary duty is to ensure that the client's interests are promoted and protected, lawyers are forbidden from misleading a court. For example, if a person accused of a crime tells his lawyer he is guilty, the lawyer would no longer be able to present evidence suggesting the client is innocent or that someone else committed the crime, and may have to withdraw from the case.

The role of defence counsel in criminal cases is not well understood or appreciated. In the public's mind, the lawyer acting for an accused person tends to be regarded as "a threat to public security who is apt to set free dangerous criminals on what everyone knows are mere technicalities."[54] One newspaper probably was not exaggerating when it published a feature exploring popular distaste for defence counsel under the headline "The Hated Lawyer."[55] This unflattering image ignores the fundamental right of everyone charged with a crime—from the most incorrigible crime boss to the first-time shoplifter—to retain a lawyer to defend their interests in court. Trials would hardly be considered fair and just if they were one-sided affairs and the accused person was not afforded the right to challenge police methods or the testimony of witnesses. Defence counsel give innocent persons a fighting chance to clear their names, and they ensure that those found guilty of crimes have asserted their full legal rights and have been given their day in court. One writer has likened defence counsel's role to that of the "shepherd" of the criminal trial process:

> They are there to ensure that if the accused is convicted, that it was done according to the proper procedure and as a result of sufficient, convincing and admissible evidence. They are there only to force the Crown to play by the rules. He/she is not there to cheat in order to obtain an acquittal for the client.[56]

Lawyers who defend those accused of a crime—particularly violent crimes and homicide—are frequently asked how they can defend someone who is guilty. The answer is, guilty in whose eyes? Even those who have clearly committed an offence have the right to challenge the state to prove them guilty. And the accused person may actually be guilty of less serious offences than those alleged by the police and Crown. Ultimately, guilt is not a matter for defence counsel to decide. In the words of British lawyer and author John Mortimer, creator of the crusty Old Bailey barrister Horace Rumpole, defence counsel must learn "to refrain from judgement. There are plenty of people whose business it is to perform this unpleasant function: judges, juries and, perhaps, God. The defender's task is to listen and suspend disbelief."[57]

Persons without the resources to retain a lawyer may qualify to be represented by counsel under publicly funded legal aid programs. Such assistance is focused on criminal matters and family law cases where children have been taken into protective custody, leaving many people unable to retain a lawyer.[58] As legal aid coverage shrinks and legal fees rise, the number of persons representing themselves in court in civil and criminal cases is increasing, creating challenges for our adversarial system of justice. And despite the old saying that people who represent themselves in court have a fool for a client, many persons choose not to hire a lawyer. But someone with no formal legal training is obviously at a serious disadvantage when it comes to presenting a case in court. Trials also tend to take longer to complete as judges do their best to guide self-represented litigants and defendants through the trial process, consuming valuable courtroom time and creating additional strain on the justice system's limited resources.

Canada's Justice System: A Summary

So the judge who incurred a public backlash by imposing a four-year prison term for manslaughter was asserting judicial independence, a cornerstone of our system of justice. The teenagers accused of involvement in the swarming declined to testify because the Crown must prove them guilty and the right to silence means they were not obliged to explain their actions. The jurors hearing the gas-bar robbery case concluded they had a duty to acquit because the evidence did not establish, beyond a reasonable doubt, that the man accused of the crime was guilty. The woman accused of murder had the constitutional right to be presumed innocent until proven guilty and to have bail set at a reasonable amount while she awaited trial. And the defence lawyer agreed to take on the case of the convicted pedophile because all persons accused of a crime—no matter how horrendous the act or unpopular the person—have the right to make full answer and defence to the charges against them.

To understand how these rights and legal principles play out in the courtroom, it is necessary to examine in more detail the criminal and civil law and how cases proceed through the courts.

NOTES

1. Quoted in Dominique Enright, compiler and ed., *The Wicked Wit of William Shakespeare* (London: Michael O'Mara Books, 2002), 47.

2. S.M. Waddams, *Introduction to the Study of Law*, 4th ed. (Scarborough, ON: Carswell, 1992), 2.

3. David Paciocco, *Getting Away with Murder: The Canadian Criminal Justice System* (Toronto: Irwin Law, 1999), x.

4. H.G. Hanbury, *English Courts of Law*, 3rd ed. (Oxford: Oxford University Press, 1960), 11.

5. Waddams, supra note 2, at 7–8.

6. *Criminal Code*, RSC 1985, c. C-46, as amended.

7. Ibid., ss. 71, 292(1), and 49(a), respectively.

8. Ibid., ss. 430(1.1), 467.1(1), and 462.31(1), respectively.

9. *R v. Lifchus*, [1997] 3 SCR 320.

10. William Blackstone, *Commentaries on the Laws of England* (Oxford: Clarendon Press, 1765–1769), quoted in Elizabeth Knowles, ed., *The Oxford Dictionary of Quotations* (Oxford: Oxford University Press, 2001), 117.

11. *Constitution Act, 1982*, RSC 1985, app. II, no. 44.

12. *Criminal Code*, s. 213(1)(c).

13. *Canadian Charter of Rights and Freedoms*, part I of the *Constitution Act, 1982*, RSC 1985, app. II, no. 44.

14. Ronald Irving, comp., *"The Law Is a Ass": An Illustrated Collection of Legal Quotations* (London: Gerald Duckworth & Co., 1999), 65.

15. Ibid., at 66.

16. Cited in Waddams, supra note 2, at 84.

17. See Dean Jobb, "Breaking Up Gets Harder To Do," *Elm Street*, November 2002, 62–69. For a more detailed discussion of equitable principles, see Waddams, supra note 2, chapter 8.

18. *Civil Code of Quebec*, SQ 1991, c. 64.

19. *Constitution Act, 1982*, s. 52(1).

20. *R v. Kporwodu and Veno*, [2003] OJ no. 2521 (QL) (SCJ).

21. *R v. Buhay*, [2003] 1 SCR 631.

22. Kent Roach, *The Supreme Court on Trial: Judicial Activism or Democratic Dialogue* (Toronto: Irwin Law, 2001), 6.

23. *Reference re ss. 193 and 195.1(1)(c) of the Criminal Code*, [1990] 1 SCR 1123, (1990) 56 CCC (3d) 65, 77 CR (3d) 1.

24. For an overview of Supreme Court of Canada rulings handed down during the first two decades of Charter litigation, see Kirk Makin, "Rights Gone Wrong?" *Globe and Mail*, April 6, 2002.

25. Roach, supra note 22, at 8.

26. *RWDSU v. Dolphin Delivery Ltd.*, [1986] 2 SCR 573; *R v. Salituro*, [1991] 3 SCR 654.

27. *Supreme Court Act*, RSC 1985, c. S-26.

28. "Role of the Court," Supreme Court of Canada, http://www.scc-csc.gc.ca.

29. For a behind-the-scenes look at how provincial courts operate, see Kirk Makin, "In the Back Halls of Justice," *Globe and Mail*, April 26, 2003.

30. *Youth Criminal Justice Act*, SC 2002, c. 1.

31. *Code of Service Discipline*, part III of the *National Defence Act*, RSC 1985, c. N-5.

32. Waddams, supra note 2, at 84.

33. Irving, supra note 14, at 100.

34. Charter, s. 11(d).

35. Speech to the annual meeting of the Canadian Bar Association, Toronto, August 20, 1994, cited in Martin L. Friedland, *A Place Apart: Judicial Independence and Accountability in Canada* (Ottawa: Canadian Judicial Council, 1995), 1.

36. See Cristin Schmitz, "Unhappy Judges 'Wait and See' on Reduced Pay Hike," *The Lawyers Weekly*, June 9, 2006, 1, 3.

37. Friedland, supra note 35, at 2.

38. *R v. Sheppard*, 2001 PESCTD 56, paragraph 16.

39. See, for example, Jacob Ziegel, "Federal Judicial Appointments: Nothing Has Changed," *The Lawyers Weekly*, November 20, 2009, 5.

40. Cristin Schmitz, "Making Canadian Judicial History," ibid., March 10, 2006, 1, 18.

41. Dean Jobb, "When Judges Are Elected, Justice Goes Down to Defeat," *Chronicle-Herald* (Halifax), March 2, 2002. See also Chris Cobb, "Canadians Want To Elect Court," *Ottawa Citizen*, February 4, 2002. A poll suggested that two-thirds of Canadians supported the idea of electing judges, even though 60 percent of respondents also said judges, not politicians, should have the final say in determining the rights of citizens.

42. See Cristin Schmitz, "Judicial Council 'Inquiry' Urges Cosgrove's Removal," *The Lawyers Weekly*, December 19, 2008, 1, 3, and Schmitz, "Cosgrove Accepts His Fate and Resigns," ibid., April 10, 2009, 1, 24.

43. *Judges Act*, RSC 1985, c. J-1, s. 65.

44. For an overview of judicial discipline in Canada, see Friedland, supra note 35, chapter 5.

45. Cristin Schmitz, "SCC Sets Minimum Constitutional Parameters for Judicial Discipline," *The Lawyers Weekly*, June 15, 2001.

46. Jack Batten, *Judges* (Toronto: Macmillan of Canada, 1986), xi.

47. Charter, s. 11(f).

48. See Lynne Cohen, "The Endangered Civil Jury" (June 2002), *Canadian Lawyer* 32–40.

49. *Borowski v. Canada (Attorney General)* (1989), 47 CCC (3d) 1 (SCC).

50. *Controlled Drugs and Substances Act*, SC 1996, c. 19.

51. Gavin MacKenzie, *Lawyers and Ethics: Professional Responsibility and Discipline* (Scarborough, ON: Carswell, 1993), 6-5.

52. *R v. Boucher* (1954), 110 CCC 263 (SCC).

53. *Rondel v. Worsley*, [1969] 1 AC 191 (HL).

54. Waddams, supra note 2, at 121.

55. Marla Cranston, "The Hated Lawyer," *Daily News* (Halifax), April 27, 1997. See also Bruce Livesey, "The Tarnished Image" (February 1995), *Canadian Lawyer* 16–20.

56. Frank P. Hoskins, "The Players of a Criminal Trial," in Joel E. Pink and David C. Perrier, eds., *From Crime to Punishment: An Introduction to the Criminal Law System*, 4th ed. (Toronto: Carswell, 1999), 169–80, at 179.

57. John Mortimer, *Murderers and Other Friends* (Toronto: Penguin Books Canada, 1994), 8.

58. For a review of legal aid funding and coverage across Canada, see "Legal Aid Was Often in the News Throughout 2002," *The Lawyers Weekly*, December 20, 2002.

CHAPTER 2

Understanding Criminal and Civil Law

Introduction

When most people think of the law, they think of the criminal law, and for good reason. Crimes are often sensational and criminal cases attract the most public attention, whether it be through media reports of a high-profile trial or an episode of a television show like *Law & Order*. Given the media's emphasis on criminal cases, it may come as a surprise to learn that civil cases account for most of the workload in Canada's courts. A high divorce rate produces a steady stream of family law actions to divide property and to decide who gets custody of the children; business deals turn sour; and the *Canadian Charter of Rights and Freedoms*[1] continues to fuel an explosion of actions challenging laws and asserting minority rights.

But, as law professor Stephen Waddams has observed, the line between criminal and civil actions is not always well defined.[2] A person convicted of theft or fraud in the criminal courts may be ordered to pay money to the victim as restitution—in effect, a form of damages. Likewise, a judge hearing a civil case may award punitive damages to the plaintiff as a way of punishing a defendant whose conduct has been flagrant or high-handed. And while imprisonment is never imposed on the losing side in a civil case, a person involved in a lawsuit could be found in contempt and jailed for failing to obey a court order. To further complicate matters, some conduct can be both a crime and a civil matter. A punch to the face that broke a person's jaw, for example, would be prosecuted as the offence of assault causing bodily harm under the *Criminal Code*.[3] But the victim also would have the right to file a lawsuit to recover the cost of medical bills and any income lost due to inability to work.

This chapter examines each branch of the law and the procedure followed as cases make their way through the court system.

The Criminal Law

What Is a Crime?

For an act to be considered a crime, two features must be present. There must be a guilty act, known by the Latin term ***actus reus***. For example, section 265(1) of the *Criminal Code* defines assault as the intentional application of force on another person, or any attempt or threat to apply such force. Consider the following scenario: as two people pass on a crowded sidewalk, one inadvertently bumps into the other. The person struck is knocked to the ground, perhaps even injured. Should an incident like this be classified as a crime? Of course not. This person meant no harm to the other pedestrian. The second element of a crime, known as ***mens rea*** or guilty mind, is missing. If, however, there was evidence that the passerby was recklessly swinging his arms or had set out to knock down other pedestrians, a charge of assault could be laid. An intention to inflict harm is fundamental to our concept of what constitutes a crime. Society has no interest in seeing people punished for accidents or honest mistakes. For someone to be convicted of a crime, the Crown must prove that the person committed an illegal act and that the conduct was reckless or intentional.

Who Can Be Charged with a Crime?

Anyone over the age of 12 can be charged with a crime, with persons under the age of 18 dealt with using special procedures set out in the *Youth Criminal Justice Act*.[4] In most cases only the perpetrator is charged, but associates and those who provide help can also become entangled in the crime. An accomplice can be charged as a **party** to the offence; the most common example is the driver of the getaway car used to rob a bank, who can be charged with robbery even though she never set foot in the bank. Anyone who helps another person to break the law can be charged under a section of the *Criminal Code* that makes it an offence to *aid* in the commission of a crime.[5] For example, a clerk who opened the back door of a stereo store to allow a thief to enter could be charged. But the assistance must be intentional—a clerk who left the back door open by mistake could not be found guilty if a theft occurred. It is also an offence to **abet** (encourage) someone to break the law, and to **counsel** (advise) another person to commit a crime.[6] And anyone who helps the perpetrator of an offence escape or destroy evidence can be charged as an **accessory** to the crime.[7]

Anyone who joins others in a *common purpose* or plan to commit one crime can be charged with any other crime committed by an accomplice.[8] For example, if three persons agreed to break into a house and one of them attacked an occupant, all three could be charged with assault because each one knew or should have known that there was a risk of encountering someone inside the house. A person can also be charged with *conspiracy* to break the law even if the crime is never carried out; the offence is established once the person agrees to commit an offence.[9] It is also an offence to *attempt* to break the law.[10]

Defences

The *Criminal Code* sets out an array of defences that, if accepted by a court, entitle an accused person to an acquittal or lead to a conviction on a reduced charge. Someone who killed an assailant in *self-defence* would be found not guilty of murder.[11] An accused murderer can raise the common law defence of *drunkenness* if he can present evidence that he was too intoxicated to have intended to kill. Likewise, someone provoked into lashing out at another person in a sudden, deadly fury can plead *provocation* as a defence to a charge of murder.[12] If a judge or jury accepts the defence of drunkenness or provocation, the person would be acquitted of murder but convicted of **manslaughter**, a less serious offence defined as an unintentional killing that results from an illegal act.

Accused persons may also be able to put forward the defence of *alibi*, presenting evidence to show they could not have committed the offence because they were somewhere else when the crime occurred. Some persons who knowingly broke the law may be able to rely on the defence of *necessity* to escape conviction; a hiker caught in a blizzard could advance this defence to justify breaking into a remote cabin in search of shelter.[13] Finally, persons found to be suffering from a mental disorder when they committed an offence would qualify for the defence of mental disorder because they would not possess the guilty mind required for a conviction. Such persons would be declared *not criminally responsible* and detained, if necessary, in a psychiatric facility.[14]

Categories of Offences

All crimes are not created equal. In Canada there are three categories of offences—summary conviction, indictable, and hybrid.

Summary Conviction

The least serious crimes are known as **summary conviction offences**—acts such as shoplifting, vandalism, impaired driving where bodily harm does not result, thefts and fraud involving less than $5,000, and minor assaults that do not cause injury. These allegations account for most of the workload of the courts; statistics compiled in seven provinces and two territories show that impaired driving and common assault combined account for more than one-quarter of all offences dealt with at the provincial/territorial court level.[15] Under the *Criminal Code*, the maximum penalty for these offences is typically a $5,000 fine and six months in jail. Provincial offences, such as illegal fishing or hunting, traffic violations, and liquor law violations, are summary conviction matters. Summary conviction charges under the *Criminal Code* must be filed within six months of the date that the offence occurred, unless the defendant agrees to extend the deadline. Some provincial legislation provides for a limitation period of a year or more for the filing of summary conviction charges. Under American law this category of minor offence is known as a misdemeanour.

Indictable

The most serious crimes—murder, manslaughter, armed robbery, violent physical and sexual assaults, thefts and fraud involving large sums of money—are classified as **indictable offences**. So are serious narcotics offences, such as the trafficking or smuggling of drugs. A conviction for these offences can bring a heavy fine and terms in custody that range from two years to life in prison. In keeping with the seriousness of these crimes and the potential for severe punishment, persons charged with an indictable offence have the right to a jury trial. There is no limit on when indictable charges can be filed, and there have been cases of persons being charged with murder and other serious crimes years or even decades after the offence occurred. A felony is the American equivalent of this type of crime.

Hybrid

Some offences fall into a third category known as **hybrid offences** (also called dual-procedure offences). As the name suggests, these crimes are a combination of summary conviction and indictable offences. The Crown attorney decides whether to pursue a hybrid offence as a summary conviction matter (known as *proceeding summarily*) or as an indictable one (known as *proceeding by indictment*).

The route taken determines the severity of the punishment that the accused can receive if convicted—a small fine or short jail sentence if the offence is prosecuted summarily, the possibility of a longer prison term if the offence is prosecuted by **indictment**. A hacker who caused minor damage to a computer database, for example, would most likely be charged with mischief and prosecuted summarily. But if the owner of the database suffered serious loss or damage, the mischief charge could be pursued by indictment and the hacker could face up to 10 years in prison if convicted.[16] When deciding how to proceed, prosecutors consider the seriousness of the offence and whether the accused has a record of previous crimes. For example, while most shoplifting offences are treated as summary conviction matters, a Crown attorney may opt to proceed by indictment against an accused shoplifter who has a long history of theft. In the case of a charge of assault causing bodily harm, the Crown will assess the severity of the victim's injuries in determining how to prosecute the offence.

Arrest and Police Powers

Citizens have the right to detain some offenders but, for the most part, the investigation of crime and the arrest of suspects are matters handled by provincial and municipal police forces and the Royal Canadian Mounted Police. In order to place someone under arrest, a police officer must have "reasonable and probable grounds"

Figure 2.1 The largest mass arrest in Canadian history occurred during the G20 Summit in Toronto in June 2010. Several journalists covering the protests claimed that their rights, along with those of many other citizens, were ignored by police, and the incident triggered broad public debate on police powers.
SOURCE: David Farrant/davidfarrant.ca

to believe that the person has committed an offence or is attempting to commit an offence. An arrest must be based on more than suspicion, but police are not expected to have absolute proof of guilt before taking someone into custody. As noted in Chapter 1, in most jurisdictions the charging decision is made by the police, usually after they have consulted a prosecutor about which charge is appropriate and whether there is enough evidence to support a prosecution.

Suspects may be apprehended at the scene of a crime or picked up on an arrest warrant. Police officers have the right to search a person who is placed under arrest but in most cases can seize evidence only after obtaining the person's consent or a court authorization known as a search warrant. To obtain a search warrant, investigators must take their suspicions to a judge or a justice of the peace, who will decide whether there is enough evidence of wrongdoing to justify a search. The Charter protects citizens from being arbitrarily detained, jailed, or searched by police.[17] If an arrest is justified and conducted properly, a suspect who struggles or refuses to co-operate could be charged with resisting arrest. The Charter also requires the police to inform those arrested of the charges they face and to allow them an opportunity to speak to a lawyer.[18] Police must provide the names of state-funded lawyers who are on call to provide legal advice to those in custody.

Charges under the *Criminal Code* and other statutes are set out in an **information**. This is a public document, filed with the provincial court, that discloses the name of the accused, the name of the victim (if there is one), when and where the offence allegedly occurred, and the precise section of the *Criminal Code* or other statute that the authorities claim has been breached. In most cases there is no arrest; police file an information and the accused is served with a summons to appear in court at a later date to answer to the charges.

Legal Rights of Accused Persons

The contest between the state and the individual accused of committing an offence is invariably an unequal one. No one, no matter how wealthy or powerful, can match the resources of the state. This is especially true for the large number of criminal defendants who cannot afford a lawyer and must rely upon legal aid to defend them. To provide a level playing field and to guard against a possible abuse of power by the authorities, the Charter and the common law afford a number of rights and safeguards to those accused of crimes. These rights are founded on the principle that no one should be convicted of a crime without **due process**—the right to be regarded as innocent until proven guilty, to remain silent, and to have a fair trial. When critics complain that the justice system puts the rights of the accused ahead of those of victims of crime, they overlook the importance of ensuring, as far as humanly possible, that only the truly guilty are convicted. It should be borne in mind, as well, that these are the legal rights of every citizen, not special rights created to shield criminals from the full weight of the law.

Presumption of Innocence and Burden of Proof on the Crown

Every accused, at every stage of a prosecution, has the right to be treated as an innocent person until declared guilty by a judge or a jury. The media often lose sight of this crucial concept, producing news reports of arrests in which police officials or community members express relief that a crime has been solved even though the accused person has yet to face a court of law. The long-established common law right to be presumed innocent is enshrined in section 11(d) of the Charter, which encompasses the principle that the Crown must present sufficient evidence to prove beyond a reasonable doubt that the defendant committed the crime.[19]

The Right to Silence

The burden on the Crown is consistent with the right to silence, which ensures that defendants are not compelled to explain or justify their actions at any stage of a prosecution. From the moment of arrest, every citizen has the right to remain silent. Suspects must provide their name and address but are not required to answer questions or to give a statement to police. Any additional information they provide can be used as evidence against them in court. The Supreme Court of Canada has ruled that the right to remain silent upon arrest is protected under section 7 of the Charter, which gives every Canadian "the right to life, liberty and security of the person and the right not to be deprived thereof except in accordance with the principles of fundamental justice."[20]

The right to silence continues in the courtroom. Section 11(c) of the Charter shields accused persons from being forced to testify at their trial. Nor are they required to prove their innocence by calling other witnesses in their defence. The right to silence is consistent with the presumption of innocence as well as the requirement that the Crown prove guilt.

The Right to a Fair Trial

Every defendant has the right to make full answer and defence to criminal charges under the Charter's guarantee of fundamental justice.[21] Section 11(d) of the Charter affords accused persons the right to be presumed innocent "until proven guilty according to law in a fair and public hearing by an independent and impartial tribunal." This right enshrines the concepts of **open justice**—that the business of the courts is open to public scrutiny—and judicial independence that are cornerstones of our justice system.

Evidence

Most of the information presented in the courtroom is **direct evidence**—what a witness personally saw or experienced. The courts also accept **circumstantial evidence**—something that links the accused to the offence, such as clothing or belongings left at the scene of a crime. All evidence must be introduced through the use of a witness. Documents and photographs may be introduced as evidence if a witness is able to vouch for their origin and contents. Similarly, weapons, clothing worn by a victim or suspect, and other physical items that the Crown or defence seeks to introduce as evidence, must first be identified by a witness. Evidence must also be relevant to the specific allegations before the court. Witnesses are not permitted to offer opinions on what may have happened, with the exception of specialists in fields such as medicine, science, and forensic techniques. Once a judge reviews their credentials and accepts

When Accused Criminals "Walk" ...

It is essential that writers understand the basic principles and rights under-lying the justice system when they tackle crime stories and criminal law issues. Otherwise, the result can be a serious distortion of how the courts operate and how crime is detected, prosecuted, and punished. Consider the opening paragraphs of this news report of a high-profile Nova Scotia trial:

> Defence lawyers for the six men accused of beating Darren Watts into a coma outside a Halifax frat house seem sure their clients will walk.
>
> So sure, in fact, they didn't call any evidence or bring any witnesses forward after prosecutor Craig Botterill closed the Crown's case yesterday in Nova Scotia Supreme Court. (Source: Halifax *Daily News*, February 17, 1996.)

The journalist who wrote this story—and the editors who allowed it to see the light of day in print—failed to grasp some of the most fundamental principles of the Canadian justice system. As a result, the story perpetuates the image of defendants getting an easy ride from courts that are soft on criminals.

Would the same report have appeared if the writer had understood the right to silence and the presumption of innocence? Accused persons are not compelled to answer police questions after arrest or to testify in court, and they have the right to call no evidence in their defence. For exercising the legal rights granted to all Canadians under the *Charter of Rights and Freedoms*, these defendants and their lawyers were portrayed as defiant, even cocky. The tenor of the article is best reflected in the use of the term "their clients will walk," which betrays the writer's distaste for a justice system that sets people free if the state fails to prove the charges against them. The Crown must prove guilt beyond a reasonable doubt, a high standard that ensures that many ac-cused persons—including some who may well be guilty—will "walk."

---

them as experts, these witnesses can present the results of scientific tests and may offer opinions that are based on the evidence before the court.

Second-hand information known as **hearsay**—what a witness overheard other people saying about a crime or the accused—is generally not usable in court. Accused persons cannot be forced to incriminate themselves or, in most cases, to testify against their spouse. These and other rules of evidence are set out in the *Canada Evidence Act*.[22] The courts also examine closely any statement that an accused person makes to a police officer or other authority figure. Judges will investigate how the interroga-tion was conducted to ensure that the confession or other statement was made vol-untarily. Statements made in response to promises or threats or as a result of prolonged or aggressive questioning may be ruled inadmissible as evidence.[23]

Procedure in Criminal Cases

When a person is charged with a crime, he or she is brought before a judge, and the courts assume control of the process. The case will be dealt with swiftly if the accused person decides not to contest a charge and pleads guilty upon first appearing in court or if charges are withdrawn. But in fact, only one in five cases is dealt with in a single court appearance. It is more common for cases to take many months to make their way through pre-trial proceedings and trial. If a verdict is appealed in the higher courts, a case may take years to complete.

The following is an overview of how a prosecution unfolds.

Arraignment

An accused person's first appearance in court is usually for a hearing known as an **arraignment**, held before a provincial court judge or a justice of the peace. The case will likely be one of many brought before the court that day; as the names of defendants are called, the judge or justice usually reads out the allegations against each one. Because defendants and their lawyers already have a copy of the information, they sometimes waive the right to a formal reading of the charges. It is common for defendants and their counsel to seek an **adjournment** of a week or two, giving them time to examine the allegations and to formulate a response.

Disclosure of Crown Evidence

Before the accused person enters a **plea** or chooses a court for trial, the Crown must disclose the evidence that the police have gathered. The Supreme Court of Canada has ruled that defendants have the right to review the evidence against them, to prevent abuses such as the production of a surprise witness to "ambush" the defence at trial. The Crown attorney must divulge all police reports, witness statements, and any other relevant evidence known to the authorities. This includes information that may exonerate the accused as well as evidence that the Crown does not intend to put before the court.[24] Judges are sometimes asked to settle disputes over how much information must be disclosed, and the courts have halted prosecutions in cases where the Crown's withholding of information has violated the defendant's Charter right to make a full answer and defence.

Disclosure in most cases is a one-way street—an accused person is not required to disclose any information to the Crown. An exception is made where a defendant claims to be innocent because he was somewhere else when the crime was committed. In this case, an accused person must notify the Crown that the defence of alibi will be raised, enabling the police to locate and interview witnesses who may support the defendant's story.

Election and Plea

"Election and plea" is the term for an accused person's formal response to the charges, but it is a bit of a misnomer. The **election**—the defendant's choice of which court will hear the trial—determines whether a plea is even made at this stage of a criminal proceeding. Pleas are entered before the court that will ultimately try the case. The classification of the offence—summary conviction, indictable, or hybrid—in turn determines which level of court can hear the trial and whether the defendant has the right to have a say in the matter.

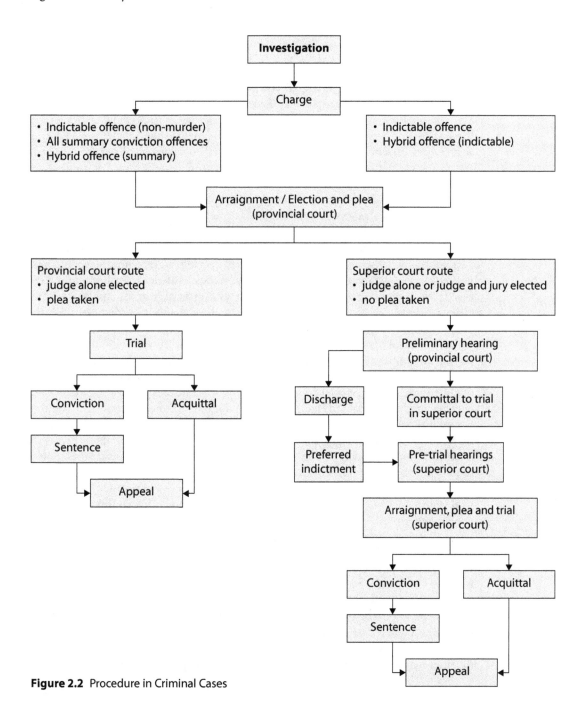

Figure 2.2 Procedure in Criminal Cases

Summary conviction offences must be tried in provincial court, so defendants have no right to elect a higher court for trial and must enter a plea upon their arraignment. If the defendant pleads not guilty, a date will be set for trial. If the defendant pleads guilty, the provincial court judge will either pass sentence immediately or set a date for a sentencing hearing.

Persons facing most indictable offences have the right to choose which court will hear their trial. Indictable offences can be heard in a provincial court or in a superior court, the latter providing a defendant with the further option of trial before a judge sitting alone or before a judge and jury. Exceptions are first- and second-degree murder and rare offences, such as piracy and treason, which once carried the death penalty; these allegations must be tried in superior court. On all other indictable charges, an accused person who selects trial before a provincial court judge will then enter a plea. If a plea of guilty is entered, the case advances to sentencing; if a plea of not guilty is entered, a date for trial is set.

An accused person's decision to face trial in superior court on an indictable charge, however, triggers a more complicated procedure. First, no plea is entered since the case is not yet before the trial court. (It is common for the media to report, erroneously, that a person facing an indictable offence was arraigned and pleaded not guilty.) Second, the judge sets a date for a preliminary hearing, an interim proceeding held in provincial court to assess whether there is enough evidence to justify sending the case to superior court for trial. Third, at the preliminary hearing, the judge either orders the trial or discharges the accused. Finally, if the judge orders the trial, the accused is re-arraigned in superior court.

In the case of hybrid or dual-procedure offences, the Crown's decision whether to pursue the summary conviction or indictable route determines the election and plea options open to the defendant. Hybrid offences prosecuted as summary conviction matters remain in provincial court, whereas hybrid offences pursued by indictment give defendants the right to elect trial in superior court. Superior court trials tend to be more expensive and take longer to complete, particularly if a jury is hearing the case. The prospect of triggering elaborate and time-consuming trials to deal with relatively minor offences helps ensure that Crown attorneys do not misuse their power to pursue hybrid charges as indictable offences.

Some accused persons who have elected trial in superior court may later re-elect trial in provincial court, a move that often signals an intention to forgo a trial and enter a guilty plea.[25]

Release Before Trial

After a person has been arrested and charged with a crime, a decision must be made whether she should be freed until a trial is held. The police release many accused persons on an **undertaking**, a recognizance, or other written promise to show up in court to answer to the charge. A defendant may have to agree to have no contact with the victim or other people connected to the crime. If the defendant is considered dangerous, has a significant criminal record, or is accused of a serious crime, the authorities may seek to have the person kept in custody pending trial.

Show Cause (Bail) Hearings

Anyone denied release on a promise to appear in court has the right to be arraigned within 24 hours so that a judge or justice of the peace can deal with the person's possible release on **bail** (also known as **judicial interim release**). Because everyone is presumed innocent until proven guilty, the Charter gives accused persons the right "not to be denied reasonable bail without just cause."[26] This right to seek bail applies even to serious crimes such as murder, armed robbery, and violent sexual assault. For all charges other than murder, bail is determined at a hearing held before a provincial court judge. In the case of murder, a judge of the superior court—the court with exclusive jurisdiction over the offence—decides whether the person can be released while awaiting trial. A person who appeals a conviction for a crime is entitled to apply for release on bail until the appeal court makes a ruling.

A bail hearing is known as a "show cause" hearing because the Crown attorney must establish that there is cause or reason to keep the person in custody. Defendants do not have to prove that they deserve to be released. The Crown presents a summary of the evidence gathered by the police, to illustrate the strength of its case, as well as information about the person's record of violence or past crimes.

The grounds for denying bail are limited. A judge must be convinced that the accused person, if released, will flee the jurisdiction, commit more offences, or try to intimidate witnesses. If the allegations are serious, a judge can deny bail if she determines that detention is justified to maintain public confidence in the administration of justice. Where there is evidence of mental instability, the accused may be remanded to a psychiatric facility for up to 30 days, where doctors will determine whether the person is capable of instructing a lawyer and therefore fit to stand trial.

If the judge rules that the accused can be released, the person may be freed with or without conditions. Release may be conditional on the accused's observing a nightly curfew, not consuming alcohol or illegal drugs, or agreeing to stay away from certain places or anyone who will be a witness at the trial. Accused persons also may be required to deposit a sum of money with the court. If the defendant does not have enough resources to post bail, a relative or friend may be able to act as a **surety**, offering their own money to meet the bail requirement or pledging their home or other property as security. If the accused fails to return to court as directed, the money or property may be forfeited to the state to cover the value of the bond.

A judge's refusal to grant bail can be appealed to a higher court for review, as can the terms of bail imposed, such as the amount of money to be posted. Some defendants who are granted bail remain in custody because they are unable to find a surety or raise the money needed to post bail.

Plea Negotiation

Defendants can plead guilty at any point during a prosecution. If they do, it is often as a result of a **plea negotiation** between the defence lawyer and the prosecutor. Such agreements are common—statistics made public in 2002 showed that 80 percent of all criminal charges filed in Ontario resulted in an agreement on plea before trial, up from 60 percent five years earlier.[27] Such arrangements can take many forms, and by one definition can encompass "any agreement by the accused to plead guilty in return for the prosecutor's agreeing to take or refrain from taking a particular course of action."[28] A typical agreement may see some charges withdrawn in exchange for a guilty plea to other charges, or the substitution of less serious charges. The defendant may agree to testify against a co-accused or provide information about other offences. There is usually an agreement on a suggested sentence that may well be lighter than normal. Although judges usually accept such recommendations on punishment, they are free to impose any other sentence that the law provides for the offence. A judge must have compelling reasons to justify a decision to ignore a joint Crown–defence recommendation and mete out a harsher penalty.

Plea negotiation is popularly known as **plea bargaining**, a term that suggests an accused person is getting a break or special treatment. But these agreements can play an essential role in keeping the court process running smoothly, saving the justice system the cost of conducting trials, and sparing victims the ordeal of testifying in court. An American legal scholar has this to say about the controversy over plea bargaining:

> To law-and-order types, it is abominable, because it lets bad guys off too easily (or so they think); to those who are interested in the rights of defendants, it is objectionable because it replaces fair trial with a kind of haggling, invisible, unfair, unaccountable. But plea bargaining is devilishly hard to get rid of. It is at least an attempt to solve a recurrent problem of criminal justice: how to handle routine cases without swamping the whole system.[29]

While plea negotiations occur in private, any agreement that results must be revealed in court and is ultimately subject to public scrutiny and the approval of a judge. For defendants, accepting a plea bargain and acknowledging guilt usually brings punishment for fewer or less serious offences, which may well have been the outcome if the case had gone to trial. For the Crown, rejecting a plea-bargain offer means giving up the certainty of a conviction on lesser charges for the possibility of a conviction on the sought-after charges. "When properly conducted, these 'resolution discussions' benefit the accused, victims, witnesses and the general public," notes one policy manual for prosecutors. "Counsel can often resolve issues of procedure, plea, fact and sentence to such an extent that running a case through the full criminal process would add little to what counsel achieve informally."[30]

Withdrawing and Staying Charges

A Crown attorney has the discretion to withdraw charges or to offer no evidence at any time as a case proceeds. This must be done in open court, and a judge will be asked to dismiss the charges, ending the prosecution. Charges may be dropped because the prosecution's case is weak, evidence has been lost, or a key witness refuses to testify. Such decisions are final—the charges cannot be revived. The Crown also has the power under the *Criminal Code* to stay a prosecution temporarily, shelving the case for up to a year to give the police more time to investigate. Unless the prosecution is reinstated within a year, however, the charges lapse and can no longer be pursued.[31] One study showed that nearly one-third of all cases dealt with at the provincial court level resulted in the charges being stayed or withdrawn.[32]

Judicial Stays Versus Crown Stays in Criminal Cases

A criminal case may end with the imposition of a **stay of proceedings**. There are two kinds of stays—Crown and judicial. Section 579 of the *Criminal Code* enables a Crown attorney to stay charges for up to a year; if the prosecution is not reactivated within that period, the charges lapse and the information or indictment cannot be revived.

Judges have the power to impose a stay before or during trial to protect accused persons if they have suffered serious violations of their rights under the *Charter of Rights and Freedoms*, or if the Crown or police have abused their powers. A judicial stay is permanent and the prosecution can be revived only if an appeal court overturns the stay. The Supreme Court of Canada has said that judges must use their power to stay charges sparingly and only where abuse of the court process is so extreme that it would offend the community's sense of decency and fair play if the prosecution were allowed to continue (*R v. Conway*, [1989] 1 SCR 1659).

The Preliminary Hearing

Also known as a *preliminary inquiry*, the **preliminary hearing** is a pre-trial proceeding held to assess the strength of the Crown's case when a person charged with an indictable offence elects trial in superior court. Preliminary hearings act as a filter, enabling the courts to stop prosecutions based on flimsy allegations and sparing citizens the expense and anxiety of an unnecessary trial. The hearing also offers the defence a chance to review the evidence gathered by police and to challenge Crown witnesses. An accused person has the right to skip the preliminary hearing and to proceed directly to trial in superior court. Many defendants do, for various reasons: the prosecution's duty to disclose evidence often provides the information needed to assess the strength of the Crown's case, the person may want to avoid paying legal fees for two proceedings, or the person may have decided to plead guilty.

A preliminary hearing unfolds much like a trial. The Crown presents its evidence and the defence has an opportunity to question each witness. Legal arguments over the admissibility of evidence are also dealt with. The defence also has the right to present evidence but it is rare for an accused person to testify or call witnesses. Although a preliminary hearing resembles a dry run for a trial, it is not a test of whether an accused person is guilty. The hurdle facing the Crown is low—the judge need only be satisfied that there is some evidence that could lead a jury, if it accepts the evidence as true, to convict. (This test is applied even if the trial is slated to be heard only by a judge.) The Crown is usually able to establish that there is some evidence of guilt, so most preliminary hearings end with a **committal**—an order for the accused to stand trial. But the judge may rule that the Crown's case is so weak that no trial is warranted. If so, the accused will be discharged. A **discharge** is like an acquittal and it ends the prosecution. A defendant facing multiple allegations could be ordered to stand trial on some charges and discharged on others. The judge also has the power to amend charges or add new ones, as the evidence dictates, before sending the case to trial.

Preferred Indictments

The Crown has the right to issue a **preferred indictment** (also known as a *direct indictment*) to take an accused person straight to trial, a procedure that can be exercised only with the approval of the attorney general or justice minister. Indictments can be preferred at any stage of the pre-trial process but they tend to be used after an accused person has been discharged at a preliminary hearing, if the Crown still believes that there is enough evidence to secure a conviction at trial.

Pre-Trial Motions

Legal arguments over the admissibility of evidence and other legal issues are usually dealt with during the trial. However, superior courts often hold pre-trial hearings weeks or months before trial to deal with lengthy and complicated matters such as Charter motions and defence applications to stay charges.

The Trial

Trials unfold in essentially the same fashion at all levels of court, with the exception of the special procedures required if a jury is hearing the case.

Superior court trials begin with the reading of the indictment, followed by the accused person's plea of not guilty. In jury trials, counsel select the jury first, and the accused enters a plea in the jury's presence.

A more streamlined approach is taken at the provincial court level. The case is called and, because the accused has already entered a plea on arraignment, the prosecutor simply calls the Crown's first witness and the trial begins.

The Crown's Case

The Crown presents its case first. Before calling witnesses, prosecutors usually make an opening statement to the jury outlining the evidence against the defendant, but they are not obliged to do so. Prosecutors must not ask leading questions, ones that suggest the answer. This rule ensures that witnesses describe, in their own words, what happened. The defence has the right to cross-examine the witnesses to challenge their testimony or to draw out information favourable to the accused. Defence counsel tend to focus on the loose ends of an investigation—the unanswered questions and missing evidence that may raise the reasonable doubt needed for an acquittal. The prosecutor can ask further questions on redirect examination, but only to explore new information brought out under defence questioning.

The Case for the Defence

Once the Crown rests its case, the defence has the right to call its own witnesses. If the prosecution's case appears weak, the accused person may ask the judge for a **directed verdict** of not guilty, but such motions rarely succeed. While defence counsel may opt to call no evidence, usually some defence witnesses are put forward. If the Crown has established a *prima facie* **case**—evidence sufficient, on its face, to meet the burden of proof beyond a reasonable doubt—a defendant who offers no evidence to contradict those facts is almost certain to be convicted.

The defence can make an opening statement outlining its position and introducing the witnesses to be called. Although the right to silence means that accused persons are under no obligation to testify, they often do—particularly in a jury trial, where a dozen citizens inundated with Crown evidence may be eager to hear the defendant's explanation. The Crown attorney has the right to cross-examine all defence witnesses, including the defendant.

Voir Dire Hearings

At any point during the trial, the Crown prosecutor or defence lawyer may ask that a *voir dire* **hearing** be convened. The judge will hear legal arguments from both sides and make a ruling on any matter that is in dispute, such as whether evidence is admissible or a question posed to a witness is proper. In jury trials, jurors will be asked to leave the courtroom during this "trial within a trial" so that they are not exposed to information that is not admissible in court or that could prejudice the accused's case.

Rebuttal Evidence

If the defence has called evidence, the Crown attorney has the right to call rebuttal evidence. This is not a chance for the prosecutor to get a second kick at the can—rebuttal evidence must relate to new information introduced as part of the defence case. The defence, in turn, has the right to introduce its own rebuttal evidence but only on subjects that arose from the Crown's rebuttal evidence.

Mistrials

At any point during a jury trial, the judge may declare a **mistrial** if it appears that the accused person's right to a fair trial has been compromised. Mistrials are usually declared if jurors have been exposed to inadmissible evidence or prejudicial information about the accused person, either through media reports or improper statements made in the courtroom. If a mistrial is declared, the accused person will be required to stand trial before a new jury at a later date, unless the prosecution decides not to pursue the charges.

Closing Arguments and Charge to the Jury

Once the evidence has been presented, lawyers for each side present a **closing argument**—a speech analyzing the evidence and suggesting how it supports the accused person's guilt or innocence. If the defence has chosen not to call evidence, the Crown attorney is the first to present a closing argument (also known as a summation) and defence counsel get the last word. When defence evidence has been called, however, the order is reversed and the Crown attorney makes the final submission.

In jury trials, the next step is for the judge to deliver the **charge to the jury**. The judge reviews the evidence for the jury and explains how the law applies to the allegations before the court. At the conclusion of these instructions, jurors file out of the courtroom to discuss the evidence in private and to try to reach a verdict.

Verdict

The judge or jury must assess whether each witness was believable and, where there are two versions of events, decide who is telling the truth. This is known as **finding the facts** of a case. These findings will be applied to the law to determine whether the accused person is guilty or not guilty.

If there is no jury, the judge may adjourn the case for days or weeks before reaching a verdict. The defendant's guilt or innocence will be announced in the courtroom and the judge may provide written reasons for her decision. Jurors deliberate in secret and the law forbids them from revealing what has been discussed in the jury room.[33] They may return to the courtroom to ask the judge for further instructions or to hear a replay of the taped testimony. Jurors are allowed to return home during the trial but, once deliberations begin, they are sequestered and billeted overnight at a hotel, if necessary, until a verdict is reached. Jurors must return a unanimous verdict; a deadlock—known as a hung jury—means a new trial will be held unless the Crown decides to withdraw the charges.

Several outcomes are possible. The judge or jury may find that there is not enough evidence to prove guilt beyond a reasonable doubt. Or the evidence may support a conviction on some charges and not others. Or an accused person may be acquitted of a charge in the indictment but convicted of an *included offence*, an offence that forms part of a more serious one. A person found not guilty is free to go and can only be tried again on the same charges if an appeal court overturns the verdict and orders a new trial. If the accused is convicted, the final step in the trial process is for the judge to pass sentence.

Sentencing and Parole

When an accused person pleads guilty or is convicted at trial, it is the judge's duty to impose punishment. The *Criminal Code* dictates the maximum custodial sentence for each offence and, for some offences, a minimum amount of time that must be served behind bars. Maximum sentences range from up to six months in jail for minor offences such as shoplifting and vandalism to terms of 10, 14 years, or life in prison for serious, violent crimes such as armed robbery, aggravated assault, manslaughter, and murder. Maximum penalties are rarely imposed and are reserved for the most heinous acts and the most incorrigible offenders. Sentences of less than two years in custody are served in jails operated by provincial or territorial governments, which is why judges sometimes impose a sentence of "two years less a day." Judges can direct that offenders serve jail terms of less than 90 days on an intermittent or part-time basis, usually on weekends.

Those sentenced to two years or more are held in federal prisons under the jurisdiction of Correctional Service Canada. Their applications for early release are heard by the National Parole Board. Federal inmates may ask to be released on day parole after six months and can seek full parole once they have served one-third of their sentence. Most of those denied parole at these early stages are released automatically after they reach the two-thirds mark of their sentence. Those considered dangerous and likely to commit further crimes may be kept in custody until they complete their full sentence. The courts sometimes bear the brunt of public criticism of early-release policies, but judges have no say in the granting of parole and must ignore the possibility of early release when deciding on an appropriate prison term.

Judges have an array of other sentencing options, and some may be imposed in combination. The offender can be required to pay a *fine* to the state that could reach into the thousands of dollars, and he may face a jail term if the fine is not paid by a certain date. The judge may order an offender to pay **restitution** to the victim to compensate for injuries or the loss of money or property. Offenders may be placed on **probation** for up to three years. During a probationary term, they must report to a probation officer and may have to fulfill other requirements, such as observing a nightly curfew, abstaining from the use of alcohol or illegal drugs, completing community service work, or undergoing treatment or counselling. Breaching a condition of probation is a criminal offence. In some cases, a judge also has the option of imposing a **suspended sentence**. Instead of passing the sentence, the judge places the offender on probation; if the offender violates the terms of probation, the judge may then impose the penalty for the original offence as well as an additional penalty for breaching probation.

When the crime is minor, first-time offenders who are unlikely to commit further crimes may be granted a **discharge**, leaving them without a criminal record. There are two types—absolute discharges, which come with no strings attached, and discharges that are conditional on the offender completing volunteer work in the community or other requirements. In 1995, Parliament amended the *Criminal Code* to require judges to consider alternatives to incarceration whenever possible, a measure intended to reduce the number of persons behind bars and to help control the cost of operating the prison system. Judges may impose **conditional sentences**, to be served in the community under house arrest, if a jail term of less than two years would have been appropriate and the offender is not considered a danger to others.[34] These sentences come with strict conditions—the offender usually can leave home only to go to work, to attend religious services or medical appointments, or to run brief errands. Violating any of these conditions could result in the offender being ordered to serve a jail term. Public and media outrage often greet a sentence of house arrest, and judges often bear the brunt of this criticism even though Parliament, not the courts, decided it is an appropriate form of punishment.

Sentencing is an art, not a science. In crafting the appropriate punishment, a judge must consider a host of factors, including the circumstances of the offender and the gravity of the offence. A number of principles are brought to bear on the sentencing decision. The fundamental purpose of sentencing is to promote public safety and to foster respect for the law. To this end, the penalty must be severe enough to deter the offender from committing further crimes while making it clear to other persons that there are consequences to breaking the law. The punishment must reflect society's denunciation of criminal acts, particularly crimes of violence and exploitation. The punishment selected must be in keeping with the seriousness of the crime and its prevalence. Justice, too, must be tempered by the need to rehabilitate offenders; it is in the long-term interest of society to help criminals become law-abiding, productive citizens.[35]

Sentences are formulated on a case-by-base basis. Judges review sentences that other courts have meted out for similar offences, to ensure that the sentence is consistent with these previous sentences and that the punishment fits the crime. They also take into account aggravating factors. For example, if the offender held a position of authority or trust, or a weapon was used to commit the offence, a harsher sentence may be warranted. On the other hand, mitigating factors such as an offender's age or lack of a previous criminal record often result in a lighter sentence. Judges may also direct probation officers to prepare a pre-sentence report that outlines an offender's background, work history, prospects for rehabilitation, and any prior record of crimes. These reports help the judge formulate an appropriate sentence. As well, the victim or members of the victim's family may present a written statement describing the impact of the crime, providing more information for the judge to consider in arriving at a suitable sentence.

If an offender is sent to prison for more than one offence, the judge has two options. In the first option, the sentence for each offence is rolled into one and served *concurrently*. For example, if a judge imposes a sentence of four years for one offence and a sentence of six years for another offence, the offender will serve six years. In the second option, the sentences are served *consecutively*, one after the other. If consecutive sentences are imposed, judges must ensure that the total sentence is not unreasonable given the nature of the crimes and the circumstances of the offender. An exception is made for multiple convictions arising from the same event or a "single criminal enterprise," which are punished with concurrent sentences.[36]

Special Cases

In certain cases, the *Criminal Code* requires judges to take special note of the nature of the crime or the circumstances of the victim. Stiffer penalties are to be imposed where the crime was motivated by racial hatred or an intolerance of minorities; where the victim was the offender's spouse or child; or where the offender was a teacher, counsellor, or other authority figure who held a position of trust in relation to the victim.[37] Special efforts are to be made to impose non-custodial sentences on aboriginal offenders, who traditionally have accounted for a disproportionately high number of prison inmates.[38]

Alternative Sentencing

Alternative means of punishing offenders have also been developed to deal with minor crimes. **Diversion programs** bypass the courts, enabling the police to refer first-time offenders who readily admit their guilt to a probation officer, who will direct the person to undertake counselling or perform community service. Those convicted of minor offences may be candidates for **restorative justice programs**. Based on the sentencing circles of aboriginal cultures, these programs enable a judge to seek input and advice from the community on the appropriate sentence. Typically, the judge, Crown attorney, defence lawyer, and offender will meet in private with police officers, social workers, and the victim to discuss the offence, why it happened, and how it should be punished. Often, the consensus will be some form of restitution to the victim, or community service, coupled with treatment or counselling, but the group may suggest a jail term as the proper punishment. The judge has the final say on the sentence imposed and is not bound to accept the recommendations of the group.

Appeals

Appeals are the justice system's mechanism for correcting the mistakes that are bound to occur in any system subject to human error and lapses in judgment. A judge may misinterpret how the law applies to the case before the court, or incorrectly explain a legal principle to a jury that then finds a defendant guilty. Because it would create an injustice to allow such verdicts to stand unchallenged, appeals can be made to a higher court. A person convicted of a crime has the right to appeal both the conviction and a sentence that appears too harsh for the crime. Likewise, the Crown has the right to appeal the acquittal of a defendant or a sentence that prosecutors consider too lenient.

Appeals for the most part focus on the trial judge's rulings on legal issues as they arose: Were Charter rights breached? Was certain evidence inadmissible? Was the jury properly instructed about how the law applied in the case? It is the role of trial judges and juries to determine what happened and to assess whether witnesses have told the truth, so appeal courts rarely disturb such findings of fact. But in extreme cases, an appeal court may find that an error is so serious that the judge or jury has reached erroneous conclusions about the facts. If so, it is proper for the appeal court to intervene.

As we have seen, trials are heard in either provincial or superior court, depending on the seriousness of the crime. For summary conviction matters dealt with in provincial court, appeals are heard by a judge at the trial level of the superior court. These decisions, in turn, can be appealed to the next level, the court of appeal of the province or territory. Challenges to the outcome of all other criminal cases heard in provincial court, as well as of trials heard in superior court, go directly to the court of appeal. Only the Supreme Court of Canada can overturn the decision of a court of appeal.

At the appeal stage, each side puts its arguments into writing and has an opportunity to make a presentation at a hearing. If the issues are not complex, the judges may retire briefly and return to announce their ruling. But it is more common for the court to reserve its judgment and to release a decision in writing at a later date. Courts of appeal in each province have established rules that set out the process to be followed for appeals. Nova Scotia's Civil Procedure Rules, for example, require that written notice of an appeal be filed with the court within 30 days of the date of the verdict or, if the penalty is being challenged, no more than 30 days after the sentence was imposed.

If the appeal court finds that a legal error has been made, it has the power to overturn a conviction and to order a new trial. The court also may rule that the error was not serious enough to have affected the outcome, and allow the verdict to stand. If the court finds that there was not enough evidence to support the conviction, it has the power to acquit the defendant. But if the Crown is appealing a verdict of not guilty, the outcome will be either a ruling that upholds the acquittal or orders a new trial. An appeal court does not have the power to convict a person who has been acquitted of a crime at trial.

Young Persons and the Criminal Law

In April 2003 the federal government introduced the *Youth Criminal Justice Act* to govern how the justice system deals with young persons who break the law. The legislation replaced the *Young Offenders Act*,[39] which was criticized as too lenient yet was harsh enough to give Canada the highest rate of incarceration of young persons in the western world. In 1999 youth court judges heard 5,000 fewer cases than in 1991 but meted out 25,000 custodial sentences, an increase of 2,300 from the beginning of the decade. Over the same period, the rate of youth crime actually dropped by almost 5 percent.[40] The new Act's objective is to ensure that young persons who break the law are dealt with in a fair and consistent fashion, while recognizing that they may lack the maturity and insight to fully understand the consequences of their actions. It also recognizes that most youth crime is non-violent—shoplifting, other minor thefts, failure to appear in court, or breaching a probation order. Minor assaults account for almost half of all offences involving violence.

Under the *Youth Criminal Justice Act*, persons between the ages of 12 and 17 who are charged with crimes are dealt with in a separate court system. Those incarcerated for their crimes are held in special youth facilities, apart from adult inmates. Publication bans and strict controls over court records are used to shield the identities of those charged. The Act emphasizes non-custodial punishments for theft, break-ins, and other offences involving property while reserving jail time for offences of violence and repeat offenders. Three years after the legislation was implemented, one study found a 40 percent decrease in the incarceration rate for young people.[41] "Extra-judicial measures" have been introduced, which require the police to consider issuing warnings to those responsible for minor offences. The restorative justice model of convening a conference, where justice officials and community members confront an offender and recommend punishments, is also encouraged. When cases are dealt with in court, youth court judges must seek alternatives to detaining accused persons while they await trial. The *Youth Criminal Justice Act* also introduced new forms of punishment, including reprimands, supervision by probation officers, and orders to attend rehabilitative programs. However, in cases of murder and other serious crimes of violence, the Act enables youth court judges to punish offenders with the same sentence that an adult would receive.[42]

The Civil Law

The civil courts provide redress for injuries or losses that an individual or corporation has suffered at the hands of another party through an accident, a business transaction, or a malicious act that falls short of a crime. Most civil cases are of little interest to anyone other than the parties, which explains their lower profile in the media. Examples include disputes over the sale or location of property; complaints of patent infringement; claims of wrongful dismissal from a job; construction liens filed by tradespeople or contractors seeking payment for work done; accusations that a teacher, corporate director, or other person in a position of trust has breached his fiduciary duty to others; and divorces and other family law disputes. Most of the civil actions that make headlines deal with controversial or politically charged issues such as same-sex marriage, or they involve high-profile litigants. Some civil cases may alter the legal rights of all citizens—for example, an action may lead to a new interpretation of child custody rights or spousal support laws.

Torts

Most well-publicized civil actions fall into a wide category known as torts. A **tort** is any wrong that one party suffers as a result of the actions or omissions of another.

Criminal Versus Civil: Using the Correct Terminology

When civil actions make news, reporters and editors often make the mistake of applying the terminology they have learned in the criminal courts. Defendants on the losing end of a lawsuit are erroneously reported to have been charged, found guilty, and sentenced. Some terms are in fact interchangeable, so this confusion is understandable. But each branch of the law has its own expressions for the parties involved, the types of cases heard, the outcome, and the penalty imposed.

The party bringing a civil action or lawsuit before the courts is the **plaintiff**, an individual, corporation, government, or government actor that claims to have suffered damages due to the conduct of another. The Crown may pursue a lawsuit on the government's behalf but otherwise plays no role in the civil courts. The party alleged to have caused the damage is the **defendant**, not the accused, and civil defendants are *sued*, they are not charged or prosecuted.

As in criminal law, the judge makes a **finding**—but the defendant is not found guilty or convicted in the criminal law sense. Instead, the losing party is found to be *negligent*, to have *breached a contract*, or to be *liable to pay damages*. Finally, an *award of damages* is not a fine and judges *order* civil defendants to pay damages, they do not impose a sentence.

(An omission is something left out or not done.) In a complex modern society, where people and businesses interact in innumerable ways, conflicts and losses are inevitable. "The purpose of the law of torts," in the words of one legal text, "is to adjust these losses and to afford compensation for injuries sustained by one person as the result of the conduct of another."[43] As society and technology change, the courts are called upon to develop new torts. For example, the advent of the motor vehicle created a major field of tort law as the drivers responsible for car crashes faced lawsuits from accident victims seeking compensation for their injuries.

There are several major types of tort. **Nuisance** is a claim that can be made against someone who interferes with a person's right to enjoy her property. Homeowners living beside a business that operates around the clock or produces a stench could sue for damages or for an injunction to stop the disruptive noise or odour. **Battery** is the tort of assault, enabling someone who is beaten to seek damages for actions that would also support a prosecution under the criminal law. **Defamation**, a tort with a direct impact on writers and their work, enables persons who have been maligned in print or in a broadcast to sue for the alleged damage to their reputation (Chapter 4 examines defamation law and its implications for journalists). Most torts are based on acts of **negligence** that cause personal injury, such as traffic accidents and medical malpractice. The courts will assess a defendant's conduct against the standard of care that is reasonable in the circumstances to determine whether the plaintiff's claim is valid. Insurance covers most successful claims for negligence, so although lawsuits may be filed in the names of the individuals involved in a traffic accident or other incident, the legal battle is usually waged between insurance companies.

Contracts

Whereas tort law applies to everyone, the law of contracts is concerned with the promises and duties that have been agreed to between parties. By one definition, a **contract** is "an agreement giving rise to legally enforceable obligations binding the parties to it. The factor which distinguishes contractual obligations from other legal obligations is that they are based on the agreement of the contracting parties."[44] So if Company A agrees to buy a certain quantity of goods from Company B, and Company B fails to deliver, Company A has the legal right to sue the supplier for breach of contract. Most contracts are set out in writing but the courts will enforce the terms of a valid verbal contract—despite the wisecrack, attributed to Hollywood mogul Samuel Goldwyn, that "a verbal contract isn't worth the paper it's written on."[45]

Remedies

The usual outcome of a successful civil action is an award of **damages**—money to compensate for the injury. Defendants may be found to share responsibility for their own injuries, reducing the amount they can recover as damages. For example, a driver who was not at fault in a car accident will have his damage award reduced if he was not wearing a seat belt to protect himself. In actions for breach of contract, the defendant is usually ordered to pay damages for the plaintiff's losses, but in certain cases a court may grant the remedy of **specific performance**, requiring the defendant to fulfill the terms of the contract. **Punitive damages** may be awarded to punish a party who has acted maliciously or abused the court process. The losing party is usually ordered to pay a portion of the other side's legal bills, known as an order for **costs**. Other remedies that a court can impose include an **injunction**—an order that restrains the defendant party from taking an action likely to cause an injury—and writs of *certiorari* and *mandamus*, which are used to review decisions of officials, administrative tribunals, and lower courts.

Procedure in the Civil Courts

The rules that determine how a lawsuit unfolds are complex and vary from province to province. The following is an overview of the major stages of a civil case.

Pleading Stage

All civil actions start with an exchange of documents known as **pleadings**. In the movie *A Civil Action*, actor John Travolta portrays a plaintiff's lawyer who likens a lawsuit to a battle and observes that all battles start with a declaration of war. The document in which a plaintiff launches a lawsuit, and declares war, is known as a **statement of claim**. It names the plaintiff (or plaintiffs, if there is more than one), identifies the defendants, sets out the facts and allegations that form the basis for the claim, and indicates the types of damages or other remedies sought from the court.

Those named as defendants face a deadline for filing a **statement of defence**. This document recites the plaintiff's allegations, denying some or all of them, and may set out the defence's version of events. Failure to file a defence may lead a judge or court official to grant an order known as a **default judgment**, requiring the defendants to pay damages to the plaintiff. A defendant may also file a **demand for particulars**, a notice calling on the plaintiff to provide further information about the allegations before a defence is filed. A defendant may file a **counterclaim** that seeks damages from the plaintiff for alleged wrongdoing, launching a parallel lawsuit in which the defendant is the plaintiff. A defendant who contends that another person or company is fully or partially to blame for the plaintiff's loss would file a **third-party action**, a lawsuit bringing those parties into the litigation.

Civil cases take one of two routes: trial or application. The procedure for each is outlined below.

Trial Route

Most civil cases are set for trial in the superior court, where there is no limit on the amount or type of damages that can be awarded to a successful plaintiff. (Small claims courts, in contrast, hear actions involving smaller amounts of money—less than $25,000 (the limit varies from province to province). Lawyers act as small claims adjudicators, there is little paperwork involved in pursuing a claim, and most parties argue their case without counsel.)

At the superior court level, after the pleading stage, the two sides exchange documents relevant to the claim, such as letters, internal memos, and experts' reports. Although a description of these documents may be filed with the court, the documents themselves usually remain private unless they are produced during the trial. Each party has the right to question the opposing side's witnesses at **examinations for discovery**—private sessions usually held in a law firm's boardroom. Witnesses testify under oath and the examinations are transcribed, but the transcripts remain private unless they are produced at trial or filed with the court as part of a pre-trial motion. Examination for discovery is the fact-finding stage of a lawsuit, where parties and their lawyers can assess the strength of each side's case.

Although some lawsuits proceed to trial, most in fact are withdrawn or end with an *out-of-court settlement*. The facts that emerge at discovery, mounting costs and legal fees, the prospect of losing at trial—all are factors that bring litigants to the negotiating table. Only a small percentage of lawsuits go to trial. Courts in some provinces require litigants to take part in *pre-trial conferences*, chaired by a judge, to explore the possibility of a settlement. In addition, mediation may be used to resolve the dispute. Details of an out-of-court settlement may be filed with the court, but it is more common for both sides to agree to keep the terms confidential.

If there is no settlement, the case will proceed to trial. Civil trials follow the same pattern as criminal ones: the plaintiff's case is presented first, the defence has an opportunity to cross-examine each witness, and the roles are reversed once it is the defence's turn to call evidence. Judges alone preside over most trials, but civil juries must be empanelled to assess certain claims, such as defamation, malicious prosecution, and false imprisonment. Verdicts can be appealed to the provincial court of appeal, and a further appeal to the Supreme Court of Canada may be possible if the case raises an important legal issue.

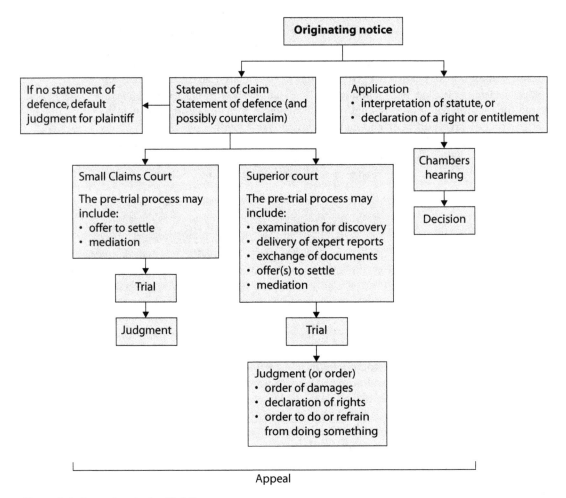

Figure 2.3 Procedure in the Civil Courts

Application Route

Application is the simpler of the two procedures and arises when the party launching the application (the applicant) seeks a declaration of a right or entitlement; the enforcement of a Charter right; or an interpretation of a statute. This route is also used in emergencies, when a swift decision is needed to prevent irreparable damage, as with the demolition of a heritage building or the broadcast of material alleged to be defamatory. In such cases, the court may agree to hear the initial application *ex parte*— without the party being sued (the respondent) being notified or present.

In applications, the focus is on legal issues, not facts. Legal arguments are presented to the court in written briefs, called **factums**, and lawyers usually confine themselves to a brief review of their positions when the application is heard. Evidence is presented in the form of **affidavits**—written statements of witnesses sworn under oath. The affidavits set out information relevant to the application, and are filed with the court. If the opposing party challenges statements made in an affidavit, the person who swore it may be required to face cross-examination in court.

Superior court judges hear applications in **chambers**, a courtroom proceeding that is open to the public. Because the issues are usually straightforward and the parties are anxious for a resolution, judges may deliver an oral decision and release a written version at a later date. The losing side has the right to appeal a chambers ruling to the court of appeal.

Applications may also arise in the course of litigation bound for trial. Either side involved in a lawsuit may file an **interlocutory application** asking a chambers judge to resolve a legal dispute. For example, a defendant may seek to quash a lawsuit as frivolous, or either side may ask a judge to require disclosure of certain documents or to order a reluctant witness to answer questions at discovery.

Criminal and Civil Law: A Summary

The criminal law is concerned with acts that harm individuals but are also an offence against society as a whole. The civil law deals with private disputes that may ultimately be resolved in the courtroom and in some cases have the potential to affect the rights of all Canadians.

The next chapter deals with another cornerstone of our justice system—openness. Openness ensures that the courts deal fairly and consistently with both criminal and civil cases. Our courts and the individuals who turn to them for justice are exposed to public scrutiny, so citizens can monitor the conduct of judges and juries, prosecutors and police officers, lawyers and litigants. In the 1920s, British lawyer and politician Gordon Hewart observed that "it is of fundamental importance that justice should not only be done, but should manifestly and undoubtedly be seen to be done."[46] To this end, Canada's courts are open courts and the Charter affords the right of freedom of expression to the journalists who cover the justice system.

NOTES

1. *Canadian Charter of Rights and Freedoms*, part I of the *Constitution Act, 1982*, RSC 1985, app. II, no. 44.

2. S.M. Waddams, *Introduction to the Study of Law*, 4th ed. (Scarborough, ON: Carswell, 1992), 61.

3. *Criminal Code*, RSC 1985, c. C-46, as amended, s. 267(b).

4. *Youth Criminal Justice Act*, SC 2002, c. 1.

5. *Criminal Code*, s. 21(1)(b).

6. Ibid., ss. 21(c) and 22(1).

7. Ibid., s. 23(1).

8. Ibid., s. 21(2).

9. Ibid., s. 465.

10. Ibid., s. 24(1). For a more detailed discussion of criminal responsibility, see Craig M. Garson, "Who Can Be Charged with a Crime?" in Joel E. Pink and David C. Perrier,

eds., *From Crime to Punishment: An Introduction to the Canadian Criminal Law System*, 4th ed. (Toronto: Carswell, 1999), 41–47.

11. *Criminal Code*, ss. 34 and 35.

12. Ibid., s. 232.

13. Alibi and necessity are common law defences preserved under s. 8(3) of the *Criminal Code*. For a more thorough analysis of defences available under the criminal law, see Eric Colvin, *Principles of Criminal Law*, 2nd ed. (Scarborough, ON: Carswell, 1991), chapters 7, 8.

14. See Brian Casey, "Guilty in Fact—Not Guilty in Law," in Pink and Perrier, supra note 10, at 85–101.

15. Canadian Centre for Justice Statistics, *The Juristat Reader: A Statistical Overview of the Canadian Justice System* (Toronto: Thompson Educational Publishing, 1999), 71.

16. *Criminal Code*, s. 430(5).

17. Charter, ss. 8 and 9.

18. Ibid., s. 10(b).

19. *R v. Oakes*, [1986] 1 SCR 103, (1985), 24 CCC (3d) 321, 50 CR (3d) 1.

20. *R v. Hebert*, [1990] 2 SCR 151, (1989), 57 CCC (3d) 1, 77 CR (3d) 145.

21. *R v. Rose*, [1998] 3 SCR 262, (1998), 129 CCC (3d) 449, 20 CR (5th) 246.

22. *Canada Evidence Act*, RSC 1985, c. C-5.

23. *R v. Oickle* (2000), 147 CCC (3d) 321 (SCC).

24. *R v. Stinchcombe*, [1991] 3 SCR 326.

25. For more detail on procedure in criminal cases, see Brian D. Williston, "Trial Procedure," and John D. Embree, "The Adversary System of Justice," in Pink and Perrier, supra note 10, at 181–98.

26. Charter, s. 10(e).

27. Kirk Makin, "Plea-Bargain Increase Worries Ontario Judge," *Globe and Mail*, November 30, 2002.

28. Law Reform Commission of Canada, *Plea Discussions and Agreements*, Working Paper 60 (Ottawa: Law Reform Commission of Canada, 1989), 3–4.

29. Lawrence M. Friedman, *Law in America: A Short History* (New York: Random House, 2002), 94.

30. "Resolution Discussions and Agreements," *Crown Attorney Manual*, Nova Scotia Public Prosecution Service, September 3, 2002 update, at 1.

31. *Criminal Code*, s. 579.

32. Canadian Centre for Justice Statistics, supra note 15, at xvii.

33. *Criminal Code*, s. 649.

34. Ibid., s. 742.1.

35. Ibid., ss. 718 and 718.1.

36. Kenneth W.F. Fiske, "Sentencing Powers and Principles," in Pink and Perrier, supra note 10, at 287.

37. *Criminal Code*, s. 718.2.

38. Ibid., s. 718.2(e).

39. *Young Offenders Act*, RSC 1985, c. Y-1. For more on the differences between the two acts, see Jim Brown, "Youth Crime Law Aims for Balance of Tough, Fair," *Chronicle-Herald* (Halifax), March 31, 2003 and Janice Tibbetts, "Young Offenders Act Dies Tomorrow," *Daily News* (Halifax), March 31, 2003.

40. *Canada Year Book 2001* (Ottawa: Statistics Canada, 2001), 531–32.

41. Kirk Makin, "Youth Jail Terms Less Common After 2003 Law, Study Says," *Globe and Mail*, June 24, 2006, A8.

42. For more information on the *Youth Criminal Justice Act*, consult Department of Justice Canada, *YCJA Explained*, at http://www.justice.gc.ca/eng/pi/yj-jj/ycja-lsjpa/ycja-lsjpa.html.

43. Cecil A. Wright and Allen M. Linden, *The Law of Torts: Cases, Notes and Materials*, 5th ed. (Toronto: Butterworths, 1970), 1.

44. G.H. Treitel, *The Law of Contract*, 3rd ed. (London: Stevens & Sons, 1970), 1.

45. Ronald Irving, comp., *"The Law Is a Ass": An Illustrated Collection of Legal Quotations* (London: Gerald Duckworth & Co., 1999), 55.

46. Elizabeth Knowles, ed., *The Oxford Dictionary of Quotations* (Oxford: Oxford University Press, 2001), 375.

CHAPTER 3

Freedom of Expression in Canada

"An Unshackled Press"

It has been hailed as "the most momentous freedom-of-the-press precedent" in early Canadian journalism.[1] On New Year's Day 1835, *The Novascotian* published a letter accusing the magistrates in charge of Halifax's police department, poor asylum, and other services of pocketing £1,000 a year at the expense of the "poor and distressed." The missive, signed with the pseudonym "The People," went on to claim that three of these officials had been fleecing the public purse for three decades. It was a brazen attack, even for an era when reputations regularly took a drubbing in the press. The outraged magistrates struck back, urging Nova Scotia's attorney general to charge *The Novascotian*'s proprietor, Joseph Howe, with criminal **libel**. In the legal jargon of the time, he stood accused of "wickedly, maliciously and seditiously desiring and intending to stir up and excite discontent among His Majesty's subjects."

After lawyers told Howe that his case was hopeless—the newspaper's rabble-rousing motives were clear and truth was not yet recognized as a defence to libel—he chose to represent himself at trial. Howe's courageous stand against the colonial powers that be has become the stuff of legend. For more than six hours he regaled the jury with fresh allegations of civic corruption. One magistrate was using the city prison as his private larder, storing vegetables in the cells and forcing inmates to make shoes for his family. The director of the poor asylum, another magistrate, was furnishing the institution with inferior, overpriced supplies. Howe ended his speech by challenging the jurors "to leave an unshackled press as a legacy to your children." Spectators peppered the speech with applause. One juryman was moved to tears. Despite the judge's stern reminder of the jurors' duty to follow the law and to find Howe guilty, they returned in 10 minutes with an acquittal. Howe and his supporters paraded through the streets in triumph; six magistrates promptly resigned in disgrace. In the next edition of *The Novascotian*, Howe declared that "the press of Nova Scotia is free."[2] While Howe's victory struck a blow for freedom of the press, it was the culmination of a struggle that had begun in the 1750s, with the publication of the first newspaper in the British colonies that would become Canada.

The Early Press

In 1752, Boston printer John Bushell published the first edition of the *Halifax Gazette*. The *Gazette* and other papers of the day were modest undertakings, typically two- or four-page weeklies that devoted most of their columns to official government announcements and European news, some of it months old and reprinted from foreign papers brought in on merchant ships.[3] These early papers have been seen as little more than agents of the government, subservient and dependent for their survival on official advertising and printing contracts. "Because the printer-editor needed government business, he carefully avoided comment on the conduct of those in authority," noted one history of the Canadian media.[4] But closer examination of surviving issues of early papers shows their proprietors did publish criticism of local administrations and the British government. Bushell, for instance, waded into a power struggle between Nova Scotia's military governor and merchants demanding the creation of an elected assembly; he published a letter in 1753 with a pointed reference to the lack of business sense among those "brought up in the military Way." He also republished attacks on the British government that were gleaned from imported opposition newspapers.[5] In 1765 Bushell's successor, Anthony Henry, mounted a campaign against Britain's *Stamp Act* duties on paper and provided *Gazette* readers with extensive coverage of anti-tax protests in the American colonies.[6] These flashes of independent reporting met with some official backlash—Henry was warned to tone down his rhetoric or risk losing government printing contracts—and became less frequent in the aftermath of the American Revolution. An influx of Loyalist refugees in the 1780s and the creation of new British colonies led to the establishment of official newspapers in colonial capitals, operated by more compliant, government-appointed King's Printers.[7]

In the 19th century, colonial governments relied on prosecutions for criminal libel to squelch criticism that might undermine their authority. Between 1786 and Joseph Howe's trial in 1835, a succession of newspaper publishers and activists were prosecuted and many were convicted, fined, or jailed. Halifax pamphleteer William Wilkie, for one, was sentenced to two years at hard labour in 1820 for alleging corruption in Nova Scotia's courts and government. In 1828 the publisher of the *Canadian Freeman* in York, Francis Collins, served 11 months behind bars for libelling Upper Canada's attorney general.[8]

Over time this draconian approach would give way to the concept of a free press as an underpinning of democracy. An early proponent, James Mill, argued that "the freedom of the press … is, in all civilized countries, among all but the advocates of misgovernment, regarded as an indispensable security, and the greatest safeguard of the interests of mankind."[9] Press freedom hinged on a key legal development. In 1792 British juries were given the right to decide not only if a statement had been published, but whether it should be considered libellous or not.[10] The same approach was instituted in the United States in 1805.[11] It would be decades before Canada's laws caught up but, as Howe's trial made clear, juries were not averse to taking matters into their own hands. Howe's acquittal was a turning point, making colonial officials across British North America wary of using the criminal law to try to stifle their critics, since a libel trial might do little more than provide a public forum for airing allegations and grievances. By 1848, in the words of Nova Scotia Lieutenant Governor Sir John Harvey, that colony's press was "as free as that of England, claiming and enjoying in fact the same privileges."[12]

The growing power and independence of the press in Britain and the United States had inevitably spilled over into Canada. The official "gazettes" were joined in the 19th century by upstarts that provided a forum for local news, political debate, and the airing of democratic ideas. William Lyon Mackenzie attacked Upper Canada's "Family Compact" in the pages of his *Colonial Advocate*, while Howe used his *Novascotian* to demand constitutional reforms and responsible government. The Tory elites that governed British North America made no attempt to disguise their contempt for the new medium and its power to shape public opinion. "It is one of the miserable consequences of the abuse of liberty," Upper Canada's attorney general, John Beverley Robinson, grumbled in 1838, "that a licentious press is permitted to poison the public mind with the most absurd and wicked misrepresentations, which the ill-disposed, without inquiry, receive and act upon as truths."[13]

But by the 1830s, notes media historian Paul Rutherford, "the very number of journals and journalists had made the press a force in the politics of the land."[14] Newspapers took either a Tory or radical bent, evolving into pro-Conservative and pro-Liberal factions of the press that dominated Canadian journalism in the decades after Confederation. Papers were, by one account, "blatantly partisan and often hysterical ... designed to pump propaganda into the national bloodstream."[15] Writers and editors attacked their political opponents with glee as they launched or promoted their own political careers. Journalists were "the hired tools of political parties, and depended on political patronage for at least some of their revenue. ... [F]ew among them may have imagined that newspapers might exist to serve any but political ends."[16]

The Press in the 20th Century

In the 20th century, the press broke free of its partisan fetters. Newspaper and magazine circulation climbed as increasing literacy and the advent of broadcasting brought new audiences. As news went mainstream, readers, listeners, and viewers demanded more than political posturing and partisan bickering. By the mid-20th century, if a newspaper's editorial columns endorsed a party or candidate, it was on the basis of platforms and policies rather than blind allegiance. Media outlets and their writers and editors came to see themselves as independent agents with a duty to safeguard and promote the public interest.[17] "Every man and woman will be better off if the transmission and reception of fact and opinion are left free from the intervention of government," the *Montreal Daily Star*'s editor, George V. Ferguson, declared in 1955. "The general will of a political society cannot be fully expressed without this freedom. Freedom of information thus becomes an essential part of any system of democracy."[18] Beland Honderich of the *Toronto Star* voiced a similar sentiment when, shortly after stepping down in 1988 as publisher of Canada's largest newspaper, he said the role of the newspaper

> is to engage in the full and frank dissemination of news and opinion from the perspective of its values and particular view of society. It should report the news fairly and accurately, reflect all pertinent facts and opinions and not only what the official establishment thinks and says.[19]

When a special Senate committee was struck in 1969 to investigate the concentration of ownership in the Canadian media, journalists across the country were asked to define freedom of the press. The committee's final report notes there was a consensus on two points. One, the press enjoys the same freedoms as any member of the public, and "press freedom is simply an extension of freedom of speech." Two, government interference poses "the gravest potential threat" to this freedom. "When a government seeks to restrict the freedoms of its citizens," the committee warned, "the press is always its first target."[20] And when the attack has come, the first line of defence for the press has been Canada's courts.

The Courts and Freedom of Expression

Pre-Charter Rulings: The Battle for Freedom of Expression

Desperate times call for desperate measures, and the hardships created by drought and economic depression in Western Canada made the 1930s one of those times. In Alberta, a Social Credit government headed by Bill Aberhart, an evangelical radio preacher, swept to power on a promise to pay residents a $25-a-month "dividend" to kick-start the economy. Social credit theory was considered dubious and Aberhart's policies were subjected to sharp criticism in the province's newspapers, which became the main political opposition. Aberhart, who dismissed newspapers as "mad dog operations" and "the mouthpiece of the financiers," introduced legislation to bring the press under the government's thumb.

An Act To Ensure the Publication of Accurate News and Information, or the Press Bill, as it was known, was an Orwellian law designed to enforce the government's version of the facts. Under the legislation, the government could demand that newspapers publish an official statement in response to any published report about a Social Credit decision or policy. Furthermore, anyone who was maligned in the official corrections was barred from suing the government for defamation. The bill also enabled the government to force newspapers to reveal their sources and to identify the author of any article, editorial, or letter appearing in their pages. Any newspaper that disobeyed such orders could be shut down, possibly for good. One observer did not exaggerate when he termed Aberhart's proposals "authoritarianism in its most overt form."[21]

The federal government, contending that the bill and other Social Credit measures were unconstitutional, referred the legislation to the Supreme Court of Canada for a ruling. The court found that the Press Bill was a clear attack on press freedom, but the court also acknowledged that the *British North America Act* (BNA Act), the constitution of the day, afforded no right to freedom of speech or expression. The Supreme Court found other means to strike down legislation that it considered "retrograde" and "autocratic." In March 1938 it declared the Press Bill *ultra vires* and an infringement on the federal government's responsibility for the criminal law. The court ruled that the *Criminal Code* already outlawed seditious libels calling for rebellion or an overthrow of the government, and that a provincial government did not have the power to criminalize the legitimate criticism and healthy political debate that the newspapers provided. The Press Bill, it opined, would stifle this debate and criticism.

Despite the BNA Act's silence on the real issue at stake, the court made some forceful pronouncements on the importance of freedom of speech in a democracy. Chief

Justice Lyman Duff described the "right of free public discussion of public affairs" as "the breath of life for parliamentary institutions."[22] But freedom of speech in Canada was not an absolute right—citizens and journalists alike who defamed others or spread sedition, he noted, would face the legal consequences. A fellow judge, Justice Lawrence Cannon, was just as adamant that a free exchange of views on political issues is

> essential to enlighten public opinion in a democratic State; it cannot be curtailed without affecting the right of the people to be informed through sources independent of the Government concerning matters of public interest. There must be an untrammelled publication of the news and political opinions of the political parties contending for ascendancy.[23]

"The Breath of Life for Parliamentary Institutions"

Chief Justice Lyman Duff, in the Supreme Court of Canada's ruling in the Alberta Press Bill case of the late 1930s, made the case for freedom of speech in Canada:

> The [*British North America Act*] contemplates a Parliament working under the influence of public opinion and public discussion. There can be no controversy that such institutions derive their efficacy from the free public discussion of affairs, from criticism and answer and counter-criticism, from attack upon policy and administration and defence and counter-attack; from the freest and fullest analysis and examination from every point of view of political proposals. ...
>
> This right of public discussion is, of course, subject to legal restrictions; those based upon consideration of decency and public order, and others conceived for the protection of various private and public interests with which, for example, the laws of defamation and sedition are concerned. In a word, freedom of discussions means ... "freedom governed by law."
>
> Even within its legal limits, it is liable to abuse and grave abuse, and such abuse is constantly exemplified before our eyes; but it is axiomatic that the practice of this right of free public discussion of public affairs, notwithstanding its incidental mischiefs, is the breath of life for parliamentary institutions. (*Reference re Alberta Statutes*, [1938] SCR 100, at 133.)

In the 1950s Justice Ivan Rand of the Supreme Court produced a pair of significant rulings on freedom of speech. In a 1951 judgment that narrowed the legal definition of "sedition," Rand declared that "freedom in thought and speech and disagreement in ideas and beliefs, on every conceivable subject, are of the essence of our life."[24] The second ruling arose from the so-called Padlock Law that the Quebec government passed in 1937 to combat the spread of communism. The legislation gave the province's attorney general the power to lock up any home or building used to "propagate communism or bolshevism by any means whatsoever." It was also an offence to print or distribute newspapers or other publications containing communist propaganda.

Although the implications for freedom of speech and a free press were obvious, the law did not come before the Supreme Court for review until the mid-1950s, when a lawsuit between a tenant and the owner of a padlocked apartment reached Ottawa on appeal.

The court once again cited the constitutional division of powers between the provincial governments and the federal government, ruling in 1957 that the Padlock Law was a criminal measure and beyond the jurisdiction of the Quebec legislature. Rand, like Duff almost two decades earlier, described freedom of speech as "little less vital to man's mind and spirit than breathing is to his physical existence." Rand went on to emphasize the link between democracy and freedom of speech:

> Whatever the deficiencies in its workings, Canadian Government is in substance the will of the majority expressed directly or indirectly through popular assemblies. This means ultimately government by the free public opinion of an open society. ... But public opinion, in order to meet such a responsibility, demands the condition of a virtually unobstructed access to and diffusion of ideas.[25]

A colleague, Justice D.C. Abbott, expressed the view—a bold view for the time—that even Parliament was powerless to fully abrogate the public's right to free speech. "The right of free expression of opinion and of criticism, upon matters of public policy and public administration, and the right to discuss and debate such matters, whether they be social, economic or political," he argued, "are essential to the working of a parliamentary democracy such as ours."[26]

Three years after the Padlock Law was struck down, in 1960, the government of Prime Minister John Diefenbaker introduced a *Canadian Bill of Rights*.[27] Section 1 set out an array of human rights and fundamental freedoms that have "existed and shall continue to exist" in Canada, including freedom of speech and freedom of the press. As an act of Parliament, however, the *Bill of Rights* did not form part of the constitution and only applied to federal laws.[28] However, the *Bill of Rights* set the stage for the *Charter of Rights and Freedoms* and the kind of constitutional protection of free speech that Abbott had envisioned in the 1950s. "Canadian judges have always placed a high value on freedom of expression as an element of parliamentary democracy," notes one constitutional scholar, "and have sought to protect it with the limited tools that were at their disposal."[29] The Charter has given the courts a new tool to protect and expand freedom of expression.

Freedom of Expression Under the Charter

Defining the Scope of Free Speech

Thomas Jefferson best summed up American attitudes toward freedom of speech when he described government as "the opinion of the people." If he ever faced a choice between "government without newspapers, or newspapers without a government," he added, "I should not hesitate a moment to prefer the latter."[30] The First Amendment to the US Constitution, ratified in 1791, sets out the fundamental freedoms of American citizens, among them a declaration that "Congress shall make no law ... abridging the freedom of speech, or of the press." In the 20th century, US courts have invoked this right to give journalists wide latitude to gather news and to protect the media against laws, government policies, and judicial rulings that inhibit the publication of information.[31]

Canadian courts, in contrast, are newcomers to the business of defining the scope of free speech. It wasn't until 1982 that the Charter appeared, guaranteeing "freedom of thought, belief, opinion and expression, including freedom of the press and other media of communication." The guarantee, set out in section 2(b), is broad, suggesting that the framers of the Charter intended a wide array of forms of expression to fall within its scope. The guarantee was also drafted to encompass the press—a term that includes television and radio as well as traditional print journalism—and all other "media of communication." Books, plays, television documentaries, websites, videos, DVDs, Internet chat groups, online magazines, social-networking sites, new forms of media technology yet to be invented—whatever the medium, Canadians are free to publish and disseminate images and ideas, subject only to laws and government restrictions that can be justified under section 1 of the Charter. Section 1 states:

> The *Canadian Charter of Rights and Freedoms* guarantees the rights and freedoms set out in it subject only to such reasonable limits prescribed by law as can be demonstrably justified in a free and democratic society.[32]

The Supreme Court of Canada has taken the view that the right to free expression was entrenched in the constitution "to ensure that everyone can manifest their thoughts, opinions, beliefs, indeed all expressions of the heart and mind, however unpopular, distasteful or contrary to the mainstream."[33] Expression, the court has said, must be given a broad definition, embracing both verbal and physical means of communication. "The content of expression can be conveyed through an infinite variety of forms of expression: for example, the written or spoken word, the arts, and even physical gestures or acts." Even the act of illegal parking could be a form of expression if the driver was engaged in a protest against unfair parking restrictions. In the court's view, "activity is expressive if it attempts to convey meaning."[34] A firm line is drawn, however, at threats or acts of violence, which the court has repeatedly said will not be granted Charter protection. "A murderer or rapist cannot invoke freedom of expression in justification of the form of expression he has chosen."[35]

In 1992 Justice Beverley McLachlin, now the court's chief justice, summarized the interests protected under section 2(b) as "truth, political or social participation, and self-fulfilment."[36] Freedom of expression is a right enjoyed not only by those making a statement, but also by those reading it or seeing it.[37] In the words of media law expert Robert Martin, the Charter protects "a process ... that extends from gathering information to publishing information, to selling and distributing information, and finally to receiving information."[38]

Political Expression

In Charter rulings on freedom of expression, the Supreme Court of Canada has reiterated its earlier pronouncements on the importance of free speech to Canadian democracy. It is nothing less than "one of the fundamental concepts that has formed the basis for the historical development of the political, social and educational institutions of western society."[39] In the view of Justice Peter Cory, writing in a 1989 judgment on media rights:

> Indeed a democracy cannot exist without that freedom to express new ideas and to put forward opinions about the functioning of public institutions. The concept of free and uninhibited speech permeates all truly democratic societies and institutions. The vital importance of the concept cannot be over-emphasized.[40]

Justice Gérard La Forest endorsed that view in a 1996 ruling, calling open discussion about government policies and practices "crucial to any notion of democratic rule. The liberty to criticize and express dissentient views has long been thought to be a safeguard against state tyranny and corruption."[41] In one application of this facet of freedom of expression, the Supreme Court of Canada ruled in 2009 that municipal transit authorities do not have the power to ban political advertisements from the sides of buses.[42] Political expression, however, has its limits. In 2004 the Supreme Court upheld limits on how much money so-called third parties—individuals and groups not affiliated with the major political parties—can spend on advertising in federal elections. The limits are $3,000 within a riding and $150,000 nationwide. The law also imposes an advertising blackout on polling day. Although these provisions of the *Canada Elections Act* clearly restrict freedom of political expression, a majority of the court ruled that the limits were justified because they "create a level playing field" and prevent wealthy interests from having an undue influence on voters and, potentially, on the outcome of an election.[43]

Commercial Expression

Under the Charter, freedom of expression is no longer limited to the political realm. The Supreme Court has ruled that the Charter protects commercial advertising, including advertising aimed at children.[44] It also protects the right of union members to stage most forms of peaceful picketing during labour disputes.[45] This right to freedom of commercial speech may also limit the ability of governments to ban or regulate the distribution of spam e-mail messages.[46] It does not, however, prevent a municipal government from using a noise bylaw to prevent a commercial enterprise from employing a loudspeaker to attract customers to its premises.[47]

Obscenity and Child Pornography

Certain forms of pornography have won Charter protection from being prosecuted as obscenity under the *Criminal Code*, but the Supreme Court has ruled that freedom of expression does not extend to depictions of explicit sex with violence, degrading or dehumanizing treatment, or the exploitation of children.[48] The offence of possession of child pornography has been upheld as a reasonable limit on free expression under section 1 of the Charter, with the exception of written or visual material created for personal use.[49]

Hate Propaganda

The court has had some difficulty grappling with the rights of those accused of spreading hate propaganda. In the case of Jim Keegstra, the Alberta schoolteacher charged under the *Criminal Code* with promoting hatred against an identifiable group,[50] the court ruled that the anti-Semitic views he was foisting on his students were "repugnant" but, since they conveyed meaning, they fit the Charter definition of expression. But Keegstra's ravings about Jewish plots were so extreme and so far removed from the core values of freedom of expression—the quest for truth, individual self-fulfillment, and participation in social and political life—that the law could stand as a reasonable limit on free speech.[51]

Ernst Zundel was more fortunate. A prominent Holocaust denier based in Toronto, he was charged with promoting hatred under a section of the *Criminal Code* that made it an offence to publish a false "statement, tale or news" that is likely to cause damage or mischief to a public interest.[52] There was no question that Zundel's pamphlet, *Did Six Million Really Die?*, was a form of expression and the Charter protects the rights of minorities to voice opinions. The Supreme Court ruled that this infringement on freedom of expression could not be justified, even though Zundel's published views were untrue. Constitutional protection must extend to such statements, since determining precisely what is true and what is false can be a difficult and subjective exercise. A majority of the court struck down the law against spreading false news as unconstitutional.[53]

Freedom of Expression and the Media

The Charter's explicit protection of "freedom of the press and other media of communication" begs a question: Do writers, publishers, and broadcasters, who make their living expressing themselves, enjoy special constitutional status? The Supreme Court has taken the view that freedom of the press and other media stands apart from the free expression rights of ordinary citizens. In a 1988 judgment Justice Antonio Lamer, who went on to become chief justice, described freedom of the press as "an important and essential attribute of a free and democratic society, and measures which prohibit the media from publishing information deemed of interest obviously restrict that freedom."[54] The court has also underscored the link between press freedom and the open exchange of information and ideas in a democratic society, stating: "It is the media that, by gathering and disseminating news, enable members of our society to make an informed assessment of the issues which may significantly affect their lives and well-being."[55] Justice Beverley McLachlin, in a dissenting judgment arising from a police search of media offices, contended that the Charter "affirms the special position of the press and other media in our society." In her opinion, the guarantee of freedom of the press "must be interpreted in a generous and liberal fashion."[56] A Canadian professor who has studied freedom of expression in Canada and the United States has disputed this view. Freedom of the press, Richard Moon has argued, "is simply an aspect or implication of freedom of expression." But, Moon concedes, "even in the absence of a special press provision, protection of press 'autonomy' may follow from the central role of the press in facilitating public debate and the exchange of information."[57]

The free-expression rights of the print media may stand apart when it comes to gaining access to the public platform needed to exchange ideas. In a pre-Charter case, the Supreme Court ruled that newspapers are not obliged to carry every advertisement submitted for publication. Because the press is free to disseminate views and to select

"The Special Position of the Press"

In 1991 the Supreme Court of Canada ruled that police can search media offices and seize evidence of wrongdoing gathered by journalists if there is no other way to obtain the information. In a dissenting judgment, Justice Beverley McLachlin (now the chief justice) argued that the Charter grants the media special status:

> By specifically referring to freedom of the press, s. 2(b) affirms the special position of the press and other media in our society. It affirms that the press and the media have the constitutional right to pursue their legitimate functions in our society. Freedom of the press under the Charter must be interpreted in a generous and liberal fashion. ...
>
> The values underlying freedom of the press, like freedom of expression, include the pursuit of truth. The press furthers that pursuit by reporting on facts and opinions and offering its comment on events and ideas—activities vital to the functioning of our democracy, which is premised on the free reporting and interchange of ideas. The press acts as the agent of the public in monitoring and reporting on governmental, legal and social institutions. ... Freedom of the press is also important to participation in the community and individual self-fulfillment. One need only think of the role of a community newspaper in facilitating community participation, or the role of arts, sports and policy publications to see the importance of freedom of the press to these goals. ... [A]n effective and free press is dependent on its ability to gather, analyze and disseminate information, independent from any state imposed restrictions on content, form or perspective except those justified under s. 1 of the Charter. (*Canadian Broadcasting Corp. v. Lessard*, [1991] 3 SCR 421, at 448–52.)

the information it reports, it follows that newspapers have the right to refuse to publish material as they choose.[58] The Charter may change this. Adbusters Media Foundation won the right in 2009 to sue the CBC and the Global Television Network for refusing to broadcast its advertisements, which promote "Buy Nothing Day," "TV Turn-Off Week," and other campaigns to reduce consumption and consumer spending. In allowing Adbusters' action to proceed, British Columbia's Court of Appeal noted the argument can be made that broadcasters, public and private alike, "have been given the power to control expression in a public space" and must comply with the Charter's guarantee of freedom of expression. The court said the issue would have to be settled at a future trial.[59]

The era of fiercely independent journalists who owned their own printing presses—the likes of Joseph Howe and William Lyon Mackenzie—is long gone. The news business is now dominated by large corporations. By 2003 two media giants—CanWest Global Communications and Quebecor—owned one out of every two daily newspapers sold in Canada, accounting for 16 million papers every week (CanWest's *National Post* and other big-city dailies were sold in 2010 to Postmedia Network Inc., making it Canada's largest newspaper chain). While the Crown-owned Canadian Broadcasting Corporation operates the country's largest radio network, 10 private companies together operated two-thirds of the country's radio stations in 2003. CBC Television and Radio-Canada compete with three privately owned national networks, two broadcasting in English and one in French. This concentration of ownership and the media's power to mould and influence public opinion have been the subject of three federal inquiries since 1969; the latest, an investigation by a Senate committee, filed a report in 2006 recommending stricter monitoring of broadcast licences and automatic investigations of most mergers involving media companies.[60] Although these inquiries have heard and expressed concerns about the concentration of media ownership in fewer and fewer hands, the federal government has been reluctant to take any action that could interfere with the media's hard-won independence.[61]

Broadcast Restrictions and the Role of the CRTC

Canada's electronic media are in a different position. As in most countries, broadcast frequencies are considered public property and their use by radio and television stations is a privilege, not a right. A federal agency, the Canadian Radio-television and Telecommunications Commission (CRTC), regulates the broadcasting industry and issues renewable licences for the use of specific frequencies. These licences carry an array of conditions. Stations must meet requirements to include certain levels of Canadian shows and music in their programming schedule. Broadcasters must devote a "reasonable amount of time" to coverage of public issues and, to ensure that this coverage is balanced, they must provide an opportunity for contrary points of view to be aired. CRTC regulations forbid licensees from airing "abusive content that … tends to or is likely to expose an individual or group or class of individuals to hatred or contempt on the basis of race, national or ethnic origin, colour, religion, sex, sexual orientation, age or mental or physical disability."[62]

Peter Desbarats, a respected commentator on media issues, credits the CRTC with showing restraint when dealing with issues that could infringe on journalistic freedom, such as complaints of bias or inaccurate news coverage. "In a regulatory climate of benevolent neglect, in a mixed system of public and private ownership," he has argued, "broadcast journalism in Canada has been marked by an extraordinary degree of editorial independence."[63] On the legal front, the courts have determined that CRTC licensing conditions and restrictions on programming do not undermine the Charter's guarantee of freedom of expression.[64] But the first major clash between the CRTC's mandate and the media's independence occurred in July 2004, when the commission refused to renew the licence of Quebec City radio station CHOI-FM after fielding dozens of complaints about program content. The CRTC ruled that the station's owner, Genex Communications, violated broadcast regulations and the terms of its licence by allowing the two hosts of a morning talk show to "use the public airwaves to make personal attacks and to harass, insult and ridicule people." The hosts described African university students studying in Canada as "sons of plunderers, cannibals" and advocated that hospital staff "pull the plug" on a psychiatric patient. Another complaint came from a female television host who was the target of lewd remarks (and later won $340,000 in damages after suing the station for defamation).[65] Genex appealed, claiming that the CRTC ruling amounted to censorship and violated its right to freedom of expression. The Federal Court of Appeal upheld the CRTC's decision in September 2005, ruling that Charter guarantees of "freedom of expression, freedom of opinion and freedom of speech do not mean freedom of defamation, freedom of oppression and freedom of opprobrium."[66] The Supreme Court of Canada denied leave to appeal in 2007[67] but the station remained on the air because, by that time, it had been sold to a new owner and relicensed.[68]

Human Rights Commissions and Freedom of Expression

Asserting the Right To Offend: The Western Standard and Maclean's Complaints

The cartoons were intended as satire, to make a point about media self-censorship when dealing with issues surrounding Islam. There were a dozen in all, the most controversial depicting the Prophet Muhammad with a bomb stuffed into his turban. They first appeared in the Danish newspaper *Jyllands-Posten* in September 2005. Representations of the Prophet's likeness are forbidden in the Islamic faith, and their republication in European newspapers in early 2006 ignited worldwide protests, attacks on western embassies in the Muslim world, and riots that caused dozens of deaths.[69]

The outrage and violence posed a dilemma for Canadian editors and producers: Should they republish or broadcast the images, which were readily available on the Internet, to illustrate the story and show their audience what the furor was about? Was it prudent and responsible to run them, when there was a risk of provoking further protests and more violence in Canada or abroad? Canada's major media outlets chose to tell, not show—they described the cartoons but did not reproduce the images. "We came to the conclusion that republishing would be both gratuitous and unnecessarily provocative," explained the *Globe and Mail*'s editor-in-chief at the time, Edward Greenspon, "especially given what we knew about how offended Muslims, not just those in the streets but those counselling calm, felt about the cartoons." The decision, he insisted, was "not a matter of self-censorship. It is a question of editing … . We will take the risk of giving offence when we deem it appropriate."[70]

It was a risk a few publications were willing to take. The Calgary-based *Jewish Free Press* and the University of Prince Edward Island's student newspaper, *The Cadre*, republished some of the cartoons.[71] Their appearance in these small publications, each with a circulation of only 2,000, attracted little attention. The *Western Standard* was a different story. The 40,000-circulation, Calgary-based magazine reproduced the cartoons to accompany a commentary on the controversy. Editor Ezra Levant, who termed the images "innocuous," said he was asserting his right to freedom of expression. "I want my readers to have the right to judge for themselves."[72] Levant became the target of two complaints to the Alberta Human Rights Commission, accusing him of publishing material intended to promote hatred and discrimination.

More complaints were filed in the fall of 2006, after *Maclean's* magazine published "The Future Belongs to Islam," an excerpt from Canadian-born writer and political commentator Mark Steyn's book *America Alone: The End of the World as We Know*

It.[73] In it, Steyn linked the threat of Muslim extremism to the growing size and power of Muslim communities within western countries. While conceding "not all Muslims are terrorists," he wrote that "enough are hot for jihad to provide an impressive support network of mosques from Vienna to Stockholm to Toronto to Seattle."[74] The Canadian Islamic Congress lodged complaints with the Canadian Human Rights Commission and its provincial counterparts in Ontario and British Columbia, accusing Steyn of discrimination and promoting hatred against Muslims.

The complaints sparked a debate over freedom of speech and whether human rights commissions should have the power to dictate what Canadians can publish and read. Human rights bureaucrats were accused of censorship and their investigations and inquiries were likened to "kangaroo courts." Critics decried the cost to publishers, in both time and money, of defending against complaints.[75] "Freedom of speech is most important when it expresses strong disapproval," observed civil liberties advocate Alan Borovoy, and writers and editors were being forced to "look over their shoulder worried about being charged or even investigated."[76] Other commentators insisted the laws clearly target only extreme expressions of hatred and contempt and better training for commission investigators would weed out frivolous complaints.[77]

While human rights restrictions on discriminatory statements and hate speech clearly infringe on the Charter right to free expression, the Supreme Court of Canada upheld them in 1990 as justifiable limits on free speech. In reviewing the federal legislation's prohibition of the promotion of hatred or contempt by telephone or other electronic means of communication, the court cautioned human rights bodies that they must target extreme statements and avoid stifling legitimate commentary and debate. The provision applies only to statements of an "ardent and extreme nature" that express "unusually strong and deep-felt emotions of detestation, calumny and vilification." In that case, the Canadian Human Rights Commission had correctly taken action against the operators of a phone line that gave callers access to recorded messages that attacked Jewish people.[78] Other courts have applied the "ardent and extreme" and "detestation, calumny and vilification" tests to assess whether statements violate provincial human rights codes.[79]

One of the complaints against Levant and the *Western Standard* was withdrawn and the other was dismissed in 2008. The Ontario Human Rights Commission dismissed the complaint against Steyn and *Maclean's* without a hearing, saying it had no power to investigate the content of media reports. But it warned of growing intolerance of Muslims since the 9/11 terror attacks and the spread of anti-Islamic attitudes. "By portraying Muslims as all sharing the same negative characteristics, including being a threat to 'the West,' this explicit expression of Islamophobia further perpetuates and promotes prejudice towards Muslims and others."[80] The Canadian Human Rights Commission also dismissed the complaint but it, too, was critical of Steyn's comments. While his writing was "polemical, colourful and emphatic" and "obviously calculated to excite discussion and even offend certain readers, Muslim and non-Muslim alike," the commission conceded his words fell short of the extreme statements its legislation targets.[81]

The BC Human Rights Commission convened a hearing but a tribunal dismissed the *Maclean's* complaint in October 2008. "The article may attempt to rally public opinion by exaggeration and causing the reader to fear Muslims, but fear is not synonymous with hatred and contempt," the tribunal concluded. The article expressed "strong, polemical, and, at times, glib opinions about Muslims" and was "hurtful and distasteful" to the complainants and other Muslims. "However, read in its context, the article is essentially an expression of opinion on political issues which, in light of recent historical events involving extremist Muslims and the problems facing the vast majority of the Muslim community that does not support extremism, are legitimate subjects for public discussion."[82]

How does the law distinguish between legitimate public discussion and extreme expressions of hatred and contempt? These cases and the review of Canada's human rights legislation that follows will help writers and editors understand where the line is likely to be drawn.

Restrictions Under Human Rights Legislation

The Canadian Human Rights Act

Under federal human rights legislation, it is an act of discrimination "to publish or display before the public or to cause to be published or displayed before the public any notice, sign, symbol, emblem or other representation" that "expresses or implies" discrimination or "incites or is calculated to incite others to discriminate."[83] Section 13 of the Act also forbids individuals and groups from using the telephone or "the facilities of a telecommunication undertaking" to distribute messages likely to expose a person or group to hatred or contempt based on their race, colour, ancestry, religion, gender, disability, and other characteristics. In 2001 this restriction was expanded to include material posted to the Internet. Information that is broadcast "in whole or in part" is exempt (reflecting the CRTC's jurisdiction over broadcasting), and the owners and operators of telecommunication services are not liable for hate messages that others distribute on their systems.[84]

As noted, the Supreme Court of Canada upheld the restriction on the dissemination of hate messages in 1990 as justified under the Charter. In 2009, however, a federal tribunal ruled that section 13 is no longer a justifiable limit on the right to freedom of expression. Prior to 1998, the commission had the power only to order offenders to cease the distribution of hate messages. In the tribunal's view, new penalties enacted that year—making offenders liable to pay a maximum fine of $10,000 and up to $20,000 in damages—transformed the legislation to such an extent that it unduly restricts free speech.[85] The Canadian Human Rights Commission appealed the ruling in the fall of 2009.[86]

In response to the controversy over the complaint against Mark Steyn and *Maclean's*, the commission asked Richard Moon, an expert in the law of free expression, to review its powers under section 13. Moon recommended that Parliament repeal the section and leave it to the police to prosecute those who distribute hate messages electronically or on the Internet, under the hate propaganda provisions of the *Criminal Code*. As well, he suggested the prosecution only of a person or group that "advocates, justifies or threatens violence."

The commission rejected that recommendation to repeal section 13, insisting it has a role to play in regulating hate speech. "In the rough and tumble of democratic debate, offence will be given and feelings will be hurt," reads its submission to Parliament on the issue. "However, freedom of expression is not a licence to hate." The commission has asked the federal government to amend its legislation to adopt the Supreme Court of Canada's definitions of the key words "hatred" and "contempt" and to repeal its power to impose fines for violations of section 13.[87] No amendments had been made by the end of 2010 and, coupled with the ruling that the section is unconstitutional, the commission's power to regulate hate messages appeared uncertain at the time of writing.

Provincial and Territorial Codes

Human rights legislation in each province and territory prohibits the publication or public display of material that discriminates against individuals or groups on the basis of race, religion, or other characteristics.[88] These provisions appear to target notices and advertisements but the wording is broad enough to apply to any material published or broadcast, including news and opinions. Quebec's *Charter of Human Rights and Freedoms*, for example, makes it a human rights violation to "distribute, publish or publicly exhibit a notice, symbol or sign involving discrimination, or authorize anyone to do so."[89] Ontario's legislation, like the federal Act, refers to the publication of a "notice, sign, symbol, emblem, or other similar representation," and similar wording is used in the codes of Prince Edward Island, Nunavut, Newfoundland and Labrador, New Brunswick, Nova Scotia, and Saskatchewan.[90] Alberta, British Columbia, and Manitoba add a published "statement" to the list of prohibited acts.[91] Human rights codes in Alberta, British Columbia, and the Northwest Territories restrict not only discriminatory publications, but those likely to expose individuals or groups to "hatred or contempt."[92]

Several jurisdictions specify that their human rights restrictions apply to material published in newspapers or broadcast on radio and television or through other mediums. This is the case in Prince Edward Island, Newfoundland and Labrador, New Brunswick, Nova Scotia, and Saskatchewan. Each of these provinces adds the caveat that these restrictions do not interfere with freedom of speech or the free expression of opinion on any subject.[93] Codes in Ontario, Alberta, and the Northwest Territories also contain provisions respecting freedom of speech.[94] As noted, the Ontario Human Rights Commission has concluded its legislation does not give it jurisdiction to investigate complaints about the content of media reports.[95] The BC tribunal that heard the complaint against *Maclean's* magazine determined that provincial human rights codes do not apply to material disseminated on the Internet because the federal government is responsible for telecommunications.[96] As well, the BC legislation specifies that it does not apply to private communications.[97]

Human rights commissions have the power to investigate complaints under these and other provisions that outlaw discrimination. An investigation may lead to a formal inquiry and anyone found to have violated the legislation can be fined or ordered to pay restitution or damages. The media have been the target of complaints besides those lodged against *Maclean's* and the *Western Standard*:

- *Alberta Report* magazine was investigated in 1998 after quoting an unidentified source who claimed commercial real estate and retailing were dominated by Jewish-owned "cliques" that would not deal with outsiders. An Alberta judge ruled the legislation's recognition of freedom of expression does not bar a complaint based on media coverage. The freedom to express "must be exercised responsibly, particularly in light of the enormous influence that the media enjoys," the judge argued. "Exempting the media from the act in this regard would be tantamount to presuming that the media is always neutral in its reporting. I am not prepared to make that presumption."[98]
- In British Columbia, a complaint was filed in 1999 against newspaper columnist Doug Collins, who questioned whether six million Jews died in the Holocaust. A judge ruled that the province's failure to specifically protect free speech within its legislation was a reasonable limit on the Charter's guarantee of free expression.[99] A tribunal later found Collins and his Vancouver-area paper, *North Shore News*, in violation of the *Human Rights Code* and ordered them to pay $2,000 in compensation to the complainant.[100]
- In 2006 the Saskatchewan Court of Appeal ruled that an advertisement, which quoted Bible passages describing homosexuality as a sin, was not discriminatory. The ad included the image of two stickmen holding hands, placed inside a red "not permitted" symbol. A complaint was filed against the man who bought the ad and the Saskatoon *StarPhoenix*, where it appeared. The newspaper had refused to run a second ad, however, and a human rights inquiry proceeded only against the ad's creator. He was found in violation of the Saskatchewan Code and ordered to pay damages totalling $4,500. The Court of Appeal overturned the finding and penalty. While the advertisement's message was "bluntly presented and doubtless upsetting to many," the court ruled it did not meet the Supreme Court of Canada's requirement for the display of "ardent emotions and strong sense of detestation, calumny and vilification."[101]
- A Muslim community leader in Nova Scotia filed a complaint in 2008 over an editorial cartoon in the *Chronicle-Herald* depicting the wife of one of the suspects in the "Toronto 18" terrorist plot, claiming the newspaper was "feeding the seeds of hatred toward a whole community."[102] The Nova Scotia Human Rights Commission does not disclose the status of investigations and it is not clear what became of the complaint. The commission receives few complaints under the section that prohibits discriminatory publications and displays, which was last invoked in 1994 in a case that arose from a caricature on a sweatshirt.[103]
- An Alberta human rights inquiry ruled a clergyman, the chair of a group called the Concerned Christian Coalition, had promoted hatred against homosexuals in a letter to the editor published in the Red Deer *Advocate* in 2002. The letter described homosexuals as a form of "evil" and "wickedness" and called on people to take a stand "against horrendous atrocities such as the aggressive

propagation of homo- and bisexuality ... . Your children are being warped into believing that same-sex families are acceptable; that men kissing men is appropriate."

An Alberta judge reversed the finding in 2009, saying the clergyman's words were "jarring, offensive, bewildering, puerile, nonsensical and insulting," but not so extreme as to risk inciting hatred or contempt. A human rights complaint against the *Advocate* was settled without a hearing, after the newspaper amended its letters policy to prevent publication of "statements that indicate unlawful discrimination or intent to discriminate against a person or class of persons, or are likely to expose people to hatred or contempt because of ... sexual orientation."[104]

Human Rights Codes: A Summary

As these examples show, human rights legislation targets statements so extreme they could incite hatred or contempt against members of minority groups or the groups themselves. While media organizations have been investigated for publishing such statements, action is usually taken against the person or group making the statement, not the messenger. Journalists and columnists who express extreme opinions about minorities face the greatest risk but, as Richard Moon has noted, human rights probes are not triggered "by everyday racist stereotypes and claims." The focus of these laws is extreme, non-mainstream, and racist expression.[105]

Open Courts

The Supreme Court of Canada has adopted a wide definition of the Charter guarantee of freedom of expression and has recognized the crucial role of the media in our democracy. And other than the regulations governing broadcasting, Canada's media face little direct state intervention in the way they gather and disseminate information. An exception is media access to Canada's courts. Judges and lawmakers use publication bans and other restrictions to impose limits on news coverage of court proceedings to protect other interests, the most important being the right of persons accused of crimes to have a fair trial. Media organizations have invoked the Charter to challenge these restrictions, leading to a seminal Supreme Court of Canada ruling—*Dagenais v. Canadian Broadcasting Corporation*—that has added new clout to the media's right to freedom of expression.

Open Courts: "The Very Soul of Justice"

Jeremy Bentham, a British philosopher of the late 18th century, was wary of judges and the power they wield. The best means to ensure that the courts act with fairness and impartiality, he believed, is to subject their work to intense public scrutiny:

> In the darkness of secrecy, sinister interest, and evil in every shape have full swing. Only in proportion as publicity has place can any of the checks applicable to judicial injustice operate. Where there is no publicity there is no justice. Publicity is the very soul of justice. It is the keenest spur to exertion and surest of all guards against improbity.[106]

Two centuries later, Bentham's call for openness still rings true. At a 1984 forum on media coverage of criminal cases, *Toronto Star* publisher Beland Honderich described secrecy as the "most sinister enemy" of justice. "If we restrict public knowledge of how justice is being administered—and to whom—we give rise to fears and suspicions of favoritism and injustice," he warned, "and slowly but surely the confidence in our courts would decline. The courts would be brought into disrepute."[107]

The Charter guarantees "a fair and public hearing" to every person accused of a crime.[108] But Canada's courts recognized the importance of open justice long before the Charter. Openness is the rule; restrictions on access to court proceedings are the exception.[109] The Supreme Court of Canada has cited with approval the British position, as set out in the authoritative *Halsbury's Laws of England*:

> In general, all cases, both civil and criminal must be heard in open court, but in certain exceptional cases, where the administration of justice would be rendered impracticable by the presence of the public, the court may sit *in camera*.[110] [Boldface added.]

The Ontario Court of Appeal has described the openness of the courts as "one of the hallmarks of a democratic society." Echoing Bentham, the court went on to declare public accessibility to be "a restraint on arbitrary action by those who govern and by the powerful."[111] Willard Estey, a Supreme Court of Canada judge from 1977 to 1988, has also stressed the importance of public oversight in keeping the court process honest:

> The governing principles of access by the public to the courtroom are based upon the theory that public surveillance of the components of the judicial system performing in the courtroom keeps the process intellectually honest, and at the same time contributes to the need for the efficiency of the judicial process. Most importantly of all, however, open access to a public trial ensures that the outcome of that trial will be just.[112]

The Media as Watchdog

The right of public access to the courts is meaningless if citizens are unable to exercise that right by monitoring what happens inside the courtroom. Few people have the time or the inclination to attend trials and hearings. Even if they did, the nation's courtrooms can only accommodate so many people at any given time. Therefore, the public must rely on the media to be its eyes and ears. "Discussion of court cases and constructive criticism of court proceedings is dependent upon the receipt by the public of information as to what transpired in court," Justice Peter Cory of the Supreme Court of Canada has observed. "Practically speaking, this information can only be obtained from the newspapers or other media."[113]

The business of the courts, then, must be open to media scrutiny. Journalists fulfill the dual role of informer and watchdog, publicizing how cases unfold while holding accountable the judges, prosecutors, lawyers, and police officers who put the justice system into action. The media's right of access, the Supreme Court of Canada has ruled, is clearly guaranteed under the Charter:

Openness permits public access to information about the courts, which in turn permits the public to discuss and put forward opinions and criticisms of court practices and proceedings. ... [The Charter] protects the freedom of the press to comment on the courts as an essential aspect of our democratic society. ... As a vehicle through which information pertaining to these courts is transmitted, the press must be guaranteed access to the courts in order to gather information.[114]

Yet the rationale for media coverage goes further than the need to keep the system honest. As Honderich noted, media coverage shields the justice system from allegations of favouritism and unfairness. News accounts play an important role in apprehending criminals and may prompt people who can implicate or exonerate a suspect to come forward. Witnesses are less likely to perjure themselves if they know their words may reach people who could expose their lies. Litigants may think twice about pursuing dubious claims in the civil courts. Finally, media reports of the sentences that judges mete out for crimes are crucial to the justice system's goal of deterring others from committing offences.

Limits on Openness

Openness, however, is not absolute. The media's right to report on the justice system and the right of citizens to attend court proceedings often conflict with competing rights. Restrictions on access to the courts and what journalists can publish about court proceedings will be examined in detail in Chapters 9 and 11.

The Proper Administration of Justice

Restrictions on media access may be justified to protect the **administration of justice**—that is, ensure that the justice system can perform its function and that justice is done. Consider the example of a child victim of sexual assault who is frightened about testifying in front of spectators and reporters in open court. If the child is too intimidated to clearly describe what happened, the prosecution's case may collapse and an abuser may go free. A similar scenario could arise in the civil courts; in order to pursue a lawsuit, a company may have to disclose financial or sales information that could benefit its competitors. To avoid having the information aired in open court, the company may drop the lawsuit and forgo a valid claim for damages. In the case of the reluctant child witness, the restrictions may take the form of an order that only counsel and the defendant be present when the child testifies. Likewise, in the civil case, the judge may grant a request to seal any sensitive financial information filed with the court. In both instances, the goal of these limits is to overcome obstacles that could stand in the way of justice being done.

Privacy Rights

There may be compelling reasons to restrict openness to protect the privacy of those involved in the court process. Judges have the power under the *Criminal Code* to make an order preventing the media from identifying victims of sexual offences, extortion, or loansharking, as well as witnesses under the age of 18 involved in such cases. These bans are intended to encourage victims, and any young witnesses who support their complaints, to come forward by shielding them from the embarrassing publicity that such prosecutions often attract. Publication bans are also issued to prevent defence counsel from disclosing confidential medical and psychiatric records or the details of a victim's sexual history. The *Criminal Code* has been amended to extend the right of privacy beyond sex-related offences. Victims of all crimes and any witness testifying in a criminal case can ask a judge for an order restricting publication of their identities.

The Right to a Fair Trial

The Charter guarantees everyone accused of a crime the right to have the allegations against them tested at a trial that is conducted fairly and impartially.[115] If the people serving on the jury were subjected to media reports offering a steady diet of gossip about the crime and slurs on the defendant's character, they would cease to be impartial triers of fact. And if the media were permitted to report freely on the evidence put forward during pre-trial hearings, jurors might come to court having already decided that the person on trial was guilty. To avoid such outcomes and to ensure fairness, judges have the power to ban publication of information that could compromise the defendant's right to a fair trial. In addition, the *Criminal Code* enables prosecutors and defendants to seek a court order delaying publication of evidence revealed at hearings in the pre-trial phase of a prosecution. Media organizations have invoked the Charter to challenge these *Criminal Code* bans, but, for the most part, the courts have found them to be reasonable limits on the right to free expression.[116]

Balancing Rights: The Dagenais Ruling

For all the solemn pronouncements about the value of a free press, and despite the stack of rulings that emphasize the importance of open courts, Canada's judges have tended to put the rights of accused persons ahead of those of the media and public. When asked to choose between a defendant's request for a publication ban and the right of access to court proceedings, judges have traditionally erred on the side of caution and granted the ban, giving precedence to fair-trial rights.

All this changed in 1994 after a legal tug-of-war between fact and fiction. The Canadian Broadcasting Corporation planned to televise the National Film Board's production of *The Boys of St. Vincent*, a gritty made-for-TV drama based on the real physical and sexual abuse of children at Newfoundland's infamous Mount Cashel orphanage. Meanwhile, in Ontario, Lucien Dagenais and three other members of the Christian Brothers—the Roman Catholic order that ran Mount Cashel—were charged with similar acts of abuse involving children at Ontario training schools where they had taught. Dagenais was the first to stand trial and the Mount Cashel drama was scheduled to air just before the jury was sent out to begin deliberations.

Lawyers for Dagenais and his co-accused appeared before a judge of the Ontario Court of Justice and obtained an injunction to block the CBC from broadcasting *The Boys of St. Vincent* anywhere in Canada until all four trials were completed. The *Globe and Mail* was forced to withdraw its TV guide insert for the week, which featured a cover story about the program. The media were even prohibited from reporting that an injunction had been granted. The *Globe* published a terse item, under the headline "Banned," that cleverly addressed the sweeping nature of the court's order:

> Somewhere in Canada yesterday, a group requested a court ban on the publication/broadcast of a certain work for certain reasons. The court granted the ban on publication/broadcast and, in addition, imposed a ban on reporting the fact of the ban.[117]

The Ontario Court of Appeal narrowed the scope of the ban, preventing the program from being broadcast in Ontario and by a Montreal-based French-language station that sent its signal into Ontario.[118] The injunction was appealed to the Supreme Court of Canada, which produced a landmark ruling in late 1994 that quashed the ban and set new ground rules for the way the courts deal with the media's right to freedom of expression.[119] By a margin of 6 to 3, the court ruled that an accused person's right to a fair trial should not trump the media's right of free expression. Writing for the majority, Chief Justice Antonio Lamer said these competing rights have equal status under the Charter and must be balanced, not regarded as a winner-take-all "clash between two titans."[120] Courts must avoid a "hierarchical approach to rights, which places some over others" when interpreting the Charter and developing the common law.[121]

Fair Trial v. Free Press: An Even Playing Field

"The pre-Charter common law rule governing publication bans emphasized the right to a fair trial over the free expression interests of those affected by the ban. In my view, the balance this rule strikes is inconsistent with the principles of the Charter, and in particular, the equal status given by the Charter to ss. 2(b) and 11(d). It would be inappropriate for the courts to continue to apply a common law rule that automatically favoured the rights protected by s. 11(d) over those protected by s. 2(b). A hierarchical approach to rights, which places some over others, must be avoided, both when interpreting the Charter and when developing the common law. When the protected rights of two individuals come into conflict, as can occur in the case of publication bans, Charter principles require a balance to be achieved that fully respects the importance of both sets of rights."

—Chief Justice Antonio Lamer, writing for the majority in *Dagenais v. Canadian Broadcasting Corporation*, [1994] 3 SCR 835, at 877

Chief Justice Lamer proceeded to set out the rights to be balanced. The Charter entrenches the right of accused persons to a fair trial, and it is in the public interest that suspects are acquitted or convicted at trials that are fair and appear to be fair. As well, the courts have an interest in protecting the reputation of the administration of justice by ensuring that justice is done and seen to be done. The publication ban imposed on *The Boys of St. Vincent*, however, had a profound impact on the right of the film director to express himself, the CBC's interest in broadcasting the film, the public's interest in viewing it, and society's interest in having an important issue—child abuse—publicly exposed and debated.[122] But, the chief justice added, these rights are not always in conflict. Persons accused of crimes have an interest in ensuring that there is "public scrutiny of the court process, and all of the participants in the court process."[123]

When considering a motion to ban publication of information, Chief Justice Lamer ruled, judges must assess the objectives of a proposed ban and whether its impact on freedom of expression is in keeping with those objectives. He articulated the test as follows:

> A publication ban should only be ordered when:
>
> (a) Such a ban is necessary in order to prevent a real and substantial risk to the fairness of the trial, because reasonably available alternative measures will not prevent the risk; and
>
> (b) The salutary [beneficial] effects of the publication ban outweigh the deleterious [harmful or detrimental] effects to the free expression of those affected by the ban.[124]

Chief Justice Lamer set out additional criteria for a ban. The ban must relate to an important objective and, if granted, the judge must ensure that it is "as limited [in scope, time, content, etc.] as possible."[125] The judge must also consider a range of options, short of banning publication, that would protect the right to a fair trial. The list includes adjourning the trial, holding the trial in another location, sequestering jurors, permitting counsel to question those called for jury duty, and issuing strong instructions to jurors to disregard media reports.[126]

Note that the *Dagenais* test does not apply to all publication bans, only those where a judge has the discretion, under the common law or under a statute, to impose or deny a ban. The precedent does not apply to mandatory bans—for example, the *Criminal Code*'s ban on publishing the evidence presented at a preliminary hearing, which must be imposed if requested by the defendant.

Applying Dagenais

The *Dagenais* ruling has been described as nothing short of "revolutionary," enhancing the openness of the courts and giving the media a powerful weapon to fight restrictions on publication and access to the courtroom.[127] And although one observer has cautioned that such hype might turn out to be "much ado about nothing," and that the ruling merely formalized the balancing of rights dictated under the Charter,[128] it is clear that *Dagenais* represents a watershed, a fundamental rethinking of how freedom of expression applies to the courts. A 1996 report of the Uniform Law Conference of Canada, a national body that lobbies for law reform, argued that the ruling is not confined to discretionary publication bans. Chief Justice Lamer "set down the fundamental principles and values which must be balanced whenever limitations may be placed upon the publication of information about what occurs in a criminal courtroom or even access to that courtroom."[129]

The Supreme Court of Canada has put the *Dagenais* approach to work in other contexts. It has applied the rights-balancing approach to the way that judges use their discretionary power under section 486(1) of the *Criminal Code* to close a courtroom to the public. As in *Dagenais*, judges must consider alternatives to excluding the public and, if an exclusion order is granted, ensure that it is as limited in scope as possible. The benefits of closing the courtroom must be weighed against the principle of openness and the right of free expression.[130]

In late 2001 the court revisited the publication ban issue in a pair of rulings (including one known as *Mentuck*) that rejected sweeping bans on police undercover operations. Declaring that Canada "is not a police state," the court said the public must be free to scrutinize the tactics used in apprehending suspected criminals. Openness and media scrutiny ensure that trials are conducted fairly and, just as importantly, help to vindicate defendants who are found not guilty by informing the public of the reasons for an acquittal. Because neither ban related to the fair-trial rights of the defendants, the court ruled that judges should apply what are now known as the *Dagenais/Mentuck* principles when faced with applications for publication bans that could protect or hinder the proper administration of justice.[131] The court has also applied this test to applications for an order sealing confidential information presented in court cases. Judges must weigh free expression and openness against the need to protect other important interests, including commercial interests.[132] The Supreme Court went further in 2005, asserting that "the *Dagenais/Mentuck* test applies to *all* discretionary court orders that limit freedom of expression and freedom of the press in relation to legal proceedings." It also ruled that the media can challenge publication bans and access restrictions "at every stage of the judicial process," including during police investigations and before criminal or other charges are filed. The court's bottom-line position, that "[i]n any constitutional climate, the administration of justice thrives on exposure to light—and withers under a cloud of secrecy," bodes well for further media challenges to restrictions on coverage of the justice system.[133]

Freedom of Expression: A Summary

The Charter guarantees the right of freedom of expression to all Canadians. Journalists, performers, artists, musicians, advertisers, political activists, concerned citizens—anyone with an agenda to promote or an opinion or point of view to express has the right to be heard. Freedom of expression, however, is not absolute. Governments can pass laws limiting free speech if the restriction is reasonable and in keeping with the freedoms afforded to the citizens of a democratic state. The constitution also protects freedom of the press and other media of communication, a recognition of the media's special role in ensuring that the public is informed and government institutions and the courts are accountable. Once again, this freedom is not absolute. The right to attend and write about court proceedings must be balanced against the right of accused persons to a fair trial, the privacy rights of participants, and the right of the courts to protect the administration of justice. Publication bans and restrictions on access—both erect barriers that limit free expression in an effort to strike this balance. These limits, and their impact on what can be written about legal issues and individual cases, will be examined in Part Three of this text.

Freedom of the Press in Canada: A Timeline

1752	John Bushell founds the *Halifax Gazette*, the first newspaper published in what would become Canada, in partnership with a Halifax lawyer and a Boston merchant. His print shop publishes laws and government proclamations as well as forms and stationery for merchants and the public.
1753	The *Gazette* publishes a letter critical of Nova Scotia's military government. Merchants lobbying for an elected legislature, the writer contends, "understand their Business better than such as have been brought up in the military Way."
1762	Nova Scotia's governing council votes to cover the cost of replacing the *Gazette*'s worn-out type. Bushell's successor, Anthony Henry, agrees to repay the loan within one year.
1764	American printers Thomas Gilmore and William Brown found the *Quebec Gazette/La Gazette de Québec*, published in English and French.
1765	*Halifax Gazette* lampoons and criticizes the British government's *Stamp Act* taxes on paper and reprints coverage of protests in the American colonies. Nova Scotia's provincial secretary warns Henry to cease his campaign against the tax or risk losing government printing business.
	The increased cost of paper under the *Stamp Act* forces the *Quebec Gazette* to suspend publication for seven months, from October 1765 to May 1766.
1766	The Nova Scotia government removes Henry as the *Gazette*'s publisher, possibly by calling in security he pledged in return for new type. London printer Robert Fletcher is recruited to publish the renamed *Nova-Scotia Gazette*, which avoids comment on local and American events.

1769	Henry founds the *Nova Scotia Chronicle and Weekly Advertiser* to compete with Fletcher's *Gazette*. The following year he regains control of the *Gazette* and merges the titles to form the *Nova-Scotia Gazette and the Weekly Chronicle*. Both of Henry's papers provide pro-American news and commentary.
1776	The Nova Scotia council issues a proclamation forbidding the "reprinting or Publishing [of] treasonable papers." By now Henry's *Nova-Scotia Gazette* is seen as reflecting the opinions of "the substantial people" of the colony, and publishes a letter denouncing the leaders of the American Revolution as villains and demagogues.
1778	Quebec's lieutenant governor, concerned that William Brown's *Quebec Gazette* is exhibiting a "Penchant to the popular cause," insists that the printer provide him with an advance copy of "whatever he intends to publish."
1779	In Montreal, publisher Fleury Mesplet and editor Valentin Jautard are jailed for three years without trial after publishing letters criticizing a judge in their paper, *La Gazette littéraire*.
1780s	An influx of Loyalist refugees after the Revolution leads to the formation of the new colonies of Upper Canada and New Brunswick and rejection of American-style democracy. King's Printers are appointed in New Brunswick (1785), Nova Scotia (1788), and Prince Edward Island (1788) to publish laws, proclamations, and official newspapers.
1786	William Lewis and John Ryan, proprietors of the *Saint John Gazette and Weekly Advertiser*, are charged with criminal libel after supporting opposition candidates in a New Brunswick election. Each man is fined £20 and ordered to post a £50 bond to ensure their good behaviour.

1791	John Graves Simcoe, governor of Upper Canada, describes the services of a printer to publish laws and other official documents as "indispensably necessary" to the administration of a new colony. Montreal printer Louis Roy is appointed King's Printer.
1807	John Ryan leaves New Brunswick to establish the *Royal Gazette and Newfoundland Advertiser* in St. John's. The governor demands he post a bond and promise not to publish anything that "may tend to disturb the peace of His Majesty's Subjects."
1818	Upper Canada reform activist Robert Gourlay is acquitted of libel after publishing attacks on the government's land-settlement policies.
	Anthony Henry Holland, publisher of Halifax's *Acadian Recorder*, is reprimanded for satirizing a member of the Nova Scotia legislature.
1820	A jury convicts William Wilkie of criminal libel for publishing a pamphlet attacking Nova Scotia's courts and all levels of local government. He is sentenced to two years in jail.
1823	The editor of the *Prince Edward Island Register*, James Douglas Haszard, attacks the actions of the colony's governor as "oppressive and illegal." His only punishment is a stern lecture from the governor.
1824	William Lyon Mackenzie founds *The Colonial Advocate* and becomes a harsh critic of Upper Canada's ruling Family Compact. Two years later a Tory mob ransacks his print shop and dumps his type into Lake Ontario.
1828	Francis Collins, publisher of the *Canadian Freeman* in York, serves 11 months in jail for libelling the attorney general of Upper Canada.
1830	In Saint John, editor John Hooper of the *British Colonist* is convicted of libel for an attack on New Brunswick's judiciary, but escapes punishment.

1833	Montreal's *Daily Advertiser* appears, the first daily published in British North America.
1835	Joseph Howe, editor of *The Novascotian*, is acquitted of seditious libel for exposing Halifax's corrupt magistrates after appealing to jurors at his trial "to leave an unshackled press as a legacy to your children." The verdict makes colonial governments wary of using the criminal law to stifle critics.
	Robert John Parsons of the *Newfoundland Patriot* is fined and sentenced to three months in jail for criticizing the colony's chief justice. A public outcry forces the government to remit the fine and free Parsons.
1838	In the wake of uprisings in the Canadas, Upper Canada Chief Justice John Beverley Robinson complains of "a licentious press ... permitted to poison the public mind with the most absurd and wicked misrepresentations."
1865	More than 375 newspapers, including 35 dailies, serve a population of 3.5 million in British North America.
1867	At Confederation, most newspapers are owned by (or support) one of the major political parties, Conservative or Reform (Liberal).
1888	John T. Hawke, editor of the *Moncton Transcript*, is found in contempt and sentenced to two months in jail for describing a judge as pompous and accusing him of being drunk in court.
1892	Parliament adopts a *Criminal Code* that formalizes the offences of defamatory, seditious, and blasphemous libel and creates defences to protect political debate and press freedom.
1900	The number of daily newspapers published in Canada reaches 121 and more than 850 other papers are published at least once a week. Partisan control and influence weakens during the first half of the 20th century as circulations and advertising revenues increase.

1914	William R. McCurdy, news editor of the *Halifax Herald*, is imprisoned for two days for contempt of the Nova Scotia legislature. He refused to identify the author of an anonymous letter, published in the *Herald*, accusing members of the government of corruption.
1914-1918	During the First World War, federal government censorship regulations restrict publication of information considered useful to the enemy.
1917	The Canadian Press wire service is formed to distribute news among member newspapers.
1918	XWA in Montreal becomes the first radio station licensed to broadcast in Canada. More than 60 stations are in operation by 1928.
1922	The Quebec legislature finds John H. Roberts, editor of the Montreal weekly paper *The Axe*, in contempt for publishing rumours that politicians are shielding those responsible for an unsolved murder. He serves five months in jail.
1929	A royal commission headed by bank president John Aird recommends public ownership of radio broadcasting.
1931	The first Canadian television station, VE9EC in Montreal, begins operation.
1932	The Canadian Radio Broadcasting Commission is established to create a nationwide broadcasting service.
1936	The Canadian Broadcasting Corporation replaces the CRBC, with greater independence from government and a clearer mandate to create a coast-to-coast network of radio stations.
1938	The Supreme Court of Canada strikes down Alberta laws curtailing freedom of the press, and describes the "right of free public discussion of public affairs" as "the breath of life for parliamentary institutions."
1939-1945	The Second World War brings the return of censorship. A network of federal censors advises editors on war-related information that can be published without risking prosecution.
1951	The Supreme Court restricts the legal definition of sedition, saying "freedom in thought and speech and disagreement in ideas and beliefs, on every conceivable subject, are of the essence of our life."
1952	The CBC begins television broadcasts.
1955	George V. Ferguson, editor of the *Montreal Daily Star*, declares that "every man and woman will be better off if the transmission and reception of fact and opinion are left free from the intervention of government."
1957	The Supreme Court strikes down a Quebec law restricting the distribution of communist propaganda. Canada's democratic system demands "government by the free public opinion of an open society," the ruling says, and "virtually unobstructed access to and diffusion of ideas."
1958	The Board of Broadcast Governors is established to oversee the granting of licences to radio and television broadcasters and to promote Canadian programming.
1960	Ottawa introduces a *Bill of Rights* to protect human rights and fundamental freedoms, including freedom of speech, but it applies only to the federal government and its laws.
1968	The CRTC, the Canadian Radio-television Commission (renamed the Canadian Radio-television and Telecommunications Commission in 1976), is created to regulate private broadcasters and the CBC.

1969	The *Report of the Special Senate Committee on Mass Media* calls government interference "the gravest potential threat" to press freedom in Canada.
	Montreal's fire commissioner jails John N. Smith for seven days after the CBC television reporter refuses to name an interviewee who claimed to be an FLQ bomber.
1977	Nova Scotia introduces Canada's first freedom of information legislation.
1980	The sudden closure of daily newspapers in Ottawa and Winnipeg prompts the federal government to set up a royal commission to investigate the concentration of media ownership and its impact on press freedom. The commission's 1981 report recommends the creation of a government agency to regulate media mergers, but no action is taken.
1981	The Supreme Court opens its doors to television cameras, permitting the broadcast of its ruling on repatriation of the constitution.
1982	The *Charter of Rights and Freedoms* is adopted as part of Canada's constitution. Section 2(b) guarantees "freedom of thought, belief, opinion and expression, including freedom of the press and other media of communication."
	The Supreme Court's landmark ruling in *Attorney General of Nova Scotia v. MacIntyre* affirms the principle of public access to court proceedings and documents.
1983	Ontario's Court of Appeal describes openness of the courts as "one of the hallmarks of a democratic society" and "a restraint on arbitrary action by those who govern and by the powerful."
	Ottawa introduces the *Access to Information Act*, allowing citizens to apply for access to the records of federal departments and agencies.

1987	The Ontario Court of Appeal effectively ends contempt prosecutions for scandalizing the courts. Its ruling in *R v. Kopyto* asserts that courts and judges "are not fragile flowers that will wither in the hot heat of controversy."
1989	In a ruling on media access to the courts, the Supreme Court concludes "a democracy cannot exist without that freedom to express new ideas and to put forward opinions about the functioning of public institutions."
1994	The Supreme Court's *Dagenais* ruling calls on judges to limit the use of publication bans and to strike a balance between freedom of the press and a suspect's right to a fair trial.
2001	In follow-up rulings, the Supreme Court says *Dagenais* restricts the use of publication bans to prevent public scrutiny of police investigations and the administration of justice.
2005	A Supreme Court ruling on access to court files declares that "the administration of justice thrives on exposure to light—and withers under a cloud of secrecy."
2006	The Senate Committee on Transport and Communications issues a report on the state of the news media that recommends automatic reviews of media mergers under the *Competition Act* and more CRTC oversight.
2008	The Supreme Court strengthens the fair comment defence to libel, ruling that Canadians "have as much right to express outrageous and ridiculous opinions as moderate ones."
	Human rights commissions dismiss discrimination complaints against the *Western Standard* magazine, for publishing controversial Prophet Muhammad cartoons, and *Maclean's*, for publishing a book excerpt warning of the Muslim threat to western societies.

| 2009 | The Supreme Court creates the defence of responsible communication on matters of public interest, which can defeat a libel claim based on factual errors or false allegations if writers and publishers demonstrate high journalistic standards. | 2010 | In a pair of rulings, the Supreme Court refuses to grant journalists a blanket right to withhold the identities of sources they have promised to protect. The court, however, recognizes the media's "special position" under the Charter and says judges should strive to "protect the media's secret sources where such protection is in the public interest," and demand disclosure of sources only as "a last resort." |

(Sources: W.H. Kesterton, *A History of Journalism in Canada* (Toronto: McClelland & Stewart, 1967); Paul Rutherford, *The Making of the Canadian Media* (Toronto: McGraw-Hill Ryerson, 1978); *Dictionary of Canadian Biography Online* (www.biographi.ca); Dean Jobb, "'The First That Ever Was Publish'd in the Province': John Bushell's *Halifax Gazette*, 1752-1761," Royal Nova Scotia Historical Society *Journal*, vol. 11 (2008), 1-22; George V. Ferguson, "Freedom of the Press," in *Press and Party in Canada* (Toronto: Ryerson Press, 1955), 1–23; James Crankshaw, ed., *The Criminal Code of Canada* (Montreal: Whiteford & Theoret Law Publishers, 1894); P.B. Waite, *The Life and Times of Confederation 1864-1867: Politics, Newspapers, and the Union of British North America* (Toronto: University of Toronto Press, 1962); John Bartlet Brebner, *The Neutral Yankees of Nova Scotia: A Marginal Colony During the Revolutionary Years* (Toronto: McClelland & Stewart, 1969); G.A. Rawlyk, *Revolution Rejected 1775-1776* (Scarborough: Prentice-Hall of Canada, 1968); J. Murray Beck, "'A Fool for a Client': The Trial of Joseph Howe," *Acadiensis*, vol. 3, no. 2 (Spring 1974), 27-44; Marie Tremaine, *A Bibliography of Canadian Imprints, 1751-1800* (Toronto: University of Toronto Press, 1952); *Royal Commission on Newspapers* (Ottawa: Supply and Services Canada, 1981); *Report of the Special Senate Committee on Mass Media*, vol. 1 *The Uncertain Mirror* (Ottawa: Queen's Printer, 1970); Standing Senate Committee on Transport and Communications, *Final Report on the Canadian News Media*, vol. 1, available online at http://www.parl.gc.ca/39/1/parlbus/commbus/senate/Com-e/TRAN-E/rep-e/repfinjun06vol1-e .htm; *Reference re Alberta Statutes*, [1938] SCR 100; *Boucher v. The King*, [1951] SCR 265; *Attorney General of Nova Scotia v. MacIntyre* (1982), 65 CCC (2d) 129; *R v. Kopyto* (1987), 62 OR (2d) 449; *Edmonton Journal v. Alberta (Attorney General)*, [1989] 2 SCR 1326; *Dagenais v. Canadian Broadcasting Corporation*, [1994] 3 SCR 835; *Toronto Star Newspapers Ltd. v. Ontario*, 2005 SCC 41; *WIC Radio Ltd. v. Simpson*, 2008 SCC 40; *Grant v. Torstar Corp.*, 2009 SCC 61; *Quan v. Cusson*, 2009 SCC 62; *R v. National Post*, 2010 SCC 16; *Canadian Bill of Rights*, SC 1960, c. 44; *Canadian Charter of Rights and Freedoms*, part I of the *Constitution Act, 1982*, RSC 1985, app. II, no. 44.)

NOTES

1. W.H. Kesterton, *A History of Journalism in Canada* (Toronto: McClelland & Stewart, 1967), 21.

2. For accounts of Howe's trial, see Dean Jobb, *Bluenose Justice: True Tales of Mischief, Mayhem and Murder* (Hantsport, NS: Lancelot Press, 1996), 23–30, and J. Murray Beck, "'A Fool for a Client': The Trial of Joseph Howe," *Acadiensis*, vol. 3, no. 2 (Spring 1974), 27-44.

3. See Marjory Whitelaw, *First Impressions: Early Printing in Nova Scotia* (Halifax: Nova Scotia Museum, 1987), 6–11.

4. Kesterton, supra note 1, at 9.

5. Dean Jobb, "'The First That Ever Was Publish'd in the Province': John Bushell's *Halifax Gazette*, 1752-1761," Royal Nova Scotia Historical Society *Journal*, vol. 11 (2008), 1–22.

6. John Bartlet Brebner, *The Neutral Yankees of Nova Scotia: A Marginal Colony During the Revolutionary Years* (Toronto: McClelland & Stewart, 1969) 135–41.

7. This was the pattern in New Brunswick (1785), Nova Scotia (1788), Prince Edward Island (1788), and Upper Canada (1791). See biographies of Christopher Sower, Anthony Henry, James Robertson, and Louis Roy in *Dictionary of Canadian Biography Online*, http://www.biographi.ca.

8. See biographies of Wilkie and Collins in ibid.

9. James Mill, "Liberty of the Press," in *Essays on Government, Jurisprudence, Liberty of the Press, and Law of Nations* (1825) (reprint ed., 1967), 18.

10. For an account of the struggle to liberalize Britain's law of criminal libel, see Lord Denning, *Landmarks in the Law* (London: Butterworths, 1984), 283–97.

11. Anthony Smith, *The Newspaper: An International History* (London: Thames and Hudson, 1979), 86.

12. Quoted in D.C. Harvey, "Newspapers of Nova Scotia, 1840-1867," *Canadian Historical Review*, vol. 26, no. 3 (1945), 279–301, at 282.

13. Quoted in Paul Rutherford, *The Making of the Canadian Media* (Toronto: McGraw-Hill Ryerson, 1978), 1.

14. Ibid., at 7.

15. Walter Stewart, "No Virginia, There Is No Lou Grant," in Stewart, ed., *Canadian Newspapers: The Inside Story* (Edmonton: Hurtig Publishers, 1980), 9–30, at 14.

16. Merrill Distad, "Newspapers, Magazines and Commercial Journals," in William H. New, ed., *Encyclopedia of Literature in Canada* (Toronto: University of Toronto Press, 2002), 809.

17. This transformation is examined in Kesterton, supra note 1, at 222–26.

18. George V. Ferguson, "Freedom of the Press," in *Press and Party in Canada* (Toronto: Ryerson Press, 1955), 1–23, at 1.

19. John Robert Colombo, ed., *The Dictionary of Canadian Quotations* (Toronto: Stoddart Publishing, 1991), 379.

20. *The Uncertain Mirror: Report of the Special Senate Committee on Mass Media*, vol. 1, 101–102.

21. Kesterton, supra note 1, at 230.

22. *Reference re Alberta Statutes*, [1938] SCR 100, at 133.

23. Ibid., at 145–46.

24. *Boucher v. The King*, [1951] SCR 265, at 288.

25. *Switzman v. Elbling and the Attorney-General of Quebec*, [1957] SCR 285, at 306. Rand used similar language to stress the importance of freedom of expression in *Saumur v. City of Quebec and Attorney-General of Quebec*, [1953] 2 SCR 299, at 330. For an analysis of Rand's contribution to the development of freedom of speech and other democratic rights, see William Kaplan, *Canadian Maverick: The Life and Times of Ivan C. Rand* (Toronto: University of Toronto Press, 2009), chapter 4.

26. *Switzman*, supra note 25, at 326. For a discussion of Abbott's ruling, see Robert Martin, *Media Law* (Concord, ON: Irwin Law, 1997), 20.

27. *Canadian Bill of Rights*, SC 1960, c. 44.

28. Robert Martin and G. Stuart Adam, eds., *A Sourcebook of Canadian Media Law* (Ottawa: Carleton University Press, 1991), 70.

29. Peter W. Hogg, *Constitutional Law of Canada*, 2nd ed. (Scarborough, ON: Carswell, 1985), 713.

30. Quoted in John Tebbel, *The Media in America* (New York: New American Library, 1976), 90.

31. See Marc A. Franklin, "An Introduction to American Press Law," in Philip Anisman and Allen M. Linden, eds., *The Media, The Courts and the Charter* (Scarborough, ON: Carswell, 1986), 63–99.

32. *Canadian Charter of Rights and Freedoms*, part I of the *Constitution Act, 1982*, RSC 1985, app. II, no. 44.

33. *Irwin Toy Ltd. v. Quebec (Attorney General)*, [1989] 1 SCR 927, at 968.

34. Ibid., at 968–70.

35. Ibid., at 970. See also *RWDSU v. Dolphin Delivery Ltd.*, [1986] 2 SCR 573, at 588.

36. *R v. Zundel*, [1992] 2 SCR 731, at 752.

37. *Edmonton Journal v. Alberta (Attorney General)*, [1989] 2 SCR 1326, at 1339–40.

38. Martin, supra note 26, at 39.

39. *RWDSU v. Dolphin Delivery Ltd.*, supra note 35, at 583.

40. *Edmonton Journal v. Alberta (Attorney General)*, supra note 37, at 1336.

41. *Canadian Broadcasting Corp. v. New Brunswick (Attorney General)*, [1996] 3 SCR 480, at 494.

42. *Greater Vancouver Transportation Authority v. Canadian Federation of Students—British Columbia Component*, 2009 SCC 31.

43. *Harper v. Canada (Attorney General)*, [2004] 1 SCR 827.

44. *Irwin Toy Ltd. v. Quebec*, supra note 33.

45. *U.F.C.W. Local 1518 v. K-Mart Canada Ltd. et al.*, [1999] 2 SCR 1083; *U.F.C.W. Local 1288P v. Allsco Building Products Ltd. et al.*, [1999] 2 SCR 1136.

46. Cristin Schmitz, "CBA Warns Anti-Spam Bill May Violate Charter Free Speech," *The Lawyers Weekly*, October 9, 2009, 2.

47. *Montréal (City) v. 2952-1366 Québec Inc.*, [2005] 3 SCR 141, 2005 SCC 62.

48. *R v. Butler*, [1992] 1 SCR 452.

49. *R v. Sharpe*, [2001] 1 SCR 45.

50. *Criminal Code*, RSC 1985, c. C-46, as amended, s. 319(3)(a).

51. *R v. Keegstra*, [1990] 3 SCR 697.

52. *Criminal Code*, s. 181.

53. *R v. Zundel*, supra note 36.

54. *Canadian Newspapers Co. v. Canada (Attorney General)*, [1988] 2 SCR 122, at 129.

55. *Canadian Broadcasting Corp. v. New Brunswick (Attorney General)*, [1991] 3 SCR 459, at 475.

56. *Canadian Broadcasting Corp. v. Lessard*, [1991] 3 SCR 421, at 449–50.

57. Richard Moon, *The Constitutional Protection of Freedom of Expression* (Toronto: University of Toronto Press, 2000), 203.

58. *Gay Alliance Toward Equality v. Vancouver Sun*, [1979] 2 SCR 435.

59. *Adbusters Media Foundation v. Canadian Broadcasting Corporation*, 2009 BCCA 148 (CanLII). See also Gary Oakes, "Charter Claim Allowed Against TV Stations for Refusal to Broadcast," *The Lawyers Weekly*, April 17, 2009, 23–24. If the Charter is found to apply to a refusal to broadcast or publish, one commentator has suggested "the long-recognized freedom of the press should trump freedom to advertise." See Ryder Gilliland, "Right To Broadcast Clashes with Editorial Freedom," *The Lawyers Weekly*, October 16, 2009, 16–17.

60. *Royal Commission on Newspapers* (Ottawa: Supply and Services Canada, 1981); and *Report of the Special Senate Committee on Mass Media*, vol. 1 *The Uncertain Mirror* (Ottawa: Queen's Printer, 1970); Standing Senate Committee on Transport and Communications, *Final Report on the Canadian News Media*, vol. 1, http://www.parl.gc.ca.

61. To date, Ottawa's only response has been to temporarily prevent newspaper proprietors from owning a television or radio station in the same city. See Canada, Standing Senate Committee on Transport and Communications, "Part II: The State of the Canadian News Media," in *Interim Report on the Canadian News Media* (Ottawa: Queen's Printer, 2004), at 30–31.

62. *Broadcasting Act*, SC 1991, c. 11: *Radio Regulations, 1986*, SOR/86-982, s. 3(b).

63. Peter Desbarats, *Guide to Canadian News Media* (Toronto: Harcourt Brace Jovanovich, Canada, 1990), 49–50.

64. Moon, supra note 57, at 208; *CJMF-FM Ltée v. Canada* (CRTC), [1984] FCJ no. 244 (QL).

65. CRTC, Broadcasting Decision CRTC 2004-271, Ottawa, July 13, 2004.

66. *Genex Communications Inc. v. Canada (Attorney General)*, 2005 FCA 283 (CanLII).

67. *Genex Communications Inc. c. Procureur général du Canada-et-Conseil de la radiodiffusion et des télécommunications canadiennes (CRTC)*, 2007 CanLII 22312 (SCC).

68. Broadcasting Decision CRTC 2006-600 (Radio Nord Communications Inc.), October 20, 2006, available online at http://www.crtc.gc.ca/eng/archive/2006/db2006-600.htm.

69. Marlene Rego, "Fear of Publishing," *Ryerson Review of Journalism*, March 5, 2006, http://www.rrj.ca/m3548/.

70. Edward Greenspon, "Self-Censorship Versus Editing," *Globe and Mail*, February 11, 2006. See also Dean Jobb, "The Right To Publish. We Should Debate Where To Draw the Line," *Media* (Spring 2006), 17.

71. Joe Woodard, "Prophet Cartoons Come to Calgary," *Calgary Herald*, February 11, 2006; "P.E.I. Student Paper Publishes Cartoons of Prophet," CBC News Online, February 8, 2006.

72. "Publisher Defends Decision To Reprint Cartoons," CTV News Online, February 14, 2006.

73. Mark Steyn, "The Future Belongs to Islam," *Maclean's*, October 20, 2006.

74. Quoted in Haroon Siddiqui, "The Weighty Matter of Hate," *Toronto Star*, March 23, 2008.

75. See Cristin Schmitz, "Human Rights Watchdog Decries 'Demonization' of Commissions," *The Lawyers Weekly*, August 28, 2009, 3, 24; Terry O'Neill, "Fire the Censors," *National Post*, January 23, 2008; and Rob Breakenridge, "Rights Commissions Biggest Clowns in Anti-Free-Speech Circus," *Calgary Herald*, February 28, 2008.

76. Arnold Ceballos, "Critics and Defenders Agree: Hate Speech Laws Need Reform," *The Lawyers Weekly*, October 31, 2008, 17.

77. Siddiqui, "Hate Laws a Reasonable Limit on Free Speech," *Toronto Star*, June 22, 2008; Ken Norman, "Human Rights Commissions *Do* Uphold Freedom of Expression," *The Lawyers Weekly*, February 8, 2008; Joy-Ann Cohen, "Regulating Hate Speech: A Balancing Act," ibid., April 17, 2009.

78. *Canada (Human Rights Commission) v. Taylor*, [1990] 3 SCR 892.

79. See, for example, *Owens v. Saskatchewan (Human Rights Commission)*, 2006 SKCA 41, and *Boissoin v. Lund*, 2009 ABQB 592.

80. "Commission Statement Concerning Issues Raised by Complaints Against *Maclean's* Magazine," Ontario Human Rights Commission, press release issued April 9, 2008. Available online at http://www.ohrc.on.ca/en/resources/news/statement.

81. "Rights Commission Dismisses Complaint Against *Maclean's*," CBC News Online, June 28, 2008.

82. *Elmasry and Habib v. Roger's Publishing and MacQueen (No. 4)*, 2008 BCHRT 378.

83. *Canadian Human Rights Act*, RSC 1985, c. H-6, s. 12.

84. Ibid., ss. 13(1), (2), and (3). The legislation's application to messages distributed on the Internet was confirmed in *Warman v. Kulbashian*, 2006 CHRT 11.

85. *Warman v. Lemire*, 2009 CHRT 26.

86. "Judicial Review Application in the *Warman v. Lemire* Case," Canadian Human Rights Commission press release, issued October 1, 2009. Available online at http://www.chrc-ccdp.ca/whats_new/default-en.asp?id=570&content_type=2.

87. "Freedom of Expression and Freedom from Hate in the Internet Age," Special Report to Parliament, Canadian Human Rights Commission, June 2009. Available online at http://www.chrc-ccdp.ca/publications/srp_2009_rsp/page1-en.asp; Richard Moon, *Report to the Canadian Human Rights Commission Concerning Section 13 of the Canadian Human Rights Act and the Regulation of Hate Speech on the Internet*, October 2008. Available online at http://www.chrc-ccdp.ca/publications/report_moon_rapport/toc_tdm-en.asp.

88. While the Yukon's legislation makes no specific reference to publications, it forbids "systemic discrimination," defined as "any conduct that results in discrimination." *Human Rights Act*, RSY 2002, c. 116, s. 12.

89. *Charter of Human Rights and Freedoms*, RSQ c. C-12, s. 11.

90. *Human Rights Code*, RSO 1990, c. H.19, s. 13(1); *Human Rights Act*, RSPEI 1988, c. H-12, s. 12(1); *Human Rights Act*, SNu 2003, c. 12, s. 14(1); *Human Rights Code*, RSNL 1990, c. H-14, s. 14(1); *Human Rights Act*, RSNB 1973, c. H-11, s. 6(1); *Human Rights Act*, RSNS 1989, c. 214, s. 7(1); *Saskatchewan Human Rights Code*, SS 1979, c. S-24.1, s. 14(1).

91. *Alberta Human Rights Act*, RSA 2000, c. A-25.5, s. 3(1); *Human Rights Code*, RSBC 1996, c. 210, s. 7(1); *The Human Rights Code*, CCSM c. H175, s. 18.

92. *Alberta Human Rights Act*, s. 3(1)(b); *Human Rights Code* (BC), s. 7(1)(b); *Human Rights Act*, SNWT 2002, c. 18, s. 13(1)(c).

93. *Human Rights Act* (PEI), ss. 12(1) and (2); *Human Rights Code* (NL), ss. 14(1) and (2); *Human Rights Act* (NB), ss. 6(1) and (2); *Saskatchewan Human Rights Code*, ss. 14(1) and (2); *Human Rights Act* (NS), ss. 7(1) and (2).

94. *Human Rights Code* (Ont.), s. 13(2); *Alberta Human Rights Act*, s. 3(2); *Human Rights Act* (NWT), s. 13(2).

95. "Commission Statement Concerning Issues Raised by Complaints Against *Maclean's* Magazine," supra note 80.

96. *Elmasry and Habib v. Roger's Publishing and MacQueen (No. 4)*, supra note 82.

97. *Human Rights Code* (BC), s. 7(2).

98. *Kane v. Alberta Report*, 2001 ABQB 570. A human rights tribunal found *Alberta Report* in violation of the Act and a second judge later ordered a new hearing. See *Alberta Report v. Alberta (Human Rights and Citizenship Commission)*, 2002 ABQB 1081.

99. *Canadian Jewish Congress v. North Shore Free Press Ltd. (No. 7)* (1997), 30 CHRR D/5. See also Canadian Newspaper Association, "B.C. Human Rights Code Declared Constitutional in Collins Hearing," *The Press and the Courts*, vol. 16, no. 6, November-December 1997.

100. *Abrams v. North Shore News (No. 3)* (1999), 33 CHRR D/435.

101. *Owens v. Saskatchewan (Human Rights Commission)*, supra note 79.

102. John Gillis, "Muslim Leader: Herald Cartoon Offensive," *Chronicle-Herald* (Halifax), May 10, 2008.

103. Presentation by Krista Daley, director and CEO, Nova Scotia Human Rights Commission, to "The Media's Right To Offend: Exploring the Legal and Ethical Limits on Free Speech," 2008 Joseph Howe Symposium at the School of Journalism, University of King's College, Halifax, November 1, 2008.

104. *Boissoin v. Lund*, supra note 79.

105. Moon, *Freedom of Expression*, supra note 57.

106. Cited by Justice Dickson in *Attorney General of Nova Scotia v. MacIntyre* (1982), 65 CCC (2d) 129, at 144–45 (SCC).

107. Ontario Press Council, *Trial by Media: An Account of an Open Forum on Pre-trial Publicity Held by the Ontario Press Council* (Ottawa: Author, May 1984), 17–18.

108. Charter, s. 11(d).

109. *Attorney General of Nova Scotia v. MacIntyre*, supra note 106.

110. *Halsbury's Laws of England*, 4th ed., vol. 10, at 316, cited ibid., at 147.

111. *Reference re: s. 12(1) of the Juvenile Delinquents Act (Canada) (sub nom. R v. Southam Inc.)* (1983), 34 CR (3d) 27, 41 OR (2d) 113 (CA).

112. Willard Z. Estey, "Freedom of Expression vs. The Individual's Right to Privacy," in Frederic L.R. Jackman, ed., *Media & Society* (Toronto: The Canadian Journalism Foundation and The Empire Club of Canada, 1994), 27–41, at 39.

113. *Edmonton Journal v. Alberta (Attorney General)*, supra note 37, at 1339–40.

114. *Canadian Broadcasting Corp. v. New Brunswick (Attorney General)*, supra note 41.

115. Charter, ss. 7 and 11(d).

116. For example, in *R v. Banville* (1983), 3 CCC (3d) 312, the New Brunswick Court of Queen's Bench found that s. 539(1) of the *Criminal Code*, which bans publication of evidence presented at preliminary hearings, is a justifiable limit on the media's freedom of expression under s. 1 of the Charter. In *Re Global Communications Ltd. and A.G. Canada* (1984), 10 CCC (3d) 97, the Ontario Court of Appeal upheld the s. 517(1) ban on publishing information presented at bail hearings.

117. "Banned," *Globe and Mail*, December 5, 1992.

118. *Canadian Broadcasting Corporation v. Dagenais* (1993), 12 OR (3d) 239 (CA).

119. *Dagenais v. Canadian Broadcasting Corporation*, [1994] 3 SCR 835.

120. Ibid., at 881.

121. Ibid., at 877.

122. Ibid., at 879–80.

123. Ibid., at 882.

124. Ibid., at 878.

125. Ibid., at 891.

126. Ibid., at 881.

127. Michael R. Doody, *Reporting on Adult Courts and Tribunals* (Toronto: Hallion Press, 1995), at 19, 21.

128. Omar Wakil, "Publication Bans on Court Proceedings in Canada," Centre for the Independence of Judges and Lawyers *Yearbook*, vol. 4 (December 1995), 101–10, at 109–10.

129. Publication Bans Committee, *Report of the Publication Bans Committee*, Criminal Law Section, Uniform Law Conference of Canada, Ottawa, November 1996. Available online at http://www.ulcc.ca.

130. *Canadian Broadcasting Corp. v. New Brunswick (Attorney General)*, supra note 41.

131. *R v. Mentuck*, [2001] 3 SCR 442, 2001 SCC 76; *R v. O.N.E.*, [2001] 3 SCR 478, 2001 SCC 77.

132. *Sierra Club of Canada v. Canada (Minister of Finance)*, [2002] 2 SCR 522.

133. *Toronto Star Newspapers Ltd. v. Ontario*, [2005] 2 SCR 188, 2005 SCC 41, at paragraphs 1, 7, and 8.

PART TWO
Journalists and the Law

CHAPTER 4

Defamation: How To Beat Libel Chill

Understanding Defamation

What Is Defamation?

The assignment was as routine as it gets. Attend a conference, then write up a story on the most interesting speaker or issue. The reporter for Halifax's *Chronicle-Herald* dutifully turned in a piece featuring a police sergeant who warned that organized crime is no longer a big-city problem. The local chapter of the Hells Angels biker gang was Nova Scotia's "most dangerous organized crime gang," the officer noted, "but it isn't alone." Asian and Eastern European gangs also operate in the province, he told a workshop at a criminal justice conference in Halifax, and he named two small-town motorcycle clubs that the police were monitoring. "Police can't say whether the members are involved in criminal activity," the newspaper reported, but the sergeant "said they are linked to the Angels."

The officer concluded his talk with a plea for citizens to report sightings of "strangers" or "suspicious activity" in their communities. The editor who reviewed the story before publication topped it with the headline: "Watch Out For Big-Time Crime: Criminal Gangs Affect Us All, Police Warn."[1]

As routine as it seemed, the story should have set off alarm bells for both the reporter and the editor. The members of the two motorcycle clubs had been branded "big-time" criminals, linked to the notorious Hells Angels. No names were reported, but in all likelihood club members were well known within their small communities. Did the newspaper have enough facts to justify publishing the damning allegation? Could members of the clubs—as individuals or as a group—sue the paper for sullying their reputations? And if the paper were sued, could the journalist and editor justify their decision to report the alleged link to Nova Scotia's "most dangerous organized crime gang"? Can disparaging comments or allegations of wrongdoing be published if the journalist can prove they are true, or if it serves the public interest to report the information? Does it make a difference whether the allegation came from an official source like the police, or whether the allegation was made during a speech at a public forum?

These questions strike at the heart of defamation, a complex area of the civil law that recognizes the importance of a person's reputation. In a passage from *Othello*, William Shakespeare captured the essence of the tort of defamation:

Good name in man, and woman, dear my lord,
Is the immediate jewel of our souls.
Who steals my purse steals trash. 'Tis something, nothing;
'Twas mine, 'tis his, and has been slave to thousands;
But he that filches from me my good name
Robs me of that which not enriches him,
And makes me poor indeed.[2]

Reputation is a precious thing and, like anything else of value, it can be lost, stolen, or destroyed. Defamation—better known as libel—is a form of tort law that gives everyone the right to protect their good name from being sullied by the unjustified allegations or criticisms of others. In the words of the Supreme Court of Canada, a good reputation

enhances an individual's sense of worth and value. False allegations can so very quickly and completely destroy a good reputation. A reputation tarnished by libel can seldom regain its former lustre. A democratic society, therefore, has an interest in ensuring that its members can enjoy and protect their good reputation so long as it is merited ... .[3]

If the damage to reputation is proven, the courts can order the journalist and media outlet responsible to pay thousands of dollars in damages to make amends. The mere threat of being sued for defamation is enough to keep journalists second-guessing their decisions. Is the criticism in the story fair? Are the facts right? Will the corporate executive or government official under attack sue? If she does, will she win in court? But the consequences for a journalist go beyond the possibility of being ordered to pay damages. "Few things do more to ruin a journalist's reputation," notes media law scholar Robert Martin, "than to write stories that lead to libel actions, especially libel actions that employers lose. The journalist gets a reputation as someone who is not thorough, who is sloppy, who is inaccurate, and so on."[4]

But the law of defamation does more than protect reputations from unfair attacks—it fosters and promotes good journalism. The common law and provincial defamation statutes offer defences that protect news stories and commentary that are factually correct, balanced, and fair. If the media could report whatever it liked about whomever it liked, readers, listeners, and viewers would find it impossible to separate fact from fiction. The impact on the media's credibility would be devastating. "If no one had any redress for libel," British journalist Paul Foot once noted, "no one would ever believe a word we wrote."[5] Although defamation law imposes limits on free speech to protect the reputations of individuals, it also defends good journalism and the media's role as public informer and government critic. If reporters, editors, producers, and news organizations conduct themselves professionally and responsibly, the risk of being sued for defamation becomes remote.

What Statements Can Be Defamatory?

Definitions

Any statement that is published or broadcast and is capable of damaging the reputation of a specific person or company could be considered defamatory. The classic British definition of a defamatory statement is one

> which tends to lower a person in the estimation of right-thinking members of society generally, or to cause him to be shunned and avoided, or to expose him to hatred, contempt or ridicule, or to convey an imputation on him disparaging or injurious to him in his office, profession, calling, trade or business.[6]

In short, a defamatory statement is one that strikes at the heart of someone's reputation, stripping away what Shakespeare called the "jewel" of the person's soul. A defamatory statement undermines someone's reputation as an honest, law-abiding, morally upright person. Any allegation of misconduct, corruption, wrongdoing, or criminal behaviour is capable of damaging or destroying someone's reputation—an accusation of belonging to a "dangerous organized crime gang" would fall into all four of these categories. It can be an attack on a person's ethics, motives, competence, trustworthiness, or morality, or a statement that a person is insolvent or financially irresponsible. Robert Martin has suggested a common-sense definition: a defamatory statement, he advises journalists, "is simply something you would not like to see said in public about yourself."[7] But an insult or abusive comment—no matter how offensive or hurtful—is not necessarily defamatory. "The words must be more than unpleasant and disagreeable," says Canadian defamation expert Raymond Brown. "Language which is simply crude, offensive and in bad taste, or which affronts a person's dignity, but does not otherwise lower him or her in the esteem of others, is generally not actionable."[8]

If a libel action goes to trial, a judge or jury ultimately decides whether words published or broadcast are defamatory. What the journalist intended the words to mean is irrelevant. It is not a defence for a writer or media outlet to claim there was no intention to defame. Likewise, the plaintiff's interpretation of what a disputed statement means will not necessarily be accepted. Judges consider the everyday, commonly understood meanings of the words in dispute, and if necessary will consult dictionaries and other reference books to obtain exact definitions. The courts strive, as one ruling put it, to "construe the words according to the meaning they would be given by reasonable persons of ordinary intelligence."[9] This can become a nit-picky exercise. A BC judge once ruled that it is not libellous to call someone a "son of a bitch," arguing that the term only takes on its meaning when coupled with an adjective. "Thus," he observed, "one has sympathy for a poor son of a bitch, admiration for a brave son of a bitch, affection for a good son of a bitch, envy for a rich son of a bitch and, perhaps incongruously, dislike for a proper son of a bitch." Adding the adjective "sick" to the term, he concluded, crosses the line—describing someone as a "sick son of a bitch" is defamatory.[10]

The courts also take into account the context of the article or broadcast item in which the words have been used. "The publication must be considered as a whole," says Brown; "a court will not dwell or concentrate on isolated passages in determining whether it is defamatory."[11] Context includes the headlines, photo captions, and artwork or visuals that accompany the item as published or broadcast. This approach can work to a journalist's benefit: in one case, a reference to a notorious Soviet defector as a "traitor" was found not to be defamatory because the description was accurate when considered within the context of the entire news story.[12] It can also create problems for journalists. A Nova Scotia court ruled that a businessman's defamation claim arising from a newspaper story should be viewed within the context of five other stories in an investigative series that made sweeping allegations of political corruption.[13]

Libel and Slander

The terms "libel" and "slander" are sometimes confused. Historically, they were considered distinct forms of defamation. Slander came first and dealt with verbal comments or attacks on the character of another person. The advent of the printing press in the 15th century created a new form of written defamation, which became known as libel and could be pursued as both a criminal offence and a civil action to recover damages. The differences went beyond the means used to disseminate the defamatory statement. In the case of slander, the law required a plaintiff to prove that a statement had damaged his reputation in some tangible way, while in the case of libel, the victim was presumed to have been harmed.

Today, the distinction has largely disappeared—most provinces and territories have introduced legislation merging slander and libel into a single tort of defamation. In the opinion of defamation expert Raymond Brown, "the law of defamation would be better served if this distinction were abolished in all jurisdictions." Many of these laws also clarify that a defamatory comment broadcast on radio or television, while in verbal form, is akin to a comment published in written form and is considered a libel. Online broadcasts would be treated in the same fashion.

(Source: Raymond Brown, *Defamation Law: A Primer* (Toronto: Carswell, 2003), Chapter 2.)

It is also important to ensure information that challenges or refutes a defamatory allegation is given prominence. In 2005, for example, British Columbia's appeal court wiped out an award of $633,000 in damages against a small-town newspaper for reporting an outbreak of food poisoning at a restaurant. The story erroneously suggested diners became sick from eating buffet food that a patron suffering from a virus had vomited on. The court found diners had been sickened, but the cause was the restaurant's failure to properly clean infected surfaces. Since the story quoted the restaurant's owner and a health official suggesting this—and not food poisoning—was the likely cause of the outbreak, the court said the overall context of the report was not defamatory. After reviewing the ruling, Vancouver libel lawyer David Crerar offered the following advice to the media: quotations or statements that offset the defamatory "sting" of a report's main allegations should be given prominence in a headline, as a stand-alone quotation (known as a pull quote), or by placing them near the beginning of the story.[14]

Allegations of Criminal Conduct

Branding someone a criminal or a person who associates with criminals has an immediate, devastating impact on the person's reputation. This is why the newspaper report linking members of small-town motorcycle clubs to Nova Scotia's "most dangerous organized crime gang" was so risky. Once the police have investigated and a person has been charged with a crime (as discussed later in this chapter), media reports that name the offender and describe the evidence produced in court are shielded from a defamation lawsuit. But it is a different story when the media, through their own investigative work, accuse a person of theft, assault, murder, or another crime. If the target of a criminal allegation sues, the media outlet must produce the evidence needed to substantiate its allegation. In 2004 a jury ordered a Halifax television station to pay $15,000 in damages for reporting that a Nova Scotia man had been arrested in connection with the 9/11 terrorist attacks in New York and Washington, DC. The allegation turned out to be groundless, leaving the station with no factual basis to support the story that labelled him a terrorist.[15] In the same way, wrongly branding someone a pedophile would have a devastating impact on the person's reputation and could result in a defamation lawsuit.

If a person is being accused of a crime, the words used do not have to point to a specific offence to be defamatory. Damages have been awarded to plaintiffs who were described as villains, rogues, rascals, or cheaters.[16] Also, there is no magic in using the word "alleged," as in describing someone who has not been charged with homicide as an "alleged killer." If journalists are levelling the allegations of wrongdoing, the term offers no protection against a defamation action—the media outlet would have to be prepared to prove the wrongdoing occurred. The "rote use of the term 'alleged' " is not a defence to a libel action, British Columbia's top court has stated, "where the whole thrust of the article is written as fact."[17]

Loaded Words

These days almost no one would take offence at being called a "fogle hunter" or a "cully," or even someone who "gammons." That's because few people have the slightest idea what these colourful terms mean. But in 18th-century England, any one of them may well have been viewed as a serious libel. Fogle hunter was slang for a pickpocket. A cully was a fool or blockhead. Gammon was a verb meaning to lie or to deceive.[18]

For words to be defamatory, they must be understood to carry a defamatory meaning—and that means words and phrases once considered libellous are no longer capable of damaging someone's reputation. As the British lawyer and writer Joseph Dean noted in the 1960s, the words in dispute at libel trials offer a "broken, distorted mirror" of their time and place: "It was libel in the seventeenth century to call a man a papist; in the eighteenth century a liberal; today a communist, and tomorrow perhaps a member of the Establishment."[19] For example, at the height of the Cold War in 1963, a British Columbia court ruled that it was defamatory to call a labour leader a communist.[20] Such a finding seems unlikely today, when the communist label would strike most people as archaic rather than damning. The flamboyant performer Liberace successfully sued a British newspaper in 1959 for libel over a column that suggested he was a homosexual. This was in an era when homosexuality was a crime; today, being labelled gay or lesbian does not carry the same stigma or potential to ruin someone's reputation. A New Jersey judge ruled in 2010 that it is no longer defamatory to falsely accuse someone of being gay; and a New York judge had reached the same conclusion a year earlier, citing a "veritable sea change in attitudes about homosexuality."[21] In these celebrity-obsessed times, words and allegations once considered libellous are as likely to make someone's reputation as to destroy it. "What used to be called shame and humiliation is now called publicity," satirist P.J. O'Rourke has noted. "If you say a modern celebrity is an adulterer, a pervert and a drug addict, all it means is that you've read his autobiography."[22]

Two centuries ago, the term "bagman" may have drawn nothing more than quizzical looks. But when a newspaper used it in 1998 to describe a prominent lawyer who was also a political fundraiser, the lawyer threatened to sue for defamation. The paper published a front-page apology. In it, the paper acknowledged that the term created a "negative characterization" and could be interpreted as suggesting that the lawyer "had been involved in improper conduct."[23] Another newspaper was forced to apologize for describing a lawyer as a "shyster," apparently unaware that the term refers to a person—and, in particular, an attorney—who is "professionally unscrupulous."[24]

So what is considered libellous in our day? David Hooper, a leading British libel lawyer, has compiled a list of allegations that "are self-evidently, according to the natural and ordinary meaning of the words, defamatory" and have led to damage awards in the British courts in recent years. They include accusations of lying, corruption, cowardice, plagiarism, professional incompetence, financial distress, and sexual misbehaviour.[25]

The following is a rundown of the allegations and loaded words that should send journalists a message, loud and clear, to handle them with care:

- *Racism* It is difficult to prove that someone's actions were motivated by racism. Is the police officer who shot the fleeing suspect a racist, as critics claim, or was the colour of the suspect's skin irrelevant? "There is arguably no more vile a label in today's parlance than to be described as a 'racist,'" a judge of Nova Scotia's Court of Appeal has observed. "It constitutes one of the most egregious attacks upon character and reputation that one could imagine. It is a human stain and for this generation a scarlet letter."[26]
- *Financial problems* Reporting that a businessperson or other individual is on the verge of bankruptcy, faces financial problems, or is avoiding paying bills can have serious consequences. Creditors are likely to demand that bills be paid; bankers may recall loans; the credit rating of the person or company may suffer; lucrative contracts and business deals may be lost. If an allegation of insolvency or sloppy business practices is wrong, such reports are highly defamatory.

- *Deceit or dishonesty* Suggesting that a politician or businessperson who denies knowledge of an event or a controversy is lying can be risky business. There could be any number of reasons why a misleading statement was made—the person may have been misinformed by her staff, taken a cursory look at her briefing notes on the subject, or simply misunderstood a reporter's question. Although journalists should point out such discrepancies, it is wise to avoid making value judgments or speculating on motives. It is also defamatory to describe someone as a hypocrite. BC-based motivational speaker Tony Robbins won $20,500 in damages from several newspapers in 2005 for portraying him as a divorcee who had "stolen" another man's wife. The inference was that Robbins "does not practice what he preaches about husband-wife relationships," a judge ruled, and "to call a person a hypocrite is defamatory." The defendants tried to justify the comment using Robbins's advice and writings on the sanctity of marriage. The judge, however, found no inconsistency between Robbins's actions and his "trite" message that people caught in unhappy situations should find the inner strength to change.[27]
- *Conflict of interest* Allegations that a politician or public official is violating a conflict of interest code, or could benefit personally from a government decision or policy, should not be made lightly. Such allegations carry the scent of corruption and, if unsubstantiated, can cause serious damage to reputation.
- *Sexual harassment and misconduct* Allegations of sexual misbehaviour carry a stigma that is almost impossible to erase. An accusation of sexual harassment could end the career of a teacher or doctor. Although harassment complaints are not as damning as a criminal allegation of sexual assault, the impact on reputation remains serious and lasting.
- *Incompetence* The careers and livelihoods of doctors, lawyers, accountants, engineers, and other professionals hinge on their reputations. News reports suggesting that a professional is incompetent or lacks proper credentials will likely have a devastating effect on the person's reputation and livelihood. A Nova Scotia engineering firm, for example, was awarded $300,000 in damages over a defamatory letter that portrayed it as lacking the competence and professionalism needed to design certain facilities.[28] Doctors and lawyers have won even larger damage awards. For example, $950,000 was awarded to a prominent heart surgeon who was accused of jeopardizing the lives of his patients.[29] The Supreme Court of Canada has described a good reputation as the "cornerstone of a lawyer's professional life."[30] It has also been found to be defamatory to report that an expert witness's opinion was influenced by his role as a paid consultant to industry.[31]

Innuendo

Innuendo—what a reader or listener may be able to read between the lines of a news report—may be defamatory. Bob Dylan captured the essence of this subtle form of defamation in the song "Idiot Wind," released on his 1975 album *Blood on the Tracks*:

Someone's got it in for me, they're planting stories in the press
Whoever it is I wish they'd cut it out but when they will I can only guess.
They say I shot a man named Gray and took his wife to Italy,
She inherited a million bucks and when she died it came to me.
I can't help it if I'm lucky.

Dylan's lucky narrator was the victim of a smear campaign, based in part on an allegation he had murdered a man and fled to Italy with the man's widow. That allegation was direct and blunt. But there was also a suggestion he had murdered the woman so he could get his hands on the money she inherited from her late husband. That is the essence of innuendo. Verifiable facts—the woman was dead and the narrator had her money—are linked in a way that suggests something illegal or nefarious has occurred.

This kind of hidden message can be conveyed in news stories, even if the journalist does not intend to suggest that more is happening than is described. A journalist, for example, could write a story noting that a municipal politician has an expensive lifestyle, even though he earns a modest salary. Those facts are true. The story could also reveal that the minutes of city council meetings show that the politician supports development proposals put forward by a prominent businessman, who is also a long-time friend of the politician. Again, all this is true. The words "kickbacks" and "bribery" do not appear in the story, but the implication is that the politician is corrupt. There could be innocent explanations for the politician's lifestyle and his support of the development proposals: he may have inherited money or done well in business before entering politics, and may support the businessman's projects because he is convinced they are good for the city. But if the politician sued for defamation, the media outlet would have to prove that the innuendo is true—that the politician was assisting the businessman in return for personal gain. If there were no evidence to support this unstated but damning conclusion, a libel action would surely succeed.

There are other examples. The CBC program *the fifth estate* was found to have libelled a heart surgeon through innuendo by implying that the doctor misused his position on a medical advisory board and received kickbacks from a drug manufacturer.[32] A bureaucrat successfully sued the CBC for suggesting—but never stating—that his actions had contributed to an oil rig worker's death in an explosion.[33] An investment banker who was reported to have given "a different version" of events during a securities investigation sued the *National Post* in 2002 for portraying him as a liar, even though the word never appeared in print.[34]

Media law expert Robert Martin offers sage advice on the issue of innuendo: "Journalists should never waste their time beating around the bush or coyly suggesting conclusions. If a reporter does not have all the details of the story verified, he should not try to make up for the gaps in it by hinting at things."[35]

Who Can Be Defamed?

Identifiable Individuals

Defamation law is concerned with protecting the reputations of identifiable individuals. For a claim to succeed, the plaintiff must establish that he or she is the person portrayed in a bad light in a media report.[36] The plaintiff need not be named in the story. The test is whether "an ordinary sensible person to whom the words were published [would] understand them as pointing to the plaintiff."[37] People who read or hear a news item must be able to figure out who the person is, either from the information reported or the context of the story. This can happen in a number of ways. The person may be referred to only by occupation or residence, but this information may be enough to reveal her identity. The person may be linked to information that has already been published (or is published later) or to a place or incident. A television news story that shows a home and reports that the suspect in a murder lives there, for example, would defame the owner if the information is untrue or the person is never charged. A story that reveals the person's association with other people, a company, or a group may also enable people to make the connection.[38] Journalists worried about being sued may be tempted to use a hypothetical situation to discuss sensitive issues or allegations. But if a plaintiff is able to establish that the supposedly fictitious scenario relates to him and to a real situation, a defamation suit could succeed.

Two lawyers who managed the prosecution office of Ontario's Ministry of the Attorney General were able to sue the *Toronto Star* in 2009 even though their names did not appear in print. The newspaper reported an allegation that officials in "the upper echelons of the attorney-general's office" had "intentionally sabotaged" a case against police officers charged with corruption, by refusing to give prosecutors the resources needed to bring the case to trial within a reasonable time. Given the nature of the plaintiffs' duties—both were members of the office's management committee and one supervised prosecutions of police officers—a judge ruled that other lawyers involved in the criminal justice system would recognize them as members of the "upper echelons" of the attorney general's office.[39]

The person defamed must be alive. It is an axiom of law that "the dead, having no rights, can suffer no wrongs." (This common law principle does not apply in Quebec, where a lawsuit claiming defamation of a deceased person may be possible—see the box titled "Defamation Law in Quebec: A Special Case" on page 124.) A reputation may survive long after death, but the legal right to defend that reputation does not. Relatives and descendants cannot pursue a libel action on behalf of an estate unless the defamatory comment reflects on them in some fashion.[40] For example, if a news report stated that a family's wealth was generated through the illegal acts of a deceased ancestor, the allegation could affect the reputation of descendants and could give them grounds to sue. In the same way, a report that a man fathered an illegitimate child before his death would reflect on the child; the statement might not be considered defamatory, however, because being born to unwed parents does not carry the stigma it once did.

Companies and Other Organizations

Plaintiffs must be "persons" in the legal sense, and this gives corporations the legal right to sue for defamation. In the case of a company, however, the allegation must relate to the way it conducts its affairs—examples are accusations of defrauding customers, mismanaging shareholders' money, or flouting environmental laws. A corporation cannot sue over allegations arising from the actions of individual officers or employees; these officials, however, are free to launch their own libel suits.[41] In 2008, for instance, both cheese manufacturer Saputo Inc. and its chairman sued three media outlets over reports about a police probe in Italy. An Italian entrepreneur accused of fraud had used the company's name to boost his credibility, and Saputo claimed the news reports unfairly linked the company to allegations of wrongdoing and its chairman to a man he had never met.[42]

Courts have ruled that other entities that are incorporated or created by statute—labour unions, school boards, non-profit organizations and associations—can also sue for libel. Entities without legal status, such as political parties and ad hoc citizen's committees, cannot sue, but individuals belonging to such groups can bring an action if a damaging statement reflected on their personal conduct.

Members of Groups

Because a plaintiff must prove that he is the specific subject of a publication, in most cases a group of people cannot sue. The statement that "all doctors are incompetent," while insulting to members of the medical profession, could not be the subject of a libel action because it is clearly false and no individual doctor could establish that the statement refers to her. This was the basis for a court's refusal to allow a group of Canadian veterans to pursue a libel action on the basis of a television documentary they claimed portrayed Second World War bomber crews as murderers.[43] In the same way, Toronto's police union lost a bid to sue the *Toronto Star* over stories that alleged a pattern of racial profiling in arrests because the stories did not single out specific officers as racists.[44] "An attack on a substantially large and indeterminate group of persons does not give rise to a cause of action to any of its members," one judge has noted, "unless there is something in the publication pointing to a particular member, or making it susceptible of special application to an individual in a class."[45]

Journalists dealing with allegations against a group of people must be conscious of the size and nature of the group. The smaller the group and the more specific the reference, the greater the chance that one or more individuals can establish that a news story defames them personally. When Halifax's *Chronicle-Herald* newspaper reported that police were targeting motorcycle gangs with connections to organized crime, for example, and named a small-town club with only a few members, those members might have been able to sue. The CBC once broadcast an interview with a prostitute who claimed that two members of a narcotics squad who were "high up—right up on top—take payoffs." A court ruled that the squad's two senior officers could sue, because they had a strong basis for claiming that the report referred to them. But seven other members of the squad were barred from taking legal action because the allegation was limited to the "top" officers.[46]

As stated above, in most cases, a group of people cannot sue for defamation. But the way an allegation is worded may enable members of a larger group to sue—journalists must ensure that an allegation against unnamed members of a group does not tar the entire group with the same brush. In one case, an Alberta court allowed 25 prison guards to sue over a story describing guards at a particular jail as "goons" and "not having the brains to be Nazis." No guards were named but the generalizations covered the facility's entire staff.[47] Casting suspicion on a single, unnamed member of a large group is safe—unless, of course, the facts as reported clearly point to a particular person. Reporting that a teacher at a large school has been accused of striking a student would not label every teacher in the school a child abuser. On the other hand, reporting that most of the employees of a trucking firm have been convicted of drunk driving would cast suspicion on all of them. One legal text warns that how the allegation is phrased is crucial: "a statement that all but one of 16 employees are felons would implicate all 16 employees; a statement that only one of 16 employees is a felon would implicate none of the employees."[48]

Quebec's civil law procedures, however, have features not found in the common law of defamation followed in the rest of Canada (see the box titled "Defamation Law in Quebec: A Special Case" on page 124) and permit large groups of people to file a class action for libel. Quebec's Court of Appeal approved a class action on behalf of about 1,000 Arab and Haitian taxi drivers against a Montreal radio host, who criticized the drivers as incompetent and ignorant and claimed they drove dirty, poorly maintained cars. The claim went to trial and a judge awarded the drivers $220,000 in damages, but this was overturned in 2008 by the Court of Appeal, which ruled the host's words were "negative and racist" but unlikely to harm the reputations of individual drivers. The drivers appealed and a Supreme Court of Canada ruling on scope of group libel claims was pending at the time of writing.[49]

Real People Described in Fictional Works or Whose Names Have Been Changed

Fiction writers must take care when creating and naming characters in stories, novels, and scripts. If the name and description match a real person, that person may have grounds to sue if the character is portrayed in a bad light. But a superficial resemblance or a common first or last name is not enough to support a defamation action: "The fictional character must be described sufficiently close to the plaintiff so that a reader or listener, knowing the plaintiff, would have no difficulty in linking the two."[50] An Atlanta woman won $100,000 in damages from a bestselling author in 2009 after establishing she was the model for a character in a novel, and was defamed by the fictional woman's portrayal as a promiscuous alcoholic.[51]

Journalists could run into a similar problem. It is common practice to rename people who have been interviewed but have asked that their real names not be used. There is usually a good reason why anonymity is requested; the person may be a drug dealer, an addict, or a victim of crime—someone who could face prosecution or embarrassment if identified. The problem arises when an innocent person's name is inadvertently given to the person who has been interviewed. The impact this can have on the innocent person's reputation can be devastating. Creating an unusual name offers no guarantee. In a 1910 case, a newspaper columnist created a character with the name Artemus Jones to criticize British tourists who misbehaved while on holiday in France. A man named Artemus Jones who holidayed in France came forward, sued, and won damages.[52]

Writers have devised strategies to avoid unintentionally defaming persons. Some fiction writers scour phone directories in the area where their stories are set or conduct online searches, looking for names that may match those assigned to their characters.[53] Journalists usually avoid surnames and look for common names like John and Susan when renaming the people in their stories, adding the phrase "not his (or her) real name" to avoid possible confusion with real people. This should be sufficient to prevent someone from coming forward. But there is still a risk that the anonymous person's occupation, age, physical description, and other details will match those of a real person who shares the made-up name. For example, a story that quotes a stockbroker named "David" who engages in insider trading, and reports his age, the city where he lives and works, how many children he has, and other details, could defame an innocent broker named David who fits this description. Journalists may find it is safer to omit personal details when dealing with anonymous sources engaged in illegal or unsavoury conduct.

Politicians and Public Figures

In Canada, politicians and other public figures have the same right to sue for defamation as any other citizen. Former prime minister Brian Mulroney sued the federal government in 1995 over an investigator's letter that linked him to allegations of kickbacks on a contract to purchase Airbus passenger jets for Air Canada (he later settled out of court in exchange for $2 million to cover his legal costs). Although Mulroney chose not to take action against the numerous media outlets that reported the contents of the letter, the law entitled him to sue them as well.[54]

American law, in contrast, makes it difficult for elected officials, celebrities, and other persons who are in the public eye to sue for libel. Even erroneous news reports are immune from legal action as long as the subject is a public figure and the journalist has not acted with malice.[55] Canada's courts have rejected arguments that the Charter's guarantee of freedom of expression should afford similar protection to the media in this country. As Justice Peter Cory of the Supreme Court of Canada remarked in a 1995 judgment: "Surely it is not requiring too much of individuals that they ascertain the truth of the allegations they publish."[56] In 2000 an Alberta judge rejected former Canadian Alliance leader Stockwell Day's bid to create a special category of "political comment" that would be immune from lawsuits as long as the defamatory statement was not made maliciously. Elected officials already face the hostility of voters and intrusive media coverage, the judge noted; allowing indiscriminate attacks on their reputations "would be a further discouragement to anyone seeking such political office."[57] In its latest pronouncement on the issue, the Supreme Court of Canada said in 2009 that politicians "cannot reasonably expect to be immune from criticism, some of it harsh and undeserved." Taking part in public life, however, does not amount to "open season on reputation."[58]

Despite this stance, journalists tend to be more aggressive when pursuing stories that involve elected officials. And rightly so. People who choose to take part in public life do so with the knowledge they will face greater public scrutiny, whether it be news reports on their backgrounds and personal life or satirical sketches lampooning their actions and mannerisms. While public life in Canada can be as rough and tumble as it is in the United States, journalists must bear in mind that there is a major difference between the two countries—allegations against politicians and other public figures in Canada must be backed up with the facts.

Governments Cannot Sue

Governments and their agencies cannot sue for libel. In two separate Ontario cases decided in 2006, judges ruled the Charter guarantee of freedom of expression protects the democratic right of citizens and the media to attack government actions and policies without fear of being sued. "If governments were entitled to sue citizens who are critical," noted one judge, "only those with the means to defend civil actions would be able to criticize government entities."[59] The other judge stressed that governments have other means at their disposal to protect their reputations:

> Governments are accountable to the people through the ballot box, and not to judges or juries in courts of law. When a government is criticized, its recourse is in the public domain, not the courts. The government may not imprison, or fine, or sue, those who criticize it ... . Litigation is a form of force, and the government must not silence its critics by force.[60]

While these rulings apply only within Ontario, judges in other provinces and the territories are likely to reach the same conclusions if a government tries to sue in its own name.

Government critics, however, must choose their words carefully and do not have the right to defame individuals within government. Elected officials, political aides, and bureaucrats and other government employees can still sue if an allegation damages their personal reputations. "Anyone entering public life does so with a certain expectation of public scrutiny and criticism," one of the judges noted, but they are not "at the mercy of defamatory statements being made about them with impunity." As well, journalists must take into account the size of the government or the public entity that is the target of criticism. In small communities where politicians and government officials "are readily known to the population," the judge added, a defamatory statement about the government "may be reasonably understood to refer to every member of that government, in which case every member may have a cause of action."[61] In other words, the federal government, a provincial administration, or a city council could not sue over a general statement that it has "lied to the public" or "stolen taxpayers' money." Individuals may be able to sue, however, if the same allegations were made against a small-town government or a public entity managed by only a few elected officials or employees, such as a school board or utility. Journalists also should bear in mind that many governments and public agencies fund libel actions launched by politicians or employees, and this may make individuals within government more likely to sue than if they were responsible for their own legal costs.[62]

Who Can Be Sued?

Writers, Editors, Publishers, and Producers

A libel action will invariably target the author or creator of an offending item, whether it is a reporter, columnist, editorial cartoonist, book or restaurant reviewer, or citizen who submitted a letter to the editor. The editor or producer who handled the copy or authorized the item to be published or broadcast can also be named as a defendant. The news organization will also be targeted. Media companies are responsible for the information they circulate and for this reason usually carry libel insurance that will cover any damages awarded. In theory, anyone responsible for the publication can be sued, including those who deliver the paper and the newsstand operators who sell it. Distributors, however, are rarely sued; if they can show they had no knowledge they were handling defamatory material, they are considered innocent disseminators and not liable for damages. Although libel insurance covers both newsroom employees and freelancers, journalists who mislead an employer or act unprofessionally run the risk of being cut adrift to fight a libel action on their own.

News Organizations and Journalists
Who Quote a Defamatory Statement

The media cannot escape a libel action by claiming they are merely passing along the statements of a source quoted in a story. As one judge has noted, it is no defence for journalists to say they are "just repeating" what others said. "There may be defences available, but the broadcaster is publishing the sting of the defamation and is liable at that point to defend it."[63] There is logic in this approach. Although a source makes the defamatory statement to a single person—the journalist—it is the news organization that makes it public, causing the real damage to reputation. A Halifax newspaper was forced to apologize to the head of an economic development body in 2008 after quoting a politician's demand for a police investigation into "white-collar crime and theft" in a controversial property sale. The newspaper retracted the story and acknowledged it was "not aware of any evidence of wrongdoing" to support the allegation.[64]

A plaintiff has the option of suing the source of the libel as well as the media outlet and the journalist who wrote the story. But plaintiffs usually ignore the source and sue the journalist and his employer, because the news organization has the resources and the insurance policy to cover any damages awarded. A plaintiff may also sidestep the media and take action directly against the party who made the offending comments. Former prime minister Brian Mulroney employed this strategy when he launched his $50-million suit over allegations of kickbacks in the Airbus affair. Numerous media outlets covered the story, but Mulroney named only the federal government, which made the allegations in a request for foreign assistance with an RCMP investigation. His decision to bypass the media was strategic. When a news organization is sued, it must take care that future reports do not repeat a libel and increase the damages awarded if the suit succeeds. Mulroney's decision ensured that the media would continue to cover his battle to clear his name.

News Organizations That Republish a Libel

Libel actions are not limited to the originating media outlet. News outlets are responsible for what they publish, and the fact that the information was previously published or broadcast is no defence to a libel claim. Anyone who reprints or rebroadcasts defamatory information already in the news runs the same risk of being sued as the originator of the report. This applies to copy picked up from news services. A federal minister who sued the Canadian Press in 2000 for accusing her of disrupting a commercial flight also filed lawsuits against several newspapers that published the story.[65] The Canadian Press was also liable for any damage that the republication of the story caused to the minister's reputation. Radio stations that "rip-and-read" stories lifted from the morning papers can also be sued.[66]

It is no defence to argue that other media outlets have published similar defamatory statements but were not sued. Plaintiffs are free to choose their targets as they see fit. The *Globe and Mail* protested that a municipal official who sued it for libel had ignored another story containing similar allegations published a day later in the *Toronto Star*. Although Ontario's Court of Appeal acknowledged that the *Star*'s article was "even more slanted" against the official, it ruled that the harm to his reputation had occurred "directly and immediately" upon publication of the original article. The *Globe* was not entitled to pay reduced damages despite its argument that "the same libel was published by others."[67]

What Kinds of Published Material Can Defame?

Print Copy and Newscasts

Any words or images that are published or broadcast can defame. This includes all elements that make up the news and feature sections of a newspaper or magazine— news stories, articles on sports and entertainment, editorials and columns, letters to the editor, as well as reviews of movies, CDs, books, and restaurants. The same goes for radio and television newscasts, from the lead story to the commentaries and audience feedback. The prominence given to an item and its placement in the publication or newscast will determine its impact—and the damage done to reputation—if it is found to be defamatory.

Headlines and Photo Captions

Headline writing is perhaps an editor's most challenging task. One editing guide describes it as akin to staging "an intricate juggling act in a five-foot-square cubicle."[68] The challenge is to find a few words that are precise enough to capture the essence of the story, but intriguing or clever enough to capture the reader's interest. More importantly, the words must fit the cramped space allotted for the headline.

Editors must choose their words carefully, to ensure that the headline conveys the substance of the story without distorting or sensationalizing the facts. A headline can be defamatory even if the accompanying story is not. Consider a news story in which a city councillor complains that the mayor's expense claims seem to be excessive. The headline "Mayor's Expenses Questioned" would be proper; the headline "Mayor Accused of Theft" would be defamatory and would not be supported by the facts of the story. Even an erroneous headline could be defamatory. The front page of one small-town newspaper was devoted to two stories, one on the purchase of land for a fast-food outlet, the other on a local drug bust. An editor somehow confused the two stories and the business story appeared under the headline "Businessman Involved in Drug Deal." Not surprisingly, the businessman sued for defamation.

"Where an article is accompanied by a headline," Raymond Brown notes, "the general rule is that they must be considered together in determining if either or both are defamatory."[69] A headline that could be construed as libellous may be saved by a story that is fair and factually correct. But a blaring headline that sends out a loud defamatory message—such as the "Mayor Accused of Theft" headline—would not be saved.

The same is true of photo captions. Although their main purpose is to identify the people or places depicted in a photo, they often also provide a synopsis of the story. Again, this summary must properly reflect the story and its nuances. Captions appear in small type and do not have the same impact as a headline, but they have the potential to defame even if the headline and story do not.

Images, Graphics, and Other Elements

Photographs, drawings, graphics, video footage, and any other visual element used to illustrate print and television reports are capable of defaming someone. In reviewing a television news report, one judge said all elements of the broadcast—"voice intonation, visual background, facial expression, gestures, background effects, scenery, music or images"—could convey defamatory meaning.[70]

In one case, a graphic depicting the scales of justice was used in a television news report that accused a government official of obstructing justice. The scales were shown tipped to one side, to illustrate the allegation of favouritism. The allegation proved false and a judge viewed the image as one of the defamatory elements of the story.[71]

Juxtaposed Words and Images

Newspaper and magazine editors must take care when designing pages. The placement of stories, photos, and headlines may harm someone's reputation. "You might have a story that is perfectly harmless and a head[line] that is also perfectly accurate and harmless," Robert Martin cautions, "but the way the page is laid out may create a libellous impression."[72] Imagine the impact if a photo of a schoolteacher receiving an award appeared above or opposite a bold headline about the conviction of a notorious sex offender. Although the placement was inadvertent, the teacher's reputation could be damaged if the layout led readers to believe that the headline and photo were part of the same story.

A photograph of a woman shopping in a store would have the same effect if used to illustrate a story on shoplifting, suggesting that the woman is a thief. File photos and video footage that depict individuals have the potential to defame if they are used to illustrate a story about crime or a controversial issue. In one case, a television news report on abortion used stock footage of a nurse at work in a hospital. The nurse, a devout Catholic, was not named but successfully sued because the accompanying script implied he supported abortion.[73]

Reviews

When Emily Brontë's novel *Wuthering Heights* was published in the 1840s, one reviewer dismissed it as "confused, disjointed and improbable." Lewis Carroll's classic children's tale *Alice's Adventures in Wonderland* was deemed a "stiff, overwrought story" when it first appeared. The influential *New York Times Book Review* described Joseph Heller's *Catch-22* as "an emotional hodgepodge" that "gasps for want of craft and sensibility."[74] As these and other writers have discovered, book reviews can be scathing. The same is true of reviews of restaurants, movies, and theatrical productions. But it is rare for a review to prompt a defamation suit. Restaurant reviews tend to be an exception, because a bad review can result in an immediate loss of business. Authors stung by a negative review are usually content to respond in a letter to the editor or to demand space to challenge the reviewer's comments.[75]

The defence of fair comment (discussed below) gives reviewers latitude to criticize and to use harsh language—in short, to call it as they see it. An Alberta judge dismissed a libel action against a radio reviewer who described a restaurant's offerings as "plain-Jane" and "overpriced," ruling that reviewers are entitled to express their opinions. However, reviewers cannot invent or distort facts and criticisms must reflect their honest opinion.[76]

Satire, Parodies, Jokes, and Cartoons

Fair comment also protects satire and parodies that poke fun at public figures. The law "must accommodate commentators such as the satirist or the cartoonist who seizes on a point of view, which may be quite peripheral to the public debate, and blows it into an outlandish caricature for public edification or merriment," the Supreme Court of Canada explained in a 2008 ruling:

> Their function is not so much to advance public debate as it is to exercise a democratic right to poke fun at those who huff and puff in the public arena. This is well understood by the public to be their function. The key point is that the nature of the forum or the mode of expression is such that the audience can reasonably be expected to understand that, on the basis of the facts as stated or sufficiently indicated to them, or so generally notorious as to be understood by them, the comment is made tongue-in-cheek so as to lead them to discount its [defamatory] "sting" accordingly.[77]

A comedy sketch that levels false allegations of wrongdoing or becomes a vehicle for mean-spirited character assassination, however, could attract a defamation suit. An allegation of criminal conduct is no less serious, in the eyes of the law, simply because it was presented in the guise of humour. A columnist who congratulated two lawyers for joining the "wife-swapping brigades" of the upper crust went too far and was successfully sued for libel.[78] In another case Tie Domi, a Toronto Maple Leafs forward with a reputation as one of the toughest players in professional hockey, failed to see the humour in an off-hand remark made about his wife during a radio talk show. The host suggested Domi's wife "could take a good punch. ... I'll bet you his idea of aerobics is to bang her around a bit once a week." A lawsuit was threatened but the host quickly apologized for the "very distasteful" comment. "It was intended to be humorous and in fun and it was neither. It was a mistake."[79]

As noted above, editorial cartoonists, who make it their business to bring politicians and other public figures down to size, are also protected under the umbrella of fair comment. New Brunswick's Court of Appeal dismissed an action against a cartoonist who compared a Holocaust denier to Nazi propaganda chief Joseph Goebbels. The court said cartoons are not to be interpreted literally and cartoonists can exaggerate and use symbolism and satire to make a point.[80] A cartoon that portrayed a businessman as breaking the law, however, was not protected because the allegation was false.[81]

Advertisements

Advertisements, too, can defame, and people with axes to grind have been quick to use them. Advertising departments need to be able to spot the warning signs of defamation and should be alerted to potentially libellous stories being shopped to the newsroom. There have been cases in which reporters and editors refused to print allegations that were clearly defamatory, only to have the source of the allegations take out an ad in their newspaper.[82] A lawyer successfully sued an Ontario newspaper for publishing a strident ad submitted by an activist who was known for making unsubstantiated attacks on other people.[83]

The Plaintiff's Case

The Three Elements of a Libel Suit

A party suing for libel does not have to prove that a defamatory statement is false. Instead, the law requires plaintiffs to prove three things:

1. the disputed statements refer to them;
2. the statements were published or broadcast, allowing them to reach a wider audience; and
3. the words used in the statements are harsh or unflattering enough to potentially harm their reputation, and are therefore *capable* of defamation. A plaintiff is not required to prove a negative—for example, persons accused of being racist or professionally incompetent do not have to prove that they are tolerant or competent.

Once the plaintiff establishes all three elements of a case, the law assumes he or she has suffered harm and the burden shifts to the defendant to prove the allegations are true or fall within the bounds of one of the other defences to libel. This presumption flies in the face of the legal principle that accusers must prove the allegations they make, and this has led to complaints that Canada's libel laws are skewed in favour of the plaintiff. "Libel law aggressively protects reputation to the point of giving plaintiffs the benefit of nearly all presumptions and placing nearly all the burdens upon the defence," media lawyers Daniel Burnett and Heather Maconachie have noted. "It is the opposite of criminal law. A reporter is not innocent until proven guilty. Rather, reporters are 'guilty' of libel unless they can prove [a defamatory statement] was true."[84] The Supreme Court of Canada alluded to the "strong criticism" of this feature of the law in its most recent defamation ruling, in 2009, but left it intact.[85]

Notices of Action, Retractions, and Apologies

Provincial and territorial defamation statutes require those who claim they have been defamed to formally notify the media that they intend to sue. The advance notice is designed to give media organizations and their lawyers a chance to review the statements and to consider how best to respond. The publisher or broadcaster may decide to stand by the story and defend against the lawsuit. If the story turns out to be flawed or wrong, the media outlet can publish a correction, retract the story, or issue a public apology.

If the mistake is minor and the story is not contentious, corrections and clarifications are usually drafted within the newsroom and published or aired the next day. But a media organization should not publish or broadcast a retraction or apology without first seeking legal advice. Defamation statutes set specific guidelines for handling such notices, which typically must be as prominent in the newspaper or newscast as the original story. As well, an apology must be genuine and express sincere regret. A statement that the newspaper "apologizes for describing Mr. Smith as a crook because there is no evidence to support such an allegation at this time" will not restore the man's reputation, nor will it get the newspaper off the hook. In the same way, a sincere apology whose text repeats the libel may compound the damage and become part of the lawsuit. For these reasons, media lawyers usually consult the plaintiff's counsel to work out the wording of a retraction or apology in advance. Many potential lawsuits are headed off by a prompt, genuine effort to set the record straight and minimize the damage to someone's reputation. The person still has the right to sue, but if the media outlet has retracted the story or apologized, the courts will restrict the amount of money that the plaintiff can recover as damages.[86]

Deadlines for Launching a Libel Action

Deadlines for giving notice of a proposed libel action and filing a lawsuit vary. In most jurisdictions, a plaintiff must notify a media outlet of the intention to sue within three months of the news report coming to the plaintiff's attention (in most cases, this will be within three months of the date of publication or broadcast). In Ontario, media outlets must be notified within six weeks. Quebec plaintiffs need only give three days' notice before filing an action, and in Saskatchewan notice must be given two weeks before an action is filed.

Ontario and Quebec have the tightest deadlines for filing an action—three months from the date the plaintiff discovers the information has been published. In Nova Scotia, New Brunswick, Prince Edward Island, and Saskatchewan, a libel suit must be filed within six months. In Newfoundland and Labrador, Manitoba, Alberta, and British Columbia, however, a plaintiff can wait up to two years before suing.

These time limits may not be cast in stone—a judge may extend the filing deadline if a plaintiff has a valid reason for a delay. Also, a claim based on dated articles may be allowed to proceed if recent stories link the plaintiff to allegations made in the older articles. As a result, many media outlets have rules that require reporters to keep their notes, documents, interview transcripts, and tape recordings, particularly if the story deals with a controversial issue or allegations of misconduct. Journalists should make it a practice to retain notes and other research materials for at least six months—longer in provinces with two-year filing deadlines—so that the information is available in the event that a libel suit is threatened or filed.

(Source: Robert S. Bruser and Brian MacLeod Rogers, *Journalists and the Law: How To Get the Story Without Getting Sued or Put in Jail* (Ottawa: Canadian Bar Foundation, 1985), appendix A, 105–106.)

Most people who complain of serious factual errors or libellous statements contact a senior editor or producer, and often through a lawyer. There are times when the person who disputes a story will phone the reporter directly. The journalist will no doubt feel defensive and the natural response is to argue the point. Even if the complaint appears to be groundless or the person complaining is abusive or rude, a journalist must remain polite and professional. "Courts are particularly interested in how concerned you are with doing a balanced story or coverage," notes veteran media law adviser Stuart Robertson. "Any cavalier attitude exhibited by you or your staff towards the interests or reputation of the plaintiff will be evidence of malice on your part in a defamation action."[87]

In most cases, people who complain about news coverage are content with a correction or clarification. A journalist who dismisses a complaint may ruin an opportunity to defuse the situation. And one who goes on the attack or makes unguarded comments may compound the libel or, worse, unwittingly provide evidence to a court that the original story was malicious or known to be false. If a reporter being grilled by a businessman blurts out something to the effect that "everyone knows you are a crook," a potential plaintiff has been handed the evidence and incentive needed to pursue a lawsuit. Journalists must keep their cool and refer the complaint to a senior editor or producer.

Injunctions To Prevent Publication or Broadcast

A person or company may try to prevent a story from being published or broadcast on the grounds that it is defamatory. Although the courts rarely grant such requests, an injunction may be imposed if the planned story appears to be highly defamatory or grossly unfair. "A defamatory publication will be restrained only for compelling reasons," notes Raymond Brown. "An injunction will be granted only in the clearest and rarest of cases, where words are clearly false and defamatory, and the plaintiff would suffer irreparable injury" if the information were published.[88] In the words of an Ontario ruling, the courts should step in to prevent the publication of a statement only when "the words complained of are so manifestly defamatory that any jury verdict to the contrary would be considered perverse by the Court of Appeal."[89] Any order forbidding publication would be temporary, and the court would convene a hearing to decide whether the injunction should be made permanent. If an injunction is denied and the article is published or broadcast, the plaintiff still retains the right to sue.

Damage Awards

Damage awards, which were once modest in Canada, increased dramatically during the 1990s. In 1982, a senior government official was awarded $125,000 in damages after the CBC accused him of obstructing justice, a baseless report that the judge described as "a form of entertainment presented in the guise of news."[90] Thirteen years later, in the landmark case of *Hill v. Church of Scientology of Toronto*, the Supreme Court of Canada upheld a jury's award of $1.6 million to a Toronto prosecutor falsely accused of misconduct.[91] Although that case did not involve a media report, it set the stage for the six-figure damage awards that have become the norm. In 1998, to cite just one example, a municipal planning official in Ontario won $780,000 in damages from the *Globe and Mail* after he was defamed in an article dealing with land development in the Toronto area.[92]

Judges and juries can award damages under several categories. **Special damages** cover the plaintiff's tangible loss—a job lost or a business deal that fell through as a result of the defamatory publication. **General damages** address a range of concerns. These usually bring the largest awards and compensate the plaintiff for injury to reputation that is assumed to have occurred from a defamatory publication, even though injury has not been proven. An additional award of **aggravated damages** may be assessed if a defendant has been subjected to humiliation, distress, or embarrassment. Finally, **punitive damages** may be awarded. These are rare and are awarded to punish a reporter or media outlet that has acted with malice or in a high-handed manner—for example, by reporting information known to be false.

Courts take a number of factors into consideration when assessing damages, including the defendant's conduct before and during the trial. A media outlet that continued to publish or broadcast unflattering stories about the plaintiff would risk being assessed additional damages. If a defendant claims that its allegations are true but fails to prove them in court, increased damages can be awarded. The status and character of the plaintiff is also a factor—a defendant could be ordered to pay additional damages for an unwarranted attack on a person with an unblemished reputation in the community. Courts also examine how the defamatory statements have been reported. Sensationalized, tabloid-style reports that use vicious or inflammatory language cause greater damage to reputation, and, as a result, more money will be awarded as compensation.[93]

Damage awards also have been linked to the size of the audience and the stature and credibility of the news organization responsible for the libel. In 2000 an Ontario judge, who awarded $950,000 to a doctor defamed by a report on CBC's *the fifth estate* on the use of a heart drug, noted the program's "remarkable potential and capacity to cause damage." *The fifth estate*'s reputation and national audience of more than a million made it "far more likely to cause damage than other less respected publications or broadcasts. Thus, there is a greater responsibility upon those who produce such programs to ensure that the content is factually correct."[94]

The Media's Defences

Truth or Justification

Truth is a complete defence to a libel action. No one wants to be branded a liar, but if there is evidence to prove that a person lies, that person cannot possibly win a defamation suit over media reports that brand him as such. Robert Martin describes truth—also known as the defence of justification—as "a pre-emptive defence." Anyone stung by the disclosures or allegations in a story would be foolish to sue if the information is true, since the libel action cannot succeed at trial.[95] But proving that information is true is not as straightforward as it may appear. The truth can be hard to establish. Facts can be slippery. Words can have unexpected shades of meaning. Witnesses may be unreliable. Chief Justice Beverley McLachlin of the Supreme Court of Canada discussed the difficulties of establishing truth in a 2009 ruling:

> A journalist who has checked sources and is satisfied that a statement is substantially true may nevertheless have difficulty proving this in court, perhaps years after the event. The practical result of the gap between responsible verification and the ability to prove truth in a court of law on some date far in the future, is that the defence of justification is often of little utility to journalists and those who publish their stories.[96]

A defendant must prove disputed statements to be true on a balance of probabilities, the standard required in civil cases. Witnesses must be produced to establish the facts to the satisfaction of the judge or jury, so journalists cannot rely on anonymous informants or sources who are unwilling or unlikely to appear in court. Witnesses must be believable; people with shady backgrounds or criminal records may be telling the truth, but if they have little credibility, their evidence alone may not be enough to prove that a story is true. As well, the defence must adhere to the rules of evidence. Hearsay—what witnesses say other people heard or saw—is generally not admissible in court. High-quality photocopiers make it easy to alter or forge documents and software programs can be used to alter photographs, and witnesses are needed to verify that any documents or images that support an allegation are authentic.

It is not enough for a media outlet to prove that someone made an allegation of misconduct or wrongdoing against the plaintiff. Proving that a source said the chief of police was corrupt is not proof that the allegation is true—the media must put forward evidence that the chief of police is corrupt. Nor are the media entitled "to repeat defamatory matters included in a report or circulated in a rumour and then succeed in a defence of justification by merely proving the existence of the rumour or report."[97] There is a final legal consideration. If a defendant relies on the defence of truth but is unable to produce the evidence needed to prove that a story is true, judges have the right to view this as evidence of recklessness and malicious intent and may respond by awarding higher damages.[98]

Michael Crawford notes that both the facts and any innuendo they create must be true. But defendants need not prove the truth of every single word used, only that the "gist of the statement" is true.[99] It is sufficient to prove the defamatory statement is "substantially true"—Daniel Burnett and Heather Maconachie point out that minor inaccuracies will not defeat the defence if the main thrust or "sting" of the libel is true.[100] For example, the wife of a white supremacist leader sued the CBC for reporting the couple had "dressed their kids in pint sized [Ku Klux] Klan uniforms" for a "celebratory cross burning." The passage, she argued, suggested she had "forcibly indoctrinated her children in racist ideology." The description of the children's attire was incorrect, but the CBC established that the children were taken to white-supremacist gatherings that featured cross burnings and people dressed in Klan robes. A judge dismissed the lawsuit, saying the report was "substantially true" and "the detail of how the children were dressed" was "immaterial" and "irrelevant."[101]

Under the defamation acts of Ontario and Nova Scotia, a plea of justification based on two or more distinct allegations can succeed even if not all of them are proven;

the remaining allegations, however, must not "materially injure" the plaintiff's reputation when reassessed in light of the proven allegations.[102] Minor inaccuracies will
not defeat the defence of truth, but journalists must report key facts and allegations
with precision. If a company is accused of having a history of ignoring environmental
protection laws, it is not good enough to establish only one instance in which the
company polluted a river. The CBC was found to have libelled New Brunswick's former
justice minister by reporting that he had halted a police investigation into "kickbacks"
to political parties; the defence of truth failed because the broadcaster could only
prove that the minister halted an investigation into "political contributions."[103] A Nova
Scotia newspaper was threatened with a libel suit and forced to apologize after publishing a headline stating that the police alleged two stockbrokers "stole millions." The
brokers were embroiled in lawsuits that claimed the misuse of investors' funds and
police were investigating, but no criminal charges had been laid and there was no
allegation of theft.[104]

While it can be difficult to establish truth to defeat a libel claim, getting the facts
and getting them right is not only the media's best defence—it's the essence of good
journalism. When journalists investigate allegations of wrongdoing, or cover a story
that involves harsh criticism of the conduct of a person or company, they must ask
themselves tough questions: Is the information capable of defamation? If it is, is it
true and is the evidence available to prove that it is true? Can the information be
verified through witnesses or documents? Are the words used in the story precise,
and do they accurately portray what is known to be true? Does the information come
from participants or people who are simply repeating what they heard from others?
Are the sources believable and are they willing to testify if a libel suit is launched?
Are there independent sources to back up the story? A journalist builds a story fact
by fact, brick by brick, creating a firm foundation to support the story's findings and
assertions.

Fair Comment

A defendant may also plead that the published statement is **fair comment**—a statement of opinion based on fact. Although this defence traditionally arose from editorials, columns, op-ed pieces, reviews, and other forms of commentary, it has come into
play for other media reports as opinions creep into news coverage. It can also be used
to defend the opinions of others as quoted and reported in a news story. Fair comment
is the defence that embodies the need to protect freedom of expression in a democratic
society. Its purpose is "the promotion of the public good and the encouragement of
useful political, social and moral criticism."[105] But there are limits to how the defence
can be used. It will not protect assertions of fact; to be considered fair comment, a
statement must express an opinion and the defence cannot be put forward to avoid
the more difficult task of proving the truth of an allegation.[106] If a columnist expressed
the opinion that a lawyer is a crook, the columnist would have to produce the evidence
needed to prove that the lawyer is a crook.

As an example of how the defence of fair comment works, consider a 1981 case
involving a CBC report on a slum landlord in Winnipeg. The item ended by describing the landlord as a person with "no morals, principles, or conscience." The man did

not deny being a slum landlord but objected to being characterized as amoral, un-principled, and without conscience. Although the court acknowledged that the journalist used "strong words," the well-researched report left no doubt that the man's tenants were living in filthy, substandard properties and the statements were judged to be fair comment.[107]

The Supreme Court of Canada modernized the fair comment defence in 2008, when it ruled that Vancouver-based radio host Rafe Mair did not defame Kari Simpson, a prominent activist against public schools using books that portray a gay lifestyle. Mair had a reputation for expressing controversial opinions—the court described him as a "shock-jock"—and in 1999 he presented an editorial on station CKNW that denounced Simpson's support of a local school board's ban on books depicting same-sex parents. "I listened to the tape of the parents' meeting … where Kari harangued the crowd," he told his listeners:

> It took me back to my childhood when with my parents we would listen to bigots who with increasing shrillness would harangue the crowds. For Kari's homosexual one could easily substitute Jew … . [I]n my mind's eye I could see Governor Wallace of Alabama standing on the steps of a schoolhouse shouting to the crowds that no Negroes would get into Alabama schools as long as he was governor. It could have been blacks last Thursday night just as easily as gays. Now I'm not suggesting that Kari was proposing or supporting any kind of holocaust or violence but neither really—in the speeches, when you think about it and look back—neither did Hitler or Governor Wallace … . They were simply declaring their hostility to a minority. Let the mob do as they wished.

Figure 4.1 The case of Vancouver radio host Rafe Mair, and his statements about activist Kari Simpson's views on homosexuals, was a turning point in modernizing Canada's fair comment defence. The court ruled that Mair had not defamed Simpson when he compared her comments to those of extreme racists.
SOURCE: Rafe Mair/thecanadian.org

Mair did not mince words. He condemned the activist as a bigot and compared her anti-gay stance with Hitler's hatred of the Jews and the suppression of civil rights in the American South. Are such extreme views protected as fair comment? In the Supreme Court's view, the answer is yes. While the *Charter of Rights and Freedoms* does not apply directly to forms of civil law such as defamation, the court said Canada's laws must reflect the values the Charter protects. A balance must be struck between freedom of expression and the need to protect people from unjustified attacks on their reputations. "An individual's reputation is not to be treated as regrettable but unavoidable road kill on the highway of public controversy," Justice Ian Binnie wrote in the court's unanimous ruling in *WIC Radio Ltd. v. Simpson*, "but nor should an overly solicitous regard for personal reputation be permitted to 'chill' free-wheeling debate on matters of public interest."[108]

The ruling reassessed and modified the four criteria that must be met to establish the defence of fair comment:[109]

- *The comment must deal with a matter of public interest* The ruling did not provide a precise definition of which issues will be considered matters of public interest. "The public interest is a broad concept," it noted, suggesting most matters that attract media attention will meet this part of the test. (The defence of responsible communication, set out below, provides a detailed definition of "public interest" that would apply to the fair comment test.) The debate over using educational material on homosexuality in schools, which prompted Mair's comments, "clearly engages the public interest," the court noted.[110] An opinion that safety inspectors should be more vigilant in their investigation of an accident-prone factory would likely be considered fair comment, because workplace safety is a matter of public interest. On the other hand, opinions on the private life of someone who plays no role in public life might be of interest to the curious but are unlikely to be considered matters of public interest. A key factor is whether the person suing for libel has invited public attention and the criticism that may come with it. In another BC case, a physician who contacted a newspaper so that he could publicly criticize the health-care system failed in an attempt to sue a columnist who subsequently criticized him. A judge said the columnist's remarks were fair comment and likened the doctor to a boxer who, "having entered the ring … must accept the blows given him provided always that none is 'below the belt.'"[111]

- *The comment must be based on fact* The evidence the CBC uncovered and reported about the slum landlord back in 1981 was crucial in establishing the defence of fair comment. Journalists must present the facts upon which opinions are based, and these facts must not be distorted or taken out of context. In its ruling exonerating Mair, the Supreme Court said the facts upon which the opinion is based must be "sufficiently stated or otherwise be known" to the audience so that those who read or hear it "are able to make up their own minds on the merits of [the] editorial comment. If the factual foundation is unstated or unknown, or turns out to be false, the fair comment defence is not available." In Mair's case, "the general facts" underlying his strong opinions were well known to his listeners, "and were referred to in part in the editorial itself." As well, Simpson's "repeated invitations to her followers to pick up the phone and call talk shows and politicians assured her views a measure of notoriety."[112]

- *The comment, while it can infer facts, must be an expression of opinion* The fair comment defence will not protect an allegation or assertion of fact that is disguised or presented as an opinion. The columnist who called a lawyer a crook, for instance, could not claim to be merely expressing a personal opinion on the lawyer's ethical standards: a person's honesty—or lack of it—is a fact, not a judgment or opinion. The Supreme Court said Mair's inference that Simpson would condone violence against homosexuals was clearly an opinion, and not an assertion she did, in fact, condone violence. This finding, in part, was based on his role as purveyor of opinion rather than as a journalist sent out to gather and report the news. "Mair was a radio personality with opinions on everything," Justice Binnie noted, "not a reporter of the facts."[113] The fair comment defence still can be claimed for news stories, including investigative reports, but only for the opinions and conclusions they contain; the facts and allegations reported would have to be proven to be true or protected under another defence.

- *Could any person honestly express the opinion based on these facts?* The traditional test for establishing fair comment was whether a fair-minded person could hold the views expressed. "The question the jury must consider," a British judge ruled more than a century ago, "is this—would any fair man, however prejudiced he may be, however exaggerated or obstinate his views, have said that which this criticism has said?"[114] And there was a crucial caveat: the person making the statement had to believe the opinion he or she expressed was true. In the late 1990s the *Globe and Mail*'s effort to use fair comment to defend a story alleging municipal corruption crumbled at trial when the reporter admitted he did not believe his story's allegations that a planning official had acted dishonestly and improperly.[115] Besides limiting who could claim the defence, this test created a dilemma for newspaper publishers, who had no means to ensure the authors of letters to the editor honestly believed the opinions they expressed.[116] In response, most provinces amended their defamation statutes to stipulate that the defence of fair comment will not fail when the actual views of a third party are not known, as long as someone could honestly hold such an opinion.[117]

The Supreme Court's ruling on Mair's comments modifies this test. The issue now is not whether the opinion is fair or whether the writer or speaker believes it to be true, but whether "any honest person, however opinionated or prejudiced, would express [the opinion] upon the basis of the relevant facts."[118] It is not in the public interest, Justice Binnie explained, "to deny the defence to a piece of devil's advocacy that the writer may have doubts about (but is quite capable of honest belief) which contributes to the debate on a matter of public interest." He continued:

> In much modern media, personalities such as Rafe Mair are as much entertainers as journalists. The media regularly match up assailants who attack each other on a set topic. The audience understands that the combatants, like lawyers or a devil's advocate, are arguing a brief. What is important in such a debate on matters of public interest is that all sides of an issue are forcefully presented, although the limitation that the opinions must be ones that could be "honestly express[ed] ... on the proved facts" provides some boundary to the extent to which private reputations can be trashed in public discourse.[119]

At his libel trial, Mair testified he did not honestly believe the implication, drawn from his words, that Simpson would condone violence. But that did not settle the issue—the question, the Supreme Court said, was whether any person honestly could say, based on the proven facts, that she would condone violence toward gay people. Simpson's public speeches, Justice Binnie noted, contained references to "war," "militant homosexuals," and other violent images, which could cause some people to believe she would condone violence toward gay people. As a result, the test was met and Mair's words—as well as the meaning others might take from them—were protected as fair comment.[120]

The fair comment defence is broad and should protect any opinion on a matter of public interest that is based on solid facts, even comments that are extreme and strident. If comparing someone to Hitler can pass muster, it would appear the precedent in *WIC Radio* has set the bar high. But columnists, commentators, and editorial writers must choose their words with care; the defence is complex, the subject must be of public interest, and opinions must flow from facts set out in the piece or already known to the audience. Journalists researching news stories must ensure the opinions of the sources they quote are based on the reported facts and relate to matters of public interest.

There is a final hurdle. An opinion expressed with malice—in a deliberate or reckless attempt to harm someone's reputation—will not be protected as fair comment, even if all other criteria for establishing the defence have been met. The type of conduct that can be considered malicious is considered later in this chapter under the heading "The Role of Malice."

Qualified Privilege

For free expression to thrive in a democracy, sometimes the right of individuals to protect their reputations must take a back seat to the public's right to know. "There are occasions when plain speaking is a public service, if not a moral duty," notes British lawyer Joseph Dean.[121] Defamatory statements may be made in certain public forums and in official documents—and publicized through the media—without fear of attracting a libel action. In the words of the leading British textbook on defamation, privilege is granted

> for the common convenience and welfare of society ... because it is in the public interest that persons should be allowed to speak freely on occasions when it is their duty to speak, and to tell all they know or believe ... . In such cases no matter how harsh, hasty, untrue, or libellous the publication would be but for the circumstances, the law declares it privileged ... . It is better for the general good that individuals should occasionally suffer than that freedom of communication between persons in certain relations should be in any way impeded.[122]

The person making the statement, in most cases, enjoys **absolute privilege**—complete immunity from being sued.[123] The media are granted a **"qualified" privilege**—immunity subject to certain conditions. News reports of what happened in a privileged forum such as a legislative chamber or courtroom must not be published with malice. There must be no suggestion that the journalist deliberately sought out privileged material out of spite or as part of a vendetta against the person whose reputation has been tarnished. The report also must be a "fair and accurate" representation of what was said. An Ontario man who was sued for libel in 2009 over an item he posted on a website was unable to claim qualified privilege because the post incorrectly described the outcome of a court action.[124] The media are not expected to produce verbatim accounts, but reports must be factually precise and reflect conflicting points of view or any contradictory information presented. "The report," Michael Crawford advises, "must be substantially correct and carry the same meaning as a word-for-word account."[125] A BC newspaper was found to have published a fair and accurate report of a court hearing when it said a company had been convicted of "deceptive business practices." The company complained that the story was incomplete and made the offence sound more serious than it was, but the province's court of appeal ruled that the wording accurately reflected the charge and news reports need not be exhaustive to be privileged.[126]

Privileged Forums

It is the forum where the information originates that dictates whether it is shielded from a libel action, not the nature of the information itself. Media reports on the public proceedings of Parliament and provincial legislatures, city and municipal councils, school boards, and other official public bodies—as well as their committees and subcommittees—are subject to qualified privilege. The same holds true for most public meetings and proceedings held in open court. But privilege does not apply to *in camera* meetings and hearings, because these are private sessions closed to the media and public.

The courts have ruled that there must be some element of public control over the proceedings for qualified privilege to apply—lectures, political rallies, and church sermons, for example, are not subject to privilege.[127] In one case, Nova Scotia's Court of Appeal ruled that the allegations of police misconduct that two lawyers made at a press conference were protected by privilege, but only because the lawyers had a duty to make the statements—there is no blanket privilege for press conferences.[128] Note, as well, that the privilege ends at the door of the courtroom or meeting room. If allegations are repeated outside the protected forum, a plaintiff could sue the speaker and any media outlet that disseminated them.

Most defamation statutes specify that reports of court proceedings must be published "contemporaneously"—usually within 30 days—to be considered privileged.[129] Even so, the common law defence of qualified privilege appears to protect reports on older cases. The media must also publish or broadcast "a reasonable statement of explanation or contradiction," if requested by the target of a defamatory comment made in a privileged proceeding.[130] But a journalist is not expected to contact the subject of an allegation or to conduct further research before publishing a report on a court ruling or hearing. "If a judge releases a decision in a court proceeding," an Ontario judge ruled in 2010, "the press need not talk to all the parties mentioned in the decision or review the entire court file before publishing a report of the judicial decision. ... the law only requires that the report be fair and accurate."[131]

Privileged Documents

Qualified privilege also applies to fair and accurate news reports based on certain documents. These include the reports and other official records produced by privileged bodies, such as the rulings of courts, tribunals, public inquiries, and royal commissions. The same protection is extended to the information in documents that have been presented or discussed at a court hearing or other privileged forum. For example, if a pre-sentence report states that an offender's parents were abusive and the allegation is published, the parents cannot sue if the report has been filed with the court or read out at a hearing. The information—the document that sets out the details of a criminal charge—is privileged once charges have been laid and the document has been filed with the courts.

In a 1995 ruling, the Supreme Court of Canada extended qualified privilege to news reports of pleadings filed with the courts in civil actions—the plaintiff's statement of claim, the defendant's written response, and other documents. But journalists must bear in mind that the report has to be fair and accurate or the qualified privilege will be lost. The Supreme Court stressed this point, warning that the media "must exercise a high degree of care in ensuring that its report is fair and accurate." Accuracy, the court noted, "is readily achieved—it is a simple matter of copying [filed documents]. So the emphasis must be on fairness."[132] Journalists must endeavour to present both sides of a lawsuit, either by quoting from defence documents filed with the courts or by seeking comment from defendants or their lawyers. A BC broadcaster was denied the defence of qualified privilege and lost a defamation action in 2000 for reporting only the plaintiff's side of a bitter lawsuit. The reports had ignored court documents in which the defendants denied the allegations.[133]

Privilege also attaches to information in "public documents," which courts have defined as the information that government agencies are required to maintain and produce for public inspection. The information must be a matter of public record, which a government body is required by law to keep on file. As well, the information must be true (allowing the publisher to plead the defence of justification) or a fair and accurate reflection of the information that the government is required to hold, and it must be disseminated without malice.[134] There have been conflicting rulings on the issue of whether qualified privilege applies to documents obtained from government agencies under freedom of information legislation. A BC judge ruled in 1997 that such documents are privileged,[135] but an Ontario judge reached the opposite conclusion the following year.[136] Journalists who find potentially defamatory information in documents obtained under access legislation should seek legal advice before airing or publishing it.

Privileged documents are the foundation for a solid, libel-proof story. Journalists should scour court files and other protected records for the information needed to substantiate tips and stories that would otherwise be too risky to publish.

Responsible Communication on Matters of Public Interest

An Ontario Provincial Police officer was hailed as a hero for taking part in the search for survivors in the rubble of the World Trade Center towers. That image crumbled within days when the *Ottawa Citizen* reported the officer had travelled to New York after the 9/11 terrorist attacks without permission, neither he nor his dog had formal rescue training, and local authorities were led to believe he was an RCMP officer. The officer sued and, at trial, a jury concluded the newspaper had proven many of its allegations but not all of them; the *Citizen* failed to establish that the officer's actions may have compromised search efforts, or that he had deliberately misled local authorities about his identity and his qualifications as a dog handler. The jury awarded $100,000 in damages against the paper and $25,000 against an OPP spokesperson quoted in its articles.[137]

In another libel case, a *Toronto Star* reporter investigated a businessman's plans to expand a private golf course on a lake in Northern Ontario by purchasing adjacent land from the provincial government. Owners of neighbouring properties and other residents opposed the development, and believed the businessman's political ties—he was a supporter of the party in power and a friend of the premier—would play a role in the government's decision on the proposal. In the words of one opponent, the businessman's "influence" appeared to make approval "a done deal." A jury rejected the *Star*'s defences that the allegations were true and the "done deal" remark was a fair comment, and awarded the businessman $1.475 million in damages.[138]

Both papers produced well-researched stories on an important issue, both could prove most of their assertions and allegations, yet both fell short of the legal requirements for establishing a libel defence. A reporter who thoroughly researches a story and endeavours to present all sides to a controversy can still lose a libel suit if some information or allegations turn out to be false. Journalists, in effect, are held to a higher standard than doctors, lawyers, and other professionals. A lawyer cannot possibly win every case for every client. Patients die on the operating table. The legal test for establishing when a lawyer or doctor is negligent is whether the steps taken to represent the client or treat the patient were reasonable in the circumstances. In the words of the chief justice of the Supreme Court of Canada, Beverley McLachlin, defamation law imposes "a standard of perfection" on the media, and this can have "a chilling effect on what is published. Information that is reliable and in the public's interest to know may never see the light of day." The law must be modernized, Chief Justice McLachlin argued, to strike a better balance between protecting reputations and the constitutional right to freedom of the press. "While the law should provide redress for baseless attacks on reputation," she explained, "defamation lawsuits, real or threatened, should not be a weapon by which the wealthy and privileged stifle the information and debate essential to a free society."[139]

To achieve this balance, the Supreme Court created a new libel defence: responsible communication on matters of public interest. In a pair of rulings handed down in 2009, the court ordered new trials in the *Ottawa Citizen* and *Toronto Star* cases and offered journalists a blueprint for how the defence works. It is based on the "responsible journalism" defence established in Britain and adopted, with slight modifications, in several Commonwealth jurisdictions.[140] The Ontario Court of Appeal's earlier rulings on the *Citizen* and *Star* libel cases imported responsible journalism to this country, and it is now embodied in the Supreme Court's renamed, made-in-Canada version.[141] The defence shifts the focus from *what* was published or broadcast to *how* the story was researched and reported. In the words of one judge, it grants the media "the right to be wrong"[142]—if a factual mistake or an unproven allegation defames someone, the media can defeat a libel claim if reasonable efforts were made to verify the information before it was made public.

To claim the defence, the media must establish that the story dealt with a subject of public interest. The definition of public interest is broad, as it is for the defence of fair comment. The term "is not synonymous with what interests the public," the Supreme Court cautioned, and does not encompass "the private lives of well-known people" or "mere curiosity or prurient interest" in a prominent person. The story must deal with a subject or issue that invites public attention, affects the welfare of citizens, or has generated controversy or gained notoriety. Stories on government and politics clearly meet this test, but the court said the public "has a genuine stake in knowing about many matters, ranging from science and the arts to the environment, religion, and morality." And the story need not be riveting or national in scope: "It is enough," the court said, "that some segment of the community would have a genuine interest in receiving information on the subject." The judge presiding over a libel trial decides whether a story deals with a matter of public interest, and must consider the story as a whole rather than focusing on isolated comments the plaintiff claims are defamatory.[143] The *Citizen's* reports on the police officer who responded to the 9/11 terrorist attacks, the court said, clearly dealt with a matter of public interest. "The Canadian public has a vital interest in knowing about the professional misdeeds of those who are entrusted by the state with protecting public safety. … the articles touched on matters close to the core of the public's legitimate concern with the integrity of its public service."[144] As for the *Star's* report on the golf course development, the court ruled it dealt with "issues of government conduct" that were "clearly in the public interest."[145]

If the public interest test is met, a jury will decide whether the media acted responsibly in researching and reporting the story (juries hear most libel trials, but the judge will make this decision if there is no jury).[146] The court drew up a list of factors to be considered when assessing the media's actions:[147]

- *The seriousness of the allegation* The more serious and damaging the allegation, the more diligent the journalist must be in researching and verifying the story. Defamatory statements, the court noted, run the gamut from "a passing irritant to a blow that devastates the target's reputation and career." The thoroughness demanded of journalists as they verify allegations of corruption or a criminal offence will not be expected for a story that makes "suggestions of lesser mischief." Thoroughness will also be expected if the story invades someone's personal privacy.

- *The public importance of the matter* Not all subjects of public interest have the same weight or importance. More diligence will be expected when journalists investigate "grave matters of national security" than when a story deals with "the prosaic business of everyday politics."

- *The urgency of the matter* "News," the court noted, "is often a perishable commodity." Jurors should take into account the media's need to file timely reports on important allegations and events. "The question is whether the public's need to know required the defendant to publish when it did." Mistakes made in the rush to score a scoop might not be forgiven if a reasonable delay and further inquiries could have prevented publication of the defamatory statement.

- *The status and reliability of the source* If a source is untrustworthy or has an axe to grind, a reporter must show extra diligence in verifying what the source says. Not all documents carry equal weight, either: an interim or draft report, for instance, may not be as authoritative or reliable as a final one. Confidential and unnamed sources can be used, but the test will be whether it was reasonable to do so. In the court's view, "publishing slurs from identified 'sources' could, depending on the circumstances, be irresponsible."
- *Whether the plaintiff's side of the story was sought and accurately reported* It is "inherently unfair," the court said, to publish a story containing defamatory statements without giving the target of the statements a chance to respond to allegations or to correct factual errors. It is not always necessary or possible to contact the target of a defamatory comment, however. A person under investigation by the police, for instance, may be unaware of the investigation and have little to contribute to the story beyond a terse "no comment." In any event, the journalist must strive to be fair and get all sides of the story, and to include denials or other information that raises questions about the facts or allegations being reported.
- *Whether the inclusion of the defamatory statement was justifiable* The defamatory statement must be relevant to the story, but the court acknowledged that juries should give "generous scope" to editorial choices made in the newsroom.
- *Whether the defamatory statement's public interest lay in the fact that it was made rather than its truth* The court termed this the "reportage" defence, and it is one of the most significant facets of the ruling. It recognizes that the public may have an interest in the allegations and counter-charges made in debates over important issues, regardless of whether these allegations can be proven to be true. As noted earlier in this chapter, those who repeat a libel can be sued as if they made the statement themselves—"one should not be able to freely publish a scurrilous libel," the court noted, "simply by purporting to attribute the allegation to someone else." However, a journalist reporting on an issue of public interest would have a defence if:

a. the statement is attributed, "preferably" to a named source;
b. the news report indicates the statement has not been verified;
c. both sides of the dispute are reported fairly; and
d. the report sets out the context in which the statement was made.

How this defence will be interpreted remains to be seen, but it may be a boon to reporters covering heated exchanges between politicians or when it is difficult to determine who's telling the truth. Such reports will have to deal with matters of public interest and must satisfy all four criteria.

- *Any other relevant circumstances* The jury can consider any other aspect of the story in assessing whether the media acted responsibly, including the tone of the article. Sensationalism or a critical tone may be appropriate, the court said, and writers should not be held to "a standard of stylistic blandness" or barred from expressing a point of view. "The best investigative reporting often takes a trenchant or adversarial position on pressing issues of the day." Jurors also should take into account what the journalist intended to say—assuming the journalist's explanation of the words used is reasonable—when assessing whether a statement is defamatory.

The court stressed that these factors provide a framework for assessing whether the test for responsible communication has been met; it is not a series of hurdles the media must clear and it will not always be necessary to satisfy all of them to defeat a libel claim. The nature of the story and the defamatory statement will determine which factors apply and whether other relevant factors should be considered. "As always," the court noted, "the ultimate question is whether publication was responsible in the circumstances." As noted, evidence the media acted with malice can defeat the defences of fair comment and qualified privilege. Malice also comes into play in the responsible communication defence: "A defendant who has acted with malice in publishing defamatory allegations," the court said, "has by definition not acted responsibly."[148]

In one of the first cases to apply the defence, a BC judge ruled it did not protect a journalist who published allegations that two police officers assaulted a man they arrested. The man was the main source used in the story and the journalist "failed to recognize in him a person with an axe to grind." The judge also cited the tone of the article—"It did not simply raise questions, but adopted allegations as fact"—and the use of "needlessly inflammatory phrases that went well beyond proper reportage." These included references to "heavily armed" officers with "the weight of the establishment on their side," an officer's boot "grinding" on the man's head, and chances of seeing justice done being "lost in the dust of the circling wagons." There was "nothing at all neutral" about the story, which omitted evidence of the man's propensity to violence. Finally, in the judge's opinion, the story could have satisfied the public interest in reports on police conduct without identifying the officers involved.[149]

The responsible communication defence is a major rethinking of Canadian defamation law. Media lawyer Richard Dearden, who argued for the new defence on behalf of the *Ottawa Citizen*, has called it "a game-changer. ... a lot of information that wasn't published, that was spiked [in the past] because of fear of not being able to prove 100 per cent of the truth of the facts, is now going to be made available to the public."[150] The defence, however, does not give journalists a licence to destroy reputations. Their actions and methods, and their news organization's code of conduct, will be placed under the microscope and measured against accepted journalistic standards. The defence will not protect "inaccurate, careless or unfair reporting," noted Kathy English, the *Toronto Star*'s public editor, and the Supreme Court has "raised the bar for standards of ethical journalism in this country." In future, she added, "journalism itself will be on trial."[151]

The full impact of the new defence will become clearer as courts apply it to libel claims and flesh out the definitions of "public interest," "reportage," and other key elements. News organizations, warned Jeffrey Dvorkin, who teaches journalism at Ryerson University, will be under greater pressure to defend their methods at a time when many are cutting newsroom budgets and devoting fewer resources to investigative journalism. "In any future libel action, the onus will now be on media organizations to prove that every reasonable effort has been made to contextualize a story," he noted. "My guess is that media law departments are now advising chief editors to restrain their journalists from doing more aggressive reporting unless they can prove that every effort (including a demonstrable commitment to editorial resources) has been made to get all sides of the story."[152] Alan Shanoff, who teaches media law at Humber College, agreed that establishing the defence "will not be an easy task" and predicted that libel cases may become more complicated and more expensive.[153] He pointed to an array of potential findings that could sabotage the defence:

> the language used was too sensationalistic; the story wasn't important enough to merit the space; the writer didn't speak to every possible source: the sources used were biased . . . more should have been done to verify the information; the other side wasn't adequately reported; the writer rushed to judgment; documents weren't properly interpreted; additional documents should have been obtained; the tone of the article was too shrill. And on and on.[154]

Despite these misgivings, the defence gives journalists a new weapon to wield in defence of their work. It encourages investigative journalism but can be used to defend any news story, even breaking news reports that are difficult to fully research and develop before publication. Journalists who are thorough in their research, rely on solid sources, and produce stories that are fair and balanced can take comfort in knowing the courts will recognize their efforts, even when the truth remains elusive.

Duty To Report

Under the common law, privilege can act as a shield against a libel action if a person has a duty to make a statement and the person to whom it is directed has a duty to receive it. For example, a witness interviewed by a police officer may accuse a third person of committing a crime. No charges may result and no crime may ever be proven. The courts have held, however, that witnesses have a duty to be candid during interviews with investigators and enjoy an absolute privilege against a defamation action brought by the third party.[155]

In most instances, however, the media are unable to avail themselves of this immunity. The Supreme Court of Canada has ruled that the privilege is lost if the person receiving the information has no interest in receiving it. The media are then left with the task of proving that the information was so compelling that every member of the public needed to be informed.[156] Consider the case of a consumer columnist who alerted readers that an importer could be distributing tainted canned goods. Even though the information proved to be false, a court dismissed a libel action because the public had an interest in being alerted to possible food poisoning and the columnist had an honest belief that the goods were tainted.[157]

An Ontario judge suggested in 1999 that the media's ability to use the privilege defence in this fashion "may be expanding," particularly when journalists can establish a "social or moral duty" to report. Courts will consider whether there was an urgent need to alert the public by disseminating the story. Examples are a news report on allegations of abuse at a home for the elderly and a story advising people how to get help for family members who have become followers of a cult leader.[158] This was one of several tentative steps that culminated in 2009 with the creation of the defence of responsible communication on matters of public interest. Responsible communication is a distinct defence, and duty to report continues to apply to when someone has a legal or moral duty to pass along information that may later be found to be false.[159] Media outlets, however, are unlikely to rely on this defence in future. Duty to report is difficult to apply to journalism and its key elements—public interest in the material and the urgency of making the news public, for instance—have been incorporated into responsible communication, a defence tailor-made for the media.

Consent

Consent, like truth, is a complete defence to a libel suit. If someone agrees to the publication or broadcast of defamatory information, the person cannot complain about any damage to reputation that results. But because people are reluctant to sully their own names, the media are rarely able to rely on this defence. Consider the following case. A Manitoba government official was defamed by a caller to an open-line radio show. The official agreed to appear on the show and made an opening statement denying a rumour that he had been charged with impaired driving. Later in the show, a caller repeated the rumour and asserted that the allegation was true. A court ruled that the defence of consent did not apply—agreeing to appear on the show was not the same as agreeing to be defamed. As well, the court said, the show's producers could have delayed broadcast long enough to delete the offending words.[160] In a similar case, a Nova Scotia judge ruled that two workers at a youth detention centre who agreed to appear on a television program to deny allegations of abuse did not consent to be defamed in a subsequent newspaper column.[161] Consent "must be clearly established," the Manitoba court said, and "consent must be given or able to be inferred with respect to each publication of defamatory material."[162]

Consider a different example, where consent was arguably given. A Nova Scotia newspaper was on firm ground when a musician phoned its entertainment reporter to announce he had just filed for bankruptcy. The reporter tried to track down the bankruptcy file to confirm the story, but the court office was closed. Calls to the musician's lawyer and agent were not returned before the story went to press. The musician quickly declared the story was a hoax designed to embarrass the paper,[163] but the story also unnerved the musician's creditors and harmed his business interests. The musician did not sue for defamation, but if he had, the newspaper would have had strong grounds to argue he had consented to publication of a libel.

Consent must be proven. If it comes down to the journalist's word against the word of the plaintiff, a judge or jury will decide whom to believe. A notation in a reporter's notebook that the person has consented may not be enough; it would be better to record the agreement on tape. And it must be clear that the person consented to the use of the defamatory information. Agreeing to an interview is not the same as agreeing to be defamed, and neither is a curt denial of a rumour or allegation. If, on the other hand, a person agrees to be interviewed to discuss rumours or allegations and invites media coverage to set the record straight, this would likely be seen as consent if the person had a change of heart and later sued for defamation.

The Role of Malice

The defences of fair comment and qualified privilege will fail if a plaintiff can prove that a journalist acted maliciously in publishing or broadcasting a story. A finding of malice also may lead to the assessment of additional damages.

Evidence of malice can be clear and can come from the mouths of those involved in producing the story. If a journalist writes a memo or tells others that his story will "get" or "nail" someone, this is solid evidence of a malicious mindset. In a ruling based on a *Toronto Sun* story accusing a politician of profiting from insider information—an allegation that turned out to be completely false—the judge did not have to look far to find evidence of malice. One of the paper's editors had referred to the politician as a "sleaze," and the reporter who fabricated the story had boasted to colleagues that he had caught the politician red-handed.[164]

Defamation Law in Quebec: A Special Case

All provinces and territories except Quebec have passed defamation statutes incorporating the main principles of the common law. These statutes outline the procedures for launching a libel suit and enshrine the common law defences—truth, fair comment, qualified privilege, and consent—available to the media. Journalists should consult the defamation act in their jurisdiction for the exact provisions that apply, as there are slight variations from province to province.

A different approach is taken in Quebec. Defamation is governed by article 1457 of the province's *Civil Code*, which makes a person liable for any harm or injury done to another "whether it be bodily, moral or material in nature." A plaintiff alleging defamation must prove he or she has suffered injury and that the defendant is at fault. The province's *Press Act*, RSQ 1977, c. P-19, extends qualified privilege to news accounts of political debates, court hearings, and official government pronouncements. The *Press Act*'s provisions apply only to newspapers, but television and radio news broadcasts are afforded similar protection under Quebec precedents (online broadcasts should be as well).

There are several features unique to Quebec's defamation laws. Publication is not necessary—a plaintiff can sue over a defamatory statement even if it has not been made to a third person or to a wider audience. There also appears to be greater latitude to sue over statements that defame the dead, particularly if the statements reflect on descendants who are still alive. But Quebec law offers an additional defence to the media and protects defamatory statements that are published or broadcast in the public interest, as long as the journalist is not motivated by malice. Truth, however, is not a complete defence; if a statement or allegation is true but was only published to injure the plaintiff—or does not deal with a matter of public interest—a defamation action can succeed.

(Sources: Michael G. Crawford, *The Journalist's Legal Guide*, 4th ed. (Toronto: Carswell, 2002), 53–56; Law Reform Commission of Canada, *Defamatory Libel*, Working Paper 35 (Ottawa: Supply and Services Canada, 1984), 11–12.)

The test, according to one defamation text, is "purity of motive."[165] The journalist must not use the cloak of privilege or fair comment as a guise to deliberately ruin someone's reputation or to settle a score. A journalist does not have to like or even respect the subject of the story, but there can be no evidence that this ill will was the motivation for publishing the story. A plaintiff may prove malice based on evidence that a journalist acted spitefully or in bad faith—in a word, unprofessionally. Journalists should refrain from passing judgment or jumping to conclusions until they have all the facts. And they should avoid making gratuitous comments about the character and motives of the people they are covering.

Even when journalists keep their thoughts to themselves, there may be evidence to indicate malice. If a journalist publishes or broadcasts information recklessly or with the knowledge that it is false, she risks having a judge find her actions to be evidence of malice.[166] Other indicators are that the story is exaggerated or given sensational treatment, or the words used are unnecessarily harsh or exaggerated. Courts also infer malice if the journalist fails to contact the target of the story, does not check the accuracy of the information reported, or leaves out key facts. An Ontario judge found that omitting key information and failing to give the plaintiff a chance to respond to criticism were evidence of malice that defeated a plea of fair comment. In the judge's view, "there was no quest for truth … . The quest was for sound bites sufficient to fit the story line."[167]

Journalists will not be seen to have acted with malice if they approach their stories with an open mind. Act professionally, investigate thoroughly, double-check facts, and strive to produce a story that is accurate, balanced, and fair.

"Politician Target of Fraud Probe": Defamatory Reporting or Responsible Communication?

How will the courts apply the defence of responsible communication on matters of public interest? Consider the following scenario:

A reporter receives an anonymous tip that a prominent provincial politician is under investigation for claiming unauthorized expenses. The journalist spends a day working the phone in an effort to verify the story. A police spokesperson confirms an investigation for expense fraud is under way, but will not disclose who the politician is. Two government officials confirm the politician's identity but refuse to be quoted by name. The premier calls a press conference late in the day to announce an independent review of the guidelines for filing politicians' expense claims. The premier says allegations an elected official has been "overbilling for expenses" have prompted the review, but refuses to identify the politician involved. The reporter makes several calls to the politician's office and home and sends an e-mail seeking an interview, but does not receive a response. Another politician agrees to comment, and insists his colleague would not intentionally file excessive expense claims. The news organization publishes a story naming the politician under the headline: "Politician Target of Fraud Probe: Expense Rules Under Review To Prevent 'Overbilling.'"

The allegation turns out to be false. The police investigation traces the suspected "over-billing" to a clerical error and the politician is cleared of wrongdoing. The politician sues the news organization for libel, claiming his reputation has been damaged. Would the responsible communication defence defeat the claim? Here are the factors a court would take into account:

- *Whether the story dealt with a matter of public interest* The allegation of expense fraud and how politicians are reimbursed are clearly matters of public interest.

- *The seriousness of the allegation* The fraud allegation is serious and required the news organization to take steps to verify who was under investigation before publishing the politician's name. Reasonable efforts were made to confirm the politician's identity.

- *The public importance of the matter* The story dealt with the conduct of politicians and the use of public money, making this a story of public importance as well as one of public interest.

- *The urgency of the matter* The premier's press conference made politicians' expense claims a pressing and newsworthy issue.

- *The status and reliability of the source* The news organization used solid sources and should be able to justify relying on unnamed sources to confirm the politician's identity.

- *Whether the plaintiff's side of the story was sought and accurately reported* Efforts were made to interview the politician who, in any event, may have had no knowledge of the investigation or the questionable claims. Quoting the politician's colleague adds balance to the story.

- *Whether the inclusion of the defamatory statement was justifiable* The story could have been published without the politician being named, but naming the politician ensured other provincial politicians were not placed under a cloud of suspicion. The report was true—the politician was under police investigation for possible fraud—even if the allegation turned out to be baseless.

- *Whether the defamatory statement's public interest lay in the fact that it was made rather than its truth* The "reportage" defence would not apply, as the fraud allegation was not the subject of dispute or debate.

- *Any other relevant circumstances* The story was not sensationalized and the report made it clear the politician was under investigation based on an allegation of fraud. It did not state that he had committed an act of fraud.

The seriousness of the false allegation compounded the damage to the politician's reputation. The story was of intense public importance, however, and the news organization took pains to verify the story and report it in a responsible manner. Allegations were not reported as fact, the reporting and sources were solid, and care was taken to present the politician's side of the story. The defence should shield the news organization from the libel claim.

Online Defamation

The Internet has been dubbed "the supreme mechanism for perpetuating libellous statements."[168] A defamatory statement is considered published if it is made available to others, and posting information to the Internet is akin to displaying it on a global billboard that invites everyone to take a look.[169] Judges have remarked on the "extraordinary capacity of the Internet to replicate endlessly any defamatory message."[170] Anyone with online access and a complaint or grudge can create a website, post a message to a listserv or blog, or tweet their comments for the world to see. "Defamatory speech ... has become commonplace as disgruntled ex-employees or consumers find that the Internet is an easy and effective way to distribute their message," notes Canadian Internet law expert Michael Geist.[171] The practice is so prevalent that it has spawned several names—flaming, cyberlibelling, and cybersmearing among them.

Publishing a libel to the Internet's vast audience has the potential to cause more damage to reputation than a report in the traditional media. Court-ordered damage awards reflect this. In 1998, in one of Canada's largest defamation awards, a judge awarded Vancouver journalist David Baines $875,000 after a Florida-based writer launched a smear campaign accusing him of manipulating stock prices. A large portion of the award—$350,000—was compensation for information disseminated to "a worldwide audience" on the Internet.[172]

The proliferation of news websites means most journalists report and write for the web, or soon will. Newspapers and broadcast outlets repost material and original content to their sites, new sites devoted to news and commentary are popping up, and blogs give journalists and ordinary Canadians alike a chance to report and comment on events. Journalists are subject to the same risks of being sued for defamation—and are protected by the same defences—as if they were writing for print or broadcast. The courts, however, are recognizing the shift in the way news is published and received, and defamation law is evolving to keep pace. The new defence of responsible communication on matters of public interest, outlined earlier in this chapter, is an example. The Supreme Court of Canada deliberately used the term "responsible communication," rather than "responsible journalism," to signal that the defence is available to anyone "who publishes material of public interest in any medium." As the court noted, "the traditional media are rapidly being complemented by new ways of communicating on matters of public interest, many of them online, which do not involve journalists. These new disseminators of news and information should ... be subject to the same laws as established media outlets." Citizen journalists will be held to the same standards as professional journalists, the court added, but these standards "will necessarily evolve to keep pace with the norms of new communications media."[173]

Internet Publishing: Libel Risks for Journalists

Blogs, Tweets, and Social Media Posts

A sports editor for a major newspaper used his private blog to denounce an Ontario businessman as a "huckster," a "two-bit shyster," and a "professional nuisance." In response, the businessman sued for $2 million, claiming damage to his character and reputation. The 2007 lawsuit, which was settled out of court after the blogger posted an apology, is one of many launched against Canadian bloggers—journalists and non-journalists alike.[174]

Many reporters and editors blog or tweet for their employers, and many more post material to personal websites, blogs, Facebook pages, and Twitter accounts. (A tweet is a text message of up to 140 characters disseminated via Twitter.) No matter what form the postings take, journalists should only publish material online if they would be comfortable publishing the same material in the traditional news media.

Comments Posted to Media Sites

An article on Halifax's fire service in *The Coast*, the city's alternative weekly paper, generated online comments—including less-than-flattering remarks about two top firefighters from people using pseudonyms such as LessTalkMoreAction and poison_pen. Halifax's fire chief and his deputy threatened to sue the posters for libel and went to court to unmask the people behind the assumed names. In April 2010 a Nova Scotia judge ordered the paper and an Internet service provider to disclose the information needed to identify the posters.[175]

People who make anonymous web postings cannot escape liability for their words. Canadian courts have ordered Yahoo! and other companies that provide Internet access to disclose the names of account holders, so that they could be sued for defamation.[176] Bloggers have also been unmasked: Canadian model Liskula Cohen secured a court order in 2009 compelling Google Inc. to identify the person responsible for posting images and defamatory comments about her on the website Skanks of NYC.[177] In 2010 a New Brunswick judge ordered Brunswick News to disclose the identity of an anonymous poster accused of defaming the author of a letter to the editor.[178] To protect a poster's privacy, the Ontario Superior Court ruled in 2010, there must be some evidence to support the defamation claim—enough to establish a *prima facie* case—before disclosure will be ordered.[179]

As the courts crack down on anonymous posters, some news organizations have responded by requiring posters to identify themselves publicly—as is the case for the authors of letters to the editor—or when they register to use an online pseudonym.[180] News outlets can be sued for defamatory statements they host on their sites, and most screen comments submitted in response to articles to weed out those that could be defamatory.[181] *The Coast* was not sued for publishing the controversial comments about the Halifax fire chiefs, but the paper removed them from its website and posted an apology in their place.[182] Promptly removing comments that draw complaints or threats of legal action may be sufficient to stave off a libel action against the media outlet itself. Some experts argue a news website should be considered an "innocent disseminator" and not legally responsible for such postings. Canadian courts are only beginning to consider this aspect of the law, however, and may hold media websites responsible for posted comments. "Media websites arguably do not play a 'passive role' in the publication of defamatory user comments," Toronto media lawyers Tony Wong and Iris Fischer have noted. "Instead, comments are actively solicited on topics raised by articles published in the media."[183] Key factors will be whether the news outlet screens or edits postings before they appear online, and whether steps are taken to promptly remove material in response to a complaint or a threat to sue.[184]

Hypertext Links to Defamatory Material

A website operator, blogger, or tweeter who posts a hypertext link to defamatory statements on another website may risk legal action. Simply posting a link to a libellous article or website does not expose the poster to a defamation suit, British Columbia's Court of Appeal has ruled. Linking could be considered republication, however, if there is evidence the person knew the linked material was defamatory, duplicated or endorsed the libellous statements, or encouraged others to click on the link to view the offensive material. The court said a number of factors should be considered, including "the prominence of the hyperlink, any words of invitation or recommendation to the reader associated with the hyperlink," and "the nature of the materials which it is suggested may be found at the hyperlink (for example, if the hyperlink obviously refers to a scandalous, or obscene publication)."[185] This will not be the last word on the issue: The BC ruling was under appeal to the Supreme Court of Canada at the time of writing.[186]

Responding to a Complaint of Online Libel

If someone threatens to sue, an online publisher should seek legal advice on the steps to take to mitigate damages if a lawsuit is filed and succeeds. Online publications, unlike the print media, have the flexibility to remove an offending item almost instantly and can promptly post a correction, retraction, or apology. Such notices, if posted, should be given the same prominence as the original statement—if not greater prominence—and should be displayed for at least the same amount of time. Steps should also be taken to remove erroneous or defamatory material from databases or archives that are accessible online. If someone retrieves or downloads an archived item, a court could consider this to be a fresh publication of the libel. When a White House aide sued Internet gossip columnist Matt Drudge in 1998 over an article falsely accusing him of spousal abuse, the Internet service provider that carried the item, America Online, quickly removed the offending edition of the Drudge Report from its archives.[187] The Canadian Press wire service, which offers a database of past news stories to its clients, has a policy of removing items that contain errors or have become the subject of a legal challenge, replacing them with revised or corrected versions.[188]

Internet News Gathering: Libel Risks for Journalists

Material Published on Social Media Sites

A Canadian poll conducted in 2009 found that more than one-quarter of respondents were unaware they were legally responsible for libellous material distributed through social network sites such as Facebook, MySpace, and Twitter.[189] This finding alone should give journalists pause before they republish controversial material or derogatory comments found on social media sites.

Rock star Courtney Love appears to be the first Twitter user sued for libel. She was accused in March 2009 of defaming a designer in a tweet.[190] In another well-publicized case, a Chicago woman was sued in 2009 for $50,000 by her landlord after posting a tweet that complained her apartment was mouldy. A judge eventually dismissed the suit, ruling the tenant's comments were too vague to be considered libellous.[191] Libel law also applies to YouTube—in 2007 a judge ordered a London, Ontario man to remove a video posted to the site in which he verbally abused his former lawyer.[192] The online, user-edited encyclopedia Wikipedia and the advertising site Craigslist have also been sued for posting defamatory content.[193]

The republication rule applies to web postings, as it does to other forms of publication. As the Supreme Court of Canada cautioned in 2009, "the fact that someone has already published a defamatory statement does not give another person licence to repeat it. ... this principle is especially vital when defamatory statements can be reproduced electronically with the speed of a few keystrokes."[194]

E-mail Messages

A derogatory statement made in a private e-mail could become the subject of a defamation action. If an e-mail containing defamatory statements about someone is sent to at least one other recipient, it has been published in the eyes of the law.[195] Because e-mail can be forwarded with ease, the person who wrote and sent the initial message also could be held responsible if it is retransmitted by others—a court would likely take the view that the writer should have anticipated that his words could be disseminated to a wider audience.[196] In 2008 an Ontario man paid a settlement of almost $8,000 for sending a defamatory e-mail that was distributed to only three people.[197]

A deliberate attempt to use an e-mail message to defame someone is likely to result in a substantial award of damages. An Ontario man who falsely accused an archaeologist of being a "grave robber" in a widely circulated e-mail—he urged recipients to forward the message to as many people and listservs as possible—was ordered to pay the archaeologist $125,000 in damages. In making the award, the judge said e-mail messages are "far more powerful than ... hard-copy letters" as a tool to defame.[198]

A writer or researcher who contacts a source via e-mail must guard against asking questions or making comments that attack someone's reputation. Internet law expert Jeffrey Schelling's advice to writers is blunt: "Do not send any messages that you would not otherwise send in a letter." The ease and brevity of communicating by e-mail, he adds, may leave a terse or poorly worded message open to misinterpretation. "What might sound reasonable in ordinary speech could be interpreted as aggressive, abrupt, or rude" in an e-mail.[199]

Newsgroup and Listserv Postings

Electronic bulletin boards, newsgroups, and listservs enable people with shared interests—everything from antiques to zoology—to exchange information via the Internet. Although these services restrict their audiences, an Australian court has ruled that comments posted in these forums are published and can become the target of a defamation claim. In this case, a professor was awarded damages after an American colleague posted an inflammatory message about him on a listserv, aimed at anthropologists, with 23,000 subscribers at universities around the world.[200] A Canadian man who used these services to accuse a mining company of theft, stock fraud, and genocide was ordered to pay $125,000 in damages.[201] And in 2004 an Iqaluit woman threatened to sue a local online forum, Rantin' and Raven, after users posted abusive comments about her.[202]

Journalists and researchers often use these services to post appeals for information. Such requests must be drafted with the same care as if they were destined for a traditional form of publication, and journalists must guard against making allegations or disparaging remarks about individuals or corporations.

Republication and Notice of Defamation Actions

The requirements for filing a defamation action based on an Internet publication are evolving. An Ontario court ruled in 2002 that an online newspaper, like a conventional one, is entitled under Ontario law to six weeks' notice of a plaintiff's intention to sue.[203] In another Ontario case, a town employee sued over information that a local councillor posted and later archived on his personal website. A judge dismissed the action because the plaintiff failed to meet the six-week deadline for notification. But Ontario's Court of Appeal reinstated the lawsuit, saying the case raised important issues that should be dealt with more thoroughly, at a trial.[204] These include whether leaving contentious material on a site, reposting it, or downloading or accessing the material should be considered a new act of publication; if so, each act would trigger a fresh deadline for a plaintiff to take legal action.[205] The Ontario case did not resolve these issues, and media law experts have called on Canada's courts to adopt the American "single-publication rule," which treats each edition of a newspaper and a single newscast as a distinct, one-time publication.[206] British Columbia's Court of Appeal, however, has suggested that defamation legislation may have to be amended to take into account the unlimited republication possible as online material is viewed, linked, downloaded, and reposted. In the meantime, it ruled, "each publication of a libel gives a fresh cause of action."[207]

Where Will a Defamation Action Be Heard?

The target of a defamatory comment disseminated over the Internet may be tempted to pursue lawsuits in several jurisdictions at once, or to sue in a country where the law is favourable to a plaintiff's case. "Libel tourism" has become popular for plaintiffs who can bear the expense of a long-distance court battle. When the owners of Harrods took offence to a tongue-in-cheek article published in the New York–based *Wall Street Journal* in 2002, the department store filed its lawsuit in London. Although the damage to reputation, if any, was done in the United States—only a dozen copies of the Internet version of the item were downloaded in Britain—the choice of court was made to take advantage of British defamation law, which, like Canada's, tends to favour plaintiffs.[208] But practical considerations come into play in cross-border defamation cases. Most plaintiffs want their name cleared where the damage was done, not in some faraway country where they are unknown to the few Internet users who have read the libellous statements. And if the plaintiff wins in a foreign country where the defendant has no assets, it may be difficult to recover any damages the court has awarded.

A leading Canadian case on the issue of Internet jurisdiction rejected a plaintiff's attempt to use an American court to win damages from a Canadian writer. The plaintiff, a technology company with a research facility in Texas, sued over statements posted on an electronic bulletin board for investors. The company filed its action in

Texas, where the courts have a reputation for granting large libel awards; the BC resident responsible for posting the information offered no defence and was ordered to pay US$400,000 in damages. British Columbia's Court of Appeal, however, refused to enforce the judgment, ruling that "the mere transitory, passive presence in cyberspace of the alleged defamatory material" was not enough to establish Texas as the proper place to file the lawsuit. There was no evidence anyone in Texas read the posting and, because the company's senior officials were based in the Vancouver area, the lawsuit should have been filed in British Columbia. "It would create a crippling effect on freedom of expression," the court ruled, "if, in every jurisdiction the world over in which access to Internet could be achieved, a person who posts fair comment on a bulletin board could be haled before the courts of each of those countries where access to this bulletin could be obtained."[209]

A key factor in where an Internet defamation suit will be heard is where the damage to reputation occurs. A person writing for an online publication based in another country, for example, can be sued here for defaming someone who lives in Canada. This situation arose in 1998 when an Ontario resident filed a lawsuit in Ontario seeking $700,000 in damages from the author of an article published in a Ugandan newspaper. The article was posted on the newspaper's Internet site, making it accessible in Ontario. The author, who also lived in Ontario, contended that the action should be filed in Uganda, not Canada. But an Ontario judge disagreed, ruling that the website's location was not the decisive factor because any damage to reputation had occurred in Ontario. The judge also took into account the expense and inconvenience that the plaintiff would face if the case had to be heard in Africa.[210]

In 2004, another Ontario judge allowed a former United Nations official living in Canada to sue the *Washington Post* over online articles accusing him of sexual harassment and financial improprieties. The lawsuit was allowed to proceed in Ontario even though the former official was living in Kenya when the stories were published. For the UN official the articles "would have the greatest impact" on his reputation in Ontario, where he had resettled and found work. "Those who publish via the Internet are aware of the global reach of their publications," the judge concluded, "and must consider the legal consequences in the jurisdiction of the subjects of their articles."[211] The ruling was appealed, with a coalition of 50 media organizations—including the *New York Times*, *Time* magazine, and CNN—describing it as a threat to "the future of global freedom of expression." The Ontario Court of Appeal overturned the ruling and found "no real and substantial connection" between the libel claim and Ontario that justified hearing the case in the province.[212]

When a writer based in another country uses the Internet to attack a Canadian's reputation, our courts have asserted their jurisdiction to hear the case. In 2002 an Ontario judge ordered three New York residents to pay $400,000 in damages to Ralph Reichmann after they used a website to defame the Toronto businessman.[213] This approach is consistent with pre-Internet rulings that enabled plaintiffs to use Canadian courts to sue over defamatory statements broadcast into Canada by American radio and television stations.[214]

Damages and Other Remedies for Online Libel

When a published statement is found to be defamatory, the Internet's ability to disseminate information to a vast audience will be reflected in the damages awarded.[215] The courts may expect a plaintiff to prove that defamatory material has been read or downloaded, rather than assuming that the Internet's global audience has been reached and the damage to reputation has been compounded. In 2008 a BC judge dismissed a libel claim after the plaintiff was unable to show that anyone in the province had read a defamatory post.[216] "The number of e-mails sent, or the number of people who read a newsgroup posting or Web page will be relevant" when a court assesses damages, one observer has noted.[217] Recall the Ontario lawsuit, discussed above, in which an article was posted on a Ugandan newspaper's website. The judge suggested that the plaintiff faced an uphill battle proving damage to reputation; only two people in Ontario accessed the site, and neither viewed the disputed article.[218]

One judge imposed additional damages because defamatory comments were made anonymously, via e-mail. "[R]eaders cannot know who the author is and that person's motives for sending the e-mail," the judge explained, and "a reader is not readily able to discount comments that are made. There is a greater risk that the defamatory remarks are believed. That aggravates the defamation."[219] In another case, a chat room user who endured years of abuse from a BC man was awarded $180,000 in damages. The judge in this case also imposed a sweeping injunction to prevent his tormentor from using the Internet to publish further defamatory comments about him.[220]

Criminal Libel

When Joseph Howe struck a blow for freedom of the press at his famous libel trial in 1835 (a milestone explored in Chapter 3), the Nova Scotia editor was acquitted of the criminal form of defamation. The offence was created in England in the 13th century to prevent people from spreading lies and unfounded rumours that might cause unrest among the populace or undermine the authority of the state. With the advent of the printing press two centuries later, the law of criminal libel gave the authorities a means to control the spread of ideas and criticism. By the 1600s it was also a crime to attack the reputation of an individual. In those days, an insult or published attack on a gentleman's character could lead to a challenge to fight a duel. By making libel a crime, the state could step in to prevent bloodshed. England's common law courts, meanwhile, were developing defamation as a civil matter, laying the groundwork for the modern tort of defamation.[221]

Today, defamation is largely a matter for the civil courts. Most plaintiffs would rather hit journalists and publishers in the pocketbook—and pocket a tidy award of damages for themselves—than prosecute them as criminals. But the criminal form of libel, known as defamatory libel, remains on the books in Canada. The *Criminal Code* makes it an offence, punishable by a prison term of up to two years, for anyone to publish a libel. The potential penalty increases to five years behind bars if the person knew the published information was false. The definition of a defamatory libel is broad, covering anything "likely to injure the reputation of any person by exposing him to hatred, contempt or ridicule, or that is designed to insult the person of or concerning whom it is published." The defences to civil defamation—truth, fair comment, qualified privilege, and consent—apply in the criminal realm, and are set out in detail in the Code.[222] Prosecutions for criminal libel are rare,[223] as Crown prosecutors are reluctant to become embroiled in private disputes over reputation that can be dealt with through the civil courts.

A separate provision of the Code makes it an offence to publish a seditious libel, which is defined as a statement advocating the use of force to overthrow the government. The provision is not aimed at stifling political dissent and there are defences that protect legitimate criticism of government policy.[224] The offence has been rarely prosecuted and there must be proof that someone deliberately set out to cause a riot or other form of unrest.[225] It is also a crime to publish a blasphemous libel—a false and malicious attack on Christianity. Opinions or arguments on religious subjects expressed "in good faith and in decent language" are exempt.[226] There appear to have been only two prosecutions for this offence in the 20th century, both in Quebec and the last one in the early 1930s.[227]

Robert Martin considers these forms of criminal libel to be as outdated as duelling.[228] A 1984 study by the Law Reform Commission of Canada dismissed the offences as "anachronistic" and predicted they would not withstand a challenge based on the Charter's guarantee of freedom of expression. As well, the commission concluded that the civil law is adequate to punish those who engage in "deliberate character assassinations."[229] Nevertheless, section 300, which makes it an offence for someone to publish a defamatory libel the person knows is false, survived a constitutional challenge and remains in force. In 1998 the Supreme Court of Canada ruled that the infringement on free expression is justified under section 1 of the Charter. But, the court said, prosecutions must be reserved for attacks on reputation that are "so grave and serious that the imposition of a criminal sanction is not excessive."[230] A related provision has been struck down as a violation of the Charter. Courts in four provinces have ruled section 301, which made it an offence to spread a defamatory libel regardless of whether the person knew the information was false, was too great an infringement on freedom of expression. In the words of one judge, prosecutors cannot use "the heavy hammer of the criminal law" against a citizen without proof the person deliberately set out to destroy someone's reputation.[231]

The Supreme Court ruling arose from a case in which two people picketed a courthouse. They brandished placards that falsely accused a police officer of facilitating the rape of a child. Another example is the 2008 prosecution of a man who stood outside an Ontario police station dressed only in his underwear and carrying a sign describing an officer as "crooked."[232] It is clear that the offence of defamatory libel is aimed at curbing this kind of deliberate, vicious attack on reputation, not the work of reputable journalists. The Code contains a defence exempting media reports on a matter of public interest, if the public will benefit from having the information discussed in an open forum (the writer or publisher must also have had reasonable grounds to believe that the defamatory statement was true).[233] No media outlet could contemplate publishing an allegation that someone sexually abused a child without first being satisfied that the story could withstand a possible defamation action under the civil law. In one of the few prosecutions of the media, a Vancouver alternative newspaper was convicted of defamatory libel in 1969 after attacking a judge as "deaf, dumb and stupid" and awarding him "the Pontius Pilate Certificate of Justice."[234] As these examples suggest, the work of a journalist would have to be exceedingly reckless and unprofessional to attract even the threat of a criminal prosecution. In the words of the Supreme Court's 1998 ruling, "defamatory libel is so far removed from the core values of freedom of expression that it merits but scant protection."[235]

Libel-Proofing the Story

Avoiding Libel Chill

Journalists and writers often gripe about **libel chill**—where important stories are toned down or ignored for fear of attracting an expensive defamation suit. Canada's media, the argument goes, should be afforded US-style protection for statements made about politicians and other public figures. And it is too easy for large corporations and the wealthy to threaten lawsuits even if their complaints of being defamed are unlikely to succeed in court.[236] There is also the problem of SLAPPs—strategic lawsuits against public participation—designed to silence critics. Citizens who speak out against the actions of corporations or controversial development projects have been hit with defamation suits, making other critics wary and shutting down public debate on important issues. Quebec passed a law to curb this abuse of the justice system in 2009; the following year, a judge used it to dismiss a libel suit filed against a man who asked municipal councillors, during a public meeting, to review a tender awarded to a company to repair a water-filtration plant. As of 2010 Ontario was considering similar legislation.[237]

There is no doubt that six-figure damage awards can have a sobering effect on journalists, media managers, and citizens alike. But the courts have made it clear that Canada's defamation laws will not be eased to make it easier to defame someone without consequences. And so the spectre remains that the fear of a lawsuit and massive legal costs will prompt media outlets to discourage investigative reporting or to suppress stories likely to attract a libel action, regardless of the strength of the evidence uncovered. The key to easing libel chill is to practise and promote good journalism (see under the heading "Good Journalism: The Best Defence to Libel," below).

The risk of a libel action should be put into perspective. Although virtually any criticism or harsh description could be seen as "capable of defamation," relatively few lawsuits are filed. Most people stung by an erroneous news report are satisfied if a correction or clarification is published. Even the more damaging statements that draw a notice of intent to sue can still be settled by publication of a correction, retraction, or apology.

Few people have the fortitude—let alone the financial resources—to mount a libel action, which can take years to reach trial. A writer in the *London Observer* once likened libel to "a profitable High Court casino" where "only the rich can play."[238] In deciding whether to publish, editors and media lawyers take into account the likelihood that the target of criticism will sue. If the allegation is serious and the person or company has deep pockets or a litigious history, extra care must be taken to ensure that the story has a solid factual foundation and will be defensible in court should a lawsuit be filed.

The Lawyering Process

Journalists should invite the chance to have a lawyer vet their stories before publication or broadcast. Once a flawed story appears, the damage is done—and the reputation of the journalist and news organization will suffer along with the reputation of the subject of the story.

Lawyers sometimes err on the side of caution and may advise against publication; if they do, request advice on how to substantiate or rework passages that may be vulnerable to a lawsuit. Think of lawyering as a dry run for the scrutiny that the story will receive from readers and, more importantly, from the person or company that is the target of the story.

Good Journalism: The Best Defence to Libel

Good journalism has always offered the best protection against a libel suit. The defence of responsible communication on matters of public interest reflects this, with its emphasis on ethical conduct and thorough, solid reporting. The following tips on how to libel-proof a story are based on court rulings and good journalism practices:

- *Be skeptical* Some stories really are too good to be true. A story that comes in a neat package with no loose ends may make a good conspiracy theory, but it is not good journalism. Journalists must avoid tunnel-vision—a tip or suspicion that appears credible may prove, on closer examination, to be overblown or unfounded. While gathering information, journalists should second-guess everything they are told and challenge their own preconceptions and assumptions.

  Not every source or tipster approaches the media out of a sense of public duty. Many have their own agendas to promote or axes to grind. Journalists should ask themselves what motivated a source to come forward. The information that the source provides may be valid, but it must be verified by consulting other sources and documents. Journalists should never hesitate to ask a source tough questions, and they should be wary of any source who objects to being challenged. If the source has documents to prove his assertions, ask for copies or an opportunity to view them. No media outlet should publish or broadcast a story based on a source's assurances that such evidence exists. Because leaked documents could be altered or forged, journalists must verify they are genuine.

- *Be realistic* Journalists should constantly analyze the information they have gathered. Is the source credible? Is a witness providing evidence of what she saw and heard, or merely repeating hearsay? If a story does not pan out, the journalist must have the courage to abandon it regardless of the effort and resources expended. One journalist who was stymied in his search for evidence that a government official was squelching prosecutions interpreted the stonewalling as proof of a coverup. The journalist's thinly researched story was broadcast and it turned out that there was a more logical explanation for the lack of evidence—the rumours of interference that had launched the story were untrue.[239]

- *Be meticulous* Double-check facts. Search for government reports, court filings, deeds, business records, and other documents that can back up a statement or assertion. Where possible, ensure that stories are grounded in documents covered by qualified privilege, such as transcripts of court hearings and political debates. Seek out at least one other person to verify information obtained from a source.

- *Be precise* Terms such as "political patronage" and "corruption" describe serious acts of misconduct. Stealing and committing fraud are crimes. Words such as these should never be used lightly to describe a person's conduct. The courts will demand proof that the assertions are true.

- *Act professionally* Copy every important document gathered while researching a story. Keep detailed, legible notes. Make an audio recording of key interviews. Most importantly, keep all of this material for at least six months, in case a defamation suit is threatened or filed. All information that a journalist gathers is subject to disclosure to the plaintiff and could become evidence in court. A journalist must not destroy notes or erase tapes if a lawsuit is filed, as this could be seen as evidence of malice or, at the very least, an indication that the journalist had something to hide.

  Because copies of notes and research materials could wind up in the hands of a plaintiff's lawyer, avoid writing derogatory comments in the margins of documents or notebooks. Even a story's slug or filename could be seen as evidence of malice. Using a word like "pervert" or "depraved" to designate a story about allegations of sexual harassment would suggest the journalist's mindset. Even comments made inside the newsroom can come back to haunt a journalist. One reporter delighted in boasting of how he would "fry up" the subjects of his stories—the kind of comment certain to be seen as evidence of malice in a lawsuit.

  Care should also be taken when conducting interviews. A poorly worded question or an accusation of wrongdoing could trigger a libel action on its own, even if the story is never written or broadcast. Avoid directly accusing someone of lying or stealing when speaking to sources—particularly sources friendly with the target of the allegation. It is safer to ask sources to explain what happened and whether they believe that what was done was proper.

- *Be fair and balanced* The old saw that there are two sides to every story is true. Strive for balance and seek out information to challenge the official line or refute an opponent's criticism. Black-and-white, good-guy/bad-guy stories are easy to produce; the truth is usually found in the grey area between such extremes. Selective presentation of information and the use of statements and comments taken out of context have been seen as evidence of malice.[240]

  Make a genuine effort to contact anyone who is being criticized in a story. A last-minute call as the newspaper is about to go to press is not sufficient. Repeated attempts must be made to contact the target of the story, so that the person has a chance to respond to an allegation or to offer an explanation. The effort may produce new information that changes the tenor of the story or spares the media outlet from publishing false or misleading statements, which would have to be corrected or retracted later. The courts have said a sincere effort must be made to contact the target of an accusation, even if it is only likely to yield a terse "No comment."[241] If an explanation is offered—even one that appears suspect or self-serving—fairness and the law demand that it be reported and given a prominent place in the story.

- *Be hesitant* Deadline pressure and the fear of being scooped can rush stories into print before they have been properly researched and verified. Be prepared to make the tough call of shelving the story for an extra day or as long as is necessary to ensure that it is correct. In one case, a newspaper's decision to publish a sensational but flawed story to beat a competing newspaper was found to be evidence of malice.[242] Law books are filled with defamation cases that could have been avoided if reporters, editors, and producers had taken more time and care before the story appeared.

- *Practise restraint* There is merit in letting facts and people speak for themselves. Jessica Mitford, whose exposés of the funeral industry, prison conditions, and other issues earned her the title "Queen of the Muckrakers," advised her fellow journalists to avoid injecting editorial comment into their stories. She preferred to let the subjects of her stories hang themselves on their own words.[243]

  Avoid speculating on the possible motives behind a statement or decision. The member of a visible minority who was denied a bank loan may have been a poor credit risk, not the victim of racism. "Idle speculation," says Robert Martin, "has no place in good journalism."[244] Avoid sensationalism and language that is unduly harsh or more judgmental than the facts will bear. Although the CBC report that condemned the Winnipeg slum landlord as a man with "no morals, principles, or conscience" was ruled fair comment, was the editorializing worth the years of litigation and hefty legal bills that were needed to stave off the defamation suit?

  Journalists are entitled to draw logical conclusions from the evidence they have uncovered, but they should never forget that readers, listeners, and viewers can think for themselves. It has been said that no journalist is completely objective; each one brings a point of view to issues and stories. Some reporters spend years plugging away at a major story, developing a thorough knowledge of the subject as well as opinions on what is happening and what should be done about it. But journalists should approach each story with an open mind. The goal should be to produce reports that are factually complete as well as balanced and objective in tone.

- *Understand your role* Defamation law imposes distinct roles on reporters and their editors and producers. Reporters gather facts; editors and producers verify those facts before publication or broadcast. "It is the editor's responsibility," one judge noted, "to know in detail before publication, the documentation to support the story and the reliability of the sources and so ensure its accuracy."

In the case of the *Toronto Sun* story discussed above, the newspaper reporter claimed he had documentation to substantiate allegations of the politician's wrongdoing, but none of his editors reviewed the material; the allegation turned out to be a fabrication.[245] In another case, a judge chastised the executive producer of a television news program who "ostensibly ... was ultimately responsible" for a broadcast, but provided "meaningless" input and failed to check a major investigative piece before it aired.[246]

- *Seek advice* Ask an editor or producer whether the story's allegations or criticisms go too far. If the answer does not appear to be clear cut, consult the lawyer who advises the news organization on media law. But libel-proofing a story should never be left solely to editors and lawyers. Journalists should flag potential problems in their stories at the reporting and writing stage. Special care must be taken with any story that involves allegations of wrongdoing or harsh criticism of someone's conduct.

Defamation: A Summary

Journalists seek the truth and strive for accuracy. Their tools are an open mind and thorough research; their watchwords are fairness and balance; their criticisms are based on fact, not conjecture. They pursue stories on matters of public interest that need to be told. These are the elements of good journalism, and they are also a journalist's best defence against a libel action. The law of defamation is complex and evolving, but what it demands of journalists is simple: get the facts right, report all sides of the story, be independent and even-handed when expressing opinions, and ensure allegations can be proven or defended. Journalists should demand nothing less of themselves.

NOTES

1. "Watch Out for Big-Time Crime: Criminal Gangs Affect Us All, Police Warn," *Chronicle-Herald* (Halifax), June 22, 2001.
2. William Shakespeare, *Othello*, III. iii. 155–61.
3. *Hill v. Church of Scientology of Toronto*, [1995] 2 SCR 1130.
4. Robert Martin, *Media Law*, 2nd ed. (Toronto: Irwin Law, 2003), 144.
5. Quoted in Robert Martin, "Ont. Paper's Coverage Shows Why We Need Law of Libel," *The Lawyers Weekly*, March 27, 1992, at 12.
6. *Halsbury's Laws of England*, 4th ed., vol. 28, at paragraph 10, cited in Robert S. Bruser and Brian MacLeod Rogers, *Journalists and the Law: How To Get the Story Without Getting Sued or Put in Jail* (Ottawa: Canadian Bar Foundation, 1985), 51.
7. Martin, supra note 4, at 148.
8. Raymond E. Brown, *Defamation Law: A Primer* (Toronto: Carswell, 2003), 26.
9. *Hodgson v. Canadian Newspapers Co. Ltd.* (1998), 39 OR (3d) 235, at 252–53 (Gen. Div.).
10. "Calling B.C. Alderman a 'Son of a Bitch' Isn't Libel, But Adding 'Sick' Is Libel," *The Lawyers Weekly*, March 27, 1992, at 12, reporting on the ruling in *Ralston v. Fomich*.

11. Brown, supra note 8, at 38.

12. *Gouzenko v. Harris* (1976), 13 OR (2d) 730 (HC).

13. *McCrea v. Canada Newspapers Co.* (1993), 126 NSR (2d) 212 (CA).

14. *P.G. Restaurant Ltd. v. Cariboo Press (1969) Ltd.*, 2005 BCCA 210; David A. Crerar, "'The Bane and Antidote Must Be Taken Together': A Recent British Columbia Court of Appeal Decision Reassures Publishers and Journalists," *Masthead*, September/October 2005.

15. Sherri Borden Colley, "TV Station Loses Defamation Suit; ATV Must Pay $15,000 for Painting Man as Terrorist," *Chronicle-Herald* (Halifax), September 30, 2004.

16. Gerald A. Flaherty, *Defamation Law in Canada* (Ottawa: Canadian Bar Foundation, 1984), 25.

17. *Reaburn v. Langen*, 2009 BCCA 465, at paragraph 24. See also Jeffrey Miller, "The Sun Will Allegedly, If Not Purportedly, Rise Tomorrow," *The Lawyers Weekly*, May 20, 2005, 5.

18. These definitions are drawn from Michelle Lovric, *The Scoundrel's Dictionary: A Copious and Complete Compendium of 18th-Century Slang* (Oxford: Past Times, 1997).

19. Joseph Dean, *Hatred, Ridicule, or Contempt: A Book of Libel Cases* (London: Penguin Books, 1964), 15.

20. *Brannigan v. S.I.U.* (1963), 42 DLR (2d) 249 (BCSC).

21. Jen Colletta, "NJ Court Rules 'Gay' Is Not Defamatory," *Philadelphia Gay News*, April 8, 2010; Debra Cassens Weiss, "Homosexuality Claim About Lawyer Is Not Defamation Per Se, Judge Rules," *ABA Journal*, August 13, 2009.

22. P.J. O'Rourke, *Give War a Chance: Eyewitness Accounts of Mankind's Struggle Against Tyranny, Injustice and Alcohol-Free Beer* (New York: Atlantic Monthly Press, 1992), 125.

23. "Apology and Retraction," *Chronicle-Herald* (Halifax), July 23, 1998.

24. According to the entry in *The New Penguin Dictionary* (Toronto: Penguin Books, 2000), 1298.

25. David Hooper, *Reputations Under Fire: Winners and Losers in the Libel Business* (London: Warner Books, 2001), 10.

26. *Campbell v. Jones*, 2002 NSCA 128. While the majority in this case found that privilege prevented a police officer from recovering damages from two lawyers who labelled her a racist, the dissenting judge called their words "a very grave defamation."

27. *Robbins v. Pacific Newspaper Group Inc. et al.*, 2005 BCSC 1634, at paragraphs 50, 52.

28. *Hiltz and Seamone Co. Ltd. v. Nova Scotia (Attorney General)* (1997), 164 NSR (2d) 161 (SC).

29. *Leenen v. Canadian Broadcasting Corp.* (2000), 48 OR (3d) 656 (SC); aff'd. (2000), 54 OR (3d) 612 (CA).

30. *Hill v. Church of Scientology of Toronto*, supra note 3.

31. *Barltrop v. CBC* (1978), 86 DLR (3d) 61 (NSCA).

32. *Leenen v. Canadian Broadcasting Corp.*, supra note 29.

33. *Thomas v. Canadian Broadcasting Corp.* (1981), 27 AR 547 (NWTSC).

34. The suit was settled out of court. See Mary Findlater, "Anatomy of a Libel" (Summer 2005), *Ryerson Review of Journalism* 72–75.

35. Martin, supra note 4, at 152.

36. Raymond E. Brown, *The Law of Defamation in Canada*, 2nd ed. (Scarborough, ON: Carswell, 1994), 298–99.

37. Brown, supra note 8, at 54.

38. Ibid., at 55.

39. *Rupic v. Toronto Star Newspapers Limited*, 2009 CanLII 500 (Ont. SC).

40. Cases on this point are discussed in Brown, supra note 8, at 79–80, and in Michael G. Crawford, *The Journalist's Legal Guide*, 4th ed. (Scarborough, ON: Carswell, 2002), 73.

41. Brown, supra note 8, at 80–83; Crawford, supra note 40, at 72.

42. Bertrand Marotte, "Saputo Launches Defamation Suit," *Globe and Mail*, March 11, 2008.

43. *Elliot v. Canadian Broadcasting Corp.* (1995), 125 DLR (4th) 534 (Ont. CA).

44. *Gauthier v. Toronto Star*, [2003] OJ no. 2622 (QL) (SC). See also John Jaffey, "Superior Court Judge Tosses Police Libel Action Against Star," *The Lawyers Weekly*, July 11, 2003, at 5.

45. Canadian Newspaper Association, "Newspaper Label of Extremist Not Grounds for Libel, B.C. Court Rules," *The Press and the Courts*, vol. 21, no. 4, August 31, 2002.

46. *Booth et al. v. BCTV* (1983), 139 DLR (3d) 88 (BCCA).

47. *A.U.P.E. v. Edmonton Sun*, [1986] AJ no. 1147 (QL) (QB).

48. Brown, supra note 8, at 61.

49. *Bou Malhab c. Métromédia CMR Montréal inc.*, 2003 CanLII 47948 (Que. CA); *Diffusion Métromédia CMR inc. c. Bou Malhab*, 2008 QCCA 1938, at paragraph 108; *Farès Bou Malhab v. Diffusion Métromédia CMR inc., et al.*, Supreme Court of Canada case no. 32931.

50. Brown, supra note 8, at 57–58.

51. Andy Peters, "Best-Selling Novel Defamed Woman, Jury Finds," *Law.com*, December 1, 2009.

52. *E. Hulton & Co. v. Jones*, [1910] AC 22 (HL), cited in Martin, supra note 4, at 152–53.

53. Susan Ferraro, "Libel & Fiction," in *Into Print: Guides for the Writing Life* (New York: Poets & Writers, 1995), 21–29, at 26.

54. Tu Thanh Ha, "Mulroney, Ottawa Settle Libel Suit," *Globe and Mail*, January 6, 1997.

55. The leading American case is *New York Times Co. v. Sullivan,* 376 US 254 (1964).

56. *Hill v. Church of Scientology of Toronto*, supra note 3.

57. *Goddard v. Day*, [2000] CarswellAlta 1516, at paragraph 54.

58. *Grant v. Torstar Corp.*, 2009 SCC 61, at paragraph 58.

59. *Montague (Township) v. Page*, 2006 CanLII 2192, at paragraph 29 (Ont. SC).

60. *Halton Hills (Town) v. Kerouac*, 2006 CanLII 12970, at paragraph 58 (Ont. SC).

61. *Montague (Township) v. Page*, supra note 59, at paragraph 28.

62. Adam McDowell, "Power vs. the People: Public Purse Used in Defamation Suits," *National Post*, February 8, 2010.

63. *Ayangma v. CBC & ors.*, 2000 PESCTD 86.

64. "Apology and Retraction," *Chronicle-Herald* (Halifax), January 5, 2008.

65. "Copps Launches Libel Suit over Flight Story," ibid., March 24, 2000.

66. Martin, supra note 4, at 159.

67. *Hodgson v. Canadian Newspapers Co. Ltd.* (2000), 49 OR (3d) 161, at paragraphs 61–62 (CA).

68. Robert E. Garst and Theodore M. Bernstein, *Headlines and Deadlines: A Manual for Copy Editors*, 4th ed. (New York: Columbia University Press, 1982), 99.

69. Brown, supra note 8, at 46–47.

70. *Myers v. Canadian Broadcasting Corp.* (1999), 47 CCLT (2d) 272 (SCJ).

71. *Vogel v. Canadian Broadcasting Corp.*, [1982] 3 WWR 97 (BCSC).

72. Martin, supra note 4, at 145.

73. Cited in Crawford, supra note 40, at 82.

74. Bill Henderson, ed., *Rotten Reviews: A Literary Companion* (New York: Penguin Books, 1987), 25, 27, and 47.

75. For one exchange between author and reviewer after a negative review, see "Who Gets In—Again," *Globe and Mail*, November 9, 2002.

76. See, for example, *Sara's Pyrohy Hut v. Brooker* (1993), 8 Alta. LR (3d) 113 (CA).

77. *WIC Radio Ltd. v. Simpson*, 2008 SCC 40, at paragraph 48.

78. *Hunter and Swift v. Fotheringham*, a 1986 ruling cited in Crawford, supra note 40, at 80.

79. Neil Stevens, "Radio Host Apologizes to Domi," *Chronicle-Herald* (Halifax), April 8, 2004.

80. *Beutel v. Ross* (2001), 201 DLR (4th) 75 (NBCA).

81. *Mapes v. Hub Publications Ltd.*, [1993] NWTR 174 (SC).

82. An example is an advertisement headlined "Justice?" that was published in a Halifax newspaper and that made sweeping, unsupported allegations against the courts and the provincial law society. The paper published a full retraction and apology the following day. *Chronicle-Herald*, June 18 and 19, 1998.

83. *Teskey v. Canadian Newspapers Co.* (1989), 68 OR (2d) 737 (CA).

84. Daniel W. Burnett and Heather E. Maconachie, "Defamation Law: Shifting Ground," in Todd L. Archibald and Randall Scott Echlin, eds., *Annual Review of Civil Litigation 2008* (Toronto: Thomson Carswell, 2008), 263–97, at 264, 273–74.

85. *Grant v. Torstar Corp.*, supra note 58, at paragraph 28.

86. These points are drawn from Crawford, supra note 40, at 57–61.

87. Stuart M. Robertson, *Robertson's Newsroom Legal Crisis Management* (Toronto: Hallion Press, 1991), 71.

88. Brown, supra note 8, at 242–43.

89. *Rapp v. McClelland & Stewart Ltd.* (1981), 34 OR (2d) 452, at 455–56 (HCJ).

90. *Vogel v. Canadian Broadcasting Corp.*, supra note 71.

91. *Hill v. Church of Scientology of Toronto*, supra note 3.

92. *Hodgson v. Canadian Newspapers Co. Ltd.*, supra note 67. In fact, the original award was higher. The appeal court reduced the trial judge's award of $880,000, which included $100,000 in punitive damages. See *Hodgson v. Canadian Newspapers Co. Ltd.*, supra note 9.

93. This synopsis of the categories of libel damages and how they are assessed is based on Brown, supra note 8, chapter 17.

94. *Leenen v. Canadian Broadcasting Corp.*, supra note 29.

95. Martin, supra note 4, at 169.

96. *Grant v. Torstar Corp.*, supra note 58, at paragraph 33.

97. Flaherty, supra note 16, at 45.

98. Brown, supra note 8, at 215.

99. Crawford, supra note 40, at 33, citing the British precedent *Walker & Son, Ltd. v. Hodgson*, [1909] 1 KB 239 (CA).

100. Burnett and Maconachie, supra note 84, at 274.

101. *Miller v. Canadian Broadcasting Corp.*, 2003 BCSC 258, at paragraph 23.

102. Robert Martin and G. Stuart Adam, *A Sourcebook of Canadian Media Law* (Ottawa: Carleton University Press, 1991), 580.

103. *Baxter v. Canadian Broadcasting Corp.* (1980), 30 NBR (2d) 102 (CA).

104. "Father–Son Stockbrokers Stole Millions, Police Allege," *Chronicle-Herald* (Halifax), June 23, 2001; "Clarification and Apology," ibid., July 7, 2001.

105. Brown, supra note 8, at 169.

106. This point is discussed in Martin, supra note 4, at 170–71.

107. *Pearlman v. Canadian Broadcasting Corp.* (1982), 13 Man. R (2d) 1 (Man. QB).

108. *WIC Radio Ltd. v. Simpson*, supra note 77, at paragraph 2.

109. The criteria are set out in ibid., paragraph 28.

110. Ibid., at paragraphs 30 and 57.

111. *Pound v. Scott*, [1973] 4 WWR 403 (BCSC).

112. *WIC Radio Ltd. v. Simpson*, supra note 77, at paragraphs 31 and 34.

113. Ibid., at paragraph 27.

114. *Merivale v. Carson*, [1887] 20 QBD 275, quoted in *Pound v. Scott*, supra note 111.

115. *Hodgson v. Canadian Newspapers Co. Ltd.*, supra note 9. See also Donn Downey, "Globe Loses Libel Case," *Globe and Mail*, July 4, 1998.

116. *Cherneskey v. Armadale Publishers* (1979), 90 DLR (3d) 321 (SCC).

117. Martin and Adam, supra note 102, at 616–21. For an example, see *Defamation Act*, RSPEI 1988, c. D-5, s. 9.

118. *WIC Radio Ltd. v. Simpson*, supra note 77, at paragraph 49, citing the Australian precedent in *Channel Seven Adelaide Pty. Ltd. v. Manock* (2007), 241 ALR 468, [2007] HCA 60, at paragraph 3.

119. *WIC Radio Ltd. v. Simpson*, supra note 77, at paragraphs 47 and 50.

120. Ibid., at paragraphs 60 and 62.

121. Dean, supra note 19, at 16.

122. *Gatley on Libel and Slander*, 9th ed. (London: Sweet & Maxwell, 1998), 327.

123. In *Prud'homme v. Prud'homme*, [2002] 4 SCR 663, the Supreme Court ruled that absolute privilege does not apply to those taking part in debates at meetings of municipal councils, but the speaker is protected by qualified privilege unless there is proof the statements were made with malice. See also *Wells v. Sears*, 2007 NLCA 21.

124. *Mudford v. Smith*, 2009 CanLII 55718 (Ont. SC).

125. Crawford, supra note 40, at 40. If the report as a whole is accurate, it will be privileged despite the existence of a few slight inaccuracies or omissions. Philip Lewis, ed., *Gatley on Libel and Slander*, 8th ed. (London: Sweet & Maxwell, 1981), 313.

126. Canadian Newspaper Association, "Fair and Accurate Reports Aren't Necessarily Complete, Judge Rules," *The Press and the Courts*, vol. 21, no. 1, February 28, 2002.

127. Crawford, supra note 40, at 40.

128. *Campbell v. Jones*, supra note 26.

129. See, for example, s. 4(1) of Ontario's *Libel and Slander Act*, RSO 1990, c. L.12.

130. For example, *Defamation Act*, RSPEI 1988, c. D-5, s. 12(2)(a).

131. *Chidley-Hill v. Daw*, 2010 ONSC 1576, at paragraph 38.

132. *Hill v. Church of Scientology of Toronto*, supra note 3.

133. *Taylor-Wright v. CHBC-TV* (2000), 194 DLR (4th) 621 (BCCA).

134. Brown, *The Law of Defamation in Canada*, vol. 2 (Toronto: Carswell, 1999), 14–62 to 14–66.

135. *Fletcher-Gordon v. Southam Inc. et al.* (1997), 33 BCLR (3d) 118 (SC).

136. *Hodgson v. Canadian Newspapers Co. Ltd.*, supra note 9.

137. *Quan v. Cusson*, 2009 SCC 62, at paragraphs 7–24.

138. *Grant v. Torstar Corp.*, supra note 58, at paragraphs 8–20.

139. Ibid., at paragraphs 39, 53, and 62.

140. See *Reynolds v. Times Newspapers Ltd.*, [1999] 4 All ER 609, and *Jameel v. Wall Street Journal Europe SPRL*, [2007] 1 AC 359. For an analysis of these rulings and how the defence has developed in Australia, New Zealand, and South Africa, see ibid., at paragraphs 68–86.

141. *Grant v. Torstar Corporation*, 2008 ONCA 796; *Cusson v. Quan*, 2007 ONCA 771.

142. Tonda Maccharles, "Media Outlets Argue for 'Right To Be Wrong' at the Supreme Court," *Toronto Star*, February 17, 2009.

143. *Grant v. Torstar Corp.*, supra note 58, at paragraphs 99–109.

144. *Quan v. Cusson*, supra note 137, at paragraph 31.

145. *Grant v. Torstar Corp.*, supra note 58, at paragraph 140.

146. One judge, Justice Rosalie Abella, endorsed the creation of the responsible communication defence but argued the judge should also decide, in all cases, if the media acted responsibly. See ibid., at paragraphs 142–46 and *Quan v. Cusson*, supra note 137, at paragraph 52.

147. *Grant v. Torstar Corp.*, supra note 58, at paragraphs 110–26.

148. Ibid., at paragraph 125.

149. *Reaburn v. Langen*, supra note 17, quoted at paragraph 16. The judge's ruling predated the creation of the responsible communication defence, but applied the similar principles of the responsible journalism defence.

150. Cristin Schmitz, "New Libel Defences of Responsible Communication and Reportage Are Game-Changers: Media Lawyers," *The Lawyers Weekly*, January 22, 2010, 2, 26.

151. Kathy English, "Defending Responsible Journalism," *Toronto Star*, November 17, 2007, and "Supreme Lessons in Journalism," ibid., January 16, 2010.

152. Jeffrey Dvorkin, "Libel Reform: Be Careful What You Wish For," *J-Source: The Canadian Journalism Project*, available online at http://www.j-source.ca.

153. Alan Shanoff, "Top Court Throws Journalists and Publishers a Lifeline," *Toronto Sun*, January 3, 2010.

154. Shanoff, "Defamation Law—We Have a Long Way to Go," *Law Times*, October 6, 2008.

155. This approach was endorsed in Britain in *Taylor & others v. Director of the Serious Frauds Office & others*, [1998] 2 All ER 801 (HL).

156. See *Globe and Mail Ltd. v. Boland*, [1960] SCR 203, and *Jones v. Bennett*, [1969] SCR 277.

157. *Camporese v. Parton* (1983), 150 DLR (3d) 208 (BCSC).

158. *Myers v. Canadian Broadcasting Corp.*, supra note 70, citing *Grenier v. Southam Inc.*, [1997] OJ no. 2193 (QL) (CA), *Silva v. Toronto Star Newspapers Ltd.* (1998), 167 DLR (4th) 554 (Ont. Ct. Gen. Div.), and *Moises v. Canadian Newspaper Co.* (1996), 30 CCLT (2d) 145 (BCCA).

159. *Grant v. Torstar Corp.*, supra note 58, at paragraphs 92–95.

160. *Syms v. Warren* (1976), 71 DLR (3d) 558 (Man. QB).

161. *Butler v. Southam Inc.* (2001), 197 NSR (2d) 97 (CA).

162. *Syms v. Warren*, supra note 160.

163. Stephanie Nolen, "Fiddler Was Just Playing with Halifax Newspaper," *Globe and Mail*, January 29, 2000.

164. *Munro v. Toronto Sun Publishing Corp.*, [1982] 39 OR (2d) 100 (HC).

165. Brown, supra note 8, at 188.

166. Ibid., at 192–94.

167. *Leenen v. Canadian Broadcasting Corp.*, supra note 29. For a rundown of the cases illustrating these points, see Brown, supra note 8, at 196–201.

168. George S. Takach, *Computer Law* (Toronto: Irwin Law, 1998), 388.

169. Brown, supra note 8, at 11.

170. *Barrick Gold Corp. v. Lopehandia*, [2004] OJ no. 2329 (CA), at paragraph 32.

171. Michael Geist, *Internet Law in Canada* (Toronto: Captus Press, 2001), 178.

172. *Southam Inc. v. Chelekis*, [1998] BCJ no. 848 (SC).

173. *Grant v. Torstar Corp.*, supra note 58, at paragraphs 96–97.

174. Tobi Cohen, "Steelback President Files Suit Against Ottawa Blogger," *Globe and Mail*, June 11, 2007; "Steelback Brewery President Drops Libel Lawsuit," *Toronto Star*, July 3, 2007; Mathew Ingram, "Media Stardom Is Pricey," *Globe and Mail*, June 16, 2007.

175. *Mosher v. Coast Publishing Ltd.*, 2010 NSSC 153. The chief and deputy chief were successful in identifying the posters, who included four current or former employees of the fire service, and sued for libel. See Clare Mellor, "Fire Chief, Deputy File Defamation Suit over Web Posts," *Chronicle-Herald* (Halifax), June 18, 2010.

176. In 1998 an Ontario judge ordered Yahoo! to identify several individuals accused of using pseudonyms to post defamatory messages about a company. See Geist, supra note 171, at 178–79. See also *Irwin Toy Ltd. v. Joe Doe*, [2000] OJ no. 3318 (QL) (SC),

in which an Internet service provider was ordered to disclose the holder of an e-mail account used to circulate a defamatory message.

177. Simon Avery, "Canadian Model Gets Google To Unmask Nasty Blogger," *Globe and Mail*, August 19, 2009.

178. *Daryl Doucette v. Brunswick News, CanadaEast Interactive and CanadaEast.com*, 2010 NBQB 233.

179. *Warman v. Fournier et al*, 2010 ONSC 2126. See also *York University v. Bell Canada Enterprises*, 2009 CanLII 46447 (Ont. SC).

180. Richard Perez-Pena, "News Sites Rethink Anonymous Online Comments," *New York Times*, April 11, 2010.

181. Dean Jobb, "Web Comments Suit Breaks New Ground," *The Lawyers Weekly*, April 30, 2010, 1, 7.

182. "Coast Must ID Commenters," *Metro Halifax*, April 15, 2010.

183. Tony Wong and Iris Fischer, "Media Must Tread Cautiously with Defamatory Web Postings," *The Lawyers Weekly*, March 21, 2008.

184. These points are discussed in David Crerar and Karen Bradley, "English Decision Makes Important Determinations on Internet Liability," *The Lawyers Weekly*, May 12, 2006, 16.

185. David Crerar and Michael Skene, "Hyperlinks to Defamatory Material: Avoiding Liability," *The Lawyers Weekly*, November 20, 2009; *Crookes v. Newton*, 2009 BCCA 392, at paragraph 60.

186. "Drawing Legal Lines on Internet E-libel," *Edmonton Journal*, April 10, 2010.

187. *Blumenthal v. Drudge*, 992 F. Supp. 44 (1998); 26 Med. LR 1717 (1998). For an overview of this case, see Roger Parloff, "If This Ain't Libel ..." (Fall 2001), *Brill's Content*, 94–113.

188. Patti Tasko, ed., *The Canadian Press Stylebook: A Guide for Writers and Editors*, 15th ed. (Toronto: Canadian Press, 2008), 94.

189. Tracey Tong, "Why the Internet Can Trap Talkers," *Metro Halifax*, October 8, 2009.

190. Garry Marr, "Tweet This: You're Being Sued," *Financial Post*, May 2, 2009.

191. Karen Sloan, "Dismissal in Early Test of Twitter Libel Liability," *National Law Journal*, January 25, 2010. Available online at http://www.law.com/jsp/nlj.

192. Gary Oakes, "Rant Against Lawyer on YouTube Ordered Removed," *The Lawyers Weekly*, September 28, 2007.

193. Cathal Kelly, "Actor Sues Anonymous Wikipedia Writer for Libel," *Toronto Star*, December 9, 2009; Neal Hall, "Metro Vancouver Woman Sues Craigslist for Libel," *Vancouver Sun*, May 31, 2010.

194. *Grant v. Torstar Corp.*, supra note 58, at paragraph 114.

195. *Rindos v. Hardwick*, [1994] ACL Rep. 145 WA 4 (Sup. Ct.). See also *Grant v. Torstar Corp.*, supra note 58, paragraph 28.

196. See, for example, *Egerton v. Finucan*, [1995] OJ no. 1653 (Gen. Div.), in which the defendant was sued for defamation for circulating a negative evaluation of the plaintiff's performance to other professors via a college's internal e-mail system.

197. Betsy Powell, "Defamatory Email Costs Sender $7,800," *Toronto Star*, September 4, 2008.

198. *Ross v. Holley*, [2004] OJ no. 4643; Colin Freeze, "Scientist Awarded Cyberlibel Damages," *Globe and Mail*, November 13, 2004.

199. Jeffrey M. Schelling, *Cyberlaw Canada: The Computer User's Legal Guide* (North Vancouver, BC: Self-Counsel Press, 1998), 20.

200. *Rindos v. Hardwick*, supra note 195.

201. Cristin Schmitz, "Pioneering Internet Libel Case Leads to $125,000 Damages," *The Lawyers Weekly*, June 18, 2004.

202. "Web Comments Prompt Threats of Legal Action," CBC Online, August 2, 2004.

203. *Weiss v. Sawyer*, [2002] OJ no. 3570 (QL) (CA).

204. *Bahlieda v. Santa*, [2003] OJ no. 291 (SC); [2003] OJ no. 1159 (CA). See also David Gambrill, "Issue of Internet as 'Broadcast' Not Settled," *Law Times*, November 3, 2003; Peter A. Downard and Berkley D. Sells, "Ont. C.A. Directs Trial of Issue in Internet Defamation Lawsuit," *The Lawyers Weekly*, October 31, 2003.

205. This is the law in Britain, in keeping with the common law principle that republication of a libel can lead to a separate lawsuit subject to its own limitation periods. The Court of Appeal for England and Wales has ruled that defamatory material was republished when a newspaper posted one of its articles on its website. *Loutchansky v. Times Newspapers Ltd.*, [2001] EWJ no. 5622, [2002] QB 783, [2002] WLR 640, [2002] 1 All ER 652.

206. Ryder Gilliland and Bryn Gray, "Courts Must Reject Infinite Liability for Online Publishers," *The Lawyers Weekly*, April 24, 2009, 5, 28.

207. *Carter v. B.C. Federation of Foster Parents Assn.*, 2005 BCCA 398, at paragraph 20.

208. Paul Kedrosky, "Harrods Lawsuit No Laughing Matter for Publishers Worldwide," *National Post*, February 17, 2004.

209. *Braintech, Inc. v. Kostiuk*, 1999 BCCA 169, at paragraphs 63 and 65. Leave to appeal denied, 1999 SCCA 236.

210. *Kitakufe v. Oloya*, [1998] OJ no. 2537 (Gen. Div.).

211. *Bangoura v. Washington Post* (2004), 235 DLR (4th) 564 (Ont. SCJ).

212. *Bangoura v. The Washington Post*, [2005] OJ no. 3849 (CA); Tracey Tyler, "Libel Case Chills World's Media," *Toronto Star*, March 8, 2005.

213. "Reichmann Wins $400,000 Libel Suit," *Chronicle-Herald* (Halifax), July 12, 2002.

214. *Jenner v. Sun Oil Co. Ltd.* (1952), 16 CPR 87 (Ont. HCJ); *Pindling v. National Broadcasting Corp.* (1984), 49 OR (2d) 58 (HCJ).

215. Raymond E. Brown, *The Law of Defamation in Canada*, 2nd ed., vol. 3 (Scarborough, ON: Carswell, 1999), 25–116 to 25–117.

216. *Crookes v. Yahoo*, 2008 BCCA 165.

217. Daniel Burnett, "Internet Defamation," May 1997 paper available online at http://www.adidem.org/Internet_Defamation.

218. *Kitakufe v. Oloya*, supra note 210, at paragraph 14.

219. *Vaquero Energy v. Weir*, 2004 ABQB 68, at paragraph 17.

220. Ian Bailey, "Injunction over Web Libel Sets Precedent," *Globe and Mail*, July 19, 2008.

221. The origins of criminal libel are discussed in Law Reform Commission of Canada, *Defamatory Libel*, Working Paper 35 (Ottawa: Minister of Supply and Services, 1984), 3–5.

222. *Criminal Code*, RSC 1985, c. C-46, as amended, ss. 298–317.

223. The Canadian Centre for Justice Statistics recorded 36 prosecutions, leading to 24 convictions, for criminal libel between 1963 and 1973. Between 1969 and 1984, only four prosecutions led to rulings published in Canadian law reports. *Defamatory Libel*, supra note 221, at 47–49.

224. *Criminal Code*, ss. 59(1), 60, and 61.

225. *Boucher v. R*, [1951] SCR 265.

226. *Criminal Code*, s. 296.

227. These cases are cited in Crawford, supra note 40, at 65–66.

228. Martin, supra note 4, at 73.

229. *Defamatory Libel*, supra note 221, at 54, 59–62.

230. *R v. Lucas*, [1998] 1 SCR 439.

231. *R v. Byron Prior*, 2008 NLTD 80, at paragraph 42. The other rulings are *R v. Finnegan*, [1992] AJ no. 1208 (QB); *R v. Lucas*, [1995] SJ no. 62 (QB); and *R v. Gill*, [1996] OJ no. 1299 (Gen. Div.).

232. "Defamatory Libel Charge Dropped Against Man in His Underwear Protesting at Police Station," *Peterborough Examiner*, October 14, 2009.

233. *Criminal Code*, s. 309.

234. *R v. Georgia Straight Publishing Ltd.* (1969), 4 DLR (3d) 383 (BC Co. Ct.).

235. *R v. Lucas*, supra note 230.

236. For discussions of libel chill, see Kimberley Noble, *Bound and Gagged: Libel Chill and the Right To Publish* (Toronto: HarperCollins, 1992), and Mary Annecchiarico, "Libel Law: The Chilling Effect" (Spring 1989), *Ryerson Review of Journalism* 6–9.

237. Luis Millan, "'Strategic Lawsuit Against Public Participation' Ruling First in Canada," *The Lawyers Weekly*, May 21, 2010, 1, 3; *Constructions Infrabec inc. c. Drapeau*, 2010 QCCS 1734; Jeff Gray, "Ontario Looks To Smack Down SLAPPs," *Globe and Mail*, July 6, 2010.

238. Ronald Irving, comp., *"The Law Is a Ass": An Illustrated Collection of Legal Quotations* (London: Gerald Duckworth & Co., 1999), 165.

239. *Vogel v. Canadian Broadcasting Corp.*, supra note 71.

240. See, for example, *Leenen v. Canadian Broadcasting Corp.*, supra note 29, and *Myers v. Canadian Broadcasting Corp.*, supra note 70.

241. For example, *Munro v. Toronto Sun Publishing Corp.*, supra note 164.

242. *Hodgson v. Canadian Newspapers Co. Ltd.*, supra note 67.

243. Jessica Mitford, *Poison Penmanship: The Gentle Art of Muckraking* (New York: Alfred A. Knopf, 1979), 24.

244. Martin, supra note 4, at 176.

245. *Munro v. Toronto Sun Publishing Corp.*, supra note 164.

246. Leenen v. Canadian Broadcasting Corp., supra note 29.

CHAPTER 5

Restrictions on Reporting and Publishing the News

Protecting Sources

The document landed on *National Post* reporter Andrew McIntosh's desk in April 2001 tucked inside that old journalism cliché, the anonymous brown envelope. Inside was a Business Development Bank of Canada loan authorization that suggested then-Prime Minister Jean Chrétien stood to benefit from $615,000 loaned to the Grand-Mère Inn in Shawinigan, Quebec. According to the document, the inn owed $23,000 to a Chrétien family holding company. As Justice Mary Lou Benotto of the Ontario Superior Court later noted, the information was political dynamite and, "if true, may have placed the prime minister in a conflict of interest."

McIntosh was the reporter responsible for breaking the so-called Shawinigate scandal—a series of stories raising questions about government loans and grants to businesses in Chrétien's home riding. When he contacted bank officials for comment, they claimed the document was a forgery and called in the RCMP. At the Mounties' request, an Ontario judge issued a search warrant to seize the document and envelope, so they could be analyzed for fingerprints and traces of DNA that might identify the leaker. Although the document had arrived anonymously, McIntosh soon learned it had come from a source he had earlier promised to protect. The *Post* handed over the document to the RCMP in a sealed envelope and, backed by the *Globe and Mail* and the CBC, challenged the legality of the seizure. Lawyers for the media organizations attacked the search warrant as a violation of the Charter guarantee of freedom of the press. Forcing journalists to expose confidential sources, they argued, deters people from coming forward with information and hinders the media's ability to inform the public. Stories on issues of intense public importance—political corruption, the sale of tainted food, the dumping of hazardous waste, to name a few—could go unexposed and unreported.

The challenge answered an important question: Do Canadian journalists have a legal right to protect confidential sources and, if so, which sources? The so-called shield laws that protect journalists' sources in many American states do not exist in

Canada,[1] and a private member's bill introduced in Parliament in 2007 to create one in criminal cases did not become law.[2] At least three Canadian journalists have been jailed for refusing to identify a source. In 1914, Nova Scotia's legislature jailed William McCurdy, news editor of the *Halifax Herald*, for 48 hours for refusing to identify the author of a letter to the editor that accused politicians of corruption. In 1969, amid FLQ bombings in Quebec that culminated in the October Crisis, Montreal's fire commissioner jailed a CBC Television reporter for seven days for refusing to name a man who claimed to be a bomber. In the third case, a camera operator with a television station in Hull, Quebec, spent 72 hours in jail in 1995 but later lost his job after acknowledging he had never promised to protect the source's identity.[3]

Courts, public inquiries, and legislatures have the power to hold a journalist in contempt for refusing to provide evidence, including the names of sources. Generally, however, judges have been hesitant to go after a journalist's sources. The Ontario judge presiding at a 1987 inquiry into allegations of conflict of interest against a federal Cabinet minister refused a motion to order two *Globe and Mail* reporters to reveal their sources. Likewise, the judge advocate presiding at a submarine commander's court martial in 1995 refused to force a Halifax reporter to name four unidentified sources cited in news stories who criticized the commander's conduct. The judge advocate ruled the names were irrelevant because military police had interviewed every submariner who had served under the commander—including, presumably, the unidentified sources.[4]

In cases where a source did not demand anonymity or later agreed to be identified, journalists have named names when called to the witness stand. Two reporters for the *Whig-Standard* in Kingston, Ontario have found themselves in this position. One acknowledged the source of a tip that sabotaged a municipal candidate's election campaign.[5] The other reporter lost a legal battle to avoid testifying in 2001 at a pre-trial hearing in a murder case. The reporter had promised anonymity to two men he interviewed about the homicide, but both sources waived their right to confidentiality.[6]

And when a news story based on unnamed sources leads to a libel suit, plaintiffs have the right to demand that journalists identify their informers so they can be summoned to court to testify. Courts in Ontario and some other provinces have adopted what is known as "the newspaper rule," which allows journalists to withhold the names of confidential sources during the pre-trial phase of a defamation case. The sources must be identified, however, if the case goes to trial.[7] This is not the case in British Columbia. When a doctor sued the *Vancouver Sun* in 2002 over articles questioning his competence, a judge ordered a reporter to name the source—an anonymous nurse who had made some of the allegations. In deference to the reporter's promise to keep the name confidential, the judge ordered that her identity be divulged only to the doctor and his lawyer.[8]

A Limited Privilege for Journalists

The *Post* won the first round in its bid to protect McIntosh's source. Justice Benotto quashed the warrant in January 2004 and recognized, for the first time in Canada, that journalists have a legal right—entrenched in the Charter's guarantee of freedom of the press—to protect the identities of their sources in certain cases. "Sources may 'dry-up' if their identities were revealed," Benotto wrote, accepting the media's position on the risks of exposing sources. She described confidential sources as "essential to the effective functioning of the media in a free and democratic society," and noted that people may have valid reasons for seeking anonymity. "They may, themselves, be breaching a duty of confidentiality. They may have stolen the information. They may fear economic reprisals. They may lose their jobs. They may fear for their safety. They may fear for the safety of their families." Benotto rejected the federal government's assertion that sources should not be encouraged to approach reporters with evidence of wrongdoing. "If employee confidentiality were to trump conscience," she argued, "there would be a licence for corporations, governments and other employers to operate without accountability."

Benotto, however, rejected a blanket protection for sources. Although the law treats most information that passes between lawyers and their clients as confidential, journalists and their sources—like doctors and patients—must establish, case by case, that their relationship should be protected from prying eyes. McIntosh's case, Benotto said, was "unique" and his story was so important—dealing, as it did, with the conduct of the country's top elected official—that the right to protect his source must prevail. Applying a legal analysis known as the **Wigmore test**, she concluded that McIntosh's relationship with his source was worthy of protection. It fit all four Wigmore criteria. One, McIntosh had promised to protect the identity of his source. Two, that promise was crucial to their relationship and the source's agreement to provide information. Three, it was in the public interest to foster this kind of confidential relationship. And finally, protecting the confidential relationship was more important than the potential benefits of forcing the journalist to identify his source. Benotto had no doubt that exposing McIntosh's informant would harm an important societal interest while doing little to advance what she felt amounted to a fishing expedition by police:

> It is through confidential sources that matters of great public importance are made known. As corporate and public power increase, the ability of the average citizen to affect his or her world depends upon the information disseminated by the press. To deprive the media of an important tool in the gathering of news would affect society as a whole.[9]

Because the judge who signed the warrant to search the *Post*'s offices had failed to consider these important issues, Benotto ruled, the seizure was invalid and both the document and McIntosh's source must be protected.

The Ontario Court of Appeal reversed Benotto's ruling in 2008, however, and ordered McIntosh and the *Post* to hand over the document and envelope.[10] The court said protecting the source would deprive the RCMP of evidence of what could be "an especially grave and heinous crime"—a criminal conspiracy designed to create controversy and possibly drive a prime minister from office. The right to protect a source, the court ruled, "loses much of its force" when used "to protect the identity of a potential criminal or to conceal possible evidence of a crime."

The *Post* appealed but in May 2010 the Supreme Court of Canada also refused to give journalists a blanket right to protect sources.[11] The constitutional protection of press freedom puts the media in a "special position," the court acknowledged, and judges should strive to "protect the media's secret sources where such protection is in the public interest." The court also accepted that confidential sources play a crucial role in news coverage, especially investigative journalism. "Unless the media can offer anonymity in situations where sources would otherwise dry up, freedom of expression in debate on matters of public interest would be badly compromised. Important stories will be left untold," Justice Ian Binnie noted in the majority ruling. Investigative journalism, he added, plays a vital role in addressing the "democratic deficit in the transparency and accountability of our public institutions," shining "the light of public scrutiny on the dark corners" of public and private institutions.

This is the good news. Attempts to shield sources, however, must be considered on a case-by-case basis. Journalists, the court ruled, must demonstrate that protecting a source is more important than uncovering information vital to a police investigation or the outcome of a legal dispute. When the claim is tied to a source accused of a crime or with information that could help solve a crime, it will be harder—but not impossible—to shield the source. "The bottom line," Binnie stated, "is that no journalist can give a source a total assurance of confidentiality. All such arrangements necessarily carry an element of risk that the source's identity will eventually be revealed." The ruling cited serious problems that could result if journalists had been given a blanket right to protect sources. The court was concerned that the definition of journalist is expanding in the Internet age, allowing people to exercise their right to freedom of expression "by blogging, tweeting ... or publishing in a national newspaper." Granting a right to protect sources to "such a heterogeneous and ill-defined group of writers and speakers and whichever 'sources' they deem worthy of a promise of confidentiality and on whatever terms they may choose to offer it ... would blow a giant hole in law enforcement and other constitutionally recognized values such as privacy." In addition, the court pointed out that journalists and media organizations disagree on when sources should be protected and whether the duty to protect evaporates if the source lies or misleads a journalist. "There is no formal accreditation process to 'licence' the practice of journalism, and no professional organization (such as a law society) to regulate its members and attempt to maintain professional standards," Binnie said, making a system of blanket source protection impossible.

In an October 2010 ruling on another source-protection case, the Supreme Court warned judges that journalists should be forced to expose sources only as "a last resort."[12] In this case, a Quebec judge hearing a civil dispute ruled that *Globe and Mail* reporter Daniel Leblanc could be questioned about a key source—known as MaChouette, a pet name that translates as "my owl"—he used to investigate the federal sponsorship program. The Gomery inquiry credited Leblanc's diligent reporting for exposing some of the worst abuses of the program, which saw tens of millions of dollars directed to politically connected Quebec advertising firms, in some cases based on inflated invoices or for work not completed. The federal government sued one of these companies, Groupe Polygone Éditeurs inc., to recover $35 million, and the company's lawyers hoped to identify the *Globe*'s source. A Quebec judge authorized the firm's lawyers to ask 22 federal employees if they passed information to Leblanc, and to question the reporter as well, depending on the outcome at the Supreme Court.

Figure 5.1 *Globe and Mail* reporter Daniel Leblanc, who reported extensively on the federal sponsorship scandal, refused to name a key confidential source. This poster reads, "I support the silence of journalist Daniel Leblanc."
SOURCE: Félix Genest/GNU-FDL

The Supreme Court used the case to set strict guidelines on when judges should order a journalist to "out" a source. First, the source's identity must deal with a central issue at stake in a court action or investigation. Another factor is whether the journalist is a witness or one of the parties directly involved in the litigation; if the journalist has a personal stake in the outcome, a source's identity is more likely to be a central issue. A "crucial" factor, the court added, is whether the information sought could be discovered without compromising the identity of a source. Other witnesses and sources of information "ought to be exhausted" and revealing a journalist's source should be "a last resort." Finally, judges must consider "the high societal interest in investigative journalism" and should demand a source's identity only when the information is "vital to the integrity of the administration of justice."

This approach is consistent with the earlier *National Post* ruling; in that case, the leaked document that could identify Andrew McIntosh's source was central to a criminal investigation and there was no other way for police to identify a suspected forger. As for Leblanc, the effort to expose his source was unresolved at the time of writing. The Supreme Court ordered a rehearing, saying the Quebec courts should decide how far Groupe Polygone's lawyers could go in questioning the reporter. The *Globe*'s lawyers were confident the Supreme Court's guidelines would make it difficult—if not impossible—to expose MaChouette's identity.[13]

The case-by-case approach to claims of privilege means journalists cannot offer an iron-clad guarantee to protect a source. To underline this point, in 2008 the Federal Court of Canada ordered two *La Presse* journalists to answer questions about the source of a secret intelligence report about a suspected terrorist, which had been leaked to the newspaper. The judge ruled the suspect's ability to fight a deportation order and defend himself against the allegations outweighed the journalists' claim their source should be protected.[14] And in 2004 an Ontario judge found *Hamilton Spectator* reporter Ken Peters in contempt for refusing to identify a source and ordered the paper to pay $31,600 in legal costs. Peters was a key witness in a multi-million-dollar lawsuit in which a nursing home claimed it had been defamed by the City of Hamilton. Subpoenaed to testify at the trial, he refused to reveal who had leaked documents to him, nine years earlier, that alleged the mistreatment of residents and staff at the home. In the words of the trial judge, Justice David Crane, the reporter's refusal to answer created a "crisis" that brought the case to a standstill and threatened to deprive the plaintiff of crucial evidence. Peters, he ruled, must reveal his source or face the consequences. "Society is about limits and citizenship is about subjecting ourselves to the law," the judge noted. "A direct challenge to the authority of the law in the face of the court when found, must be met and defended against on behalf of the administration of justice."[15]

The *Spectator* appealed and in 2008 the Ontario Court of Appeal overturned the finding of contempt as well as the assessment of legal costs.[16] The court faulted Crane for moving too swiftly and imposing an "excessive" penalty, and warned other judges that citing a journalist for contempt should be a last resort. Peters's source came forward on his own, the court noted, and journalists trying to protect a source should be treated with respect, not as if their goal is to defy the court or subvert justice. That ruling was not appealed but the Supreme Court of Canada, in its *National Post* ruling, also cautioned judges to be hesitant to cite journalists for contempt if they refuse to identify a source. "The courts," it noted in that ruling, "have long accepted the desirability of avoiding where possible putting a journalist in the position of breaking a promise of confidentiality or being held in contempt of court."[17]

Negotiating Confidentiality Agreements

Professional ethics demand that journalists keep their promises; they have a duty to honour any promise to protect a source unless the source agrees to be identified. The clear message in the *National Post* and *Globe and Mail* rulings is that journalists should avoid making promises that could land them in legal hot water—and leave them facing a fine or jail time. In the words of veteran Vancouver media lawyer David Sutherland: "Don't make unqualified promises and, if you do, bring your toothbrush."[18]

When someone demands anonymity, a journalist should first determine what assurances the source is seeking in exchange for revealing information. Does the person want the information attributed to "an unnamed source," or is the person seeking a promise that his identity will never be revealed? Journalists should carefully negotiate the terms of any agreement to protect a source's identity. It should be made clear that the journalist is obliged to disclose the source's identity to an editor or producer—as noted in Chapter 4, under defamation law, newsroom managers have a duty to verify all information that a reporter gathers before it is published or broadcast.

Sources who demand confidentiality should understand that the law does not offer absolute protection. In the *Hamilton Spectator* case, Justice Crane advised journalists to stop giving unconditional promises of confidentiality. In his view, journalists should agree to protect a source's identity "to the full extent of the law" or promise to "exert all lawful means to protect the confidence."[19] Journalists, in other words, should level with their sources and tell them that it is impossible to give a guarantee of complete confidentiality. It may even be prudent to negotiate some form of exit strategy—to seek assurance from the source that he or she will come forward in the unlikely event the journalist is facing a fine or jail term for refusing to testify. A journalist who is too quick to promise confidentiality runs the risk of facing a gut-wrenching legal and ethical dilemma down the road. "If it seems harsh that courts would order someone to give up the identity of a confidential source," media lawyer Peter Jacobsen has noted, "perhaps the message to journalists is 'don't promise what you can't deliver.' "[20]

The Journalist as Witness

Journalists who witness an accident or crime or have information about the events at the heart of a criminal case or lawsuit are in the same position as any other citizen—they can be compelled to testify. Reporters and photographers must obey a subpoena to appear in court and can be ordered to bring any documents, notes, or other materials in their possession that might be relevant to a case. Nova Scotia's Court of Appeal, for example, ordered four CBC journalists to testify in 1997 about their interviews with women who accused a former Nova Scotia politician of molesting them (*CBC et al. v. The Hon. Judge Batiot and Regan*, February 13, 1997, court file CA no. 131906 (NSCA)). But the courts are wary of allowing lawyers to go on a fishing expedition. When journalists are subpoenaed to testify, the overriding question is whether the information they have collected while doing their jobs is relevant to the case before the court.

The grounds for forcing a journalist to testify were outlined in a 1998 ruling in a BC case. Judges must assess whether the journalist's evidence is relevant to the case. They must consider whether there are other means to obtain the evidence. And finally, they must balance the pros and cons of forcing a journalist to testify and whether the need for the evidence outweighs any negative impact on the media's ability to gather and report the news (*R v. Hughes*, [1998] BCJ no. 1694 (QL) (SC)).

These principles were put to the test in 2004 when Holocaust denier Ernst Zundel was fighting deportation from Canada and sought to force investigative journalist and author Andrew Mitrovica to testify. Mitrovica's book *Covert Entry*, which examines the operations of the Canadian Security Intelligence Service, alleged that CSIS may have been aware of a plot to send a letter bomb to Zundel but took no action to warn him. A judge of the Federal Court agreed with Mitrovica's position that his evidence would amount to nothing more than hearsay. Mitrovica "has no direct evidence of CSIS activities, only what has been reported to him," the judge noted, and could contribute little or nothing to the case "beyond what is already part of the public domain through his book." Forcing Mitrovica to produce notes and other documents would be "unduly intrusive," the judge added, and in any event he was likely to invoke journalistic privilege to protect his sources. The subpoena was quashed (*Re Zundel*, 2004 FC 798).

Finally, journalists should make sure they—and their sources—understand the exact terms of their agreement. "If you are willing to go to jail to protect a source, say so," the Canadian Association of Journalists (CAJ) advises in its *Statement of Principles and Ethics Guidelines* for investigative journalism. "Otherwise, spell out the conditions." Whatever promise is made, journalists must ensure they can follow through and their employer is willing, if necessary, to absorb the legal costs of defending a promise of confidentiality. Journalists also should heed the lessons of the Maher Arar case, where unnamed government sources used the media to smear Arar—a Canadian detained and tortured in Syria—as a terrorist. The CAJ believes sources should be on notice that, if they lie or knowingly provide false information, all deals are off and the journalist is free to expose them.[21] The *Professional Code of Ethics for Quebec Journalists* also requires journalists to honour a promise of anonymity "unless they have been intentionally deceived by their sources."[22]

Invasion of Privacy

Privacy Law in Canada

A person who takes any actions that invade the personal privacy or personal life of another person can be sued for invasion of privacy. Publishing a compromising photo of the person or disclosing extracts from the person's diary are examples of acts that would clearly invade privacy. There have been few precedents to establish the scope of this tort under Canadian common law, and fewer cases still that involve the actions of the media.[23] In 2009, after reviewing a number of cases in which a violation of privacy had been claimed under the common law, a Nova Scotia judge concluded such claims were likely to succeed only if there is evidence of "harassing behavior or an intentional invasion of privacy."[24] The *Globe and Mail* and its reporter Jan Wong were sued for invasion of privacy in 2008, over Wong's descriptions of a messy home she had cleaned while posing as a maid for a series of articles on the working poor. The homeowners were not named but claimed the information published had identified them and they had suffered embarrassment and mental distress. The action also claimed damages because Wong had gained entrance to the home under false pretenses. A judge turned down the *Globe*'s motion to strike out the claim, ruling that a trial was needed to balance privacy interests against the rights of journalists to gather news. The suit was settled out of court, however, and the newspaper published an apology for any harm the article had caused.[25] While the legal issues were not resolved, the case offers some guidance to journalists who go undercover for a story: they should tell as few lies as possible and avoid detailed descriptions of people and places that could identify innocent parties.

In four provinces—British Columbia, Saskatchewan, Manitoba, and Newfoundland and Labrador—privacy legislation defines the kinds of acts that can be considered invasion of privacy. This legislation delineates the tort of invasion of privacy in these jurisdictions and protects citizens from a range of intrusive acts: illegal wiretaps on phones, eavesdropping on private conversations, being stalked or followed, unauthorized use of diaries or other personal papers, and using someone's name or likeness to advertise products without the person's consent.[26] Although privacy legislation appears aimed primarily at stalkers and overzealous private investigators, a journalist could stray into this territory. A reporter might overhear a private conversation by chance or a source might offer access to someone's private letters; publishing or broadcasting such information would likely be an invasion of privacy.

At the same time, the legislation provides protection for legitimate forms of newsgathering, and restrictions on publication do not apply where there is a public interest in the information or the material is considered privileged under defamation law.[27] Although it would be up to a judge or jury to decide whether information is a matter of public interest, these provisions provide a solid defence for most media news coverage. Saskatchewan's law goes a step further and specifically exempts the newsgathering activities of journalists.[28] The New Brunswick government introduced a stringent privacy bill in 2000 that could have made it possible to sue the media for covering events that occurred in a public place or if "undue publicity" were given to a private matter. The government later backed down in the face of media protests and scrapped the proposals.[29]

Quebec's *Civil Code* provides a general right to sue for injuries, including injuries caused by an invasion of privacy.[30] The province's *Charter of Human Rights and Freedoms* also guarantees every resident the right to "respect" for their "private life," protection from the release of confidential information, and the right to safeguard their "dignity, honour and reputation."[31]

As noted above, such provisions have seldom been put to the test. But in British Columbia and Quebec, several cases have provided insight into the scope of privacy legislation.

- In 1985 a judge ruled that a television news crew did not invade the privacy of a businessman while covering a labour dispute. The crew members were working in the parking lot of a building being picketed when a scuffle broke out with the man, who was trying to stop them from filming. The judge said the station had been entitled to air footage of the scuffle—the parking lot, while private property, was clearly visible to passersby and the labour dispute was a matter of public interest.[32]
- A BC man sought an injunction to prevent the CBC from airing an ambush interview in which a reporter had asked him about his past conviction for a drug offence. The judge found that the man's criminal record and the fact he had received a pardon were matters of public record and did not invade his privacy.[33]
- In 1996, a television station was sued for broadcasting video of a bald man undergoing a procedure to restore his hair. The company that offered the service (and provided the video) was found liable for invasion of privacy but a court dismissed the man's claim against the station, which had sought assurances that the footage could be used before putting it on the air.[34]
- A woman who witnessed a murder sued Vancouver's daily newspapers and the CBC for identifying her in news reports. The woman agreed to be interviewed and photographed but later regretted the decision, fearing she would be a target of the assailants who were still at large. The case was settled out of court

before trial, so it is unclear how a judge would have interpreted the media's actions. One media law expert has suggested that the woman's initial consent to be interviewed and the public interest exemptions under British Columbia's *Privacy Act* offered the media a strong defence.[35]

- In a Quebec case, a doctor who wrote to complain about a television program won $3,000 in damages after the show's host broadcast his name and address and invited his audience to contact the doctor to "cheer him up." The doctor was deluged with letters and calls—some of them offensive and harassing—and was forced to disconnect his phone.[36]

- In 1991 a teacher successfully sued the *Montreal Gazette* for $37,500 in damages for identifying him as being afflicted with AIDS. Although the report did not name the teacher, a court ruled that enough detail was provided to identify the man and violate his right to keep his illness and sexual orientation private. The court viewed the report as exploitive and found the newspaper liable for the damage caused by other media outlets that picked up the story.[37]

- Lawyers for Karla Homolka, who served 12 years for manslaughter in the deaths of two teenage girls, sought a sweeping injunction to prevent the media from reporting on her movements and private life after her release from prison in July 2005. Her lawyers cited an avalanche of media coverage of her release and death threats circulating on the Internet, but a Quebec judge refused to impose any restrictions. Homolka must face the public and media after her release, the judge said, and "the public has the right to know the nature of the crimes committed." The judge added, however, that the courts could revisit the issue "if the media becomes too insistent or behaves badly."[38] As it turned out, upon her release Homolka went directly to the Montreal studios of Radio-Canada to tape an exclusive television interview that was broadcast from coast to coast.[39]

- In 2009 a Quebec man was ordered to pay $17,500 in damages after he posted a provocative photograph and profile of his ex-girlfriend, a television personality, on a dating website.[40]

In an era when the Internet displays words and images to a global audience, when ever-smaller electronic gadgets enable anyone to make a secret audio or video recording with ease, calls to protect personal privacy are certain to increase. The federal government responded in 2000 with a new law to control the use of personal information in the hands of private businesses.[41] Greater awareness will likely result in more efforts to restrict media coverage using privacy legislation and the common law. Even so, journalists will likely face few legal barriers when they disclose information about individuals as they explore stories and issues that are of public importance. The line appears to be drawn if a journalist uses illegal or covert methods to collect personal information, subjects a person to unwarranted harassment, or discloses information about an individual when there is no wider public interest in the person's private life. The CBC's reporting handbook advises that intrusions into the private lives of individuals are warranted only when the person's private life spills over into his or her public life or when private matters become relevant to the discussion of a public issue.[42]

Taking and Using Photos and Video

When photographing or filming people in public places, it is standard practice to seek the person's consent before the image is published or broadcast. A newspaper photographer looking for a picture of a sunbather, for example, should approach the person, identify herself as a member of the media, and ask permission to take and publish the photo. It is not always possible to obtain permission, such as when photographing a crowd or filming a busy street. Photographs of crowds are often taken from a distance, so individuals are not readily identifiable. But, singling out one person in a crowd—particularly if the story deals with a controversial event or issue—could be seen as unfair or lead to a complaint or legal action.

The Ontario Press Council, which adjudicates public complaints against Ontario newspapers, upheld a complaint against the *Toronto Sun* for running a photograph of a woman entering her apartment building, where a murder suspect also lived. The council criticized the publication of the photo as "a thoughtless act" that caused the woman to fear for her safety, even though she was not identified by name.[43] In another privacy-related case, a Quebec television station was ordered to pay $5,000 in damages in 1987 for repeatedly airing file footage showing a Sherbrooke man being led into court with several offenders accused of murder. The man was not prosecuted but when the footage was reused no captions or other explanations were used to make it clear he was not involved in the murder case.[44]

In another Quebec case, a woman was awarded $2,000 in damages under Quebec's privacy legislation after an arts magazine published a photo of her sitting on a doorstep on a sunny day. The magazine did not seek her permission, and the Quebec courts ruled that publishing the photo subjected her to humiliation and teasing from relatives and friends. The Supreme Court of Canada upheld the damage award and, in the process, discussed when images captured in a public place can be published or broadcast without consent. It ruled that artists, politicians, and other people whose professional lives depend on publicity must expect that some aspects of their personal lives will be in the public eye. So must people who were previously unknown but find themselves playing a central role in a matter of public interest, such as a trial, an environmental disaster, or a political scandal. Other people may unwittingly place themselves in the limelight by being in the crowd at a sporting event or a demonstration when a news photo is taken, or they may be part of the scenery in a photograph taken in a public place. In such cases, photographers and those who publish their photos do not invade the person's privacy. The line is crossed—and consent is required to publish or broadcast an image—when "the public nature of the place where the photograph was taken is irrelevant," the court said, and "the place was simply used as background for one or more persons who constitute the true subject of the photograph."[45]

When a person consents to be photographed or filmed, it is also prudent to ensure the subject understands how the image will be used. A Quebec model won $35,500 in damages from a publisher and a photographer in 2004 after her photograph appeared on a magazine cover with one of her breasts exposed. The model had been assured the image would be altered before publication and her breasts would not be revealed.[46] Many media outlets have developed a consent form for subjects to sign, to prevent such misunderstandings. The consent of a parent or legal guardian is required to take and use images of children and young people under the age of majority. Journalists may find that schools with experience dealing with media requests for images have obtained parental permission in advance, making it easier to gather the photos and footage needed to accompany a story on education or youth issues. The legal and ethical concerns that arise when interviewing, photographing, and filming young people are dealt with in greater detail in Chapter 12.

Criminal Voyeurism

Section 162 of the *Criminal Code*, introduced in 2005, makes it an offence to surreptitiously watch, photograph, or make a video recording of someone—including a public figure or celebrity—at a time or in a place where the person is entitled to believe their privacy will be respected. The law targets peeping Toms and those trying to secretly capture pornographic images of adults or children. In what is believed to be the first prosecution under the section, a Nova Scotia man pleaded guilty in 2006 to standing on a ladder outside a home to videotape a young girl as she showered.[47] But the law is also designed to curb the excesses of the paparazzi and tabloid journalism. A news photographer who uses a telephoto lens to take pictures of a woman sunbathing topless at a backyard pool, for instance, could face up to five years in prison. Under section 162(4) it is also an offence—punishable by up to five years behind bars—for an editor or media outlet to possess, sell, publish, or distribute such images if they know they were illegally obtained.

The law makes it an offence to watch, photograph, or film someone for a sexual purpose and defines two situations in which people are entitled to believe their privacy will be respected: when people are observed, photographed, or filmed in a bathroom, bedroom, hotel room, or other place where they could be expected to be nude, partially nude, or engaged in sexual activity; and when people are intentionally watched, photographed, or filmed for the purpose of catching them nude, partially nude, or engaged in sexual activity. Although the law absolves photography and videotaping that "serves the public good,"[48] media law experts have suggested the defence is unlikely to protect tabloid-style journalism or other sensationalized media reports. But a celebrity, indeed anyone, remains fair game when in a public place—for example, when walking along the street or while entering or leaving a building.[49]

Recording and Using Phone and Private Conversations

Canadian journalists can make an audio recording of interviews they conduct over the phone without the knowledge or consent of the person on the other end of the line. Although secretly recording a phone conversation is illegal in some American jurisdictions, in Canada it is legal to record a private conversation as long as one of the people taking part in the conversation consents to the recording.[50] In this case, the consenting party is the journalist who has decided to record the conversation. A journalist is under no obligation to inform a source that an interview is being recorded. But if the source asks whether a recording is being made, the best response is to say yes and explain that doing so ensures that the resulting article is as accurate as possible. Most sources appreciate knowing that a journalist is making every effort to get the facts right. It would be unethical for the journalist to lie and deny an interview is being recorded. And it is a criminal offence for a media outlet to publish or broadcast a phone conversation that was illegally recorded by another person.[51]

There is no restriction on how print journalists use recorded telephone interviews—they can be transcribed and reported as they would be if the journalist took handwritten notes of what was said. But radio and television reporters face an additional restriction. Canadian Radio-television and Telecommunications Commission (CRTC) regulations forbid media outlets from broadcasting an interview or conversation conducted on the phone without the consent of the person who was on the other end of the line. The same would hold true for an audio interview posted to the Internet. An exception is made if the person phoned the station to participate in a program.[52] When an Ottawa radio station was convicted of this offence in 1978, the Supreme Court of Canada rejected the argument that this was a restriction on freedom of expression—broadcasters are barred from airing an interview without consent. But the court added that hosts and reporters are free to repeat what a person interviewed has said.[53]

It is also illegal to secretly record any "oral conversation" that takes place in a situation where it is reasonable to expect that no one else will hear.[54] Again, the consent of at least one of the people involved in the conversation is required. Media law expert Michael Crawford uses the example of a conversation picked up by a tape recorder secretly left running in a room where a private meeting was taking place. In his view, it would be an offence to disseminate what was said, because no one involved consented to the tape being made.[55] A BC judge has stated that the *Criminal Code* does not prevent the clandestine videotaping of persons speaking as long as no sound is recorded.[56]

Recorded conversations that journalists discover by chance or through the recklessness of the person who made the recording, however, appear to be fair game. Journalists who were able to eavesdrop on a political party election strategy session in 2007 published what they heard without repercussions. The reporters, who were meeting in an adjoining conference room, discovered that a speaker was piping in what was being said next door.[57] In another case, a Nova Scotia judge ruled in 2009 that the media were entitled to publish conversations between a federal minister and an aide, which had been inadvertently captured on the aide's digital recorder. The aide misplaced the recorder and it wound up in the hands of a reporter for the Halifax *Chronicle-Herald*, who tried without success to return the device before reviewing the audio files it contained. The conversations were not private—they had occurred during a long car ride and the driver overheard at least some of what was said—and dealt with an important public issue, a shortage of the isotopes needed to make medical diagnoses. "It is wrong to deprive the press, and the public it serves, of remarks made privately, but not confidentially," the judge concluded, "after those remarks became available because of poor record keeping or management."[58]

In another case decided in 2009, an aide to a Quebec labour union was unable to prevent the broadcast of a conversation recorded without his knowledge. The person who made the recording had supplied it to a journalist. The conversation disclosed nothing about the aide's private life and a judge concluded the media did not obtain the recording by illegal means. Significantly, the judge applied the *Dagenais/Mentuck* test and concluded the public interest in disclosing the conversation outweighed any privacy rights at stake, making this a useful precedent when disputes arise over the media's use of recorded conversations.[59]

This is a complex area of the law, one in which ethical considerations also come into play. The CBC's policy manual states that a broadcaster "operates openly where it can see and be seen," and, as a rule, hidden cameras and microphones are not to be used to gather information. Exceptions are made for stories that should be told in the public interest, such as exposés of illegal activity, fraud, or abuse of the public trust. A senior CBC newsroom official must authorize any use of a hidden camera or microphone.[60] Any journalist who intends to make secret recordings or to use recordings obtained by chance or through a source should consult an editor or producer or seek the advice of the news organization's legal advisers before proceeding.

Intercepted Cellular Calls

It is a criminal offence to use or disclose the contents of an intercepted conversation on a cell phone, unless the information is revealed in a courtroom. The *Criminal Code* protects the privacy of cellular calls—the Code refers to them as "radio-based telephone communications"—which can be picked up on a police-radio scanner. It is even an offence to disclose the existence of a cell phone conversation unless one of the parties to the conversation agrees to the disclosure. A journalist convicted of the offence would face up to two years in jail and could be ordered to pay up to $5,000 in damages to the victim of this invasion of privacy.[61] A federal law, the *Radiocommunications Act*, makes it a separate offence to divulge or use cellular calls, or information gathered from them, without permission.[62] The maximum punishment for anyone convicted of the offence is a $25,000 fine and a year in jail, while a corporation can be fined up to $75,000.

The *Criminal Code* allows the media to report the details of cellular calls that are disclosed during a court proceeding. As well, the prohibition does not apply to conversations overheard on a police-radio scanner or a citizen's band radio because such communications are not expected to be private.[63] Broadcasting such conversations without permission, however, would be a violation of the *Radiocommunications Act*.

Disclosing Wiretaps

Reporters must tread carefully if they discover the existence of wiretaps or of information collected through a wiretap. The *Criminal Code* outlaws the use or disclosure of the information collected through a wiretap and further prohibits the media from disclosing that a wiretap or intercepted phone conversation exists. The restriction covers "the substance, meaning or purport" of the intercepted conversation. But the existence of wiretaps and their contents can be reported once the information is revealed in court during a criminal or civil case. However, in 2003 an Ontario Superior Court judge rejected media arguments that this exception extends to details of wiretap evidence disclosed in search warrants months or years before a trial. "The wiretap regime is intended to be confidential," the judge ruled. "To argue that because reference has been made to information obtained through a wiretap in an application to obtain a search warrant suddenly transforms the information into the public domain cannot be sustained."[64] A BC judge has taken a more flexible approach, ruling in 1999 that the media could disclose the fact that wiretap evidence was used to obtain a search warrant for the home of the province's premier.[65]

Legal Restrictions on Newsgathering

Trespassing

The media's right to gather news does not give journalists the right to enter private property. **Trespassing**—entering, crossing, or using someone else's property without the permission of the owner (or a person in control of the property, such as a security guard)—is a tort and trespassers can be sued for damages. In most cases, a complaint of trespassing is prosecuted as a summary conviction offence under provincial trespass laws; violators are punished with a modest fine and may be ordered to compensate for any damage caused to the property. These laws make it an offence to walk or drive onto private property when the person has been given a verbal or written warning not to enter, when "No Trespassing" signs are clearly posted, and when a fence has been erected to keep people out. In general, private homes, lawns, gardens, orchards, and farm fields under cultivation are considered to be off-limits unless a person has permission to enter.[66] Ontario's trespassing law forbids anyone from entering a body of water that is on private property, as well as a ship, vehicle, train, or aircraft.[67]

Reporters and camera operators must respect "No Trespassing" signs and fences, or an order to leave a property, even if a newsworthy event is occurring on the property. More than a dozen journalists who climbed a fence surrounding an Ontario nuclear power plant in 1980, in order to cover a demonstration inside, were charged with trespass. Three years later, in another case, a number of reporters and camera operators were convicted and fined $200 each after scaling the fence around the Toronto airport to reach the site of a plane crash.[68] The *Criminal Code* gives a person in control of a property the right to forcibly remove a trespasser from the property. The person ejecting a trespasser must use "no more force than is necessary," and could be charged with assault for roughing up a trespasser who did not resist. A trespasser who resists removal, on the other hand, can be charged with assault.[69] This power to remove trespassers does not entitle a property owner or security guard to seize or destroy a journalist's notebooks or any audio recordings or video footage collected on the property. Notes and audio or video recordings can be seized by police as evidence—but not destroyed—if a journalist or camera operator is arrested and charged with trespassing.[70]

Despite these restrictions, journalists have some freedom of movement when pursuing a news story that requires them to gain access to private property. A walkway to the front door of a home is considered an invitation to a journalist or any other person to approach, knock on the door, or ring the doorbell (unless a "No Trespassing" sign has been posted). If the person who answers the door orders a reporter or camera operator to leave the property, though, a journalist who fails to comply could be ejected by force and charged with trespassing. Streets and sidewalks, as well as roads that do not cross private land, are public property and journalists can use them as vantage points to observe or to take photographs or video footage (as long as they are not blocking traffic). Journalists can also work from a neighbouring property if its owner gives them permission to be there.

Journalists—like any other visitor—are entitled to enter stores, other businesses that serve the public, and the reception areas of offices. Again, the owner or person in control of the premises has the right to order a journalist to leave or a camera operator to stop filming. Although shopping centres and their parking lots may appear to be public spaces, these are private property and journalists must obey an order to leave. When interviewing shoppers or covering news stories inside a shopping mall, journalists should seek the permission of the owner or the mall's head of security. Government offices, while publicly owned, are also considered private property. Railway tracks, railway yards, airports, and port facilities are private property, and there are obvious safety and security reasons to restrict access to these facilities. Airport terminals, train stations, and bus depots are private property and although members of the public are invited to use them, permission can be withdrawn and a trespasser can be prosecuted. However, flying an aircraft over a property to take photographs or video footage is permissible because intruding into airspace is not considered trespassing.[71]

A journalist who is unsure whether a location is public or private property should ask permission to enter or take steps to contact the owner. Journalists may decide that some stories are important enough to take the risk of being charged with trespassing. In 2005 a Radio-Canada reporter and camera crew accessed and filmed an unguarded Hydro-Québec dam and power plant, exposing serious security lapses. The journalists were not charged, and their reports forced Hydro-Québec to hire additional security guards and utilities in other provinces to review their security systems.[72]

Trespassing at Night

A journalist caught lurking around someone's home at night, in a misguided attempt to collect information or take a photograph, could be charged with the offence of trespassing at night. It is a crime for someone to loiter or prowl on another person's property if the intruder is found near a home on the property.[73] The provision is aimed at peeping Toms and people who are about to break into a house, but it could capture a journalist who has no business skulking around someone's property. Unlike trespassing in the daytime, trespassing at night is a criminal offence. A conviction would bring a criminal record as well as a penalty of up to six months in jail and a maximum fine of $2,000. Criminal trespass, however, only relates to private homes and can only occur at night. It would not be a crime to trespass near a home in daylight or on property adjacent to a factory or other business during the nighttime, but these acts could still be prosecuted under a provincial trespass law.

Stealing Information

Theft and possession of stolen goods are crimes.[74] Hence, a journalist can be charged with stealing a document or possessing a report or document that has been stolen. But confidential information in itself has no value and cannot be stolen. For example, a journalist who photocopied a stolen document was not charged with possession of

Working Undercover: Three Crimes To Bear in Mind

Stalking

A journalist who shadows the subject of a story or stakes out someone's home or business may risk being arrested as a stalker. The offence is known as criminal harassment and section 264 of the *Criminal Code* defines it as repeatedly following or communicating with someone or "besetting or watching" the person's home or workplace. In order for someone to be convicted of the offence, there must be evidence that the acts of harassment caused the person targeted to fear for his safety, and these concerns must be reasonable in the circumstances.

Similarly, the actions of a journalist engaged in surveillance might not be considered harmless. There are two key elements of the offence. First, the surveillance must have been conducted in such a way that the person's fears were reasonable or justified. Second, it must be proven that the person accused of harassment either knew the conduct would cause such fears or did not care whether the person felt harassed (*Criminal Code* sections 264(1) and (2)). A judge might conclude that a person who saw a car parked across the street from his home day after day, and did not recognize the car or its occupants, had reason to fear the worst. There is no exemption for newsgathering activities, but a journalist who drives by someone's house a few times, parks on the person's street, or follows the person to work once or twice runs little risk of being prosecuted.

Impersonating a Police Officer

While journalists may at times assume another identity in pursuit of a story—posing as customers or job applicants, for example—they must not pretend to be a police officer. A person who claims to be an officer, or uses a uniform or badge to try to convince others that she is a police officer, is guilty of a criminal offence under section 130 of the *Criminal Code*.

Communicating with a Prostitute

It is an offence to communicate or to try to communicate "in any manner" with another person, in a public place, in order to obtain the sexual services of a prostitute (*Criminal Code*, section 213(1)(c)). This means that a journalist must take care when researching a story on prostitution—an attempt to speak to a prostitute on the street could be misunderstood. If the prostitute turned out to be an undercover police officer, a charge could be filed and the journalist would have to convince a judge that the contact was made to gather information for a story. The courts rejected a Nova Scotia man's claim that he tried to speak to an officer posing as a prostitute while researching a paper for a university course, and the man was convicted. A journalist should avoid speaking to prostitutes on the street and should instead contact them through support groups or social agencies. In 2010 an Ontario judge struck down this and several other prostitution-related offences as violations of the Charter (*Bedford v. Canada*, 2010 ONSC 4264). The ruling was under appeal at the time of writing, and communicating with a prostitute in a public place will remain an offence until the ruling is upheld or Parliament repeals or alters this provision.

stolen goods, because the information transferred to the copy was not a "good" that could be stolen.[75] Another case further illustrates this point. Ottawa television reporter Doug Small obtained a leaked pamphlet summarizing the upcoming federal budget. To the government of then-prime minister Brian Mulroney, the embarrassing breach of budget secrecy was a crime. A month after Small read details of the budget on Global Television's national newscast in April 1989, he was charged with possession of stolen goods. A provincial court judge later stayed the charge as an abuse of the court process, after concluding that the RCMP and prosecutors pursued the charge in order to please elected officials. The judge also found that although goods can be stolen, information cannot, and Small had been prosecuted for possessing the almost worthless paper that the information was written on.[76]

Information stored in electronic form is another matter. It is illegal to hack into a computer service or system in order to access data or programs. It is also an offence to use a password to hack into a computer system or to supply a password to another person to enable that person to break into the system.[77] So far the most serious breach of a computerized system by a journalist occurred in the United States. In 1998 the *Cincinnati Enquirer* launched a series of stories investigating the overseas operations of food giant Chiquita Brands International, which is based in Cincinnati. The paper retracted the stories and paid a US$14-million settlement to the company after acknowledging that one of its reporters had obtained access codes to Chiquita's voicemail system and had used them to intercept and record the private messages of company officials. The *Enquirer* fired the reporter, who later pleaded guilty to illegally accessing a computer system and unlawfully intercepting communications, and was put on probation for five years.[78]

Obtaining and Using Confidential Information

In 2010 the Supreme Court of Canada established that the media have the right to publish confidential information obtained from a source—even when the source has no right to divulge the information or has obtained it by illegal means. The issue arose as part of the bid to protect *Globe and Mail* reporter Daniel Leblanc's sponsorship scandal source (discussed earlier in this chapter). A Quebec court issued a publication ban that prevented Leblanc from reporting on out-of-court negotiations to settle the federal government's lawsuit against Groupe Polygone Éditeurs inc., one of the advertising firms that received sponsorship funds. The Supreme Court overturned the ban as a violation of the media's right, under the Charter, to gather news. While the court stressed the importance of protecting confidential settlement negotiations, it stated that promises to keep these discussions secret "bind only the parties to settlement negotiations and their agents." It would be "a dramatic interference with the work and operations of the news media to require a journalist … to ensure that the source is not providing the information in breach of any legal obligations. A journalist is under no obligation to act as legal adviser to his or her sources of information." If the media "obtains truthful information about a matter of public importance, and does so in a lawful manner … the state cannot punish the publication of that information."[79]

Despite this ruling, when a journalist obtains confidential information, the courts may have the power to prevent its publication and may even order the information to be returned. The Canadian Press was ordered to hand over a leaked draft report of the investigation into a 1998 ferry accident, as well as all copies that its journalists had made. The judge also imposed an injunction barring the news service from publishing stories based on the report, which is considered confidential under federal law.[80] The judge noted that the final report of an accident investigation is made public and said the board was "entitled to a measure of confidentiality as it gathers facts and confirms its information. … Ultimately, transportation safety benefits more from a thorough and accurate and public report than by transforming every investigation into a public inquiry."[81] In another case, Nova Scotia's Court of Appeal upheld an injunction preventing the CBC from broadcasting the contents of two letters and a report about a controversial development project. The documents disclosed legal advice shielded by solicitor–client privilege, the court ruled, and the client—in this case, a municipal government—had the legal right to force a third party such as the media to keep the information confidential.[82]

Harassing Phone Calls

Journalists should be persistent in their efforts to track down information and to hold public officials accountable for their actions. But the media do not have the right to hound people relentlessly for information or comment.

It is a crime to make repeated telephone calls that are intended "to harass any person."[83] How many calls can be made before the law is violated is a matter of common sense. A half-dozen attempts to reach a key player in a story seems reasonable. Dozens of calls made to the same person at all hours of the day or night could be considered harassment. Although a person who has a "lawful excuse" for making the harassing calls will not be convicted, the courts may not see newsgathering as a legitimate defence. The key issue would be whether the number of calls that the journalist made was reasonable and whether the annoyance caused was minimal.

Disrupting a Religious Service

Journalists frequently cover funerals, memorial services, and other events held in a place of worship. The *Criminal Code* makes it an offence to intentionally disturb or interrupt an assembly held for religious worship or any gathering for "a moral, social or benevolent purpose." It is also an offence to do "anything … at or near" such a meeting "that disturbs the order and solemnity of the meeting."[84] An innocent act, such as a camera crew inadvertently making noise while entering a church, would not run afoul of the law. But a journalist who deliberately interrupted a service, or created a scene outside a church after being denied access, could be prosecuted. Journalists covering such events should contact a church official in advance to work out the details of media access.

Legal Restrictions on Publishing Information

Obscenity and Child Pornography

The reader who complained to the Halifax police about "Savage Love," a syndicated column published in the city's alternative weekly *The Coast*, thought that its frank advice about sexual practices was obscene. In response, the police investigated in the fall of 1996 but found no basis for charging the paper or the columnist with violating obscenity laws. Why? Under Canadian law, the notion of what words and images are obscene is based on the concept of community standards, not individual taste. The police took the view that the people of Halifax, like those living in any other modern urban centre, considered the column to be acceptable.

But what the community will tolerate is a moving target. Canadians have proven willing to accept—or at least to tolerate—increasingly explicit language and images in the media. As a result, obscenity prosecutions have become extremely rare. The *Criminal Code* defines a publication as obscene if its "dominant characteristic ... is the undue exploitation of sex," or the undue exploitation of sex when it is linked to crime, horror, cruelty, or violence.[85] It is an offence to print, publish, distribute, post to the Internet, or circulate—or to possess for the purpose of publishing or distributing—"any obscene written matter, picture, model, phonograph record or other thing whatever." The Code makes an exception if "the public good was served" by the publication or distribution of the obscene matter, a provision intended to protect works with literary or other merit.[86] In balancing these provisions against the Charter right to freedom of expression, as noted in Chapter 3, the Supreme Court of Canada has severely restricted the types of publications that the courts could find obscene. The court identified three categories of pornography that could be considered obscene: depictions of explicit sex acts combined with acts of violence; depictions of explicit sex that subjects people to degrading or dehumanizing treatment; and portrayals of explicit sex that include children.[87]

It is also an offence to publish, import, distribute, sell, or possess child pornography. The Code defines child pornography as any photo, video, or other image depicting a child under the age of 18 engaged in explicit sexual activity. The prohibition extends to images that focus on a child's genitals and any "written material or visual representation that advocates or counsels sexual activity" with a person under the age of 18.[88] A journalist working on a story about child pornography must bear in mind that it is an offence to simply *possess* such materials—and, in one case, a judge ruled viewing images on a computer meets the definition of possession, even if the images are not downloaded from a website or saved on a computer or storage device.[89] If the materials have been viewed or collected in the course of newsgathering, a journalist might be able to take advantage of the defences set out in the Code, which exempt material that has "a legitimate purpose related to the administration of justice or to science, medicine, education or art."[90] In 1999, however, an American journalist who distributed child pornography online was convicted and sentenced to 18 months in jail, despite his claim he did so as part of his research into a story on child molesters.[91] The Supreme Court of Canada has upheld the offence of possessing child pornography as a reasonable limit on free expression, with the exception of writings or images—but not photographs—that someone has created for personal use.[92]

As well, broadcasters must comply with a CRTC regulation prohibiting the airing of "obscene or profane" words or images.[93] Again, what is obscene or profane is a matter of individual taste and the test is what the audience as a whole considers appropriate. The CBC and other broadcasters routinely warn in advance if an upcoming news report contains coarse language or graphic images, to ward off complaints from listeners and viewers.

Counselling Others To Commit a Crime

It is an offence to counsel—to "procure, solicit or incite," in the words of the Code—another person to commit an offence.[94] Accordingly, journalists, publishers, and broadcasters cannot urge members of their audiences to break the law. A news item describing in detail how a crime was committed would not run afoul of this provision. But a how-to item offering people step-by-step instructions on cheating on their taxes or breaking into homes—and urging them to do it—would likely cross the line. It is also an offence to counsel, urge, or advise a member of Canada's Armed Forces (or foreign military personnel stationed in Canada) to mutiny, to disobey their superiors, or to refuse duty.[95]

In what appears to be the only counselling conviction based on a media report, the Vancouver alternative newspaper *Georgia Straight* was found guilty of counselling readers to grow marijuana in a 1969 article headlined "Growing and Cultivating Pot."[96] A prosecution for running a similar article today seems unlikely, however. A separate section of the Code that made it illegal to create, advertise, or sell literature that promoted the production or use of illicit drugs remains on the books, but has been struck down by the courts as a violation of the Charter right to free expression.[97]

Advertising Rewards

It is an offence to advertise a reward for the return of lost or stolen goods if the offer promises that "no questions will be asked" if the item is returned. The restriction also applies to anyone who "prints or publishes" an advertisement that includes such a promise. The law appears to be designed to discourage people from striking deals that would allow thieves to evade justice, while pocketing a reward for their trouble. There are no known instances of journalists or media organizations being prosecuted for this offence.

Hate Propaganda

It is a crime in Canada to publish or broadcast statements that advocate genocide or incite or promote hatred against an identifiable group based on the race, colour, religion, or ethnic origin of the members of the group. To violate the law, statements inciting hatred must be so extreme that they are likely to lead to civil unrest or acts of retribution against the group. To convict someone of promoting hatred, the Crown must prove that the person intended his remarks to inflame hatred.[98] The Code recognizes several defences to an allegation of promoting hatred. A defendant will be acquitted if the person can establish that the statements were true or that she had reasonable grounds for believing they were true. The law also excludes statements made in good faith as part of an argument over religion, for the public benefit, or to combat hatred against minority groups.[99]

Hate propaganda laws have little effect on how journalists do their jobs, because even the most opinionated columnists in the mainstream media are unlikely to express such extreme views. The most high-profile prosecution under the criminal law to date involved an Alberta teacher, Jim Keegstra, who taught his students that the Holocaust was a hoax.[100] Keegstra was convicted of wilfully promoting hatred against an identifiable group, and his conviction was upheld by the Supreme Court. More recently, native leader David Ahenakew was prosecuted after a media interview in which he called Jews "a disease" and claimed Hitler had "fried six million of them" to prevent their takeover of Germany and Europe. Saskatchewan's Court of Appeal described the comments as "shocking, brutal and hurtful" and the judge at his second trial in 2009 considered them "revolting, disgusting, and untrue." Ahenakew was acquitted, however, because he had not sought out the interview and the prosecution could not prove he had intended to promote hatred.[101]

Broadcast journalists face a broader restriction on statements that amount to hate propaganda. CRTC regulations forbid radio and television stations from airing "abusive comment"—and in the case of television, an "abusive pictorial representation"—that is likely to expose a person or a group of people "to hatred or contempt on the basis of race, national or ethnic origin, colour, religion, sex, sexual orientation, age or mental or physical disability."[102] Again, the mainstream media are unlikely to broadcast such abusive material.

Spreading False News

As noted in Chapter 3, the *Criminal Code* offence of publishing a "statement, tale or news" that is false[103] has been struck down as unconstitutional.[104] Despite the ruling, radio and television stations are restricted under a similarly worded CRTC regulation that forbids them from broadcasting "any false or misleading news."[105] However, harmless on-air pranks, spoofs of news reports, and satirical pieces are not subject to sanction.

The prosecution of an underground Montreal newspaper for spreading false news in 1969, before the *Criminal Code* provision was struck down, suggests how a judge today might interpret the broadcasting regulations. The newspaper, *Logos*, published a parody of the *Montreal Gazette* that included a story reporting that the city's mayor had been shot by a "dope crazed hippie." The publisher was fined $100, but Quebec's Court of Appeal overturned the conviction even though the report came "very close" to violating the letter of the law. The story was "stupid, pointless and in bad taste," the court ruled, but there had been no harm to the public interest because no one could possibly have thought the story was true.[106]

Reproducing Images of Paper Currency

It is a criminal offence to publish, print, or distribute the likeness of a banknote. Distribution "by electronic or computer-assisted means"—in other words, via television and the Internet—is also forbidden. The law exempts certain types of images, allowing the media to reproduce banknotes to illustrate stories. The law applies only to "current" notes—bills that are in circulation. Currency can be reproduced if the image is in black and white, appears on only one side of a page, and is either at least 75 percent smaller or more than 50 percent larger than the actual note.[107]

Police Powers

Obstructing a Police Officer

To reporters and camera operators, traffic accidents, riots, hostage-takings, and armed standoffs are news. To police, they are crime scenes that must be cordoned off to preserve evidence or to protect the public from harm. When the goals of law enforcement collide with the media's pursuit of information and images, journalists need to know the legal limits on their movements.

It is an offence to obstruct a peace officer or public officer who is engaged "in the execution of his duty."[108] In most cases, journalists deal with police officers, but they may also encounter **peace officers**, a category that includes sheriff's deputies, prison guards, military police officers, customs agents, and fisheries officers.[109] The offence covers a wide range of possible actions, from getting in the way of an officer who is trying to apprehend a suspect, to ignoring an order to stay at a certain distance from a crime scene. To convict, a judge must be satisfied that a journalist's conduct interfered with the officer's efforts to do his job. As well, the Crown must prove that the journalist meant to obstruct the officer. "Obstruction involves more than mere passive resistance," advises one legal guide for journalists, "it must involve actively getting in the way or frustrating the police's duty in a situation."[110] Taking notes and videotaping at a crime scene or in the midst of a violent protest do not obstruct the police. But disobeying a police officer's orders or crossing the warning tape that surrounds an accident scene is likely to lead to an obstruction charge. If an arrest is made, police have the right to seize equipment such as cameras and audio recorders as evidence.

The prosecutions of two news photographers in Ontario offer insights into where the line may be drawn. One photographer was taking photos of a disturbed man who was being taken into custody by police. The camera's flash agitated the man, making him more difficult to subdue, and the officers ordered the photographer to stop taking pictures. The photographer continued taking photos and was arrested, charged with obstruction, and convicted.[111] In the second case, a photographer tried to push his way past a police officer to reach a public area cordoned off to protect a foreign head of state during a visit to Canada. The photographer was convicted for obstruction, and the Supreme Court of Canada upheld his conviction. The court noted that the dignitary had been assaulted at a previous stop during his visit and ruled that the police were justified in restricting access to the area to protect him.[112]

As the above cases show, when an officer orders a reporter, photographer, or camera operator to stop what he is doing or to move to another location, the wisest course is to comply. Refusing such demands is almost certain to lead to the journalist's arrest on a charge of obstruction. A journalist who struggles or refuses to comply could face further charges of resisting arrest or assaulting a police officer.[113] If there is no urgency to an officer's request to move or to stop taking pictures, it may be possible to discuss the officer's concerns and work out a compromise that will enable both sides to do their jobs. If the officer appears to be in no mood to negotiate, journalists would be well advised to back off and take up their complaints with a superior officer or the officer in charge of media relations.

Officers may overreact or exceed their powers when restraining the media. There have been repeated incidents of reporters and photographers being detained or pepper-sprayed while covering demonstrations and street protests that have turned violent.[114] In 2001 Halifax police considered filing charges against several journalists who tried to reach a cordoned-off area inside the Nova Scotia legislature (an area normally open to the public) so that they could interview politicians about controversial legislation stripping nurses of the right to strike. In the end, no charges were laid.[115] In April 2005 the RCMP arrested and briefly detained a photographer for a Nova Scotia newspaper who had ignored an order to stop taking photos at the scene of a traffic accident that involved a police officer. The photographer was detained for 15 minutes in the back of a police cruiser but was released when it became clear that there were no grounds for charging him with obstruction. The force later apologized for the officer's actions.[116] Winnipeg police appear to have gone too far in 2007 when a CBC cameraman was arrested and charged with obstructing an officer. The cameraman, it turned out, had complied with an order to step back from a police cordon and was arrested because he continued to film, even though he was standing on private property. Crown attorneys withdrew the charge shortly afterward.[117]

Newsroom Searches

A newsroom, like any other office, can be searched by police if there is reason to believe that a search will yield the evidence needed to help build a criminal case against an offender. Not even a journalist's home is off-limits, as *Ottawa Citizen* reporter Juliet O'Neill discovered in January 2004, when RCMP officers rummaged through her personal belongings to find the source of leaked information about Maher Arar, the Canadian jailed and tortured in Syria.[118] Photographs, videotape, outtakes (film footage that has not been broadcast), reporters' notes—all might furnish proof that a crime has been committed or help the police to identify suspects. A journalist might have interviewed a key witness to a crime who refuses to speak to the police. Video footage shot during a violent protest may establish who was responsible for damaging property and which protestors are innocent of wrongdoing.

Media outlets have argued that newsrooms are not like other offices and should be protected by the Charter, which guarantees freedom of the press and gives journalists the right to gather information without government interference. The Supreme Court of Canada has grappled with this issue in several cases sparked by searches of media offices. The answer has always been the same—the police have the right to search newsrooms. But these intrusions into the media's affairs should be rare and there are restrictions on when searches can be conducted and what can be seized.

In a pre-Charter case decided in 1977, a BC judge quashed a search warrant used to seize notes, a reporter's list of contacts, and photographic negatives from the *Vancouver Sun* and *Vancouver Province* as part of an investigation into illegal picketing. The search disrupted and delayed publication of the papers, and the judge ruled that searches of newsrooms should be undertaken only as a last resort. In his view, the authorities must exhaust alternative sources before being permitted to search media offices.[119] Courts in other provinces were not obliged to follow British Columbia's lead, but the Supreme Court of Canada later endorsed this reasoning. "Where a search would interfere with rights as fundamental as freedom of the press," Justice Antonio Lamer wrote in a 1982 ruling, a justice of the peace "should refuse to issue the [search] warrant" unless the police have tried, without success, to obtain the information from other sources.[120]

In a pair of 1991 rulings, however, the Supreme Court eased the restrictions on newsroom searches, and made the following points. A judge or justice of the peace should take extra precautions when authorizing media searches and impose conditions, if necessary, to minimize any disruption to the work of gathering and reporting the news. But the police are not always required to identify and explore other possible sources of the information sought from the media. And once information has been published or video footage has been broadcast, the material passes into the public domain and a search warrant should be issued. In fact, the court suggested that the media should voluntarily hand over incriminating videotapes to the police once the footage has been aired.[121] Two dissenting judges argued in favour of greater protection of the media's rights. Justice Gérard La Forest warned that the ruling could have a "chilling effect" on people who deal with the media and that it could hamper journalists' ability to gather information and cover events. He was particularly concerned about the possible seizure of a journalist's notes or information that would reveal the media's sources. "The press," he said bluntly, "should not be turned into an investigative arm of the police." The other dissenter, Justice Beverley McLachlin, argued in vain for special constitutional status for the media and strict safeguards, including affording the media a chance to argue against the issuing of a warrant.[122]

The Supreme Court of Canada's position has left media lawyers with little room to manoeuvre when trying to challenge the validity of a search warrant. Unless there are glaring errors in the wording of a warrant, courts have found that police searches of newsrooms are reasonable. Warrants have been upheld even when the police have failed to disclose or pursue other sources of information. In 2001, for example, Ontario's Court of Appeal refused to quash warrants used to seize videotapes and photographs from Toronto's major media outlets that covered an anti-poverty riot outside the Ontario legislature. The court said it was "fanciful" to suggest that a justice of the peace would have refused to issue the warrants simply because police failed to acknowledge they already had security camera footage of the riot.[123] The police, perhaps emboldened by this trend, have begun to use "assistance orders" to force journalists to help search newsrooms. An **assistance order**, when coupled with a search warrant, requires a person in control of a premises—the editor-in-chief or the executive producer, in the newsroom context—to obtain and hand over the information or images sought. For example, the RCMP used an assistance order to seize the Shawinigate-related banking document leaked to the *National Post*. The media have decried their use, complaining that they turn editors into officers of the state.[124] But in upholding the *Post* warrant, the Supreme Court of Canada ruled it is reasonable for police to use them to help locate evidence.[125]

Police searches of newsrooms have little of the drama of a television cop show. Investigators usually call ahead to arrange a time to serve the warrant and conduct the search. The media outlet should contact its legal advisers and may want to have a lawyer present to check the warrant for defects. If the news organization plans to challenge the warrant, it is good practice to place the seized documents, photos, or tapes in a sealed envelope—police are not entitled to review the materials until the courts have decided whether the search was justified. Journalists must take no action to thwart a police search. An attempt to prevent an officer from opening a file drawer or accessing a computer hard drive could result in a charge of obstructing or assaulting a police officer. Similarly, a journalist who hides or destroys information once a warrant has been issued could be charged with obstruction of justice. But there is no requirement for the media to retain archival materials that are not subject to seizure under a warrant, even if it appears likely that the police may seek out the material in future. Some news organizations erase tapes of footage that was not broadcast and delete digital photographs or destroy negatives that were not published, in part to ensure that the police can gain access only to material already made public.[126]

Copyright Law

Copyright and Plagiarism

In most cases, journalists, writers, photographers, artists, filmmakers, and others who produce words and images own what they create. The law of copyright, as set out in the federal *Copyright Act*, prevents the unauthorized use, duplication, or public display of such works. The legislation protects forms of artistic expression as diverse as sculpture, architectural plans, computer programs, and any work of journalism that is broadcast or published in a newspaper, review, magazine, or other periodical.[127] Journalists and news organizations do not have to apply for copyright protection—the protection is automatic—and it covers stories made public as well as unpublished articles and scripts that have not been broadcast. Copyright protection remains in effect for 50 years after the death of the person who created the work.[128] Copyright does not extend to facts and ideas. "Copyright protects only the form of expression. It does not protect the message in the words," notes Stuart Robertson.[129] As the leading textbook on copyright in Canada puts it, copyright protects the "embodiment" of ideas.[130] "However good or valuable an idea or plan is," adds another copyright guide, "it becomes public property once it is publicly disclosed."[131]

Copyright infringement is a serious offence. Offenders can be sued for damages, barred from publishing a pirated work, and forced to hand over any profits earned from its sale. An Ottawa man, for example, was ordered to pay $100,000 in damages in 2004 for selling hundreds of copies of computer software manuals on an online auction site.[132] The police can also be asked to investigate a copyright infringement as a criminal matter, and a conviction could lead to a fine and even a jail term.[133]

Violating copyright can also cost journalists their jobs. Passing off someone else's work as your own is **plagiarism**, a form of intellectual theft. Readers have been quick to spot plagiarism by writers, and there are numerous instances of reporters and columnists being disciplined or fired for the offence. "Plagiarism," states an American text on media ethics, "is unacceptable in news."[134] Nick Russell has identified three types of plagiarism: deliberate theft by journalists who are too lazy to produce their own work, deliberate theft by journalists who are too pressed for time to produce their own work, and the accidental repetition of someone else's words. The key to combatting plagiarism, he says, is to ensure that it is "denounced loudly and heavily punished" whenever it is detected.[135] Plagiarism is copying without attribution the way ideas are expressed, not the ideas themselves. Testifying in defence of a reporter fired for plagiarism, Peter Desbarats outlined the following test:

> [T]he greater the length of the work being copied, the more conclusive the evidence of plagiarism … . [T]he more original the expression in the passage allegedly being plagiarized, the more apparent it would be that the writer intended to copy someone else's work and pass it off as his own.[136]

Who Owns the News?

There is no copyright over the news—the facts that form the raw material of news stories. Copyright protects only the words that the journalist uses to express and convey this information. Not surprisingly, then, rewriting a competitor's story is common practice in newsrooms (journalists have even coined terms for it, and speak of "matching" and "scalping" a rival's scoop). As long as the story is rewritten from beginning to end, this practice is not a breach of copyright. "Making a few changes in expression is not sufficient," *The Canadian Press Stylebook* warns, "the presentation must be substantially original."[137] Newspapers and broadcasters are also free to use verbatim copy that has been purchased or obtained under contract from wire services such as the Canadian Press, the Associated Press, and Reuters.

"Hot News": Too Hot To Copy?

Rolling Stone magazine set off a political firestorm in Washington and brought down a top US military commander. Its June 2010 article revealing General Stanley McChrystal's unflattering assessment of White House leadership forced President Barack Obama to replace him as head of military operations in Afghanistan. Unfortunately for the magazine, other media outlets broke the story before it appeared in print or on *Rolling Stone*'s website.

Two media outlets, *Time* magazine's website and *Politico*, obtained a PDF copy of the *Rolling Stone* article and posted it without seeking permission or waiting for the magazine to publish it online. "It was a clear violation of copyright and professional practice, and it amounted to taking money out of a competitor's pocket," media critic David Carr noted in the *New York Times*. When *Rolling Stone* objected, *Time* and *Politico* removed their posts and replaced them with links to the story after it appeared on the magazine's website.

The incident underlined an important legal issue in the age of instant news on the Internet: can a media organization claim ownership of news—and the right to be the first to report it—if it has a scoop? Content, no matter how novel, is not subject to copyright law in Canada or the United States—how the information is worded and presented belongs to its creator, not the raw information itself. But American competition law recognizes a doctrine known as "hot news." The concept dates to the First World War and a dispute between rival wire services over whether one could paraphrase and circulate the dispatches of another. The US Supreme Court ruled in 1918 that copyright does not extend to the facts of news reports but repackaging those facts in a way that could cause financial harm to a competitor amounts to "unfair competition in business." The underlying philosophy, media law expert Sam Bayard noted, is the need to ensure companies have a financial incentive to produce a product or service that the public needs. Arguably, *Rolling Stone*'s McChrystal scoop—a report on a matter of intense public interest that required considerable time and expense to research and write—would meet this definition.

The "hot news" concept was imported into today's Internet world in March 2010 when a New York federal judge ordered a stock market research website, theflyonthewall.com, to delay posting the recommendations and stock analyses of three Wall Street brokerage houses. The ruling did not explore whether such restrictions can override the constitutional guarantee of press freedom, Bayard noted, and this may limit its impact as a precedent for the mainstream media. The ruling was under appeal at the time of writing and major media outlets, including the *New York Times* and the Associated Press, argued in favour of protecting "hot news." "Unless generalized free-riding on news originators' efforts is restrained," they argued in a brief filed with the appeal court, "originators will be unable to recover their costs of news gathering and publication, the incentive to engage in the news business will be threatened and the public will ultimately have fewer sources of original news."

Commercial news aggregators oppose any attempt to restrict the flow of breaking news. "In a world of modern communications technology, where anyone with a cell phone may disseminate news throughout the world even as it is occurring," Google and Twitter argued in a brief filed in support of theflyonthewall.com, "the notion that a single media outlet should have a monopoly on time-sensitive facts is not only contrary to law, it is, as a practical matter, futile."

If the "hot news" doctrine is found to apply to Internet news, Bayard predicted there would be little if any risk it would affect postings by bloggers and users of social media tools such as Twitter and Facebook. Since the people who use social media to share information are not in direct competition with media outlets, the commercial argument underlying the concept is missing.

The lesson for editors and producers in this country? While "hot news" is not recognized under Canadian law, this legal battle over American news is worth bearing in mind when publishing or distributing a story based on a competitor's scoop. Ensure the original story has been published or broadcast, or has appeared online, and give credit where credit is due.

(Sources: Michael Hastings, "The Runaway General," *Rolling Stone*, June 25, 2010; David Carr, "Heedlessly Hijacking Content," *New York Times*, June 27, 2010; Sam Bayard, "The Barclays Case: Will "Hot News" Limit the Right To Aggregate News?" *Nieman Journalism Lab*, available online at http://www.niemanlab.org; Edvard Pettersson, "Google, Twitter Oppose Theflyonthewall.com Injunction," *Bloomberg.com*, June 22, 2010; *Barclays Capital Inc. v. TheFlyOnTheWall.com*, 06 Civ. 4908 (SDNY March 18, 2010); *International News Service v. Associated Press*, 248 US 215 (1918).)

With the exception of copy purchased or obtained under contract from wire services, reprinting a newspaper story as it was written or reading it verbatim on a radio or television newscast is a blatant violation of the newspaper's copyright. Imitation may be the sincerest form of flattery (to paraphrase 19th-century British clergyman and writer Charles Caleb Colton) but it is also a violation of copyright. The *Copyright Act* forbids the unauthorized reproduction of a complete work such as a news story or "a substantial part" of it.[138] There is no firm rule on how much of an original work can be copied without violating copyright. The courts may not consider the repetition of a few minor passages in a news story to be enough to constitute a violation of copyright (even though this would likely be sufficient to support an allegation of plagiarism). On the other hand, regurgitating the key wording of another story would likely be seen as a "substantial" use. "The first test," says Stuart Robertson, "is whether or not the major thrust of the story is copied in substantially the form it originally appeared."[139] Journalists also have copyright over the notes and recordings they make during interviews with the subjects of their stories.[140]

Freelanced Stories and Images

When a freelance journalist sells an article or image to a media outlet, the outlet is buying "first rights" and the article can be used only once. Copyright remains with the journalist.[141] Unless there is a verbal agreement or a written contract authorizing additional uses, the publication must pay for **subsequent rights** to republish the article or image or to resell it to another user. Care must be taken not to reuse a story or image that is on file without the freelancer's permission, which may require payment of an additional fee.

Works by Staff Writers and Photographers

Journalists and photographers on the staff of a media outlet are in a different position. Employees of newspapers, magazines, and broadcasters write stories and record images on company time, so their employer owns the copyright.[142] Staff journalists are paid for their work when they cash their paycheques; an employer can reprint articles and images and rebroadcast reports without providing further compensation unless the employee and employer have agreed to some other arrangement. Journalists on the payroll even lose the right to reuse their own material—a staff writer who wants to publish his columns in a book, for example, must seek permission from his employer, the copyright holder. So would a staff photographer who seeks to reuse or sell images taken while on the job.

Stock Images

Agencies such as Corbis and Getty Images are in the business of supplying media outlets with stock images to illustrate articles. While these agencies supply some images royalty-free, in most cases the rights to use them are sold. Fees vary, depending on how the image is used and how many times it is reproduced. Stock agencies routinely search the web for unauthorized uses of images, and media firms that reuse images without payment risk being sued for copyright infringement. Media outlets should keep a record of the rights and permissions they have purchased, in case their use of an image is questioned.[143]

Electronic Rights

The reuse and resale of published stories and images on the Internet or in electronic databases sparked a major copyright battle pitting freelance writers and photographers against Canadian media corporations. Toronto writer Heather Robertson, the named plaintiff in a class action suit, objected to the *Globe and Mail*'s reuse of two pieces of her work in a database and on CD-ROM. After a decade of litigation, the Supreme Court of Canada ruled in 2006 that copyright was violated and freelancers are entitled to be paid for use of their work in electronic form without their permission. An $11-million settlement with several publishers was reached in 2009, with the money allocated to freelancers whose work was used in electronic form, without their consent, after 1979.[144] In response, media outlets introduced contracts that require freelancers to authorize the reuse of their work in electronic form and on websites. Freelancers may be able to negotiate a higher fee—typically an additional 10 or 15 percent—in exchange for providing the electronic rights to stories and photos. Staff writers have no claim to the electronic rights to their stories, as these are the property of their employers.

Fair Dealing

Under a concept known as **fair dealing**, a journalist can use excerpts or portions of a copyrighted work as part of a news report or in the course of writing a book review or other form of criticism. The *Copyright Act* stipulates that credit must be given to the author of the material being reproduced.[145] Other forms of fair dealing are the use of copyrighted material for educational purposes, research, and private study.

The term "fair dealing" is not defined in the legislation, leaving the courts to determine whether the use falls within these exemptions. Judges will examine the amount of material copied and the number of copies made to assess whether the use is indeed fair. Canadian copyright expert Lesley Ellen Harris suggests that it is acceptable to use a "very small" portion of a copyrighted work in a review or news story. If a journalist is in doubt about how much is too much, permission to use the material should be sought from the copyright holder.[146]

Moral Rights

When reproduction rights are granted, freelancers and staff journalists retain some control over how their work is published or broadcast. These so-called moral rights enable a writer to insist on having her byline placed on the article as well as the right to remain anonymous or to use a pseudonym.[147] As well, moral rights are infringed if the work is "distorted, mutilated or otherwise modified" before publication or broadcast. For infringement to occur, the changes must be sufficient to alter the thrust of the work or to belittle its creator. The legislation also states that the right to protect the integrity of a work applies only to changes that prejudice "the honour or reputation of the author." Moral rights are also infringed if a work is used commercially to promote a product or service, or associated with a cause or institution, without the authorization of its creator.[148]

Publishers and broadcasters can edit or shorten an article without violating the moral rights of the writer. No journalist would object to having typos fixed or errors corrected before an article appears in print. But a journalist can object to wholesale changes that substantially alter an article, and can demand that the article be withheld or published with the byline removed. Journalists can waive their moral rights or may be asked to sign a contract relinquishing these rights, giving a publisher or broadcaster free rein to alter an article or script. The Canadian Association of Journalists took issue with the CanWest News Service in January 2005 for forcing freelancers to sign away moral rights to their work, characterizing the move as a threat to press freedom and the writers' independence.[149]

Parodies

Reproducing the design and distinctive look of a publication in a parody edition might provoke more than laughter—it could be the basis for an allegation of copyright violation. Media giant Canwest, owner of the *Vancouver Sun*, sued the publishers of a fake edition of the newspaper in 2007 that copied the *Sun*'s name and layout. The fake papers were placed in *Sun* vending boxes and contained articles critical of Canwest's coverage of the Israeli-Palestinian conflict in the Middle East. The BC courts rejected motions to toss out the lawsuit, ruling the Charter right to freedom of expression and the fact the four-page copycat was intended as a parody are not defences to a claim of copyright infringement.[150] While parodies of publications and broadcasts are common, the Canwest suit shows there may be legal risks in producing them.

Copyright and the Internet

The Internet has been described as the world's largest photocopier,[151] disseminating words, images, and sounds to a vast audience in electronic formats that can be downloaded and reproduced with ease. Can copyright be enforced in a medium that affords instant access to newspapers, magazines, and even books for anyone with a computer and a modem? Hypertext links, the highlighted words and phrases that enable users to skip from one website to another as they explore a subject, are one of the Internet's most convenient features. Are website designers and bloggers obliged to seek permission from the owner of the target website before they create such links?

The Internet appears, at first glance, to make copyright obsolete. As a British media law text notes, "virtually anything that can be reduced into digital form can be transferred to any user of the Internet free of charge."[152] Other writers have dubbed it "the ultimate copyright infringement technology"[153] and "a mecca for copyright infringement."[154] Despite the ease of access and copying, original works posted on the Internet—articles, books, comments, e-mail messages, music, and images—remain the property of their creators. The federal government introduced legislation in 2010 designed to crack down on the unauthorized copying of music, movies, video games, and other forms of commercial media.[155] The concept of fair dealing enables material to be copied for private study or research purposes if the source is attributed, but Internet users must seek permission if material is republished or used for commercial purposes. The Internet is also a plagiarist's dream, providing access to an unlimited supply of ready-made copy for student essays and journalists scrambling to meet a deadline. The flip side of this ease of access, however, is ease of detection. A freelance contributor to a Halifax newspaper was fired in 2003 after lifting much of a column from an Internet posting. The column acknowledged that "some" of the material came "from the Internet," but the newspaper discovered, after being tipped off by a reader, that in fact virtually the entire column had been lifted from an American website.[156]

Internet service providers, or ISPs, are not liable when their clients post material that infringes on copyright, the Federal Court of Canada ruled in 2002. As is the case with defamatory statements, however, an ISP could be held responsible if it was notified of a copyright infringement and failed to take steps to remove the offending posting within a reasonable time.[157]

Copying or Reusing Website Content

The act of viewing or "browsing" material posted on the Internet is, in itself, a form of copying. When journalists and other Internet users access a website, their computers copy at least a portion of the content so that it can be displayed. Web pages are also temporarily stored or "cached" in the user's computer as each one is accessed and reviewed. Existing copyright law does not address this limited form of copying, which is an unavoidable result of Internet technology.[158] In any event, most Internet users are oblivious to the fact that copying is occurring as they surf the Web.

Unauthorized copying or reuse of website content, other than for purposes permitted under the fair-dealing exemption, is a violation of copyright. This restriction does not apply to the use of facts or ideas gleaned from a site or content that is in the public domain (copyright expires when more than 50 years have passed since the creator's death). Many websites include a notice asserting copyright over their contents, while others state that their contents can be used for educational or other non-commercial purposes without formal authorization.[159] Quoting passages or paraphrasing a small amount of material for a news story or opinion piece is permissible as fair dealing, as long as the amount of material reused is not substantial and full credit is given to the source of the material. It is a violation of copyright to repost an entire article or an image from a website on a website or blog, but it is common—and permissible—to post a description or brief extract along with a hyperlink directing users to the original work. It is also an infringement of copyright to send an article or image to others via e-mail or to post it to a newsgroup or Facebook page, even if the audience able to receive or view the work is limited. As long as some segment of the public can access the copied work, permission must be sought or copyright must be waived before such reuse.[160]

Linking and Framing

Linking has been described as "a defining characteristic of the Internet,"[161] enabling users to skip from one site to another with ease. The practice, while widespread, may raise copyright issues. In a British case, the *Shetland Times* accused a rival newspaper, the *Shetland News*, of violating copyright by creating links between websites that each paper maintained. The *News* reproduced headlines from the *Times* on its website, which, when clicked, took Internet users directly to the full story as posted on the

Times site. The *Times* objected to links being made to content within its site because readers were able to circumvent its home page and the accompanying advertisements, threatening the paper's ad revenues. The case was settled out of court but serves as a warning to media that links made to content deep within a site could be considered an infringement of copyright, particularly if the link undermines a site's financial viability.[162] This is not simply a concern for commercial and media websites—in 1999 an Ottawa film buff was forced to remove links from his personal website to movie trailers on the Universal Pictures site after the studio's lawyers threatened legal action.[163] The leading text on Canadian copyright law offers some advice on the practice of linking. It suggests that links to the home page of another site are acceptable, but it would be prudent to seek permission before making deeper links to pages within a site.[164]

A related practice, known as framing, involves one website providing a link to another website but displaying the content within the page design or "frame" of its own site. Framing has obvious copyright implications because outside content is incorporated into the site providing the link, making it appear to be part of that site. In one of the few cases to address the practice, the Federal Court of Canada issued an injunction preventing a movie theatre operator from framing the website materials of a rival.[165] To avoid a claim of copyright infringement, frames should be designed to ensure that Internet users are not misled about the source of the framed content.[166]

Reproducing E-mails, Tweets, and Content Posted to Social Media Sites

Messages posted on newsgroups, listservs, and electronic bulletin boards—as well as material posted to the "friends" or "members" areas of Facebook and other social-networking sites—are the creations of their authors and meet the definition of literary works under copyright law.[167] Such postings should not be reproduced or republished without the author's consent. An e-mail message is also subject to copyright, and the author may not intend or expect that its contents will be made public. *The Canadian Press Stylebook* advises journalists to obtain the permission of the author of an e-mail before publishing quotations or extracts from the message.[168] Although forwarding an e-mail to someone else could be seen as a technical breach of copyright, one guide to Internet law observes that "the generally accepted custom implies that such use is acceptable."[169]

Comments posted via Twitter and to the public areas of social media sites such as Facebook, however, can be reproduced for a news story or a commentary, as long as the fair-dealing requirements are met: there is no substantial reuse and the source is credited. Photos and other images are difficult to fit within this framework—any reproduction is likely to require reuse of a substantial portion of an image—but credit still must be given to the source. Journalists also can seek permission from the tweeter or Facebook page creator, to ensure no complaints or copyright issues will arise. Given the public nature of such postings, the risk of copyright infringement is likely remote, but this is a developing area of the law and journalists should not assume such material is fair game.

In any event, someone who posts material to the public areas of social media sites will likely have difficulty claiming copyright infringement, or invasion of privacy for that matter. Facebook's "Statement of Rights and Responsibilities," for instance, warns users that, when they "publish content or information using the 'everyone' setting, it means that you are allowing everyone, including people off of Facebook, to access and use that information, and to associate it with you (i.e., your name and profile picture)." While Facebook users "own all of the content and information" they post, they are cautioned to use the site's privacy settings if they want to restrict access to all or some of their information.[170]

NOTES

1. As of 2005, shield laws in at least 30 states offered journalists varying degrees of protection against being forced to reveal the identities of sources. Despite such protections, dozens of American writers and journalists have been jailed for refusing to identify sources, including the 189-day imprisonment in 2001 of Texas writer Vanessa Leggett for refusing to cooperate with a grand jury investigating a murder. The jailing of *New York Times* reporter Judith Miller in 2005, after she refused to identify the source of a leak that exposed an undercover CIA agent, led to proposals for a federal shield law to protect sources but one had not been enacted as of 2010. In jurisdictions without shield laws, American courts review claims to protect sources on a case-by-case basis employing the Wigmore test, as Canada's courts do. The party seeking disclosure must show the information is relevant to a case, unavailable from other sources, and there is a "compelling" need to override the constitutional right to freedom of the press. *Branzburg v. Hayes*, 408 US 665, 1 Media L Rep. 2617 (1972). See also Kent R. Middleton, William E. Lee, and Bill F. Chamberlin, *The Law of Public Communication, 2005 Edition* (Boston: Pearson Education, 2005), chapter 11; Guillermo X. Garcia, "The Vanessa Leggett Saga" (2002), *American Journalism Review* 20–7; Alan Freeman, "U.S. Court Jails Reporter for Refusing To Name Source," *Globe and Mail*, July 7, 2005.

2. Bill C-426, introduced by Bloc Québécois MP and former journalist Serge Ménard, would have amended the *Canada Evidence Act* to give journalists the right to refuse to name a confidential source or to produce records that would identify one. This right would not be absolute—a judge could order disclosure if it was in the public interest to identify the source, if all other means of identifying the source had been exhausted, and after considering the impact on the source. Journalists would also have the right to withhold unpublished information unless it was deemed to be of vital importance and could not be obtained by other means. Also, the legislation would require a judge or justice of the peace to be satisfied, before issuing a warrant to search a journalist's materials or a media outlet, that the public interest in investigating and prosecuting an offence takes precedence over a journalist's right to gather and report information.

3. William March, *Red Line: The Chronicle-Herald and The Mail-Star, 1875–1954* (Halifax: Chebucto Agencies Ltd., 1986), 119–22; Sidney N. Lederman, Patrick O'Kelly, and Margaret Grottenhaler, "Confidentiality of News Sources," in Philip Anisman and Allen M. Linden, eds., *The Media, the Courts and the Charter* (Toronto: Carswell, 1986), 234; André Picard, "Journalist Fired over False Report: Hull Camera Operator Served Jail Sentence for Contempt of Court in Protecting Source," *Globe and Mail*, September 29, 1995.

4. Donna-Marie Sonnichsen, "Reporter's Sources Irrelevant to Case, Military Judge Rules," *Chronicle-Herald* (Halifax), September 15, 1995.

5. Frank Armstrong, "Reporter's Admission Saved Case: Defence," *Whig-Standard* (Kingston, Ontario), June 24, 1999.

6. Canadian Newspaper Association, "Kingston Reporter Ordered by Court To Testify and Turn Over Notes," *The Press and the Courts*, vol. 20, no. 1, February 28, 2001.

7. The rule was set out in *Reid v. Telegram Publishing Co. Ltd. and Drea*, [1961] OR 418 (HC).

8. *Bouaziz v. Ouston et al.*, 2002 BCSC 1297.

9. *R v. The National Post et al.*, [2004] OJ no. 178 (QL) (SC). The Supreme Court of Canada acknowledged in a 1989 ruling that journalists can make a case to protect their sources under the Wigmore test, when the need to protect the confidential relationship outweighs the information's value to a court proceeding. In that case, however, the court was dealing with a reporter who was fighting a tribunal's order to testify about information she had apparently *given* to a source. The identity of a confidential source was not at stake and the journalist could be forced to testify. *Moysa v. Labour Relations Board et al.* (1989), 60 DLR (4th) 1 (SCC).

10. *R v. National Post*, 2008 ONCA 139.

11. *R v. National Post*, 2010 SCC 16.

12. *Globe and Mail v. Canada (Attorney General)*, 2010 SCC 41.

13. See Dean Jobb, "Media Confidentiality Gets Big Boost by Supreme Court," *The Lawyers Weekly*, November 5, 2010.

14. *Charkaoui (Re)*, 2008 FC 61.

15. *St. Elizabeth Home Society v. City of Hamilton et al.*, ruling on show cause hearing December 1 and 2, 2004 (Ont. SC). For discussion of the impact of this ruling, see Rebecca Caldwell, "Media Fear Chill from Ruling," *Globe and Mail*, December 3, 2004, and Dean Jobb, "On the Level: The Case of *Hamilton Spectator* Reporter Should Teach Us That It's Important To Spell Out What Kind of Protection We Can Offer Sources," *Media* (Winter 2005), 13, 20.

16. *St. Elizabeth Home Society v. Hamilton (City)*, 2008 ONCA 182.

17. *R v. National Post*, supra note 11, at paragraph 30.

18. Quoted in Michael Wilhelmson, "Third Annual Workshop Looks at Media Law Issues," *The Lawyers Weekly*, December 5, 2003.

19. *St. Elizabeth Home Society v. City of Hamilton et al.*, supra note 15.

20. Peter Jacobsen, "Should the Courts Protect the Journalist's Promise of Confidentiality? Don't Count on an Answer in the Affirmative," *Media* (Winter 1995), 13–14, at 13.

21. *Statement of Principles and Ethics Guidelines—Investigative Journalism*, available online at http://www.caj.ca/?p=155. For more on concerns over the use of confidential sources in coverage of the Arar story, see Andrew Mitrovica, "Hear No Evil, Write No Lies," *The Walrus* (December 2006/January 2007), available online at http://www.walrusmagazine.com.

22. Cited in *Charkaoui (Re)*, supra note 14.

23. For a comprehensive, but dated, overview of Canadian privacy law, see Gordon F. Proudfoot, *Privacy Law and the Media in Canada* (Ottawa: Canadian Bar Foundation, 1984). See also Michael G. Crawford, *The Journalist's Legal Guide*, 4th ed. (Toronto: Carswell, 2002), chapter 5.

24. *MacDonnell v. Halifax Herald Ltd.*, 2009 NSSC 187, at paragraph 15.

25. *Nitsopoulos v. Wong*, 2008 CanLII 45407 (Ont. SC); "Apology," *Globe and Mail*, January 2, 2010. For more on the implications of this lawsuit, see Dean Jobb, "The Charter Collision Course: Where Privacy Rights and Freedom of the Press Meet Head-On," *Media* (Winter 2009), 25.

26. See, for example, Saskatchewan's *Privacy Act*, RSS 1978, c. P-24, s. 3.

27. An example is British Columbia's *Privacy Act*, RSBC 1996, c. 373, s. 2(3).

28. *Privacy Act*, Saskatchewan, s. 4(1)(e).

29. See Carolyn Ryan, "Privacy: A Vehicle for Censorship" (Spring 2001), *Media*.

30. This point is made in Crawford, supra note 23, at 131–32.

31. *Charter of Human Rights and Freedoms*, RSQ c. C-12, ss. 4, 5, and 9.

32. *Silber and Value Industries Ltd. v. British Columbia Television Broadcasting System Ltd.* (1985), 69 BCLR 24 (SC).

33. *John Doe v. Canadian Broadcasting Corp.* (1993), 86 BCLR (2d) 202 (SC).

34. *Hollingsworth v. B.C.T.V.* (1996), 34 CCLT (2d) 95 (BCSC).

35. Crawford, supra note 23, at 127, citing *Pierre v. Pacific Press Ltd.* (1994), 113 DLR (4th) 511 (BCSC).

36. *Robbins v. Canadian Broadcasting Corp.* (1957), 12 DLR (2d) 35 (Que. SC).

37. *Valiquette v. Gazette (The)* (1991), 8 CCLT (2d) 302 (Que. SC).

38. Ingrid Peritz and Colin Freeze, "Attempt To Muzzle Media Fails," *Globe and Mail*, June 30, 2005; LuAnn LaSalle, "Homolka Fair Game: Judge Rejects Killer's Request To Block Media from Reporting on Her Whereabouts," *Chronicle-Herald* (Halifax), June 30, 2005.

39. Ingrid Peritz, "'I Will Never Really Be Free': Jail Sentence Over, Homolka Heads Directly to TV Studio and Says She's Sorry," *Globe and Mail*, July 5, 2005.

40. *A. v. B*, 2009 QCCQ 14676 (CanLII) B., 2009 QCCQ 14676 (CanLII).

41. *Personal Information Protection and Electronic Documents Act*, SC 2000, c. 5. Note, though, that s. 2 of the legislation exempts anyone who "collects, uses or discloses" personal information for "journalistic, artistic or literary purposes."

42. *Journalistic Standards and Practices* (Toronto: Canadian Broadcasting Corporation, 2001), 63.

43. "Press Council Upholds Privacy 'Rights,'" *Toronto Star*, March 14, 2005.

44. Canadian Newspaper Association, "Repeated Use of File Photos Costs TV Station $5,000," *The Press and the Courts*, vol. 6, no. 1, February 13, 1987.

45. *Aubry v. Editions Vice-Versa*, [1998] 1 SCR 591.

46. *Podolej v. Rodgers Media Inc.*, 2004 CanLII 49429 (QCCS).

47. Tom McCoag and Michael Lightstone, "Advocate: 90 Days Slap on Wrist for Voyeur, Slap in Face for Victims," *Chronicle-Herald* (Halifax), September 1, 2006.

48. *Criminal Code*, ss. 162(6) and (7).

49. Cristin Schmitz, "Publishers' Lawyers Beware of Anti-Voyeurism Bill," *The Lawyers Weekly*, March 11, 2005, at 3, 8.

50. *Criminal Code*, RSC 1985, c. C-46, as amended, s. 184(2)(a).

51. Crawford, supra note 23, at 117.

52. Section 3(e) of the *Radio Regulations, 1986*, SOR 86-982, forbids the broadcast of "any telephone interview or conversation, or any part thereof, with any person unless

    (i) the person's oral or written consent to the interview or conversation being broadcast was obtained prior to the broadcast, or

    (ii) the person telephoned the station for the purpose of participating in a broadcast."

53. *CKOY Ltd. v. The Queen* (1978), 90 DLR (3d) 1 (SCC).

54. *Criminal Code*, s. 183.

55. Crawford, supra note 23, at 118.

56. *R v. Biasi (No. 3)* (1981), 66 CCC (2d) 566 (BCSC).

57. "Conservatives Warn Organizers To Be Election-Ready," Canadian Press, November 4, 2007.

58. *MacDonnell v. Halifax Herald Ltd.*, supra note 24, at paragraph 18.

59. *Audette v. Société Radio-Canada*, 2009 QCCS 4241.

60. *Journalistic Standards and Practices*, supra note 42, at 85.

61. *Criminal Code*, ss. 193.1(1) and 194.

62. *Radiocommunications Act*, RSC 1985, c. R-2, ss. 9(1.1) and (2).

63. *R v. Gasper*, [1976] WWD 93 (Sask. Dist. Ct.).

64. *National Post Co. v. Ontario*, 2003 CanLII 13 (Ont. SC), at paragraph 17.

65. *Criminal Code*, s. 193(1); Stewart Bell, "Wiretaps 'Integral Part' of Getting Search Warrants, Media Can Report," *National Post*, August 14, 1999.

66. Robert S. Bruser and Brian MacLeod Rogers, *Journalists and the Law: How To Get the Story Without Getting Sued or Put in Jail* (Ottawa: Canadian Bar Foundation, 1985), 14.

67. *Trespass to Property Act*, RSO 1990, c. T.21, s. 1(1).

68. Both trespass cases are cited in Bruser and Rogers, supra note 66, at 14.

69. *Criminal Code*, ss. 41(1) and (2).

70. Crawford, supra note 23, at 140.

71. See *Bernstein of Leigh (Baron) v. Skyview and General Ltd.*, [1977] 3 WLR 136 (QB), a British precedent cited ibid., at 137.

72. Rhéal Séquin, "Security Flaws at Hydro-Québec Prompt Countrywide Checks," *Globe and Mail*, February 18, 2005.

73. *Criminal Code*, s. 177.

74. *Criminal Code*, ss. 322 and 354.

75. This was the conclusion of the Supreme Court of Canada in *R v. Stewart*, [1988] 1 SCR 963.

76. Sean Upton, "The Judge's Decision Was Unequivocal," *Ottawa Citizen*, July 16, 1990.

77. *Criminal Code*, s. 342.1. It is also an offence, under s. 430, to alter or destroy computer data or to block someone from accessing a computer system that the person is authorized to use.

78. Alicia C. Shepard, "Bitter Fruit: How the Cincinnati Enquirer's Hard-Hitting Investigation of Chiquita Brands International Unravelled" (September 1998), *American Journalism Review*; Nicholas Stein, "Banana Peel" (1998), *Columbia Journalism Review*; Dan Horn, "Former Enquirer Reporter Guilty," *Cincinnati Enquirer*, September 25, 1998.

79. *Globe and Mail v. Canada (Attorney General)*, supra note 12, at paragraphs 81, 84–85. In 2009 Quebec's highest court lifted a similar publication ban that prevented Montreal's *La Presse* from reporting on confidential talks to settle the lawsuit. The court said "banning journalists from using confidential information would seriously limit, if not crush, their ability to probe and gather information" on such abuses. See Tu Thanh Ha, "Quebec's Top Court Overturns Gag Order," *Globe and Mail*, August 14, 2009.

80. *Canadian Transportation Accident Investigation Safety Board Act*, SC 1989, c. 3, s. 24(3).

81. *Canadian Transportation Accident Investigation Safety Board v. Canadian Press*, 2000 CanLII 4353 (NSSC). See also Judy Monchuk, "Court Grants Injunction To Block Cat-Report Stories," *Chronicle-Herald* (Halifax), February 4, 2000, and Mark Fitzgerald, "Court Spikes Canadian Press Story: Justice's Decision Drives a Stake into Heart of a Free Press," *Editor & Publisher*, April 3, 2000.

82. *Amherst (Town) v. Canadian Broadcasting Corp.*, [1994] NSJ no. 291 (QL) (CA).

83. *Criminal Code*, s. 372(3).

84. Ibid., ss. 176(2) and (3).

85. Ibid., s. 163(8).

86. Ibid., ss. 163(1) and (3).

87. *R v. Butler*, [1992] 1 SCR 452. See also "Obscenity To Be Judged on Its Harm to Society, Not Immorality: S.C.C.," *The Lawyers Weekly*, March 20, 1991, at 1, 16.

88. *Criminal Code*, ss. 163.1(1), (2), (3), and (4).

89. *R. v. Daniels, Patrick*, 2004 NLSCTD 27. See also Tonda MacCharles, "Child Porn Viewers on Net May Be Charged," *Toronto Star*, March 15, 2001.

90. *Criminal Code*, s. 163.1(6).

91. James Franklin, "Journalist Sentenced for Child Porn," Associated Press wire service, March 8, 1999.

92. *R v. Sharpe*, [2001] 1 SCR 45.

93. *Radio Regulations, 1986*, SOR/86-982, s. 5(1)(c) and *Television Broadcasting Regulations, 1987*, SOR/87-49, s. 5(1)(c).

94. *Criminal Code*, s. 22. "Counsel" is defined in s. 22(3).

95. Ibid., s. 62. A conviction for counselling a member of a military force to commit these crimes is punishable by up to five years in prison.

96. *R v. McLeod et al.* (1971), 1 CCC (2d) 5 (BCCA).

97. *Iorfida v. MacIntyre* (1994), 93 CCC (3d) 395, 21 OR (3d) 186 (Gen. Div.). The provision is s. 462.1 of the Code.

98. *Criminal Code*, ss. 318, 319(1), and 319(2).

99. Ibid., s. 319(3).

100. *R v. Keegstra*, [1990] 3 SCR 697.

101. *R v. Ahenakew*, 2008 SKCA 4 (CanLII); *R v. Ahenakew*, 2009 SKPC 10 (CanLII).

102. *Radio Regulations, 1986*, SOR/86-982, s. 5(1)(b) and *Television Broadcasting Regulations, 1987*, SOR/87-49, s. 5(1)(b).

103. *Criminal Code*, s. 181.

104. *R v. Zundel*, [1992] 2 SCR 731.

105. *Radio Regulations, 1986*, SOR/86-982, s. 5(1)(d) and *Television Broadcasting Regulations, 1987*, SOR/87-49, s. 5(1)(d).

106. *R v. Kirby* (1970), 1 CCC (2d) 286 (Que. CA), cited in Bruser and Rogers, supra note 66, at 74.

107. *Criminal Code*, s. 457.

108. Ibid., s. 129(a).

109. Ibid., s. 2.

110. Bruser and Rogers, supra note 66, at 15.

111. *R v. Kalnins* (1978), 41 CCC (2d) 524 (Ont. Co. Ct.).

112. *Knowlton v. The Queen* (1973), 33 DLR (3d) 755 (SCC).

113. *Criminal Code*, s. 270.

114. For examples, see Jay Somerset, "Gotcha: Police Have More Power Over Reporters Than Most of Us Realize. Whatcha Gonna Do When They Come for You?" (Summer 2001), *Ryerson Review of Journalism* 11–15.

115. Amy Smith, "Cops Hold Back Media," *Chronicle-Herald* (Halifax), June 28, 2001; Rachel Boomer and Cathy Nicoll, "Police Consider Laying Charges Against Media: Journalists 'Pushed Past' Officers—Cops," *Daily News* (Halifax), June 29, 2001.

116. Dan Arsenault, "Herald May File Cop Complaint: Photographer Arrested at Crash," *Chronicle-Herald* (Halifax), April 13, 2005; Arsenault, "RCMP Official Apologized to Herald for Arresting Photographer," ibid., April 14, 2005.

117. Aldo Santin, "Police Charges Against CBC Cameraman Dropped," *Winnipeg Free Press*, January 23, 2008.

118. Jeff Sallot, "Police Raid Journalist in Hunt for Arar Leaks: Mounties Search the Home and Office of Reporter Who Wrote al-Qaeda Story," *Globe and Mail*, January 22, 2004.

119. *Re Pacific Press Ltd. and The Queen* (1977), 37 CCC (2d) 487 (BCSC).

120. *Descoteaux v. Mierzwinski*, [1982] 1 SCR 860.

121. *Canadian Broadcasting Corp. v. Lessard*, [1991] 3 SCR 421; *Canadian Broadcasting Corp. v. New Brunswick (Attorney-General)*, [1991] 3 SCR 459.

122. *Canadian Broadcasting Corp. v. Lessard*, supra note 121.

123. *R v. Canadian Broadcasting Corp.* (2001), 52 OR (3d) 757. See also John Jaffey, "Appeal Court Upholds Media Office Searches After Queen's Park Riot," *The Lawyers Weekly*, March 16, 2001.

124. See editorial, "The Editor Is Not an Arm of the State," *Globe and Mail*, September 4, 2002.

125. *R v. National Post*, supra note 11, at paragraph 90.

126. This trend is discussed in Somerset, supra note 114, at 14.

127. *Copyright Act*, RSC 1985, c. C-42, s. 2.

128. Ibid., s. 6.

129. Stuart M. Robertson, *Newsroom Legal Crisis Management: What To Do When a Crisis Hits* (Dunedin, ON: Hallion Press, 1991), 41.

130. Lesley Ellen Harris, *Canadian Copyright Law*, 3rd ed. (Toronto: McGraw-Hill Ryerson, 2001), 8.

131. Peter Burns, *Copyright and Trade Mark Law in Canada* (Toronto: Coles Publishing, 1978), 3.

132. Cristin Schmitz, "Ottawa Man Fined $100,000 for Selling Pirated Copies on Web," *The Lawyers Weekly*, October 1, 2004, 6.

133. For more details of potential penalties, see Harris, supra note 130, chapter 13.

134. Clifford C. Christians, Mark Fackler, Kim B. Rotzoll, and Kathy Brittain McKee, *Media Ethics: Cases and Moral Reasoning* (New York: Longman, 2001), 73.

135. Nick Russell, *Morals and the Media: Ethics in Canadian Journalism*, 2nd ed. (Vancouver: UBC Press, 2006), 135.

136. *Globe and Mail and Southern Ontario Newspaper Guild (Kelly), Re* (1994), 40 LAC (4th) 289, at 314. This passage reflects Desbarats's expert testimony as paraphrased in the ruling.

137. Patti Tasko, ed., *The Canadian Press Stylebook*, 15th ed. (Toronto: The Canadian Press, 2008), 233.

138. *Copyright Act*, s. 3(1).

139. Robertson, supra note 129, at 41.

140. This principle was established in *Gould Estate v. Stoddard Publishing* (1998), 161 DLR (4th) 321 (Ont. CA) and *Hager v. ECW Press Ltd.*, [1999] 2 FC 287 (TD).

141. *Copyright Act*, s. 13(1).

142. Ibid., s. 13(3).

143. Jenna Wilson, "Avoiding the Legal Pitfalls of Stock Imagery," *The Lawyers Weekly*, June 5, 2009, 7–8.

144. *Robertson v. Thomson Corp.*, 2006 SCC 43; Richard Blackwell, "Globe Settles Freelancers' Lawsuit," *Globe and Mail*, May 5, 2009.

145. *Copyright Act*, ss. 29.1 and 29.2.

146. Harris, supra note 130, at 126–29.

147. *Copyright Act*, s. 14.1(1).

148. Ibid., ss. 28.2(1)(a) and (b).

149. "CanWest Contract Bad for Journalism: CAJ," Canadian Association of Journalists press release issued January 11, 2005, available online at http://www.canadiandemocraticmovement.ca/ canwest-contract-bad-for-journalism-caj.

150. *Canwest v. Horizon*, 2008 BCSC 1609; *Canwest Mediaworks Publications Inc. v. Murray*, 2009 BCSC 391.

151. Jeffrey M. Schelling, *Cyberlaw Canada: The Computer User's Legal Guide* (North Vancouver, BC: Self-Counsel Press, 1998), 72.

152. Peter Carey, *Media Law*, 2nd ed. (London: Sweet & Maxwell, 2003), 201.

153. George S. Takach, *Computer Law* (Toronto: Irwin Law, 1998), 113.

154. Harris, supra note 130, at 237.

155. See Andy Blatchford, "Digital Copyright Bill Tabled: Companies Could Sue People Who Copy Music, Movies, Games," *Chronicle-Herald* (Halifax), June 3, 2010.

156. See Jane Kansas, "I Need the Pope's Advice," *Daily News* (Halifax), August 10, 2003 and "Plagiarism Concerns" and "Kansas Apologizes," ibid., August 16, 2003.

157. *Society of Composers, Authors, and Music Publishers of Canada (Socan) v. Canadian Association of Internet Providers*, [2002] 4 FC 3. See also John Cotter and Tara James, "Tariff 22 Decision Provides Some Guidance on Internet Liability," *The Lawyers Weekly*, May 17, 2002.

158. Harris, supra note 130, at 227.

159. Ibid.

160. Chris Bennett and Jeannine Tse, "Copyright Liability for Electronic Postings," *The Lawyers Weekly*, March 13, 2009, 12–13.

161. Schelling, supra note 151, at 95.

162. *Shetland Times v. Shetland News*, 1997 SLT 669. See also Carey, supra note 152, at 201. In a 1997 American case, also settled out of court, the online ticket-ordering service Ticketmaster sued Microsoft Corporation over links that bypassed its home page. See *Ticketmaster Corporation v. Microsoft Corporation*, no. CV97-3055 RAP (CD Ca.), cited in Takach, supra note 153, at 133, note 255.

163. Carl S. Kaplan, "Is Linking Always Legal? The Experts Aren't Sure," *New York Times*, August 6, 1999. Reproduced in the *Cyber Law Journal* and available online at http://www.nytimes.com/library/tech/99/08/cyber/cyberlaw/06law.html.

164. Harris, supra note 130, at 228.

165. *Imax Corp. v. Showmax Inc.*, [2000] FCJ no. 69 (QL) (TD).

166. Harris, supra note 130, at 228.

167. Schelling, supra note 151, at 73.

168. Tasko, supra note 137, at 29.

169. Schelling, supra note 151, at 82.

170. See Facebook's "Statement of Rights and Responsibilities," available online at http://www.facebook.com/terms.php?ref=pf.

CHAPTER 6

Using Freedom-of-Information Laws

Access Laws: An Overview

David Rabinovitch has proven that freedom-of-information laws work. In just four years the Ontario man submitted some 2,500 requests for access to government files. He got his hands on information about radioactive materials, the debate over the goods and services tax, foreign policy issues such as Middle East politics and the most recent war in the Balkans, and the quality of drinking water in his community. Rabinovitch even managed to obtain a copy of the blueprints to the maximum-security Oak Ridge hospital for the criminally insane in Penetanguishene, Ontario, where he was being held in 1992 after a court found him not guilty by reason of insanity for setting a string of fires.[1]

If a confessed arsonist can use access laws to get the plans to his prison, no journalist or researcher should doubt the value of such legislation. Since 1977, when Nova Scotia became the first Canadian jurisdiction to introduce a freedom-of-information law, the legislation has offered a window on government and how it works. The federal *Access to Information Act*[2] is designed to "facilitate democracy," the Supreme Court of Canada has declared, "by helping to ensure that citizens have the information required to participate meaningfully in the democratic process and that politicians and bureaucrats remain accountable to the citizenry." The court went a step further in 2010, ruling the *Charter of Rights and Freedoms* gives Canadians the right to demand information from public bodies when the information is required to promote "meaningful public discussion on matters of public interest."[3] One study described the federal law as having "more potential than any statute to harass, embarrass, distract and annoy the government of the day."[4] And the media and others have done just that. Journalists, researchers for political parties, and academics have used access laws to reveal wasteful spending, patronage abuses, and the results of government-commissioned polls and audits of government programs. They have uncovered reports on the safety of the food and drugs we consume and the trains and planes we use for travel. They have exposed the motives behind decisions to establish new policies and programs or to dispense with old ones. They have used access laws to dig into topics as diverse as the cleanliness of restaurants, training standards for police SWAT teams, and safety violations in coal mines and other workplaces.[5]

Examples abound. The media's relentless pursuit of information about the role of Canadian peacekeepers in the death of a young Somali man exposed a coverup within the military.[6] *National Post* reporter Andrew McIntosh used access legislation to investigate former prime minister Jean Chrétien's role in securing federal grants and loans for businesses in his home riding, the so-called Shawinigate affair.[7] The *Globe and Mail*'s Daniel Leblanc and Campbell Clark used a succession of access requests to uncover waste and mismanagement in the federal advertising sponsorship program, setting the stage for a damning audit and the Gomery inquiry into kickbacks to the Quebec wing of the Liberal Party of Canada.[8] A team of CBC investigative reporters used the legislation to access a Health Canada database that tracks adverse reactions to medications. Using computer-assisted reporting techniques, they analyzed the data and produced award-winning stories that exposed serious shortcomings in the agency's systems for monitoring drugs after their approval for use in Canada.[9]

Barriers to Access

Yet access laws can be a source of frustration for users. The legislation is complex, broad categories of information can be withheld, and many agencies are not required to disclose their records. Many officials of the agencies that must disclose err on the side of caution or deliberately apply exemptions to records that should be released. Canada's former information commissioner, John Reid, criticized a culture of secrecy within the federal government and bureaucracy and complained in 2005 of a "deep distrust" of the legislation "at all levels in government."[10] His successor, Robert Marleau, warned in 2009 that resistance from government officials and delays in processing requests had created a "major information management crisis"; he cited the departments of National Defence, Foreign Affairs, and Public Works, the RCMP, and Canada Border Services Agency as the least open and cooperative federal institutions.[11]

Delays, fees, and heavy-handed editing pose other obstacles to access. It can take months for an application to be processed, frustrating authors and academics working on long-term projects, let alone journalists facing tight deadlines. Kirk LaPointe, former Ottawa Bureau chief for the Canadian Press, frequently used access laws during his tenure but has described them as a "last resort for reporters" and a "better tool of history than of journalism."[12] Government agencies sometimes quote hefty fees for locating and copying documents, creating a further disincentive for users.

A Canadian Newspaper Association freedom-of-information audit released in 2009—a compilation of more than 200 requests—found glaring inconsistencies in the way federal, provincial, and municipal agencies handle access applications. "Information freely available from some government agencies was denied by others," noted Fred Vallance-Jones, a journalism professor at the University of King's College in Halifax who conducted the audit in collaboration with the association. "And when it wasn't denied, prohibitive fee estimates often took it out of the reach of all but the wealthiest requesters." One request was for access to the use-of-force reports police officers file after using a taser. Winnipeg police demanded a $4,500 fee to view the reports, while police forces in Regina, Saskatoon, and Saint John, New Brunswick refused access. Police in Halifax, Calgary, and Victoria, in contrast, released the records for free. Requests for basic financial information exposed similar discrepancies. The City of Windsor demanded a fee of $103,000 for access to a list of its payments for goods and services, information three other cities made public at no charge. The

Canadian Broadcasting Corporation said it needed six months to release a list of its top employees, their classifications, and their salary ranges, while most other federal institutions audited disclosed that information in a month or less.[13]

And when documents are released, they may be edited to remove information that the government considers confidential or otherwise exempt from disclosure. For example, the *Ottawa Citizen* once applied to Ontario's Ministry of Food, Agriculture and Rural Affairs for records dealing with the mistreatment of animals at provincially funded laboratories. The ministry supplied about 50 heavily censored documents, including a couple of pages that contained only scattered references to frogs, mice, rabbits, guinea pigs, and rats, and were otherwise blank.[14]

Journalists writing about an event or issue that involves government—and most do—should know how to overcome these obstacles. Despite the horror stories, access laws are an essential tool for unearthing information and holding governments and public agencies accountable. This chapter explores how to make the best use of them.

The Federal Access to Information Act

The *Access to Information Act*, in force since 1983, gives members of the public a right of access to records held by most federal institutions.[15] The legislation's guiding principles are that information should be available subject to "limited and specific" exemptions, and that decisions to withhold documents should be subject to an independent review by an information commissioner and the courts.[16] The Act is designed to facilitate public access, not to create barriers to access. "Access should be the normal course," in the words of one court ruling. "Exemptions should be exceptional and must be confined to those specifically set out in the statute."[17]

Records Available

Access can be sought to a wide range of records—letters, internal memos, reports, notes and minutes of meetings, e-mails, and information stored in computer databases. The Act's broad definition of a record includes any "book, plan, map, drawing, diagram, pictorial or graphic work, photograph, film, microform, sound recording, videotape, machine readable record, and any other documentary material, regardless of physical form or characteristics."[18] A request for "records" is sufficient to capture all forms of information on file with a department or agency.

Departments and Agencies Covered

The Act applies to records held by all federal departments, from Agriculture and Agri-Food to Veterans Affairs. It also covers the records of some 140 other federal agencies, including financial institutions (the Bank of Canada and the Business Development Bank of Canada), the Canadian Forces, the RCMP, the Canadian Security Intelligence Service, the federal prison system (the Correctional Service of Canada and the National Parole Board), 18 Crown corporations and regulatory bodies such as the Canada Revenue Agency, the Canadian Firearms Centre, and the Canadian Food Inspection Agency. Cultural institutions (including the Canada Council for the Arts, the Canadian Radio-television and Telecommunications Commission, and national museums) are subject to the Act, as are the Immigration and Refugee Board, regional development programs such as the Atlantic Canada Opportunities Agency, and some harbour and bridge authorities. A complete list of departments, agencies, commissions, and other federal institutions subject to the legislation is set out in schedule 1 of the Act, which is available online at http://laws.justice.gc.ca/en/A-1/index.html.

In 2007 Ottawa expanded the scope of the legislation to include the records of officials who report to Parliament, including the information commissioner, the privacy commissioner, the auditor general, and the chief electoral officer, and foundations created under federal laws, including the Canada Millennium Scholarship Foundation. The legislation's disclosure requirements were also extended to the Canadian Wheat Board and seven Crown corporations: the Canadian Broadcasting Corporation, VIA Rail Canada Inc., Atomic Energy of Canada Limited, the National Arts Centre, the Public Sector Pension Investment Board, Export Development Canada, and Canada Post Corporation.[19] While the CBC's administrative and financial records are accessible, the broadcaster retains the right to withhold information relating to "its journalistic, creative or programming activities."[20]

Agencies Not Subject to the Act

The *Access to Information Act* does not apply to records held in the offices of members of Parliament and Cabinet ministers and in the prime minister's office. Records of these offices, however, may be accessible through a department that is subject to the Act and holds duplicates. As the federal government has created agencies, or shifted responsibility for government services to outside organizations, the new entities have tended not to be subject to the access law. Among the agencies exempt are Nav Canada, which provides air-traffic control at airports, Canadian Blood Services, and the Nuclear Waste Management Organization, which decides how to store spent fuel from nuclear reactors. Alasdair Roberts, an authority on Canada's access laws, has accused Ottawa of conducting "a low-level campaign of attrition" to shield federal bodies from scrutiny.[21]

Information Exempt from Disclosure

Cabinet Records

The Act bars access to the records of the federal Cabinet and its committees for 20 years from their date of creation. The restriction applies to agendas and minutes, memos setting out proposals or recommendations, discussion papers providing background information on issues or policies, draft legislation, and records that would disclose discussions between ministers on government decisions or policies. The exclusions reflect the tradition of Cabinet secrecy, but there are exceptions. Discussion papers will be released if they relate to decisions that have been made public. If the decision has not been made public, they will be released four years after their creation.[22] The exclusion of Cabinet records has been described as "the most notable shortcoming" of the legislation, creating a loophole so large and so open to abuse by government that it has been dubbed the "Mack Truck clause."[23] A claim of Cabinet confidentiality was final and could not be challenged until 2002, when the Supreme Court of Canada ruled the courts have the right to review such claims.[24]

Published Information

The Act does not apply to information that has been published or will be published within 90 days, or is already available for purchase.[25]

Mandatory Exemptions

The Act designates three categories of information that the government must not release, except under certain conditions.

1. Business and Third-Party Records

Information submitted to government by companies, consultants, and other third parties must be withheld to protect trade secrets, information that could undermine a firm's competitive position, or confidential financial, scientific, or technical information. These records can be made public, however, if the third party does not oppose their release. As well, the government retains the right to release third-party information dealing with health, safety, or environmental protection, because these are matters of public interest.[26] Despite these restrictions, an access request will produce detailed information about government contracts and the businesses involved. Corporations, in fact, file close to half of all requests under the federal law to keep tabs on competitors or to find out why contracts were won or lost.[27]

2. Government Confidences

Ottawa is also bound to protect the secrets of other governments, and must withhold information received in confidence from foreign governments and their agencies, international organizations, and provincial and municipal governments.[28]

3. Personal Privacy

The most important mandatory exemptions relate to personal privacy. The government cannot release information about its citizens without their consent. Businesses may be able to spy on each other, but one person cannot use the legislation to spy on another person. Information that can be linked to identifiable persons is off-limits, including information that reveals race, age, religion, marital status, education and employment history, medical records, and financial transactions.[29]

Privacy does not completely trump access, however. If a record relates to an individual, the document may be released after the name and any information that could identify the person are deleted. And journalists and researchers can request information about an individual if they have the person's consent.

The Act protects the personnel records of government employees, but not the identities of civil servants who produced documents or are named in them. Individuals who work for the government under contract and those who receive grants, licences, or permits also waive their right to privacy.

Discretionary Exemptions

Other categories of records may be released or withheld at the government's discretion. These include records dealing with federal–provincial relations, the safety of individuals, details of certain testing and auditing methods, and privileged information passed between lawyers and clients.[30] Officials can also block the release of information that could harm Canada's relations with other countries or national defence, including diplomatic correspondence and information about weapons, military tactics, and intelligence operations.[31] The federal government also has the right to shield information that could have an impact on the economy (such as proposed changes to interest rates or customs duties) or undermine its operations or financial interests (including negotiating positions and research conducted by government scientists).[32] Finally, records of the RCMP and other law enforcement agencies can be withheld to protect investigative methods, the identities of informers, and information that could compromise an ongoing investigation. Access can be denied to information gathered or prepared during an investigation, but only for 20 years. The government can also withhold information that would assist criminals, such as details of the security measures used to protect buildings or computer systems.[33]

Disclosure of Edited Documents

If portions of a record contain information that falls within an exemption, government officials are obliged to release an edited version that discloses the remaining information.[34] For example, the RCMP would be obliged to release documents showing the cost of an investigation—an administrative matter—but would be entitled to block out references to the evidence gathered.

How To Apply for Access

Any Canadian citizen or permanent resident can apply for access to records. Although corporations do not have a right of access, a person may submit an application on behalf of a company or a media outlet. The application must be in writing and the records sought must be described in enough detail to enable agency officials to locate them without much effort.[35] Applicants are not required to explain why they are seeking the information or how it will be used.[36]

Application forms can be downloaded from the website of the Treasury Board of Canada Secretariat at http://www.tbs-sct.gc.ca/tbsf-fsct/350-57-eng.asp or requests can be submitted by letter. Info Source, a comprehensive guide to the records on file at each department or agency, is available from the Treasury Board Secretariat, at most libraries, and on the Internet at http://infosource.gc.ca. Info Source also lists mailing addresses and other contact information for **access coordinators** (the officials who process requests). It is prudent to first touch base with one of these officials by phone or by e-mail to ensure that the agency has the records being sought.

Fees

There is a $5 application fee for each request. Payment must accompany the application, with the cheque or money order made payable to the Receiver General for Canada. There may be additional charges for search time (the first five hours are free) and photocopying (the first 150 pages are usually free). The agency will provide an estimate of these costs in advance, so that applicants will not be stuck with an unexpectedly high bill. Although the $5 application fee is mandatory, applicants can ask that other fees be waived if the information should be released in the public interest. Requests for a fee waiver should be made when the application is filed.

Time Limits for Response

Departments have 30 days to respond, although they can request more time. Most requests are dealt with within 60 days. Agencies have the right to seek an extension of time if a request involves large numbers of records or requires notification of third parties who have a financial or privacy interest in the records.

Reviews and Appeals

It is rare for an applicant to receive all records sought. Government officials must justify decisions to withhold some documents or to delete information from others, in each instance citing the exemption they are claiming.[37]

A refusal to disclose information or an exorbitant fee estimate can be appealed to the Information Commissioner of Canada, an independent official appointed by Parliament to investigate complaints arising from the administration of the Act. An appeal costs the applicant nothing and must be filed within one year of the government receiving the request. The commissioner's recommendations are not binding, but often persuade the government to reduce fees or to release more information. If the information commissioner agrees that records are exempt from disclosure or the government ignores a recommendation to make more information public, applicants have the right to appeal to the Federal Court of Canada, which can order that the records be released. The information commissioner may go to court on an applicant's behalf if a case could set a precedent for improved access. For more information on the appeal process, consult the information commissioner's website at http://www.infocom.gc.ca.

Government Records in the Public Domain

Freedom-of-information laws give Canadian citizens the right to demand access to the internal records of government. A host of other documents and reports are made public or released upon request, including the annual reports of departments, agencies, and Crown corporations, studies and advisory reports, statistical information, and the reports of inquiries, royal commissions, and government auditors. Much of this material is available in electronic format through government websites; hard copies are available at the Library of Parliament in Ottawa or the legislative library in each provincial capital. Many public and university libraries also boast extensive collections of federal and provincial government documents.

Other records and sources of information in the public domain include:

- *Debates* Transcripts of the proceedings of Parliament and provincial legislatures, as well as their committees, are available in hard copy or through government websites. These transcripts are known as Hansard.
- *Orders in council* Federal and provincial Cabinet orders are available through the office of the Cabinet clerk or secretary and, in some cases, online.
- *Ministerial expenses* Most governments make public the monthly expense accounts of Cabinet ministers and high-ranking members of their staffs.

The federal government, for example, publishes details of the travel, hotel, and restaurant expenses of senior officials.

- *Public accounts* Each year the federal and provincial governments disclose the amounts paid to contractors and the salaries and expenses of politicians and public servants.

- *Lobbyists* Consultants and companies paid to lobby the federal government or the governments of Ontario, British Columbia, Quebec, and Nova Scotia are required to disclose the names of their clients and details of their activities.

- *Political donations* Political parties at the federal and provincial level must disclose their sources of funding. For donations exceeding a certain level—$50 or $100 are typical starting points—parties must identify the individual or corporate donor and the amount donated. Political candidates must identify contributors to their election campaigns, and, in some jurisdictions, party leadership candidates are also required to disclose the sources of donations. At the municipal level, candidates for elected office may be required to identify their financial supporters.

- *Assets of politicians* To expose potential conflicts of interest, ministers and senior officials at the federal level and most provincial politicians must disclose their assets and business interests.

- *Municipal records* Members of the public have the right to inspect property assessment rolls, minutes of meetings of municipal councils and their committees, building permits, and zoning records. The salaries of elected officials and most municipal employees are also public information.

Provincial, Territorial, and Municipal Freedom-of-Information Laws

Public Bodies Covered

All provinces and territories have freedom-of-information laws. Prince Edward Island, long a holdout, adopted an access law in 2002.[38] These laws provide access to the records of departments, Crown corporations, and government-appointed agencies, boards, and commissions. Nova Scotia's *Freedom of Information and Protection of Privacy Act*, for example, applies to about 250 entities that regulate a range of activities, from pest control to theme parks.[39] In some jurisdictions, the records of hospitals, school boards, universities, and community colleges are also accessible, with the exception of confidential material such as patient records and files on individual students. British Columbia's freedom-of-information law is the only one in the country that applies to self-governing societies that regulate lawyers, doctors, and other professionals.[40] Records of most municipal governments are also accessible, either under the provincial law or separate access legislation that applies to cities, towns, and regional governments.

Records Available

Like the federal *Access to Information Act*, provincial and territorial access laws provide access to records in a variety of forms. Under Alberta's legislation, for example, the definition of "record" includes "notes, images, audiovisual recordings, X-rays, books, documents, maps, drawings, photographs, letters, vouchers and papers and any other information that is written, photographed, recorded or stored in any manner."[41]

Information Exempt from Disclosure

Many of the exemptions in provincial and territorial legislation mirror those in the federal Act. Records must be withheld or edited to protect the privacy of individuals. Cabinet records tend to be more accessible at the provincial level than at the federal level, protecting information that would reveal Cabinet deliberations but in some cases providing access to background information as soon as decisions have been implemented or made public. The time period for keeping Cabinet documents under wraps ranges from 10 years in Nova Scotia to 30 years in Manitoba. Other records can be withheld if their release would undermine law enforcement efforts, breach solicitor–client confidentiality, or harm relations with the federal government or other provinces. Agencies can also refuse to disclose the trade secrets of businesses and information that could affect the financial interests of the province or territory. Many laws specify that they do not apply to a judge's personal files, court administration records, or a prosecuting agency's files about cases that are still before the courts. Most acts also shield the advice and recommendations that ministers receive from their officials, an exemption that often gives departments and agencies wide latitude to deny access. The provisions of each jurisdiction's legislation can be accessed on the Canadian Legal Information Institute's website, at http://www.canlii.org.

How To Apply for Access

Applications must be submitted in writing, either by letter or by application forms available through government offices or websites. Requests are usually made to the head of the department or agency involved. The work of preparing documents for release will be delegated to an official within the department or agency, and this person should be able to offer advice on how and where to file an application.

Fees

A filing fee of $5 per request is typical but some provinces charge no fee at the application stage. The fee in Alberta is $25. A cheque or money order to cover the application fee must accompany the request. Search fees ranging from $15 to $30 per hour may be charged for assembling and processing documents, as well as a per-page charge for photocopying. Some jurisdictions do not charge for the first two hours of search time. Applicants can ask the department or agency to waive fees if the information should be released in the public interest. Some acts also allow for fees to be waived if the applicant is a student or other person with limited financial resources. Typically, the public body must provide a fee estimate before any work is done.

Time Limits for Response

In general, government agencies have 30 days to respond to a request. Institutions can extend the deadline by 30 days or more if additional time is needed to collect and review records or to notify a third party.

Reviews and Appeals

Each jurisdiction has an independent official (an information commissioner, review officer, or ombudsman—titles vary from province to province) to investigate complaints about how requests are handled. Applicants can appeal an agency's refusal to release information as well as delays or fee estimates. The official conducting the review has the right to examine undisclosed records to determine whether they fit within the exemptions the government has claimed.

Information commissioners in Alberta, British Columbia, Ontario, and Quebec have the power to order the government to reduce fees or to release records that have been improperly withheld. Information watchdogs in the remaining jurisdictions, like their federal counterpart, can only recommend fee reductions or the release of additional information.[42] Applicants in all jurisdictions have the right to appeal to a judge of the superior court, who has the power to order the release of additional information.

American Access Laws

In the United States, the federal and state governments tend to be more open than their Canadian counterparts and applicants do not have to be American citizens. Some departments and agencies publish, or make public, records that are available in Canada only through an access request. Other records can be requested under the *Freedom of Information Act*, which came into force in 1966 and establishes a right of access to records in the possession of federal departments, the military, government-owned corporations, and regulatory agencies.[43] Among the agencies covered are the Food and Drug Administration, the Federal Bureau of Investigation, the Central Intelligence Agency, the Federal Aviation Administration, the Environmental Protection Agency, and the executive office of the president. The legislation does not apply to elected officials (including the president, vice-president, and members of congress), federal judges, the recipients of federal contracts and grants, or tax-exempt organizations.

Upon taking office in 2009, President Barack Obama pledged to create "an unprecedented level of openness in government" and declared government information "a national asset" to be shared with citizens. He issued a series of orders and directives that require federal agencies to administer freedom-of-information legislation in a way that ensures timely release of as much information as possible. His administration also committed to making more federal government information available on the Internet.[44]

There is no fee for filing an application under the *Freedom of Information Act*. Most requests are processed free of charge, but applicants should request a fee waiver, citing the public interest in having the records disclosed. Records can be withheld or edited before release to protect law enforcement efforts, national security and defence interests, confidential business information, personal privacy, inspection reports on banks and other financial institutions, geological data relating to oil and gas development, personnel records, and information exempt from disclosure under other laws. The government has 20 days to respond and can seek a 10-day extension. A refusal to release records can be appealed to an official within the department or agency, who has 20 days to reconsider a decision to deny access. Applicants then have the right to file an appeal with the courts.[45] A guide to using the Act and a list of contacts is available through the US Department of Justice website at http://www.usdoj.gov/04foia.

Each US state and many local governments have access laws. Consult their websites for a description of the records subject to disclosure and details of how to make a request.

Tips for Using Access Laws

- *Think before you file* Applicants should have a clear idea about the information they are seeking and where it is most likely to be found. Consult government websites and guides or flow charts that show how governments are structured to determine which department or agency is responsible for the issue or incident being researched. For example, a journalist might request the details of a contract to privatize prisons or ask a department what studies were done to determine the impact of new welfare rules.

- *But don't overthink* Never assume that it is not worth applying because records appear likely to be shielded by an exemption. Many requests produce far more information than the applicant expects.

- *Make a call* Before filing a request, touch base with the official responsible for processing access requests. It's a good way to ensure that the application is headed to the right department or agency, and applicants sometimes discover that records will be released without a formal request. But be wary of offers to handle a request for information outside the Act—these side-deals are not subject to deadlines or appeal provisions, enabling officials to stall access or withhold documents with impunity.

- *Be specific* The wording of the request is crucial. A request that's too broad may take months to process and fishing expeditions may be met with an estimate of high search fees. Provide as much information as possible about the records being sought. For a specific report or letter, provide the name of the author, the title, and the approximate date it was completed, if such details are known. If the report itself is lengthy, consider requesting access to only the executive summary, introduction, and conclusions. Dean Beeby, a journalist with the Canadian Press, recommends an initial request seeking the title page and table of contents of internal audits and reports, followed by a second round of requests for the full version of those documents that look promising.[46] Another approach is to cast a wide net but to narrow the time frame, to ensure that the number of records subject to the request is manageable. For example, an applicant may seek inspection reports for all bridges within a province, but only for the past two months.

- *Be a little greedy* If a particular report or audit is being sought, apply for access to records created in response to its findings. Memos, briefing notes, follow-up reports, and e-mails will reveal whether government officials take the findings seriously and what they plan to do about them.

- *Consider multiple applications* Access coordinators are bound to have differing opinions on whether an exemption applies to a particular record. If two or more departments or agencies have a copy of a record, a request to all of them may result in one releasing more information than the others.

- *Don't be deterred by delays* Departments and agencies respond to most access requests within a month or two. No matter how long it takes to obtain documents, the material should still be newsworthy. Even if the information released is somewhat dated, *The Canadian Press Stylebook* points out, it "can shed new light on key issues and developments and provide an opportunity to revisit important stories."[47]

- *Avoid fees* Applicants should never be shy about asking for a waiver of search and photocopying fees. Unlike corporations seeking information to improve their bottom line, writers and researchers who plan to publish the results of their research can make a strong case to have fees waived in the public interest. Most access laws specify that persons can apply free-of-charge for information about themselves. A writer or researcher who has permission to apply for access to someone's personal information could use this rule to avoid paying fees by having the person file the request in her own name.

- *Create a file* Photocopy the application form or letter before submitting it and keep any correspondence received in response to the request. These documents will be needed if an appeal is filed.

- *Follow up* Touch base with access coordinators as deadlines approach— some gentle prodding may speed up the release of information. And be prepared to negotiate to reduce fees or to scale back a request that involves more records than expected.

- *Check the results* Carefully review every record that's released. Letters or memos may refer to documents that are missing from the paper trail, due either to oversight or design. The information released may reveal other sources of information or identify records that should be the subject of a follow-up request.

- *Don't take "no" for an answer* If an application is denied, or records or parts of documents appear to have been withheld without justification, file an appeal. Critics such as access expert Alasdair Roberts and former federal information commissioner John Reid have warned of a growing trend toward secrecy in government. Delays, fee increases, and the abuse of exemptions have become the weapons of choice as ministers and bureaucrats strive to keep a lid on information that may be politically sensitive or will embarrass the government. Those using the Act can fight back by ensuring that decisions to withhold documents are not left unchallenged.

NOTES

1. Ian MacLeod, "Ontario's No. 1 Data Demon," *Ottawa Citizen*, January 25, 1992.

2. *Access to Information Act*, RSC 1985, c. A-1.

3. *Dagg v. Canada (Minister of Finance)*, [1977] 2 SCR 403; *Ontario (Public Safety and Security) v. Criminal Lawyers' Association*, 2010 SCC 23.

4. *The Access to Information Act: 10 Years On* (Ottawa: Information Commissioner of Canada, 1994), 23.

5. See, for example, David Pugliese, "Armed and Dangerous—SWAT, You're Dead" (Summer 1999), *Media*, at 14; Robert Cribb, "Dirty Dining" (Summer 2001), *Media*, at 12–13; Dean Jobb, *Calculated Risk: Greed, Politics and the Westray Tragedy* (Halifax: Nimbus Publishing, 1994).

6. See David McKie, "The General's Mea Culpa" (Fall 1996), *Media* 5–6, 23–24.

7. Andrew McIntosh, "Into the Rough" (Summer 2000), *Media* 6–7.

8. Edward Greenspon, "Four Years of Dogged Digging Unravelled Sponsorship Scandal," *Globe and Mail*, February 14, 2004.

9. More information on the CBC's "Faint Warning" series is available online at http://www.cbc.ca/news/adr.

10. Scott Deveau, "Access to Information Not Always Accessible," *Globe and Mail*, June 6, 2005.

11. Canadian Press, "Watchdog Attacks Federal Cult of Secrecy," *Chronicle-Herald* (Halifax), February 27, 2009.

12. Quoted in *The Access to Information Act: 10 Years On*, supra note 4, at 16.

13. Canadian Newspaper Association, *National Freedom of Information Audit—2008*, available online at http://www.cna-acj.ca/en/news/public-affairs/cna-releases-4th-annual-freedom-information-audit. The association's 2005 audit found that federal departments, school boards, public health agencies, municipal governments, and police forces complied with less than two-thirds of requests for basic information about their operations. The requests covered such routine subjects as classroom sizes, reports of schoolyard bullying, the annual cost of sick leave for civil servants, plans for street repairs, the results of restaurant inspections, and the number of public complaints filed against police officers. Robert Cribb and Fred Vallance-Jones, "Access Denied: Access Laws Are Supposed To Help Canadians Get Information from Government. But a Cross-Country Audit Has Found Many Agents of Government Are Just Saying No," *Toronto Star*, May 28, 2005.

14. Cited in John Wicklein, "Canada: How Government Foils Investigative Reporters" (July/August 1998), *Columbia Journalism Review* 61–62.

15. For a comprehensive guide to the Act and court rulings interpreting its provisions and disclosure exemptions, see Michel W. Drapeau and Marc-Aurele Racicot, *The Complete Annotated Guide to Federal Access to Information 2002* (Toronto: Carswell, 2001).

16. *Access to Information Act*, s. 2(1).

17. *Canada (Information Commissioner) v. Canada (Minister of Employment and Immigration)*, [1986] 3 FC 63, at 69 (TD), cited in Robert Martin, *Media Law*, 2nd ed. (Toronto: Irwin Law, 2003), 67–68.

18. *Access to Information Act*, s. 3.

19. *Federal Accountability Act*, 2006 c. 9, ss. 141–72.

20. *Access to Information Act*, s. 68.1.

21. Alasdair Roberts, "The Politics of Open Government" (May 2003), *Fraser Forum* 5–6, at 5.

22. *Access to Information Act*, ss. 69(1) and (3). Thirty years after their creation, all Cabinet records are transferred to the National Archives of Canada, where they are catalogued and available for inspection without the requirement of an *Access to Information Act* application.

23. *The Access to Information Act: A Critical Review* (Ottawa: Information Commissioner of Canada, 1994), 7.

24. This ruling and its implications are discussed in the *Annual Report of the Information Commissioner 2002-2003* (Ottawa: Information Commissioner of Canada, 2003), 12–16. See also Kirk Makin, "Tenets of Cabinet Confidentiality Upheld," *Globe and Mail*, July 12, 2002.

25. *Access to Information Act*, s. 68.

26. Ibid., s. 20.

27. In the fiscal year 1992–93, for example, businesses filed 43 percent of all requests, compared with 39 percent for individuals. Journalists filed just 7.6 percent of the 9,729 requests filed that year. *The Access to Information Act: 10 Years On*, supra note 4, at 14–17.

28. *Access to Information Act*, s. 13.

29. As defined in the *Privacy Act*, RSC 1985, c. P-21, s. 3.

30. *Access to Information Act*, ss. 14, 17, 22, and 23.

31. Ibid., s. 15.

32. Ibid., ss. 18 and 21.

33. Ibid., s. 16.

34. Ibid., s. 25.

35. Ibid., ss. 4(1) and 6.

36. "At no stage of the process is the applicant required to establish that she wishes the information for some useful or legitimate purpose, nor, indeed, should the applicant even be asked why she wants the information." Martin, supra note 17, at 66.

37. *Access to Information Act*, s. 10(1)(b).

38. *Freedom of Information and Protection of Privacy Act*, RSPEI 1988, c. F-15.01.

39. *Freedom of Information and Protection of Privacy Act*, SNS 1993, c. 5. See schedule of public bodies.

40. *Freedom of Information and Protection of Privacy Act*, RSBC 1996, c. 165, schedule 3.

41. *Freedom of Information and Protection of Privacy Act*, RSA 2000, c. F-25, s. 1(q).

42. Alasdair Roberts, *Limited Access: Assessing the Health of Canada's Freedom of Information Laws*, Freedom of Information Research Project, April 1998, School of Policy Studies, Queen's University, Kingston, Ontario, 58–59.

43. *Freedom of Information Act*, 5 USC § 552.

44. See "The President's Memorandum on Transparency and Open Government" and "The Open Government Directive," available online at http://www.whitehouse.gov/Open.

45. For more information on government records available in the United States and how to use American freedom-of-information legislation, see Brant Houston, *The Investigative Reporter's Handbook: A Guide to Documents, Databases and Techniques*, 5th ed. (Boston and New York: St. Martin's Press, 2009), 41–42, 52, 121–78; and William Gaines, *Investigative Reporting for Print and Broadcast* (Chicago: Nelson-Hall Publishers, 1995), 59–61, 227–35.

46. Dean Beeby, address to the forum "Freedom of Information and Privacy in Nova Scotia," School of Journalism, University of King's College, October 1997.

47. Patti Tasko, ed., *The Canadian Press Stylebook: A Guide for Writers and Editors*, 15th ed. (Toronto: Canadian Press, 2008), 68.

PART THREE

Covering the Courts, Publication Bans, and Restrictions on Access

CHAPTER 7

Covering the Criminal Courts

The Media and Public Perceptions of Justice

At the end of 2002, the *Globe and Mail* published poll results that gauged the public mood on a range of topics, from politics and work to fashion and sex. On the subject of justice, a poll found that 63 percent of Canadians believe that judges do not deal harshly enough with criminals.[1] This notion that courts are soft on crime is not new. Polls conducted since the 1960s have consistently shown that between two-thirds and four-fifths of the population believes that judges are too lenient when they sentence offenders.[2]

Why have a majority of Canadians come to believe that justice is not being done? Why are so many people convinced that judges are not doing enough to protect them from criminals, when few of these Canadians have ever set foot in a courtroom? The answer lies, in large measure, in what they learn about crime and court cases from news reports. Too often, the media send a message, loud and clear, that the justice system is not working. If a judge stays charges because the police have violated a defendant's constitutional rights, the public is likely to be told that a criminal has been "freed on a technicality." If a sentence of house arrest is imposed, the penalty is dismissed as a "slap on the wrist." And when offenders are put behind bars, the media

Figure 7.1 Despite statistical evidence to the contrary, many Canadians maintain that crime is rising and the justice system is failing to address it, making the accurate reporting of crime and the courts that much more important. Here, a videographer films a crime scene.
SOURCE: John Hanley/ johnhanleyphoto.com

give victims of crime and their supporters a platform to complain that the sentence was not severe enough, sometimes without comment or context.

The public has a right to know what is happening in the courts and citizens are free to judge whether justice has been done. But for criticism in media reports to be fair and constructive, it must be informed. Some news reports on court cases are guilty of distorting facts or inflaming emotions. The media have a duty to report accurately and to criticize fairly, not to feed the popular belief that the courts are soft on crime or that every crime must be punished with a long prison term. The court of public opinion should operate with a full understanding of the facts and the law behind a jury's verdict, a judge's sentence, or a Charter ruling—an understanding that can only come through fair and accurate news coverage.

Reporting on the Justice System

Ensuring Accuracy

Emmerson Weagle was someone who valued accurate reporting on court cases. In 1954 he dashed off a letter to the editor of his local newspaper—preserved for posterity by Nova Scotia writer Harry Bruce—demanding the following correction:

> In last week's paper you announced that I was arrested in Danesville at a Garden Party on Thursday. I would like to inform you that I was not arrested at a Garden Party, nor was I arrested in Danesville. … I was arrested at a dance held at Harry Whynott's at Italy Cross, and at no Garden Party.[3]

Here was someone so concerned about setting the record straight that he was willing to draw more attention to his arrest. But Weagle's indignation at being portrayed as a dandy who frequented garden parties pales in comparison to the damage that an inaccurate news report can inflict. For example, failing to fully identify an accused charged with an offence could sully the reputation of an innocent person with the same or similar name. And unless media descriptions of charges are accurate and specific, it may appear as if a defendant faces allegations that are more serious than they really are. "No area of reporting requires greater care than crime," notes *The Canadian Press Stylebook*. "People's reputations and livelihoods are at stake."[4] The practices discussed in this chapter will help writers produce accurate coverage of court cases.

Check the Paperwork

Examine informations, indictments, or other court documents to double-check basic facts such as names, dates, charges, and the circumstances surrounding an offence. After a document is referred to in court or read into the record, journalists should seek permission to view the document to check the accuracy of their notes. If the court clerk is unable to arrange prompt access to the court file or an exhibit, prosecutors or defence lawyers may allow a journalist to refer to their copies during a break or once a hearing is over.

Clearly Identify Defendants and Charges

When identifying persons accused of crimes, report their full name, age, and street address. One newspaper was forced to publish an apology after reporting that "a convicted crack dealer" had posted bail for a stabbing suspect; it turned out to be a woman with the misfortune of having the same first and last name as a drug dealer convicted a decade earlier.[5] The more common the surname of the accused person—Smith, Jones, or MacDonald, for example—the more effort that must be made to provide further identifying details such as a middle name or initial and exact address.

Similar care must be taken in describing allegations. Manslaughter, the unintentional killing of another person through an unlawful act such as mishandling a rifle, is not murder; possessing stolen goods is not the same as committing a theft; possessing a narcotic is far less serious than selling illegal drugs.

Care, too, must be taken in the use of language. Although the *Criminal Code* or other statute involved will provide the proper wording, avoid legal terminology that means little to the average reader or listener. Someone charged with "intentionally or recklessly causing damage by fire or explosion" is accused of arson; taking a person's money or property "by deceit, falsehood or other fraudulent means" is an allegation of fraud. But avoid being too vague—describing an offence simply as "an attack," for example, could cover everything from a minor assault to attempted murder. The heading that precedes each provision of the Code offers a guide to putting criminal allegations into plain language, but there's no need to cite the actual section number. In the words of *The Globe and Mail Style Book*, charges "should be reported accurately but in standard English, not in the convoluted language of the statute or in the cryptic, ungrammatical language of the police blotter."[6]

Avoid Legal Jargon

The law is replete with Latin terms and phrases that come naturally to lawyers and judges but mean nothing to the average person. Translate such jargon into plain language and, if in doubt, consult a dictionary of legal terms, such as John A. Yogis, *Canadian Law Dictionary*, 6th ed. (Hauppauge, NY: Barron's, 2009). There is a glossary of common legal terms at the end of this textbook.

Attend Hearings Whenever Possible

Never rely on second-hand information about what happened in the courtroom, even from lawyers, court officials, or others who were present. Journalists who miss a hearing or are juggling other assignments must avoid the temptation to reconstruct events or quotations on the basis of followup interviews—the result is usually a flawed and distorted version of what occurred. Interviews and court documents may provide enough information for a brief report on an arraignment or other routine proceeding, but the devil is in the details. If a journalist discovers after the fact that a hearing was newsworthy and deserves more detailed coverage, the best approach is to seek access to a taped or written transcript of the proceeding.

Double-Check Facts and Quotations

Misquotations are nothing new. Back in 1838, reporters covering a trial for rival Halifax newspapers produced different accounts of one witness's testimony. According to the writer for the *Acadian Recorder*, a man who came upon a farmhouse and discovered the wounded victims of an assault testified he "heard heavy groaning and I thought they were asleep." The *Novascotian*'s less-accurate account was laughable in comparison, reporting that the man told the court: "I heard heavy groaning—I thought it was a sheep."[7]

Most courtrooms seem designed to frustrate a journalist's efforts to be accurate. Acoustics tend to be poor, the public gallery is far removed from the action, and lawyers tend to be facing away from listeners when they speak. Microphones record what participants say but do not amplify their voices. To compound the problem, few journalists have been trained to take shorthand. A 1980s study of the extensive news coverage of a Saskatchewan murder trial found that up to one-quarter of the quotations used by some journalists were wrong.[8]

Fortunately, there are steps a writer can—and should—take to ensure accuracy. Where taping is permitted in the courtroom, key submissions and testimony can be recorded for later reference. Important facts and statements are often repeated several times as lawyers explore the evidence, giving a writer an opportunity to check his notes. If there is uncertainty about precisely what was said, it is better to paraphrase statements than to risk publishing a misquotation. Also, as mentioned above, it may be possible to ask court officials for an opportunity to review the taped transcript.

Tell Court Stories with Precision and Thoroughness

Stories about court cases are stories—writers must have an eye for the dramatic turning point, key testimony, or crucial legal ruling that explains the outcome. But news reports also must clearly convey where the case stands in the court process, as well as other important information. What is the stage of the prosecution or the reason for the hearing? Is the defendant being arraigned, undergoing a preliminary hearing, or standing trial? Is there a ban on publishing a name or certain evidence? What level of court is involved? Who is the judge? Is there a jury? What is the next step in the proceedings? Where was a statement made: in the courtroom or during a media scrum in the lobby after the hearing ended? Are the allegations based on documents or testimony or on a lawyer's closing arguments to the jury? These details must be woven into accounts of court cases and the audience must be clear about the source of the writer's information.

The following account of the opening day of a trial, adapted from a newspaper article but using fictitious names, is an example of good court reportage:

Abuse Accuser Recalls Being "Scared" Teen

A 38-year-old man says he spent almost half his life scared and ashamed to tell anyone that his probation officer sexually assaulted him, a Halifax court heard Wednesday.

"I was a 15-year-old kid … I knew about sex but I didn't know what he was doing," the man told the Nova Scotia Supreme Court jury trial for John Arthur Smith, 63, of Dartmouth.

The man, whose identity is banned from publication, was the first witness at the trial, which is expected to last six to 12 weeks. Justice David Wise is presiding.

Mr. Smith faces 26 charges involving 12 complainants. All of the offences are alleged to have occurred between September 1972 and November 1989 at various locations in Halifax, as well as at a camp, in a cottage and in cars.

The witness told Crown Attorney Susan Andrews that his introduction to the criminal justice system came when he was 15 in 1980 and was sentenced to probation for possessing a stolen car.

His case was assigned to Mr. Smith, a trained social worker and youth probation officer with an office in the family court building.

Back then, the witness was a scrawny five-foot-four teen who weighed only about 130 pounds. From his vantage point, Mr. Smith was "a big man" who stood nine inches taller and had a good 100 pounds on him.

At the first appointment, "we sat down and talked about school," the man said. "He could tell I was nervous and said he wanted to help me relax." Mr. Smith moved behind the man's chair and began to massage his shoulders, he said.

It seemed to last forever, he said, "but now that I think about it, it was probably five or 10 minutes." Two weeks later, he had his second—and final—visit.

Mr. Smith greeted the boy in his office and then shut the door. "He said he wanted to try a method to relax me so he told me to close my eyes."

Again, he said, Mr. Smith moved in behind his chair. He rubbed his shoulders, then his chest, and then his crotch. "I was scared. I sat there like a dummy and let him do it."

He testified he didn't resist Mr. Smith's actions or consent to them. The man, who wore a black leather jacket and blue jeans to court, said he spent the next 20 years in and out of jail.

According to Ms. Andrews, there will be more witnesses in the next few weeks with similar stories. In an opening statement, she told the jurors that Mr. Smith is charged with performing sexual acts on boys in his care.

Sometimes the children were threatened with a stay in a youth detention facility and sometimes they were offered gifts, she said.

Defence lawyer Robert Jones also addressed the jury, an unusual move he explained as getting an early chance to speak. Mr. Jones told the seven women and five men in the jury box that "the alleged offences simply didn't happen" and the trial was "mainly based on (the) credibility" of witnesses "who may have an interest in the outcome."

"Eleven of the 12 witnesses are in the process of suing for compensation ... which is delayed pending the outcome of criminal charges."

According to the first witness, though, the compensation issue came up only after he had given statements to police. The trial continues today.

This account identifies the who, what, where, when, why, and how of the court proceedings while telling the story. The context—the stage of the trial, the charges before the court, the level of court hearing the case—is clear. Events described to the court are vivid. The defence position is explained, adding balance to a story built around the most newsworthy aspects of the trial's first day—the witness's disturbing testimony and the allegations made in the Crown attorney's opening statement.

Report Sentences and Maximum Penalties Appropriately

At the beginning of a prosecution, it is appropriate to refer to the maximum penalty that can be imposed on a person convicted of the crime. (This is not the case once a trial is imminent or under way, when this information could prejudice the right to a fair trial and may be punished as a contempt of court, as discussed in Chapter 8.) But the maximum sentence, while an indication of the severity of a crime, may be misleading to readers and raise unreasonable expectations. The maximum penalty is rarely imposed and is reserved for the most serious crimes and the worst offenders.[9] For example, the *Criminal Code* stipulates that a person who commits robbery while armed with a gun faces a minimum four-year term and a maximum sentence of life in prison,[10] but most sentences are in the range of four to nine years in prison.[11] Manslaughter covers a range of possible offences, from a careless act that proves fatal to a provoked or drunken assault that falls just short of a deliberate murder. The maximum penalty for manslaughter is life in prison but sentences run the gamut from a brief stint in jail to prison terms of a dozen years or more.

The *Globe and Mail*'s style guide considers it "misleading sensationalism" to refer to the maximum sentence if it is highly unlikely that such a sentence will be imposed.[12] The Canadian Press recommends that the media report the maximum sentence in important cases "but also mention that the maximum penalty is rarely imposed and prison terms are rarely served in full." When substantial prison terms are imposed, *The Canadian Press Stylebook* suggests that journalists specify how much of the sentence must be served before the person can apply for release on parole.[13] Parole authorities will verify the timelines and criteria for early release in specific cases. If a court imposes sentences to be served concurrently, news reports should relate the actual time to be served and not a cumulative total that is misleading. For example, an offender convicted of two counts of sexual assault and ordered to serve concurrent four-year prison terms for each offence has been sentenced to four years in prison. If the judge imposed consecutive four-year terms, the sentence would be eight years.

Journalists should bear in mind, as well, that policies regarding incarceration have changed. Parliament has directed judges to seek alternatives to jail sentences, particularly for non-violent offences, but the media have been slow to recognize this policy shift. Too often, restorative justice initiatives and sentences of house arrest are met with a torrent of media criticism and editorial outrage. In some instances, the punishment may not fit the crime, but the media should not portray incarceration as the only option in sentencing offenders. This attitude fuels public dissatisfaction with the justice system and ignores the reality that prisons can be a fertile training ground for rookie criminals.

Understanding Court Rulings

Writers who tackle legal issues or court cases should be aware of how rulings are structured and catalogued. Rulings provide a detailed review of the issues and evidence before the court, the legal precedents that apply, and the bottom-line decision of the court or individual judge. Rulings are edited and published in bound volumes known as **case reports** or, increasingly, collected in electronic databases. Each ruling is prefaced with a brief summary, known as a headnote, that provides a synopsis of its facts and legal issues.

Cases are cited by the title of the case or **case name** (formerly known as the style of cause), a unique identifier usually drawn from the identities of the parties involved. *Dagenais v. Canadian Broadcasting Corp.*, for example, is the case name of Lucien Dagenais's action to prevent the CBC from broadcasting information he claimed would prejudice his trial on charges of abusing children. The "*v.*" stands for *versus*, and separates the names of the opposing parties. If there are multiple plaintiffs or defendants, one or two names will be given, followed by "*et al.*," Latin for "and others."

Cases are cited and indexed using a standardized system. The following citations are typical:

Dagenais v. Canadian Broadcasting Corp., [1994] 3 SCR 835.

Nova Scotia (Attorney General) v. MacIntyre (1982), 65 CCC (2d) 129 (SCC).

Grant v. Torstar Corp., 2009 SCC 61.

In the *Dagenais* example, "SCR" refers to the reporting series—the publisher of the ruling—in this case, the Supreme Court Reports. The "3" that precedes it is the volume number and "835" is the page at which the ruling begins. So *Nova Scotia (Attorney General) v. MacIntyre* is reported in volume 65 of Canadian Criminal Cases (CCC), beginning at page 129. Other major reporting series are Ontario Reports (OR), Western Weekly Reports (WWR), Criminal Reports (CR), Nova Scotia Reports (NSR), and Dominion Law Reports (DLR). References to "(2d)," "(3d)," or "(4th)" indicate that the volume is found in the second, third, or fourth series of a long-running case report. Sometimes, the name of the reporting series indicates which level of court made the ruling, as in the *Dagenais* example—"SCR" tells us that the ruling was made by the Supreme Court. Other times, as in the *MacIntyre* example, the name of the reporting series does not provide this information, and so it is provided in parentheses at the end of the citation—"SCC" stands for the Supreme Court of Canada. When the year is given in square brackets, as in the *Dagenais* citation, it indicates when the case report was published and not necessarily when the ruling was made. A date given in round brackets correlates to the year that the ruling was made.

As cases are increasingly stored in databases, courts and electronic reporting services like Quicklaw use pared-down case citations. For example, in *R v. Brown*, [1999] OJ no. 4870 (SC), "OJ" refers to Quicklaw's Ontario Judgments collection, and the ruling of the Ontario Superior Court is given a number for easy reference: "no. 4870." Since 1999 courts and tribunals have adopted simplified "neutral citations" that consist of three elements–the year the ruling was handed down, an abbreviation for the court or tribunal, and a number identifying the individual ruling. The *Grant v. Torstar Corp.* ruling cited above is an example—it is the 61st ruling the Supreme Court of Canada released in 2009.

The judge who wrote the ruling is usually identified only by surname, followed by "J," "CJ," "ACJ," or "JA." These must not be mistaken for the judge's initials—"J" stands for the title Judge or Justice, while "CJ" and "ACJ" denote Chief Justice and Associate Chief Justice. "JA" identifies a justice of a court of appeal and "JJA" is the plural form used when two or more are named. Similarly, justices of the Supreme Court of Canada use "J" after their names and "JJ" when two or more are listed. The Chief Justice of the Supreme Court of Canada is identified as "CJ." To verify a judge's full name and title, consult the court's website, law reports, or reference books.

In cases argued at the Supreme Court of Canada or before a court of appeal, one judge will be designated to write the judgment and the other judges on the panel will indicate they agree. Sometimes one or more judges will agree with the main judgment but will offer their own analysis of the law in a separate **concurring judgment**. If a ruling is not unanimous, the court will issue a **majority judgment**, which decides the outcome of the case, followed by a **dissenting judgment**, which offers the minority's opinion of how the case should have been decided.

Ensuring That Reports Are Fair and Balanced

Present Both Sides of the Story

Criminal cases tend to be one-sided affairs. During the pre-trial stage, the Crown's allegations are front and centre and the defendant's response is usually limited to a plea of not guilty. When a trial finally begins, the initial focus is on the prosecution's opening statement, and then Crown evidence may dominate the proceedings for days or weeks.

Journalists should strive to bring balance to this inherently unbalanced situation. When the evidence is contradictory, or if witnesses disagree on events or the description of a suspect, these flaws in the Crown's case should be highlighted. Space should be devoted to points that the defence raises in cross-examination. The same even-handed approach should be taken if the defence calls evidence and relegates the prosecution's case to the sidelines. *The Canadian Reporter*, a textbook used in reporting courses in many Canadian journalism schools, advises journalists to remain objective as evidence and legal arguments emerge: "Drawing too much from one side and ignoring the other can create a credible version of events—but an erroneous one. Snap judgments by a reporter are dangerous."[14]

Strive for reports that strike a balance between Crown and defence. Be on the lookout for alternative explanations or answers given during cross-examination that will add depth and fairness to stories. A Crown attorney may emphasize how an assault occurred, but details favourable to the accused may only come out under cross-examination. If the media ignore evidence that contradicts the prosecution's case or raises a reasonable doubt about guilt, they have overlooked the accused person's right to be presumed innocent. The public is poorly served by one-sided media reports that suggest acquittals are unwarranted and justice has not been served.

Track Cases from Start to Finish

Charges, accusations, and convictions often rate front-page treatment. Acquittals are sometimes relegated to an inside page or the end of a newscast, if they are reported at all. A Halifax newspaper once reported that a Nova Scotia man was charged with sexual assault but neglected to cover the man's trial two years later. News that a jury acquitted the man was published only after his lawyer contacted the paper in a bid "to have his name cleared."[15] Instances of the justice system working as intended—freeing persons that the Crown cannot prove guilty beyond a reasonable doubt—should be as newsworthy as a conviction. Media organizations should strive for consistency, reporting only on criminal cases they intend to cover from start to finish. If an arraignment is covered, fairness demands that the outcome of the prosecution be given prominence. The CBC's journalistic standards call on reporters to be sensitive to the potential damage that an innocent person may suffer if coverage is incomplete.[16]

Provide Legal Context

Journalists should explain the legal principles that apply to the case being covered. Never assume that members of the public understand how the standard of proof differs in criminal and civil cases, an accused person's right to remain silent, the presumption of innocence, and other fundamentals. Although it may not be feasible to explain such concepts in every case, prosecutions that attract widespread publicity offer an opportunity to inform and educate the public. If a court throws out damning evidence because of a violation of the defendant's Charter rights, make sure that the public understands the Charter rights involved, how they were violated, and why they are important. If the family of a crime victim criticizes the sentence handed to an offender, take the time and allot the space to explain the precedents and sentencing options that the judge faced. When politicians criticize judges for being soft on offenders, put their comments into context by explaining the rule of law and judicial independence.

Writers should seek out lawyers and legal experts who understand the law and are willing to explain its intricacies, both for attribution and in background briefings. In this era of live news coverage and instant analysis, media outlets, in their rush to be first to publish, often distort trial evidence and court rulings. Look no further than coverage of the US Supreme Court's ruling on the results of the 2000 presidential election, when television correspondents fumbled through the court's complicated judgment on-air while politicians and experts contacted for reaction were monitoring the same TV news reports for details of the ruling. The law and its nuances make poor sound bites, and legal experts are hesitant to comment on rulings they have not seen. Journalists should line up commentators in advance and provide them with copies of the rulings they are being asked to assess. Most importantly, journalists must strive to get the facts and the law straight before going public.

Mention Race, Religion, or Ethnic Origin Only When Appropriate

A defendant's race, religion, or country of origin should be reported only if it is relevant to the case before the court. Witnesses may have referred to an assailant's race when providing a description to police. Defence lawyers may claim that their clients are victims of a police crackdown on suspected members of Asian gangs, or a defendant may cite her strong Catholic beliefs to justify the illegal picketing of an abortion clinic. A convicted offender may face deportation to his homeland or a racial slur may have provoked an assault. In situations such as these, race or ethnic origin becomes an integral part of the story. But a reference to an offender as Asian or Muslim, for example, is not appropriate if the person's race or religion has nothing to do with the crime.

Avoiding Sensationalism and Distortion

Don't Promote Misconceptions About Crime

Media accounts have tremendous power to mould public opinion and can create an erroneous impression that a city or region is facing a crime wave. Studies have shown that a steady diet of crime stories makes people more fearful for their safety even when the crime rate is in decline. One study, which tracked Canadian network news coverage of homicides during 1999 and 2000, concluded that "when television news downplays crime, public fear of crime decreases. … Conversely, when coverage of [homicide in] a region increases, people there become uneasier, despite the statistical evidence that indicates that they are not in greater danger."[17] Another study, which followed two decades of press coverage of homicides in Britain up to 2003, found that murders with sexual overtones or murders committed during a robbery or theft tended to attract coverage, while killings that resulted from a quarrel were unlikely to be publicized.[18] In fact, in some years the country's major newspapers ignored four out of five cases. One criminologist has underscored the danger of media coverage that does not provide a balanced portrayal of crime:

> If the media reports that most sexual assaults are committed by strangers jumping out from behind bushes in parks, then that stereotype is more likely to be believed. … If a crime wave is constructed around kids who swarm or muggers in dark alleys with knives, then people will not worry about bid-rigging, insider trading or environmental pollution. A steady diet of sensationalistic crimes hides more mundane and harder-to-detect crimes.[19]

Of the hundreds of thousands of criminal cases that pass through Canada's courts each year, only a fraction attract media attention. These cases will be singled out because they involve serious allegations, prominent defendants, or shocking acts of violence. Others may be published because they test the fairness of the courts or establish important legal principles. In short, the public learns about cases that the media think are notable and newsworthy and important. As reporters and editors decide which cases are covered and which are ignored, they should bear in mind how their choices affect public attitudes toward crime and public safety. Take burglaries as an example—while most break-ins at empty homes are ignored, there is extensive coverage of home invasions in which the occupants are robbed and brutalized, even though these comprise a small percentage of all break-ins. The media should put crimes into context and emphasize that most offences are minor and non-violent, rather than creating a distorted impression that people are not safe in their own homes. A simple reference to statistics on break-ins or the fact that the offence is not typical would help provide a more balanced picture to the public. Harold Levy, who has combined the professions of law and journalism, has offered the following warning about the dangers of media distortion:

> The reporter of specific cases and of the criminal justice system generally has a wide range of responsibilities to the accused person, to the prosecution, to the community and ultimately to the reader to report in an accurate, balanced and informed manner. Departing from this standard can harm individuals and can create misconceptions which may lead to unwarranted public unrest and to the enactment of extreme, unwarranted policies.[20]

Portray Courtroom Drama Fairly

Court proceedings have been a staple of media reports since lurid accounts of crimes and trials began appearing in England's earliest newspapers in the 16th century. "The journalists who were feeding the early printing presses learned what all journalists have learned," notes media historian Mitchell Stephens, "that crime news is prime news."[21] The courts supply the media with a steady stream of dramatic fodder, neatly packaged and ready for publication or broadcast—tales of good and evil, acts of hatred, greed, and lust interspersed with examples of heroism and compassion. The law "shows us at our very worst, and sometimes at our very best," legal commentator Jeffrey Miller has observed. "It distills the human condition in the way of good fiction, editing out all of the 'one damn thing after another' of everyday life and shining its high beam on whether we have demonstrated grace under pressure."[22]

Good court reportage conveys the horror of a crime and the reality of court proceedings, but with restraint. Writers who unduly exploit drama and emotion run the risk of distorting reality and may expose the media as a whole to accusations of sensationalizing events to attract readers, viewers, or listeners. "Courtrooms are natural theatres of human drama and good court reporting takes the reader to the heart of the drama," *The Canadian Press Stylebook* advises, "but always with fairness and objectivity in the recording of testimony and the description of witnesses."[23]

While court business is serious business, occasionally a witty remark or humorous case will shatter the solemnity, however briefly. The inept robber who robs a bank but leaves his wallet and identification cards behind always makes good copy. A humorous comment or event may be worth reporting, but writers should not mock those involved or belittle a crime. An example of a clumsy attempt to inject humour into a court case is the reporter who poked fun at an assault victim, writing that the man "lost the tooth, the whole tooth and nothing but the tooth" after being punched in the face.[24] A violent act should never be treated as a laughing matter.

Avoid Assumptions of Error

Journalists and commentators sometimes conclude that the justice system has failed when closer examination reveals that it has not. The media should apply the same healthy skepticism to the allegations of lawyers and the complaints of crime victims—persons with a stake in the outcome of a case—as they would to a politician's criticism of a rival. Our adversarial system ensures that there will be winners and losers and journalists should cast a critical eye on the assertions of those on the losing end. The concerns of victims and other critics should not be ignored, but the media should present contrary opinions and explain the law and precedents that apply.

It is also important to ensure that the justice system is not portrayed as a monolith. If police officers or Crown attorneys make mistakes that cause a prosecution to go off the rails, responsibility rests with the individuals and agencies involved, not the system as a whole. Too often the media create the impression that the justice system failed when defence counsel, judges, or other players in the system performed their roles as intended—and perhaps prevented a miscarriage of justice.

Sentencing: A Flashpoint

When a British Columbia judge refused to put two young men behind bars for taking part in a street race that left a bystander dead, the result was a public free-for-all. Critics attacked Justice Linda Loo's decision to impose a two-year conditional sentence instead of a prison term. The media gave the victim's supporters and average citizens a forum to vent their outrage. The province's attorney general, Geoff Plant, lamented the "loss of public confidence in the justice system."

It's a scenario repeated in media coverage of cases across the country. A sentence is imposed and the media seek out the reaction of victims, politicians, and other critics, most of it negative. This time, however, a judge took the extraordinary step of writing a long letter to the editor of the *Vancouver Sun* in 2003. Judge Jerome Paradis defended his colleague and complained bitterly about the attorney general's intervention and what he considered the hysterical tone of the newspaper's coverage.

Paradis accused Plant of inciting disrespect for the courts in an effort to please voters, but he reserved much of his criticism for the "court-bashing" media. He accused the *Sun* of pandering to public opinion to boost circulation and failing to provide a detailed account of the reasons for the judge's sentence. The media use victims of crime or their survivors as "poster people to enhance the emotional appeal of the story," he wrote, and the public is being led to believe that the only fair and just sentence for a crime is one that pleases them. By doing so, he warned, the media "slowly and inexorably create in the collective mind the perception of a zealously indifferent judiciary" and "significantly erode confidence in the one institution that is constitutionally empowered to settle disputes between citizens or, far more to the point, between the state and its citizens."

Judges recognize that their decisions may be controversial, and that they may provoke criticism and even anger. "Members of the public have a right to express their views about sentences they feel do not reflect society's concerns about particular crimes. Judges should know what those concerns are," Judge Donna Martinson of the British Columbia Provincial Court noted in an article published almost a decade before Judge Paradis's outburst. "But members of the public should also be aware of all the circumstances that are considered in choosing a particular sentence so they can make an informed decision about the appropriateness of the sentence."

When an offender is sentenced, media accounts rarely focus on the substance of the judge's decision—the principles of sentencing, the penalties imposed for similar crimes, the evidence of guilt, and the prospects for rehabilitating the offender. Often these details are ignored or downplayed in the media's rush for reaction. One study of more than 800 accounts of sentencing hearings, drawn from newspapers in nine Canadian cities, found that more than two-thirds of the stories failed to mention the judge's reasons for the sentence imposed. The sentence imposed is no longer the story; the focus has become what people are *saying* about the sentence. The media have a responsibility to provide accurate, balanced accounts of sentencing decisions. Reaction to a sentence is part of the story, but not the whole story.

Two Canadian criminologists once conducted a study to determine how media reports influence public opinion. They recruited two groups that reflected a cross-section of the public. One group was given a newspaper account of a sentencing, the other a compilation of the evidence and arguments that were put before the judge. More than 60 percent of the group relying on the newspaper account thought the sentence was too lenient, compared with just 13 percent who felt it was overly harsh. In contrast, only 19 percent of the group relying on the information put before the judge felt the sentence was too lenient, compared with more than 50 percent who considered it too harsh. One of the criminologists, Anthony Doob of the University of Toronto, conducted similar experiments with other groups. The findings were consistent. As he told a 1995 law conference, "newspapers appear to make sentences look more lenient." Such findings make a solid case for more balanced media coverage of sentencings.

In the street-racing case, Justice Loo was sentencing two young men who had no record of previous criminal offences. She ordered them to spend two years under house arrest and to complete 240 hours of community service. Both men were required to serve a further three years on probation and were banned from driving for five years. The British Columbia Court of Appeal later upheld the sentence, ruling that it was "within the acceptable range" for the offence.

(Sources: Judge Jerome Paradis, "A Law-and-Order Rodeo," *Vancouver Sun*, February 18, 2003; Judge Donna J. Martinson, "Some Thoughts on Public Perceptions of the Role of Judges in the Administration of Justice in Canada," in Jean Maurice Brisson and Donna Greschner, eds., *Public Perceptions of the Administration of Justice* (Montreal: Les Éditions Thémis, 1995), 35–55, at 42; Anthony N. Doob, "Criminal Justice Reform in a Hostile Climate," ibid., 253–75, at 256–60.)

Know When To Use Graphic Language and Evidence

"The criminal court is an innately tough arena," Justice Gérard La Forest of the Supreme Court of Canada has noted. A criminal trial "often involves the production of highly offensive evidence, whether salacious, violent or grotesque. Its aim is to uncover the truth, not to provide a sanitized account of facts that will be palatable to even the most sensitive of human spirits."[25] Victims of sexual assault must describe what happened to them in precise detail. Words and photos will be used to convey the horror of a murder victim's wounds. Witnesses must repeat comments and threats as they were said or heard, complete with profanities or racial insults.

The media have always struggled to walk the fine line between reporting sensational facts about court cases and sensationalizing those facts. An early journalism textbook of the 1920s recommended that writers err on the side of caution:

> [T]he reporter should guard against writing a story that will exert an unwholesome, anti-social influence. Testimony often deals with grewsome [sic] details, minute accounts of methods of crime and vice, and illicit sex relations, which, if reproduced in news stories ... unquestionably will have a bad effect on many readers. The greatest care must be taken to present objectionable matter in such a way that it will not give offense and will not injure any member of the family when printed in a paper that goes into the home.[26]

Public attitudes have changed dramatically since this advice was offered. Television, newspapers, and magazines now bring words and images into the home that were once considered objectionable and unsuitable for a mass audience. Media outlets no longer see themselves as protective parents and audiences no longer expect to be treated like children. But writers continue to grapple with how much intimate or graphic detail to include in stories about court cases. The tabloid-style media may have few qualms about using as many details as possible. Mainstream media outlets, on the other hand, may have internal guidelines or policies that limit the use of graphic details or require the removal of profanities from quotations. In the absence of such guidance, the writer should assess the relevance of the information. Is a graphic description of a victim's wounds needed to convey the severity of the crime? Should profanity be included to preserve the context of what was said? Will the explicit details of a sexual assault help the public assess whether the complainant is telling the truth?

Dealing with the Players

It was long the practice in Canada that those involved in the justice system refused to comment publicly about legal issues and specific cases. Lawyers or Crown attorneys who granted media interviews were seen as grandstanding. Judges took the view that the impartiality of their office forced them to remain silent and above the fray. Lawyers argued their cases in the courtroom. If a judge had something to say about the law, she said it from the bench.

Times have changed. The work of the courts is attracting more media attention than ever as the Charter diverts debate over public policy and social issues into the courtroom. Judges and lawyers recognize that a rigid "no comment" policy will not satisfy media demands for facts and opinion. Media interviews are seen as an opportunity to inform the public about the justice system. Ottawa law professor David Paciocco has argued that the legal profession's traditional reticence has contributed to Canadians' waning confidence in the courts. "We have an obligation to explain in understandable terms why the system is the way it is and why we do what we do," he has written. "We would go a long way towards restoring the credibility of the administration of justice if only we would seek to explain the system to the general public."[27] Claire L'Heureux-Dubé, a former justice of the Supreme Court of Canada, once put it more bluntly: "If we don't help, how can we criticize reporters who get the story wrong?"[28]

How much help and cooperation the media receive from the players in the justice system is determined by ethical rules, communications policies, and the need to ensure that public comments do not prejudice cases or defame innocent persons.

Police

Police forces across the country provide the media with routine reports on offences and arrests. Larger forces have an officer or civilian official assigned to field media inquiries, and significant arrests and decisions to file charges are announced through press releases or at press conferences. Also, police recognize the value of news coverage of their work, using the media to make public appeals for information on unsolved crimes, to publicize photographs or composite sketches of suspects, or to alert the community that an offender who is considered dangerous has been released from prison. But the police have also been known to mislead the media or the public to aid an investigation. Detectives in Toronto once circulated a sketch of a suspect that had been deliberately doctored to resemble a man under investigation, in hopes that the bogus sketch would put pressure on their target.[29]

Privacy concerns have prompted many police forces to withhold the names of those charged with offences until the defendants are arraigned in court. It is also common for police to refuse to confirm that an investigation is under way and to withhold the names of anyone under investigation. The operational manual of the Royal Canadian Mounted Police, for example, directs that information may be provided to "accredited media" unless its release would compromise privacy legislation, an ongoing investigation, investigative techniques, or the rights of a suspect or victim of crime. The manual directs officers to withhold the names of suspects until charges have been laid and to ensure that information released to the media does not cause "injury, injustice or embarrassment to the innocent or accused." RCMP in Manitoba were ordered to pay $65,000 in damages to a businessman and his company after an officer breached these policies and tipped off three journalists about a search that did not result in charges.[30]

Police have also been criticized for releasing information that may jeopardize a defendant's right to a fair trial. Defence lawyers in Ontario have accused the police of convening press conferences to display seized drugs or weapons in order to create "an atmosphere of guilt around the accused."[31] In a guide to news coverage of the criminal justice system, Harold Levy advised journalists to be wary of the motives behind the release of information about crimes and suspects. "Although the police may have legitimate reasons for communicating with the public through the media," he cautioned, "public statements by the police can, if abused, jeopardize accused or potential accused persons by stirring up the public to support personal police views about the guilt of a particular accused person." He used the example of Guy Paul Morin, who was charged with murdering a young girl in a small Ontario town in 1984. When Morin was arrested months later, the chief of police declared the community was now "safe" and revealed information that the police knew was inadmissible in court—that Morin fit an FBI profile of the suspected killer.[32] Levy's example of potential prejudice was astute: Morin was wrongly convicted of first-degree murder and served 18 months in prison before DNA evidence exonerated him a decade later.[33]

Lawyers

British author and lawyer John Mortimer once observed that there is a fundamental difference between his two professions. "If you're a writer, you're trying to find out the truth or tell the truth. If you're a defence barrister, your business is trying to prevent the truth obtruding at all times."[34] Truth is, lawyers have good reason to be wary about what they say and when they say it, not least because their primary duty is to protect the interests of their clients. When dealing with the media, a lawyer must steer a course through a thicket of rules that govern the conduct of members of the legal profession. And lawyers, like writers, can be prosecuted for contempt of court or sued for defamation based on their public statements. Toronto media law specialist David Brown has advised his fellow lawyers to approach the making of public comments on court cases "with a caution approaching reserve, prudence and a strong dose of common sense."[35]

Until the mid-1980s, lawyers considered it unprofessional and even unethical to be interviewed in the media. Attitudes began to change in 1984, when the chief justice of the Supreme Court of Canada, Brian Dickson, challenged lawyers to help the media and the public "make sense of legal issues of current interest."[36] At about the same time, the courts recognized that silencing lawyers was a violation of their Charter right to free expression. In striking down a prohibition on media contact, an Ontario judge said a lawyer has "a moral, civil and professional duty to speak out where he sees an injustice." As well, lawyers have the expertise "to provide information and stimulate reasons, discussion and debate" on legal issues.[37]

The Canadian Bar Association and provincial law societies have introduced ethical rules that permit lawyers to speak publicly, within limits, about their cases and legal issues. Lawyers must treat prosecutors, judges, and other lawyers with the same respect and courtesy as they would inside the courtroom. Criticism of rulings or the conduct of other players in the justice system must be fair and constructive. The Nova Scotia Barristers' Society took disciplinary action in 2009 against a lawyer who had been elected mayor and complained in a media interview that the province's judges were political appointees and not the "tree shakers" needed to rule favourably on his city's claim for increased tax revenues. While a disciplinary panel condemned the comments as "intemperate" and "offensive," it ruled the profession can punish its members only for remarks made when acting as lawyers and not when serving in other capacities, such as political office.[38] Ontario's rules of professional conduct demand that lawyers encourage public respect for the administration of justice while striving to improve it. Public comments must not be made to attract attention to the lawyer or to drum up new business. Lawyers must ensure that it is in the client's best interests to release information or to grant interviews, and must obtain the client's consent before speaking publicly.[39]

Lawyers also must refrain from expressing an opinion on whether a client's case has merit. This prohibition is set out in the Canadian Bar Association's code and is reflected in the rules governing lawyers in Manitoba, Saskatchewan, and Nova Scotia. Rules in British Columbia and Prince Edward Island specify that lawyers must not comment publicly on the validity or possible outcome of a client's case.[40] Ontario's rules are less stringent, forbidding lawyers from conveying to the media any information they know will have a "substantial likelihood of materially prejudicing a party's right to a fair trial or hearing."[41] New Brunswick's handbook of professional conduct offers examples of inappropriate comments that suggest where other law societies would be likely to draw the line. Lawyers must not comment on the evidence to be presented in court, the credibility of a party or witness, or a defendant's character or criminal record. Nor can lawyers discuss possible pleas or speculate on whether a defendant is guilty or innocent.[42]

These rules serve a single purpose—to avoid the grandstanding and post-hearing press conferences that have become a feature of court cases in the United States. Canadian judges frown on the practice of arguing cases in the media and lawyers are well aware that what they say outside the courtroom may have an impact on their client's case. "A lawyer who freely expresses a personal opinion to the media about a client's case in advance of a hearing risks antagonizing the judges who ultimately hear the case," David Brown has warned. "Judges are being asked to listen to and decide upon the case, and many have little patience for counsel who attempt to preempt or influence a hearing by making advance statements to the media."[43] Given the risks and the ethical pitfalls, writers may find that lawyers are reluctant to provide background information about a case or to grant interviews. The lawyer's personal experience in dealing with the media, including whether the writer involved has proven to be reliable and trustworthy in the past, will also affect the level of cooperation. A lawyer's reticence should never be mistaken for evasiveness or seen as evidence that the lawyer or client has something to hide.

Most lawyers will accommodate media requests for information and interviews, particularly when doing so will advance a client's case. There may be times when a lawyer has a duty to speak in the public forum—for example, to correct inaccurate or misleading media coverage about a client.[44] Because broadcast journalists cannot use cameras and audio recorders inside the courtroom, much of their material is gleaned from interviews with lawyers conducted before and after hearings. Most lawyers are willing to explain the nature of the proceeding and the legal issues involved, or to summarize the arguments or evidence presented. Some lawyers will indicate that their client denies the allegations before the court, particularly if the defendant stands accused of an indictable offence and cannot formally enter a plea of not guilty until a trial date is set. Although some provinces forbid lawyers from discussing possible pleas or the merits of their case, Ontario's lawyers defeated a proposal put forward in 1999 that would have restricted their right to proclaim a client's innocence. Lawyers who handle criminal cases argued they must be able to respond to the negative publicity generated by police press conferences and media reports.[45] Edward Greenspan, a media-savvy Toronto lawyer who routinely takes on high-profile clients and causes, has urged other lawyers to employ "spin" to advance their cases: "The aim of your dealings with the media is to put forward as good an image of your client as possible in the circumstances and as good an image of yourself as a fair-minded and responsible lawyer."[46] Journalists, of course, should be wary of being manipulated by lawyers seeking to advance their careers or a client's case.

On occasion a judge will tell lawyers not to discuss a specific case outside the courtroom. In one hard-fought Nova Scotia case, a judge ordered lawyers for the Crown and defence to put an end to "reciprocating allegations of impropriety" that he feared could taint a jury. While counsel were free to criticize each other in the courtroom, he said, "there should be no reason to [do] so out of court."[47] Another Nova Scotia judge slapped a "no-interviews" order on lawyers involved in a politically sensitive wrongful dismissal suit, but backed down within days in the face of media criticism and the lawyers' request that the order be rescinded.[48] One media law text suggests that such restrictions are binding only on the parties, leaving the media free to report the comments of any lawyer who deliberately or mistakenly violates the order.[49]

Lawyers are freer to discuss cases in which they are not directly involved, but they are still bound to treat judges and their fellow lawyers with respect. Codes of professional conduct recognize that lawyers have a duty to help members of the public understand the law and how the justice system works. They can comment on the adequacy of existing laws and proposed legislation, and can discuss the issues involved in legal actions under consideration or already before the courts. Lawyers who act for special interest groups or who are experts in an area of law are free to share their views and expertise with the media.[50]

A final note about dealing with lawyers. Writers seeking legal advice about information they intend to publish or broadcast should consult their media organization's legal advisers, either directly or through an editor. It is not the job of the prosecutor or defence lawyer involved in a case to provide advice on the scope of a publication ban or whether certain information could prejudice the right to a fair trial.

Crown Attorneys

Not long ago, journalists waiting outside a courtroom for a comment from a Crown attorney were usually out of luck. Prosecutors routinely brushed off reporters' questions about witnesses' testimony, trial procedure, or how a case would unfold in the days ahead. In the 1970s a *Toronto Sun* columnist complained that Crown attorneys offered a terse "no comment" in response to straightforward requests to see documents filed with the court.[51]

Such brush-offs have become rare as Crown attorneys and their superiors recognize that ignoring media inquiries may result in one-sided news coverage and a perception that prosecutors are not accountable to the public. Crown attorneys are subject to the same ethical standards as other lawyers when they deal with the media. In addition, prosecuting agencies across the country have developed written guidelines that set out what Crown attorneys can say about their cases. Some guidelines offer general advice to avoid statements that could prejudice a case while others provide specific guidance or suggested answers to common inquiries. In general, Crowns are forbidden to discuss police investigations, possible charges, or whether a verdict or sentence is likely to be appealed. They must not discuss a defendant's character or criminal record, the credibility of witnesses, the merits of a verdict, or the strength of the Crown or defence case. Questions about prosecution policies or the shortcomings of the criminal law are to be referred to superiors or to the agency's communications officer. In cases that have attracted significant media attention, prosecuting agencies in some jurisdictions convene a press conference to announce the withdrawal of charges or a decision to appeal a verdict.[52]

The Public Prosecution Service of Canada has a media relations policy that urges staff prosecutors and lawyers acting for the federal Crown to provide journalists with "timely, complete and accurate information." The policy reminds prosecutors to avoid offering personal opinions on the merits of a case or the wisdom of specific laws or government policies. Lawyers are also directed not to reveal privileged information, advice offered to investigators or the attorney general, or whether an accused has entered into plea negotiations or is likely to plead guilty. "The goal is to foster understanding, not to create sensation," the policy advises.[53]

Nova Scotia's Public Prosecution Service invites prosecutors to view media inquiries as "opportunities to speak to Nova Scotians." But Crowns should not make statements that could prejudice a case, reveal their strategy, violate a publication ban, or be interpreted as arguing their case in the media. Nor should they reveal the existence of police investigations or comment on whether a verdict or finding might be appealed. Those exceptions aside, the policy states, "the public has a legitimate interest in hearing the Crown's side in cases currently before the courts" and prosecutors are "encouraged to respond to media inquiries about cases in which they are involved."[54]

Saskatchewan's policy tells Crown attorneys to bear in mind that, when they speak in public, they are seen as representing their department and the justice system as a whole. Although prosecutors are warned never to reveal information to the media before it is introduced in court, they can provide a "factual synopsis" of the status of their case when they emerge from the courtroom. The policy even offers tips on handling specific questions: "If the media asks for your opinion, a comment such as 'it is the Crown's job to present the evidence, the court must weigh the evidence,' can be effective in answering the question by reminding the audience what the prosecutor's job is during the trial."[55]

In British Columbia, the *Crown Counsel Act* specially mandates prosecutors to "provide liaison with the media and affected members of the public on all matters respecting approval and conduct of prosecutions of offences or related appeals." In 1998 the Criminal Justice Branch of British Columbia's Ministry of the Attorney General went a step further, assigning a Crown attorney to deal with media inquiries. The media policy for Newfoundland and Labrador authorizes prosecutors to provide explanations and factual information but draws the line at offering comments or opinions about what has occurred.[56]

Ontario's guidelines authorize Crown attorneys to explain court procedures, clarify issues that a reporter did not understand, or provide "a brief outline" of what was said in court. Further elaboration may be "unwise," it cautions, as the Crown attorney has no control over how such comments play out in the media. While the policy urges caution in most media dealings, it states that "defence counsel are not permitted to engage in unfair or misleading criticism or commentary about cases before the courts. Nothing in this guideline should be construed as preventing Crown counsel from responding by way of correction to false or misleading information being circulated in the media."[57]

A former chief justice of the Ontario Superior Court, Patrick LeSage, has urged prosecutors to draw a line between educating the public and arguing cases in the media. In his view, it is proper for Crown lawyers to respond to journalists' questions on their way into the courtroom and to distribute copies of legal arguments filed with the court, but they should not use the media to argue their case in advance of a hearing. "Explain, if necessary," he recommends, and "inform the media what your case is, but don't plead with the media. That, I can assure you, is an absolute turn-off to judges."[58]

Judges and the Courts

Judges, traditionally the most tight-lipped players in the justice system, are also speaking out. A leading proponent of a higher public profile for judges was the Supreme Court of Canada's Justice John Sopinka. "No longer can we expect the public to respect decisions in a process that is shrouded in mystery and made by people who have withdrawn from society," he warned in 1995.[59] Judges also recognize that they should not expect lawyers or politicians to come to their defence as their rulings, their conduct, and their role are debated. "The judiciary has no voice and no champion," former Chief Justice Antonio Lamer of the Supreme Court of Canada noted in 1998, expressing alarm at examples of "judge-bashing" in the media. "I would be certainly reluctant to see judges enter the political fray. ... On the other hand, I worry that there is also a risk in having judges hold their tongues."[60]

Judges are best suited to serve as champions for the judiciary. The Canadian Judicial Council adopted ethical principles in 1998 that highlight a judge's obligation to educate the public, particularly about judicial independence.[61] The Judicial Council also produced a 1999 report calling on judges to assume a leadership role in dealing with the public and the media. The document urges judges to take advantage of invitations to speak to students and community groups about the role of judges. Courts are also encouraged to develop plans to respond to unfair criticism or inaccurate media reports, either through interviews, press releases, letters to the editor, or informal meetings with journalists or editorial boards. "In the world of the Charter, judges are indeed makers of news and controversy," the report concluded. "Contact with the media ... is an appropriate mechanism for explaining the role of the courts and judges."[62]

Judges frequently give speeches at meetings and conferences that attract media coverage.[63] It has also become common for judges to grant journalists' requests for interviews, and a Supreme Court of Canada judge has fielded calls on an open-line radio show.[64] A few have even published books on legal issues and appeared on talk shows to promote them.[65] But judges will not explain or defend their rulings to journalists or in other public forums, regardless of the significance of the decision or the controversy it may create. It is a long-standing practice to allow rulings to speak for themselves; if a judge has made a mistake in interpreting the law, it is up to a higher court to correct the error on appeal. When judges speak publicly, they are also expected to steer clear of political issues, cases before the courts, and other subjects that could be seen as compromising their independence and impartiality. The Canadian Judicial Council's ethical principles advise that judges should "avoid deliberate use of words or conduct, in and out of court, that could reasonably give rise to a perception of an absence of impartiality." Among the topics that judges can freely discuss are legal principles, the impact of the Charter, the administration of the courts, and the role and conduct of judges. Also open for discussion are controversial and politically sensitive subjects that are matters of legitimate interest to the judiciary—such as judges' salaries, government funding for the courts, and the process for selecting judges.[66] Judges remain wary of media contacts, however, as comments made in interviews and other public forums have prompted complaints of bias and demands for disciplinary action.[67] An Ontario judge was disciplined in 2008 for leading a group opposed to a real estate development near his home and encouraging the media to cover the controversy. While the Canadian Judicial Council noted judges "do not surrender their rights as citizens on appointment to the bench," it warned they cannot misuse their positions and must avoid words and actions that undermine their reputation for fairness and impartiality.[68]

Many courts have designated a communications officer to help journalists locate court files and to respond to requests for information or interviews. And courts in many jurisdictions have established committees of judges and media representatives to improve communications and to resolve disputes over access to the courts.[69]

Victims of Crime

In the past, victims of crime and their families had a voice in the criminal justice process only if they testified at trial. Now, victims or surviving relatives are afforded an opportunity to address a judge before an offender is sentenced, so that they can describe the physical and emotional impact of the crime on their lives. The media provide a wider forum for victims and relatives to express their anger or frustration: reporters routinely solicit their views on the verdict or on whether the sentence imposed is adequate. One observer has accused the media of transforming victims into "the new royalty of the court system."[70]

Crime victims and their relatives and supporters have an interest in the outcome of a case, and their views are valid. What is surprising, however, is how many journalists report their comments without context or comment, no matter how bitter or outlandish or uninformed they may be. Victims and relatives are given free rein to lash out at a judge's sentence as inadequate, even when the law and circumstances of the crime clearly dictate that a longer prison term would be unjustified. No journalist should be surprised that a murder victim's family feels a stiffer sentence was warranted; indeed, it would be truly newsworthy if relatives considered a sentence to be too harsh. And although a victim's tearful plea for justice may make for riveting television or good newspaper copy, it may emphasize vengeance and denunciation of crime at the expense of other goals of the justice system—objectivity, fairness, and the rehabilitation of offenders. A Prince Edward Island judge, confronted with protesters demanding that he impose the maximum penalty for a man convicted of killing his common law spouse, offered this response:

> [J]udges and courts cannot respond to the public perception of what should be justice when the law clearly sets forth the road that the judge or court must follow. … Vengeance is not an integral part of our legal system. We are not living in a country where an 'eye for an eye' theory of justice is carried out … . I must follow the law. I cannot strike out and make new laws where the law is clear.[71]

Victims and their supporters should not be ignored in court coverage. But their views should be subjected to the same critical analysis and skepticism as any other piece of information conveyed to the public. When a victim calls for a longer prison term, the media should balance those comments by reporting the typical penalty for the offence and the judge's rationale for the sentence imposed. Reporters and editors should consider whether the trend toward victim-oriented coverage informs the public or merely exploits the emotional turmoil of vulnerable persons.

A Guide to Online Legal Resources
Basic Legal Information
Duhaime.org

Maintained by British Columbia lawyer Lloyd Duhaime, this site offers detailed information on Canadian and American law, including specific fields such as criminal law, family law, contracts, and defamation, and offers links to law-related websites in all provinces. There's even a dictionary of legal terms.

http://www.duhaime.org

Media Law and Ethics
J-Source

Also known as the Canadian Journalism Project, the J-Source site was created by Canada's journalism schools to provide news, commentary, and advice on a wide range of journalism subjects. The "Rights & Wrongs" section deals with media law and ethical dilemmas and explores the latest rulings on libel, publication bans, confidential sources, and other media-related legal issues.

http://www.j-source.ca

Legislation
Federal

The Government of Canada's website features electronic versions of the Charter and all federal statutes and regulations, including the *Criminal Code* and the *Youth Criminal Justice Act*. The legislation is in full text and searchable by keyword.

http://laws.justice.gc.ca/en/index.html

Provinces and Territories

Links to searchable, full-text versions of statutes and regulations for each jurisdiction are available through the Canadian Legal Information Institute website.

http://www.canlii.org

Rulings

Canadian Legal Information Institute (CanLII)

This fully searchable site provides free access to the full text of judgments of the Supreme Court of Canada, the Federal Court, and courts and tribunals in all provinces and territories. Coverage of current rulings is comprehensive, but access to older decisions varies from court to court. The database includes rulings of courts and tribunals that do not provide access through their own websites.

http://www.canlii.org

Quicklaw

This subscription service offers access to more than 2,500 databases of legal news and business sources and rulings of courts, boards, and tribunals in Canada, the United States, the United Kingdom, and the Commonwealth, as well as statutes and expert commentary.

http://www.lexisnexis.ca

Links to Law-Related Websites

Alan Gahtan's Canadian Legal Resources

This site provides comprehensive links to sites offering contact information for lawyers and legal experts, statutes, case law, legal publishers, law libraries, and a host of other resources.

http://www.gahtan.com/cdnlaw

Access to Justice Network Canada

This site provides legal information as well as links to the websites of Canadian law firms, bar societies, legal education societies, and other justice system organizations.

http://www.acjnet.org/nahome

Canadian Forum on Civil Justice

This site includes a list of useful links to court, government, and other law-related websites.

http://www.cfcj-fcjc.org/links

American Legal Links

FindLaw

This site provides an array of US legal resources, including news on cases and law-related issues, law journals, and links to databases of rulings from federal and state courts. Includes a search engine for finding US lawyers.

http://www.findlaw.com

Finding Lawyers and Legal Experts

Canadian Law List

Use this site, maintained by legal publisher Canada Law Book, to find the phone numbers and e-mail addresses of lawyers, judges, law professors, and law society officials across the country. Searchable by name, law firm, location, title, and legal specialty.

http://www.canadianlawlist.com

Criminal Lawyers' Association

"A voice for criminal justice and civil liberties in Canada," the Criminal Lawyers' Association offers contact information for more than 1,000 members across the country.

http://www.criminallawyers.ca

Ad IDEM

Ad IDEM—Advocates in Defence of Expression in the Media—is a national organization of media lawyers, also known as the Canadian Media Lawyers Association. The site features new developments in the law of defamation, publication bans, and access to the justice system, with contact information for members.

http://www.adidem.org

The Legal Profession

Canadian Bar Association

The CBA, a 37,000-member organization of legal professionals, lobbies for changes to the law and keeps its members informed of new developments and rulings. There are CBA branches in each province and territory, and the association is divided into sections that concentrate on specific areas of law, such as criminal, family, environmental, bankruptcy, and immigration. The site provides contact information for branches and sections, offering writers quick access to experts in specific fields.

http://www.cba.org

Federation of Law Societies of Canada

This umbrella group provides links to Canada's 14 law societies and to legal organizations in other countries.

http://www.flsc.ca

Law Schools
Jurist Canada

Designed for law professors, this site provides access to academic studies of legal issues and other legal resources.

http://jurist.law.utoronto.ca

The Judiciary
Canadian Judicial Council

This body of senior superior court judges is responsible for judicial education programs and handles complaints against federally appointed judges. The site outlines the council's activities and provides press releases on disciplinary rulings.

http://www.cjc-ccm.gc.ca

Statistics on Crime and Justice
Juristat

Juristat, a joint venture of Statistics Canada and the Canadian Centre for Justice Statistics, crunches the numbers on crime rates, charges filed, conviction rates, sentencing trends, and justice system spending. While a subscription is required to access the full range of studies, some statistics are available online without charge.

http://www.statcan.gc.ca/bsolc/olc-cel/olc-cel?catno=85-002-XIE&lang=eng

NOTES

1. Murray Campbell, "What We're Really Like," *Globe and Mail*, December 28, 2002.

2. Anthony N. Doob, "Criminal Justice Reform in a Hostile Climate," in Jean Maurice Brisson and Donna Greschner, eds., *Public Perceptions of the Administration of Justice* (Montreal: Les Éditions Thémis, 1995), 253–75, at 255–56.

3. Harry Bruce, *Down Home: Notes of a Maritime Son* (Toronto: Key Porter Books, 1988), 94.

4. Patti Tasko, ed., *The Canadian Press Stylebook: A Guide for Writers and Editors*, 15th ed. (Toronto: Canadian Press, 2008), 207.

5. "Convicted Drug Dealer Convinces Judge To Spring Accused Stabber," *Daily News* (Halifax), September 27, 2001; "Correction & Apology," *Daily News* (Halifax), September 28, 2001.

6. J.A. (Sandy) Mcfarlane and Warren Clements, *The Globe and Mail Style Book: A Guide to Language and Usage* (Toronto: McClelland & Stewart, 1998), 71.

7. Dean Jobb, *Bluenose Justice: True Tales of Mischief, Mayhem and Murder* (Lawrencetown Beach, NS: Pottersfield Press, 1993), 137.

8. Cited in Nick Russell, *Morals and the Media: Ethics in Canadian Journalism* (Vancouver: UBC Press, 1994), 65–66.

9. This principle is set out in *R v. M. (C.A.)* (1996), 105 CCC (3d) 327, at 347 (SCC).

10. *Criminal Code*, RSC 1985, c. C-46, as amended, s. 344(b).

11. This is the range of sentences imposed by judges in British Columbia. See *R v. Bernier*, 2003 BCCA 134, at paragraph 26.

12. Mcfarlane and Clements, supra note 6, at 209.

13. Tasko, supra note 4, at 208.

14. Catherine McKercher and Carman Cumming, *The Canadian Reporter: News Writing and Reporting*, 2nd ed. (Toronto: Harcourt Brace & Company, 1998), 224–25.

15. "Inquiry Date Set in Sex-Assault Case," *Chronicle-Herald* (Halifax), April 15, 1999; "Timberlea Man Cleared of Sex Crime," *Chronicle-Herald* (Halifax), June 20, 2001.

16. Canadian Broadcasting Corporation, *Journalistic Standards and Practices* (Toronto: Author, 2001), 65.

17. Lydia Miljan, "Murder, Mayhem, & Television News," *Fraser Forum*, March 2001, 17–18.

18. "Unbalanced Newspaper Coverage Is Teaching the Public the Wrong Lessons About Homicide Cases," Economic and Social Research Council press release, January 22, 2003, available online at http://www.esrc.ac.uk/esrccontent/news/jan03-5.asp.

19. Chris McCormick, *Constructing Danger: The Mis/Representation of Crime in the News* (Halifax: Fernwood Publishing, 1995), 5.

20. Harold J. Levy, *A Reporter's Guide to Canada's Criminal Justice System* (Ottawa: Canadian Bar Foundation, 1986), 14.

21. Mitchell Stephens, *A History of News* (Toronto: Harcourt Brace College Publishers, 1997), 99.

22. Jeffrey Miller, *Where There's Life, There's Lawsuits: Not Altogether Serious Ruminations on Law and Life* (Toronto: ECW Press, 2003), x.

23. Tasko, supra note 4, at 207.

24. "Man Changes Plea, Given Probation," *Daily News* (Halifax), October 16, 1990.

25. *Canadian Broadcasting Corp. v. New Brunswick (Attorney General)*, [1996] 3 SCR 480, at paragraph 40.

26. Willard G. Bleyer, *Newspaper Writing and Editing*, rev. ed. (Boston: Houghton Mifflin Company, 1923), 165–66.

27. David Paciocco, *Getting Away with Murder: The Canadian Criminal Justice System* (Toronto: Irwin Law, 1999), 9, 11–12.

28. Quoted in Pierre A. Michaud, "The Media and the Courts," address to Lord Reading Law Society, Montreal, October 6, 1994, 11.

29. Canadian Newspaper Association, "Police Give Fake Sketch to Media To Squeeze Suspect, Officer Testifies," *The Press and the Courts*, vol. 21, no. 4, August 31, 2002.

30. *Uni-Jet Industrial Pipe Ltd. v. Canada (Attorney General)*, 2001 MBCA 40. The RCMP's operational manual is cited at paragraph 11.

31. Canadian Newspaper Association, "Lawyer Says Police News Conferences Jeopardizing the Fairness of Jury Trials," *The Press and the Courts*, vol. 19, no. 5, October 31, 2000.

32. Levy, supra note 20, at 58.

33. Morin's ordeal is chronicled in Kirk Makin, *Redrum the Innocent* (Toronto: Penguin Books, 1998).

34. Dean Jobb, "Your Mr. Rumpole Could've Got Me Out … ," *Novascotian* (insert to the *Chronicle-Herald*), December 7, 1985.

35. David M. Brown, "What Can Lawyers Say in Public?" (1999), vol. 78, nos. 3 & 4 *Canadian Bar Review* 283, at 325.

36. Quoted in Beverley G. Smith, *Professional Conduct for Canadian Lawyers* (Toronto: Butterworths, 1989), 90.

37. *Re Klein and Law Society of Upper Canada* (1985), 50 OR (2d) 118 (Div. Ct.).

38. Dean Jobb, "Mayor's Remarks Against Judges Not 'Misconduct': Disciplinary Tribunal," *The Lawyers Weekly*, February 26, 2010, 1, 27.

39. Brown, supra note 35, at 291–93.

40. Ibid., at 292–93.

41. *Rules of Professional Conduct*, Law Society of Upper Canada, Public Appearances and Public Statements, rule 6.06(2).

42. Brown, supra note 35, at 296–98.

43. Ibid., at 292.

44. See, for example, *Legal Ethics and Professional Conduct: A Handbook for Lawyers in Nova Scotia* (Halifax: Nova Scotia Barristers' Society, 1990), commentary 22.15, at 99.

45. Bill Rogers, "LSUC Quietly Deletes Guideline Against Proclaiming Clients' Innocence," *The Lawyers Weekly*, November 26, 1999; Canadian Newspaper Association, "Ontario Law Society Rejects Gag Law for Lawyers Talking to Media," *The Press and the Courts*, vol. 19, no. 4, August 31, 2000.

46. Edward Greenspan, "Winning with the Media," address to the Criminal Lawyers' Association, April 4, 1998, 2, 14–15.

47. *Re "The Chronicle-Herald" et al. and The Queen* (indexed as *R v. Regan*) (1997), 124 CC (3d) 77 (NSSC).

48. Susan Hughes, "Judge Revokes Gag on Lawyers in Fiske Case," *Chronicle-Herald* (Halifax), May 16, 2000.

49. Michael Crawford, *The Journalist's Legal Guide*, 4th ed. (Toronto: Carswell, 2002), 204.

50. Gavin MacKenzie, *Lawyers and Ethics: Professional Responsibility and Discipline* (Scarborough, ON: Carswell, 1993), at 13-2.

51. Alan Anderson, "In the Matter of the Crown vs. the Press," in Barrie Zwicker and Dick MacDonald, eds., *The News: Inside the Canadian Media* (Ottawa: Deneau Publishers, 1982), 189–93.

52. See Dean Jobb, "Crownspeak," *Canadian Lawyer*, April 2003, 22–27.

53. "Principles Governing Crown Counsel's Conduct," *The Federal Prosecution Service Deskbook*, part III, chapter 10, available online at http://www.justice.gc.ca.

54. "Policy on Media Inquiries and Public Statements," Nova Scotia Public Prosecution Service, September 24, 2002.

55. Saskatchewan Justice, Public Prosecutions, "Media Relations: Guidelines for Crown Prosecutors," *Policy and Practice Directive*, June 1, 1998.

56. Jobb, supra note 52, at 24, 27.

57. Province of Ontario, Ministry of the Attorney General, "Media Contact by Crown Counsel," *Crown Policy Manual*, January 15, 1994, policy no. M-1.

58. David Gambrill, "Crown Should Explain, Not Plead, Cases in Media," *The Law Times*, September 9, 2002.

59. John Sopinka, "Must a Judge Be a Monk—Revisited," speech to the Canadian Association of Provincial Court Judges, Moncton, NB, September 14, 1995, at 3.

60. Stephen Bindman, "Judges Have 'No Voice, No Champion': Chief Justice Says It May Be Time To Break the Vow of Silence," *Ottawa Citizen*, August 24, 1998.

61. Canadian Judicial Council, *Ethical Principles for Judges* (Ottawa: Author, 1998), 10.

62. Canadian Judicial Council, *The Judicial Role in Public Information*, Report of the Special Committee on Public Information, September 1999. See also Cristin Schmitz, "Time To Go Public, Judicial Council Decides," *The Lawyers Weekly*, February 4, 2000.

63. See, for example, coverage of Supreme Court of Canada Chief Justice Beverley McLachlin's speech to the Canadian Club on judicial activism and other subjects: Joseph Brean, "Judges Not Writing the Laws: McLachlin," *National Post*, June 18, 2003.

64. Cristin Schmitz, "Iacobucci Scores a First: Appears on Open-Line Radio Show," *The Lawyers Weekly*, June 21, 2002. For examples of media interviews with judges, see Kirk Makin, "Lamer Worries About Public Backlash," *Globe and Mail*, February 6, 1999; Kirk Makin, "No Life Like It," *Globe and Mail*, January 5, 2002; Cristin Schmitz, "McMurtry Third Senior Judge To Rebuke Canadian Alliance for Attacks on Judicial Activism," *The Lawyers Weekly*, May 4, 2001; Cristin Schmitz, "SCC's Major Sees Potential Merit in Opening Appointments Process," *The Lawyers Weekly*, January 10, 2003.

65. Christopher Guly, "Judges Moving Out from Behind the Bench To Be Seen and Heard," *The Lawyers Weekly*, September 18, 2009, 26–27.

66. Canadian Judicial Council, supra note 61, at 32, 39.

67. For example, the Canadian Judicial Council investigated two complaints in 2001 after Supreme Court of Canada Justice Michel Bastarache stated in an interview that he disagreed with his court's controversial ruling on aboriginal Canadians' access to the

fishery in Atlantic Canada. The complaints were dismissed, but the judge was reminded that judges must "exercise restraint when speaking publicly." See John Jaffey, "Judicial Council Rejects 2 Complaints over Bastarache Interview Comments," *The Lawyers Weekly*, March 30, 2001.

68. Cristin Schmitz, "Matlow Stays on Bench: Media Contact OK with Limits," *The Lawyers Weekly*, December 12, 2008, 1, 15.

69. For an overview of these initiatives, see Dennis Orchard, "Involving Citizens with Courts and Tribunals: Initiatives in Canada," in Stephen Coughlan and Dawn Russell, eds., *Citizenship and Citizen Participation in the Administration of Justice* (Montreal: Les Éditions Thémis, 2001), 45–53.

70. Susan Musgrave, "A Poet's Lament" (Summer 2003), *Ryerson Review of Journalism*, 94–95, at 94.

71. *R v. Sheppard*, 2001 PESCTD 56, at paragraphs 16, 18.

CHAPTER 8

Contempt of Court

Understanding Contempt of Court

Preventing "Trial by Media"

An American satirical weekly once envisioned what might happen if guilt and innocence were decided in the court of public opinion rather than in a court of law. In an item headlined "Murder Suspect To Be Tried by Media," *The Onion* claimed that the overworked Los Angeles courts were embarking on an innovative program designed to reduce caseloads. In selected cases, the media would serve "not only as judge and jury, but also as executioner," saving time and money. In the inaugural case, a newspaper columnist, who had described a murder suspect as "human garbage who must pay dearly" for his crimes, had been selected to preside at the man's trial.[1]

Although *The Onion*'s scenario was tongue-in-cheek, the spectre of "trial by media" and its implications for the pursuit of justice are real. Justice and fairness demand that legal disputes are resolved through an impartial and reasoned consideration of the admissible evidence and the applicable law, not on the basis of rumour, spite, emotion, or popular opinion. Much is at stake for persons accused of crimes and for civil litigants; they must be assured that published comments attacking their characters, disclosing information not admissible in court, or demanding a particular outcome will not influence their fate. "If there is undue publicity or the speculation is unfair, there is a chance that eligible jurors who read the newspaper or look at television will be prejudiced before the trial even starts," explained a former Supreme Court of Canada justice, Willard Estey.[2] Without limits on what is said publicly about a case, the court process would become superfluous. "Why have a trial when the press knows (and is only too willing to disclose) the answer to the very question the jury will be asked to decide?" one observer has asked. "Moreover, as public pressure grows, it becomes increasingly difficult for a court to ignore the clamor and do its duty."[3]

Guilt and innocence are matters for judges and juries to decide, and courts have the power to punish—with a fine or a jail term—anyone who usurps their role or attempts to influence the outcome of a case. This power under the common law flows from the judge's duties to ensure a fair trial, to protect the rights of the parties involved in a case, and to uphold the integrity of the administration of justice—in short, to ensure that justice is done. While Canadian court proceedings are open to public scrutiny, the law of contempt insulates the process from outside influences by imposing restrictions—temporary restrictions, for the most part—on what can be written or broadcast about them.

Contempt: A Grey Area of the Law

The courts' centuries-old power to cite for contempt is preserved under section 9 of the *Criminal Code*—the only common law crime still in force in Canada.[4] The Code, however, does not define the offence, making this a troublesome and intimidating area of the law for anyone writing about court proceedings. The distinction between legitimate accounts of court proceedings and contemptuous ones is not always clear. Legal texts invariably describe the law of contempt as nebulous and vague—cold comfort for anyone pondering what they can publish or broadcast with confidence.[5]

The publication of certain information, however, is clearly high-risk. Any suggestion that a suspect is guilty as charged—if published before a court has passed judgment—is likely to invite a contempt action. Revealing the criminal record of a person accused of a fresh crime, disclosing the fact that a suspect has confessed to police, and publishing other evidence that may never be presented in court are the acts most likely to be punished as contempt. The status of the case within the legal process is also an important factor. In the words of an Ontario judge who found a newspaper in contempt, "it's a question of timing."[6] Information published at the time of a suspect's arrest, such as the person's previous criminal convictions, is unlikely to be fresh in the minds of jurors when the case comes to trial many months later. Publication of the same facts immediately before or during a trial would pose a much greater risk of influencing a jury and is far more likely to be punished as contempt. But judges are reluctant to wield their formidable contempt powers, so prosecutions are relatively rare in Canada. As one media law text observes, technical breaches of the law of contempt "will not inevitably lead to a prosecution. The timing and character of the breach, the size of the community, the place of publication or broadcast or whether the matter is to be decided by a judge or a judge and jury can all have a bearing."[7] As a result, there are relatively few court rulings to offer guidance to writers.

To add to the uncertainty, the law of contempt in Canada has undergone dramatic changes in recent years and remains in a state of flux. News organizations have become bolder in their coverage of court proceedings, pushing traditional limits on what can be reported and when. "Once upon a time there was innocence until proven guilty … and the media didn't trade in wild speculation, innuendo and rumour before a trial," Klaus Pohle, who teaches media law at Carleton University in Ottawa, has noted. Yet media reports on murder and sexual assault charges against a high-ranking military commander in early 2010, in his view, portrayed the suspect as "the devil incarnate" and included reports the man had confessed and led police to a victim's body. "Given the feverish coverage," he noted, "is there anyone out there who still believes him to be innocent?"[8] At the same time, judges have recognized that their decisions must be open to criticism and that media-savvy jurors are able to think for themselves. The line between what can and cannot be published has become a moving target, and to complicate matters, courts in different jurisdictions draw the line at different places. Courts in some areas tolerate or ignore the publication of information that judges in other jurisdictions view as prejudicial and grounds for contempt.[9] Courts and prosecutors in Western Canada tend to take a harder line on what constitutes prejudicial pre-trial publicity. According to one study, 24 contempt prosecutions were launched against the media in Canada between 1985 and 1999. Alberta and British Columbia each accounted for 5 prosecutions, almost half the total.[10] The best defence for those writing about the courts or court cases is to have a thorough understanding of the law of contempt, how it is evolving, and where it is most likely to be enforced.

Defining Contempt

In the absence of a statutory definition, contempt remains a creature of the common law. Its essence and scope are found in court judgments that have shaped the offence since it was first invoked by a British court in 1631. The classic definition—one Canadian courts often cite with approval—comes from *R v. Gray*, a British case decided at the turn of the 20th century:

> Any act done or writing published calculated to bring a Court or a judge of the Court into contempt, or to lower his authority, is a contempt of Court. … Further, any act done or writing published calculated to obstruct or interfere with the due course of justice or the lawful process of the Courts is a contempt of Court.[11]

A 1960s Canadian judgment offers a more modern and concise definition, stating that contempt encompasses "any conduct that tends to bring the authority and administration of the law into disrespect or disregard" or tends to "interfere with or to prejudice" parties or witnesses involved in a case before the courts.[12]

Such affronts to the court process can be committed directly or indirectly. Acts of contempt committed directly include disrupting a hearing or refusing to answer questions on the witness stand. A writer's refusal to testify or to reveal the identity of a source would be an act of direct contempt, an issue that was examined in Chapter 5. This chapter will focus on what is sometimes termed **publication contempt**—indirect or external acts of contempt committed through the publication of information that is not part of a court proceeding, or that attacks the character of a participant in a legal action.[13] Another form of contempt, one committed by breaching a court-ordered ban on publishing specific information, will be examined in Chapter 9.

Prejudicing Court Cases: The Sub Judice Rule

The courts have created two distinct forms of publication contempt. The first is designed to protect cases that are *sub judice*, a Latin term meaning "under a court" or "before a court or judge for consideration."[14] Courts have a duty to ensure that published accounts of cases do not misrepresent the proceedings or prejudice the parties involved until the case has been adjudicated, or decided. This is known as the ***sub judice* rule**. To quote a British judgment from the mid-1700s, "there cannot be any thing of greater consequence, than to keep the streams of justice clear and pure, that parties may proceed with safety both to themselves and their characters."[15] Published information does not have to create prejudice against a defendant to be considered a contempt. Reports that interfere with the trial process by causing undue delay and expense or "by creating an appearance of substantial unfairness at any stage of the proceedings" may lead to a conviction for contempt, a British Columbia court noted in 1987. "This will be so regardless of prejudice to the accused."[16]

Canadian courts have set a high standard for judges to apply when deciding whether a published report has the potential to taint the "streams of justice." To be contemptuous, British Columbia's Court of Appeal has stressed, a publication must "present a real risk, as opposed to a mere possibility of interference with the due administration of justice."[17] In the words of Britain's House of Lords, "the prejudice must be more than trifling or trivial but less than a certainty."[18]

Whether such declarations clear up the uncertainty that pervades the law of contempt is open to debate. "What information will, if published, cause real prejudice to the administration of justice?" asks media law scholar Robert Martin. "The honest answer is that no one really knows for sure."[19] Allegations of contempt through publication are assessed on a case-by-case basis and courts take into consideration all surrounding circumstances, making it vital that reporters and editors are able to weigh the risks before publication.

Lord Reid on Publication Restrictions

In a 1974 judgment, Lord Reid of Britain's House of Lords offered the following rationale for restricting publicity surrounding cases that are before the courts:

> I think that anything in the nature of prejudgment of a case or of specific issues in it is objectionable not only because of its possible effect on that particular case but also because of its side effects which may be far reaching. Responsible "mass media" will do their best to be fair, but there will also be ill-informed, slapdash, or prejudiced attempts to influence the public. If people are led to think that it is easy to find the truth, disrespect for the processes of the law could follow, and, if mass media are allowed to judge, unpopular people and unpopular causes will fare very badly. ... I do not think that freedom of the press would suffer and I think that the law would be clearer and easier to apply in practice if it is made a general rule that it is not permissible to prejudge issues in pending cases.

(*Attorney-General v. Times Newspapers Limited*, [1974] AC 273, at 300 (HL).)

Criticism of Rulings, Judges, and Courts: Scandalizing the Courts
The second form of publication contempt looks beyond individual cases and is concerned with upholding the reputation of the court process. Courts traditionally have considered it a contempt to publish comments that may undermine the reputation of

an individual judge or court, or that could erode public confidence in the fairness of the entire justice system. This brand of contempt is known as **scandalizing the courts**.

Judges, however, do not enjoy a licence to punish their critics or to stifle debate about their rulings. In the words of the seminal case *R v. Gray*: "Judges and Courts are alike open to criticism, and if reasonable argument or expostulation is offered against any judicial act as contrary to law or to the public good, no Court could or would treat that as a contempt of Court."[20] A Canadian court has made clear that the offence of scandalizing the courts is not designed to protect judges from scrutiny, but to "prevent interference with the due course of justice, and to prevent suitors from having their confidence in the court shaken or destroyed."[21]

The highest Canadian court to consider a scandalizing allegation since the introduction of the *Canadian Charter of Rights and Freedoms* found that the offence violates the guarantee of freedom of expression. The Ontario Court of Appeal's 1987 ruling observed that courts must be subject to vigorous, even unreasonable, criticism of their work. In the words of Justice Peter Cory, courts "are not fragile flowers that will wither in the hot heat of controversy."[22] Although the ruling is not binding on courts outside Ontario, some commentators believe that it has sounded the death-knell for the offence of scandalizing the courts in Canada.[23] Extreme, unfounded attacks on the motives or integrity of judges and courts, however, remain open to contempt proceedings.

Sub Judice Contempt in Criminal Cases: Assessing the Risks

To find solid ground in the midst of this uncertain area of the law, the writer must assess an array of factors. The stage of the court proceedings, the nature of the published information or opinions and their potential to undermine a fair trial—all determine whether a publication carries the risk of contempt.

Is There a Case Before the Courts?

Unless there is a court case to prejudice, there can be no contempt. So the writer's risk of committing an act of contempt arises only when a live case is under the jurisdiction of a court. In criminal cases, the *sub judice* rule comes into play the moment an individual is accused of a specific offence. The line is crossed once someone is arrested, when police or prosecutors formally file charges, or when a justice of the peace or a judge summons an accused to appear in court or issues a warrant for a suspect's arrest. In the United Kingdom, the risk of contempt arises as soon as it becomes clear that an arrest or charge is "imminent."[24] Although this practice has not been extended to Canada, media lawyer Stuart Robertson advises that once it becomes evident that a prosecution is about to be launched against an individual, "a reporter would be prudent to ensure that any statements made will not interfere with a future proceeding."[25]

Before a prosecution formally commences, other legal concerns may come into play. Writers must exercise great restraint when writing about allegations of wrongdoing that involve the reputation of an individual. A person who is accused of a crime, identified as a suspect, or reported to be under investigation for an offence may have grounds to sue for **defamation** if no charges are laid or the allegations turn out to be unfounded. During an investigation, police may question and even arrest people who have no connection to the crime; media reports naming them as suspects or suggesting they are guilty could be highly defamatory. In 2004 a jury ruled that a television station defamed a Nova Scotia man by airing footage of his arrest at gunpoint shortly after the September 11, 2001 terrorist attacks on New York City and Washington, DC. The station was ordered to pay $42,500 in damages and legal costs for reporting that the man was "being watched by police" in connection with the attacks, an allegation that proved false.[26]

Reports on Arrests and Charges

Is the Suspect Linked Directly to the Offence?

For the presumption of innocence to have any meaning, persons charged with crimes must not be convicted in the media—and in the public mind—before a court passes judgment on the allegations against them. Contempt law and journalistic standards have come a long way from the 19th century, when newspapers brazenly declared suspects guilty as charged. An example is a crime report published in 1875 that oozes prejudice: "The murder was evidently premeditated. ... He has been ill-treating his wife for some time. He was not given to drink but was an innate fiend."[27]

This is the most blatant way to prejudice someone's right to a fair trial—telling the world, flat out, that the person committed the offence. Compare the impressions created by the following two headlines, which appeared over the same Canadian Press story about a British Columbia man charged with using stolen debit cards to defraud $1.2 million from bank accounts. The *Vancouver Sun* headlined the story "Debit-Card Scam Leads to 100 Charges." This headline reports the facts—a fraud has been committed and a suspect has been charged. On the Canada.com website, the same story appeared under the heading "Debit Fraud Artist Faces 100-Plus Charges." By referring to the suspect as a "fraud artist," the second headline jumps the gun and declares the man guilty as charged.[28] An Alberta weekly also jumped the gun when it ran a front-page report that a suspect had been charged in the murder of a teenager named Moen, under the headline "Moen Murderer Arrested."[29] In a similar vein, a Nova Scotia newspaper managed to proclaim a suspect's guilt and possible innocence in the same breath through the ill-conceived headline "Thief Pleads Not Guilty."

Prejudice can be created in more subtle ways. Prominent criminal defence lawyer Edward Greenspan tells of a Toronto newspaper that published a list of murders "solved" by police while a client charged with one of the crimes was still awaiting trial. Despite the newspaper's wishful thinking, the man was acquitted. Greenspan has accused the media of disregarding the principle of presumption of innocence by describing those charged with crimes as "the gunman, the holdup man, the killer, thus implying that that individual is the proven perpetrator of the crime before there is an actual guilty verdict."[30]

Journalists should endeavour to distance the person accused of the crime from the crime itself. A published report can outline the charges filed, reconstruct events before and after an offence, and describe in detail the crime scene and the investigative work of the police. But the act at the heart of the charges—the shooting, theft, kidnapping, or other crime—should be attributed to an unspecified "man," "woman," or "suspect." The accused person should be identified in a separate paragraph, and is typically described as charged "in connection" with the incident or as the person "alleged" to have committed the offence. One strategy is for writers and editors to approach crime stories as if the person charged is not the perpetrator—in other words, put the presumption of innocence into action. "Read a story with this mindset," *The Globe and Mail Style Book* suggests, "and any prejudicial information or implications of guilt fairly jumps out."[31]

One newspaper's coverage of a stabbing death provides a good illustration of how to insulate named suspects from their alleged crimes. The paper revealed that the victim and the man accused of his murder lived in the same rooming house. In an interview, the suspect's wife confirmed that the men were drinking together on the night of the murder. The fact that police had found the suspected murder weapon—a large kitchen knife—near the scene was duly reported. Withheld from the account, however, was a damning piece of information: a large knife was missing from the suspect's room.[32] That information, if published, would have forged a direct link between the suspect and the crime and suggested that the man was guilty.

Interviewing Witnesses to a Crime

Writers are free to interview and quote anyone who witnessed a crime or has information about an offence, even though such sources will likely become important witnesses at trial. "The courts frown on amateur investigations of crimes by reporters," notes media law expert Michael Crawford. "But a factual presentation of the events can still be produced."[33] In a 1950s case, a court refused to cite two Vancouver newspapers for contempt for running stories quoting eyewitnesses to a hostage-taking and describing the assailant as a "crazed gunman." One paper took the precaution of not naming the man under arrest while the other identified the accused in the concluding paragraph. The judge said that the stories were "factual reports" of what the witnesses saw and that they expressed no opinion on the suspect's guilt. "It is the business of newspapers to gather and publish information to their readers of matters of public importance," the judge noted, "and that right will not be interfered with unless the higher right of the Courts to determine the guilt or innocence of an accused is thereby prejudiced or interfered with."[34]

After a high-profile arrest, journalists often seek out shocked neighbours or co-workers, who almost invariably describe the suspect as quiet or unassuming. The published assessments tend to be positive because the comments of people who feared that the suspect was a walking time bomb or a threat to others, if published, would invite an action for contempt.

Quoting Police Sources

Law enforcement agencies may make public statements during the course of their investigations, either to confirm that a probe is under way or to report on its progress. In high-profile cases or at the conclusion of a major probe, it has become common for investigators to hold a press conference to reveal who has been charged and the allegations they face. Bundles of illegal narcotics, seized weapons, or other evidence may be displayed for the benefit of the cameras. If a suspect is at large or considered dangerous, a description or photograph may be circulated to the media to help apprehend the person.

Publication of this kind of factual information does not create a risk of contempt. The substance of the charges, the duration of the probe, the investigative agencies involved, how many witnesses were questioned, the evidence seized—such details are routinely disclosed in media accounts. But statements made by police, like any other public comment on a case before the courts, should not impute guilt or attack a suspect's character. Writers should proceed with caution if investigators stray from a "just-the-facts" approach and offer opinions on the strength of their case or the character of those charged. At a police press conference called to name suspects rounded up in a crackdown on drug trafficking, for example, it could be risky to quote an investigator who denounced all drug pushers as "scum" or "lowlifes" who prey on schoolchildren. Although the words may be intended as a comment on the morals of traffickers in general, a court could view such inflammatory statements as prejudicial to those named in the charges.

In a leading case on contempt arising from a police statement, an officer was convicted for issuing a press release announcing charges against a Montreal firm under the city's food-safety bylaws. The release noted that the force's organized crime section was involved, promised that more charges would be filed "in the near future," and said that the firm's owners had been observed in the company of "many well known American Mafia figures." Though no action was taken against Montreal newspapers that published the accusations, Quebec's Court of Appeal made it clear that a contempt charge could be brought against a third party who "helped or encouraged" the publication of such prejudicial information.[35] That case dates to the early 1970s and there now seems to be greater tolerance for police statements that implicate suspects, at least at the arrest stage of a prosecution. At a post-arrest press conference in 2004, the chief of an Ontario force displayed a photograph of a man charged with first-degree murder and stated: "Ladies and gentlemen, this is not just a murderer. This is the most despicable of criminals. This is a child murderer." The comment was widely reported and generated some public debate over whether it could prejudice the suspect's right to a fair trial. But no contempt proceedings appear to have been contemplated against the police chief for making the statement or the media for reporting it.[36]

A Suspect's Criminal Record and Reputation

Reporting Prior Convictions
It is a fundamental principle of our criminal justice system that people are punished for what they have done, not for who they are. Everyone charged with an offence, regardless of his character or past conduct, is entitled to the presumption of innocence and so a finding of guilt must be based on fact rather than reputation. One judgment has described the strict limits on the use of a criminal record at trial as "one of the most deeply rooted and jealously guarded principles of the criminal law."[37]

Jurors may never learn that the person on trial has previously been convicted of a crime. In fact, a prosecutor or police witness could trigger a mistrial by merely suggesting that the defendant has a criminal record. This information can be revealed only if the accused person chooses to testify. Even then, the judge must consider the relevance and prejudicial impact of the defendant's record and may order that all or some of the prior convictions be suppressed.[38] A defendant's conviction for a minor crime such as shoplifting, for example, would have little bearing on his trial on a charge of murder and would likely be excluded as evidence.

This is why Canadian courts have long considered it highly prejudicial for the media to publish the criminal record of someone charged with an offence. Some courts take a zero-tolerance approach; a typical example is the 1987 contempt conviction of a Winnipeg newspaper for revealing the criminal histories of two men just two days after they were charged with murder.[39] In 1990, *Alberta Report* was convicted and fined $5,000 for a story published 10 days after a law professor was charged with murdering his wife. The magazine described the "explosive, moody and unpredictable" accused as possessing "a hair-trigger temper" that had earned him the nickname Rambo among students. The story also revealed a previous conviction for a criminal offence involving a shotgun. In the judge's opinion, such "irresponsible journalism" portrayed the accused as "a person of very bad character, capable of committing the crime with which he was charged" and created a "real and substantial" risk of interference with the course of justice.[40]

The British Columbia Court of Appeal takes the position that it is "a grave contempt" for anyone to publish "before or during a trial, any statements, comments, or information which reflect adversely upon the conduct or character of an accused person, or to suggest directly or indirectly that he has been previously convicted of any offence."[41] An Alberta judge has drawn a distinction between publication of "anecdotal accounts and opinions" of an accused person's neighbours or friends and details of a criminal record:

> A criminal record ... represents judicial pronouncement upon prior conduct; it is likely to be given considerable credence and weight by members of the community and, accordingly, its publication poses a much more significant and substantial risk to a fair trial.

The judge went on to say that the publication of the criminal record of any accused "who is not at large and does not constitute a danger to the community" is, on its face, a contempt of court.[42] Statements that a defendant consorts with criminals, has a bad reputation, or is "known to police"—a hackneyed staple of crime reporting—likely fall into the same category.

At what point the disclosure of a criminal record becomes a contempt of court, however, is no longer clear. The information is not secret—a journalist need only review court files, search a media database, or contact the National Parole Board to reconstruct someone's criminal history. In some jurisdictions, the media have begun publishing details of an accused person's criminal record upon arrest, taking the position that there is little risk of prejudicing a trial that is unlikely to be held for a year or more.[43]

The practice has become routine in Ontario and Nova Scotia.[44] Crown decisions not to prosecute newspapers and broadcasters for aggressive coverage of high-profile defendants appear to have emboldened the media in each province. In 1993 Ontario's attorney general decided that it was not in the public interest to prosecute media outlets over their investigations into the background and character of then-accused double-murderer Paul Bernardo. And in another case, in 1998, the Halifax media reported that a man charged with several brutal assaults in Halifax was an American fugitive who had killed his mother. Nova Scotia's justice department circulated a letter warning media outlets of the potential prejudice but turned down a request by the defendant's lawyer to prosecute for contempt.[45] Manitoba, too, has become more tolerant of media reports disclosing a suspect's criminal record at the time of arrest. A 2004 media law workshop, sponsored by the Canadian Judicial Council, was told that Manitoba authorities have shown "no inclination to initiate contempt citations where … the publication of the prior record is restricted to the time period immediately following the laying of charges or the arrest of the accused."[46]

When the *Globe and Mail* revealed the criminal past of a man charged in 1999 with a string of rapes in the Toronto area, the newspaper felt compelled to explain its decision to readers. "Traditionally that was beyond the pale," wrote crime reporter Sean Fine. "Reporting a criminal record was seen as tantamount to saying the accused lacks credibility. If he did this other terrible thing, he must have done the new one. … The rules have changed."[47] But change has not been uniform. The risk of being prosecuted for disclosing a defendant's criminal record has become akin to the value of real estate: It depends on location. "What flies in a big city may not fly in a small town," cautions one lawyer who specializes in media law. "Publication contempt is still a roll of the dice and may depend more upon where a newspaper is published than the content of a publication."[48]

The Alberta courts, for example, have routinely punished the media for disclosing an accused person's criminal record, even at the time of arrest. The only daily newspaper in the northern Alberta community of Fort McMurray was convicted of contempt in 1995 for publishing two stories disclosing that a man charged with murder had a prior conviction for assaulting the victim. The front-page stories appeared the day after the man was arraigned on the charge, under the headlines "Father Says Daughter Was Being Stalked" and "Accused Murderer Had Attacked Woman Before: Court Document." In the judge's view, disclosure of the criminal record "served no useful community, social or legal purpose" and the risk of prejudice to a fair trial "was an almost virtual certainty." The paper and two of its editors were found in contempt and fined a total of $5,000.[49]

More recently, in March 2000, the *Sun* newspapers in Edmonton and Calgary were fined $5,000 for revealing that a man charged with the murder of a four-year-old boy had been previously convicted of assaulting the child. The stories, published two days after the man was charged, questioned the decision of provincial child welfare authorities to return the boy to the man's care despite the assault. The judge characterized the coverage as "highly inflammatory" and "a clear example of 'trial by newspaper,'" adding:

> Common sense leads inevitably to the conclusion that the accused beat the child to death—that he is guilty. … Were a juror to read these articles, I am satisfied that it would be extremely difficult, if not impossible, to disabuse himself/herself of the idea—conscious or subconscious—that the accused killed the child.[50]

The convictions and fines were overturned on appeal, however, signalling an easing of this hard-line approach. A January 2003 ruling of the Alberta Court of Appeal cited several factors as reducing the risk of prejudice: the limited circulation of both newspapers in Red Deer, where the trial would be held; the expected delay between publication and trial; and the likelihood that the man's criminal record would have become evidence at trial. While "some risk" existed, the court ruled, "that risk was not of the seriousness targeted by criminal contempt." A key factor was that neither paper offered home delivery in Red Deer, minimizing the potential impact on the jury pool. Publication of an accused person's criminal record closer to the date of trial and "in the locality from which the jury pool is drawn," the court warned, "would almost invariably result in a finding of contempt, because the harm caused both to the administration of justice and the fairness of trial would be obvious."[51]

Given the divergent approaches that have developed across the country, journalists must understand how prosecutors and courts within their jurisdiction view pre-trial disclosure of an accused person's criminal record. If there is uncertainty about local practice and attitudes, it is vital to seek legal advice before publishing details of a person's criminal record at the time of arrest.

Escapees, Parole Violators, and Sexual Predators

Some exceptions to the criminal record taboo appear to be recognized in all jurisdictions. When an escapee is captured and charged with being unlawfully at large, it is permissible to report that the accused was in prison and for what crime; this background information is an integral part of the new charge. The same logic applies to the arrest of offenders charged with crimes committed behind bars, and to offenders who have violated probation, parole, or the terms of a conditional sentence imposed for a previous conviction. When a parolee is charged with a fresh offence, the media routinely report that the suspect was on parole and for what crime. Police forces sometimes issue public alerts identifying convicted sex offenders who have been released from prison after serving their sentences but are still considered dangerous. If these persons are arrested and charged with new crimes, it is common for media reports to reveal the offender's criminal record and the fact that an alert had been issued. It is increasingly risky, however, to repeat details of such previous offences as the date for trial approaches.

Prosecutions on Unrelated Charges

It is considered proper to report that a person accused of a crime is also before the courts on other charges that are unrelated to the case at hand. There is a vast difference between reporting unproven allegations in a related, ongoing case and reporting a previous conviction, which carries the stigma of a finding of guilt. A judgment call, however, may be in order before publication—for example, is it relevant or even newsworthy to reveal that a businesswoman charged with fraud is also before the courts on a charge of driving while impaired? Relevance and ethical considerations, not the law of contempt, may determine whether such information is published.

Confessions and Statements to Police

Publishing the confession or other damning admission of a person accused of a crime carries a high risk of prejudice, no matter who hears the words. And if suspects admit their guilt to a police officer or other authority figure, the risk is even greater because there is no guarantee that the confession will be admitted in court. Judges must convene a *voir dire* hearing to examine where, when, and how a confession was obtained, to ensure that the accused was not pressured or threatened to make an incriminating statement. If a judge rules that the statement was voluntarily made, the Crown can introduce it as evidence at trial.

In the meantime, publishing details of an accused person's admissions—or even revealing that a confession or statement to police exists—would undoubtedly be considered a contempt of court. Confessions are considered so prejudicial that a provision of the *Criminal Code*, section 542(2), forbids publication of the fact that a confession has been presented as evidence at a preliminary hearing. An Ontario newspaper was found in contempt in the 1950s for publishing a story that a man charged with fraud had "allegedly admitted" to selling advertisements for a bogus magazine. The judge viewed publication of the information, which came from a senior police officer, as a "direct interference" with the right to a fair trial.[52] The judge also found that the use of the word "alleged" did not reduce the risk of prejudice, ruling that, "to the reader it clearly means that the accused had admitted to the police officer that element [of the offence] that entered into the question of his guilt."[53]

Linking Suspects to Crimes: A Case Study

"Holly Murder Suspect ... BUSTED," blared a fat headline on the front page of the June 21, 2003 edition of the *Toronto Sun*. Forty days after someone abducted and murdered 10-year-old Holly Jones, then dumped her dismembered body in Lake Ontario, Toronto police made an arrest. Michael Briere, a 35-year-old computer software developer who lived a block from the girl's home, was charged with first-degree murder.

His arrest set off a media frenzy, one that provides insights into where Canada's media draw the line when reporting on crime. In high-profile, sensational cases, news coverage at the time of arrest is forging a close connection between crimes and the persons accused of committing them.

Coverage of Briere's arrest was intense. The *Sun* devoted 12 pages to reports on the arrest and community reaction. Nine news stories and columns appeared in the *Toronto Star*. In the *Globe and Mail* and the *National Post*, the story dominated the front page and earned a two-page spread inside.

All four papers quoted police chief Julian Fantino's statement that Briere "became more and more obvious" as a suspect during the investigation. The *Star*, *Sun*, and *Post* went further, reporting that Briere was among a small group of neighbourhood men who refused to provide a DNA sample. Readers were told that police officers had him under surveillance for two weeks and recovered a soft-drink can he discarded, giving them traces of saliva to be tested for DNA. Officers who visited his apartment observed green mats that appeared to match fibres found on the girl's body, the papers disclosed.

Police withheld Briere's photograph for three days, buying time to search for witnesses who might recognize him from the night of the murder rather than from media reports. In the meantime, the picture emerging in the press was not pretty. Neighbours described him as quiet, a loner, a computer nerd. Inquiries in his hometown, Montreal, revealed that he had been raised by a single mother who was in ill health and emotionally unstable. His dreams of becoming an actor or stand-up comic had fizzled. And although Briere had no criminal record and was not listed on Ontario's registry of sex offenders, his ex-wife described him as obsessed with violent video games and slasher films. The local video store furnished reporters with a list of 184 movies Briere had rented, ranging from the gore of *American Psycho* to the romantic schmaltz of *Kate and Leopold*. On June 28 the *Globe* reported that he had spent more than $100 on Internet pornography in the month Holly was killed.

Sun columnist Mark Bonokoski boldly contemplated Briere's guilt and compared him to one of Canada's most notorious killers. "If Briere is indeed her killer, then it is impossible to look upon him in any other way than that of a depraved sicko reminiscent of Paul Bernardo," he opined on June 23. "It's a prejudgment that's inescapable."

There were also the requisite stories and columns expressing a collective sigh of relief. "Holly's Neighbourhood Comes to Life After the Arrest," read a typical headline in the *Sun* on June 23. In the avalanche of media accounts, one of the few notes of caution was sounded in response to a *Star* poll, published June 25, that asked readers whether the arrest made them feel safer. "I would just like to point out that in our system this man is innocent until proven guilty," said a Mississauga man. "So I will feel safer when someone is actually convicted of the crime."

Whether this aggressive reporting and blunt commentary prejudiced Briere's right to a fair trial became a moot point. He pleaded guilty to first-degree murder in June 2004, admitting that he abducted and killed Holly Jones after viewing child pornography.

Pre-Trial Phase

Proceedings in Open Court

The well-established principle of open justice demands that what happens in the courtroom is the public's business. All information presented in court at any stage of a criminal case may be published, as long as there is no statutory or court-ordered ban on its publication. Everything that takes place while court is in session is publishable—discussion of procedure and dates for upcoming hearings, any information, testimony, or evidence presented, the legal arguments of counsel, rulings by the judge.

As will be examined in Chapter 9, however, publication bans are likely to prevent or delay publication of evidence presented during the pre-trial phase of a prosecution, to suppress information that could prejudice a fair trial. As well, in jury trials, there is an automatic ban on publishing information presented at *voir dire* hearings held in the jury's absence.

Court Documents

The contents of case-related documents can also be published once the papers have been filed with the court registry or submitted as evidence in the courtroom. There is no risk of contempt in disclosing the basic facts set out in the charging document, or information—the accused person's name, occupation, and address, the time and place of the incident, the identity of the victim, and the wording of the *Criminal Code* or other statute that the Crown alleges has been breached.

If police seize evidence in the course of an investigation, the search warrant and its supporting documents are filed with the courts. This information is open to public scrutiny, but its publication may pose a serious contempt risk for journalists. Search warrant files disclose the offence under investigation and describe in detail the evidence implicating the suspect—information that could be highly prejudicial if the person is before the courts on charges.

Timing: How Close Is the Trial?

This may well be the single most important factor to take into consideration when assessing the risk of contempt. The same information that was made public without repercussions when an offence was committed, such as the accused person's reputation or criminal record, is likely to be viewed as prejudicial if republished shortly before or during a trial. The rule of thumb is that the contempt risk increases as the date of trial approaches and is highest when the trial is under way.[54] The reasoning is that people selected for jury duty are unlikely to recall the details of media reports that appeared up to a year or more before trial. "The passage of time tends to make memories dim," one judge has noted, "and it frequently occurs that even where there has been wide publicity at a much earlier stage, a court does not consider that a fair trial will be impaired."[55]

So how does the writer determine whether it is too close to trial to safely publish certain information? The Supreme Court of Canada was asked to decide whether news reports that appeared 9 to 10 months before a Winnipeg murder trial had the potential to influence the jury. Despite "some media speculation" on the background of the man accused of the murder, the court ruled that the pre-trial coverage did not pose a realistic risk of destroying the impartiality of jurors, in part because the trial was held "a substantial period of time" after the information was published. The court also stressed the nature of the coverage, which focused on the search for the body and the involvement of the victim, a pimp known as Tommy T., in killings in the United States.[56] In another case, an Ontario man claimed that pre-trial coverage of his prosecution for murdering his common law wife would taint the jurors at trial. The Ontario Court of Appeal described most of the coverage as factual reports of court proceedings leading up to the trial. The lone exception was a news story, published three days after the homicide, based on court records of the couple's custody dispute. The man was accused of committing violent acts and threatening the victim—information that the court viewed as "potentially prejudicial" and not admissible as evidence at trial. However, the fact that the information was published almost two years before trial provided "an adequate antidote against any realistic possibility of prejudice." The court added that it was "farfetched" to suggest that jurors "would remember, much less be prejudiced by," such coverage.[57] The same court has ruled that intense media coverage of an Ontario police officer's murder a year before the trial of the alleged killer was too remote to have any impact on the trial.[58]

In covering court cases, timing is everything. Any potentially prejudicial information that a writer proposes to publish should be assessed with an eye to the date of trial. The more months between publication and trial, the better. If a contempt prosecution is triggered, it will ultimately become a judge's decision whether enough time will pass to insulate the upcoming trial.

Will the Accused Stand Trial Before a Jury?

When assessing the contempt risk of publishing information not already before the court, an overriding consideration for journalists is whether the accused person will stand trial before a jury. "A chemist would not make a test with test tubes contaminated with waste materials," Edward Greenspan has noted. "The minds of the jurors are the test tubes of the judicial system. They must be kept clean of extraneous matter if justice is to be done."[59] Unlike judges, citizens chosen for jury duty are not accustomed to ignoring information from outside sources when assessing the evidence presented in court, nor are they expected to be completely immune from such influences. As the Supreme Court of Canada cautioned in *Dagenais*:

> Impressions may be created in the minds of the jury that cannot be consciously dispelled. The jury may at the end of the day be unable to separate the evidence in court from information that was implanted by a steady stream of publicity.[60]

For this reason, if a defendant is to be tried by a jury, there is a far greater risk that a court will find that a published report creates real prejudice and make a finding of contempt.

The courts have other means to insulate the trial from potentially damaging publicity. If a case has been the subject of extensive or sensational coverage, the defendant has the right to apply for a change of venue—to have the trial held at another location within the province or territory, where jurors are less likely to have been exposed to the coverage. The process is used sparingly, however, since it entails delays and additional costs. Each juror swears an oath to decide the guilt or innocence of the accused person solely on the evidence presented in court. Jury candidates can be questioned to find out what they know about the case and whether they can assess the evidence with an open mind. In the course of a trial, judges frequently remind jurors to disregard anything they may have heard about the case through the media. If necessary, the judge can issue specific instructions that certain information or past media reports must be ignored. But such measures may not alleviate concerns that published information has tainted the process. One judge used the example of the headline "Fugitive

Was Adept Liar," which appeared at the time of a suspect's arrest. If the same headline appeared during a trial, the judge said, the defendant might not receive a fair trial "because certain impressions will have been created which the jury may not be able to dispel despite the strongest form of judicial direction to disregard what has not been placed in evidence before them."[61]

Mark Twain once remarked that the only drawback of the jury system was "the difficulty of finding twelve men every day who don't know anything and can't read."[62] Given the media's pervasive presence in modern society, it is unrealistic to expect jurors to have no advance knowledge of the case before them. The Supreme Court of Canada has recognized this, taking the position that "negative publicity does not, in itself, preclude a fair trial" in jury cases. In a 1995 ruling arising from the deadly Westray coal mine explosion in Nova Scotia, the court said the definition of an impartial jury must take into account the realities of media coverage and the procedures available to screen jurors for bias: "It comes down to this: in order to hold a fair trial it must be possible to find jurors who, although familiar with the case, are able to discard any previously formed opinions" and will reach a verdict "based solely on the evidence presented at trial."[63] In another case, a Newfoundland judge refused to stay the prosecution of a man charged with abusing boys at the notorious Mount Cashel orphanage, even though seven of the man's accusers had told their stories at a public inquiry broadcast province-wide on television. Careful questioning of jurors and instructions from the bench to disregard such publicity, the judge ruled, would neutralize any damage.[64]

As early as 1968 an Ontario report on civil rights expressed "grave doubts" that media reports disclosing evidence before trial create "a real risk" of tainting jurors. "Vicious and inaccurate gossip and rumour" spread through a community, it suggested, are more likely to cause damage to a defendant's case than "a fair and accurate report by news media."[65] Studies of juror bias have concluded that, while people soon forget most of the facts they hear or read about cases, graphic or lurid details and information about a suspect's past crimes or bad character tend to stick in their minds.[66] Despite these findings, one judge of the Supreme Court of Canada has described the possibility that pre-trial media coverage will taint a jury as "highly speculative." Another conceded that "extensive publicity can prompt discussion, speculation, and the formation of preliminary opinions in the minds of jurors," but added the courts should rely on "the good will and good sense" of individual jurors to ignore information not presented in the courtroom.[67]

Although these studies and rulings suggest that Canadian courts are becoming more tolerant of pre-trial publicity, even in jury cases, it remains prudent for journalists to exercise extreme caution and avoid publication of material that could be seen as influencing a jury. The issue in both the Westray and Mount Cashel cases was the impact of pre-trial publicity, not whether media outlets should be prosecuted for contempt. The law books are laden with contempt-law precedents in which judges underscore the necessity of shielding potential jurors from prejudicial publicity.

Logic suggests that there is less risk of contempt in publishing information about cases that will not be heard by a jury. Judges pride themselves on being immune to publicity; in court they routinely decide whether evidence is admissible and, if it is not, they are expected to banish it from their minds when reaching a verdict. "Our entire system of non-jury trials is built on the theory that judges can ignore highly prejudicial and inadmissible evidence," noted a 2009 judgment of the Ontario Court of Appeal.[68] Trial by judge alone, however, does not give journalists free rein to publish whatever information they consider newsworthy. Were that the case, a Quebec court has observed, it "would open the doors to general and unlimited confusion and interference with the judicial machine from anyone," undermining the independence and impartiality essential to the proper administration of justice.[69] Another court said it would be "exceedingly dangerous" to allow the media to publish whatever comments they pleased simply because the trial will be heard by a judge sitting without a jury. Disclosure of information not before the court can place judges in an awkward position and may, unconsciously, influence their decisions.[70] That was the case in March 2000 when a judge declared a mistrial after the *Ottawa Citizen* revealed the criminal record of the accused in the midst of a trial for attempted murder. Even though there was no jury, and even though the accused's past might never become part of the evidence, the judge said a mistrial was necessary to preserve "the appearance of fairness." The newspaper was asked to explain its actions but was not prosecuted for contempt.[71] An Ontario appeal court upheld another judge's decision to stay a charge of failing to provide a breath sample after a newspaper ran an editorial describing the case as "open and shut" and calling for a conviction. The judge said the editorial placed him in an untenable position and made a fair trial impossible: "If I convict, it could well be perceived that I was bowing to pressure," the judge complained. "If I acquit, it can be perceived that I overreacted."[72]

The distinction between jury and non-jury trials may be of little help to the journalist, particularly in the early stages of a prosecution. The right to a jury trial is available for murder and most serious crimes—the kinds of cases most likely to attract media attention. As well, an accused person may choose trial by jury at the outset and re-elect to be tried only by a judge closer to the date for trial. If so, the reduced risk of prejudicing a non-jury trial would have to be weighed against the increased danger of publishing prejudicial information closer to the date of trial.

Sensationalism and Presentation

How information is presented is a factor in whether it is likely to be considered prejudicial. Reports about a crime or an accused person that play high in a newscast or are given sensational treatment are more likely to raise concerns about creating prejudice. In one case, a judge decided that there was no need to fine a newspaper for a contemptuous report that was "not given any great prominence or published in a provocative way."[73] At the other end of the spectrum would be a lurid, front-page report delving into the previous misconduct of the accused. A related factor is the notoriety of the case—the more high-profile and newsworthy the crime, the more likely the information could influence people who may wind up on the jury.

The Supreme Court of Canada has observed that it would be impossible to formulate rigid guidelines for assessing the potential of pre-trial publicity to influence a jury. But the court has said that a distinction can be drawn "between mere publication of the facts of a case and situations where the media misrepresents the evidence, dredges up and widely publicizes discreditable incidents from an accused's past or engages in speculation as to the accused's guilt or innocence."[74]

Information Favourable to the Accused

Defendants, either personally or through their lawyers, often proclaim their innocence on the courthouse steps or reveal their intention to plead not guilty; such comments can be published without risk of contempt and may add needed balance to accounts of pre-trial proceedings, which tend to be dominated by the prosecution's side of the story. The defence may go further and publicly criticize the tactics of the police or prosecution, or complain of being unfairly targeted. The publication of such comments is unlikely to pose a risk of prejudicing the defendant's right to a fair trial, but journalists should still consider what weight and credence to give to them.

Photographs and Video Images of the Accused

A key issue at trial may be identification—the defence may seek to show that witnesses have mistakenly identified the accused as the person seen committing the crime. As a result, in a few cases the courts have ruled that it is prejudicial to publicize pictures of the accused. If the suspect's face becomes widely known through media reports, the thinking goes, the images may influence witnesses who are not certain that the accused is the person they saw. This poses a dilemma for the media, which routinely depict an accused person using police mug shots, file photos, or archived video footage, or through fresh images of the person entering or leaving the courtroom. It may not become clear until trial that identification is a factor in the case.

Contempt prosecutions on this basis are rare, but British Columbia's highest court issued a recent warning that this form of contempt is far from dead:

> It seems not uncommon for newspapers and television programs to portray the accused, sometimes in prison garb, being hustled by a group of officers from a steel doorway to a secure vehicle or vice versa. Such scenes are capable of creating a real risk of prejudice. That may be particularly so when the pictures are shown shortly after arrest when they carry the risk of compromising identification issues and of conveying the message that "the police have got their man."[75]

Although other courts may not take such a strict approach, editors should be cautious about publishing a likeness of the accused if the prosecution or defence has made it clear that identification is in dispute.

The Trial Stage

Republishing Background Information on the Case

In reports on a case as it proceeds through the courts, care must be taken when repeating information about a crime or investigation that was published when the accused was arrested or charged. As noted, timing is a crucial factor in assessing whether information has the potential to create prejudice. It is also risky to regurgitate eyewitness interviews or crime-scene accounts, because this information may be inaccurate or inadmissible as evidence. The risk is greatest on the eve of a jury trial, when media outlets often publish or broadcast a background story in advance of the start of the trial. An example is a television news report on the start of a major cocaine-smuggling trial in British Columbia. One of the accused was described as the ringleader of the operation and "the subject of numerous police investigations over the years involving drugs and stolen property mainly, but no significant charges have stuck so far." The report was found to be in contempt and, in the opinion of the province's Court of Appeal, a clear example of a report that creates a real risk of prejudice.[76]

Once a jury is empanelled and the trial is under way, screening jurors and other procedural safeguards are no longer an option to deal with the publication of prejudicial information. In the words of one court, "the contempt power is more readily invoked during a trial, after a jury is chosen, because it is then almost the only weapon remaining in the judicial arsenal to assure justice for all."[77]

Disclosing the Accused's Criminal Record

Disclosing the accused's criminal record shortly before or during the trial, unless the information is put before the jury in open court, is likely to cause a mistrial and is almost guaranteed to bring a contempt charge. A television news program was found in contempt for reporting that a man on trial for murder had been previously convicted of shooting a prison guard during a hostage-taking incident. The station also aired file footage of the previous incident.[78] Another TV station pleaded guilty to contempt for reporting, on the opening day of a trial, that "a convicted murderer" known as the "Abbotsford Killer" was back in court.[79] In 2005 the *Prince George Citizen* and two of its journalists were found in contempt for publishing details of a suspect's criminal record on the day the man's jury trial on new charges was set to begin. In levying $12,000 in fines, a judge noted "there was no delay at all between the publication and trial" and it was unlikely the man's criminal record would have been admitted as evidence.[80]

Retrials and Parole Reviews

Retrials are a sensitive area, because reporting that the accused was convicted of the same charges but won a new trial on appeal, or rehashing evidence from the first trial, could influence the second jury. The fact that an accused was previously convicted of the crime is not admissible evidence. A Kamloops, BC newspaper caused a mistrial by reporting that a man on trial for murder had been convicted of the killing two years before but had won a new trial on appeal.[81]

Parole reviews similarly require careful handling by journalists. Section 745.6 of the *Criminal Code* permits those convicted of murder and those who have served 15 years of a life sentence to apply to the courts for early release on parole. The application must be heard by a jury. When the procedure was first used in the early 1990s, the *Edmonton Journal* and three of its employees were convicted of contempt for publishing details of a convicted murderer's crime on the day that a jury was empanelled to hear his application for early release. Alberta's Court of Appeal later overturned the conviction, ruling that there was no prejudice because the newspaper's story only contained information that the jury would later hear in court.[82] But had the report gone further and expressed an opinion on whether the offender should be granted early release, the appeal court likely would have viewed the story in a different light.

Portrayals of the Accused and Security Measures

It is not considered contemptuous to report that the accused is in custody pending trial, or to show images of the defendant under guard. How the information is presented, however, may make a difference. If the accused is portrayed as someone who had to be locked up to protect the community, there may be a risk of prejudicing the jury. According to one ruling, such reports must not be seen as "reflecting adversely upon the conduct or character of the accused or as suggesting that he had previously been convicted of an offence."[83]

Descriptions of security measures not seen by jurors, such as the accused in handcuffs, also may pose a risk. One court has offered some guidance on this point by observing that the risk of contempt increases with the scale of the security efforts. If the authorities felt it necessary to surround the courthouse with a heavily armed SWAT team, for example, it would "unavoidably carry an implication that the accused is a dangerous criminal."[84] At the other end of the spectrum, the media frequently report on routine precautions, such as screening spectators with metal detectors before they enter the courtroom. A judge concerned about the risk of prejudice has the power to impose a ban on publication of the details of security measures. This was done in an Ontario case, and a newspaper that reported that the accused was "led away yesterday in handcuffs and leg irons" was found in contempt for disobeying the court order.[85]

Information Not Before the Court

When a trial is in progress, writers must guard against the disclosure of information that has not been aired in court. A British Columbia newspaper pleaded guilty in 1997 to contempt for reporting what a key Crown witness, a police officer, said during a discussion in the courthouse corridor while a murder trial was in progress.[86] In another case, a judge declared a mistrial after the *Globe and Mail* reported that a man accused of extortion was linked to a motorcycle gang—a fact that did not form part of the case before the jury.[87]

The maximum penalty for a conviction set out in the *Criminal Code* should not be reported during a jury trial, as this information is never presented to the jurors. The maximum penalty, which is rarely imposed, may lead jury members to believe that the accused's crime is more serious than it actually is.

Reaction and Followup Stories

It is extremely risky to publish stories that solicit reactions to what is happening in the courtroom or provide additional information to flesh out the evidence presented. Such reports may be seen as an attempt to enhance the credibility of a witness or to undermine a defendant's case. In one case, a reporter followed up on the revelation at trial that a drug courier's bag, containing a large amount of money, went missing after being inspected by RCMP officers. In the subsequent story, published in the midst of a jury trial, a police spokesman was quoted as saying that an internal investigation had found no wrongdoing on the part of the officers involved. The presiding judge rebuked both the journalist and the police spokesman but the trial continued. Another court later denounced the interview as an improper attempt to bolster the credibility of police witnesses and an exercise in damage control conducted without regard to the fairness of the trial.[88]

Journalists may also be tempted to wade into issues in the midst of a trial without a jury. For example, consider the following Nova Scotia case, in which a man charged with sexual assault exercised his right to cross-examine his accuser. The man, who stood accused of the violent attack, subjected the female victim to more than six hours of questioning. Media reports promptly examined the issues involved, including the accused's right to a full defence, legal aid cutbacks that have increased the number of defendants forced to represent themselves, and amendments before Parliament to enable defence counsel to be appointed for such questioning. The media also reported the complainant's outrage at the "mockery of the justice system," the Nova Scotia justice minister's description of the questioning as "like double rape," and criticism that the judge should have done more to protect the woman.[89] The fact that the case was not before a jury was undoubtedly a major factor in the media's decision to publish while the trial was still in progress. But a similar media frenzy in the midst of a jury trial would be unlikely, given the far greater risk of contempt.

Followup reports on any controversy during trial could be seen as an attempt to interfere with the trial, even one without a jury. Writers are free to investigate such matters, and the results can be safely published after the jury retires to deliberate or the trial is over. When a key Crown witness posted comments on the Internet during the 2005 trial of three youths charged with murdering an Ontario boy known only as Johnathan, the *National Post* prudently waited until the jury had begun deliberations before publishing the information. The comments, which suggested that the witness had perjured herself, prompted the judge to declare a mistrial. By publishing the information at the proper time, the newspaper was able to inform the public—and have a profound effect on the case—without being accused of tainting the jury.[90]

Comment on Evidence and Proceedings

Some journalists, led by columnist Christie Blatchford of the *Globe and Mail*, have produced colourful and opinionated accounts of trials, peppered with personal reactions to what happens in the courtroom. One Blatchford column, typical of the style she developed while writing for the *National Post*, described a woman seeking early parole for strangling her young son as a "child-killing, baby-making sex machine." When the woman testified, Blatchford wrote of having to suppress the urge "to leap into the witness box and slap her hard across her pretty face."[91] This personalized "play-by-play" approach is a new trend in Canadian journalism, assessing the evidence and the conduct of courtroom players with a critical eye. Blatchford once offered a less-than-flattering critique of traditional reporting on court cases:

> Historically, court reporters merely report what the witnesses of the day say and what the lawyers ask them. … Add a few lines about the demeanor of the accused ("He sat impassively in the prisoner's box" is a classic) and any remarks the judge might make, and you have the typical story.

This "objective" formula, she added, does not ensure fairness and may lack the context needed for an accurate portrayal of what is happening in the courtroom. Blatchford has used the term "informed observation" to describe her approach, and says she strives to ensure that her comments are based solely on what is said or done in court. "Whatever conclusions I might draw are conclusions that any of the jurors might also reasonably have reached."[92]

Blatchford's work has raised concerns among some defence lawyers and judges, who accuse the media of eroding the right to a fair trial—"usurping the jury's function," in the words of prominent Ontario defence counsel Irwin Koziebrocki.[93] The issue became the subject of public debate in late 1999, when *National Post* media columnist John Fraser suggested that these "melodramatic" accounts of trials could be considered a contempt of court. In his view, judges and lawyers have become "more forbearing, even timid," but he quoted an anonymous judge as predicting "a terrible reckoning one day," when the courts realize they have been too lenient.[94] A month later, then-chief justice Patrick LeSage of Ontario's Superior Court of Justice voiced his concern about "the general content and tone" of some newspaper reports on criminal cases. He urged Ontario's attorney general to "take appropriate action when required" to ensure that the right to a fair trial is not jeopardized by "inappropriate comments and opinions before the case is concluded."[95] LeSage later implored journalists to "stick to the facts" and avoid expressing opinions that could taint or "poison" the minds of jurors or even judges, who can be "intimidated, cajoled, pressured or improperly swayed, like everyone else."[96]

Blatchford wrote a column in response, accusing judges of paying lip service to the notion that jurors can think for themselves and will honour their oaths to decide cases on the basis of the evidence. "Every day, in the criminal courts across Canada, judges sing the praises of jurors. They laud their collective common sense and life experience," she wrote. "And then the judges proceed to treat them like children in short pants."[97] Although LeSage's comments fall far short of a "terrible reckoning," the media have been put on notice that Canada's judges are closely monitoring how trials are covered. The jury is still out on how far writers can go in commenting on a trial-in-progress without inviting a prosecution for contempt. Straightforward factual reporting carries no risk. Commentary may carry some risk, depending on whether a court might see the opinions as prejudicing the accused, prejudging the issues, or otherwise interfering with the trial. Ridiculing a witness or speculating on the motives of the prosecution or defence is clearly dangerous. Blatchford's practice of drawing the line at commenting solely on what jurors have seen or have been told is clearly a prudent approach.

Opinions on Guilt or the Accused's Character

The line also must be drawn at expressing an opinion on the accused's guilt or publishing comments that could be seen as goading a court to return a particular verdict. In the words of a former Ontario chief justice, "no judge or juror should be embarrassed in arriving at his decision by an expression of opinion on the case by anyone."[98] In a 1991 case that clearly crossed the line, a columnist was convicted of contempt after describing a trio of murder defendants as "violent, base persons" in the midst of a jury trial. The column also described one of the accused as a "small-time cocaine dealer" and noted that the trial had exposed "the sleazy underbelly of Oshawa's parasitic drug culture." While no mistrial was declared, the newspaper, its publisher and managing editor, and the columnist were ordered to pay the defendants $5,000 in costs.[99]

It is also dangerous to attack or ridicule the accused. British Columbia's highest court considers it a contempt for the media to "comment adversely or at all upon the strength or weakness" of an accused person's defence.[100] Consider the following case in point. A front-page Blatchford column appeared in the *National Post* in September 1999, headlined "A Butcher Asks Jury To Believe His Story." The column appeared nine months into Taghe Savojipour's murder trial and just days before the judge was to charge the jury. The facts were horrific—the victim, a teenage boy, had been raped, murdered, and dismembered. Savojipour testified that two thugs forced him to commit the rape and claimed they murdered the boy; he admitted cutting up the corpse, an act that explained the "butcher" reference in the headline. Blatchford described the defence as "bizarre" and ridiculed Savojipour's clumsy attempt to explain away DNA evidence linking him to the victim's body.[101] Defence lawyer David Bayliss complained that the headline and column amounted to "an argument for conviction" and portrayed Savojipour's defence as "simply unbelievable." At the defence's request, the judge questioned each juror to gauge the column's impact. It turned out that two jurors had read the column and five others were aware of it, but all of them assured the judge that Blatchford's comments would not influence their assessment of the evidence. The case proceeded and the jury convicted Savojipour of first-degree murder.[102] Defence counsel sought to have the newspaper cited for contempt, but no action was taken.

Interviewing Prosecutors and Defence Counsel

Prosecutors and defence lawyers can be interviewed as a criminal case progresses and during the course of a trial, but journalists should be aware that what they are willing or able to say may be limited. Law societies in each province and territory have established ethical guidelines that recognize the importance of disseminating accurate information through the media to improve public understanding of the justice system.[103] Counsel for the Crown and defence are free to explain courtroom procedure and the legal issues before the court. But lawyers, like the media, are at risk of being cited for contempt if their words prejudice a case that is *sub judice*. As a result, counsel are careful to avoid questions about the strength of an opponent's case, whether a particular witness is believable, or the likely outcome of a proceeding. The Law Society of Upper Canada's guidelines, for example, forbid lawyers from conveying information to the media or making public statements that have "a substantial likelihood of materially prejudicing a party's right to a fair trial or hearing."[104] In addition, defence counsel must have the consent of the accused before speaking to the media and must be satisfied that such contact is in the client's best interests. Prosecuting agencies across the country also have policies that limit what Crown attorneys can say about cases before the courts. The Public Prosecution Service of Canada, for example, warns Crown attorneys not to argue their cases in the media and directs that "all comments which prejudice the right of an accused to a fair trial must be avoided."[105]

Some judges have cautioned counsel to make their arguments in the courtroom, not on the courthouse steps.[106] During one high-profile trial, the judge criticized counsel's practice of holding daily press conferences to put their spin on the evidence, saying this practice had given the public a distorted view of the proceedings. In another case, the judge, fearing that a bitter war of words being waged outside the courtroom could taint the jury, threatened contempt action if the sides continued to accuse each other of improper conduct.[107] In the face of such warnings from the bench, counsel often err on the side of caution and merely repeat what has already been said in the courtroom or in documents filed with the court.

Publishing Related Stories

In rare cases, judges have taken the media to task for publishing stories about issues that are the subject of an ongoing trial. In one instance, the *Ottawa Citizen* published a feature on a child abuse case in the United States while a local woman was on trial for the murder of a toddler. The presiding judge rejected a defence motion for a mistrial but criticized the newspaper for displaying "colossal poor judgment" in running the report, which dealt with allegations similar to those before the court. The judge's recommendation that the Crown bring a contempt charge against the newspaper was never pursued.[108] Care should also be taken in positioning stories—running an account of a murder trial alongside a feature story decrying the rising homicide rate could be seen as prejudicial.

Publication During a Jury's Deliberations

Section 648(1) of the *Criminal Code* imposes a ban on publication of all evidence and legal issues presented at *voir dire* proceedings in the jury's absence. The ban expires as soon as jurors leave the courtroom to begin their deliberations, because jurors are sequestered while they try to reach a verdict and so are isolated from media reports. Unless a judge extends the ban and orders the media to delay publication until a verdict is reached, the media are free to report information about a case once the jury is sequestered. A judge acquitted a Vancouver newspaper of contempt for reporting, during a jury's deliberations, that the man on trial for murder was a suspect in another killing. In the judge's opinion, "publishing prejudicial material after sequestration but before verdict does not present a real and substantial risk of trial unfairness."[109]

Books, Plays, and Television Dramas Based on Court Cases

Contempt concerns may arise in the publication of a work based on a court case—a non-fiction book, a novel, a stage or radio play, a television documentary, or a movie-of-the-week. For example, a book published at the conclusion of a high-profile murder trial may disclose details of the evidence against a co-accused who has yet to stand trial. Fictional accounts also carry the risk of prejudice. A television drama based on real-life events, for example, could create a risk of prejudice to ongoing cases based on similar facts. An example is the *Dagenais* case, which arose from the National Film Board production of *The Boys of St. Vincent*, a fictionalized account of child abuse at a Roman Catholic orphanage. As discussed in Chapter 3, the mini-series was scheduled to air on CBC Television in late 1992, just as an Ontario jury was set to begin deliberations at Dagenais's trial on charges of abusing young boys at a Catholic training school. A judge granted an injunction preventing the program from being aired anywhere in Canada until the trial and the upcoming trials of three co-accused were completed. The Ontario Court of Appeal narrowed the scope of the ban to prevent broadcast within Ontario and by a Montreal station serving the area where the trials were held.[110] The Supreme Court of Canada later ruled even this ban was too broad, since the Dagenais jury could have been sequestered and steps could have been taken to minimize the prejudice to the other defendants, including delay or moving their trials.[111]

The crucial factor for a court is timing. James Keegstra, the Alberta schoolteacher convicted of promoting hatred against Jews in the classroom, obtained an injunction in 1985 to prevent the CBC from broadcasting a television drama about an Ontario teacher who advocated anti-Semitism in the classroom. The judge who blocked the show from being aired in Alberta described it as "a thinly disguised characterization" of Keegstra—whose conviction was under appeal at the time—and a possible contempt of court. Alberta's Court of Appeal lifted the injunction, however, ruling that there had been no real risk of prejudice because the outcome of Keegstra's appeal was unknown and a new trial, if ordered, would not be held for at least three years.[112] The situation had changed by 1992, when the same court upheld an injunction against the staging of a play featuring a hate-mongering teacher named Jim Keegstra. By now the real Keegstra had won a new trial, which was under way when the play's promoters asked the court for a ruling on whether they could be held in contempt. In the court's view, the risk of prejudice was now real. Even though the performances were scheduled for small venues in Edmonton and Calgary, some distance from the site of the trial in Red Deer, Alberta, the court noted that promotional efforts and theatre reviews would bring the production to the attention of a wide audience, possibly even jurors hearing the case.[113]

Writers may be able to take precautions to avoid the threat of contempt or the expense of a court battle to try to strike down an injunction. Delaying release of the work until all related trials have ended is one option. In the fall of 2003, Random House Canada published a book on biker gangs but delayed its distribution to bookstores in Nova Scotia, where members of the Hells Angels motorcycle gang were awaiting jury trials. Customers within the province were still able to purchase the book through the Internet.[114] Another approach is to revise the manuscript to remove references to persons still before the court or evidence suggesting their guilt. A 1986 book on Helmuth Buxbaum's sensational trial for the murder of his wife was set for publication while one of Buxbaum's co-accused was awaiting trial. The co-accused sought an injunction that would have blocked publication or forced the publisher to alter the text at enormous cost. The author had taken the precaution of not naming the co-accused in the book, a factor that figured prominently in the judge's refusal to grant the injunction. The judge also said the courts should not block republication, in book form, of information already widely disseminated through media coverage of a trial.[115]

Post-Trial Coverage

Once the courts have completed their work, there is no longer a case to prejudice. The risk of contempt virtually disappears once the accused pleads guilty, a court delivers a verdict, or the judge stays the prosecution or accepts a Crown motion to dismiss or withdraw all charges. But a few precautions are still in order. If the accused pleads guilty or is convicted, the law considers the case to be *sub judice* until the offender has been sentenced. In the period between conviction and sentencing, care should be taken when publishing information or editorial comment that could be seen as an attempt to influence the judge's decision on the appropriate punishment. Examples would be reporting evidence of an accused's bad character that may never be put before the sentencing judge or an editorial demanding a harsh penalty. In a 1997 case, a judge delayed the sentencing of a man convicted of sexual assault, citing a spate of publicity in the small community of Williams Lake, BC. The local paper ran an editorial, a man-on-the-street feature, and a column written by a local politician, all demanding a jail sentence. The judge said the comments were "wrong headed," possibly contemptuous, and went beyond legitimate comment on court proceedings. "An impartial reader, and certainly the accused in this case, would be justified in concluding that the paper and the politician were trying to influence me in the decision I am about to make."[116]

At the appeal stage, the risk of contempt is considered to be at an end. "Appeal judges are supposed to be less easily influenced by the press than are juries or, for that matter, lower court judges," notes one media law guide.[117] Although a retrial could be ordered by an appeal court, this is only a possibility. Timing is also a factor—it will be months before an appeal court reviews the case and, if a new trial is ordered, it will be many more months before it is held.[118] If a new trial is ordered, however, the *sub judice* rule once again applies to the case.

Contempt of Court and the Internet

The proliferation of blogs and social-networking sites and tools on the Internet means information about crimes and suspects—as well as opinion, rumour, and speculation—can be distributed quickly and easily. While the courts have dealt with violations of publication bans on the Internet, as explored in the next chapter, it is less clear how the law of contempt of court applies in cyberspace. Information about a crime or an offender posted to the Internet, even if published long before a trial, "is always accessible, right up to the time of the trial," Ontario's Court of Appeal noted in a 2009 ruling on publication bans. The permanence of material published online and the ease of finding it using a search engine mean judges concerned about the potential impact of prejudicial information on jurors "cannot always simply rely upon the fact that time will have passed from when the information was first published and that this passage of time will lessen any prejudicial effects of the information." One of the judges hearing that case suggested it was "no longer appropriate or realistic" to assume jurors will no longer remember what they have read or heard about a case by the time a trial is held. "Once something has been published, any juror need only 'Google' the accused on the Internet to retrieve and review the entire story." The court offered no opinion on what this means for enforcement of the law of contempt of court.[119]

Courts and police have responded to specific concerns about Internet publications that could have an impact on a case before the courts. In a 2006 ruling on a motion to move a trial to another community due to pre-trial publicity, for instance, an Ontario judge was asked to consider the impact of blog posts that speculated on whether the man facing trial had killed his wife. The judge dismissed the concerns, noting: "A reading of the material on that author's website is enough to persuade me that no right thinking individual would consider the source to be credible." The judge also noted there was no evidence the blogs had been read by anyone in the area where the trial would be held.[120] Ontario police investigated a Facebook group set up in 2007 after a North Bay woman was charged with infanticide. Contributors posted comments describing the woman as a "babykiller," "sick," and "twisted," and encouraging people to attend her next court appearance to express their "hate" for her. The investigation was prompted by fears for the woman's safety, rather than concerns over possible prejudice to her right to a fair trial, and the site's administrator voluntarily deleted the offensive comments and began to screen postings.[121]

Material published on Facebook and other personal websites does not appear to carry the same weight—or create the same level of concern—as a media report. By quoting or reposting this material, however, a media organization could lend credibility to information and opinions and, in turn, raise concerns about prejudice to a case before the courts. When assessing the contempt risk of reproducing material gleaned from the Internet, the factors to be taken into consideration remain the same—the nature of the information, the timing of publication, and whether a jury will hear the case.

Defences

Truth is not a defence to an allegation of contempt. If the information published or broadcast is true—for example, that the accused has a record of committing violent acts—its publication would be all the more damaging to the trial process. Erroneous or false information also may be contemptuous if it has the potential to interfere with the right to a fair trial. In 1992 the *Barrie Examiner* was found in contempt for a front-page headline that said a man on trial had confessed to raping and murdering a woman; a mistrial was declared and the paper was fined $2,500 because the accused had admitted only to killing the victim.[122]

A court can convict for contempt even if the offending publication does not result in a mistrial.[123] It is also no defence to show that a police officer or prosecutor provided the prejudicial information.[124] Similarly, it is not a defence to claim that the prejudicial information was simply reproduced from another publication or broadcast. Contempt can also arise from prejudicial information or comments relating to a case made in Parliament, in a provincial legislature, at a meeting of a municipal council, or during an unrelated court proceeding. Although qualified privilege prevents those who publish comments made in such forums from being sued for defamation—an issue examined in Chapter 4—the protection does not apply to the law of contempt of court.[125] If a politician rose in Parliament to proclaim that an accused person is a notorious criminal and guilty as charged, the politician and anyone publishing the comments could be cited for contempt.

Robert Martin, an advocate of more rigorous news coverage of the courts, has downplayed the seriousness of a conviction for publication contempt. If the writer is engaged in "serious professional reporting" and acts in good faith, he suggests, it is unlikely that a contempt conviction "will result in his career being ruined." Instead, he argues, "It might well make someone's reputation."[126] It is equally possible, however, that a writer found in contempt will earn an unwanted reputation for carelessness and disrespect for the law.

In any event, it appears that publishers have more to fear from the law of contempt than do writers. Traditionally, the courts have cast a wide net in punishing those responsible for contemptuous publications—editors, publishers, and the publishing company have been convicted as well as the reporter. This approach is changing, however, as judges recognize that the offence is committed when prejudicial information is published, not when it is written. A BC judge endorsed this rationale in a 2001 ruling that dismissed a contempt charge against a newspaper reporter who "played no role in the decision to publish." Contempt proceedings continued against his employer, the corporation that owned the newspaper.[127] In 2009 the Canadian Press wire service was found in contempt and fined $4,000 for distributing a report that revealed the first name of an undercover police officer, in violation of a publication ban. The reporter who filed the story was also charged but his only punishment was an order to speak to a journalism school class about the importance of publication bans.[128] A BC television reporter was convicted of breaching a publication ban as a party to the offence, however, even though he did not have the final say on what information was broadcast. The reporter "created the report and went on air as the person at the scene," British Columbia's Court of Appeal ruled in 2005, and "played a prominent and crucial role in the broadcast." Not everyone involved in preparing a story for publication or broadcast will be held responsible, the court added, citing a cameraman as an example of someone too remote from the decision to broadcast to be held liable under the criminal law.[129]

Penalties

The penalty for a contempt conviction is usually a fine, and the amount varies—from several hundred dollars for inadvertent acts to $10,000 for serious acts of contempt. Although a jail term is an option, it is unlikely that such a harsh punishment would be imposed in a case of publication contempt. When the report causes a mistrial, some media outlets have been ordered to pay the defendant's legal costs or the cost of a new trial, which could exceed $10,000. In 2005 a British Columbia daily was fined $10,000 and an editor and reporter were fined $1,000 each for publishing details of the criminal record of a man on trial, triggering a mistrial and forcing the new trial to be moved to another community.[130] Minor violations often draw a stern lecture from the bench and a reminder to the jury to ignore media coverage. In such cases, the judge may consider an apology to be sufficient punishment to purge the contempt. In each instance, the context, the degree of sensationalism, and the judge's assessment of the risk of prejudice will determine the scale of the response.[131]

The Impact of the Charter and Dagenais

Media law experts predict that the Charter's guarantee of freedom of expression will ease traditional restrictions on what can be published about court cases. Robert Martin, for one, has described *sub judice* contempt as "a systematic affront" to the Charter and its underlying philosophy.[132] The advent of aggressive, opinionated coverage of trials is one reflection of the changes under way; another is the routine disclosure, in many jurisdictions, of a suspect's criminal record at time of arrest.

The Supreme Court of Canada's ruling in *Dagenais*, putting the media's right to freedom of expression on a par with the accused's right to a fair trial, could bring about further changes.[133] The **Dagenais test** holds that publication bans should be imposed only when information poses a "real and substantial risk" to a fair trial, and judges must limit the scope of the ban to ensure that the public receives as much information about the case as possible. A similar approach to *sub judice* contempt could redefine what can be published about a case, particularly in the early stages. The issue was argued in 2000 before a judge of Alberta's Court of Queen's Bench, who convicted Alberta's *Sun* newspapers of contempt for revealing the criminal record of a man accused of murdering a child. Justice M.A. Binder rejected "the wholesale importation of the *Dagenais* test to publication contempt law." In his view, "the inevitable result would be the triumph of freedom of expression over the right to a fair trial and the integrity of the administration of justice."[134] The province's Court of Appeal agreed, ruling that *Dagenais* applies to publication bans and other court-imposed restrictions on free expression but not to the criminal offence of contempt. In any event, the court concluded that contempt is a reasonable limit on freedom of expression under section 1 of the Charter, because the law seeks to punish only publications that create a real risk of prejudice to a fair trial or the administration of justice.[135]

In a dissenting judgment, however, Justice Ronald Berger advocated the adoption of a public-interest defence to contempt charges. He noted that the man accused of murder had previously been convicted of assaulting the victim, the son of his common law spouse—a fact the *Sun* newspapers disclosed in questioning the decision of social services officials to return the child to his care. The papers were not motivated by mischief or sensationalism, Justice Berger concluded, but by a desire to draw attention to an important issue. Media outlets, he said, should not be convicted of contempt for publishing information "in good faith in order to inform the public of a legitimate, compelling and pressing issue of public importance."[136]

It remains to be seen whether other courts will follow Justice Berger's lead. Ultimately, the Supreme Court of Canada may be asked, in a future case, to determine how the law of *sub judice* contempt should be modified in light of the Charter.

Sub Judice Contempt: American, Canadian, and British Approaches

Shortly after the arrest of two suspects in the DC sniper shootings in the fall of 2002, the *Washington Post* reported that John Lee Malvo had confessed to killing some of the 14 people gunned down during the shooting spree. Quoting anonymous law enforcement sources, the newspaper reported that the teenager had admitted to pulling the trigger in several of the murders and was "talkative, smiling and even bragging" during a seven-hour interrogation. Lawyers for Malvo and his co-accused, John Allen Muhammad, accused police "cowards" of "poisoning the jury pool." The leak was flashed around the globe and legal experts on CNN and other networks debated whether the police tactics—questioning a juvenile despite defence demands to stop—would render the confession inadmissible in court.

The incident underscores the stark contrast in the Canadian and American approaches to pre-trial publicity. In Canada, reporting that a suspect had confessed to a crime would be considered highly prejudicial and a blatant act of contempt.

Coverage of criminal cases in the United States is fought on a similar constitutional battleground to Canada's. In the United States, the media's First Amendment right to freedom of the press competes with the Sixth Amendment right of every accused person to a fair trial. The key difference is that any form of restraint on media coverage before the coverage is published or broadcast is anathema under American law. The counterpart to Canada's "real risk of prejudice" test is found in a 1947 US Supreme Court ruling, which decreed that comments punishable by contempt must pose an imminent threat to the administration of justice: "The danger must not be remote or even probable; it must immediately imperil" (*Craig v. Harney*, 331 US 367, at 376).

While Canadian courts use the threat of contempt to suppress pre-trial publicity that could taint the jury pool, American courts allow the media wide latitude to report on allegations and potential evidence. To ensure that an impartial jury is selected at trial, US judges rely on rigorous questioning of potential jurors to reveal their knowledge of the case and any prejudice toward the accused. In Canada, jurors are allowed to return home at the end of the day's proceedings and are only sequestered once deliberations begin, which is why the *Criminal Code* bans publication of trial proceedings held in the jury's absence. In the United States, the practice is to sequester jurors for the duration of the trial to shield them from unfettered media coverage and commentary.

American writers face restrictions, however—grand jury proceedings are secret, but witnesses can be interviewed after they have completed their testimony. The American Bar Association's code of conduct forbids lawyers from making statements that have a "substantial likelihood of prejudicing a criminal proceeding." But the courts have loosened this restriction, particularly when the lawyer is replying to the out-of-court comments of an opposing lawyer. One observer has likened American restrictions on lawyers' pre-trial comments to "a sieve with very large holes," which explains media free-for-alls like the one at the O.J. Simpson murder trial.

In Britain, the common law of *sub judice* contempt was formalized in 1981 in the *Contempt of Court Act*, which preserves the power of the courts to punish published reports on pending cases that threaten the administration of justice. Under the statute, the test is whether the publication "creates a substantial risk that the course of justice in the proceedings in question will be seriously impeded or prejudiced." In 1984 the Canadian government used similar wording to draft an amendment that would have added the offence of publication contempt to the *Criminal Code*; the proposal died on the order paper and has not been revived.

(Sources: *Washington Post*, November 10, 11, 2002; S.L. Alexander, *Covering the Courts: A Handbook for Journalists* (Lanham, MD: University Press of America, 1999); C.W. Wolfram, "Lights, Camera, Litigate: Lawyers and the Media in Canada and the United States" (1996), 19 *Dalhousie Law Journal* 373; *Contempt of Court Act 1981* (UK), 1981, c. 49. The differences between the Canadian and American approaches are discussed in *Re Global Communications Ltd.* and *A.-G. Can.* (1984), 44 OR (2d) 609, 5 DLR (4th) 634, 10 CCC (3d) 97 (Ont. HC).)

Criticism of the Courts: Assessing the Risks

In the 1880s the chief justice of the Supreme Court of Canada threatened to find the *Ottawa Citizen* in contempt for publishing an editorial that deplored a growing back-log of cases awaiting a hearing or a final decision. Chief Justice Sir Henry Strong was not amused and dispatched a prominent lawyer to tell publisher P.D. Ross he would be jailed unless the paper apologized. The threat fizzled once the intermediary discovered that the offending newspaper item represented the verbatim comments of one of the chief justice's Supreme Court colleagues. As Ross dryly noted in his memoirs, "I never heard any more about it."[137] A New Brunswick editor was not as careful as Ross, or as fortunate. John T. Hawke, editor of the *Moncton Transcript*, was found in contempt and sentenced to two months in jail in 1888 for referring to a judge as "Mr. Justice Pooh-Bah"—after the pompous Gilbert and Sullivan character—and accusing him of being drunk in the courtroom.[138]

In the 1930s the Judicial Committee of the Privy Council—the British tribunal that was then Canada's final court of appeal—upheld the right to criticize the courts, ruling that a newspaper article examining unequal sentences imposed for similar crimes was not in contempt:

> [N]o wrong is committed by any member of the public who exercises the ordinary right of criticizing, in good faith, in private or public, the public acts done in the seat of justice ... . [P]rovided that members of the public abstain from imputing improper motives to those taking part in the administration of justice, and are genuinely exercising a right of criticism, and not acting in malice or attempting to impair the administration of justice, they are immune. Justice is not a cloistered virtue: she must be allowed to suffer the scrutiny and respectful, even though outspoken, comments of ordinary men.[139]

Canadian judges recognize that their rulings and their conduct must be open to public comment and criticism. To understand the line between legitimate criticism and comments traditionally seen as contemptuous, consider the following comments that have been found in contempt: A city councillor who said a trial "stinks from the word go"; a student reporter who referred to New Brunswick's courts as "instruments of the corporate elite"; a federal Cabinet minister who believed that no "sane" judge could make a ruling he described as "silly" and "a complete disgrace."[140] The courts also have used the law of contempt to protect jurors from unfair attacks. In the 1950s, when capital punishment was still the ultimate penalty under Canadian law, a Vancouver writer was found in contempt for saying a jury had "planned the murder" of a man sent to the gallows after his conviction for murder.[141]

It is doubtful whether such comments would still be prosecuted as contempt of court. As noted earlier, in 1987 the Ontario Court of Appeal in the case of *R v. Kopyto* dealt a potentially fatal blow to the offence of scandalizing the court, striking it down as a violation of the Charter right to freedom of expression. In that case, a frustrated lawyer had publicly lashed out at a small claims court ruling against his client, saying the decision "stinks to high hell" and proved the courts and police were "sticking so close together you'd think they were put together with Krazy Glue." His words were quoted in the *Globe and Mail* but contempt proceedings were not taken against the newspaper. One judge dismissed Kopyto's comments as disgraceful, unprofessional, and "no more than the whining of an unhappy loser." Although the conviction was overturned, the court left open the possibility of future prosecutions for scandalizing the courts if the Crown could prove that an offender intended to bring the administration of justice into disrepute and created a real and serious risk to the administration of justice.[142] The Canadian Judicial Council's guidelines on the use of contempt powers, issued in 1992, advise judges that "scandalizing by words will rarely be an offence, particularly with regard to completed [court] proceedings. Generally speaking, judges must henceforth be prepared to endure almost any form of out of court criticism."[143]

But there are limits to criticism of the courts. Scathing attacks on individual judges or the courts in general continue to be prosecuted as contempt. In 2000 a Manitoba court drew a distinction between legitimate criticism of judges and attacks that amount to "direct interference with the administration of justice." On that basis, a man was found in contempt for making vulgar and abusive comments, in a letter and by phone, that were clearly designed to intimidate a judge into ruling in his favour.[144] Journalists who publicize such extreme comments run the risk of being prosecuted along with the source of the remarks. A radio news reporter in Vernon, BC was charged with contempt in 1989 after airing an interview with a man who called a judge an incompetent "anarchist" who was responsible for the death of a teenager. The man responsible for the comments was convicted and sentenced to 30 days in jail. But the journalist was acquitted because he had been unaware of the man's involvement in an adoption case being handled by the same judge. The court hearing the contempt allegation ruled that, in light of *Kopyto*, there must be clear evidence that the journalist intended to interfere with the administration of justice.[145] In contrast, no action was taken against a Halifax newspaper for publishing a column a week before a high-profile jury trial. The column predicted that the proceedings would be a "sick charade" that would dispense "vengeance, not justice."[146] While lawyers are unlikely to face contempt proceedings over criticism of the courts, the ethical codes of their profession require them to avoid intemperate or petty remarks, to treat the courts with courtesy and respect, and to encourage public respect for the administration of justice. A lawyer who described a judge as a "bigot" in a letter circulated to other counsel involved in a case, for instance, was disciplined for breaching these ethical duties. Manitoba's Court of Appeal ruled in 2007 that such sanctions do not violate a lawyer's Charter right to freedom of speech.[147]

Editorial writers and columnists are free to comment on rulings and judicial conduct, but such criticism should be fair, balanced, and based on fact. Journalists must avoid personal attacks on a judge or comments that call into question a judge's competence, motives, integrity, or impartiality. One media scholar offers the following advice:

> Journalists can criticize individual decisions, but they should do so with some moderation. As a rule of thumb, they should not conclude that the judges involved are either generally incompetent or prompted by hidden and improper motives.[148]

Journalists must also bear in mind that judges have the same right as any other citizen to sue for defamation over criticisms that are inaccurate or unfair. The writer would have to prove an allegation that a judge is biased or corrupt.

Sub Judice Contempt in Civil Cases: Assessing the Risks

A civil case is *sub judice* once the plaintiff files a statement of claim with a court, which commences the action. As in criminal cases, the chances of a publication being found in contempt increase as the date for trial approaches. Any information revealed in documents filed with the court, or presented in open court during chambers motions or at trial, can be published unless it is subject to a publication ban. The contempt risk is considered to be lower than in criminal cases, for two reasons. First, in relative terms, there is less at stake—money as opposed to a citizen's loss of liberty. Second, jury trials are less common in civil cases and many jurisdictions are moving to further restrict the types of actions that can be heard by jury.[149]

Nevertheless, the following contempt concerns arise when accounts of civil cases are published.

Damages

A statement of claim sometimes puts a dollar figure on the damages that a plaintiff is seeking. The amount is often inflated and is never revealed to jurors, so the information has the potential to influence a jury's verdict. The amount sought, if known, is routinely disclosed in the media when lawsuits are filed but the risk of creating prejudice increases as the date for trial approaches. One judge saw nothing improper about media reports that a plaintiff had filed a lawsuit seeking $500,000 in damages, but ruled that a newspaper was in contempt for publishing the same information 18 months later, once a jury trial was under way.[150]

Allegations in Pleadings

At the pleadings stage, the statement of claim that is filed provides a wish list of the allegations that a plaintiff hopes to prove in court. Revealing details of these allegations is permissible early in the court process, but repeating them shortly before and during a trial may invite a citation for contempt unless the allegations have been repeated to the jury.

Insurance Coverage

In civil jury trials, references to a defendant's insurance coverage are off-limits to lawyers and reporters alike unless the existence of a policy or the insurer's role in opposing the claim is revealed in court. The courts fear that jurors may award higher damages if they know that a civil defendant is insured and will not personally bear the burden.[151]

Criminal Records of Parties or Witnesses

The criminal record of a plaintiff, defendant, or a witness involved in a civil case is unlikely to become an issue at trial or form part of the evidence. This information could seriously damage the credibility of the players and should not be reported in the midst of a civil trial unless it has been disclosed to the jury.

Contempt of Legislative Bodies

Parliament and provincial and territorial legislatures have the power to punish those who attack the integrity of the body or its members. This contempt power is rarely used, but there have been instances of journalists being threatened with punishment for failing to retract criticism or refusing to identify a source. When the *Halifax Herald* published an anonymous letter in 1914 accusing members of the Nova Scotia government of corruption, the paper's news editor, William R. McCurdy, was imprisoned for two days for contempt for refusing to identify the letter's author.[152] In 1922 John H. Roberts, editor of the Montreal weekly paper *The Axe*, served five months in jail after being found in contempt of the Quebec legislature for publishing rumours that politicians were shielding those responsible for an unsolved murder.[153] The Charter guarantee of freedom of the press is likely to make legislators think twice about wielding such powers against today's journalists.

Contempt of Court: A Summary

When a criminal case is before the courts, writers must guard against disclosing information that portrays accused persons in a bad light or that implies they are guilty as charged. Opinions about the accused's guilt, the strength of the defence's case, or what the judge's ruling should be—in short, any comment that prejudges the issues—must be withheld until the trial is over.

In both criminal and civil cases, the timing of a publication is crucial, because the risk of contempt increases as the date of the trial approaches. The risk is greatest once the trial is under way. Whether the case is to be heard by a judge or by a judge and jury is a key consideration, given the courts' overriding objective to shield jurors from prejudicial pre-trial publicity. Informed and balanced public criticism of judges and their decisions is not only proper, it is considered to be vital in ensuring the fairness of the justice system.

The law of publication contempt in Canada is in a state of flux. This chapter has examined the danger zones, the information generally viewed as prejudicial to the fair-trial rights of an accused person, and how the law is evolving. Writers who are unsure whether they can safely publish specific information about a court proceeding should seek legal advice before publication or broadcast.

NOTES

1. *The Onion*, June 15, 2000, cited in Stephen Bindman, "The Interplay Between Individual Citizens and the Courts: How Decisions Get Played Out in the Press," in Stephen Coughlan and Dawn Russell, eds., *Citizenship and Citizen Participation in the Administration of Justice* (Montreal: Les Éditions Thémis, 2002), 219–25, at 219–20.

2. Willard Z. Estey, "Freedom of Expression vs. the Individual's Right to Privacy," in *Media & Society* (Toronto: The Canadian Journalism Foundation and The Empire Club of Canada, 1994), 27–43, at 39.

3. Colin Wright, "Issues of Law and Public Policy," in *Royal Commission on Newspapers Research Publications*, vol. 3, *Newspapers and the Law* (Ottawa: Minister of Supply and Services, 1981), 49–73, at 61.

4. *Criminal Code*, RSC 1985, c. C-46, as amended.

5. Robert Martin, for one, notes the "gelatinous, mystical nature" of contempt and describes the law as "exceedingly vague." Martin, "Contempt of Court: The Effect of the

Charter," in Philip Anisman and Allen M. Linden, eds., *The Media, the Courts and the Charter* (Toronto: Carswell, 1986), 207–22, at 207–208.

6. *Bielek v. Ristimaki* (1979), unreported (Ont. HC), reproduced in Stuart Robertson, *Courts and the Media* (Toronto: Butterworths, 1981), 287–92, at 290.

7. Robert Martin and G. Stuart Adam, *A Sourcebook of Canadian Media Law* (Ottawa: Carleton University Press, 1989), 204.

8. Klaus Pohle, "Presumptions of Guilt: The Notion That an Accused Person Is Presumed Innocent, Regardless of What We Think We Know About the Case, Has Taken a Beating in Recent Years," *Ottawa Citizen*, February 24, 2010.

9. See Dean Jobb, "The New Court Coverage," *Canadian Lawyer*, February 2001, 42–46.

10. Alan Shanoff, "Publication Contempt of Court After *Dagenais*," Advocates in Defence of Expression in the Media, 1999, available online at http://www.adidem.org.

11. *R v. Gray*, [1900] QB 36, at 40. For a list of cases that have cited Lord Russell of Killowen's definition in *Gray*, see Jeffrey Miller, *The Law of Contempt in Canada* (Scarborough, ON: Carswell, 1997), 11–12.

12. *Hébert v. Quebec (Attorney General)* (1967), 2 CCC 111, at 131 (Que. QB).

13. The Latin terms for the two forms of contempt are *in facie curiae* (in the face of the court) and *ex facie curiae* (not in the face of the court). See Miller, supra note 11, at 17–19.

14. John A. Yogis, *Canadian Law Dictionary*, 4th ed. (New York: Barron's, 1998), 256.

15. *Roach v. Garvan* [*St. James's Evening Post* case] (1742), 2 Atk. 469.

16. *R v. CHEK TV Ltd.* (1987), 33 CCC (3d) 24, at 30 (BCCA).

17. Ibid.

18. *Attorney-General v. Times Newspapers Limited*, [1974] AC 273, at 300.

19. Martin, "Contempt of Court," supra note 5, at 208.

20. *R v. Gray*, supra note 11, at 40.

21. *Fournier v. Attorney General* (1910), 17 CCC 108 (Que. CA).

22. *R v. Kopyto* (1987), 62 OR (2d) 449, at 463 (CA).

23. Robert Martin has declared that "scandalizing the court is effectively dead in Canada. Its burial was long overdue." Martin, *Media Law* (Concord, ON: Irwin Law, 1997), 79.

24. *R v. Savundranayagan and Walker*, [1968] 3 All ER 439 (CA).

25. Robertson, supra note 6, at 49.

26. Sherri Borden Colley, "TV Station Loses Defamation Suit; ATV Must Pay $15,000 for Painting Man as Terrorist," *Chronicle-Herald* (Halifax), September 30, 2004; Sherri Borden Colley, "CTV Ordered To Pay More in Defamation Case; Company's Offer Insulting—Judge," *Chronicle-Herald* (Halifax), December 1, 2004.

27. Walter Stewart, "No Virginia, There Is No Lou Grant," in Stewart, ed., *Canadian Newspapers: The Inside Story* (Edmonton: Hurtig Publishers, 1980), 9–30, at 14–15.

28. "Debit-Card Scam Leads to 100 Charges," *Vancouver Sun*, December 5, 2002; "Debit Fraud Artist Faces 100-Plus Charges," Canada.com, December 6, 2002 (http://www.canada.com).

29. "Moen Murderer Arrested," *Brooks & County Chronicle*, July 17, 2006.

30. Ontario Press Council, *Trial by Media: An Account of an Open Forum on Pre-Trial Publicity Held by the Ontario Press Council* (Ottawa: Author, 1984), 11, 27.

31. J.A. Mcfarlane and Warren Clements, *The Globe and Mail Style Book: A Guide to Language and Usage* (Toronto: McClelland & Stewart, 1998), 76.

32. Barry Dorey and Amy Smith, "Victim Stabbed 40 Times," *Chronicle-Herald* (Halifax), September 20, 1996.

33. Michael Crawford, *The Journalist's Legal Guide*, 4th ed. (Toronto: Carswell, 2002), 158.

34. *Fortin v. Moscarelle et al.* (1957), 11 DLR (2d) 606, at 608 (BCSC).

35. *R v. Carocchia* (1973), 15 CCC (2d) 175 (Que. CA); aff'g. 14 CCC (2d) 354.

36. James Cowan, "Police Chief Assailed for Comments," *National Post*, July 23, 2004; Christie Blatchford, "A Police Chief's Alleged Offence," *Globe and Mail*, July 24, 2004.

37. *Alberta v. The Edmonton Sun*, 2000 ABQB 283, at paragraph 48.

38. *R v. Corbett*, [1988] 1 SCR 670.

39. *Attorney-General for Manitoba v. Groupe Quebécor Inc.* (1987), 45 DLR (4th) 80; Canadian Newspaper Association, "Winnipeg Sun Fined $2,500 for Contempt of Court," *The Press and the Courts*, vol. 6, no. 1, February 13, 1987.

40. *Re Attorney-General of Alberta and Interwest Publications Ltd.* (1990), 58 CCC (3d) 114 (Alta. QB).

41. *R v. CHBC Television*, 1999 BCCA 72, at paragraph 23, quoting the ruling in *R v. Froese and British Columbia Television Broadcasting Systems Ltd. (No. 3)* (1979), 50 CCC (2d) 119, at 121 (BCSC); aff'd. (1980), 54 CCC (2d) 315 (BCCA).

42. *Re Attorney-General of Alberta and Interwest Publications Ltd.*, supra note 40, at 132.

43. Jobb, supra note 9.

44. For examples, see Kim Honey, "Police Pursue Stabbing Investigation," *Globe and Mail*, August 8, 1998; "Murderer Faces Sex Charges," *Daily News* (Halifax), February 12, 1999; Patricia Brooks, "Robbery Suspect Led Storied Life of Crime," *Chronicle-Herald* (Halifax), November 14, 2002.

45. Canadian Newspaper Association, "Ontario Attorney-General Abandons Notion of Contempt Charges in Bernardo Case," *The Press and the Courts*, vol. 12, no. 2, May 7, 1993; Bruce Erskine, "No Shrubsall Case Contempt Charges," *Chronicle-Herald* (Halifax), August 22, 1998.

46. Robert Sokalski, "Contempt Law Update—Issues for Media: 2004 'Whither Goest We Now?'" paper prepared for The Media and the Courts: A one-day workshop examining the relationship between the media and the justice system, Winnipeg, April 17, 2004.

47. Sean Fine, "Print and Prejudice No Longer Last Word on Right to a Fair Trial," *Globe and Mail*, September 10, 1999.

48. Shanoff, supra note 10.

49. *R v. Bowes Publishers Ltd.*, [1995] AJ no. 489, at paragraphs 37–38 (QL); Canadian Newspaper Association, "Fort McMurray Today Fined $4,000 for Contempt," *The Press and the Courts*, vol. 14, no. 4, June 23, 1995.

50. *Alberta v. The Edmonton Sun*, supra note 37, at paragraphs 50–51, 53–54.

51. *Alberta v. The Edmonton Sun*, 2003 ABCA 3, at paragraphs 65–66.

52. *Steiner v. Toronto Star Ltd. et al.* (1955), 1 DLR (2d) 297, at 299 (Ont. HC).

53. Ibid., at 300.

54. As Michael Crawford has said, "The closer a civil or criminal action gets to trial, particularly when a jury is involved, the more cautious a journalist must be in his or her reports." Crawford, supra note 33, at 156.

55. *Bielek v. Ristimaki*, supra note 6, at 290.

56. *R v. Sherratt*, [1991] 1 SCR 509, (1991), 63 CCC (3d) 193.

57. *R v. Merz*, [1999] OJ no. 4309, at paragraphs 34–36 (QL), (1999), 46 OR (3d) 161.

58. *R v. Collins*, 1989 CanLII 264 (Ont. CA). This approach was endorsed in *R v. Sandham*, 2008 CanLII 84099 (Ont. SC).

59. Ontario Press Council, supra note 30, at 11.

60. *Dagenais v. Canadian Broadcasting Corp.*, [1994] 3 SCR 835, at 886.

61. *R v. Shrubsall (W.C.)* (2000), 187 NSR (2d) 310, at 317.

62. Ronald Irving, comp., *"The Law Is a Ass": An Illustrated Collection of Legal Quotations* (London: Gerald Duckworth & Co., 1999), 138.

63. *Phillips v. Nova Scotia (Commission of Inquiry into the Westray Mine Tragedy)*, [1995] 2 SCR 97, at 168.

64. *R v. Kenny*, [1991] 92 Nfld. & PEIR 318 (Nfld. SCTD).

65. *Ontario Royal Commission Inquiry into Civil Rights*, Report Number One, vol. 2 (Ottawa: Queen's Printer, 1968), 763.

66. See studies cited in *Toronto Star Newspapers Ltd. v. Canada*, 2009 ONCA 59, at paragraphs 87–88.

67. See comments quoted in ibid., at paragraph 93.

68. *Toronto Star Newspapers Ltd. v. Canada*, supra note 66, at paragraph 125.

69. *R v. Carocchia*, supra note 35, at 184.

70. *R v. McInroy, Re Whiteside* (1915), 25 CCC 49, at 54, 26 DLR 615, at 620 (Alta. SC).

71. "Newspaper Story Causes Mistrial of Attempted Murder Case," Canadian Press wire service, March 22, 2000.

72. Canadian Newspaper Association, "Stay of Proceedings Upheld as a Result of Editorial," *The Press and the Courts*, vol. 6, no. 1, February 13, 1987.

73. *Steiner v. Toronto Star Ltd. et al.*, supra note 52, at 304.

74. *R v. Sherratt*, supra note 56, at 536.

75. *R v. CHBC Television*, supra note 41, at paragraph 32.

76. Ibid., at paragraphs 23, 73.

77. *Canadian Broadcasting Corp. v. Keegstra* (1986), 35 DLR (4th) 76, at 78 (Alta. CA).

78. *R v. CHEK TV Ltd.*, supra note 16.

79. *R v. BCTV, a division of WIC Television Ltd.*, [1999] BCJ no. 1558 (QL) (CA).

80. *HMTQ v. Peebles & Others*, 2005 BCSC 1387 (CanLII). See also Gary Oakes, "Newspaper Fined for Contempt After Stating Man on Trial Had Been in Prison for Murder," *The Lawyers Weekly*, October 21, 2005, 14.

81. Canadian Newspaper Association, "Judge Declares Mistrial over Newspaper Article During Murder Hearing," *The Press and the Courts*, vol. 10, no. 6, December 19, 1991.

82. Canadian Newspaper Association, "Appeals Court Quashes Contempt Convictions Against Journal," *The Press and the Courts*, vol. 14, no. 3, June 21, 1995.

83. *R v. CHBC Television*, supra note 41, at paragraph 30.

84. Ibid., at paragraph 31.

85. *R v. Scozzafava*, [1997] OJ no. 4576 (QL) (Gen. Div.).

86. *R v. The Daily Courier Estate*, 1997 BCSC 35396. The Kelowna, BC newspaper was fined $4,000.

87. Canadian Newspaper Association, "Judge Orders Mistrial After Story Links Accused to Motorcycle Gang," *The Press and the Courts*, vol. 10, no. 5, October 25, 1991.

88. *R v. Innocente et al.* (2000), 183 NSR (2d) 1 (SC).

89. Richard Foot and Mary Vallis, "Clash in Courtroom: Rape Suspect Quizzes Victim," *National Post*, January 7, 2003; "Cross-Examination 'Like Double Rape,' Muir Says," *Chronicle-Herald* (Halifax), January 17, 2003.

90. Joseph Brean, "Johnathan Mistrial: Judge Says Post Story Casts Doubt on Witness," *National Post*, February 16, 2005.

91. Cited in Mike Drach, "Trial by Journalist" (Summer 2002), *Ryerson Review of Journalism* 50–55, at 54.

92. Christie Blatchford, "Jurors Deserve Better Than This," *National Post*, January 12, 2000. For an example of a Blatchford column that weighs the evidence and arguments before the court, see "Jury Sees Two Faces of Star Witness," *National Post*, January 13, 2003.

93. See Jobb, supra note 9.

94. John Fraser, "There Will Soon Be a Terrible Reckoning," *National Post*, December 11, 1999.

95. Kirk Makin, "Judge Warns Journalists About Views," *Globe and Mail*, January 11, 2000.

96. Tracey Tyler, "Save Opinion Till End of Trial, Chief Justice Tells Journalists," *Toronto Star*, March 27, 2000.

97. Blatchford, supra note 92.

98. J.C. McRuer, "Criminal Contempt of Court Procedure: A Protection of the Rights of the Individual" (1952), 30 *Canadian Bar Review* 225, at 227–28.

99. Canadian Newspaper Association, "Oshawa Times, Columnist Pay $5,000 in Court Costs on Contempt Charges," *The Press and the Courts*, vol. 10, no. 3, June 21, 1991.

100. *R v. Froese and British Columbia Television Broadcasting Systems Ltd. (No. 3)* (1979), supra note 41.

101. Christie Blatchford, "A Butcher Asks Jury To Believe His Story," *National Post*, September 10, 1999.

102. Jobb, supra note 9; *R v. Savojipour* trial transcript, September 14, 1999, at 53.

103. See, for example, Nova Scotia Barristers' Society, *Legal Ethics and Professional Conduct: A Handbook for Lawyers in Nova Scotia* (Halifax: Author, 1990), rules 22.5 and 22.6, at 99.

104. Law Society of Upper Canada, *Rules of Professional Conduct*, rules 6.06(1) and 6.06(2), available online at http://www.lsuc.on.ca/regulation/a/profconduct/rule6/.

105. "Communications with the Media," *The Federal Prosecution Service Deskbook*, part III, chapter 10. Available online at http://www.justice.gc.ca.

106. David Gambrill, "Crown Should Explain, Not Plead, Cases in Media," *The Law Times*, September 9, 2002, at 1. For more detailed examinations of the rules governing lawyer–media contact, see Gavin MacKenzie, *Lawyers and Ethics: Professional Responsibility and Discipline* (Scarborough, ON: Carswell, 1993), chapter 13; David M. Brown, "What Can Lawyers Say in Public?" (1999), vol. 78, nos. 3 and 4 *Canadian Bar Review* 283.

107. *R v. Ludwig*, [2000] AJ no. 509 (QL) (QB); *Re The Chronicle-Herald et al. and The Queen* [indexed as *R v. Regan*] (1997), 124 CCC (3d) 77 (NSSC).

108. Canadian Newspaper Association, "Judge Suggests Citizen Should Be Charged with Contempt," *The Press and the Courts*, vol. 7, no. 2, March-April 1988.

109. *R v. Dawson et al.*, 2001 BCSC 178, at paragraph 19.

110. See *Dagenais v. Canadian Broadcasting Corp.*, supra note 60.

111. Ibid., at 881.

112. *Canadian Broadcasting Corp. v. Keegstra*, supra note 77.

113. *One Yellow Rabbit Theatre Association v. R and James Keegstra* [indexed as *R v. Keegstra (Alta. CA)*] (1992), 91 DLR (4th) 532, 2 Alta. LR (3d) 162, 6 CPC (3d) 1, 20 WAC 232, 127 AR 232, [1992] AJ no. 330 (QL) (CA).

114. Patricia Brooks, "Legal Potholes Sink Road to Hell; Book About Biker Gangs Not for Sale in N.S. Pending Court Cases," *Chronicle-Herald* (Halifax), November 6, 2003.

115. *Foshay v. Key Porter Books Ltd. et al.*, [1986] OJ no. 197 (QL), (1986), 58 OR (2d) 566, 36 DLR (4th) 106 (HC).

116. *R v. Mitchell*, [1997] BCJ no. 2707, at paragraph 6 (QL) (Prov. Ct.).

117. Robert S. Bruser and Brian MacLeod Rogers, *Journalists and the Law: How To Get the Story Without Getting Sued or Thrown in Jail* (Ottawa: Canadian Bar Foundation, 1985), 64.

118. For a discussion of the risk of contempt at the appeal stage, see Crawford, supra note 33, at 166–67.

119. *Toronto Star Newspapers Ltd. v. Canada*, supra note 66, at paragraphs 105–107 and 177.

120. *R v. Glover*, 2006 CanLII 8036 (Ont. SC), at paragraph 6.

121. "Police Investigate Facebook Group," *Daily News* (Halifax), June 15, 2007.

122. Canadian Newspaper Association, "Barrie Examiner Fined $2,500 for Headline That Causes Mistrial," *The Press and the Courts*, vol. 11, no. 4, September 4, 1992.

123. *R v. CHEK TV Ltd.*, supra note 16.

124. *Attorney-General for Manitoba v. Groupe Quebécor Inc.*, supra note 39; *R v. Bowes Publishers Ltd.*, supra note 49.

125. The points about republication and qualified privilege are made in Bruser and Rogers, supra note 117, at 60, 71–72.

126. Martin, *Media Law*, supra note 23, at 73.

127. *R v. Dawson et al.*, supra note 109, at paragraph 23.

128. *R v. The Canadian Press*, 2009 BCSC 988 (CanLII).

129. *R v. Daly*, 2005 BCCA 389 (CanLII).

130. *HMTQ v. Peebles & Others*, 2005 BCSC 1387 (CanLII).

131. Martin and Adam, supra note 7, at 204, 275–76.

132. Martin, supra note 5, at 214. Among those espousing this view was M. David Lepofsky, *Open Justice: The Constitutional Right To Attend and Speak About Criminal Proceedings* (Toronto: Butterworths, 1985), chapters 5–6.

133. One author who has predicted that *Dagenais* will overhaul the law of *sub judice* contempt is Michael R. Doody, *Reporting on Adult Courts and Tribunals* (Toronto: Hallion Press, 1995), 19, 21.

134. *Alberta v. The Edmonton Sun*, supra note 37, paragraphs 36–37; Dean Jobb, "Creating Some Limits for Contempt of Court?" *Canadian Lawyer*, February 2001, 45.

135. *Alberta v. The Edmonton Sun*, supra note 51.

136. Ibid., at paragraphs 119, 124.

137. Philip Dansken Ross, *Retrospects of a Newspaper Person* (Toronto: Oxford University Press, 1931), 42–44.

138. See Hawke's biography in *Dictionary of Canadian Biography Online*, http://www.biographi.ca.

139. *Ambard v. Attorney General for Trinidad and Tobago*, [1936] AC 322, at 335 (HL).

140. These and other examples are cited in Crawford, supra note 33, at 147; Robert Martin, "Criticizing the Judges," 28 *McGill Law Journal* 1, 13–20, reproduced in Martin and Adam, supra note 7, at 274–78.

141. *Re Nicol*, [1954] 3 DLR 690 (BCSC).

142. See the discussion of *R v. Kopyto* (1987), supra note 22, in Miller, supra note 11, 111–14.

143. Cited in Martin L. Friedland, *A Place Apart: Judicial Independence and Accountability in Canada* (Ottawa: Canadian Judicial Council, 1995), 32.

144. *R v. Gillespie*, 2000 MBQB 149.

145. Canadian Newspaper Association, "Vernon Radio Station Contempt Charge Dismissed," *The Press and the Courts*, vol. 9, no. 4, August 17, 1990.

146. Brian Flemming, "The Tricks Memory Plays: They Threaten To Put Gerald Regan Behind Bars for Things He Didn't Do," *Daily News* (Halifax), October 28, 1998.

147. *Histed v. Law Society of Manitoba*, 2007 MBCA 150 (CanLII).

148. Wright, supra note 3, at 59.

149. See Lynne Cohen, "The Endangered Civil Jury," *Canadian Lawyer*, June 2002, 32–40.

150. *Bielek v. Ristimaki*, supra note 6, at 290.

151. The possibility of prejudice to civil cases arising from media reports of insurance coverage and pleadings is discussed ibid., at 291.

152. William March, *Red Line: The Chronicle-Herald and The Mail-Star, 1875-1954* (Halifax: Chebucto Agencies Ltd., 1986), 119-22.

153. John Kalbfleisch, "Feisty Editor Was Jailed in a 1920s Battle over Press Freedom," *Montreal Gazette*, November 2, 2008.

CHAPTER 9

Publication Bans in Criminal and Youth Cases

The Rationale for Publication Bans

"Gag order." The term sometimes crops up in news reports about court-imposed publication bans, and it speaks volumes about media attitudes toward these restrictions and how journalists feel muzzled by them. Journalists report. Writers tell stories. Publishers and broadcasters inform. Publication bans throw a cloak of secrecy over proceedings, delaying disclosure of information for months or years and, in some cases, permanently preventing the facts from being made public.

Publication bans, by their very nature, infringe on the right to freedom of expression under the *Canadian Charter of Rights and Freedoms*.[1] They also conflict with the principle of open courts. As has been noted, however, free expression and openness are not absolutes and must be balanced against other rights and interests. Canada's system of selective openness stands in stark contrast to the no-holds-barred American approach to covering crimes and trials. The rationale for our web of publication bans, journalism professor G. Stuart Adam has noted, is that publicity is viewed "as a means in a system in which justice is the end. … In short, publicity is a necessary component of the system, but it should not interfere with the administration of justice."[2]

Bans restrict the publication or broadcast of prejudicial information about a pending case. Criminal records, confessions, aspersions about a defendant's character—the publication of any of these could lead to a citation for contempt under the common law. Bans are also invoked to protect the proper administration of justice. In essence, **publication bans** are *sub judice* restrictions reduced to the tangible form of a law or court order that stipulates what can be reported and when. As a result, they eliminate some of the uncertainty that pervades the law of contempt of court. Increasingly, bans are also imposed to protect the privacy of victims of crime and other persons caught up in the court process.

Bans fall into two broad categories: statutory bans and non-statutory bans. **Statutory bans** prevent the disclosure of prejudicial information presented in the pre-trial phases of a prosecution or are imposed to protect the privacy of persons connected with the case. Statutory bans, in turn, are of two types. Mandatory bans are either automatically in place or imposed by a judge when a party involved in a case seeks the court's protection and a judge has no choice but to grant the ban. Most statutory bans, however, are left to the discretion of the judge. Superior court judges can also create and impose a second form of publication ban as the need arises, a **non-statutory ban**, drawing on their inherent power to control proceedings and to ensure that justice is done. All non-statutory, judge-made bans are discretionary. Before imposing these optional bans, judges must strive to achieve a balance between privacy interests and fair-trial rights on one hand, and freedom of expression and the imperative of open justice on the other.

When assessing how a ban applies to situations as they arise in court, writers and editors should bear in mind the underlying intent of a ban to balance rights and interests and, in most instances, to delay publication until those rights and interests are no longer at risk. This chapter will explore the scope of each ban, using court rulings and published reports to illustrate the information that can be revealed without violating the provisions of each ban. The goal of this chapter is to help journalists, publishers, and broadcasters understand what can be made public and when, enabling them to inform the public about court proceedings to the fullest extent that the law allows.

Statutory Bans

Parliament has created statutory publication bans that apply to certain information or specific stages of a prosecution. These provisions temporarily restrict the broadcast or publication of information that could prejudice a defendant's future trial. In the 1980s, new bans were introduced to protect the identities of complainants and young witnesses involved in prosecutions of sexual offences—a protection now offered to every witness or victim, regardless of the crime. The *Youth Criminal Justice Act* opens juvenile justice to public scrutiny, subject to bans on identifying young persons involved as defendants, victims, or witnesses.

A few general observations can be made about statutory bans. The principle of open justice demands that restrictions on publication should be as limited as possible in scope. Although a few bans are automatically put in place, in most cases the judge must formally impose the ban in the courtroom, and journalists will be notified of the restrictions that apply. Judges have the discretion not to impose certain bans if they are sought by the Crown, but have no choice if the defendant makes the request. Even when a ban is imposed, members of the public are entitled to remain in the courtroom and reporters can take notes for future use. This is an important right, since most bans are delays on publication, not outright prohibitions. Most bans expire once charges are dismissed, a defendant pleads guilty, or a verdict is reached—once there is no longer a need to protect the right to a fair trial. This frees the media to report evidence, legal arguments, and other previously banned information vital to understanding how a case unfolded, although this is often cold comfort to journalists, who equate timeliness with newsworthiness. But this is not the case for bans on identifying crime victims, witnesses, or young persons accused of a crime. Unless a judge lifts the ban or the young person is in a position to waive anonymity, these bans are permanent.

Statutory Bans Under the Criminal Code

Bans on Identities

Sex-Related Offences, Extortion, and Loansharking: Section 486.4(1)

Section 486.4(1) of the *Criminal Code* empowers a judge to ban publication of the name and "any information that could disclose the identity" of victims of sex-related crimes and witnesses younger than 18 involved in such cases. The ban is designed to encourage victims of sexual offences—and young witnesses who support their allegations—to come forward without fear of public embarrassment. The ban applies to charges of sexual assault, sexual exploitation and interference, indecent assault, and some prostitution-related offences (sections 151, 152, 153, 155, 159, 160, 170, 171, 172, 173, 271, and 273 of the Code). It applies to charges of rape in cases where the allegations predate the adoption of a wider definition of sexual assault in 1983. The ban is also available in prosecutions involving allegations of charging a criminal rate of interest—a rate in excess of 60 percent—and extortion (sections 347 and 346 of the Code). If other offences are being dealt with in the same hearing, the identity of a victim or young witness can be banned in connection with all charges, under section 486.4(1)(b). Another section, 486.4(3), empowers a judge to ban publication of information that could identify a person represented in any form of child pornography.

Some news organizations have a policy of not naming complainants in sexual assault cases even if no ban is sought or if the victim's name is discovered in court documents before a ban is requested.[3] The ban has even been applied after the victim has been identified in the media. In 2010, police identified a missing New Brunswick woman and news outlets published her name and photograph. She was found a month later, after escaping from a man accused of kidnapping and sexually assaulting her. Despite the widespread publicity, the woman was entitled to request a publication ban that prevented her from being identified in future media reports.[4] A photograph or television image could run afoul of the ban, even if the person's face is obscured or not shown. The *Hamilton Spectator* was fined $4,500 in 2010 for publishing a photo of a victim of sexual assault as she left the courthouse with her husband. Even though the photo was taken from behind and from a distance, people who knew the couple were able to identify them.[5]

Crown attorneys usually make a motion to have a ban imposed in sexual assault cases during the defendant's first appearance in court. A Quebec court has ruled that a complainant must ask that the ban be imposed before beginning to give testimony.[6] The ban must be imposed when it is requested by a prosecutor, complainant, or young witness[7] and no evidence is needed to justify imposing it.[8] As well, judges have a duty, under section 486.4(2) of the *Criminal Code*, to inform complainants and witnesses under the age of 18 "at the first reasonable opportunity" of their right to seek the ban.[9] A defendant can apply under the section to ban publication of the identity of the complainant or a witness, but in these circumstances the judge has the option of refusing the request. Some victims of sexual offences do not want their identities shielded, and a Saskatchewan judge has ruled that it is not mandatory for a court to impose a publication ban if a prosecutor seeks it without the complainant's consent.[10]

Judges also have the power to ban publication of the identity of a complainant or witness on their own motion, if they consider this step necessary to ensure a fair trial or to maintain proper control of the courtroom.[11] Although this ban infringes on the media's right to freedom of expression, the Supreme Court of Canada has ruled that the limitation is justified because it ensures that serious crimes are prosecuted.[12]

The ban is permanent unless rescinded by a judge. The victim or witness can never be named, even after the person dies.[13] But the person can be identified in the media, even in connection with other crimes, as long as the news report does not refer to the person as a victim of sex-related offences, loansharking, or extortion. A British Columbia television station that aired file footage of a woman who was rescued from a kidnapper, without revealing that she was the victim of a previous sex crime, was acquitted of violating the ban.[14] Some victims of sexual assault decide to go public about their ordeals; if they do, journalists must bear in mind that the ban is a court order and remains in force despite the wishes of the person involved.[15] In a case that confirms the courts have the final say over whether a ban is lifted or remains in place, the CBC was convicted and fined $2,000 in 2004 for broadcasting an interview with a victim of sexual assault even though the woman consented to being identified.[16] A judge must be asked to rescind the order and a Crown attorney will often agree to make the motion on a victim's behalf. In May 2005 Quebec entertainer Natalie Simard, who was sexually assaulted by her former manager, asked a judge to lift a ban protecting her identity so that she could "share her sad experience with the public." She promptly went on television to describe her ordeal and launched a lawsuit seeking damages from her assailant.[17] A judge can only rescind the ban with the consent of both the prosecution and the complainant.[18] Judges should ignore an accused person's opposition to having the ban lifted, Ontario's Court of Appeal has ruled.[19] When a ban is rescinded, the media must also take care not to publish details that could identify relatives, witnesses, or other persons whose names remain banned from publication.

Accused persons are not entitled to apply under section 486.4(1) for an order banning publication of their names and information that could identify them.[20] Yet some defendants benefit from anonymity because naming them could identify someone protected under the ban. This situation clearly arises in allegations of incest, in sex-related offences where assailants, victims, and witnesses share the same surname, and where the person accused of the crime is the victim's step-parent, foster parent, or common law spouse. In such cases, the defence lawyer or the prosecutor may claim that the identity of the accused person must be banned to ensure that the victim is not identified. The judge may have the same concern and be the first to raise the issue. However, there must be evidence to support the contention that identifying the defendant could identify a complainant or witness.[21] An Ontario judge overturned a ban on identifying a man convicted of sexually assaulting children who were close friends of his own children. The judge said the ban should only be expanded to shield the identity of defendants in incest cases where the accused person shares a surname with the victim or is a parent or guardian.[22] An Alberta judge took a similar approach in 2007, ruling a man who abused his common law wife's four-year-old daughter could be named because he had a different last name and was not the child's legal guardian.[23]

The size of the community may also play a role—a judge banned publication of the identity of a Nunavut man accused of molesting 13 children because he and his victims lived in a small northern community.[24]

Unless the judge has banned publication of the defendant's identity on this basis, the media can name the accused person as long as the relationship to the victim is not revealed. If the defendant's identity is shielded under a wider ban, however, the media are free to report the nature of the relationship between the unnamed parties. An argument can be made that there is merit to adopting the latter approach, even if the defendant's name is not explicitly banned. It ensures that media reports do not create the distorted impression that only strangers commit sex-related offences.

What Information Could Identify a Victim or Witness?

The *Criminal Code*'s restrictions on identifying victims and witnesses are more than a ban on names; the law prohibits the publication or broadcast of any information that "could disclose the identity" of a person. The challenge for the writer is to figure out how much information can be divulged without making someone's identity known and violating the ban. One judge has suggested that there must be "more than a slight degree of possibility" that a media report will make the person's identity known (*A.B. v. College of Physicians*, 2001 PESCTD 75). Describing a victim as "a 32-year-old Vancouver man," for example, does nothing to reveal his identity. At the other extreme, reporting that "the mayor's teenage daughter" has been sexually assaulted obviously gives away her identity. Also, the more detailed the description of the victim or witness, the greater the chance of violating the ban, particularly in a small community.

There have been few court rulings to clarify how much detail is too much detail. In one Nova Scotia case, a television station was prosecuted for revealing the city where a young victim of a sexual assault lived, her age, and the fact that her father was a member of a specialized unit of the local police force. Those facts, while sketchy, enabled relatives in another province who heard the news report to deduce who she was (*R v. Atlantic Television System*, NS Prov. Ct., unreported, July 19, 1996). On the other hand, the *Ottawa Citizen* was not prosecuted for naming the accused in a sexual assault case, reporting that the complainant was his former fiancée and a co-worker, and stating their occupations, despite concerns that her anonymity had been compromised (Canadian Newspaper Association, "Judge Reverses Himself on Ban After Media Intervention," *The Press and the Courts*, vol. 19, no. 6, December 31, 2000). It is safe to reveal a person's age, gender, and community of residence, and the person's general job or profession. But journalists must carefully consider the impact of combining information with specific references to the person's street address, employer's name and location, or, if the person is a student, the school attended. Compare the description of "a 20-year-old student who was sexually assaulted in her residence room at the University of Halifax" with "a 20-year-old University of Halifax commerce major from Sherbrooke, Quebec who was sexually assaulted in her third-floor room at Palmer Hall."

There may also be a professional or community relationship that links defendant and victim. If the accused person is a clergyperson, teacher, doctor, or sports coach, or the victim is a babysitter or other employee, journalists must consider whether specifying the defendant's job and relationship with the victim, coupled with details such as the victim's age and the location of the offence, could be sufficient to violate the ban. Identifying a man accused of sexually assaulting a teenage girl and describing her as a babysitter, for example, may identify the victim within a circle of neighbours and relatives who know that the girl routinely cares for the man's children. An important factor may be whether the crime occurred in a city or large town as opposed to a rural hamlet, where readers and viewers may be able to figure out who was involved. Reporting that "John Smith, a Toronto man who coaches minor hockey, is charged with sex-related offences involving a player" is safe; reporting that "Toronto minor hockey coach John Smith is charged with sexually assaulting an 11-year-old player," and naming the team and the boy's neighbourhood or school, likely goes too far.

Writers must carefully assess each piece of information and the likelihood that it will reveal the victim's identity, both on its own and when published in combination with other details about the victim, the crime, or the defendant. Sometimes judges take the matter into their own hands and specify the kinds of information that, in their opinion, could identify a victim. In a New Brunswick child pornography case, for instance, the judge banned publication of the names, ages, likenesses, addresses, and occupations of the young victim and the couple facing charges, the schools the girl attended, and how she knew the couple. In addition, the media could only report that the offences had occurred in "the Moncton area" (Craig Babstock, "Child Porn Couple Makes Tearful Apology," *Times & Transcript* (Moncton), January 9, 2009).

Victims of Crime and Witnesses: Section 486.5(1)

This provision gives victims and witnesses involved in all crimes—not just those specified in section 486.4(1)—the right to seek an order banning publication of their names and information that could reveal their identities. A prosecutor can make the application for the ban on the person's behalf. The provision requires the judge to weigh the risk to the person's safety and the goal of encouraging the reporting of crime against the rights to open hearings and freedom of expression.[25] It is not mandatory for judges to impose the ban. The application must be in writing, and the judge may direct the applicant to notify others "affected by the order"—in most cases, the media—that the ban is being sought. A judge may hold a hearing to review the request and must consider several factors before imposing a ban: the impact on free expression, security concerns, and alternatives to restricting publication. The judge has the right to hold the hearing in private and the media can only report what happened if the ban is denied. If the judge forbids disclosure of the person's identity, "the contents of the application" are banned from publication, essentially imposing a blackout on the procedure. Journalists must choose their words carefully if the ban is imposed and ensure that descriptions of victims and witnesses do not provide enough information to disclose the person's identity.

Few crime victims and witnesses take advantage of this right to seek anonymity, perhaps to avoid triggering a legal battle with the media. As well, judges have ruled that there must be a solid basis for imposing the ban, so there is no guarantee the request will be granted. A Nova Scotia judge refused to ban publication of the identities of two young assault victims and the accused, their mother's boyfriend, ruling that persons who report crimes must expect public scrutiny and that a ban should not be granted to avoid "simple embarrassment."[26] In an Ontario case, a judge allowed the media to identify the owner of an apartment building where a murder occurred, ruling that the landlord's fear of financial loss did not justify a ban.[27] The wife of an Ontario man who stood trial in 2008 on charges of possessing child pornography was also unable to secure the ban, despite claims that harassing phone calls and taunts had forced her to move to another city. A judge refused to ban her identity when she testified at her husband's trial, ruling the courts must be open "despite the inconvenience, damage, humiliation, and even danger to witnesses." Media outlets were notified of the application and lawyers for two newspapers opposed shielding her identity, but the entire motion was subject to a publication ban for almost a year; the issues and outcome could be reported only after the woman decided not to appeal.[28]

A judge can formulate a ban that protects identities while granting the media considerable latitude in their reporting. At the high-profile trial of a Prince Edward Island nun charged with assaulting children in her care, the judge invoked this section to ban publication of the names of the five child victims and their parents. But the judge specified that the ban was limited only to their names and to "any other information that could lead a person that has no knowledge of any of the relevant circumstances to ascertain the names" of the children and parents. This significantly reduced the scope of the ban. Media outlets were free to name the defendant, to delve into the history of the small commune she led in rural PEI, and to explore allegations that the authorities had failed to protect the children.[29]

Note that the *Criminal Code* does not impose an automatic ban on identifying victims or witnesses who are 17 or younger, while the *Youth Criminal Justice Act* does when the person accused of the crime is also 17 or younger (as discussed later in this chapter). This creates an anomaly in the law: Young victims of crimes committed by adults—and young witnesses to such crimes—can be identified unless a judge imposes a ban, yet there is an automatic *Youth Criminal Justice Act* ban on identifying them if the perpetrator is under the age of 18.

Bans on identity are not new. Before the Code made a ban available to victims and witnesses, regardless of the crime involved, judges drew on their inherent powers to order that certain witnesses not be identified. In 1991 a jailhouse informant who testified against Guy Paul Morin, an Ontario man eventually exonerated of murder, was ordered to be identified only as "Mr. X" after complaining of being harassed and threatened. Ontario's Court of Appeal later upheld the ban.[30] In a 1998 ruling, the British Columbia Court of Appeal endorsed a publication ban on the identities of three gay men who testified at a murder trial, describing them as "vulnerable witnesses" who would suffer if their sexual orientation were exposed.[31] Likewise, Alberta's Court of Appeal found that it was proper to ban publication of the identities of people who were named in court as potential targets of a blackmail scheme—allegations that were not before the court. Though trials must be open, the court noted in its 1985 judgment, "where there is no public interest advanced by the publication of names, the trial process should not be used as a springboard for embarrassing revelations, or, worse, unfounded allegations concerning the private lives of citizens."[32] Bans have also been granted to prison inmates and other witnesses who feared retaliation if they testified[33] and to protect undercover officers.[34]

Justice System Participants: Section 486.5(2)

Section 486 was amended in 2002 to enable justice and law enforcement officials to apply for an order keeping their identities secret if they are taking part in cases that involve allegations of intimidation, terrorism, spying, or offences by members of criminal organizations such as biker gangs. Among those that the Code categorizes as "justice system participants" entitled to request the ban are politicians, judges, lawyers, jurors, court administrators, police officers, prison guards, parole officials, informants, and customs officers. The procedures for notifying the media and assessing the impact of a ban on freedom of expression must be followed.

As with the expanded ban on identifying crime victims and witnesses, there must be compelling grounds for shielding the person's identity. In one case, correctional officers who saw their co-workers assault inmates sought the ban, contending they might be persecuted by their colleagues if they were identified as witnesses. A judge refused the request, noting there was no risk the officers would suffer serious harm and the accused guards already knew their identities.[35]

Jurors: Sections 631(3.1) and 631(6)

Section 631(3.1), added to the *Criminal Code* in 2002, allows a prosecutor to apply to have persons called for jury duty referred to in court by a number rather than by name. The judge, who has the right to make the motion without being asked, must be satisfied that the procedure is "in the best interest of the administration of justice" and necessary "to protect the privacy or safety of the members of the jury." Under section 631(6), if an order has been made to use numbers as identifiers, the judge may impose a ban on publication of any information that could disclose a juror's identity if the ban "is necessary for the proper administration of justice."

Should Defendants' Names Be Banned from Publication?

When an Ontario man charged with a sex crime killed himself rather than endure humiliating publicity, the *Globe and Mail*'s legal affairs reporter, Kirk Makin, questioned the wisdom of publicly identifying persons accused of crimes. "Had some social imperative truly been served by publishing that name?" Makin asked in a column published in the *Ryerson Review of Journalism* (Spring 1989). "What was the hurry? Could it not have waited a few months until his trial?"

Lawyers who defend clients accused of crimes have asked the same question. Publicity magnifies the stigma of being charged with a crime—particularly a sexual offence—and strips many accused persons of the support of family, friends, and employers at a time when they need it most. And the damage is done despite the presumption of innocence and long before a court has passed judgment on whether the accusations have merit.

It is well established under the common law, however, that criminal defendants have no right to have their identities banned from publication. In *Re Regina and Unnamed Person* (1985), 22 CCC (3d) 284, Ontario's Court of Appeal lifted a ban on the identity of a young woman charged with infanticide, saying that judges do not have the power to shield accused persons or their families from embarrassment and possible loss of employment. And in *R v. Several Unnamed Persons* (1983), 44 OR (2d) 81 (HC), an Ontario judge refused to ban publication of the names of several defendants charged with gross indecency.

The Ontario Court of Appeal has ruled that bans on identifying young offenders and the victims of sex-related offences do not discriminate against adults accused of crimes, who have no such protection (*R v. D.(G.)* (1991), 2 OR (3d) 498 (CA)). Concerns for a suspect's safety and the integrity of a police investigation have also been found to be insufficient to justify a ban. A justice of the peace cited those grounds in banning the identity of a Toronto police officer charged with murder, but a judge lifted the ban within days at the media's request (Estanislao Oziewicz, "Constable Faces Murder Charge," *Globe and Mail*, June 18, 2002). A man who pleaded guilty to sexually abusing a child, however, was able to secure a ban on further publication of his photograph. The judge cited concern for the safety of the man, who was in a fragile emotional state and tried to commit suicide when his photograph was first published. The media remained free to publish the man's name (*R v. Roy*, [1998] OJ no. 3523 (QL) (Gen. Div.)).

In a Nova Scotia case, *R v. Prosper*, 2001 NSPC 33, a judge rejected a bid to ban the identity of a woman charged with a prostitution-related offence, despite her fears that publicity would cost her the support of her family, make it impossible to find work, and possibly compromise her safety. Despite the presumption of innocence, the judge said members of the public have a right to know about pending criminal charges, parents have a right to know who is associating with their children, and employers have a right to know whether employees and job applicants are facing criminal charges. In overturning a ban on the identity of a clergyman charged with sexual assault, an Ontario judge offered other compelling reasons for identifying persons accused of crimes:

> [T]he public has a genuine interest in knowing the identity of the accused. It is entitled to be advised that the police have conscientiously pursued a criminal investigation or put at ease where there has been a rash of crimes and an individual has been charged. The name of the individual is important as it is the only means of verifying the accuracy of the report. Furthermore, publication of the name of the accused will prevent speculation and damaging rumours against innocent parties and ensure the rights of the accused to a fair trial. The essential quality of the criminal process in a democracy is the absence of secrecy (*R v. Southam Inc.*, (1987), 37 CCC (3d) 139 (HC)).

> Consider the implications of not naming those charged with crimes. People would be arrested and essentially disappear into the black hole of the justice system, their fate known only to the authorities, family members, and close friends. Media accounts of court cases would feature the same anonymous, faceless defendants. The public's ability to monitor trials and to assess whether defendants are the victims of discrimination or the beneficiaries of favouritism would be severely eroded. As a Quebec judge noted in *Southam Inc. v. Brassard* (1987), 38 CCC (3d) 74 (SC), "secret justice is a social evil much more serious than the momentary inconvenience suffered by an accused whose identity has been revealed."

The ban, designed to protect jurors from intimidation or threats, is rare but may be sought when suspects are charged with serious violent crimes or have links to a motorcycle gang or other criminal organization. An Ontario judge imposed it at the 2004 trial of two men charged with a murder committed during a home invasion, based on allegations the suspects' associates had shot a witness to prevent the man from testifying. The ban was deemed necessary to protect jurors "and to provide them with the peace of mind required to enable them to fulfill their duties."[36] Two years later, another judge refused to impose the ban when two former members of the Hells Angels motorcycle gang stood trial for attempted murder. In that case, the judge pointed out there was no evidence the men were still active in the Hells Angels and police were not concerned about the safety of jurors.[37]

Bail Hearings: Section 517(1)
Bail hearings invariably produce information that could prejudice a defendant's trial—hearsay evidence, descriptions of past criminal behaviour, as well as debate over whether the suspect is likely to harm others or flee if released. To preserve the

right to a fair trial, section 517(1) authorizes a sweeping, temporary publication ban on the proceeding. Although a judge has discretion to deny a prosecutor's request for the ban, it must be imposed if the defendant seeks it. The restriction has withstood two media challenges under the Charter.[38] The most recent was decided in 2010, when the Supreme Court of Canada said the ban must continue to be imposed at a defendant's request in order to protect the liberty of suspects and their fair-trial rights. The ban prevents prejudicial allegations and evidence from being aired before trial, the court concluded, and ensures defendants do not face the additional burden of fighting for a publication ban. The court acknowledged the ban prevents the media from producing timely reports on why a suspect is detained or released, in some cases fuelling public outrage because the judge's reasons for granting or denying bail cannot be explained in the media. "Although not a perfect outcome," the court ruled, the bail hearing ban "represents a reasonable compromise."[39] The court also overturned an earlier Ontario ruling that would have limited the ban to cases slated to be heard before a jury, so the ban can be imposed on any bail hearing—even when a judge will hear the trial and there is no risk that the information presented could influence jurors.[40]

Although the ban is routinely sought, some defendants see a strategic advantage in allowing media coverage of the bail hearing. For example, no ban was sought at the January 2003 bail hearing for a Montreal woman charged with a murder committed two decades earlier, enabling the media to publicize an elaborate police undercover operation that the defence claimed had unfairly entrapped her.[41] In another Quebec case, the defence did not seek the ban because a man charged with murdering a police officer during a drug raid wanted the evidence to be aired; the man claimed he had mistaken the raid for a home invasion and he had acted in self-defence.[42]

The ban covers all evidence and information presented, as well as the submissions of the prosecutor and defence lawyer. As noted, it even prohibits disclosure of the judge's reasons for granting or denying bail, since the ruling will turn on whether there is evidence that the suspect is dangerous or likely to flee. Journalists can describe, in general, the factors a judge must consider before granting or denying bail—whether a person is considered dangerous or unlikely to show up for trial, for instance—and some media reports have done so.[43] But this should be done with caution and the report must not suggest or disclose the reasons a specific suspect has been released or detained. A BC television station and its reporter were convicted under section 517(1) in 2003 for paraphrasing a judge's comments that the two defendants faced charges that were "breathtaking in their seriousness" and that they must be denied bail to maintain public confidence in the justice system.[44] But courts have ruled that the fact that a hearing is held, whether bail is granted or denied, and the amount of a surety and other conditions of release can be published without violating the ban.[45] The suspect's name, a description of the charges and procedural matters, such as the progress of the hearing and the number of witnesses called to testify, can also be reported. A Quebec court has ruled that section 517(1) does not prevent the media from reporting information about a case gleaned from police or other sources, but warned that if such reports created prejudice they could bring a prosecution for contempt of court.[46] The ban does not appear to extend to what is said or occurs in the courtroom when court is not in session. No action was taken against a Halifax newspaper for reporting on a testy exchange between a court clerk and spectators that took place during a break in a bail hearing that was subject to a publication ban.[47] If a bail hearing is held for multiple suspects and some defendants seek a publication ban while others don't, the ban still applies to each of them and to all information presented. The ban will be effective "only if it applies to all the accused," the Supreme Court of Canada has ruled, since "the evidence against the parties will overlap to a great extent."[48]

If the ban is imposed, the bail hearing remains open to members of the public. Journalists can attend and take notes for future use. The ban can be imposed "before or at any time during" the hearing—a unique provision, because most bans must be sought before proceedings begin. Because this ban can be applied retroactively, journalists who duck out of a hearing early must ensure that the ban is not imposed in their absence. The ban can also be imposed on an array of other bail proceedings:

- hearings to review a judge's decision to grant or deny bail under sections 520(9) and 521(10);
- superior court bail applications held in murder cases under section 522(5);
- applications to vary the terms of bail under section 523(3);
- hearings into violations of bail conditions under section 524(12); and
- reviews of detention orders under section 525(8).

The ban is temporary and remains in force only while the defendant's right to a fair trial is in jeopardy. If no trial is held, the need for the ban disappears and the media are free to report what was revealed at the bail hearing. Section 517(1) specifies that the ban expires if the defendant is discharged after a preliminary hearing or, if a trial is ordered, once "the trial is ended." The ban also expires once a defendant pleads guilty, when the Crown withdraws the charges, or when a judge imposes a stay of proceedings to end the prosecution.

The media can report bail hearing information once it is presented as evidence at trial, and in most cases that is when the information sees the light of day. If the prosecution ends before trial, the hearing may be the only source of details about the defendant or related police investigations. Journalists who did not cover the bail hearing should be able to obtain a written or taped transcript of the proceeding from court officials.

Preliminary Hearings

Ban on Evidence: Section 539(1)

A preliminary hearing is held to assess the strength of the Crown's case, and the defence rarely calls witnesses to provide a balanced picture of the evidence. To ensure that potential jurors are not exposed to potentially distorted and prejudicial information, the judge presiding at the hearing has the power under section 539(1) of the *Criminal Code* to ban publication of "the evidence taken." The ban has been upheld under the Charter despite its restriction on the right to freedom of expression,[49] and it applies even if the case is not slated to be heard by a jury.

Like the restriction on publicizing bail hearings, this ban is mandatory if sought by the defendant but is imposed at the discretion of the judge if requested by the prosecution. Unlike the bail hearing ban, however, the order must be requested at the outset—the Code specifies that it must be sought "prior to the commencement of the taking of evidence." In a Quebec case, where a defendant did not seek the ban until a key witness was called to testify, the court ruled that a ban can be imposed during a proceeding but the judge has the right to deny the request. If the ban is imposed belatedly, it only applies to evidence presented from that point on.[50] It is rare for a preliminary hearing to be held without a ban in place.

The ban, introduced in 1969, restricts publication of the evidence presented—the testimony of witnesses and any information contained in documents presented as exhibits. Media reports can name the witnesses who testify (unless, of course, disclosure of their identities has been banned) and procedural matters, such as scheduling and motions. Legal arguments and the judge's rulings also can be reported, as long as no evidence is revealed.[51] Journalist Stevie Cameron was able to report background information about the case of Robert William Pickton, the BC man accused of murdering 27 Vancouver women and later convicted of murdering six of them—including the number of witnesses heard at his preliminary hearing, the cost of the prosecution, and the massive operation to excavate his farm in search of the DNA of missing women—without violating the ban.[52]

As is the case for bail hearings, journalists can attend preliminary hearings and take notes. The ban expires if the defendant is discharged or, if a trial is ordered, once there is a verdict, a guilty plea, or a stay of proceedings. It remains in force, however, if a defendant is discharged on some charges but ordered to stand trial on others. If multiple defendants are being prosecuted together, one or more of the co-accused may be discharged or plead guilty before trial. In such cases, the ban remains in place, as long as one of the defendants is still awaiting trial.

Should the case proceed to trial, evidence heard at the preliminary hearing becomes publishable when it is repeated at trial. Media outlets sometimes staff preliminary hearings in high-profile cases in the event that the accused is discharged or later pleads guilty. Likewise, a writer working on a book about a case can take advantage of this preview of the evidence to gather material and have the book ready for print soon after the trial or when the ban is lifted.[53]

Ban on Confessions and Admissions: Section 542(2)

If no ban is imposed, the media still must respect section 542(2) of the Code, which makes it an offence to reveal that "any admission or confession" was presented at a preliminary hearing. The ban is rarely mentioned in the courtroom and writers are expected to know that it is automatically in place. There is no restriction on attendance or taking notes when a confession or statement is being discussed in the courtroom.

The ban applies to the information contained in a confession or statement and even prohibits the media from reporting that a confession or statement exists. The concern is that members of the public will perceive any statement to be an admission of guilt, even though the defendant may have denied responsibility or offered an alibi. And there is no guarantee that the information will be admissible as evidence—the judge must hold a hearing to ensure that the statement or confession was not made under duress. Without the ban, there is a risk that potential jurors will be exposed to highly prejudicial information that, by law, cannot be used against the defendant at trial. As with the publication restrictions on bail proceedings and evidence presented at preliminary hearings, the ban expires if an accused person is discharged or when the trial ends. And once a confession or statement is presented at trial, its existence and contents can be published.

Prosecutions for violations of this section are rare, no doubt because most preliminary hearings are subject to an overriding ban on publishing the evidence presented. There were only two prosecutions in the decade after the ban was instituted in 1959, both involving news reports on cases heard in the Manitoba courts.[54]

It appears that this ban does not apply at the bail hearing stage. When a Montreal woman charged with murder waived her right to a ban on information revealed at her bail hearing, the *Globe and Mail* duly reported that she had been "enticed … to brag about the killing to an RCMP agent posing as a crime boss," and the exchange was recorded on videotape.[55] Although the *Globe* ran the risk of being cited for contempt for revealing the confession, the woman had just been arrested and the information was unlikely to prejudice a trial that would not be held for a year or more.

Jury Trials and the Voir Dire Rule: Section 648(1)
The ban under section 648(1) of the Code is perhaps the best-known but least-understood publication ban imposed in criminal cases. Some reporters and editors assume that no information disclosed at a *voir dire* hearing can be published, even after the trial is over and regardless of whether a jury is involved. But the ban, which is automatically in place, is far more limited in scope and duration. Section 648(1) stipulates that "no information regarding any portion of the trial at which the jury is not present" shall be published "before the jury retires to consider its verdict." As the wording makes clear, the ban is temporary and applies only to jury trials.

It is common for jurors to be asked to leave the courtroom from time to time during a trial. In their absence, the judge and lawyers for the Crown and defence will convene a *voir dire* hearing to discuss procedural issues or deal with motions or legal issues. Information disclosed at these hearings, which may never be put before the jury, has the potential to prejudice the defendant's case. The defence may challenge the validity of a search warrant, argue that police used illegal tactics to obtain a confession, or seek to have the defendant's criminal record or other information excluded as evidence. The ban is intended to ensure that jurors are not influenced by information found to be irrelevant or inadmissible. But the hearing remains open, and journalists can take notes for future use. And if information presented in a *voir dire* is found to be admissible, it becomes publishable once it is presented to the jury.

The *voir dire* ban highlights one of the fundamental differences between the Canadian and American approaches to coverage of the courts. The American practice is to sequester jurors for the duration of a trial while allowing unfettered media coverage of proceedings held in their absence. In Canada, jurors are allowed to return to their homes each night during a trial and are sequestered only when deliberations begin. Although our judges routinely warn jurors to ignore media coverage, the *voir dire* ban is an additional safeguard to prevent jurors from being exposed to information that does not form part of a case.

The ban stipulates that "no information" can be revealed—a term that encompasses all court business transacted in the jury's absence, evidence and legal argument alike. The fact that a hearing is being held in the jury's absence can be reported, since jurors are usually told that discussions will be held while they are excused from the courtroom. But reporting the subject or substance of the hearing, even in vague terms, is sufficient to violate the ban. A BC newspaper was convicted in 1997 for reporting that a *voir dire* was held to discuss "the admissibility of evidence" and that evidence was ruled inadmissible. The judge declared a mistrial and fined the paper $2,000, saying the report could have led jurors to engage in "improper speculation and conjecture" about the excluded evidence and its possible importance. In the same trial, a radio station was charged for reporting that counsel had announced that the defence would call no witnesses. Although the statement was made during a *voir dire*, the judge ruled that the information was "innocuous," accurate, and posed no risk of prejudicing the trial. Despite the technical breach of the ban, the radio station was acquitted of contempt.[56]

In one of the few rulings to interpret the scope of this provision, the media were able to report that the victim's father tried to attack the accused during a recess. Even though the jury was absent, Ontario's Court of Appeal said the incident did not occur during a "portion of the trial," as required for the section 648(1) ban to apply.[57] In another case, a BC television station was charged with contempt for broadcasting a *voir dire* discussion of the defendant's transfer to another jail. The province's Court of Appeal ruled that the ban applies not only to evidence but also to "housekeeping matters" discussed in the jury's absence. The ruling offered this rule of thumb: "If the judge is in the courtroom, and if court is still in session however informally, that is a portion of the trial."[58]

Once deliberations begin, jurors are kept together until they reach a verdict. Court officials must ensure they are insulated from news coverage of the case, even if this means covering up newspaper boxes in hotel lobbies and disconnecting the televisions in jurors' rooms. At this stage, media reports can no longer prejudice a defendant's right to a fair trial, so the section 648(1) ban expires the moment the jury is sequestered. All *voir dire* proceedings—the judge's rulings, testimony heard in the jury's absence, even evidence or statements ruled inadmissible—can be published and broadcast. As long as enough sheriffs' deputies are available to shield jurors from media reports, one judge ruled, "publishing prejudicial material after sequestration but before verdict does not present a real and substantial risk" to a fair trial.[59]

In high-profile trials, the start of deliberations is usually marked by news stories revealing the evidence not presented to the jury.[60] Sometimes the information is sensational, linking the defendant to other crimes. The *voir dire* may have been a turning point in a trial; the judge may have chastised the police for acting improperly or ruled that crucial evidence was tainted. The right to publish such information once the threat to a fair trial has passed reflects the openness of the courts and the media's watchdog role. The media must be free to explain the basis for a defendant's conviction or acquittal, and the key may be a ruling made during a *voir dire*. The public has the right to know what information was withheld from a jury and why. And if a prosecution collapses because of misconduct on the part of prosecutors or police officers, the circumstances and the identities of those responsible are obviously matters of public interest.

Despite the letter of the law, judges sometimes make an order extending the *voir dire* ban until the jury announces a verdict. There may be a concern that, in spite of the best efforts of court officials, sequestered jurors will be exposed to media reports about inadmissible evidence. Even a glimpse of a "What the Jury Didn't Hear" headline on a newspaper rack could interfere with deliberations by giving jurors a sense they have not heard the whole story. The highest authority for extending the ban comes from a 1985 ruling of the Alberta Court of Appeal, which says judges can restrict publication of *voir dire* evidence until a verdict is reached, drawing on their inherent power to control the proceedings before them.[61] If the ban is extended in this fashion, however, it does not prevent publication of information about a case that was not revealed in a *voir dire*, or information that the media have obtained from another source, such as the police.[62]

In rare cases, a defendant may plead guilty or have all charges withdrawn or stayed in the midst of a jury trial; if so, the ban on publishing *voir dire* evidence ends. Where two or more persons are being tried together, however, the situation is more complicated. If charges are stayed against one of them, the ban on *voir dire* evidence remains in place to protect the trial of the remaining defendant or defendants. When this situation arose in an Ontario case, the judge ruled that the media could publish a court-approved summary of the decision to stay the charges that did not implicate those still facing trial.[63] A similar restriction would likely apply if a defendant pleaded guilty but others were still on trial.

In trials heard without juries, *voir dire* hearings are convened to settle legal issues and to determine whether evidence is admissible. Counsel make their arguments or present the evidence in dispute, the judge hands down a ruling, and the trial continues. Because there is no jury to influence, there is no publication ban and the information presented at these hearings can be published without delay.[64]

Pre-Trial Hearings in Jury Cases

Charter challenges and other motions can take days or weeks to argue, resulting in lengthy *voir dire* hearings that inconvenience jurors and delay trials. To alleviate this problem, section 645(5) was added to the *Criminal Code* to enable complex legal issues to be dealt with at pre-trial hearings before a jury is empanelled. This change begged an important question for the media: If a jury has yet to be selected, does the *voir dire* ban under section 648(1) apply? The Code is silent on the issue and judges have differing opinions. Judges presiding over high-profile trials in Ontario and Nova Scotia have ruled that the *voir dire* ban applies to pre-trial hearings in cases slated to be heard by a jury.[65] Two Alberta judges have rejected this approach and ruled that section 648(1) applies only after a jury has been chosen. To prevent the disclosure of information that could prejudice a trial, however, the Alberta judges invoked their inherent powers to ban publication of pre-trial hearings dealing with the admissibility of evidence. This ban, like the section 648(1) ban, was to remain in place until the jury was sequestered.[66]

Media challenges have succeeded in opening some aspects of pre-trial hearings to public scrutiny. In the Nova Scotia case, the judge ruled that the word "information" in section 648(1) must be given a narrow interpretation when applied to pre-trial hearings. The judge banned publication only of evidence or allegations of wrongdoing on the part of the prosecution or accused that could prejudice the upcoming trial.[67] In the Ontario case, the judge ordered that pre-trial hearings were subject to a ban modelled on the Code's restriction on publicizing preliminary hearings—evidence was banned but the media could report on procedural matters.[68] As noted, the Alberta courts have restricted publication of pre-trial hearings involving the admissibility of evidence, enabling the media to report on procedural matters and legal issues aired at these proceedings.[69]

At some pre-trial hearings, the issue of a publication ban has not been raised and the media have covered the proceedings in detail, including testimony and legal arguments, while avoiding information bearing directly on the allegations against the defendant. At pre-trial hearings for a Nova Scotia probation officer facing dozens of charges of abusing young offenders, for example, the media reported details of a related investigation into unsubstantiated claims of widespread abuse in youth detention centres.[70]

Evidence of Sexual Conduct: Section 276.3(1)

Section 276.3(1) of the Code creates a ban that is automatically in place whenever a defendant charged with a sex-related offence applies to introduce evidence of the complainant's sexual history. These are sometimes referred to as *Seaboyer* applications, after the Supreme Court of Canada ruling that established the process to be followed in such cases.[71] The media can report that the defence has asked to present evidence of previous sexual conduct, but there is an automatic ban on the "contents of an application," the legal arguments presented, and any evidence of prior sexual activity put forward. If a judge agrees to hear the application, the hearing must be conducted in private.

The outcome of the application determines what information, if any, can be publicly disclosed. If the evidence is ruled admissible, the result of the hearing and the judge's reasons can be published. The actual evidence of sexual conduct can be reported once it is presented at trial. If the evidence is not found to be admissible, the ban remains in place and no details of the application or the hearing can be published. A judge has the power to lift this residual ban after weighing "the complainant's right of privacy and the interests of justice." Otherwise, the ban is permanent.

Confidential Records: Section 278.9(1)

The ban on publication of confidential records under section 278.9(1) is similar to the ban on evidence of sexual conduct and applies to applications for access to the private records of a complainant or witness. These include personal journals and diaries; medical, psychiatric, counselling, education, and employment records; and adoption or social services records. Lawyers often refer to this as an *O'Connor* application, after the Supreme Court of Canada precedent on access to such records.[72]

The ban is automatic. The media can report that an application has been made for access to records, but the "contents of the application" and all other details are banned. A judge must hold an *in camera* (private) hearing to determine whether the records are relevant and should be produced. If they meet this initial test, the judge must review the records and may convene a second *in camera* hearing to determine whether they should be provided to the defendant. The media are prohibited from publishing "any evidence taken, information given or submissions made" at these hearings. The ban covers the rulings at both stages, but the judge can permit publication of the outcome of the application after balancing the interests of open justice against "the right to privacy of the person to whom the record relates."[73] If the judge decides that the records can be used as evidence, any information they contain can be published once it is produced at trial.

Reviews of Mental Fitness of Offenders: Section 672.51(11)

A judge or a provincial review board may be asked to release a person who has been declared unfit to stand trial or found not criminally responsible for an offence because of a mental disorder. Although these hearings are open to the public, section 672.5(6) authorizes a judge or board to hold the session *in camera* if doing so is "in the best interests of the accused and not contrary to the public interest." The person involved may be excluded from the hearing in order to protect the safety of others or to further the person's treatment and recovery. If so, section 672.51(11) imposes a ban on publication of any information disclosed in the person's absence. There is also an automatic ban on the publication of information contained in an assessment report if the report has been withheld from the person. In addition, a judge or review board has the power to ban publication of an assessment report if the information would be "seriously prejudicial" to the person and the circumstances dictate that "protection of the accused takes precedence over the public interest in disclosure."

When these provisions were examined in an Ontario case, the judge said the principles set out in the *Dagenais* ruling demand that the ban, if imposed, must be limited in scope. A newspaper, *Oshawa This Week*, challenged a blanket prohibition on media coverage of the 2001 review hearing of a man released into the community after being found not criminally responsible for murder. The man was a suspect in a subsequent murder and the authorities were concerned that publicity would compromise the police investigation and prejudice the man's fair-trial rights if charges were laid. But the judge said a prosecution was "highly speculative" and that the risk of tainting the jury pool was "remote." The media were permitted to report that the man was a suspect in the killing, was alleged to be involved in illegal drug use, and had lived in the same crack house as the victim. The judge also lifted a publication ban on details of the man's medical treatment over a 14-year period, saying there was a legitimate public interest in knowing why he had been released into the community despite concerns over his drug use and criminal behaviour. But the judge upheld the ban on other details of the murder investigation, saying there was a real and serious risk that the information could compromise efforts to solve the crime.[74]

Search Warrant Documents: Sections 487.2(1) and 487.3(1)

When the authorities use a warrant to search a home, business, vehicle, or other location, three documents are created and filed with the courts. Investigators must submit a detailed affidavit to a judge or justice of the peace that describes the allegations being probed and sets out the evidence justifying a search. If the judge or court official authorizes the search, a warrant will be issued. If the search is successful, a document known as a **return** will be filed with the court, listing all of the items seized. In the landmark *MacIntyre* ruling on access to court files, the Supreme Court of Canada said that once a search has been conducted, and as long as evidence has been seized, these documents are open to public scrutiny.[75]

In an effort to restrict the scope of the *MacIntyre* ruling, Parliament added section 487.2(1) to the *Criminal Code* in 1985, creating a publication ban on certain details contained in search warrants if no charges had been laid. The provision barred the media from identifying locations searched, the persons who occupied or controlled those premises, and the identity of anyone named in a search warrant as a suspect in the offence under investigation. An exception was made if the publisher obtained the permission of those searched or named as suspects—an unlikely scenario, given the reluctance of most people to confirm they are the targets of an investigation. Superior courts in Ontario and Manitoba quickly struck down the amendment as a violation of the Charter guarantee of freedom of expression.[76] Quebec's Court of Appeal later confirmed that the provision is unconstitutional.[77] Although section 487.2(1) remains in the Code and these rulings are not binding in other provinces, the ban is no longer considered to have the force of law.[78]

The courts have the power, however, to curtail the right of public access to search warrants to protect other interests. Section 487.3(1) of the Code empowers a judge to seal warrants and associated documents if "the ends of justice would be subverted" by their disclosure or if the information they contain "might be used for an improper purpose." Grounds for sealing a warrant include the risk of compromising an ongoing investigation; the need to protect the identity of a **confidential informant**; the risk of prejudice to the interests of an innocent person; and the possibility that a person engaged in undercover operations will be endangered. Courts are also granted broad discretion to seal warrants "for any other sufficient reason," but the need to suppress the information must outweigh the importance of granting access to the court process.[79] A third party such as the media has the right to apply at any time to the judge who sealed the warrant, asking that it be made public.[80]

Restriction on Interviewing Jurors: Section 649

In high-profile trials in the United States, it is routine for jurors to hold a press conference to discuss their verdict. Contrary to popular belief, Canadian journalists are not forbidden from interviewing jurors once a case is over. The practice is rare, however, because the *Criminal Code* imposes strict limits on what jurors can say about a case. Section 649 makes it an offence for jurors to reveal "any information relating to the proceedings of the jury when it was absent from the courtroom." Jurors can only discuss what happened in the jury room if they are questioned by police during an investigation of possible obstruction of justice or, if jury tampering charges are laid, when called to testify in court. The Supreme Court of Canada has upheld this restriction as a reasonable limit on freedom of expression.[81]

The section covers everything said in the jury room—comments, opinions, arguments, and votes cast in the process of reaching a verdict. Journalists can ask jurors about their personal experiences, their impressions of the process, even their impressions of the evidence and the defendant—anything that does not disclose the jury's discussions or what fellow jurors said or did. Jurors have been interviewed in many high-profile Canadian cases without straying into the substance of the deliberations.[82] A journalist who serves on a jury is also free to write about the experience, as long as care is taken not to disclose what was said in the jury room.[83]

Writers must not try to contact or interview jurors before the verdict is announced—doing so could cause a mistrial or lead to an accusation of jury tampering. Although the prohibition on discussing deliberations only applies to jurors, a journalist who induced a juror to disclose what was said in the jury room could be charged as a party to the offence.

Interviewing Jurors

Jurors who convicted Paul Bernardo of first-degree murder in 1995 for the sex slayings of two Ontario teenagers made a pact not to speak publicly about their experience. But two weeks after the verdict, Eric Broadhurst broke ranks and spoke out at a media scrum when Bernardo returned to court to face other charges. The *Globe and Mail*'s report on the interview illustrates how far writers can go when interviewing jurors.

Broadhurst offered his views on a wide array of issues connected to the trial. Bernardo's ex-wife Karla Homolka was "as guilty" of murdering the girls, he said, and should serve the full 12-year sentence imposed when she pleaded guilty to manslaughter. Homolka testified at the trial, but Broadhurst said he did not believe her claims that she was a battered woman who was blackmailed and intimidated into participating in the murders.

The juror commented on trial tactics, including defence lawyer John Rosen's "gutsy call" to put Bernardo on the witness stand. He described Bernardo's performance as "cold and steely … . I don't know how he could remain so distant and cool and reserved." Intense media coverage of the trial, coupled with the presence of the victims' parents in the courtroom, made Broadhurst feel "very much in a fishbowl." He also discussed the emotional impact of having to view videos of the victims being sexually assaulted. "It was terribly difficult," he said, and, as a result of the viewing, most of the jurors were taking advantage of court-sponsored counselling sessions.

Broadhurst stressed that he was speaking only for himself. Had he described what other jurors said or how they reacted to the evidence, he would clearly have crossed the line between personal observation and improper disclosure of what happened in the jury room.

(Source: Kirk Makin, "Homolka Just as Guilty as Bernardo, Juror Says," *Globe and Mail*, September 16, 1995.)

Penalties

A breach of a *Criminal Code* ban is a summary conviction offence, punishable upon conviction by a maximum fine of $2,000 and up to six months in jail for an individual, and by a maximum fine of $25,000 for a corporation.[84] The media have also been prosecuted under a section of the Code that makes it an indictable offence, punishable by up to two years in prison, to disobey a court order.[85] A violation can also be prosecuted as a contempt of court, leaving the judge free to impose a higher fine. For example, a British Columbia newspaper convicted of contempt in 1999 for reporting *voir dire* evidence was fined $5,000.[86] Six years earlier, the *North Bay Nugget* pleaded guilty to a contempt charge for breaching the same ban and was fined $2,500 and ordered to pay $1,750 in costs for publishing information that triggered a mistrial.[87] There appears to be no precedent for a Canadian journalist or other writer being jailed for violating a publication ban.[88] One Manitoba judge took direct and immediate action after a publication ban was breached: the newspaper reporter responsible was barred from the courtroom for the remainder of the hearing, but the media outlet was allowed to send another journalist to cover the case.[89]

Statutory Bans Under the Youth Criminal Justice Act

The *Youth Criminal Justice Act*, which replaced the *Young Offenders Act* in April 2003, establishes procedures for prosecuting youths between the ages of 12 and 17 who are accused of crimes. The provinces and territories have passed similar legislation to deal with young persons charged with offences under their statutes, such as those concerning trespassing, driving infractions, and possession of liquor. Although youth courts are open to the media, the Act shields the identities of most of the persons involved—children and young persons who are victims of crime or witnesses, as well as the young defendants themselves. The Act's underlying principles stress the need to rehabilitate offenders and reintegrate them into their communities while protecting their rights, including their right to privacy.[90] The former *Young Offenders Act* accomplished these goals by imposing a strict ban on publishing identities. The current Act, in contrast, provides some flexibility. The names of most youths convicted of serious crimes can be disclosed, and there are provisions for offenders, victims, and witnesses to consent to having their identities revealed.

Identifying Accused Persons

Ban on Identifying Information: Section 110(1)

Section 110(1) of the *Youth Criminal Justice Act* makes it an offence to publish the name of a young person or "any other information related to a young person" if it "would identify" that person as being accused of an offence. This is similar to *Criminal Code* bans on identifying victims of crime and witnesses. But where the Code uses the words "any information that *could* disclose the identity," this section bans publication of information that "*would* identify," suggesting that there must be more than a possibility that the details will compromise the person's anonymity. Newspapers and television stations have used photos or video clips of young suspects who are shot from behind, or in which the person's face is digitally altered, without violating the ban; however, care must be taken to obscure tattoos or other features that could identify the person.

Writers must consider whether the young person's age and neighbourhood can be disclosed in combination with other details, such as school attended, grade, or other personal or family details, without identifying the young person, particularly in smaller communities. In some cases, judges will specify information they believe would identify the suspect if released. When a 17-year-old hockey player was charged with the on-ice assault of a teenage opponent in 2008, for instance, a Quebec court extended the ban to include the names of their teams.[91] The courts, too, must grapple with the privacy of young offenders in publishing rulings. In these rulings, names are replaced with initials and details that could identify the offender are obscured.

In upholding a similar provision in the *Young Offenders Act*,[92] an Ontario court said the goal of allowing youths to enter adulthood with a clean slate justifies the limit on freedom of the press.[93]

Exceptions for Serious Crimes: Section 110(2)

1. *Adult Sentences* Under this provision of the *Youth Criminal Justice Act*, the media have the right to identify youths convicted of an offence if a youth court judge sentences them as if they were adults. The Supreme Court of Canada approved of this provision in a 2008 ruling, noting: "When an adult sentence is imposed, the young person loses the protection of a publication ban."[94]

2. *Presumptive Offences* The ban also may be lifted for offenders over the age of 14 who have been convicted of a **presumptive offence**—so-called because, based on the youth's age and the seriousness of the offence, it is *presumed* an adult sentence is appropriate. Presumptive offences include murder, attempted murder, manslaughter, and aggravated sexual assault. Other serious violent crimes fall within the definition if it is the youth's third conviction for such an offence. The Act allows provincial and territorial governments to stipulate an age greater than 14 as the point at which a crime may be treated as a presumptive offence (in Quebec, for instance, this provision applies at age 16).[95]

   The Supreme Court ruling quoted above altered this provision, and a young offender is no longer expected to justify keeping the ban in place. Instead, the Crown must establish that the ban should be lifted.[96] The judge must weigh the importance of rehabilitation against the public interest in publication of the offender's identity.[97] If a prosecutor gives notice that the Crown will not seek an adult sentence for a presumptive offence, section 65 requires the judge to continue the ban on the offender's identity. How youth courts handle violent offenders and when their identities will be protected remain controversial issues; in early 2010 the federal government introduced legislation to loosen the restrictions on identifying those convicted of violent acts, but the amendments had not been passed at the time of writing.[98]

Lifting the Ban: Sections 110(3) and (6)

When young persons who were prosecuted under the *Youth Criminal Justice Act* or the *Young Offenders Act* reach the age of 18, they have the right under section 110(3) to authorize the media to disclose their identities. The only requirement is that the person must no longer be in custody for a youth crime at that point. It would be prudent for a journalist to obtain the consent in writing or to ask the person to record their consent on an audio or video recording, so that proof is available if needed. Offenders who are under the age of 18 or still in custody can apply, under section 110(6), to a youth court judge for an order lifting the ban. But the judge must be satisfied that disclosure is not contrary to the person's "best interests or the public interest."

Lifting the Ban To Apprehend Suspects: Section 110(4)

To help apprehend a suspect who is considered dangerous, the police can apply under section 110(4) of the *Youth Criminal Justice Act* for an order allowing the youth's identity and photograph to be publicized in the media for five days. The ban is reinstated at the end of this period, so media outlets must ensure that images and stories identifying the youth are removed from websites and electronic archives when the order expires.

Identities of Young Victims and Witnesses

Ban on Identifying Information: Section 111(1)

Section 111(1) of the *Youth Criminal Justice Act* bans publication of any information that "would identify" a child or a young person under the age of 18 who is the victim of a crime prosecuted under the Act or who is a witness to such an offence.

In 2001 an Alberta court ruled that a similar provision in the *Young Offenders Act*[99] was an unjustified infringement on freedom of expression because the ban was mandatory. The ruling overturned the convictions of two newspapers for revealing the name of a youth wounded in a 1999 shooting at a high school in Taber, Alberta. Charges were laid even though police had staged a press conference to present the injured youth with gifts and the papers had sought permission from the boy's parents before publishing his name. A judge of the Alberta Court of Queen's Bench ruled it is "illogical" to shield victims of youth crime while allowing the media to identify a young person injured or killed by an adult.[100] Although the judge's decision struck down the ban on victims and witnesses as unconstitutional, the ruling is not binding outside Alberta. Courts in other provinces may take a different view of the provision as retained in the *Youth Criminal Justice Act*. Until the provision is successfully challenged, the ban is mandatory.

Lifting the Ban: Sections 111(2) and (3)

Children and young persons who are victims or witnesses have the right, under section 111(2) of the *Youth Criminal Justice Act*, to authorize the media to disclose their identities, if they have the permission of their parents or once they reach age 18. If the victim or witness is deceased, the media can identify the person with the parents' permission. It appears that the consent of both parents is required, and journalists are advised to seek consent in writing or in an audio or video recording. Section 111(3) allows other young victims or witnesses to apply to a youth court judge to lift the ban. The judge must find that identification is in the person's best interests or the public interest.

Republication Once Ban Lifted: Section 112

When a young offender, victim, or witness grants permission to be identified or a judge lifts the ban, section 112 of the *Youth Criminal Justice Act* authorizes other media, once the person's identity has been made public, to republish the information without seeking permission or further court approval.

Permanency of Bans

Unless the ban on identity is waived or lifted, it is permanent. In the words of one judge, the ban "is absolute and continues even after the young offender becomes an adult."[101] So if an adult offender was convicted of crimes as a youth, the media are barred from reporting that the prior convictions exist, even if they are revealed in court. One newspaper was convicted of breaching the ban for publishing a report on a tribunal hearing into a man's complaint against the police. The report named the complainant, who was 20, and revealed that he had been convicted of robbery at age 17. Although the media were entitled to cover the hearing, naming the man and linking him to the robbery conviction was a violation of the ban.[102]

Penalties for Breaching a Ban: Section 138(1)

Under section 138(1) of the *Youth Criminal Justice Act*, violating any of the Act's bans on identifying young persons can be prosecuted as an indictable offence, punishable by up to two years in prison, or as a summary conviction matter. Convictions under the *Young Offenders Act* were generally punished with a fine; a television station that broadcast details identifying a teenage rape victim, for example, was sentenced to pay $990 in fines and court costs.[103]

In a high-profile prosecution under the *Young Offenders Act*, the editor-in-chief of the *Hamilton Spectator*, Kirk LaPointe, was granted an absolute discharge in 2001 for publishing the name, photograph, and youth court criminal record of a violent suspect. The breach was intentional; LaPointe wrote an editorial to accompany the coverage and argued that the law should no longer shield the man, who was 19 and the subject of a police manhunt.[104] LaPointe maintained that he broke the law out of concern for public safety, and the judge, in granting the discharge, made reference to his "very honourable intentions."[105]

Non-Statutory Bans

Statutes do not envision all situations where the publication of information could jeopardize a defendant's rights, someone's privacy, or other interests. As has been noted, superior court judges have inherent powers to formulate bans to deal with specific situations as they arise. Such bans must conform with the principles set out in the Supreme Court of Canada's ruling in *Dagenais v. Canadian Broadcasting Corp.* (and refined in *R v. Mentuck* and subsequent rulings) and must accommodate the media's right to freedom of expression.

Applying the Dagenais/Mentuck Test

The *Dagenais/Mentuck* test decrees that the fair-trial rights of an accused no longer trump freedom of expression—and that these competing rights must be balanced when devising bans. As noted in Chapter 3, for a ban to be imposed there must be a "real and substantial risk" to the fairness of the trial, and the judge must be satisfied that alternative measures—such as screening jurors, adjourning the trial or moving it to another location, or sequestering jurors before deliberations begin—do not provide reasonable options for alleviating the risk. Also, the benefits of imposing the ban must outweigh the harm caused by limiting freedom of expression. Finally, the prosecutor, defendant, or other party seeking the ban must prove that the restriction is necessary.

This balancing of rights is not restricted to judge-made bans, and is to be undertaken when a provision of the *Criminal Code* or other statute gives the judge the discretion to deny application to ban publication. The *Dagenais/Mentuck* test does not apply if the ban is mandatory—when a statute directs that the judge "shall" impose the ban if it is sought. (While these bans can still be challenged under the Charter, the Supreme Court of Canada's 2010 ruling upholding the mandatory bail hearing ban used another legal test to assess the impact on freedom of the press.)[106]

Banning Publication: Pros and Cons

In writing the majority judgment in *Dagenais v. Canadian Broadcasting Corp.*, Chief Justice Antonio Lamer discussed the factors that a judge should take into account when deciding whether a ban is appropriate.

Although imposing a ban will limit freedom of expression, he noted, it may also shield jurors from inflammatory media reports and inadmissible evidence. Bans may be an important factor in ensuring that reluctant or vulnerable witnesses, such as children and police informants, will testify. The anonymity that a ban affords protects the privacy of innocent parties, aids the *Youth Criminal Justice Act*'s goal of rehabilitating young offenders, and may encourage the reporting of sexual offences. Imposing a ban may be preferable to the expense and emotional costs of alternative measures such as delaying or moving a trial. In some cases, a ban may be necessary to protect national security.

Publicity, on the other hand, makes it more likely that persons with knowledge of a case will come forward. It makes witnesses less likely to lie in court and publicly denounces criminal behaviour, which may help reduce crime. Media coverage also promotes discussion of important public issues while providing the scrutiny needed to "prevent state and/or court wrongdoing."

Chief Justice Lamer said his list was not comprehensive, but illustrated the factors that judges should take into consideration before banning publication. If a ban is ordered, he added, "the judge must consider all possible ways to limit the ban and must limit the ban as much as possible." The judge must ensure that the restriction on the right of freedom of expression is in line with the benefits gained in protecting the right to a fair trial or other interests.

(*Dagenais v. Canadian Broadcasting Corp.*, [1994] 3 SCR 835, at 882–83, 891.)

Notifying the Media

In *Dagenais*, Chief Justice Lamer recognized that the media have a stake in any decision that leads to a restriction on publication. In light of this, judges may require the party seeking a ban to notify the media of an application for a discretionary ban, he said. Any media outlet that responds should be given an opportunity to appear in court to argue against banning publication. He did not specify which media outlets should receive notice, saying it was up to the courts in each jurisdiction to devise rules governing such notice.[107] Alberta implemented a practice note in 1997 that requires those seeking a publication ban to notify the media at least 14 days in advance, by posting written notice of the application at the courthouse where the motion is to be heard.[108]

When a publication ban is sought in other provinces, most judges recognize a journalist's right to rise and request a brief adjournment so that counsel can be retained to challenge the ban. To formalize the process and minimize the disruption to trials, the Nova Scotia courts launched an Internet-based system in 2001 that enables the media to be notified via e-mail of applications for bans. The Alberta provincial court introduced an e-mail notification system in 2004, British Columbia followed suit in 2005, and courts in other provinces have considered instituting a similar system.[109] The BC courts have also created a website page where information about judge-made bans is posted soon after they are imposed, and it includes a search function so journalists can find out whether a ban applies in a particular case. As of 2010 it only recorded bans imposed by the province's Supreme Court in the cities of Vancouver and New Westminster.[110] The Supreme Court of Canada's 2001 rulings in *R v. Mentuck* and a companion ruling, *R v. O.N.E.*, require judges to consider a ban's impact on freedom of expression even if media organizations do not challenge the ban. In these rulings, the court also called on Parliament to amend the *Criminal Code* to simplify the process for appealing discretionary bans after they have been imposed. Provincial courts of appeal have no right to review a ban issued by a superior court judge, forcing media outlets to pursue a costly and time-consuming appeal directly to the Supreme Court of Canada.[111]

When Judge-Made Bans Are Likely in Criminal Cases

Separate Trials for Co-defendants

Judge-made bans are commonly imposed when two or more persons are accused of the same crime but face separate jury trials. Because the evidence will be similar, information presented at the initial trial or trials could incriminate those still awaiting their day in court, undermining their rights to a fair trial and an impartial jury. In pre-Charter days, judges often slapped a complete blackout on any media coverage of the initial trial—a highly effective measure, but one that sacrificed the principles of open courts and freedom of expression.[112]

In keeping with the Charter and *Dagenais/Mentuck*, such bans are now crafted to allow trials to be publicized as they occur. Typically, to prevent prejudice to future trials, only the names of the co-accused and evidence or statements suggesting their guilt will be banned from publication, and only until all trials are completed. Another approach is to impose a so-called sunset ban that comes into effect shortly before a trial and prevents further publication of evidence disclosed at related trials or that has previously appeared in media reports. In 2009, for instance, a judge banned publication of information about the criminal records of those charged in a murder and any evidence, drawn from a previous trial, that would implicate them in the crime. With jury selection in the case slated for January 2010, the judge directed that the ban would come into effect on December 1, 2009.[113] If defendants still awaiting trial testify at the trial of a co-accused, their evidence will likely be banned until all trials are over.[114]

Guilty Pleas and Stays Involving Co-defendants

A similar approach is taken when a person pleads guilty and is sentenced while one or more co-defendants are awaiting trial. The most controversial example is the 1993 ban on publishing details of Karla Homolka's sentencing after she pleaded guilty to manslaughter in the deaths of two abducted teenage girls. The ban was designed to protect the fair-trial rights of her estranged husband, Paul Bernardo, who was awaiting trial for murder.[115] When a Nova Scotia woman pleaded guilty to being an accessory to murder, the judge rejected a defence request for an outright ban. The media could report that the woman had pleaded guilty to helping someone escape after a murder was committed, but publication of the identities of two men accused of the murder was banned until their trials were over.[116]

If charges are stayed against an accused person, a temporary ban may be imposed on the disclosure of information that could prejudice the future trials of co-defendants.[117]

Multiple Trials for the Same Defendant

Concerns that publicity will taint a future jury trial also arise if a defendant faces two or more trials for different offences. In one Nova Scotia case, a man facing back-to-back jury trials on charges of robbery, assault, and sexual assault sought a blanket ban on publishing the evidence and outcome of the first trial until the completion of the second. A third trial was pending, but no ban was sought because it was not slated to be heard by a jury. The judge applied the *Dagenais* test and imposed a limited ban that enabled most of the evidence from the initial trial to be reported. The only exceptions were two pieces of evidence likely to surface at both trials and the defendant's testimony if he took the witness stand at the initial trial.[118]

When a BC man stood trial for murder in January 2000, the judge imposed a temporary ban on publication of "the fact of and the circumstances surrounding" a second murder charge against the same man, which was slated to go to trial in another city the following year. The ban remained in place until the completion of the first trial.[119]

Change of Venue Applications

Trials are usually held in the area where the offence occurred. But section 599 of the *Criminal Code* enables a court to move the trial to another part of the province—known as a change of venue—to protect the defendant's right to a fair trial. Applications to move trials rarely succeed. There must be evidence that pre-trial publicity about the case has been so intense, or popular sentiment is running so strongly against the accused, that it may not be possible to empanel an impartial jury.[120]

Although the Code makes no provision for a publication ban on these hearings, it is common for judges to ban publication of the information presented—and even the fact that an application for a ban has been made—until the end of the trial. The concern is that further publicity surrounding the application may defeat the goal of moving the trial to an area where potential jurors are less familiar with the case. It is also possible that information presented at the hearing will be prejudicial or inadmissible as evidence at trial.[121] A temporary ban on any information about a change of venue application, even an unsuccessful one, is in keeping with the *Dagenais* principles and a justifiable limit on freedom of expression, according to an Alberta ruling. In that case, the judge said disclosure of a bid to move a trial from Edmonton could suggest that the defendants had no faith that the city's residents would treat them fairly or, worse, that the defendants were playing the system to "get a better deal elsewhere."[122]

Not all change of venue hearings are subject to a publication ban, however. An Ontario judge refused to order a ban in a case where the pre-trial publicity was not considered to be extensive or prejudicial.[123]

Prior Restraint

In rare cases, a court will issue an order restricting someone from publishing or broadcasting information that could prejudice a trial that is pending or under way. Quebec's Court of Appeal barred the CBC from airing a videotape made by security cameras as a gunman stormed the province's National Assembly. Although the footage had already been shown at the man's trial on three charges of first-degree murder, the court ruled that the broadcast should be delayed because it was possible that the man's convictions would be overturned and a new trial ordered. During 1999 the Saskatchewan courts twice barred CTV from showing a movie that dramatized the case of David Milgaard, who was wrongfully convicted of murder and served 23 years in prison before being freed. The temporary bans were imposed to protect the trial of the man accused of the crime, who was eventually convicted.[124]

Appeals

Appeal courts have the power to ban publication of evidence or documents, but such bans are rarely imposed at the appeal stage of a criminal case. A new trial is only a possibility and, if one is ordered, the risk of prejudice is low because it will be months before a new jury will be empanelled. The Quebec Court of Appeal's ban on broadcasting videotapes of the gunman who stormed the province's legislative chamber, imposed while the man's appeal was before the court, is an exception rather than the rule. A judge of British Columbia's Court of Appeal refused to ban publication of fresh evidence suggesting a romantic relationship had developed between a juror and a defendant during a murder trial. The judge said publicizing the evidence when it was put before the appeal court would not prejudice the outcome of the appeal or any future trial.[125]

Retrials

If a person convicted of an offence wins a new trial on appeal, a news report rehashing evidence from the first trial—by now a distant memory for most people—could prejudice the upcoming retrial. The risk would be greatest if the information were published shortly before or during the new trial. As noted in Chapter 8, such reports could be punished as a contempt of court. A judge has the power to settle the issue by banning publication of any information about the first trial until the second trial is complete.[126]

Enforcement of Publication Bans

Assessing Liability

As is the case with contempt law, some courts are recognizing that decisions to publish or broadcast information are made at the corporate and managerial level, not by the reporter. In the words of one judge, "it is publication, not authorship, that is the *actus reus*" of the offence.[127] At three newspapers, reporters were acquitted in 1999 of violating the privacy provisions of New Brunswick's *Family Services Act* in stories that identified a child and parents involved in a custody battle with social workers. There was evidence that their editors and publishers made a conscious decision to publish the names in spite of the law. Although the reporters wrote the offending stories, a judge ruled that "they played no part ... in publishing the articles."[128] In another case, a television news anchor who read a report that breached a publication ban was prosecuted for contempt, but the Crown withdrew the charge because the anchor was not involved in preparing the story or deciding that it should be broadcast.[129] The Ontario Court of Appeal ruled in 2007 that journalists can be convicted of violating a ban only if there is proof they intended to do so, but the media outlet that employs them can still be convicted and fined.[130]

In other cases, however, the journalist has been found responsible and convicted. A Saskatchewan reporter was found guilty in 2003 of violating a ban after taking part in newsroom meetings to discuss how much information could be included in his story. The judge said the reporter's supervisors had decided to publish based on his input.[131] British Columbia's highest court says a journalist can be convicted even if he or she did not make the ultimate decision to publish or broadcast banned information. A television journalist who prepared a story and presented it on air was found to have played "a prominent and critical role" in its broadcast and was convicted of violating the *Criminal Code* ban on bail hearings.[132]

The courts also take the view that owners and senior officials are responsible for ensuring that their staff members are properly trained and comply with the law. "It is no answer to blame a junior employee," warned a British Columbia judge who ordered the company operating a television station to pay $4,000 to charity as punishment for breaching a ban. "There is an onus on senior management to properly supervise and educate junior employees about the principles underlying the criminal justice system, including media rights and responsibilities."[133] In another case, a judge criticized media bosses for putting "economic concerns" ahead of proper news coverage by not staffing trials on a full-time basis. In this trial, a television station was charged with violating a ban that had been imposed when its reporter was not present in the courtroom.[134]

Prosecutors and judges have excused journalists and publishers who have inadvertently breached a ban through an editing error or other mistake.[135] But it is no defence to plead ignorance. The courts have ruled that journalists have a duty to know the law and to make reasonable efforts to determine whether a publication ban has been imposed.[136] Though courts in some jurisdictions flag case files and rulings that are subject to publication bans, practices vary and the failure of court staff to warn that a ban is in place will not absolve the media of blame. A judge of British Columbia's Supreme Court has put it bluntly: "[T]here is absolutely no obligation on the court, prosecutors, defence counsel or anyone for that matter, to advise members of the media whether there is a publication ban in place."[137] Once a ban's existence becomes known, failure to take steps to minimize the damage may be viewed as further evidence of contempt for the court process. The same BC judge chastised the publisher of a community newspaper for failing to halt delivery after being warned that a ban had been breached. The judge said the publisher's "callous disregard" for the administration of justice and rights of the defendant was "unacceptable and intolerable in the extreme."[138] The same logic would apply to a radio or television station that deliberately continued to broadcast a story containing banned information.

Publication Bans and Information Obtained from Other Sources

Writers and publishers may be uncertain whether information already in the public domain, or obtained from sources other than the courtroom, becomes off-limits once a publication ban is imposed. Basic facts about the accused person, the charges, and the circumstances of the offence can still be published, even if this information is repeated at a bail or preliminary hearing that is subject to a ban.

The status of banned information gleaned from outside sources is less clear. The *Vancouver Province* was acquitted in 2001 of breaching a ban by publishing information that duplicated what had been disclosed during a *voir dire* hearing. The paper reported that a BC man awaiting the jury's verdict in a murder case was a suspect in a slaying in Edmonton. The judge found that the information had been previously reported and "was derived entirely from other sources"—a spokesman for the Edmonton police—and not from the hearing. Section 648(1) of the *Criminal Code* restricts the publication of information presented during "any portion of the trial" held in the jury's absence. But, in the judge's view, it does not prohibit publication of information gleaned "from sources other than what is said and done in the courtroom." However, this is not an invitation for writers to thwart a ban by stepping into the courthouse lobby to interview police officers, lawyers, or witnesses. The judge said a report based on information supplied by outside sources could be punished as a contempt of court if it created a real risk of prejudice to a fair trial (*R v. Dawson et al.*, 2001 BCSC 178, at paragraphs 10, 11, and 17).

A Saskatchewan judge rejected this reasoning in convicting the Saskatoon *Star-Phoenix* and one of its reporters in 2003 for violating a ban on publishing information presented at a sentencing hearing. The newspaper argued that "the bulk" of its information came from a previous hearing that was not subject to the ban. The judge, however, said the information was being published for the first time and the reporter and his editor knew the facts were essentially the same as those subject to the ban. The journalists were aware of the ban, the judge added, and understood that it was intended to protect the rights of a co-defendant yet to stand trial (*R v. The Star-Phoenix*, 2003 SKQB 2).

Another judge, this one in Quebec, ruled that section 517(1) of the Code, which provides for a ban on bail hearings, does not bar the media from reporting information gleaned from police or other sources. The judge overturned a lower court's ban on publishing certain information supplied by police—in this case, the defendants' names and addresses. This was hardly a victory for openness, however. The police routinely identify who is charged with crimes, and making this basic information public does not prejudice the right to a fair trial. As well, the judge issued a stern warning that published reports based on outside information may still be punished as a contempt of court (*Southam Inc. v. Brassard* (1987), 38 CCC (3d) 74 (Que. SC)). An Ontario judge faced with intense media coverage of the case of a nurse charged with murder disagreed with this approach. In his view, the ban at the preliminary hearing stage prevents the publication of information produced as evidence at the hearing, even if the same facts were published previously or obtained from other sources (see M. David Lepofsky, *Open Justice: The Constitutional Right To Attend and Speak About Criminal Proceedings* (Toronto: Butterworths, 1985), 71).

Judges would undoubtedly use their contempt power to punish anyone who published information from outside sources in a deliberate effort to flout a ban, particularly if the information was sensational or prejudicial. Take the example of a news report revealing a defendant's criminal record despite a ban imposed when the information was presented at a bail hearing. If court files were consulted to confirm the previous convictions, a journalist could argue that the ban, which covers "the information given" at the hearing, was not breached. But this would not prevent a court from convicting the reporter of contempt if the information was found to create a real risk of prejudice to the defendant's future trial.

It is clear, however, that a publication ban does not apply retroactively to information published before it was imposed. A journalist who reported the criminal record of a person accused of murder, for example, could not be charged with violating a ban imposed days or weeks later when the same information was introduced at a bail hearing. In the view of one media law scholar, a ban prevents the media "from publishing information which has already been introduced into evidence and that is all" (Lepofsky, at 72). But journalists must always be aware of the risk of *sub judice* contempt. The *Vancouver Province* was convicted of contempt and fined $8,000 in 2001 for reporting that a man charged with two murders had notified the media of a motion to ban publication of his trials until both were complete. The report appeared the day the first trial began and, when it did, the judge ordered a temporary ban on publishing any reference to the second murder allegation. Although no ban was in place when the *Province*'s story appeared, the judge found it "fundamentally inexplicable" that the newspaper would pre-empt the very issue before the court by publishing information that was "utterly prejudicial" and clearly in contempt of court (*R v. Pacific Press*, 2001 BCSC 115, at paragraphs 12 and 18).

The lesson for journalists is that once a publication ban has been imposed or notice of a ban application has been given, any effort to skirt it using information from outside sources is fraught with risk. Even if the information appears to be beyond the scope of a ban, legal advice should be sought before it is published because there remains the possibility of a prosecution for contempt of court.

Civil Liability for Breaching a Ban

If a statutory or court-ordered ban shielding a person's identity is breached, those responsible could face a lawsuit seeking damages in the civil courts. Judges or juries have found that publishers and their employees owe a duty of care to persons whose identities have been shielded, and have awarded damages exceeding $10,000 to victims of sexual assault.

In an Ontario case, the *Kitchener-Waterloo Record* identified a female police officer who was sexually assaulted during an undercover investigation of a doctor accused of abusing patients. The newspaper named the officer despite an order, under section 486(3) of the *Criminal Code*, banning publication of her identity and the identities of eight other complainants. Because the case involved allegations of sexual assault, the judge said the reporter knew that a ban was likely to be in place and had a duty to ensure that there was no ban before publishing the name. The judge rejected the newspaper's position that a police officer is not entitled to the benefit of a publication ban. The officer's work suffered as a result of the revelation, she withdrew from friends and family, and she sought psychiatric help to cope with feelings of embarrassment and humiliation. A judge ordered the newspaper and the reporter who wrote the story to pay her $12,000 in damages. The newspaper's owner, Southam Inc., was assessed a further $5,000 in punitive damages after suggesting that it might once again flout the ban and identify the officer.[139]

Two civil claims have succeeded in British Columbia. The *Nelson Daily News* and one of its writers were ordered to pay $19,000, including $15,000 in punitive damages, to a woman who was sexually assaulted and seriously injured by her common law spouse. The newspaper reported the woman's name, leaving her so ashamed she was forced to move from Nelson and abandon plans to open a business in the community.[140] In the other case, the *Duncan Citizen* was ordered to pay $10,000 in damages to a woman who had been sexually abused by her stepfather. The paper published a report naming the stepfather, violating a ban on identifying either the defendant or the victim. The stepfather was well known within his small community, but another factor was a competing newspaper's report, published the same day, which withheld both names—in keeping with the terms of the ban—but revealed the relationship between the man and his victim. The woman sued the *Citizen*, and a judge ruled that the cumulative effect of the reports was to identify her, forcing her to quit her job and move away in shame. Since the *Citizen* had clearly breached the ban, the judge said the paper could not complain that a competitor's report had "fleshed out" the information needed to identify the victim. The paper also argued that its reporter had consulted records supplied by court staff, which did not disclose that a publication ban was in effect. But the judge said this was not sufficient to fulfill the duty of care to the woman, because the paper should have known such a ban was possible in a sexual assault case.[141]

Although these cases deal with the ban regarding sex-related offences under section 486(3) of the *Criminal Code*, any crime victim or witness identified in violation of a ban would have the right to sue. The same would be true if a published report breached a *Youth Criminal Justice Act* ban on identifying a young victim or witness.

Publication Bans and the Internet

The Internet's instant global reach, disregard for national borders, and the ease of retrieving material posted online create new challenges for Canadian courts and lawmakers bent on controlling what's published about criminal cases before trial. Some judges have questioned whether traditional methods of controlling pre-trial publicity—publication bans and contempt law—have been rendered unenforceable or obsolete. One frustrated New Zealand judge, faced with repeated breaches of publication bans on that country's websites, suggested the Internet has rendered such orders "stupid" and "futile."[142] And just days after Justice John Gomery imposed a temporary ban in March 2005 on evidence given at the inquiry into federal contracts awarded to Quebec advertising firms, a blogger based in Minnesota brazenly posted the banned information on his website for all to see.[143]

In the landmark *Dagenais* ruling, former chief justice Antonio Lamer noted that the Internet, like cable television and satellite transmissions, creates "considerable difficulties for those who seek to enforce bans .... In this global electronic age, meaningfully restricting the flow of information is becoming increasingly difficult." The Internet's vast audience, he added, is a factor to be considered when a judge decides not only whether a publication ban is justified, but whether it will ultimately prove effective.[144] While grappling with the effectiveness of the *Criminal Code* ban on information presented at bail hearings, judges of Ontario's Court of Appeal pointed out that any juror inclined to find out more about a case need only type the name of the defendant into a search engine such as Google. Archived media reports and material posted to social media sites such as Facebook are readily accessible "regardless of location or time," the court noted in 2009, making it "no longer appropriate or realistic to rely on jurors' faded memories of any pre-trial publicity by the time of the trial as the basis for confidence that they will not remember what they have read or heard."[145] The judge presiding over a high-profile Nova Scotia murder case in 2010 thought it prudent to remind jurors not only to disregard media reports on the case, but also to avoid checking out anything posted on Facebook, MySpace, YouTube, or Twitter.[146]

Bans and Canadian Online Media

Enforcing bans in the Internet age can be difficult, but it is not impossible. Publication bans and other restrictions on publicizing Canadian court proceedings apply to websites and Internet postings that originate within Canada.

Media outlets have been prosecuted for violating publication bans through online reports, and these cases suggest the steps news organizations should take to minimize the damage caused when a ban is breached in today's online world. The CBC was fined $7,500 in 2007 after material identifying an undercover police officer involved in the investigation of serial killer Robert William Pickton was posted on its website for almost two weeks, breaching a ban imposed by the BC Supreme Court. The broadcaster removed the information once the violation was discovered and asked search engine provider Google to remove all cached versions of the original posting. The judge imposed a higher fine than usual for a ban violation, noting "the medium of an Internet posting provided worldwide continuous access to the identity of the undercover officer over a 13-day span."[147] In another case, the Canadian Press pleaded guilty and was fined $4,000 in 2009 for violating a ban on identifying an undercover officer who testified at another BC murder trial. When the violation was discovered the following day, CP issued an advisory to its media and other clients to kill the article. A new story was circulated, with the officer's name deleted, and the original version was

Figure 9.1 Restricting the flow of information that might be viewed by jurors is becoming increasingly difficult, but some media outlets have been successfully prosecuted for violating bans through online reports.

removed from CP's in-house archival database, to make sure it could not be used again. CP also conducted an online search to find where the offending article had been posted, and contacted the operators of these websites to ensure the article was removed. In imposing the fine, the judge noted that publication of the information "to the world" via the Internet compounded the seriousness of the violation.[148]

In rare cases, a ban may be imposed on information after it has been published online. In 2010 a New Brunswick judge banned publication of the identity of the victim of a kidnapping and sexual assault, even though her name and photograph were widely reported over the course of the month-long search for her. While the ban prevented further publication of information that could identify her, it was not retroactive. Archived and cached media reports identifying her, but posted before the ban was imposed, remained accessible on the Internet.[149]

Bans and Foreign Media Coverage

If American reporters show up to cover a preliminary hearing in Canada, can they ignore the ban routinely imposed on publishing or broadcasting the evidence? Can news organizations based in other countries post details of the evidence on their websites for anyone—including Canadians who may serve on the jury—to see? And if a publication ban is breached in this fashion, do Canadian judges have the power to enforce their orders outside Canada?

The American media, accustomed to few restrictions on pre-trial coverage of cases at home, often report banned names and evidence with impunity when reporting on Canadian cases. After a Montreal teenager known as Mafiaboy was charged in 2000 with hacking into computer databases, the *New York Times*, the *Washington Post*, and other major American newspapers identified his father, who had been arrested on unrelated charges. Although Mafiaboy himself was not named, the reports violated the ban, under Canadian law, on publishing information that identifies minors charged with crimes. The name appeared in copies of papers distributed in Canada and on the newspapers' websites, but no action was taken against the papers involved.[150] In most cases, enforcement is impossible. Writers and publishers can be prosecuted for contempt or breaching a ban only if they are within our borders or agree to come to Canada to face charges.[151] In 1982 a reporter for the *Bangor Daily News* who covered a preliminary hearing in New Brunswick voluntarily returned to Canada to contest a charge of publishing banned evidence. He was ultimately convicted.[152]

In any event, most American media reports have no impact on a suspect's right to a fair trial in Canada. If a television station in Arizona chooses to broadcast details of the evidence presented at a preliminary hearing in Calgary, the chances are slim that one of the viewers is a vacationing Calgarian who will be called for jury duty. However, if the Arizona signal is rebroadcast in Alberta or the evidence is reported on the station's website, the risk of tainting jurors becomes real, as does the risk of a prosecution. The *Bangor Daily News* report revealing banned evidence led to a prosecution because the newspaper was circulated in the New Brunswick town where the case was destined to go to trial.

Although Canadian authorities are unable to prosecute foreign media outlets for breaching publication bans, judges have employed other means to prevent banned information from reaching the Internet. During a hearing in the Paul Bernardo murder case in 1993, the judge barred foreign journalists from the courtroom to prevent the American media from following through on a threat to ignore a sweeping publication ban.[153] In 2002, lawyers for Robert Pickton, the BC man convicted of murdering six women, tried to have all journalists and spectators barred from their client's preliminary hearing to prevent the American media from reporting banned evidence via the Internet. The request was denied but, after Seattle-based media outlets published the opening day's evidence on their websites, the presiding judge specified that the publication ban included material posted on the Internet.[154] He also put the three American reporters involved on notice that they would be barred from the courtroom, and could be fined or jailed, if the violations continued. The website coverage ceased.[155]

The Pickton case highlighted problem areas that may arise for the Canadian media when banned evidence appears on the Internet. During Pickton's preliminary hearing, lawyers suggested that Canadian media reports drawing attention to American websites where banned evidence could be found were, in themselves, a violation of the publication ban.[156] When pre-trial hearings in the Pickton case began in June 2005, the judge barred the Canadian media from publishing or broadcasting "information that would tend to identify websites or other sources" (such as blogs) where banned information about the hearings was posted—effectively preventing end-runs around the ban. Simply revealing the names and addresses of websites and blogs posting the information, the judge in the Pickton case warned, would violate the ban.[157] As well, a Canadian media website that created a hypertext link to reports containing banned information, or reposted them, would risk being prosecuted. The RCMP launched an investigation in 2004 when it appeared that an American television report disclosing evidence against Pickton had been posted on a website maintained by the University of British Columbia.[158]

Social Media Sites, Blogs, and Publication Bans

Everyone who posts to a personal website or blog, uploads a video to YouTube, maintains a Facebook or Twitter account, or uses other social media tools could be considered a publisher in the eyes of the law. So anyone who uses the Internet to post or disseminate information in violation of a ban imposed by the courts or set out in the *Criminal Code, Youth Criminal Justice Act*, or other statute risks being prosecuted. "Social media sites, like all other forms of media, are subject to and governed by publication bans," a spokesperson for Ontario's Ministry of the Attorney General asserted in 2010.[159] The federal Justice Department has also taken the position that publication bans apply to Facebook and other social media.[160] Charges have been filed against Internet users who ignore bans. In 2001 an Ontario judge cited a Cornwall man for contempt for posting banned evidence on his website in the midst of a jury trial. Although the judge stopped short of ordering the website to be shut down, he discharged the jury and issued an injunction to prevent further postings that would interfere with the trial.[161] The following year, a Quebec man was convicted of contempt after flouting a ban and publishing pre-trial evidence on several websites and newsgroups, and through e-mails.[162] Ontario writer Stephen Williams was charged in 2003 with more than 50 counts of violating publication bans imposed to protect the victims of murderer and rapist Paul Bernardo, based on information posted on Williams's personal website. He pleaded guilty and was sentenced to serve three years on probation.[163] And in 2006 an Ontario woman involved in a child protection case was found in contempt for identifying herself and her children on her personal website, in violation of a publication ban. She was ordered to remove the material or face arrest.[164]

Despite prosecutions such as these, the proliferation of Facebook, Twitter, and other social media sites—and the sheer volume of posted material that could violate a publication ban—makes enforcement difficult. In January 2010, after a judge banned publication of the identity of an Ontario toddler and the man accused of murdering him, people posted photographs and tributes identifying the boy on a Facebook page that attracted 2,400 members within days. A media challenge led to the ban being lifted, making the possible Facebook violations a moot point.[165] Later in 2010, an Ontario man created a Facebook page that identified a defendant accused of sexual assault, in violation of a publication ban. The man, who argued he had a duty to warn people that the suspect had been previously convicted of sexual offences, vowed to fight any attempt to shut down the site.[166] The judge who imposed a publication ban on the trial of some of those charged in a high-profile Toronto murder case seemed to acknowledge that the courts can do little to enforce bans on social media users. The judge's 2009 ruling stipulated that the ban applied "to publications, electronic and otherwise by organizations in the business of providing news" and not to "comment by individuals."[167]

Journalists, who must obey the law even when they feel a ban is unnecessary or goes too far, are understandably frustrated at seeing banned information published with impunity. A few media outlets have demanded that the authorities crack down on social media users and overhaul publication bans to take into account the impact of the Internet.[168] One thing is clear—a journalist or news organization that republished banned material from a social media site could be prosecuted, even though the information is already widely available on the Internet.

Tips for Dealing with Publication Bans

When a ban is imposed, journalists need a clear understanding of what can and can't be reported. Here are some tips on how to get the story without violating a ban.

Statutory Bans

- *Read the section* Check the *Criminal Code* or *Youth Criminal Justice Act* for the precise wording of the ban. Consult media law guides like this one for more detail on what each ban covers and how the courts have interpreted its scope.

- *Seek legal advice* If in doubt, check with an editor or producer who has experience dealing with the ban and, if necessary, ask to consult your media organization's lawyer to clarify what can and can't be reported.

- *Don't ask counsel* Crown attorneys and defence counsel routinely apply for publication bans, but may not understand how the wording of a ban translates into news coverage. Don't expect them to act as your legal adviser—and don't be surprised if their advice is to err on the side of withholding information. Their primary interest is their client and their case, and not necessarily the public's right to know.

- *Watch for expanded bans* Judges may expand the scope of a statutory ban to cover specific information, such as the hometown or occupation of a victim of crime. Unless the media succeed in challenging such a ban as excessive, its terms must be followed.

- *Learn when to expect a ban* Bans are routinely imposed on bail hearings and preliminary inquiries; victims of sexual assault, with few exceptions, ask the courts to protect their identities. When covering cases and hearings such as these, assume there's a ban until you have confirmed the case is an exception to the rule.

Non-statutory (Judge-Made) Bans

- *Consider a challenge* The *Dagenais* precedent gives the media the right to challenge non-statutory bans—the ones judges craft to deal with specific concerns about evidence, privacy, or fair-trial rights. The law demands that such bans allow as much information as possible to be reported, and courts must give serious consideration to arguments in favour of a limited ban. If you're in court when such a ban is being discussed, most judges will accommodate a journalist's polite request for a short break so editors and legal counsel can be consulted about a possible legal challenge.

- *Get it in writing* Make sure you understand the exact terms of the ban. Ask a court official or the judge's office to supply a written version of any ban announced in the courtroom. And make sure editors and producers know the terms as well, so they don't inadvertently add material from previously published stories that may now be subject to a ban.

- *Learn when to expect a ban* High-profile cases attract more media attention, so judges are more likely to face applications for common law bans on evidence or the identities of those involved. When co-defendants stand trial separately or one pleads guilty, a ban is likely to be sought on evidence implicating those still awaiting trial.

- *When in doubt, check* Tight deadlines and smaller newsroom staffs make it tough for journalists to be in the courtroom for every moment of a hearing or trial. Check with court officials and counsel to make sure you have not missed a motion for a publication ban in your absence. Notices of bans are prominently displayed on judges' written rulings and, in some jurisdictions, court officials flag the case file or post a notice at the court-room door when a ban is in place.

- *Request a notification system* The Nova Scotia courts pioneered a system that notifies media outlets by e-mail when a judge-made ban is sought, to give them a chance to argue against the ban or to limit its scope; courts in other jurisdictions have implemented or are considering similar notification systems. An online registry of publication bans has been established for some BC courts, enabling journalists to quickly check whether there's a ban on a particular case. And many courts have established a media-liaison committee, where judges and journalists can discuss publication bans and other access issues. Find out what's being done in your province or territory, and lobby court officials and judges for better ways of ensuring everyone knows when bans are sought and imposed.

Criminal and Youth Court Publication Bans: A Summary

In spite of the maze of publication bans, much of the business of Canada's courts is open to public scrutiny. The effect of the *Dagenais/Mentuck* rulings has been profound, ending some restrictions on publication, curbing others, and giving the media new tools to challenge attempts to limit openness. But it is an ongoing struggle. Bans continue to be sought and imposed, and newsrooms don't have enough reporters to cover every case or the money to mount a legal challenge to every ban. Critics accuse the courts of paying lip-service to the principle of open courts while ignoring the spirit and the letter of the *Dagenais/Mentuck* precedents.[169] In the fall of 2003, the *Globe and Mail* discovered that a case had been before the Ontario courts for close to three years under a shroud of secrecy so intense that even the order banning publication was sealed. The newspaper sounded an alarm about the excessive secrecy and, within a week, the judge convened an open session to reveal what the case was about and who was involved.[170] The media widely condemned a near-total blackout imposed in 2010 on the prosecution of two people charged with murdering an eight-year-old Woodstock, Ontario girl, led by a front-page *Toronto Star* editorial bearing a large, one-word headline: "Gagged."[171] A judge who spoke to the *Globe and Mail* in response to the outcry acknowledged there can be "a huge disconnect" between lofty court rulings espousing more openness and the daily struggle to balance the rights of the media and defendants in the courtroom.[172]

Secrecy, however, will continue to be the exception rather than the rule. "[T]he courts are taking a very rational, case-by-case approach and are increasingly insisting that exemptions to the openness rule will only be permitted sparingly and on the clearest of evidence," notes Toronto media lawyer Peter Jacobsen. "For journalists this is good news. It means that life is being breathed into freedom of expression as set out in section 2(b) of the Charter."[173]

NOTES

1. *Canadian Charter of Rights and Freedoms*, part I of the *Constitution Act, 1982*, RSC 1985, app. II, no. 44.

2. G. Stuart Adam, "The Thicket of Rules North of the Border: Canadian Perspectives on a Free Press and Fair Trials" (1998), vol. 12, no. 1 *Media Studies Journal* 24–30, at 26–27.

3. The stylebook of the Canadian Press wire service, for example, advises that if no ban is sought on the identity of a victim of sexual assault, editors "should still weigh whether using the name will send a signal to readers that the media are indifferent to the problems of sexual assault victims in general." If the name is used, the report should also explain why the person is being identified in this instance. Patti Tasko, ed., *The Canadian Press Stylebook,* 15th ed. (Toronto: Canadian Press, 2008), 219.

4. "Missing Woman Was Held in Basement," *Chronicle-Herald* (Halifax), March 25, 2010; Craig Babstock and Aloma Jardine, "Man Charged in Bizarre Case of Missing N.B. Woman," *Times & Transcript* (Moncton) (republished at canada.com), March 25, 2010.

5. Barbara Brown, "Spectator Fined $4,500 for Violating Court Identity Ban," *Hamilton Spectator,* June 1, 2010.

6. *R v. Calabrese and Renard (No. 3)* (1981), 64 CCC (2d) 71, at 72 (Que. SC).

7. Ibid., at 71.

8. *R v. Southam Inc.* (1989), 47 CCC (3d) 21, at 24 (Ont. CA).

9. *Criminal Code*, RSC 1985, c. C-46, as amended.

10. *R v. Canadian Broadcasting Corp.*, [2003] SJ no. 400 (QL) (PC). This provincial court ruling is not binding but it is well reasoned, firmly based on Charter precedents, and likely to be followed by other courts.

11. Ibid., at paragraph 73.

12. *Canadian Newspapers Co. Ltd. v. Canada (Attorney General)* (1988), 43 CCC (3d) 24 (SCC).

13. *R v. Canadian Broadcasting Corp.*, [1996] NWTJ no. 115 (QL) (SC).

14. *R v. BCTV* (1999), 131 CCC (3d) 414 (BCCA).

15. The ban remains in force until varied by a court with jurisdiction to do so. See *R v. K.(V.)* (1991), 68 CCC (3d) 18 (BCCA).

16. *R v. Canadian Broadcasting Corp.*, 2004 SKQB 320. The Supreme Court of Canada denied leave to appeal the ruling. See "Supreme Court Turns Down CBC Publication Ban Case," CBC News Online, June 21, 2007.

17. Ingrid Peritz, "Assault Victim 'X' Steps into the Light," *Globe and Mail*, May 25, 2005; Peritz, "Former Quebec Child Star Sues Ex-Manager for Sexual Abuse," *Globe and Mail*, May 26, 2005.

18. *R v. Adams*, [1995] 4 SCR 707.

19. *R v. Betker* (1997), 33 OR (3d) 321, at 324 (CA).

20. *R v. London Free Press Printing Co.* (1990), 75 OR (2d) 161 (HC).

21. *R v. Southam Inc.*, supra note 8, at 24.

22. *R v. Southam Inc.* (1987), 37 CCC (3d) 139 (HC).

23. Paul Simons, "Ruling a Victory for Freedom of the Press: Naming Accused Doesn't Identify Victim: Judge," *Edmonton Journal*, May 8, 2007.

24. Greg Younger-Lewis, "Court Gag Order Protects Name of Accused Molester," *Nunatsiaq News*, April 30, 2004.

25. *Criminal Code*, s. 486.5(7).

26. *R v. Rhyno et al.* (2001), 193 NSR (2d) 250 (Prov. Ct.).

27. *R v. Brown*, [1999] OJ no. 4870 (QL) (SC).

28. *R v. Carswell*, 2008 ONCJ 518; Tracy McLaughlin, "Publication Ban Rejected for Accused's Spouse in Child Porn Case," *The Lawyers Weekly*, October 3, 2008, 3.

29. *R v. Poulin*, 2002 PESCTD 68. For an example of media coverage of the case, see Kevin Cox, "PEI Commune Death Probed," *Globe and Mail*, November 30, 2002.

30. *Morin v. R* (1997), 32 OR (3d) 265 (CA). See also Monique Conrad, "Morin Nemesis 'Mr. X' Remains a Mystery Man," *The Lawyers Weekly*, February 21, 1997.

31. *R v. Paterson*, [1998] BCJ no. 126 (QL) (SC). See also Brad Daisley, "Sexual Orientation Not To Be Revealed by Media," *The Lawyers Weekly*, March 6, 1998.

32. *Toronto Sun Publishing Corp. v. Alberta (Attorney General)*, [1985] AJ no. 543, at paragraph 17 (QL) (CA).

33. *R v. McArthur* (1984), 13 CCC (3d) 152 (Ont. HC) involved inmates. In *R v. Friebus* (1988), 62 CR (3d) 378 (Sask. QB), a ban was imposed to protect a witness who feared reprisals and feared for his safety.

34. In *R v. Mentuck*, 2001 SCC 76, the Supreme Court of Canada ruled that the identities of police officers involved in an undercover sting operation could be banned from publication, but only for one year.

35. *R v. Cutherbert*, cited in Sheldon Gordon, "Silence by Decree," *The National*, May 2003, 40–43, at 41.

36. *R v. Jacobson*, 2004 CanLII 20531 (Ont. SC), at paragraph 64.

37. *R v. Vickerson*, 2006 CanLII 2410 (Ont. SC).

38. *Re Global Communications and Canada (Attorney General)* (1984), 10 CCC (3d) 97 (Ont. CA); *Toronto Star Newspapers Ltd. v. Canada*, 2010 SCC 21.

39. *Toronto Star Newspapers Ltd. v. Canada*, supra note 38. Media outlets challenged the ban in the case of 18 Toronto-area men charged with terrorism-related offences in 2006 and the 2005 Alberta case of a man accused of murdering his wife. For more on the ruling's impact on public understanding of the justice system, see Dean Jobb, "Supreme Court Muzzles Media and Public's Right To Know," *Toronto Star*, June 11, 2010.

40. *Toronto Star Newspapers Ltd. v. Canada*, 2009 ONCA 59. In contrast, the Alberta Court of Appeal—like the Supreme Court of Canada—upheld the ban. See *R v. White*, 2008 ABCA 294.

41. Tu Thanh Ha, "RCMP Sting Found Alleged Contract Killer, Bail Court Told," *Globe and Mail*, January 8, 2003.

42. Paul Cherry, "Laval Cop Shot Four Times, SQ Officer Testifies," *Montreal Gazette*, May 4, 2007.

43. See, for instance, "Filmmaker Accused of Murder Denied Bail," *National Post*, July 25, 2009.

44. *R v. Daly*, 2003 BCSC 1143, upheld by the BC Court of Appeal in *R v. Daly*, 2005 BCCA 389.

45. *R v. Forget* (1982), 65 CCC (2d) 373 (Ont. CA).

46. *Southam Inc. v. Brassard* (1987), 38 CCC (3d) 74 (Que. SC).

47. Andrea MacDonald, "Teens Jailed Until Trial," *Daily News* (Halifax), November 7, 2002.

48. *Toronto Star Newspapers Ltd. v. Canada*, supra note 38.

49. *R v. Banville* (1983), 3 CCC (3d) 312 (NBQB).

50. *R v. Harrison* (1984), 14 CCC (3d) 549 (Que. Ct. Sess.).

51. See Dean Jobb, "Driving Blind: The Gerald Regan Sex Case Helped Define How Far Reporters Can Push a Publication Ban" (Summer 1997), *Media*, at 6.

52. Stevie Cameron, "The Missing Women," *Elm Street*, November 2003, at 22.

53. See, for example, Stephen Kimber, *"Not Guilty": The Trial of Gerald Regan* (Toronto: Stoddart Publishing, 1999). By attending the lengthy preliminary hearing into sexual assault charges against a former Nova Scotia premier, the author was able to produce a book quickly and incorporate details of allegations that did not proceed to trial.

54. Wilfred H. Kesterton, *The Law and the Press in Canada* (Ottawa: Carleton University Press, 1984), 15.

55. Tu Thanh Ha, supra note 41.

56. *Re Daily Courier, a division of Thompson Canada Ltd.*, [1997] BCJ no. 1840 (QL) (SC).

57. *R v. Dobson* [1985], 19 CCC (3d) 93 (Ont. CA).

58. *R v. CHBC Television*, 1999 BCCA 72, at paragraph 44.

59. *R v. Dawson et al.*, 2001 BCSC 178, at paragraph 19.

60. See, for example, Peter Cheney, "Just Desserts: What the Jury Didn't Hear," *Globe and Mail*, December 7, 1999, which took advantage of the ban's expiry to report details of a confession ruled inadmissible during a *voir dire* in a high-profile Toronto murder trial.

61. *Toronto Sun Publishing Corp. v. Alberta (Attorney General)*, supra note 32, at paragraph 5.

62. *R v. Dawson et al.*, supra note 59, at paragraph 11.

63. *R v. Brown* (1998), 126 CCC (3d) 187 (Ont. Ct. Gen. Div.).

64. A request for a publication ban on *voir dire* evidence presented at a trial heard by judge alone was rejected in *R v. Muise* (1993), 124 NSR (2d) 98 (SC).

65. *R v. Bernardo*, [1995] OJ no. 247 (QL) (Gen. Div.); *Re The Chronicle-Herald et al. and The Queen (R v. Regan)* (1998), 124 CCC (3d) 77 (NSSC).

66. *R v. Cheung (Donald) et al.* (2000), 150 CCC (3d) 192 (Alta. QB); *R v. Trang*, 2001 ABQB 437.

67. *Re The Chronicle-Herald et al. and The Queen*, supra note 65, at 89–90. See also Dean Jobb, "Regan Coverage Ruling Partial Victory for Media," *Chronicle-Herald* (Halifax), October 22, 1997.

68. *R v. Bernardo*, supra note 65. Another judge of the same court, the Ontario Court of Justice (General Division), took the view that s. 648(1) stands as an "absolute prohibition" on publication of pre-trial hearings in jury cases. See *R v. Ross*, [1995] OJ no. 3180 (QL) (Gen. Div.).

69. *R v. Cheung (Donald) et al.* and *R v. Trang*, supra note 66.

70. See Dean Jobb, "400 Abuse Claims Given OK Without Proof—Officer," *Chronicle-Herald* (Halifax), June 13, 2000; Dean Jobb and Donna-Marie Sonnichsen, "Some Abuse Claimants Never Lived at Centres," *Chronicle-Herald* (Halifax), May 31, 2000.

71. *R v. Seaboyer*, [1991] 2 SCR 577.

72. *R v. O'Connor*, [1995] 4 SCR 411.

73. *Criminal Code*, ss. 278.4(2), 278.6(2), and 278.9(1).

74. *Oshawa This Week v. Ontario (Review Board)*, [2002] OJ no. 554 and OJ no. 5383 (QL) (SCJ).

75. *Nova Scotia (Attorney General) v. MacIntyre*, [1982] 1 SCR 175.

76. *Canadian Newspapers Co. v. Canada (Attorney General)* (1986), *(sub nom. Canadian Newspapers Co. v. Canada)* 53 CR (3d) 203, 29 CCC (3d) 109 (Ont. HC); *Canadian Newspapers Co. v. Canada (Attorney General)* (1986), 28 CCC (3d) 379 (Man. QB).

77. *Girard v. Ouellet* (2001), 198 DLR (4th) 58 (Que. CA), cited in Michael Crawford, *The Journalist's Legal Guide*, 4th ed. (Toronto: Carswell, 2002), 185, at footnote 12.

78. Crawford, ibid., at 185. See also *Martin's Annual Criminal Code 2002* (Aurora, ON: Canada Law Book, 2002), 801–2.

79. *Criminal Code*, s. 487.3(2).

80. *Criminal Code*, s. 487.3(4).

81. *R v. Pan; R v. Sawyer*, [2001] 2 SCR 344.

82. For examples of juror interviews, see Ian Bailey, "Jurors Should Have Convicted Me If They Thought I Was Guilty, Murrin Says," *National Post*, January 29, 2000; Michael Harris, *Justice Denied: The Law Versus Donald Marshall* (Toronto: Macmillan of Canada, 1986), 139.

83. See, for instance, Stephen Kimber, "Nothing We as a Jury Could Do Would Make Their Lives Right Again," *Daily News* (Halifax), January 22, 1999.

84. *Criminal Code*, ss. 735(1)(b) and 787(1).

85. *R v. The Star-Phoenix*, 2003 SKQB 2.

86. Noted in *R v. CHBC Television*, supra note 58, at paragraph 3.

87. Canadian Newspaper Association, "North Bay Nugget Fined $2,500 Over Mistrial," *The Press and the Courts*, vol. 12, no. 3, July 5, 1993.

88. In a 1999 contempt ruling arising from the breach of a publication ban, British Columbia's Court of Appeal noted that no one in the province had been jailed for such an offence "over the past several decades." *R v. CHBC Television*, supra note 58, at paragraph 61.

89. Dean Pritchard, "Judge Bans Free Press Reporter," *Canoe* online news, June 26, 2009. The ban was under a provincial statute prohibiting the identification of those testifying at a child protection hearing. These restrictions are examined in chapter 10.

90. *Youth Criminal Justice Act*, SC 2002, c. 1, ss. 3(1)(a)(ii) and (b)(iii).

91. Sidhartha Banerjee, "Lawyer for Quebec Player on Trial for Assault Cites Unwritten Hockey Code," Canadian Press report, July 30, 2009.

92. *Young Offenders Act,* RSC 1985, c. Y-1, s. 38(1).

93. *Southam Inc. v. R* (1984), 48 OR (2d) 678 (HCJ).

94. *R v. D.B.*, 2008 SCC 25, at paragraph 83.

95. Presumptive offence is defined in the *Youth Criminal Justice Act*, ss. 2(1)(a) and (b).

96. *R v. D.B.*, supra note 94. The ruling has been criticized for shrouding youth justice in excessive secrecy. See Alan Shanoff, "Supreme Court Wrong To Tinker with YCJA," *Edmonton Sun*, June 15, 2008.

97. *Youth Criminal Justice Act*, s. 75(3).

98. Caroline Alphonso, "Tory Bill Proposes Publicizing Names of Violent Young Offenders," *Globe and Mail*, March 17, 2010.

99. *Young Offenders Act*, s. 38(1).

100. *R v. Thomson Canada Ltd.*, 2001 ABQB 962. See also Darcy Henton, "Naming Names: Teenage Crime Victim Waives Publication Ban, But Prosecutors Charge Newspapers Anyway," *Sunday Herald* (Halifax), November 18, 2001.

101. *R v. Sun Media Corporation*, 2001 ABPC 108, at paragraph 12.

102. Ibid., at paragraphs 5 and 6.

103. Amy Pugsley Fraser, "ATV Guilty of Violating YOA," *Chronicle-Herald* (Halifax), July 20, 1996.

104. Kirk LaPointe, "We Have a Duty To Tell the Public the Whole Story," *Hamilton Spectator*, November 5, 1999.

105. Canadian Newspaper Association, "Spectator Editor's 'Good Intentions' Brings Absolute Discharge for Breaching YOA," *The Press and the Courts*, vol. 20, no. 2, April 28, 2001.

106. *Toronto Star Newspapers Ltd. v. Canada*, supra note 38, at paragraph 18.

107. *Dagenais v. Canadian Broadcasting Corp.*, [1994] 3 SCR 835, at 868–69. An Ontario judge has ruled that there is no obligation to notify the media, even though such notice is vital if media outlets are to exercise their right under *Dagenais* to challenge the ban. David Gambrill, "Should Courts Have To Notify Media of Publication Bans?" *Law Times*, June 11, 2001. Leave to appeal the decision to the Supreme Court of Canada was denied. *United States of America v. D.J.M.*, [2001] SCCA no. 352 (QL).

108. *Publication Bans for the Court of Queen's Bench of Alberta*, Criminal Practice note 4, January 1, 1997.

109. See Dean Jobb, "Notes on Publication Ban Notices," *Canadian Lawyer*, October 2001, 20–24; James Rossiter, "Discretionary Publication Bans" (2002), vol. 27, no. 3 *Nova Scotia Law News*, at 67, 91; Cristin Schmitz, "CBA, Media Seeking Notice," *The Lawyers Weekly*, February 28, 2003; and Heather J. Innes, "Alberta's Provincial Court Sets New Rules on Publication Bans," *The Lawyers Weekly*, April 30, 2004, 8. Details of the BC system are available on the province's Supreme Court website, at http://www.courts.gov.bc.ca/supreme_court/publication_bans/notification.aspx.

110. The web address is http://www.courts.gov.bc.ca/supreme_court/publication_bans/search.aspx.

111. *R v. Mentuck*, [2001] 3 SCR 442, 2001 SCC 76; *R v. O.N.E.*, [2001] 3 SCR 478, 2001 SCC 77.

112. The practice persisted even after the Charter came into force, until the *Dagenais* test established that competing rights must be balanced. See, for example, the ban on all evidence presented at the trial of the first two co-accused in *R v. Doyle* (1988), 86 NSR (2d) 26 (SC).

113. *R v. Valentine*, 2009 CanLII 46171 (Ont. SC).

114. For an example of this approach, see *R v. Wood* (1993), 124 NSR (2d) 128 (SC).

115. The Homolka ban is discussed in Omar Wakil, "Publication Bans on Court Proceedings in Canada," *Yearbook*, vol. 4, December 1995, 101–10, published by the Centre for the Independence of Judges and Lawyers. A similar approach was taken when a co-accused pleaded guilty in the case of *R v. Church of Scientology of Toronto* (1986), 27 CCC (3d) 193 (Ont. HC).

116. *R v. Wournell*, 2002 NSSC 270.

117. *R v. Brown*, supra note 63.

118. *R v. Shrubsall (W.C.)* (2000), 187 NSR (2d) 310 (SC).

119. *R v. Pacific Press*, 2001 BCSC 115, at paragraph 7.

120. This test was established in *R v. Charest* (1990), 57 CCC (3d) 312 (Que. CA).

121. These reasons were cited by a judge of the Northwest Territories Supreme Court in *R v. Atsiqtaq*, [1987] NWTJ no. 123 (QL) (SC).

122. *R v. Trang*, supra note 66, at paragraph 44. A temporary ban was also imposed on an unsuccessful bid for a change of venue in *Southam Inc. v. R (No. 2)* (1982), 70 CCC (2d) 264 (Ont. HC).

123. *R v. Reid*, [1994] OJ no. 3064 (QL) (Gen. Div.).

124. *R v. Fisher*, [1999] SJ no. 726 (QL) (QB); Thomas Claridge, "Milgaard Film Banned To Avoid Sequestering Fisher Jury," *The Lawyers Weekly*, December 3, 1999.

125. *R v. Budai*, 2000 BCCA 226, at paragraphs 31 and 32.

126. *R v. Barrow*, [1989] NSJ no. 121 (QL) (SC).

127. *R v. Dawson et al.*, supra note 59, at paragraph 23.

128. *R v. Dimmock* (1999), 211 NBR (2d) 138 (QB). For media coverage, see Richard Duplain, "Custody Case: Reporters Acquitted," *Fredericton Daily Gleaner*, March 9, 1999; Canadian Newspaper Association, "Reporters Acquitted of 'Publishing' Names Under Ban," *The Press and the Courts*, vol. 18, no. 2, April 30, 1999.

129. *R v. BCTV, a division of WIC Television Ltd.*, [1999] BCJ no. 1558, at paragraph 2 (QL) (SC).

130. *R v. Helsdon*, 2007 ONCA 54. See also Dean Jobb, "Publication Bans the Responsibility of News Outlet, Not Just Reporter," *The Lawyers Weekly*, February 9, 2007, 3.

131. *R v. The Star-Phoenix*, supra note 85, at paragraph 17.

132. *R v. Daly*, 2005 BCCA 389, at paragraph 25.

133. *R v. BCTV, a division of WIC Television Ltd.*, supra note 129, at paragraph 27.

134. *R v. CHBC Television*, supra note 58, at paragraph 49. The station's conviction was overturned on appeal. The judge ruled that the offending report, which revealed a discussion of the defendant's transfer between jails, did not pose a real risk of prejudicing the trial.

135. See, for example, Canadian Newspaper Association, "Toronto Sun Avoids Contempt Charge for Breaking Publication Ban," *The Press and the Courts*, vol. 18, no. 6, December 31, 1999.

136. Ibid., at paragraph 69.

137. *R v. The Maple Ridge, Pitt Meadow Times Newspaper*, 2001 BCSC 1357, at paragraph 12.

138. Ibid., at paragraphs 23 and 26. The newspaper was fined $5,000 for breaching the *voir dire* ban. The jury was discharged but the prosecution and defence agreed to have the trial continue before a judge sitting alone.

139. *R.(L.) v. Nyp* (1995), 25 CCLT (2d) 309 (Ont. Gen. Div.).

140. *J.M.F. v. Chappell*, [1998] BCJ no. 276 (QL) (CA). See also Brad Daisley, "Violating Publication Ban Costs Newspaper $19K," *The Lawyers Weekly*, March 6, 1998.

141. *P.R.C. v. Canadian Newspapers Co.*, [1993] BCJ no. 741 (QL) (SC). See also Daisley, "Newspaper Must Pay $10,000 for Identifying Assault Victim," *The Lawyers Weekly*, April 16, 1993.

142. David McLoughlin, "Court Suppression Orders Futile—Judge," *Dominion Post* (Wellington, New Zealand), May 16, 2005.

143. Elizabeth Thompson, "U.S. Blogger Defies Publication Ban," *Gazette* (Montreal), April 5, 2005; Jane Taber, "Testimony at Gomery Published on Blogs," *Globe and Mail*, April 4, 2005; Rondi Anderson, "Borderless Blogs vs. Canada Press Ban," *Christian Science Monitor*, April 13, 2005.

144. *Dagenais v. Canadian Broadcasting Corp.*, supra note 107, at paragraphs 89–92. See also Willard Z. Estey, "Freedom of Expression vs. the Individual's Right to Privacy," in Frederic L.R. Jackman, ed., *Media & Society* (Toronto: Canadian Journalism Foundation and The Empire Club of Canada, 1994), 27–43, at 42; Justice John Sopinka, "Freedom of Speech and Privacy in the Information Age," address to the University of Waterloo Symposium on Free Speech and Privacy in the Information Age, November 26, 1994, Waterloo, Ontario, cited in George S. Takach, *Computer Law* (Toronto: Irwin Law, 1998), at 185, note 156.

145. *Toronto Star Newspapers Ltd. v. Canada*, 2009 ONCA 59, at paragraphs 177 and 221.

146. Ian Fairclough, "Stay Off Twitter, Judge Tells Jury," *Chronicle-Herald* (Halifax), June 15, 2010.

147. *R v. Canadian Broadcasting Corporation*, 2007 BCSC 1970.

148. *R v. The Canadian Press*, 2009 BCSC 988.

149. See James Keller, "Social Media Presenting New Challenges for Publication Bans, Experts Say," *Globe and Mail*, April 28, 2010.

150. Canadian Newspaper Association, "Identity of Accused—Open Borders Make Mockery of YOA Secrecy Rules," *The Press and the Courts*, vol. 19, no. 4, August 31, 2000.

151. Canadian courts' lack of jurisdiction over the American media is discussed in *R v. Bernardo* [*Publication ban—Proceedings against co-accused*], [1993] OJ no. 2047, at paragraphs 112–19 (QL) (Gen. Div.). The sensational Bernardo case attracted widespread media attention outside Canada, in violation of court-imposed publication bans. See Warren Bass, "The Silence of the Press" (September/October 1993), *Columbia Journalism Review*; Debby Waldman and Mary McIntosh, "The Ban Follow-up" (July/August 1994), ibid.; Canadian Newspaper Association, "Media Lawyers Say Publication Ban Violates Charter: Roundup of Media Reports on Details of Homolka's Manslaughter Trial," *The Press and the Courts*, vol. 12, no. 6, December 17, 1994.

152. *R v. Banville* (1982), 69 CCC (2d) 520 (NB Prov. Ct.); aff'd. (1983), 3 CCC (3d) 312 (NBQB).

153. *R v. Bernardo* [*Publication ban—Proceedings against co-accused*], supra note 151.

154. *R v. Pickton*, [2002] BCJ no. 2830 (QL) (Prov. Ct.).

155. Jane Armstrong, "Judge Berates Media over Pickton Ban," *Globe and Mail*, January 16, 2003; Greg Joyce, "Pickton Judge Issues Warning to Reporters," *National Post*, January 16, 2003.

156. See ibid.

157. *R v. Pickton*, 2005 BCSC 836; Robert Matas, "Pickton Judge Imposes Unique Media Ban," *Globe and Mail*, June 9, 2005.

158. "Fox News, UBC Probed over Alleged Breach of Pickton Media Ban," Global BC news report, February 6, 2004.

159. Douglas Quan, "Do Social Media Make Publication Bans Useless?" *Montreal Gazette*, May 12, 2010.

160. Howard Elliott, "Facebook Poses Dilemma," *Hamilton Spectator*, January 7, 2008.

161. Tracey Tyler, "Judge Curbs Internet Content: Ruling Restricts Web Comment on Sex Abuse Case," *Toronto Star*, February 16, 2001.

162. *R v. Turmel*, (2002-09-27) QCCS 550-01-003994-011.

163. Williams, who pulled the disputed information from his website within 24 hours, pleaded guilty to one count of breaching a publication ban. See Kirk Makin, "Bernardo Author Faces 94 New Charges: More Than 50 Indictments Focus on Web Site Maintained by Investigative Writer," *Globe and Mail* (online edition), October 23, 2003; Shannon Kari, "Police Accused of Being on Vendetta: Author of Books About Bernardo, Homolka's Crimes Pleads Guilty," CanWest News Service, January 25, 2005; Aviva West, "Police Brutality: Is Stephen Williams Taking Freedom of Expression Too Far?" (Summer 2004), *Ryerson Review of Journalism* 22–27.

164. *Frontenac Children's Aid Society v. C.M.N.*, 2006 CanLII 31295 (Ont. SC).

165. Jesse McLean, "Does Facebook Page Break the Law?" *Toronto Star*, January 11, 2010; Emily Mathieu, "Publication Ban Lifted in Oshawa Toddler's Death," ibid., January 12, 2010.

166. Quan, supra note 159.

167. *R v. Valentine*, supra note 113, at paragraph 23.

168. See, for instance, Elliott, supra note 160, and "New Media Leave News Bans in Dust," *Edmonton Journal*, May 14, 2010.

169. See, for example, Shannon Kari, "Courts Pay 'Lip Service' to Open Access," *National Post*, January 8, 2008, and Alan Shanoff, "Hallmark of Democracy Is Open Courts," *Law Times*, July 14, 2008.

170. Kirk Makin, "Secrecy Over Case in Court Surprises Experts," *Globe and Mail*, September 27, 2003; Kirk Makin, "Secrecy Unnecessary, Court Told," *Globe and Mail*, October 4, 2003.

171. "Gagged," *Toronto Star*, May 1, 2010. The *Globe and Mail* also ran a front-page editorial—bearing the headline "This Ban Goes Too Far" and describing the ban as "absurd"—on May 1, 2010.

172. Kirk Makin, "One Law, Many Views on Keeping the Public Informed: As Media Faces Publication Ban in Stafford Trial, Jurists Warn of 'Huge Disconnect' in How They're Taught To Decide Press Access," *Globe and Mail*, May 25, 2010.

173. Peter Jacobsen, "Gag the Gag Orders" (Summer 1999), *Media* 27–28, at 28.

CHAPTER 10

Publication Bans in Other Proceedings

Bans in Civil Cases

Publication bans often crop up in cases or at hearings that do not involve allegations of crime. Judges presiding over civil cases can impose publication bans to protect someone's personal privacy or information considered sensitive or confidential.

Legislation in Ontario gives provincial and superior court judges the power to exclude the public from the courtroom if there is "the possibility of serious harm or injustice to any person." If a hearing is closed, judges have the power to issue an order prohibiting the disclosure of the information presented.[1] Judges in Prince Edward Island and Manitoba have the same powers.[2] In civil cases, as in criminal ones, superior court judges also can use their inherent powers to impose publication bans. This principle was reiterated in *Dagenais v. Canadian Broadcasting Corp.*[3] Although the *Dagenais* precedent arose from a criminal proceeding, bans applied in civil cases must strike the same balance between protection of the rights or interests of a party in a case and the guarantee of freedom of expression under the *Canadian Charter of Rights and Freedoms*.[4]

Before a ban is imposed, three criteria must be met. The ban must be necessary to prevent a real and substantial risk of serious harm to a person or to the fairness of a trial, the court must consider alternatives to restricting publication, and the benefits must outweigh the limit on free expression. In the words of one judge, publication bans in civil cases should "only be granted in a narrow range of circumstances."[5] At least one court has taken the position that the party seeking a ban in a civil case must notify the media and other affected parties who may wish to argue against the proposed restriction.[6]

Bans on Identities of Parties and Witnesses

When a civil claim is based on allegations of sexual abuse or other conduct with the potential to cause humiliation or to seriously damage someone's reputation, judges have banned publication of information that would identify the person at risk. If a plaintiff, defendant, or witness is granted the ban, courts have ordered that the party be identified only by initials or by a pseudonym such as Smith, Jones, or Doe.[7] This trend is becoming common when allegations of sexual assault arise in divorces and custody disputes, and when doctors, teachers, therapists, counsellors, or other professionals are sued based on accusations of sexual abuse. But the courts have said that anonymity should be granted sparingly. "[S]ecrecy can only attend a private system of justice, not a public one," an Ontario judge noted in making a forceful case for openness in the civil courts in a 1987 ruling. "[P]ublicity is a necessary consequence of the obvious benefits that are derived from a public system put in place to serve society in general, including private litigants."[8]

The Supreme Court of Canada has established as a general rule that "the sensibilities of the individuals involved" in a case do not justify a departure from the principle of openness.[9] Most plaintiffs seeking to recover monetary damages in the courts abandon their right to privacy, and patients alleging malpractice cannot assert that their medical records are confidential.[10] In some cases, however, the fear of embarrassment or humiliation may deter plaintiffs from pursuing a court action unless their anonymity is protected.[11] A man who sued an Ontario doctor for negligence after undergoing cosmetic surgery to enlarge his penis was granted a publication ban, shielding him from an expected onslaught of media coverage. Psychiatrists warned that publicity would cause the plaintiff further trauma and emotional harm.[12]

As the above case shows, evidence of potential harm is necessary to justify a ban. Another man who planned to sue the same doctor, after undergoing a similar operation, was denied a ban after a judge was not satisfied he would suffer serious harm if identified. In this case, the judge observed that "the public interest demands openness, including the public identification of the parties, as the norm."[13] Judges, in denying bans, often cite the need to ensure that plaintiffs and their allegations are subjected to public scrutiny and that defendants receive a fair trial. In one Manitoba case, however, a man suing a clergyman for sexually abusing him as a boy was granted anonymity, even though the order hindered the defendant's ability to find witnesses with knowledge of the allegations and the plaintiff's reputation.[14]

The rationale for shielding defendants is that allegations are easy to make—there is no police investigation to weed out malicious or unsubstantiated civil claims—and may never be proven in court. In a lawsuit that branded some employees of a BC reform school as pedophiles, the judge banned publication of their names to prevent "untold harm" to their reputations "before any finding of misconduct has been made against them in a court of law." The ban was applied to the identities of defendants who were deceased, but the judge refused to ban the name of the facility or the names of defendants who were accused of failing to prevent abuse by others.[15]

Other considerations may come into play in the decision to impose or deny a ban. After an Alberta man was cleared of murder charges, he sued a group of undercover policemen for malicious prosecution. A judge rejected a motion to ban the names of the officers, ruling that there was no evidence they would be put at risk by the disclosure of this information. But the judge banned disclosure of their photographs, their physical descriptions, and the false names they used in their undercover roles, citing the "very grave" risk of harm if that information were made public. The judge also refused to protect the identities of three jailhouse informants who claimed the man had confessed, noting they were no longer in custody and there was no evidence their safety was at risk.[16]

Bans on Evidence

Judges have issued orders in civil cases to ban publication of testimony or to seal documents filed with the court. According to a leading BC case on the issue, these restrictions can be justified to protect a child, the safety of a witness, the details of a patent, or a company's trade secrets; they are also justified when "the administration of justice would be rendered impracticable by the presence of the public."[17] The purpose of an action claiming theft of a trade secret or other confidential information, for example, would be defeated if the plaintiff were required to reveal the information in court.[18] When a New Brunswick pathologist accused of misdiagnosing patients went to court in 2007 in a bid to overturn the suspension of his licence to practise medicine, a publication ban was imposed on details of a medical society investigation that were inadmissible in court. The ban was lifted nine months later, when a judge concluded the information could no longer prejudice the doctor's appeal.[19]

The Supreme Court of Canada has said that the party seeking to shield evidence or to seal documents in a civil action must show that there is a serious risk to an important interest, and this interest must be recognized as worthy of protection in the wider public interest. In the case of a business or commercial interest, the court said,

> the interest in question cannot merely be specific to the party requesting the order; the interest must be one which can be expressed in terms of a public interest in confidentiality. For example, a private company could not argue simply that the existence of a particular contract should not be made public because to do so would cause the company to lose business, thus harming its commercial interests. However, if … exposure of information would cause a breach of a confidentiality agreement, then the commercial interest affected can be characterized more broadly as the general commercial interest of preserving confidential information. Simply put, if there is no general principle at stake, there can be no "important commercial interest" for the purposes of this test.[20]

Divorce and Other Family Law Cases

Publication bans are commonly sought in family law cases—a divorce or child-custody dispute may reveal intimate details of a couple's private life or disclose personal financial information. Provincial legislation governs access to family court hearings and case files and, in some jurisdictions, gives judges specific powers to ban publication of names and evidence (these restrictions are explored in more detail in the "Family Courts" section of Chapter 11). Such bans, however, are usually imposed on a case-by-case basis and the open courts principle applies, as it does in other civil matters. In 2010 British Columbia's Court of Appeal refused to use that province's access rules to seal financial information filed in a divorce case. "In matrimonial proceedings, as in other court proceedings" the court observed, "public access is the norm."[21] In an Ontario case decided in 2003, a judge refused to ban publication of the names of a divorcing couple despite allegations of sexual abuse. Only the husband sought the ban and he was unable to present evidence that publicity would damage his reputation and business interests. "Humiliation of one party," the judge concluded, "does not warrant the right to anonymity."[22] And in 2010 a Quebec judge lifted a ban on the divorce of a Montreal financial adviser convicted of defrauding tens of millions of dollars from investors, ruling creditors and the public had a right to know how the couple's assets were being dealt with.[23]

Despite rulings such as these, the need to protect privacy or confidentiality may outweigh the openness principle. A sweeping ban was imposed in 2004 on names, ages, occupations, addresses, and other information that could identify an Ontario couple believed to be the first same-sex couple to divorce in Canada, based on concerns that media coverage would damage the professional reputation of one of the parties. There was no ban, however, on other evidence presented.[24]

Voir Dire Hearings in Jury Trials

The restriction on publication of information disclosed in a *voir dire* hearing applies to civil trials heard by a jury.[25] The ban is in place until deliberations begin, unless the judge issues an order extending the ban until a verdict is returned. In some jurisdictions, the ban is formalized by statute; Prince Edward Island's *Jury Act*, for example, imposes an automatic ban on the publication of "any information regarding any portion of the trial at which the jury is not present" until deliberations begin.[26]

Penalties for Breaching a Ban

In most cases, a violation of a ban imposed in a civil case would be prosecuted as a contempt of court and punished, upon conviction, with a fine. Where the ban is based on a statute, the legislation may stipulate the potential punishment. A breach of Prince Edward Island's statutory ban on disclosing *voir dire* evidence in jury cases, for example, could bring a maximum $5,000 fine and up to three months in jail.[27]

Bans Under Federal Statutes

Criminal Code procedures and publication bans apply when charges of possession, trafficking, or importing narcotics are filed under the *Controlled Drugs and Substances Act*.[28] The same is true of *Food and Drugs Act*[29] charges of improper handling or sale of food and prescription drugs, and prosecutions of quasi-criminal offences under the *Fisheries Act*[30] and the *Canadian Environmental Protection Act*.[31]

Other federal statutes have provisions restricting publication of certain information or empowering the judge presiding at a hearing to issue a publication ban.

Election Results and Public Opinion Polls

The *Canada Elections Act* makes it an offence to publicize, on the day of a federal election, the results of a public opinion poll or survey in electoral districts where the polls are still open. The Act creates two offences—transmitting poll results and knowingly causing them to be transmitted. An exception is made for the republication or rebroadcast of poll results that had previously been made public.[32] The one-day blackout is a considerable easing of the previous, three-day restriction, which the Supreme Court of Canada struck down as an unjustifiable restriction on freedom of expression.[33]

As well, broadcasters and Internet publishers who disseminate information across time zones must comply with a provision of the Act that prohibits the transmission of election results from areas where polls have closed to electoral districts where voting is still under way. The provision forbids transmission of "the result or purported result of the vote," apparently encompassing partial and unofficial tallies as well as the final numbers.[34]

In February 2003 a judge of the British Columbia Provincial Court ruled that this temporary ban on reporting election results was a reasonable limit on free expression, because it ensures that all citizens have access to the same information before they cast their votes.[35] The decision led to the conviction of a BC man who posted election results from Atlantic Canada on his website before the polling booths closed in British Columbia. On appeal, a judge of the province's Supreme Court disagreed and used the Charter to strike down the law, enabling the media to provide coast-to-coast coverage of the results of the 2004 federal election. However, the British Columbia Court of Appeal, the highest court in the province, reversed the ruling in May 2005 and reinstated the restriction on publishing poll results.[36] The Supreme Court of Canada put an end to the confusion in 2007, when it upheld the Court of Appeal's ruling and endorsed the delay on publicizing election results. The legislation's goal of "ensuring informational equality among voters," the court ruled, justified its infringement on freedom of speech and freedom of the press.[37]

Extradition Proceedings

The *Extradition Act* allows a judge to ban publication or broadcast of evidence presented both at a bail hearing for a person facing extradition and at the extradition hearing itself. The judge must be satisfied that publicity "would constitute a risk to the holding of a fair trial" in the country seeking extradition. The ban, if granted, remains in place until the defendant is discharged or, if extradition is ordered, until the conclusion of the person's trial in the foreign state.[38]

Immigration Hearings

The Immigration and Refugee Board holds public hearings but has the right to conduct sessions in private or to take "any other measure that it considers necessary to ensure the confidentiality of the proceedings." Access can be restricted to protect the life, liberty, or security of a person, to protect information relating to public security, or if publicity could undermine the fairness of a proceeding. Refugee claims are to be heard in private, but the panel hearing the claim has the discretion to grant "appropriate access to the proceedings."[39] An immigration adjudicator used these provisions to ban publication of the names of 76 migrants arrested on a ship off the coast of British Columbia in 2009, after allowing journalists to attend their detention hearings.[40]

The minister of public safety and the minister of immigration have the power under the *Immigration and Refugee Protection Act* to issue a certificate seeking to expel a permanent resident or foreign citizen who is considered undesirable or a security threat—a power that has invited increased media scrutiny in the wake of the September 11, 2001 terrorist attacks in the United States. Grounds for issuing a certificate include security concerns, violations of international human rights, a serious criminal record, and involvement in organized crime.[41]

A judge of the Federal Court of Canada must hold a hearing to review the certificate and decide whether it is lawful and reasonable. Sections 83 and 84 of the Act direct that the judge conducting the review—and judges hearing any appeal that results—"shall ensure the confidentiality" of information presented to support the certificate. The section also directs the judge to keep confidential any other evidence put forward, "if, in the judge's opinion, its disclosure would be injurious to national security or endanger the safety of any person." The judge, if satisfied that security or safety concerns exist, must assess the information in private and exclude it from the case summary released to persons facing expulsion and their lawyers.

The minister of immigration also has the power to apply for an order of non-disclosure of security and intelligence information presented at immigration hearings, detention reviews, and appeals before the Immigration Appeal Division. The board involved must take the same steps as a judge to protect the confidentiality of such information. If a court is asked to review a decision of an immigration panel, the minister may apply for an order of non-disclosure of security and intelligence information presented at earlier stages of the process as well as of information relating to claims for refugee protection and the issuing of a visa to enter Canada.[42]

Protecting National Security, Defence, and Sensitive Government Information

The federal government can invoke special measures to prevent the disclosure of information relating to Cabinet secrets, terrorist acts, or national security. The *Canada Evidence Act* gives a minister or other federal official the right to object to the disclosure of certain information to "a court, person or body" with the power to force someone to testify or produce evidence. Such objections may be based on "a specified public interest," a term that encompasses Cabinet secrets, military secrets, and intelligence information. Once the objection is made, the court or tribunal has a duty to ensure "that the information is not disclosed other than in accordance with this Act." A superior court judge has the power to deal with the objection but a tribunal or other body must refer it to a Federal Court or superior court judge. The court must convene an *in camera* hearing to determine whether the objection is valid, and any appeals of an order to disclose or withhold the information also must be held in private.[43]

However, even if the judge finds that revealing the information would affect the specified interest, she has the discretion to order disclosure of some or all of the information if "the public interest in disclosure outweighs in importance the specified public interest." After imposing conditions to minimize the impact on the interest at stake, the judge may order disclosure of "all of the information, a part or summary of the information, or a written admission of facts relating to the information." If the information is withheld, the judge must impose an order prohibiting its disclosure.[44]

The Act also sets out a procedure to be followed when a witness summoned to testify at a criminal trial, court martial, or other hearing is asked to disclose information that the person believes could compromise Canada's defence or national security. The procedures apply to information that could be "potentially injurious" to international relations, national defence, or national security if made public, and "sensitive information" relating to foreign affairs, defence, or security interests that the federal government "is taking measures to safeguard."[45]

The person summoned to give evidence, or a government official who believes that sensitive information could be revealed, must notify the federal justice minister and the judge or person presiding at the hearing. The Act forbids any person, including the media, from disclosing that notice has been given and the information involved. The ban also extends to any mention of a voluntary agreement by the government or witness to disclose the information. The ban does not apply if the federal government authorizes disclosure of the information, in writing or by agreement, or if a court has ordered its disclosure and the decision is not subject to an appeal.[46] If the disclosure issue is referred to a judge of the Federal Court for a ruling, the Act stipulates that the application is confidential, that it must be heard *in camera*, and that a judge may order the court file to be sealed and stored in a location where there is no public access.[47]

Even if the courts order that sensitive information should be disclosed in a courtroom or other hearing, the matter may not be settled. The justice minister has the power to issue a certificate overriding an order to disclose information, citing the need to protect national defence, national security, or information obtained in confidence from a foreign government or agency. The certificate, which is valid for 15 years and can be reissued, can be appealed to a judge of the Federal Court of Appeal for review, but the process is again dealt with at a private hearing and the court file can be sealed to ensure confidentiality. The certificate itself, and any court order to cancel it or vary its terms, must be made public through a notice published in the government's official publication, the *Canada Gazette*.[48]

A public inquiry into Ottawa engineer Maher Arar's deportation in 2002 to Syria, where he was tortured as a suspected terrorist, has tested this legal tug-of-war between openness and secrecy. The federal government objected to the disclosure of thousands of pages of documents about the case and a summary of the testimony of agents of the Canadian Security Intelligence Service, citing national security concerns.[49] The inquiry cleared Arar's name but the federal government used the *Canada Evidence Act* provisions to remove about 1,500 words from the commissioner's final report, citing national security concerns. In 2007 a Federal Court judge found the government had the legal right to withhold most of these passages.[50]

Protected Witnesses

The *Witness Protection Program Act* makes it an offence, punishable by a fine of up to $50,000 and imprisonment for up to five years, to "disclose, directly or indirectly, information about the location or a change of identity" of anyone protected under the program. Persons in the program now or in the past have the right to disclose their identity or location, and the person receiving this information has the right to pass it along to others, but doing so would be risky. This exception only applies if disclosing the information "does not endanger the safety" of anyone else in the program "and does not compromise the integrity of the program"—leaving the authorities plenty of room to decide whether to prosecute those responsible for the disclosure. As well, the commissioner of the RCMP can disclose this information with the person's consent or after the protected person has disclosed the information, and if disclosure "is essential in the public interest" to investigate or prevent a serious crime, to establish someone's innocence, or for reasons of national security or national defence. If the commissioner releases the information to an investigator or other person under these provisions, however, that person is not authorized to pass along the information to anyone else.[51]

These provisions prevented the *Globe and Mail* and *Ottawa Citizen* from revealing the new identity of a protected witness who committed murder after receiving a $100,000 payment and being placed in the program. The ban also prevented the newspapers from revealing who had been killed and the circumstances of the offence. This is not the case in the United States, where a protected witness who commits murder or another serious crime can expect this information to be revealed during the trial process. In 2008 the *Globe* demanded amendments "allowing protected witnesses to be outed when they commit major crimes," but Canada's permanent ban remains in place.[52]

Canadian Judicial Council Inquiries

When the Canadian Judicial Council holds an inquiry into whether a judge of the superior court or the Tax Court of Canada should be removed from office because of advanced age, infirmity, or misconduct, the hearing may be conducted in public. If the hearing is open, the *Judges Act* gives the council the discretion to prohibit publication of "any information or documents" placed before it as part of the inquiry if the council "is of the opinion that the publication is not in the public interest."[53]

Courts Martial

The judge advocate presiding at a court martial has the power to impose a publication ban on all or part of the evidence presented. The issue arose in 1994, when a group of Canadian soldiers faced military trials on charges of murder, torture, and assault in the death of a Somali looter who died in their custody during a peacekeeping mission. At the trial of the first soldier, the judge advocate banned publication of any evidence that would reveal the role that other soldiers may have played in the death. The ban was to remain in place until the last soldier stood trial, to ensure that the panel of officers chosen as a jury would not be influenced by media reports. Publication of photographs taken as the youth was being tortured was also banned. The Federal Court rejected a CBC challenge to the ban, ruling that military judges have the power to impose publication bans and civilian journalists must obey them.[54]

Tribunals and Public Inquiries

Federal tribunals, parliamentary committees, and public inquiries into disasters, scandals, or public policy issues may have the authority to restrict the publication of certain evidence. The statute creating a tribunal or authorizing the appointment of an inquiry should stipulate the scope of these powers.

Justice John Gomery, the commissioner of an inquiry into federal contracts awarded to Quebec advertising firms, issued a ban in March 2005 to temporarily withhold the testimony of three witnesses who were awaiting trial on fraud charges related to the contracts. The judge lifted his ban on most of the testimony after it was heard, ruling that the information would not damage their right to a fair trial. Citing the Charter's guarantee of freedom of expression, he said it was "in the public interest that this evidence with few exceptions be made available." Bans should be "imposed rarely," he added, "particularly in the context of a public inquiry."[55]

Bans Under Provincial and Territorial Statutes

Child Protection Cases

When social workers intervene with a family or assume custody of a child considered at risk of being abused, the courts review attempts to supervise the parents or to take the child into temporary or permanent foster care. In these cases, the identities of the child and the child's family are shielded under a publication ban. This restriction exists in most jurisdictions and the wording of Ontario's *Child and Family Services Act* is typical, banning publication of information "that has the effect of identifying" the child, any other child who testifies or participates in the hearing, and the child's parents, foster parents, or other family members.[56] Nova Scotia's *Children and Family Services Act* contains an identical provision.[57] In Alberta, the ban covers names and "any information serving to identify a child" or a guardian of the child, but the child can consent to being identified once he or she reaches age 18.[58] The ban continues even after the child's death, which prevented journalists covering a 2007 fatality inquiry from identifying an Alberta teenager killed while in the care of a social worker.[59] In Ontario a judge has ruled the ban remains in force even if a child consents to being identified.[60] These bans, however, apply only if a person is linked to an ongoing child protection case. An Ontario court ruled that the CBC could rebroadcast a documentary about a family's parenting struggles that named the parents and child, since there was no reference to the fact that a custody proceeding had begun after the original broadcast.[61] Likewise, a family that is under the scrutiny of social workers can be publicly identified if no formal action has been taken to seize a child.[62]

The media are free to report details of child welfare cases that do not identify those involved, ensuring that the actions of government officials are subjected to public scrutiny. But the hearings themselves are generally deemed to be private unless the judge rules that journalists and spectators can attend. In Prince Edward Island, for example, access is restricted to the parties, their lawyers, and "such other persons as the court may consider appropriate."[63] An exception is Nova Scotia, which deems a hearing to be public unless the judge closes it to prevent emotional harm to a child, to ensure that a witness gives "full and candid" testimony, or to protect the administration of justice.[64]

Evidence heard in hearings may be subject to a publication ban. The Ontario legislation requires the judge to take into consideration the wishes and interests of the parties and possible emotional harm to the child before holding a public hearing. The judge retains the right to exclude reporters from portions of the hearing or to impose a publication ban on portions of the evidence to prevent possible emotional harm to a child.[65] In a case that attracted national media attention in 2002, a judge imposed a sweeping ban on a hearing into allegations that Christian fundamentalist parents had used excessive force to discipline their children. The ban encompassed the evidence presented and even prohibited references to the demeanour of the parents as they testified. The order was struck down on appeal as too broad, with an admonition that judges are "not at liberty to impose such a ban based on speculation" and without evidence of possible emotional harm to a child.[66]

Fatality Inquiries

When a judge or coroner undertakes an inquiry into the cause of a sudden death, publication bans may apply. Legislation in Alberta and Nova Scotia, for example, makes it an offence to publish any testimony or document presented at any portion of a fatality inquiry held *in camera*. The ban does not apply to information incorporated into the judge's findings or official report.[67] In Quebec, coroners have wide powers to ban publication of photographs of a victim's body, the identities of young witnesses, and other information related to inquests. If criminal charges have been filed in connection with the death, there is a ban on publishing any evidence presented at the inquest until the trial is over and all appeals have been exhausted.[68] Other provinces allow coroners to hold *in camera* hearings to restrict publication of information if the death is also the subject of a criminal prosecution.[69]

Judicial Council Inquiries

In most provinces, judicial councils may hold public hearings and have the power to restrict publication of certain information. Ontario's council has the power to ban publication of the name of the judge under scrutiny and the identities of complainants and witnesses when there are allegations of sexual misconduct or sexual harassment.[70] The Ontario council declined to invoke these powers during a 2004 hearing into allegations of sexual misconduct against an Ontario court judge—there was no ban on publication of the judge's name and the media were free to report the testimony of women who accused him of inappropriate touching and of making sexual comments.[71]

Inquiries into the conduct of provincially appointed judges are conducted in private in Alberta. The judges conducting an inquiry may make public the fact that an investigation is under way but have the power to ban publication of information or documents relating to their work.[72]

Disciplinary Hearings for Members of Professions

Lawyers, doctors, engineers, and many other professionals belong to self-governing societies created under provincial laws. These bodies have internal disciplinary panels that investigate complaints about the conduct of their members and punish acts of misconduct. Although access rules vary, many bodies have opened their discipline hearings or have given the member being disciplined the right to request a public hearing. The disciplinary panel may have the power to ban publication of complainants' names and the disclosure of sensitive or confidential information.[73] For example, in May 2005 a discipline panel of the Nova Scotia Barristers' Society convened a public hearing to disbar a lawyer accused of misappropriating $1.3 million from clients' trust funds. The panel turned down a request to withhold the lawyer's name but imposed a publication ban on details of the allegations and the names of the clients involved.[74]

Tribunals and Public Inquiries

Provincial boards and tribunals may have the authority to ban publication of evidence or restrict public access in certain situations. Refer to the statute creating the public body to determine its powers to restrict access or coverage. Ontario's Criminal Injuries Compensation Board, for example, has the power to ban publication of all or part of the evidence presented at hearings to assess compensation claims.[75] When the Nova Scotia Human Rights Commission held a public inquiry in 2009 into allegations that co-workers harassed an employee of a youth correctional facility because they suspected he was gay, a publication ban shielded the name of the complainant, who was referred to in media reports only by the initials A.B. The inquiry chair ruled the ban was justified because the complainant's children did not know he was gay.[76]

NOTES

1. *Courts of Justice Act*, RSO 1990, c. C.43, ss. 135(2) and (3).

2. *Supreme Court Act*, RSPEI 1988, c. S-10, ss. 57(2) and (3); *The Court of Queen's Bench Act*, CCSM c. C280, ss. 76(2) and (3).

3. *Dagenais v. Canadian Broadcasting Corp.*, [1994] 3 SCR 835, at 916.

4. This position predates *Dagenais*. See *John Doe v. Canadian Broadcasting Corp.*, [1993] BCJ no. 1875 (QL) (SC); aff'd. [1993] BCJ no. 1862 (QL) (CA). For a post-*Dagenais* example of a case applying this approach, see *Edmonton (City) v. Kara*, [1995] AJ no. 5 (QL) (QB).

5. *Dix v. Canada (A.G.)*, 2001 ABQB 838, at paragraphs 27 and 28.

6. *Doe v. Roe*, 1999 ABQB 281.

7. For example, a judge allowed a woman suing a major-league baseball player for sexual assault to file the lawsuit under the name Jane Doe. John Jaffey, "Plaintiff Can Use 'Doe' Pseudonym," *The Lawyers Weekly*, October 17, 2003, at 5.

8. *P.S. v. D.C.* (1987), 22 CPC (2d) 225, at paragraph 14 (Ont. HC).

9. *Nova Scotia (Attorney General) v. MacIntyre*, [1982] 1 SCR 175, at 185.

10. *Doe v. Smith*, 2001 ABQB 277, at paragraph 11.

11. This point was made in *DC v. 371158 Ontario Ltd.* (1994), 113 DLR (4th) 150 (Ont. Gen. Div.).

12. *T. (S.) v. Stubbs* (1998), 38 OR (3d) 788 (Gen. Div.).

13. *A.B. v. Stubbs*, [1999] OJ no. 2309, at paragraph 12 (QL) (SCJ).

14. Lynn Niedzwiecki, "Privacy Rights Trump Public Interest, Pseudonyms Used in Sex Abuse Case," *The Lawyers Weekly*, August 8, 1997.

15. *B.G. v. British Columbia*, [2002] BCJ no. 2246 (QL) (SC).

16. *Dix v. Canada (A.G.)*, supra note 5, at paragraph 55.

17. *John Doe v. Canadian Broadcasting Corp.*, [1993] BCJ no. 1869, at paragraph 34 (QL) (SC).

18. This point was made in *A.B. v. Stubbs*, supra note 13, at paragraph 39.

19. *Menon v. College of Physicians and Surgeons of New Brunswick*, 2007 NBQB 247 (CanLII); *Menon v. College of Physicians and Surgeons of New Brunswick*, 2008 NBQB 80 (CanLII).

20. *Sierra Club of Canada v. Canada (Minister of Finance)*, [2002] 2 SCR 522, at paragraph 55.

21. *Michie v. Michie*, 2010 BCCA 232 (CanLII). See also Cristin Schmitz, "Public Access 'the Norm' in Family Law Cases," *The Lawyers Weekly*, May 28, 2010, 3.

22. *T. v. T.*, 2003 CanLII 1998 (Ont. SC).

23. Anne Sutherland, "Judge Lifts Publication Ban on Jones Divorce," *Montreal Gazette*, January 19, 2010.

24. Tracey Tyler, "Now It's Divorce, Same-Sex Style," *Toronto Star*, July 21, 2004.

25. Michael Crawford, *The Journalist's Legal Guide*, 4th ed. (Toronto: Carswell, 2002), 203.

26. *Jury Act*, RSPEI 1988, c. J-5.1, s. 32(3).

27. Ibid., s. 32(4).

28. *Controlled Drugs and Substances Act*, SC 1996, c. 19.

29. *Food and Drugs Act*, RSC 1985, c. F-27.

30. *Fisheries Act*, RSC 1985, c. F-14.

31. *Canadian Environmental Protection Act, 1999*, SC 1999, c. 33.

32. *Canada Elections Act*, SC 2000, c. 9, ss. 328(1) and (2).

33. *Thomson Newspapers Co. v. Canada (Attorney General)*, [1998] 1 SCR 877.

34. *Canada Elections Act*, s. 329.

35. *R v. Bryan*, [2003] BCJ no. 318 (QL) (Prov. Ct.).

36. *R v. Bryan*, 2005 BCCA 285.

37. *R v. Bryan*, 2007 SCC 12, [2007] 1 SCR 527.

38. *Extradition Act*, SC 1999, c. 18, s. 26.

39. *Immigration and Refugee Protection Act*, SC 2001, c. 27, s. 166.

40. "Hearings Begin for Migrants Arrested off B.C. Coast," *Montreal Gazette*, October 21, 2009.

41. *Immigration and Refugee Protection Act*, SC 2001, c. 27, s. 77.

42. Ibid., ss. 86 and 87.

43. *Canada Evidence Act*, RSC 1985, c. C-5, ss. 37(1), (1.1), (2), and (3).

44. Ibid., ss. 37(4.1), (5), and (6).

45. Ibid., s. 38.

46. Ibid., ss. 38.02(1) and (2).

47. Ibid., ss. 38.04(4) and 38.12(2).

48. Ibid., ss. 38.13(1), (7), and (9), and ss. 38.131(1), (6), (8), (9), and (12).

49. Jeff Sallot, "Effort To Stop Judge Releasing Arar Data Is Normal, PM Says," *Globe and Mail*, December 17, 2004; Daniel Leblanc, "Ottawa Lashed Over Arar Secrets—Not Quite Full Disclosure: Summary of CSIS Testimony Censored," *Globe and Mail*, December 21, 2004.

50. *Canada (Attorney General) v. Canada (Commission of Inquiry into the Actions of Canadian Officials in Relation to Maher Arar)*, 2007 FC 766, [2008] 3 FCR 248. See also Colin Freeze, "Arar Commission Won't Appeal Secrecy Decision," *Globe and Mail*, July 27, 2007.

51. *Witness Protection Program Act*, SC 1996, c. 15, ss. 11(1), (2), (3), and (4), and s. 21.

52. "An Informant and His Immunity," *Globe and Mail*, January 3, 2008; Greg McArthur, "Protected Witnesses Who Kill Unmasked in U.S.," ibid., March 31, 2007.

53. *Judges Act*, RSC 1985, c. J-1, ss. 63(5) and (6).

54. *Canadian Broadcasting Corp. v. Boland*, [1995] 1 FC 323 (TD).

55. Daniel Leblanc and Tu Thanh Ha, "Gomery Muzzles the Media at Sponsorship Inquiry," *Globe and Mail*, March 30, 2005; Allison Dunfield, "Gomery Partially Lifts Ban on Volatile Testimony," *Globe and Mail*, April 7, 2005. The text of Justice Gomery's March 29, 2005 ruling is available online at http://www.gomery.ca/en/ rulingonapplicationsforpublicationban.

56. *Child and Family Services Act*, RSO 1990, c. C.11, s. 45(8).

57. *Children and Family Services Act*, SNS 1990, c. 5, s. 94(1).

58. *Child, Youth and Family Enhancement Act*, RSA 2000, c. C-12, ss. 126(1) and (2).

59. "The Law Lets Children Die Nameless," *Edmonton Journal*, May 11, 2007.

60. *R v. Davies* (1991), 87 DLR (4th) 527 (Ont. Prov. Div.).

61. *Children's Aid Society of Hamilton-Wentworth v. D.-G. (E.)* (1995), 21 OR (3d) 643 (Div. Ct.).

62. See, for example, Brian Flinn, "Child Protection Cracks Down on Noah's Bus Family," *Daily News* (Halifax), September 6, 2003.

63. *Child Protection Act*, SPEI 1988, c. C-5.1, s. 35(1).

64. *Children and Family Services Act*, SNS 1990, c. 5, s. 93.

65. *Child and Family Services Act*, RSO 1990, c. C.11, ss. 45(4) and (7).

66. Canadian Newspaper Association, "Judge Quashes Sweeping Publication Ban on 'Spanking Case' After Appeal by Seven Media Outlets," *The Press and the Courts*, vol. 21, no. 3, June 30, 2002. For criticism of the ban, see Christie Blatchford, "Spanking Trial Starts with Muzzle," *National Post*, May 29, 2002.

67. *Fatality Investigations Act*, SNS 2001, c. 31, s. 34; *Fatality Inquiries Act*, RSA 2000, c. F-9, s. 46.

68. See Crawford, supra note 25, 205–206.

69. See, for example, *Coroners Act*, RSBC 1996, c. 72, s. 28.

70. *Courts of Justice Act*, RSO 1990, c. C.43, ss. 51.6(7), (8), (9), and (10).

71. Shannon Kari, "Panel Rules Ontario Judge Engaged in Sexual Misconduct," *The Lawyers Weekly*, October 8, 2004, at 2.

72. *Judicature Act*, RSA 2000, c. J-2, ss. 34(5) and 36.

73. See, for example, Nova Scotia's *Land Surveyors Act*, RSNS 1989, c. 249, s. 26(4), which gives a discipline committee the power to hold a public hearing upon request.

74. *Nova Scotia Barristers' Society v. Pillay*, 2005 NSBS 2; Sherri Borden Colley, "Lawyer Disbarred for Tapping into Trust Funds," *Chronicle-Herald* (Halifax), May 31, 2005. The Nova Scotia Barristers' Society's formal discipline hearings into a lawyer's conduct are held in public unless a private hearing is ordered. Discipline panels have wide powers to ban publication of information that is privileged, confidential, or could jeopardize someone's safety. *Legal Profession Act*, SNS 2004, c. 28, ss. 44(1) and (2).

75. *Compensation for Victims of Crime Act*, RSO 1990, c. C.24, s. 13.

76. "Ex-Jail Worker Says He Was Victim of Anti-Gay Harassment," *CBC News Online*, July 21, 2009.

CHAPTER 11

Access to Hearings and Documents

Access to Justice

The CBC reporter was cooling his heels in the corridor for only a short time, maybe 20 minutes. Meanwhile, inside the courtroom, a judge was hearing details of sex-related offences before sentencing a prominent New Brunswick man. The prosecutor had sought an exclusion order under section 486(1) of the *Criminal Code*—which gives a judge the power to clear the courtroom—citing the "very delicate" nature of the evidence and the fact that the victims were "young females." The CBC fought the order all the way to the Supreme Court of Canada and, in 1996, won access to a transcript of the closed portion of the hearing.

Writing for the court in *Canadian Broadcasting Corp. v. New Brunswick (Attorney General)*,[1] Justice Gérard La Forest reiterated the importance of public access to court hearings and documents. "Courts are and have since time immemorial been public arenas," the forum where "the rights of the powerful state are tested against those of the individual," he wrote. "As a vehicle through which information pertaining to these courts is transmitted, the press must be guaranteed access to the courts in order to gather information."[2] Secrecy and closed hearings are the exception, openness and judicial accountability are the rule.

But there are limits to the openness of the justice system. The Supreme Court's 1982 precedent in *Nova Scotia (Attorney General) v. MacIntyre*, which opened search warrants to scrutiny, directs that access to the courts can be curtailed "to protect social values of superordinate importance," such as the rights of innocent parties.[3] In 2007 the Supreme Court ruled that *in camera* hearings are justified to protect the identities of police informants, despite the open-court rule. "[T]hose who choose to act as confidential informers must be protected from the possibility of retribution," Justice Michel Bastarache wrote in the majority judgment. "Information which might tend to identify a confidential informant cannot be revealed, except where the innocence of a criminal accused is at stake. Open courts are undoubtedly a vital part of our legal system and of our society, but their openness cannot be allowed to fundamentally compromise the criminal justice system."[4] A judge also has the power to banish an unruly person who disrupts the court's business. As well, some stages of the court process must occur behind closed doors. Members of the public are not entitled to sit in on jury deliberations or to eavesdrop while appeal court judges hammer out their rulings. And there is no right to be physically present—if a courtroom is too small to accommodate everyone who shows up for a hearing, some will be excluded and they will have to find out what happened from the people who were inside.[5]

An array of laws, rules, and guidelines govern access to court hearings and files. Although the business of the courts is overwhelmingly conducted in the open, anyone writing about the justice system must understand the exceptions to the openness rule.

Restrictions on Access to the Courts

Criminal Code Restrictions

Exclusion Orders

Any Proceeding: Section 486(1)

Although section 486(1) of the *Criminal Code* states that criminal proceedings must be held in open court, a judge may, under an **exclusion order**, exclude "all or any members of the public" from the courtroom for "all or part" of a hearing. The courtroom may be closed on three grounds: "in the interest of public morals," to maintain order, or to protect the administration of justice. This power is most often invoked on this last ground, when the witness is a child who may be intimidated by the presence of spectators. Section 486(1.1) specifies that the "proper administration of justice" includes protecting witnesses under the age of 18 in cases of sexual or violent offences. A related provision, section 486(1.5), enables judges to clear the courtroom to protect the identities of "justice system participants" involved in the case, such as politicians, judges, lawyers, jurors, court officials, and police officers and informants. The Code also empowers judges to allow witnesses who are young or disabled, and witnesses involved in cases of terrorism, spying, or organized crime, to testify via a closed-circuit video link or behind a screen that shields their identity.[6]

The New Brunswick case of the CBC reporter excluded from a sentencing hearing defined the scope of this provision and established the procedure to be followed in the decision to grant or deny an exclusion order. The Supreme Court of Canada says the *Dagenais* test applies—the party seeking a closed hearing under section 486(1) must present evidence to justify the infringement of freedom of expression. "Mere offence or embarrassment" or the fact that a case involves sex offences or young persons who are female is not a sufficient ground to warrant public exclusion.[7] As well, invoking section 486(1) at a sentencing hearing will rarely be justified. The sentencing process serves a "critically important social function," the court noted; it enables the public to assess whether the punishment fits the crime.[8]

The Quebec Court of Appeal has ruled that, to justify excluding the public, the presence of spectators must be so stressful that witnesses will not testify or the quality of their evidence will suffer.[9] The Supreme Court of Canada has endorsed this approach.[10] A Manitoba judge's use of this section to exclude a newspaper reporter while allowing other spectators to stay was overturned on appeal. The judge's purpose, to prevent publication of the names of witnesses, was found to be beyond the scope of protecting the proper administration of justice.[11] However, an order excluding the public while a judge questioned several jurors about their impartiality was upheld as a proper exercise of the discretion to clear the courtroom.[12]

The media's right to be heard before a judge closes the courtroom is less clear. In the New Brunswick case, the CBC called in a lawyer and, once the courtroom reopened, the judge was asked to provide reasons for excluding the public. Those reasons became the basis for the legal challenge that followed. While judges are to apply the *Dagenais* approach when deciding whether to exclude the public, the Supreme Court's ruling is silent on whether the media should be notified and given standing to oppose a closed hearing. A journalist faced with a motion to close the court could ask for a brief adjournment to consult a superior about a possible legal challenge, but the judge may not be obliged to grant the request.

Preliminary Hearings: Section 537(1)(h)

A similar provision of the *Criminal Code*, section 537(1)(h), enables a judge at a preliminary hearing to order everyone—except the prosecutor, the defendant, and the defence lawyer—to leave the courtroom if "the ends of justice will be best served by so doing." This power cannot be used to remove some members of the public but not others. One Ontario judge, concerned that foreign journalists would ignore the publication ban on a preliminary hearing, ruled that he must exclude all members of the public to ensure a fair trial for the defendant.[13]

Publication Not Banned

Exclusion orders prevent writers from being present to record what happened. They do not, in themselves, ban publication of the information presented at the hearing. A journalist can interview lawyers involved in the case or consult a taped or written transcript of a closed proceeding. Before publishing, however, the journalist must ensure that the information is not also subject to a publication ban.

In Camera Hearings

Some hearings in criminal cases must be held in private. For others, the judge has the discretion to convene a closed hearing. Interests that can take precedence over public and media access include national security, personal privacy, solicitor–client privilege, and the need to protect the integrity of ongoing police investigations. Many of these provisions are coupled with one of the publication bans discussed in Chapter 9.

Search Warrant Applications

When investigators apply to a judge or a justice of the peace for a search warrant under section 487(1) of the *Criminal Code*, the request must be heard *in camera*. In the words of the Supreme Court of Canada, secrecy is vital to ensure that evidence is not hidden or destroyed: "The effectiveness of any search … will depend much upon timing, upon the degree of confidentiality which attends the issuance of the warrant and upon the element of surprise which attends the search." As a result, the court ruled, "the proceeding must be conducted *in camera*, as an exception to the open court principle." But some public scrutiny of the process is necessary, the court noted, to ensure that police and court officials do not abuse their powers. If evidence is seized, the search warrant and its related documents are made public unless a judge seals the file. But if no evidence is found, the public's right to know must yield to the need to protect the innocent and the documents remain secret.[14]

Hearings To Issue a Summons or Arrest Warrant Under Section 507(1)

Under section 507(1) of the *Criminal Code*, when the police ask a judge or a justice of the peace to issue a summons or arrest warrant for a suspect, the hearing must be held *in camera*. The Ontario Court of Appeal has ruled that closing these hearings is a reasonable limit on the right to freedom of expression.[15]

Applications for a Ban on Identity: Section 486.5(1)

A judge asked to ban disclosure of the identity of a victim of crime or a witness under this section of the *Criminal Code* has the option under section 486.5(6) of holding an *in camera* hearing to consider the request.

Evidence of Sexual Conduct: Sections 276.1(3) and 276.2(1)

Sections 276.1(3) and 276.2(1) of the *Criminal Code* require a judge to exclude "the jury and the public" from the courtroom when a defendant applies to produce evidence of a complainant's sexual history. If a hearing is held to assess whether the information is admissible, it too must be held in private. These restrictions operate in concert with a publication ban, under section 276.3(1), that applies to most facets of these applications.

Production of Confidential Records: Sections 278.4(1) and 278.6(2)

In prosecutions involving sex-related offences, private hearings must be held when a judge is asked to order the production of the personal or confidential records of a complainant or witness. There is a two-stage process. An initial hearing must be held *in camera* to determine whether the complainant, witness, or other person who possesses the record should be ordered to produce it for review. If production of the record is ordered, the judge must review it in private or at a hearing held *in camera* to determine whether some or all of the information should be provided to the defendant. Again, a publication ban applies to the information presented at these hearings.

Privilege Claims Relating to Seized Documents: Section 488.1(10)

Lawyers and their clients enjoy a confidential relationship, and most of the information that passes between them is protected by solicitor–client privilege. So when investigators seize files from a lawyer's office or a law firm, the documents cannot be examined or copied without a judge's approval. The documents must be placed in a sealed envelope until a prosecutor applies for access or the lawyer or client seeks an order to keep them confidential. Under section 488.1(10) of the *Criminal Code*, these applications must be heard in private.

Reviews of Mental Fitness of Offenders: Section 672.5(6)

Under section 672.5(6) of the *Criminal Code*, a court or board reviewing the status of a person found unfit to stand trial, or not criminally responsible for an offence because of a mental disorder, can hold all or part of a hearing *in camera*. This power can be exercised when the judge or board considers a private session to be "in the best interests of the accused and not contrary to the public interest."

Applications in Terrorism Cases: Sections 83.05(6), 83.06(1), 83.06(3), 83.13(1), and 83.28(5)

Provisions added to the *Criminal Code* in 2001, in response to the September 11, 2001 terrorist attacks in the United States, require judges to assess a number of terrorism-related issues in private. Any organization or group placed on the government's list of terrorist organizations can apply to the courts to have the designation rescinded. Under section 83.05(6), the judge must examine any relevant security or criminal intelligence reports in private. A summary of the information is to be provided to the organization or group after the removal of any information that, in the judge's opinion, "would injure national security or endanger the safety of any person." As well, section 83.06(1) gives federal officials the right to appear before a judge in private to present information provided in confidence by a foreign government or agency or an international body. If the judge decides that disclosure of the information would harm national security or endanger others, section 83.06(3) requires that the information remain secret. The government can apply to the Federal Court for an order to seize or freeze assets or property belonging to an organization accused of supporting terrorism. Section 83.13(1) requires the judge to hear the application in private.

One of the most controversial provisions creates a pre-charge procedure, known as an **investigative hearing**, in cases of suspected terrorism. If the authorities have reason to believe that a person has information about a terrorist act or plans to commit such an act, a superior or provincial court judge can be asked to convene an investigative hearing. If one is ordered, the person can be forced to appear before a judge to answer questions and to produce evidence. Under section 83.28(5), the judge can impose any "terms or conditions" needed to protect the interests of the witness, other persons, or "for the protection of any ongoing investigation." This provision was subject to a sunset clause and expired in 2007. As of 2010, the federal government had made two attempts to reinstate investigative hearings and they may be revived in future.

Initially, the courts were prepared to go to great lengths to suppress information about this process. The first investigative hearing was sought in July 2003 in connection with the 1985 bombing of Air India Flight 182, which killed 329 people. The witness involved challenged the law as a violation of the right to silence and other Charter protections. A judge of the British Columbia Supreme Court heard the challenge *in camera* and, although she made public a brief synopsis of her decision, she sealed her complete ruling and other details of the case.[16] The witness sought leave to appeal to the Supreme Court of Canada, where a judge sealed the file once again despite media demands for the right to challenge the sealing order and any decision to hear the leave application *in camera*.[17] The Supreme Court later ruled that the secrecy was excessive and unnecessary and that the challenge could have been heard in public without disclosing the identity of the witness or jeopardizing the investigation. Judges must now make public as much information as possible about investigative hearings and, once the evidence has been heard, they should review whether any sealing orders or publication bans that were put in place are still justified.[18]

Youth Courts

Access to Hearings
Under section 132(1) of the *Youth Criminal Justice Act*, a youth court judge may exclude "any person from all or part" of a criminal case involving a young person. This power can be used if the judge "considers that the person's presence is unnecessary to the conduct of the proceedings," or if the information presented at a hearing would be "seriously injurious or seriously prejudicial" to the defendant or a child or young person who is a witness or the victim of a crime. As is the case under the *Criminal Code*, "any or all" members of the public can be excluded "in the interest of public morals, the maintenance of order or the proper administration of justice."[19] The provinces and territories have enacted similar provisions to exclude the public when young persons have been charged with quasi-criminal offences under their statutes.[20] Section 132(3) of the Act deals with hearings held after a young person has been convicted of a crime. A judge or a provincial board established to review the custody arrangements for youths, when hearing information that could seriously harm or prejudice a young offender, has the power to exclude the media and public. Similar provisions of the previous *Young Offenders Act* were upheld as a reasonable infringement on the Charter right to free expression.[21]

Access to Records
There are tight controls on access to the files of cases prosecuted under the *Youth Criminal Justice Act*. Written or electronic records relating to a case (including cases dealt with under the previous *Young Offenders Act*[22]) are accessible only to court and correctional officials, lawyers, judges, and police investigators. Journalists, researchers, and other members of the public must apply to a youth court judge, who has the power under section 119(1)(s) to grant access if the person has "a valid interest in the record." The judge must be satisfied that disclosing the record is "desirable in the interest of the proper administration of justice." In a Nova Scotia case that interpreted a similar provision of the *Young Offenders Act*, the media were deemed to have a valid interest in the transcript of a youth court trial and were granted access.[23] The media have had success gaining access to records since the enactment of the *Youth Criminal Justice Act*. In 2006 a Nova Scotia judge granted media access to exhibits—including psychological and correctional services reports and a pre-sentence report—presented at the sentencing hearing of a youth who received an adult sentence.[24] And in 2008 an Ontario judge ruled the media had "a valid interest" in accessing exhibits presented at hearings for a teenager charged, along with 17 other Toronto-area men and youths, with terrorism-related offences.[25]

Section 119(2) of the current Act imposes strict time limits on applications for access, with the deadlines ranging from two months to five years after the completion of the case, depending on the outcome and the sentence imposed. An exception is made where youths have been convicted of serious crimes and sentenced to the same punishment as an adult; once all avenues of appeal have been exhausted, section 117 provides that records of these cases are open to public scrutiny like any other criminal file.

These restrictions pose serious obstacles for journalists attempting to cover youth court cases. Although hearings are open, section 118(1) forbids the disclosure of any information contained in a youth court record that would identify a defendant. As a result, court officials in some jurisdictions delete the names of defendants from the docket, leaving only the time for the hearing, the courtroom, and the charges involved. Reporters are also unable to check material in the court file, to ensure that their notes are complete and accurate, without making a formal application to the court for access.

Family Courts

General Restrictions

The laws and rules governing access to hearings and court files in family law cases, such as divorce and custody disputes, vary from jurisdiction to jurisdiction. (The specific laws and rules for each province and the territories are discussed in the sections below.) In general, a hearing is open to the public unless a judge decides that an *in camera* session is justified. The court file is likewise open to public scrutiny unless a statutory provision, a court rule, or a judge's order requires that all or some of the documents be sealed.

Alberta

In Alberta, judges have the discretion to hear family court matters in private.[26] But there is no formal restriction on public access to documents filed with the courts in these cases.

British Columbia

Family court matters are to be heard in open court, but the judge can exclude anyone whose presence might prejudice the interests of a child or adult or otherwise interfere with the administration of justice. There is a ban on publishing any information likely to disclose the identity of a party or child involved in a case.[27] As well, a provincial Supreme Court judge must approve requests to review the court file in a divorce or custody case—only the parties and their lawyers have a right to access these documents.[28]

Manitoba

In Manitoba, superior court judges have the power to exclude the public from hearings in any civil case, including family disputes.[29] But there is no restriction on access to documents filed with the court in such cases.

New Brunswick

Judges of the family division of the New Brunswick Court of Queen's Bench have the option of closing all or part of a hearing. As well, judges may order that financial and income statements filed in divorce cases be treated as confidential if "public disclosure … would create hardship."[30]

Newfoundland and Labrador

Family court judges in Newfoundland and Labrador can hold all or part of a hearing in private to prevent the disclosure of "intimate financial or personal matters," and they may take the further precaution of banning publication of the information. Judges can also order that financial and property statements presented in family law matters be kept confidential and not made part of the court file. Supreme Court judges hearing family law cases have the power to exclude members of the public from the courtroom to protect the parties and children, or in the interest of "public morals, the maintenance of order or the proper administration of justice."[31] As well, Supreme Court rules prevent anyone other than lawyers, judges, and the parties involved from viewing the court file in a family law case.[32]

Nova Scotia

Two levels of court deal with family law matters in Nova Scotia. The first level, the Family Court, is not a public forum—the law requires judges to restrict attendance at hearings to the parties involved and to "guard against any publicity."[33] The second level is the family division of the Nova Scotia Supreme Court, which sits in some areas and is slated to replace the Family Court. Hearings in this court are open to the public. Judges, however, can hear all or part of a case *in camera* after weighing the public interest in openness against "any potential harm that may be caused to any person if matters of a private nature were disclosed in open court."[34] There is no restriction on access to the family division's case files.

Ontario

Ontario legislation imposes no specific restrictions on family law proceedings. The province's *Courts of Justice Act*, however, allows a judge to exclude the public from any hearing if "the possibility of serious harm or injustice to any person" justifies a departure from the principle of openness. A judge also has the power to seal any document filed in a civil proceeding.[35]

Prince Edward Island

In Prince Edward Island, the public can be excluded from family court hearings if the judge believes that guarding against "the consequences of possible disclosure of intimate financial or personal matters" outweighs the right of access. When financial statements are produced as evidence, judges can order that the information be treated as confidential and removed from the public record if its disclosure "would be a hardship on the person giving the statement."[36]

Quebec

Family law proceedings are private in Quebec unless the judge rules that it is "in the interests of justice" to hold a public hearing. Special provision is made for the media, however. When the public is excluded, the judge may allow journalists to remain in the courtroom unless, under the *Code of Civil Procedure*, the media's presence would be "detrimental to a person whose interests may be affected by the proceedings." Judges retain the right "in a special case" to ban publication of any information presented in court, and financial information and details of support payments are kept confidential.[37]

Saskatchewan

Judges of Saskatchewan's Court of Queen's Bench have the discretion to hold any family law proceeding in private.[38] In cases dealing with support payments and family property, judges must weigh the desirability of holding an open hearing against the consequences of personal or financial information being disclosed.[39] Only the parties involved in family law cases and their lawyers have the right to see transcripts, exhibits, support and separation agreements, and other records filed with the Court of Queen's Bench. Journalists and other members of the public must apply to a judge for an order granting access to all or part of a file.[40]

The Territories

In the Yukon, Supreme Court judges have the right to seal any document filed in a family law dispute if public disclosure of the information would cause someone hardship.[41] There is also provision to restrict public access to hearings and court documents that would disclose intimate financial or personal matters. Publication of the information can also be banned.[42] In the Northwest Territories and Nunavut, judges can order that details of spousal and child support be kept confidential.[43]

Child Protection Cases

Most provinces limit access to court proceedings commenced when social workers take action to seize a child who is at risk of abuse or neglect. Approaches vary. Some jurisdictions require an open hearing unless a judge orders it to be closed. Others declare the court closed unless a judge opts for an open hearing. In some provinces, the law stipulates that hearings are closed but allows media representatives to attend or to apply for access. If a hearing is open or access is granted, child protection laws in all provinces, as discussed in Chapter 10, forbid publication of any information that could disclose the identity of a child or parent involved in a proceeding.

Legislation in British Columbia requires these proceedings to be held in open court but gives judges the right to exclude the public to protect the interests of the child or the parties.[44] In addition, a court rule prevents anyone from viewing the file of a child protection case without the authorization of the judge or a party or lawyer involved in the case.[45] In Nova Scotia, judges have the right to close all or part of a hearing to protect a child from emotional harm, to ensure that a witness gives "full and candid" testimony, and to promote the proper administration of justice. Access to the case file is restricted, but journalists and other persons can apply to a judge for an order granting access.[46] New Brunswick allows judges to decide on a case-by-case basis whether a hearing will be public or private. The decision must take into account the positions of the parties involved, the public interest in open proceedings, and whether "matters of a private nature" would be disclosed that would cause "potential harm or embarrassment" to a person.[47] In Saskatchewan, judges have the discretion to hear cases *in camera* and can impose a publication ban on all or part of a hearing if disclosing the information would cause adverse effects or hardship for a child.[48] Alberta's legislation also implies that hearings are open but empowers a judge to exclude any person whose presence "may be seriously injurious or seriously prejudicial" to a child involved in the case, or to restrict access on the grounds of "public morals, the maintenance of order or the proper administration of justice."[49]

Ontario hearings are closed unless the judge, after considering the wishes and interests of the parties involved and whether the presence of the public would cause emotional harm to a child, orders an open hearing. If a hearing is closed, Ontario law still permits a pool of two journalists to attend to cover the proceedings. If journalists are unable to agree among themselves who should attend, the judge has the right to select the media representatives. The judge has the option of allowing more than two journalists to attend, and the court reserves the right to exclude all members of the media from all or part of a hearing.[50] Manitoba hearings are closed to the public but open to journalists, unless the judge grants a motion to bar them from the courtroom on the basis that the media's presence would be "manifestly harmful to any person involved in the proceeding."[51] In Quebec, hearings are held *in camera* but any journalist who seeks access must be allowed to attend unless the media's presence "would cause prejudice to the child."[52]

Legislation in Newfoundland and Labrador requires a private hearing unless the judge orders it to be open.[53] In Prince Edward Island, hearings are closed but other persons the judge "may consider appropriate" can attend,[54] offering a possible route for the media to gain access.

General Access Restrictions

Provincial laws and court rules may give judges the power to close any hearing to the public, regardless of the issues involved. In British Columbia and the Yukon, for example, Supreme Court rules require all motions to be heard in open court unless the application for restriction is urgent or the judge finds that there are "special reasons" that justify hearing it in private.[55]

In Nova Scotia, legislation allows Supreme Court judges to bar the public from attending any hearing in the interest of protecting public morals, to maintain order in the courtroom, or to ensure the proper administration of justice.[56] Although Ontario law mandates that all hearings are open to the public, judges have the right to exclude the public when "the possibility of serious harm or injustice to any person" justifies a departure from the openness rule. As well, Ontario court rules permit private hearings of urgent motions, of applications at pre-trial conferences, and of issues that are argued before a single judge of an appellate court.[57] Judges of Prince Edward Island's Supreme Court are required to hold public hearings unless a statute allows for a private hearing. As in Ontario, exceptions are made when an open hearing might cause serious harm or injustice to someone.[58] In Quebec, court sessions are deemed public "wherever they may be held," but a judge may exclude the public "in the interests of good morals or public order."[59] All hearings of the Federal Court of Canada, with the exception of pre-trial or settlement conferences, are to be open to the public but judges have the power to hear all or part of a case *in camera*.[60]

Media Access Rules

Access to Court Facilities

Courthouses

Most courthouses have an office set aside for the media's use. Local court rules or practices may designate that the areas adjacent to courtrooms cannot be used for media interviews or scrums, either as a security measure or to ensure that access is not blocked as people enter and leave a courtroom.

Courtrooms

Restriction on Movement Beyond the Bar

Courtrooms are divided into two areas, a public gallery and the main body of the court, where lawyers, judges, and juries do their work. A rail or bar separates these areas, and journalists and other members of the public are not permitted beyond this point without an invitation from the judge or, when court is not in session, the permission of the court clerk. That's why, when lawyers are licensed to practise, they are said to have been "called to the bar"—they have earned the right to enter the body of the courtroom. Journalists must not pass beyond the bar without permission, even if the courtroom is empty. In May 2003 a reporter for an Albany, New York newspaper was sentenced to two days in jail for contempt and lost his job after going behind the judge's bench during a break in a trial. The courtroom was vacant but a security camera showed the journalist using the phone and perusing a copy of instructions that the judge had given to the jury.[61]

Judges may set aside a special table or seating area for journalists inside the bar or in the gallery, particularly if a case has attracted significant public attention and there may not be enough seats for spectators.

Decorum

Journalists and members of the public must adhere to some basic rules of decorum when attending court hearings. There is no dress code but spectators cannot bring food or beverages into the courtroom. Nor should they show disrespect by chewing gum, chatting with neighbours, or reading during the proceedings. Cellular phones and pagers must be turned off and the devices cannot be used in the courtroom. Spectators may enter or leave while court is in session, but must do so as quietly and unobtrusively as possible to prevent disruption. In some instances, the judge may direct court officials to forbid anyone to enter or leave while witnesses are testifying or during the judge's instructions to the jury. The judge has the power to eject any spectator who interrupts or disturbs a hearing. Serious infractions can be punished as a contempt in the face of the court, with the offender facing a fine or a jail sentence.

Camera Access

Inside Courthouses

Most provinces have laws or rules that ban the use of cameras inside courthouses. The most rigid restrictions are found in Ontario, where the *Courts of Justice Act* forbids photographing or filming within any building that houses a courtroom and makes it an offence to photograph or film any person entering or leaving a hearing. It is also an offence, punishable by a maximum $25,000 fine and six months in jail, to publish, broadcast, or reproduce such images.[62] The CBC challenged a similar prohibition found in an earlier version of the Act, after a television reporter was charged with filming a witness as he left an Ottawa courtroom. In 1992 a majority of the Ontario Court of Appeal ruled that restricting camera access inside courthouses was a reasonable limit on freedom of expression. One judge argued that decorum and the dignity of court proceedings must be preserved beyond the courtroom door:

> The presence of photographers and television cameramen in the corridors outside the courtroom is bound to create noise and confusion. [The prohibition] is designed to preserve the calm, quiet atmosphere which is essential for the proper administration of justice. A courthouse is not a place of entertainment or education; it is a place where people come to obtain a just resolution of their legal disputes.[63]

Courts in other provinces have taken a less draconian approach, with some allowing judges to consider requests to bring cameras into courthouses on a case-by-case basis. Cameras are banned from all court facilities in Manitoba unless the chief justice or chief judge of the court involved approves their use.[64] In the Yukon, journalists must seek the court's permission to use cameras inside the Whitehorse Law Courts building and an adjacent atrium used as a waiting area.[65]

Courts in Quebec and Nova Scotia permit cameras to be used in approved areas within the lobbies and other public areas of courthouses. Quebec's rules, which restrict cameras and interviews to designated areas, survived a Charter challenge in 2008, with the province's Court of Appeal finding the media do not have a right to gather "the most gripping news" as it occurs in a courthouse.[66] In Nova Scotia, camera operators must take care not to film or photograph the interior of a courtroom through an open door or a window. As well, cameras are banned from some public areas of specific courthouses for security reasons or to keep hallways clear.[67]

Areas Surrounding Courthouses

Judges may rely on court rules or their inherent powers to restrict camera use in the vicinity of a courthouse. The rules of New Brunswick's Court of Queen's Bench, for example, allow a judge to ban cameras from being used on "the precincts or grounds of the property at which the courtroom or courthouse is located" if such a step is necessary in the interests of justice.[68] The Yukon courts bar cameras from being used on the steps and vehicle ramps used to gain access to the courthouse in Whitehorse.[69]

Inside Courtrooms

With few exceptions—and in stark contrast to practices in many American courts—cameras are banned from Canadian courtrooms. According to a 1992 ruling, it is a long-standing, unwritten rule of the British Columbia courts that cameras cannot be used to record trials or hearings. "Its origins may be said to be lost in the mists of time," the judge said of this restriction, "but its existence, rather than its origins, is what is significant."[70]

Other jurisdictions have put the prohibition into writing. A practice rule of the Quebec Superior Court forbids "the practice of photography, cinematography, broadcasting or television ... during sittings of the court."[71] Ontario is the only province that makes it an offence to film or take photographs during a court hearing. A judge can make an exception for official ceremonies or if the parties and witnesses involved agree to have the proceeding recorded for instructional or educational purposes.[72] Courts in most other jurisdictions permit cameras to be used in the courtroom when the media cover swearing-in ceremonies for judges, and will grant requests to photograph or videotape weddings held in courtrooms. The media may also be able to make arrangements to use a vacant courtroom for photo shoots or to record stand-ups for a television report.[73] Despite the general rule against camera access, judges in Ontario, Newfoundland and Labrador, and Manitoba have authorized the filming of portions of hearings for documentaries and television news reports. Other courts have experimented with pilot projects.[74]

Several superior courts have introduced policies that permit television coverage of their proceedings. Appeals before the Supreme Court of Canada are recorded and broadcast on the Cable Public Affairs Channel (CPAC). The court installed the recording equipment and controls all aspects of filming. The Federal Court of Appeal also permits video recording of its proceedings. Since 1996 the Nova Scotia Court of Appeal has allowed media outlets to apply, on a case-by-case basis, to record and broadcast hearings. The parties to the appeal have the right to object to camera access but the court has approved most applications, even in the face of opposition from a defendant in a murder case.[75] The media outlet that is granted access must use a single camera and share the footage with other television stations. When access is approved, newspaper photographers are permitted to take still photographs of the participants for up to two minutes before the hearing begins. Television camera operators also have the right to enter and shoot footage in the courtroom during this period.[76] The Ontario Court of Appeal launched a pilot project to televise hearings in 2007, including a 10-day review that exonerated Steven Truscott, who was wrongly convicted of murder in 1959.[77] The video was broadcast live on the Internet and appeal courts in Nova Scotia and New Brunswick have webcast selected hearings since 2009.[78] Media law scholar Robert Martin has attributed the lack of controversy about camera access to appeal courts to the fact that such proceedings attract little public attention:

> Nobody seems to care seriously about whether journalists record proceedings before appellate courts, largely because these proceedings are not very interesting .... there are no ordinary people there, no witnesses. All that happens before appellate courts is lawyers arguing points of law.[79]

This approach is changing, but slowly. British Columbia has rectified its lack of a written policy on camera access and, in the process, has jumped to the forefront of the debate. The catalyst was the July 2000 decision of Justice Ronald McKinnon of the province's Supreme Court, who granted a media request to allow television and still cameras to record portions of the trial of nine Korean seamen charged with smuggling illegal immigrants into Canada. Access was limited to recording the lawyers' closing arguments and the judge's charge to the jury; filming of defendants, jurors, and witnesses was forbidden. Justice McKinnon said the common law provided no basis "for excluding modern technology from the courtroom" and, in the spirit of the *Dagenais* precedent, he granted access as an "experiment."[80]

In response, the British Columbia Supreme Court introduced a policy in March 2001 to regulate camera access in future cases. The policy bans the use of cameras in courtrooms "or areas immediately adjacent" to them when court is in session and during recesses. Cameras will only be admitted if the parties to the case give their consent and the judge grants permission. If access is approved, the judge has the power to impose conditions "to protect the interests of justice and to maintain the dignity of the proceedings." The court also announced that it would develop detailed guidelines for camera access in consultation with the legal profession and the media.[81] The policy was put to the test in September 2001, when the media applied to televise the criminal trial of the province's former premier, Glen Clark, who was accused of breach of the public trust. The presiding judge denied access, expressing serious reservations about the possible impact of cameras on the fairness of trials. Justice Elizabeth Bennett, who described camera access to courtrooms as an issue of "grave significance" to the justice system, said further research and supervised access were needed before an informed decision could be made on easing restrictions.[82] British Columbia's attorney general revived the debate in 2010 and promised to launch a pilot project to televise some proceedings, including trials.[83]

There is no shortage of experience with cameras in the courtroom in other countries. In the United States, as of 1998, 48 states permitted camera access on a permanent or experimental basis. Thirty-nine of these states allowed camera coverage of trials and appeal hearings, providing plenty of fodder for Court TV, a cable network devoted to broadcasting court proceedings. In 1996 the US federal courts relaxed a long-standing ban on cameras, allowing coverage of many trials and appeals.[84] Courts in Scotland, New Zealand, and Australia have permitted camera access on an experimental basis or have drafted guidelines to control their use.[85]

The Camera on Trial

The debate over cameras in the courtroom has raged since 1935, when 120 cameramen descended on a New Jersey courthouse to chronicle Bruno Hauptmann's trial for the kidnapping and murder of aviator Charles Lindbergh's young son. Here's a summary of the arguments for and against televising trials:

Arguments For Televising Trials

Television coverage ...

... opens trials to public scrutiny, making them more fair and boosting public confidence in the justice system by exposing the participants to scrutiny and criticism

... merely "watches," portraying what happens accurately and without distortion, providing more accurate, balanced, and complete reports than other media

... causes lawyers to prepare their cases thoroughly to avoid looking foolish, ensuring more effective advocacy and improving the administration of justice

... ensures that the courts are seen as public institutions, not the private preserve of judges and lawyers

... increases public understanding of the system, engendering respect and reducing cynicism

... reaches citizens who have no direct access to courtrooms

... produces tapes of proceedings to be used as an educational tool

Arguments Against Televising Trials

Television coverage ...

... may make witnesses reluctant to testify in the glare of publicity

... may distract witnesses or make them nervous, affecting the ability of a judge or jury to assess their credibility

... will widely disseminate what has been said in court, possibly influencing witnesses who have yet to testify

... may prompt witnesses to embellish their testimony to attract media attention during their "15 minutes of fame"

... puts pressure on jurors and could affect their judgment

... may tempt lawyers to grandstand and influence how they approach their questioning

... may stress sensational evidence or emotional testimony that has little bearing on the outcome of a trial, conveying incomplete or inaccurate information to the public

... may focus on sensational trials, distorting the reality of the justice system, diminishing the dignity of the courts, and fostering disrespect

... may make victims reluctant to report crimes if they face testifying on television

... may deter litigants from filing lawsuits or force them to accept unfair settlements to avoid publicity

... will make witnesses well-known, possibly exposing them or their families to acts of revenge or intimidation

... will compromise the safety of judges, lawyers, and court officials, who will become more recognizable

... may attract activists and even terrorists to the courtroom, increasing security risks

(Source: Adapted from *Supreme Court of British Columbia Policy on Television in the Courtroom*, adopted March 9, 2001. Available online at http://www.llbc.leg.bc.ca/ public/PubDocs/bcdocs/358159/courtroom.pdf.)

But televised trials remain controversial, even in the United States, where tabloid-style, gavel-to-gavel coverage of the O.J. Simpson trial and other sensational cases has sparked a renewed debate on the issue.[86] Despite the conflicting British Columbia rulings, in 2001 the Canadian Judicial Council rejected a proposal that the country's senior judges reconsider their position that "televising court proceedings would not be in the best interests of the administration of justice."[87] While cameras are making their way into some courtrooms, for the foreseeable future most Canadians will have to rely on American television for a glimpse inside a courtroom. Ontario's chief justice, Roy McMurtry, may have captured the prevailing opinion among judges in a 2003 speech when he asked a legal audience: "Why would any rational society want to risk polluting the justice system as the price for the entertainment value of 20-second soundbites on the evening news?"[88]

Artists' Sketches

With cameras barred from most courtrooms, the media have long relied on artists' sketches to depict what happens in the courtroom. The practice is not regulated but legislation in Ontario specifically recognizes the right to make drawings during court proceedings.[89] But artists must abide by any restrictions on identifying those they depict. Two Vancouver newspapers covering the Air India bombing trial in 2003 were taken to task for publishing sketches of a key witness—a woman who feared for her life and was in a witness-protection program—whose identity was protected under a publication ban. In one sketch, her face was obscured but her hairstyle and clothes were recognizable. The other drawing showed the woman with her hand partly obscuring her face. The judge presiding over the trial prohibited further sketches and asked British Columbia's Attorney General's Office to consider filing contempt charges.[90]

Audio Recorders and Laptop Computers

Most courts allow journalists to make audio recordings of trials and hearings. The recordings are intended only for reference and as a supplement to written notes—broadcast of what has been said in the courtroom is prohibited.[91] Journalists are also permitted to use laptop computers to take notes in some courtrooms. Electronic note-taking is a privilege, not a right, and judges may restrict or prohibit use of this equipment during specific hearings.

In Nova Scotia, all levels of court allow the use of audio recorders and laptops under comprehensive guidelines for media access to the courts.[92] Ontario's *Courts of Justice Act* authorizes lawyers, journalists, and anyone who is a party to a case to "unobtrusively" make "an audio recording at a court hearing, in the manner that has been approved by the judge, for the sole purpose of supplementing or replacing handwritten notes."[93] Judges of New Brunswick's Court of Queen's Bench issued an order in 1990 authorizing "bona fide representatives" of the news media to use tape recorders in their courtrooms, unless "expressly prohibited by the judge presiding over any proceeding."[94] In Manitoba, both the Court of Queen's Bench and the provincial court permit taping "provided it is for the sole purpose of supplementing or replacing handwritten notes."[95] The British Columbia Supreme Court followed suit in 2002, adopting a policy that allows accredited journalists to use tape recorders "to assist them to report accurately on the proceedings."[96] Courts in other jurisdictions may have informal rules governing the use of audio recorders and computers, or judges may field requests to use them on a case-by-case basis. Any writer who is uncertain about local rules or practices should consult the court clerk or a sheriff's deputy before operating this equipment in a courtroom.

Twitter in the Courts: Covering Trials, 140 Characters at a Time

Twitter, the micro-blogging network, allows journalists to publish online reports on trials in real time, in bursts of up to 140 characters filed from inside the courtroom. The courts authorized the use of the social media tool in two high-profile trials in 2009 and courtroom "tweets" may become a routine part of coverage of the justice system.

"Tweeting is an instant way to get the proceedings out there," says Kate Dubinski of the *London Free Press*, who covered the Ontario murder trial of six men convicted of murdering eight members of the Bandidos biker gang. "Many people have told me they felt like they were in the courtroom with me throughout the trial." *Ottawa Citizen* reporter Glen McGregor filed more than 2,000 tweets during the two-week trial of Ottawa Mayor Larry O'Brien, who was acquitted of influence peddling. "You're basically putting your notebook online in real time," he says, and at one point some 600 people were following his steady stream of mini-reports.

Inviting Twitter into the courtroom is a logical extension of existing media access rights. Many courts already allow journalists to take notes on laptop computers. The only difference is Twitter allows a steady stream of brief reports to be filed directly to the Internet. The judge presiding over the O'Brien trial granted the *Citizen*'s request to use BlackBerrys and laptops to file from the courtroom. Justice Douglas Cunningham of the Ontario Superior Court ruled in May 2009 that "instant text transmission to the blogosphere ... will be permitted so long as any texting is done in an unobtrusive way and does not affect the running of the trial." In the Bandidos case, there was no formal ruling but a court official told Dubinski she had permission to blog the trial. Security concerns meant electronic devices were banned from the courtroom, so she used her laptop to file from an overflow room as she watched the trial via a live video feed.

The American media also are using Twitter to cover the courts. Journalists in Kansas and Colorado have tweeted trials but a judge in Georgia refused access, ruling the practice amounts to broadcasting a judicial proceeding and that's prohibited under US federal court rules. Canada's judges are taking a case-by-case approach—Justice Cunningham stressed his ruling was not "a broad policy statement" by his court, and applied only to the O'Brien trial. The

Figure 11.1 *Ottawa Citizen* reporter Glen McGregor used Twitter to report on the 2009 court case of Ottawa Mayor Larry O'Brien.
SOURCE: Glen McGregor. Used by permission.

decision might have been different if the case were being heard by a jury, he suggested, because "jury trials may present a whole set of different problems." In contrast, Dubinski says no concerns were raised about live-blogging the Bandidos trial, which was heard by a jury. In October 2010 an Ontario judge authorized journalists to file tweets and live text reports from the sentencing hearing for Russell Williams, a disgraced Armed Forces colonel who pleaded guilty to murdering two women, sexually assaulting two others, and breaking into dozens of homes to steal lingerie. The ruling enabled media outlets to post detailed, up-to-the-minute online reports as the shocking evidence of Williams' crimes was revealed in court.

Whether journalists can capture the nuances of a complex legal proceeding in 140 characters or less using Twitter is another matter. McGregor found he could give readers an almost verbatim account of the evidence. Despite the strict word limit, Dubinski was able to add colour and depth to her reporting—when a witness mentioned a certain firearm, for instance, she tweeted a hyperlink to an image of the weapon. Ottawa-based Internet law expert Michael Geist told *The Lawyers Weekly* that using Twitter is the same as "taking notes, with faster dissemination … . Any steps taken to increase the level of transparency [in the courts] are typically good things."

(Sources: Luigi Benetton, "Twitter in the Courtroom: A Fad or Here to Stay?" *The Lawyers Weekly*, June 12, 2009, 20-21; Daniel Leblanc, "Media Can File from Inside Mayor's Trial," *Globe and Mail*, May 5, 2009; Kate Dubinski, "Bandidos Trial Tweets Critical," *London Free Press*, October 16, 2009; "Ruling on Use of Recording Devices," Ontario Superior Court, May 4, 2009 (available online at http://www.adidem.org/File:R._v._O'Brien_re_Blackberry.pdf); Jim Rankin, "Judge Permits Live Text Reports from Russell Williams Sentencing," *Toronto Star*, October 14, 2010; Dean Jobb, "Social Networking Inside the Courtroom," *Media*, vol. 14, no. 2 (Winter 2010), 33.)

Access to Court Files and Documents

The principle of open courts extends to the paperwork of the justice system. Pleadings in civil cases, indictments alleging criminal offences, exhibits, transcripts of hearings, the judge's ruling—all are presumed to be open to public scrutiny. This is an ancient right, enshrined as early as the 14th century in a British statute that granted "any subject" the right to access the "records of the King's Courts … for his necessary use and benefit."[97] But as is the case with access to the courts themselves, exceptions may be made to protect privacy and other important interests.

Certain records, though filed with the courts, are sealed to prevent public inspection. These include adoption records,[98] contingency fee agreements between lawyers and clients,[99] applications to register a person as a child abuser,[100] and records of private conferences designed to settle disputes before trial.[101] In some jurisdictions, it may be necessary to apply to a judge for access to copies of victim impact statements and pre-sentence reports on offenders, even if the documents have been cited or read aloud in court.[102] The British Columbia Supreme Court has adopted a policy of unrestricted access to three classes of documents in criminal files—informations, indictments, and rulings—but a judge's permission is required to view other records. "The governing legal principle is that there is a presumption in favour of public access," the policy notes, "but that access must be supervised by the court to ensure that no abuse or harm occurs to innocent parties."[103]

Court administrators in at least two provinces implemented policies that denied reporters and citizens the right to view files if there was a publication ban on the case—in effect, transforming a ban on publication into a sealing order. The Ontario government introduced the restriction in 2006 but rescinded it three years later, after journalists produced a newsletter that documented how the policy blocked access to information and files that are, by law, open to public scrutiny. In response to a 2010 investigation by journalists at the Victoria *Times-Colonist*, British Columbia's attorney general promised to change a similar policy and to improve access to other court records.[104]

Dockets

Every court makes public its **docket**—a schedule of its upcoming hearings. A basic docket sets out the name of the case, the file number of the case, the type of hearing, the courtroom, and the date and time that the hearing will be held. Some are more detailed, providing background information about the case and identifying the judge and lawyers involved. Dockets are available at court registry offices and are posted in courthouses.

Case Files

When criminal charges are laid or a lawsuit is launched, the court opens a file and assigns a number to the case. A journalist or writer, like any other member of the public, can inspect the file at the court's registry during office hours. A retrieval fee may be levied for each file requested, and documents can be photocopied for a per-page fee. The file accompanies the case to court, and a journalist should be able to make arrangements with the court clerk to examine it during a break or after the proceeding ends.

A Court Documents Primer

An understanding of court files and what they contain is essential for any writer or researcher, whether it is a journalist looking for the details of a case, an author researching a true-crime book, an investigative reporter digging for information about a person or company, or an academic seeking the stories behind crime statistics. Below is a guide to tracking down files on criminal and civil cases and what writers and researchers can expect to find.

Criminal Case Files

Provincial Courts

Charges are filed with the court registrar's office in the city, town, or district where the offence occurred. Files are indexed using the surname of the defendant.

What's on File

- *Informations* These documents provide the name, address, age, and some-times the occupation of the person accused of the offence. The date and place of the offence and the victim's name are also disclosed. As a case proceeds, an information becomes the permanent record of the case. The judge or court clerk uses it to note the defendant's plea, any conditions of release pending trial, whether bans on publication apply to the case, and the date of the next hearing. If the case remains in provincial court, the date of conviction and the sentence imposed are also recorded.

- *Summonses, Arrest Warrants, Undertakings, Subpoenas* Some documents may be filed with the information, including a summons for the defendant to appear in court; an arrest warrant, if the defendant is at large or has failed to appear in court; any undertakings the defendant has signed to gain release before trial; and subpoenas directing witnesses to testify.

- *Search Warrants* Once police have completed a search, three documents become public (unless sealed to protect an investigation):

  — the warrant reveals the location searched and the evidence sought;

  — the information to obtain the warrant sets out details of the investigation, the names of suspects, and the offences being alleged; and

  — the return lists items and documents seized.

  Search warrant files may be stored in centralized registries or kept in the office of the judge or justice of the peace who issued it. Practices vary from province to province and sometimes within a jurisdiction.

Superior Trial Courts

Provinces and territories are divided into judicial districts, each with a superior court registry that is usually housed in the area's main courthouse. Files are indexed by the surname of the defendant and are available for inspection at the registry office.

What's on File

- *Indictments* This document, a redrafted version of the information, restates the charges once the case reaches the superior court level for the taking of a plea and the trial. A copy of the information drafted and used at the provincial court level will be included in the superior court file.

- *Court Orders* This file could contain a variety of orders, including the provincial court judge's committal to stand trial, the exact wording of any bans on publication, and orders for the prosecution to disclose evidence to the defence.

- *Transcripts* If the prosecution or defence has ordered a transcript of the preliminary hearing or any bail proceedings, a copy should be included in the file. If a publication ban has been imposed, the contents cannot be reported until the prosecution ends.

- *Summonses, Arrest Warrants, Undertakings, Subpoenas* One or more of these orders may appear in the superior court file.

- *Rulings* Most of the decisions that a judge makes as a case proceeds are delivered from the bench. The verdict and the ruling on sentence are usually produced in writing, but it may be weeks or even months before they are transcribed and added to the file.

- *Pre-sentence Reports* These reports are prepared by probation officers and outline the offender's family background, employment history, criminal record, and other information. In some jurisdictions, judges reserve the right to seal these reports if they include sensitive medical information or psychological assessments.

Civil Case Files

Small Claims Courts

The registry for these courts, which hear disputes involving relatively modest amounts of money (typically less than $25,000), is usually in the same building as the provincial court.

What's on File

- *Forms* Forms outline the plaintiffs' claims and the ruling of the adjudicator.

Superior Trial Courts

As with criminal cases, documents are filed with the superior court registry in the area where the lawsuit's allegations occurred. A civil action based on events in more than one jurisdiction may be filed where the plaintiff or defendant resides. Files are indexed under the names of the plaintiff and defendant or, in the case of an application, under the names of the applicant and respondent.

What's on File

- *Statements of Claim or Originating Notices* These documents set out the plaintiff's version of events, the allegations against the defendant, and the court order or damages sought.
- *Demands for Particulars* Before responding to a lawsuit, a defendant may formally demand more details of the plaintiff's allegations.
- *Statements of Defence* Defendants have a deadline for filing a defence refuting the allegations and providing their version of events.
- *Counterclaims* Defendants may countersue plaintiffs, alleging wrongdoing and seeking their own order or damages.
- *Lists of Documents* As part of the civil trial process, each side must disclose all documents relevant to the claim. Lists of these documents are filed with the court in some provinces, but the documents themselves remain private until produced as evidence at trial.

- *Affidavits* These are the sworn statements of a witness, setting out the facts as the witness sees them.

- *Transcripts of Examinations for Discovery* Although discovery hearings are held in private, transcripts may be filed with the court to support an application for an order forcing a witness to answer questions or to produce documents.

- *Motions* This type of application is made to a chambers judge to resolve legal disputes that may arise during the pre-trial stage.

- *Rulings* In most civil cases, the judge will hand down a written ruling, which will be incorporated into the file. Once a verdict has been reached, the judge may be asked to make a further ruling on the legal costs that the successful party is entitled to recover from the losing side.

Appellate Court Files

The Supreme Court of Canada and provincial and territorial courts of appeal hear both criminal and civil cases. There is only one appellate court for each jurisdiction, so all files are housed in a central registry office located in the provincial or territorial capital. The Supreme Court of Canada's registry is in Ottawa. Files are indexed by the names of appellants and the names of respondents.

What's on File

- *Trial Documents* An appeal court file includes copies of all documents filed with the court at the trial level.

- *Transcripts and Exhibits* A complete transcript of the trial—testimony, legal arguments, and rulings—is prepared for appellate judges to review. Bound volumes containing the transcript and copies of all documents and photographs presented as trial exhibits will be filed.

- *Factums* These are written submissions in which the lawyers for each side review the evidence and put forward the legal arguments to support their positions.

- *Rulings* Most appeal court rulings are produced in writing; those delivered from the bench are transcribed and added to the file.

Exhibits

As a trial unfolds, witnesses are asked to identify the physical evidence that relates to the crime or civil dispute. The possibilities are endless—experts' reports; photos taken at the scene of a crime or an accident; a suspect's videotaped statement to police; maps and diagrams; bundles of seized narcotics; financial records and other documents; the clothing that a suspect or victim wore or the gun or knife that an assailant wielded.

Once each item has been identified, it is given an exhibit number and becomes part of the evidence before the court.

Journalists need access to exhibits in order to properly cover court proceedings. Being able to photocopy the documents used as exhibits—or at least take notes on their contents—ensures accurate reporting. The publication of police photos or the broadcast of a videotaped interrogation conveys the reality of crime and investigative methods in a way that a written description cannot match.

The courts have the power to deny or control access to exhibits to protect other rights or interests. Ownership may be an issue—some exhibits belong to the defendant or to someone with little connection to the case, and these items will be returned to their owner after the courts make a final ruling.[105]

In the leading case on access to exhibits, *Vickery v. Nova Scotia Supreme Court (Prothonotary)*, a CBC television producer sought the videotape of a suspect confessing to a murder and re-enacting his crime. Nova Scotia's Court of Appeal overturned the man's conviction, ruling that the confession was inadmissible because it was obtained after police denied him the Charter right to speak to a lawyer. Court officials refused to provide a copy of the tape to the journalist, who was researching a story about how police use video recordings to record statements and gather evidence. The CBC fought for access all the way to the Supreme Court of Canada but lost in 1991.

In *Vickery*, the court reiterated the principle of access to court hearings and documents, but a majority of judges found that the suspect's privacy interests should prevail. The suspect had been acquitted and must be treated as innocent, the majority stressed. As well, the confession had been improperly obtained and the public's right of access had been fulfilled when the tape was presented at the man's trial. Before granting access to any exhibit, the court said, a judge should take into account the type of evidence involved, whether it has been produced in a courtroom, and the privacy interests of those involved in the case. As well, judges reserve the right to ask how the exhibit will be used and to impose conditions on access. In the dissenting ruling, Justice Peter Cory argued that all court records and exhibits are in the public domain—even evidence ruled inadmissible—unless there is an overriding interest at stake. "There should not be a priestly cult of the law whereby lawyers and judges exclusively determine those items of the appeal record which can be seen and heard by members of the public."[106]

Many media law experts question whether the process set out so long ago in *Vickery* should still be followed, in light of subsequent Supreme Court rulings expanding the media's access rights under the Charter, but it remains the basis of court rules and practices for dealing with requests to view or copy exhibits. The law, however, is evolving: in 2010 the Ontario Court of Appeal ruled the *Dagenais/Mentuck* test applies to requests to access and copy exhibits. The media's access rights extend "to anything that has been made part of the [court] record"—all documents and recordings tendered as evidence, even those not read or played in the courtroom—and those opposing access must show compelling reasons why the materials should be withheld.[107] During a trial or other hearing, the presiding judge decides whether access will be granted. Exhibits are made available only after they have been identified, numbered, and entered into evidence. Requests to view them are usually made informally to the court clerk, who will consult the judge. Access is usually granted and arrangements are made for the journalist to view the item during a break or adjournment, with the clerk on hand to ensure that the evidence is not tampered with or removed from the courtroom. Often, the lawyers involved in the case will allow journalists to review or photocopy their versions of documents being used as exhibits.

A formal hearing and court order may be necessary in some provinces, or if privacy or other concerns could arise from making documents, photographs, and videotapes available to the media. In the *Vickery* case, the Supreme Court was not asked to take into account the Charter right of freedom of expression, and the media have been successful in using the Charter to persuade other judges to follow Justice Cory's liberal approach to access. In 1995 the CBC and the *Edmonton Journal* were allowed to copy and disseminate photographs, hundreds of pages of transcribed interviews, and the videotaped confession of a man convicted of planting a bomb that killed nine Yellowknife miners during a bitter labour dispute. Likewise, a Nova Scotia judge released a murderer's videotaped confession for duplication and broadcast, noting that the man had pleaded guilty and could no longer claim his privacy interests would be harmed. Each judge delayed access until the completion of any appeals arising from the case.[108] The media were also allowed to broadcast a videotaped interview with convicted murderer Paul Bernardo in 2008, despite concerns that posting it on news websites could lead to its reproduction or misuse on YouTube and other websites.[109] And in 2010 British Columbia's Court of Appeal granted access to video recordings of an undercover police operation that induced suspects to confess to their previous offences to a purported "crime boss." The video had been presented during a trial and the court said concerns for the safety of the officers involved could be met by altering the recordings to delete their names and information that could identify them.[110]

Courts have also granted the right to reproduce controversial exhibits, such as the audiotapes of a murder victim's anguished calls to 9-1-1 dispatchers[111] and a videotape of a police officer carrying a corpse into a police station.[112] A freelance writer covering a BC child pornography case was allowed to view and describe a book of photographs depicting nude children, on the condition that he not publish any information that could identify anyone in the photos.[113] Calgary newspapers were able to duplicate photographs, a 9-1-1 tape, letters, X-rays, and patient care records used as evidence in a high-profile attempted murder trial.[114] But there are limits. A columnist for the *National Post* was denied access to autopsy photographs showing injuries to Reena Virk, the victim of a violent swarming by other youths. Even though the paper was only seeking the right to view the photos, not to publish them, the judge said the emotional harm to the girl's parents outweighed the right of access.[115] At Paul Bernardo's murder trial, journalists were barred from viewing explicit videotapes depicting the assault and torture of two teenage victims. When the footage was presented to the jury, video screens facing the gallery were switched off but journalists and members of the public were allowed to hear the audio portion of the tapes.[116] In 2009 a Saskatchewan judge also opted for limited access to an audio recording of police radio transmissions made just before two RCMP officers died in a gun battle with a fleeing suspect. The judge refused to allow duplication and broadcast of the recording, citing concerns this would cause further distress to the families of the slain officers, but released a transcript for publication.[117]

Transcripts and Audio Recordings of Hearings

An audio recording is made of all proceedings and many courts provide copies for a fee. The recordings are not intended for broadcast and there may be specific laws or court rules restricting such use.[118] A typed transcript may be filed with the court if the outcome of a hearing has been appealed. In some jurisdictions, a journalist who has missed a hearing may be able to arrange to listen to the recording the same day. Typically, the judge who presided at the hearing will have to approve the request.

Electronic Access to Rulings

Most court rulings are produced electronically as well as in writing and released to the media, with a copy earmarked for inclusion in the court file. The exceptions are rulings of little legal significance or routine decisions made during the course of a trial, which are announced publicly in the courtroom but may be reduced to writing only if an appeal is launched. Rulings provide a snapshot of the evidence presented in a case, the law that applies to those facts, and the court's reasons for its ruling. Because precedents are the fuel that drives our common law justice system, significant decisions have been collected into bound volumes, known as case law reports, for future reference as legal issues arise. As noted above, almost all rulings are released in electronic form, so most lawyers and journalists search for cases in online or commercial databases. Courts across the country post and archive rulings on their own websites and CanLII, the Canadian Legal Information Institute website (http://www.canlii.org), offers free access to a comprehensive collection of rulings and laws drawn from all jurisdictions (see the box below). It is common for the courts to notify the media of the release of decisions in high-profile cases, and procedures may be in place to make other rulings public soon after the parties involved have been notified.[119]

During 2002, in response to privacy concerns, courts in British Columbia and Alberta moved to restrict Internet access to rulings in family law cases. British Columbia adopted a policy of posting only those rulings that may set a legal precedent, while Alberta chose to no longer provide online access to judgments.[120] Both courts continued to make family law rulings available to commercial legal publishers, but such policies threaten to erode access to rulings just as new technology promises to make the courts more open and transparent.

Electronic Access to Court Files

Electronic access to rulings is just the beginning. Canada's courts are in the midst of a transition from paper records to computerized systems to file and store documents. Most courts also post dockets and case summaries on the Internet. Procedures to permit the electronic filing of at least some documents in criminal and civil cases are in place or are being contemplated. In the words of a Canadian Judicial Council discussion paper on computerized access to court records, compiled by senior judges in 2003, "it is not a question of whether the electronic environment will dominate the administration of justice. It is a question of when."[121]

Making files and documents widely available in databases and via the Internet makes the courts far more accessible to the public. Although paper records have always been open to scrutiny, few people had the time, money, or inclination to visit a courthouse and wade through indexes and files. But the ease of electronic access creates new problems and privacy concerns. Sexual predators can glean information about children from divorce files; court records may disclose personal and financial information that could make litigants vulnerable to identity theft; a few mouse clicks could enable anyone to scour court files for dirt on their neighbours, friends, or enemies. Ease of access, combined with the ability to search countless records by the name of any person or company, has removed what has been termed the "practical obscurity" of paper records, which are more cumbersome to search. In the United States, where electronic filing is more advanced—among the records offered online are arrest warrants, divorce files, liens for unpaid taxes, sex offender registries, and speeding tickets—courts have ordered that sensitive information be sealed or removed from Internet sites.[122] Here in Canada, the federal privacy commissioner has cautioned the courts to take steps to protect personal information that may be found in court filings. "The open-court principle is extremely important," she told a meeting of the Canadian Bar Association in 2008, "but it wasn't meant for the age of Google."[123]

Finding Court Rulings and Case Information Online

Canadian Legal Information Institute (CanLII)

This site offers free online access to the full text of more than 500,000 rulings of courts and tribunals in all provinces and territories, as well as laws and regulations. New rulings are posted daily and older ones are being added, making this a comprehensive site for finding precedents and information on legal trends and issues.

http://www.canlii.org

Court Websites

Canadian courts maintain their own websites. The resources offered vary from jurisdiction to jurisdiction, but typically these sites provide access to dockets, news releases, background information about the justice system, and a searchable database of rulings.

Supreme Court of Canada

This site provides access to news releases and weekly bulletins that track the status of hearings, reserved decisions, and applications for leave to appeal. There is also a full-text archive of all rulings since 1983.

http://www.scc-csc.gc.ca

Federal Court of Canada

This site provides online access to a database of rulings dating to 1992.
http://www.fct-cf.gc.ca

Superior and Provincial Courts

Courts in the provinces and territories maintain websites, most offering electronic access to recent and archived rulings. They also provide contact information for registry offices and court staff, plus links to statutes and regulations and other legal resources.

Alberta	**http://www.albertacourts.ab.ca**
British Columbia	**http://www.courts.gov.bc.ca**
Manitoba	**http://www.manitobacourts.mb.ca**
New Brunswick	**http://www.gnb.ca/cour**
Newfoundland and Labrador	**http://www.court.nl.ca**
Northwest Territories	**http://www.nwtcourts.ca**
Nova Scotia	**http://www.courts.ns.ca**
Nunavut	**http://www.nucj.ca**
Ontario	**http://www.ontariocourts.on.ca**
Prince Edward Island	**http://www.gov.pe.ca/courts**
Quebec	**http://www.tribunaux.qc.ca**
Saskatchewan	**http://www.sasklawcourts.ca**
Yukon	**http://www.yukoncourts.ca**

The 2003 discussion paper on the issue called on the Canadian Judicial Council to take the lead role in the development of new policies to govern electronic access and to ensure that courts across the country adopt consistent practices. According to the authors of the discussion paper, the starting point for the debate must be the principle "that the right to open courts generally outweighs the right to privacy."[124] The council released an electronic access policy, intended as a model for courts across the country, in 2005 that recommended measures to prevent the use of court records "for improper purposes, such as commercial data mining, identity theft, stalking, harassment and discrimination." The report's main concern was restricting online access to "personal data identifiers" included in court records, such as birthdates, street addresses, e-mail accounts, phone numbers, social insurance numbers, and bank account information. The policy calls on everyone who creates or handles court records—lawyers, clerks, and judges alike—to ensure such information is included only when it is relevant to the case.[125] The policy was drafted with little media input and has been criticized for creating an "Internet roadblock" to public access at a time when technology should be making it easier and cheaper to locate and view court records. "Public, but not too public—that's the Canadian position," the *Globe and Mail* complained in an editorial.[126]

Not surprisingly, the courts are moving slowly and cautiously as they consider posting records other than rulings, dockets, and bare-bones case information. The Supreme Court of Canada provides background information about cases and the legal issues on its website, and began posting factums (written legal arguments filed in advance of appeal hearings) in February 2009.[127] British Columbia has emerged as the leader in providing online access to court records. Court Services Online, launched in 1999, is a web-based service offering selected records of court cases for a fee of $6 per file. More than 200,000 documents filed in civil cases—with the exception of family law matters—were available by mid-2008. Electronic indexes with "tombstone" information about criminal and civil cases—names of parties, dates of filing, disposition—are also available. Affidavits and exhibits found in court files are not posted, however, because they may contain sensitive information or unproven allegations.[128]

Restrictions on Access

Orders Sealing Documents and Files

At least three provinces—Ontario, Manitoba, and Prince Edward Island—give superior court judges sweeping powers to seal any document filed in a civil case.[129] Under the rules of the Federal Court, a party can apply to a judge for an order to keep any filed document confidential. The judge must be satisfied that the information should be sealed "notwithstanding the public interest in open and accessible court proceedings."[130] Judges of other superior courts can use their inherent powers to seal documents that are presented as evidence or filed with the court. While such orders are more common in civil actions, they have been imposed in criminal cases.

From a media perspective, a sealing order is indistinguishable from a publication ban or an exclusion order. When a judge declares that certain information is confidential and segregates documents within the court file, the Charter right to freedom of expression is curtailed. Recognizing this, the Supreme Court of Canada has called on judges to apply the *Dagenais/Mentuck* test when asked to use their discretionary powers to seal documents—to balance competing rights of privacy or commercial interests against the right of access. In reviewing a sealing order sought by a defendant under the Federal Court rules, the court ruled in 2002 that confidentiality should be granted only to prevent "a serious risk to an important interest," when there are no other means to alleviate the risk, and when the benefits of preventing disclosure (such as ensuring a fair trial for the litigants) outweigh the public interest in keeping the courts open and accessible.[131] In this case, the federal government was trying to prevent an environmental group from seeing information about the sale of nuclear reactors to China. The Supreme Court ruled that the information should be sealed because an important commercial interest, one with wider implications for the public interest, was at stake—a confidentiality agreement under a commercial contract. The information was the property of the Chinese government and the reactor contract required Atomic Energy of Canada, a federal Crown corporation, to keep it confidential.

Applying the *Dagenais/Mentuck* test to sealing orders promises to have a profound impact on how judges deal with applications to seal documents and files. The Supreme Court's reasoning suggests that, as in the case of publication bans, the media should be notified of these motions and be afforded a chance to challenge or minimize any restriction on access. But most confidentiality concerns arise in civil cases that attract little or no media attention, and sealing orders have been sought and imposed with little regard to the public interest. In one Saskatchewan case, a judge sealed the entire file of a civil case in order to protect the contents of some of the documents. The order, intended as a short-term measure, stood for nine years before another judge of the province's Court of Queen's Bench found no basis for the sweeping denial of access. The second judge reiterated the "fundamental principle that a court file is not sealed other than in exceptional circumstances."[132] In May 2003 an Ontario judge tried to retroactively seal a ruling after it had been made public and circulated to the media. Legal observers said the incident highlighted the need to establish systems to notify the media of applications for sealing orders.[133]

Lifting Sealing Orders on Search Warrant Documents

Although search warrants are accessible to the public once a search has been completed, judges have the power to seal warrants and related documents, under section 487.3(1) of the *Criminal Code*, at the time that these documents are issued. The documents can be sealed if "the ends of justice would be subverted" by making them public, if the information could be used for an improper purpose, and for "any other sufficient reason." Grounds for sealing warrants include protecting the identity of innocent persons, informants, undercover officers, and ongoing police investigations. Under section 487.3(4), media outlets can ask the judge who sealed the documents to rescind the order and to make public all or part of the file. Ontario's Court of Appeal has described orders sealing a search warrant or other document as a "significant intrusion" on freedom of expression. Applying the *Dagenais/Mentuck* test, the court ruled in 2003 that warrants should be sealed only when there is a serious risk to fair-trial rights or the administration of justice. Police concerns that publicity might hinder their efforts to question witnesses, the court said, were too vague and a fundamental right such as freedom of expression cannot be "sacrificed to give police a 'leg up' on an investigation." The *Toronto Star* won access to warrants used to search a meat packing plant under suspicion of processing tainted meat, with minor editing to shield the identity of a confidential informant. The court also said the media have a right to intervene on motions to seal search warrants and to make the case for keeping all or part of a file in the public domain. The Supreme Court of Canada upheld this ruling in 2005, and used the case to confirm the *Dagenais/Mentuck* test applies to "all discretionary court orders that limit freedom of expression and freedom of the press in relation to legal proceedings." This includes search warrant sealing orders made at the investigative stage.[134]

Media outlets have successfully challenged sealing orders on search warrant files in a number of high-profile cases. For instance, warrants used during the investigation of fraud allegations tied to a federal government helicopter purchase were unsealed in 2003, with the exception of information that would expose a confidential informant.[135] Two years later the *Ottawa Citizen* was able to gain access to search warrants related to Maher Arar's rendition to Syria, despite concerns for the privacy of people searched but not charged and the government's claim that disclosure could pose risks to national security.[136] And in 2007 the *Citizen* won access to search warrant records after a judge ruled the public had a right to be told of the unreliable "rumour mill of hearsay allegations" police relied on to investigate Ottawa's mayor on allegations of influence peddling.[137] Access, however, is not guaranteed. An Alberta judge refused access to warrants used to build a murder case against an Edmonton filmmaker in 2009, ruling they contained evidence that would be banned from publication at the man's upcoming preliminary hearing.[138] There are also administrative hurdles: search warrants are issued in secret and the file created is stored separately from other case files, making it difficult for journalists to find out which judge or justice of the peace issued the warrant, where it was issued, and where the file is kept. Reporters may have to rely on tips or police contacts to track them down. And these problems may be compounded if the file has been sealed, because the sealing order itself may be sealed.[139]

Discovery Transcripts and Documents Produced in Civil Cases

Testimony and documents produced at the pre-trial stage of a civil action are subject to an implied undertaking (agreement) that they will be kept confidential and used only for purposes related to the litigation. Plaintiffs and defendants, as well as their lawyers, face punishment for contempt of court if they are found to have used this information for a "collateral" or ulterior purpose. An example would be leaking the information to the media to pressure or publicly embarrass the other party to the litigation. This undertaking applies in most provinces to the documents exchanged between the parties as they assess the evidence and prepare to examine witnesses during discovery hearings.[140] As for transcripts of the testimony given under oath at discovery hearings, there is either an implied undertaking or a formal agreement between the parties that the transcripts will not be used for other purposes.[141] The Supreme Court of Canada has ruled that this undertaking, which exists under the common law and is reflected in the court rules of Quebec and other jurisdictions, is justified because discovery hearings are private and not part of the court process.[142] If a lawyer or a party involved in a lawsuit makes a disclosed document or a discovery transcript available to a journalist, the law (as noted in the privacy law section of Chapter 5) does not prevent the publication of the information. The courts, however, may punish the person who leaked the information. A lawyer who breached the undertaking could also face disciplinary action from the provincial law society.

If documents and discovery transcripts are filed with the court or presented in the courtroom, either during a pre-trial motion or at trial, they are in the public domain unless the court imposes a publication ban or makes an order restricting access.[143]

Access to Other Proceedings

Administrative Tribunals and Human Rights Inquiries

Administrative tribunals at the federal and provincial level may have the power to restrict access to their hearings. The legislation establishing the tribunal and its procedures will dictate whether such powers exist and how they are applied. When a human rights commission convenes a formal inquiry into a complaint of discrimination, the proceedings are usually heard in public. Nova Scotia's human rights law, for example, requires open hearings.[144] In Manitoba, inquiries are open but the adjudicator may ban publication of the identity of any party or witness, to protect the person from "undue prejudice," until a final decision is made on the complaint.[145] Under federal law, the Canadian Human Rights Commission must hold its inquiries in public. A hearing can be closed, however, to prevent hardship to those involved or to protect public security, the fairness of the hearing, or the "life, liberty or security" of a person.[146]

Adoption Applications

Provincial legislation restricts access to adoption applications that come before a court. Legislation either requires an application to be heard in private, unless the judge orders an open hearing, or states that the hearing is open to the public unless the judge orders the court closed.[147] Access to adoption files is either prohibited or permitted only by court order.[148]

Coroner and Fatality Inquiries

Inquiries into the causes of a sudden or suspicious death are generally open to the public. The coroner or judge, however, may have the power to conduct all or part of the inquest in private. In Alberta and Nova Scotia, an inquiry can be closed to protect information relating to public security or to prevent the disclosure of "intimate or personal matters," if these interests outweigh the public interest in open hearings. Under Alberta's legislation, the judge must consider factors such as the privacy of the victim's family, the interests of medical personnel who treated the victim, and the harm that might be caused by the release of information in a patient's file.[149] Manitoba's legislation requires a judge to take similar factors into account, as well as whether "the professional reputation of an individual would be damaged unjustifiably."[150] In one of the few tests of these powers, Manitoba's Court of Appeal upheld a decision to deny the CBC access to documents disclosed at an inquest into a teenager's suicide while in the custody of child protection services. Access to the records was prohibited under provincial law and the court ruled this confidentiality was not lost when they were presented as evidence at the inquiry.[151] Coroners in New Brunswick have the right to close any inquest at any time and for any reason.[152] In Prince Edward Island, an inquiry must be heard *in camera* if someone has been charged in connection with the death or could face prosecution, and if that person requests that the hearing be closed.[153] The law in Ontario and British Columbia empowers a coroner to close a hearing when national security might be endangered or when a person has been charged with a criminal offence in connection with the death.[154] The government of the Northwest Territories has wide discretion to direct that an inquest be held in private to protect national security or when the "possibility of prejudice to the public interest" outweighs the desirability of holding an open hearing.[155]

Courts Martial

Military trials are to be held in public but all or part of a hearing can be closed to prevent the disclosure of information that could jeopardize public safety, public morals, or national defence. Hearings can also be closed to protect international relations, to maintain order in the hearing room, and to ensure "the proper administration of military justice." The Court Martial Appeal Court has the option of sitting in public or *in camera* when hearing evidence, including new evidence relating to the case before it.[156]

Extradition Proceedings

A judge hearing an extradition application or a bail application for a person facing extradition has the power to exclude any person from all or part of the hearing on the basis of protecting public morals, order in the courtroom, or the proper administration of justice.[157]

Immigration and Refugee Hearings

Hearings of adjudicative panels of the Immigration and Refugee Board—the Refugee Protection Division, the Immigration Division, and the Immigration Appeal Division—are open to the public. (Public hearings are also contemplated for the proposed Refugee Appeal Division, which was created in 2001 but had not been constituted as of 2010.) Proceedings may be held in private, however, if publicity would create "a serious possibility that the life, liberty or security of a person will be endangered." Hearings can also be closed to prevent "a real and substantial risk" to the fairness of the proceeding or the disclosure of "matters involving public security." Alternative measures must be considered before a hearing is closed. Hearings into claims for refugee protection are to be held in private unless those presiding are satisfied it would be appropriate to conduct an open hearing.[158]

Judicial Council Inquiries

A Canadian Judicial Council inquiry into the conduct of a superior court judge can be held in public or in private, unless the federal minister of justice orders a public hearing.[159] Practices vary for inquiries involving provincially appointed judges. In Ontario, inquiries can be closed only in "exceptional circumstances" and when the council concludes that it is more desirable to maintain confidentiality and hold all or part of a hearing in private. In 2006 the council ordered a public hearing into allegations a Brampton judge had insulted and denigrated his fellow judges and also made public letters and e-mails documenting the abuse.[160] If the hearing is closed to the public, however, the name of the judge under scrutiny must not be disclosed.[161] If Nova Scotia's judicial council considers it more desirable to maintain confidentiality than to hold an open hearing, it can convene all or part of an inquiry in private.[162] In British Columbia, an inquiry must be open unless the investigating tribunal believes that it is in the public interest to close the hearing or part of the hearing.[163] In Alberta, in contrast, the judicial council must hold its inquiries in private. The council may make public the fact that an investigation is being conducted, and the inquiry report is a public document.[164]

Parole Hearings

Access to Hearings and Records

Parole hearings for federal inmates (those sentenced to two years or more in prison) are open to any journalist or other member of the public. Requests for observer status must be submitted in advance of a hearing and in writing. Because most hearings are conducted inside prisons, security is a concern and the Parole Board of Canada may require up to 30 days to process an application and to conduct a security check on the applicant. The board has the right to deny access to anyone who poses a security risk or whose presence is likely to disrupt the hearing or adversely affect someone who has supplied information to the board, including victims of crime, their families, and relatives of the offender. If any of these concerns surface during the course of a hearing, the board has the power to exclude an observer from a portion of the hearing.[165]

The Parole Board of Canada maintains a registry of all parole applications dealt with after November 1, 1992. The registry is accessible online to the media and members of the public, at http://pbc-clcc.gc.ca/media/dec-eng.shtml. Applications for access must be made in writing and must state the reason for the request. These files, which outline an offender's personal history and criminal record, are edited to remove information that might jeopardize someone's safety, identify a confidential informant, or adversely affect efforts to rehabilitate the offender.[166]

Court Reviews of Parole Eligibility

A conviction for first-degree murder carries an automatic penalty of life in prison with no right to apply for parole for at least 25 years. Second-degree murder is also punished by life in prison, but the judge who passes sentence can require the offender to serve between 10 and 25 years before being eligible for release. Convicted murderers who have served 15 years, and are still not eligible for parole, can apply for a review of their parole status. The application is made to a superior court under section 745 of the *Criminal Code*, the so-called faint hope clause, and a 12-member jury is empanelled to decide whether the offender can apply for early release. Courts in Ontario, New Brunswick, and Prince Edward Island have introduced rules that enable judges to hold review hearings *in camera* and to impose a partial or total ban on the evidence presented.[167]

Police Disciplinary Hearings

Provincial legislation and municipal bylaws govern access to disciplinary hearings for police officers. Access rules vary but restrictions on access have been challenged with some success. Under Ontario law, there must be compelling reasons to exclude the public, such as security or privacy concerns.[168] In one case, a judge refused to order an *in camera* hearing for an Ottawa police officer accused of discreditable conduct, citing the open court rule and the public interest in how police officers use their law enforcement powers.[169] In 1999 the Prince Edward Island Supreme Court struck down a municipal regulation that required private disciplinary hearings. The judge said there is a strong public interest in such hearings and mandatory exclusion rules violate the right to freedom of expression. An adjudicator has the discretion to hold a hearing *in camera*, the judge said, but only after balancing any need to protect privacy against the public's right of access.[170]

Professional Disciplinary Hearings

Most self-governing bodies that oversee the conduct of lawyers, physicians, engineers, and other professionals hold their disciplinary hearings in public, subject to provisions to close a hearing or portions of a hearing. Law societies in all provinces permit public access to formal discipline hearings, but the investigative stages of the process remain private.[171] In Manitoba, for example, discipline hearings for lawyers accused of misconduct are open, but members of the public can be excluded to prevent the disclosure of privileged communications with a client or when private interests outweigh the public interest. There is also a ban on publishing the name of a lawyer who is the subject of an investigation or complaint until there has been a finding of incompetence or professional misconduct.[172] Open disciplinary hearings are mandatory for Ontario doctors, but the public may be excluded from all or part of a hearing to protect public security or someone's safety, to prevent the disclosure of personal or financial information, or to avoid prejudice to a person facing a criminal prosecution or lawsuit. The disciplinary panel also has the power to impose a publication ban to prevent the disclosure of such information.[173]

Public Inquiries and Royal Commissions

Inquiry commissioners have broad investigative powers but, oddly, in most provinces they are not required by law to hold public hearings.[174] Most proceedings are conducted in public, however, and Ontario's legislation requires inquiries to hold public sessions unless the need to protect public security or intimate personal or financial matters justifies a closed hearing.[175] Between the late 1970s and 1994, more than 20 inquiries and royal commissions permitted the televising of their hearings, in whole or in part.[176]

Access to Hearings and Documents: A Summary

Justice cannot be seen to be done if it occurs behind closed doors. Although open proceedings are the rule, some hearings can be convened *in camera* and documents may be sealed to protect privacy, confidential information, and other interests. Media challenges to closed hearings and orders to seal court documents and search warrants have established that compelling grounds are needed to curtail the rights of public access and freedom of expression. But most restrictions on access to the justice system have yet to be subjected to Charter challenges. As they are, and as the courts further narrow the grounds for denying access, fewer citizens and journalists should find themselves cooling their heels outside the courtroom door.

NOTES

1. *Canadian Broadcasting Corp. v. New Brunswick (Attorney General)*, [1993] 3 SCR 480.

2. Ibid., at paragraphs 20, 26, and 28.

3. *Nova Scotia (Attorney General) v. MacIntyre*, [1982] 1 SCR 175, at 186–87.

4. *Named Person v. Vancouver Sun*, 2007 SCC 43, at paragraphs 4 and 16.

5. *Canadian Broadcasting Corp. v. New Brunswick (Attorney General)*, supra note 1, at paragraph 27.

6. *Criminal Code*, RSC 1985, c. C-46, as amended, ss. 486(2.1) and (2.101).

7. *Canadian Broadcasting Corp. v. New Brunswick (Attorney General)*, supra note 1, at paragraphs 41, 73, and 84.

8. Ibid., at paragraph 88.

9. *R v. Lefebvre* (1984), 17 CCC (3d) 277 (Que. CA).

10. *Canadian Broadcasting Corp. v. New Brunswick (Attorney General)*, supra note 1, at paragraph 77.

11. *F.P. Publications (Western) Ltd. v. R* (1979), 51 CCC (2d) 110 (Man. CA).

12. *R v. Musitano* (1985), 24 CCC (3d) 65 (Ont. CA).

13. *R v. Sayegh (No. 1)* (1982), 66 CCC (2d) 430 (Ont. Prov. Ct.), and *R v. Sayegh* (No. 2) (1982), 66 CCC (2d) 432 (Ont. Prov. Ct.).

14. *Nova Scotia (Attorney General) v. MacIntyre*, supra note 3.

15. *Southam Inc. v. Coulter* (1990), 60 CCC (3d) 267 (Ont. CA). See also the annotations in *Martin's Criminal Code 2010* (Aurora, ON: Canada Law Book, 2009), 992–93.

16. *In the Matter of an Application Under s. 83.28 of the Criminal Code*, 2003 BCSC 1172.

17. John Jaffey, "Secrecy Surrounds First Test at SCC of Anti-Terrorism Law," *The Lawyers Weekly*, August 15, 2003; Mark Bourrie, "Supreme Court Seals File in Secret Witness Case," *Law Times*, August 11, 2003.

18. *Vancouver Sun (Re)*, [2004] 2 SCR 332.

19. *Youth Criminal Justice Act*, SC 2002, c. 1, s. 132(1)(b).

20. See, for example, Alberta's *Young Offenders Act*, RSA 2000, c. Y-1, s. 25(1) and the Yukon's *Young Persons Offences Act*, SY 1987, c. 22, s. 33(1).

21. *Young Offenders Act*, RSC 1985, c. Y-1, ss. 39(1) and (3). The exclusion power was found to be constitutional in *R v. Southam Inc.* (1984), 48 OR (2d) 678 (HC); aff'd. 53 OR (2d) 663 (CA).

22. See *Youth Criminal Justice Act*, s. 163.

23. *Halifax Herald Ltd. v. Sparks* (1995), 142 NSR (2d) 321 (SC). See also Barry Dorey, "Judge Violated Freedom of the Press, Court Rules," *Chronicle-Herald* (Halifax), April 26, 1995. The comparable provision of the *Young Offenders Act* was s. 44.1(1)(k).

24. *R v. A.A.B.*, 2006 NSPC 16.

25. *R v. N.Y.*, 2008 CanLII 23498 (Ont. SC).

26. *Provincial Court Act*, RSA 2000, c. P-31, s. 20.

27. *Provincial Court Act*, RSBC 1996, c. 379, s. 3.

28. *Supreme Court Rules*, BC Reg. 221/90, rule 60(41).

29. *Court of Queen's Bench Act*, CCSM c. C280, s. 76(2).

30. *Judicature Act*, SNB, c. J-2, s. 11.3(1); *Rules of Court*, rules 72.14(8) and 73.11(6).

31. *Family Law Act*, RSNL 1990, c. F-2, ss. 25, 48(3), and 58.

32. *Unified Family Court Act*, RSNL 1990, c. U-3, s. 11; *Rules of the Supreme Court*, 1986 NR 52/97, rules 56A.03 and 56A.04(1).

33. *Family Court Act*, RSNS 1989, c. 159, ss. 10(2) and (3).

34. *Judicature Act*, RSNS 1989, c. 240, s. 32D.

35. *Courts of Justice Act*, RSO 1990, c. C.43, ss. 135(2) and 137(2).

36. *Family Law Act*, RSPEI 1988, c. F-2.1, ss. 2(4) and 41(2).

37. *Code of Civil Procedure*, RSQ c. C-25, ss. 13, 815.4, 827.5, and 827.6.

38. *Queen's Bench Act*, 1998, SS 1998, c. Q-1.01, s. 99.

39. *Family Maintenance Act*, 1997, SS 1997, c. F-6.1, s. 18; *Family Property Act*, SS 1997, c. F-6.3, s. 47.

40. *Queen's Bench Rules*, rules 587(1) and (3).

41. *Supreme Court Rules*, BC Reg. 221/90, rule 60D(36).

42. *Family Property and Support Act*, RSY 1986, c. 63, s. 54(1)(5).

43. *Family Law Act*, SNWT 1997, c. 18, s. 27(3.2). This provision also applies to Nunavut.

44. *Provincial Court Act*, RSBC 1996, c. 379, ss. 3(1) and (3).

45. *Provincial Court (Child, Family and Community Service Act) Rules*, BC Reg. 417/98, rule 8(15).

46. *Children and Family Services Act*, SNS 1996, c. 3, s. 93; *Civil Procedure Rules*, rule 69.16.

47. *Family Services Act*, SNB, c. F-2.2, s. 10(1).

48. *Child and Family Services Act*, SS 1989-90, c. C-7.2, ss. 26(1) and (2).

49. *Child Welfare Act*, RSA 2000, c. C-12, s. 24(1).

50. *Child and Family Services Act*, RSO 1990, c. 11, ss. 45(4), (5), and (6).

51. *Child and Family Services Act*, CCSM c. C80, s. 75(1).

52. *Youth Protection Act*, RSQ, c. P-34.1, s. 82.

53. *Child, Youth and Family Services Act*, SNL 1998, c. C-12.1, s. 50(1).

54. *Child Protection Act*, RSPEI 1988, c. 5.1, s. 35(1).

55. *Supreme Court Rules*, BC Reg. 221/90, rule 52(9).

56. *Judicature Act*, RSNS 1989, c. 240, s. 37.

57. *Courts of Justice Act*, RSO 1990, c. C.43, ss. 135(1) and (2); *Rules of Civil Procedure*, RRO 1990, Reg. 194, amended to O. Reg. 19/03, rule 37.11(1).

58. *Supreme Court Act*, RSPEI 1988, c. S-10, ss. 57(1) and (2).

59. *Code of Civil Procedure*, RSQ, c. C-25, s. 13.

60. *Federal Courts Rules*, 1998, SOR/98-106, rule 29(1).

61. "Herald Reporter in Contempt of Court," *Albany Herald*, May 29, 2003. The reporter was given the option of completing 48 hours of community service to avoid serving the jail term. I am indebted to Michael Fitz-James, former executive editor of *Canadian Lawyer* magazine, for bringing this incident to my attention.

62. *Courts of Justice Act*, RSO 1990, c. C.43, ss. 136(1) and (4).

63. *R v. Squires* (1992), 11 OR (3d) 385 (CA).

64. *Court Policies/Practices Affecting Media Coverage*, Manitoba Courts, available online at http://www.manitobacourts.mb.ca/media.html.

65. *Policy Governing the Use of the Law Courts, the Adjacent Atrium and Contiguous Property*, Practice Direction no. 9, Yukon Supreme Court, January 17, 2005.

66. *Société Radio-Canada c. Québec (Procureur Général)*, 2008 QCCA 1910; Luis Millan, "Quebec Judges Eying Limits on TV in Province's Courthouses," *The Lawyers Weekly*, July 16, 2004; *Rules of Practice of the Superior Court of Quebec, Criminal Division, 2002*, s. 8(b).

67. *Guidelines for Media and Public Access to the Courts of Nova Scotia*, Appendix A, available online at http://www.courts.ns.ca/media_access/media.htm. Click on the "Media Guidelines" link.

68. *Bench Rule in Respect of Making of Video and Audio Recordings in Courtrooms*, Court of Queen's Bench, New Brunswick, February 20, 1990, rules 4 and 5.

69. *Policy Governing the Use of the Law Courts, the Adjacent Atrium and Contiguous Property*, supra note 65.

70. *R v. Vander Zalm*, [1992] BCJ no. 3065, at paragraph 3 (QL) (SC).

71. *Rules of Practice of the Superior Court of Quebec, Criminal Division, 2002*, s. 8. The rule also prohibits "the reading of newspapers" during a hearing but permits audio recording for note-taking purposes "unless the judge decides otherwise."

72. *Courts of Justice Act*, RSO 1990, c. C.43, ss. 136(1) and (3).

73. See *Bench Rule in Respect of Making of Video and Audio Recordings in Courtrooms*, supra note 68, rules 4(a) and (b), and *Guidelines for Media and Public Access to the Court in Nova Scotia*, supra note 67, *Part 5: Media-Related Rules*.

74. Daniel J. Henry, "Electronic Public Access to Court—An Idea Whose Time Has Come" (1985), paper available online at http://www.adidem.org/Category:Articles.

75. Canadian Newspaper Association, "N.S. Supreme Court [sic] Allows Camera To Record Hearing To Reactivate 33-Year-Old Murder Charge," *The Press and the Courts*, vol. 15, no. 1, February 28, 1996.

76. *Guidelines for Media and Public Access to the Courts of Nova Scotia*, supra note 67, *Appendix B: Cameras in the Nova Scotia Court of Appeal*.

77. Tracey Tyler, "Truscott Case Offers Rare TV Peek into Courtroom," *Toronto Star*, January 30, 2007; Susan Goldberg, "The Public Eye," *The National* (the Canadian Bar

Association magazine), July/August 2007, 46-50; and Jim Middlemiss, "Smile, You're on CA Camera," *Canadian Lawyer*, March 2007, 11-12.

78. "Court Hears Appeal in Morgentaler's Fight Against N.B. Government," CBC News Online, January 13, 2009; "Nova Scotia Streams First Live Court Hearing," *The Lawyers Weekly*, February 6, 2009.

79. Robert Martin, *Media Law* (Concord, ON: Irwin Law, 1997), 69.

80. *R v. Cho*, 2000 BCSC 1162, at paragraphs 27, 37–40.

81. The policy is reproduced in *R v. Pilarinos and Clark*, 2001 BCSC 1332, at paragraph 4.

82. Ibid., at paragraph 227. Several BC television stations applied to the Supreme Court of Canada and were granted leave to appeal. In December 2002, however, the court declined to hear the appeal, ruling that since Clark's trial was over, the issue was moot. See *Global B.C. et al. v. Her Majesty The Queen et al.* (B.C.) SCC file 28823 (motion to quash granted December 2, 2002).

83. Louise Dickson, Rob Shaw, and Lindsey Kines, "Put Trials on TV: Attorney General," *Times-Colonist* (Victoria), February 11, 2010; Robert Matas, "B.C. Ponders Letting Cameras in Court," *Globe and Mail*, March 18, 2010.

84. S.L. Alexander, *Covering the Courts: A Handbook for Journalists* (Lanham, MD: University Press of America, 1999), 19–22.

85. These initiatives are examined in *Supreme Court of British Columbia Policy on Television in the Courtroom*, adopted March 9, 2001, available online at http://www.llbc.leg.bc.ca/public/pubdocs/bcdocs/358159/courtroom.pdf.

86. See, for example, Ronald L. Goldfarb, *TV or Not TV: Television, Justice and the Courts* (New York: New York University Press, 1998). One scholarly journal devoted an entire issue to the fallout from the O.J. Simpson trial: "Covering the Courts" (Winter 1998), vol. 12, no. 1 *Media Studies Journal*.

87. Cristin Schmitz, "Judicial Council Divided Over TV Cameras in Court," *The Lawyers Weekly*, October 5, 2001.

88. Cristin Schmitz, "Ontario's Chief Justice Rejects Televising Trial Proceedings," *The Lawyers Weekly*, March 7, 2003. For an overview of the arguments for and against televising court proceedings, see Dean Jobb, "Cameras: Coming to a Courtroom Near You," *The Lawyers Weekly*, September 19, 2008.

89. *Courts of Justice Act*, RSO 1990, c. C.43, s. 136(2)(a).

90. Robert Matas, "Air-India Court Sketches Restricted," *Globe and Mail*, November 7, 2003.

91. One Quebec judge has proposed that the media should be permitted to broadcast audio recordings of the testimony of some witnesses. See *Société Radio-Canada c. Québec (Procureur Général)*, supra note 66.

92. *Guidelines for Media and Public Access to the Courts of Nova Scotia*, supra note 67.

93. *Courts of Justice Act*, RSO 1990, c. C.43, s. 136(2)(b).

94. *Bench Rule in Respect of Making of Video and Audio Recordings in Courtrooms*, supra note 68, rules 3(b) and (c).

95. *Court Policies/Practices Affecting Media Coverage*, Manitoba Courts, available online at http://www.manitobacourts.mb.ca/media.html.

96. *Accreditation Process for Journalists Re: Supreme Court Policy on Recording Devices*, British Columbia Supreme Court, July 12, 2010. Available online at http://www .courts.gov.bc.ca.

97. Cited in *Southam Publishing Company v. Mack* (unreported), [1959-60] 2 CLQ 119 (Alta. SC). I am grateful to Toronto media lawyer and author Stuart Robertson for bringing this reference to my attention.

98. See, for example, British Columbia's *Adoption Act*, RSBC 1996, c. 5, s. 43, and New Brunswick's *Family Services Act*, SNB 1980, c. F-2.2, s. 91(1).

99. For example, *Alberta Rules of Court*, AR 390/68, rule 617.

100. See *Guidelines for Media and Public Access to the Courts of Nova Scotia*, supra note 67.

101. See *Court of Queen's Bench of Alberta Civil Practice Note No. 1, Case Management*, rule 36.

102. See, for example, *Guidelines for Media and Public Access to the Courts of Nova Scotia*, supra note 67.

103. *Criminal Law Practice Direction (Consolidated)*, British Columbia Supreme Court, November 2, 1998, available online at http://www.courts.gov.bc.ca/supreme_court/ practice_and_procedure/criminal_practice_directions.aspx. Click on the link "Con-solidated Criminal Practice Direction."

104. See Dean Jobb, "Access to Information: Law and Reality Miles Apart," *The Lawyers Weekly*, March 6, 2009; Tracey Tyler, "Journalists Win Access to Files," *Toronto Star*, April 2, 2009; Jobb, "Rolling Back Secrecy on Court Files," ibid., April 9, 2009; Lindsay Kines, Rob Shaw, and Louise Dickson, "Rules Cloak Some of B.C.'s Most Serious Criminal Cases," *Times-Colonist* (Victoria), February 5, 2010; Shaw, Dickson, and Kines, "B.C. Attorney General Mike de Jong Promises Changes to Courts Access After Investigation," ibid., February 11, 2010.

105. Ownership and the return of exhibits are discussed in *Halifax Herald Ltd. v. Nova Scotia (Attorney General)* (1992), 7 Admin. LR (2d) 46 (NSTD).

106. *Vickery v. Nova Scotia Supreme Court (Prothonotary)*, [1991] 1 SCR 671.

107. *R v. Canadian Broadcasting Corporation*, 2010 ONCA 726. For discussion of the shortcomings of the *Vickery* precedent, see David Crerar and Majda Dabaghi, "Media Access to Court Exhibits," available online at http://www.j-source.ca/english_new/ detail.php?id=229. For more information on Ontario's policy on accessing court exhibits, see "Attorney General's Ministry Blocks Access to Exhibits," *The Lawyers Weekly*, December 10, 2004, 5, 26, and Shannon Kari, " 'Gut Feelings' Often Trump Open Courts: Ontario Arguably Most Closed Court System in Country," *Law Times*, June 30, 2008.

108. *R v. Warren*, [1995] NWTJ no. 9 (QL) (SC); *R v. Thornton [Canadian Broadcasting Corp. v. Nova Scotia (Supreme Court, Prothonotary)]*, [1999] NSJ no. 317 (QL) (SC).

109. *R v. Canadian Broadcasting Corporation*, 2008 CanLII 28062 (Ont. SC).

110. *Global BC, a Division of Canwest Media Inc. v. British Columbia*, 2010 BCCA 169.

111. *R v. Dunlop*, ruling of the Manitoba Court of Queen's Bench, May 2, 2001, available online at http://www.adidem.org/case/dunlop.html.

112. *R v. Van Seters* (1996), 31 OR (3d) 19 (Gen. Div.).

113. *R v. Sharpe*, [1999] BCJ no. 2581 (QL) (CA).

114. *Calgary Sun, a Division of Toronto Sun Publishing Corp. v. Alberta*, [1996] AJ no. 536 (QL) (QB).

115. "Judge Denies Bid To View Virk Autopsy Photos," *Chronicle-Herald* (Halifax), May 5, 1999.

116. *R v. Bernardo*, [1995] OJ no. 1472 (QL) (Gen. Div.).

117. Betty Ann Adam, "Playing Tapes of Dagenais Chase Would Re-victimize Families: Judge," *Star-Phoenix* (Saskatoon), March 17, 2009.

118. See, for example, Prince Edward Island Supreme Court *Practice Note 23: Transcripts and Tapes of Evidence*, which directs that taped transcripts "shall not, either in whole or in part, be used for broadcast, audio reproduction or re-taping."

119. Prince Edward Island's Supreme Court, for example, has a practice of making rulings public 24 hours after lawyers and their clients have been notified of the outcome. See *Practice Note 25: Release of Judgments*, available online at http://www.gov.pe.ca/courts/supreme/notes/note25.pdf.

120. *Open Courts, Electronic Access to Court Records, and Privacy*, discussion paper prepared on behalf of the Judges Technology Advisory Committee for the Canadian Judicial Council, May 2003, available online at http://www.cjc-ccm.gc.ca.

121. Ibid., at 22.

122. Jennifer Lee, "Dirty Laundry, Online for All To See," *New York Times*, September 5, 2002.

123. Kirk Makin, "Online Tribunal Evidence Leaves Citizens' Data Open to Abuse," *Globe and Mail*, August 20, 2008.

124. *Open Courts, Electronic Access to Court Records, and Privacy*, supra note 120, at 2–3.

125. Judges Technology Advisory Committee, "Model Policy for Access to Court Records in Canada" (Canadian Judicial Council), September 2005, available online at http://www.cjc-ccm.gc.ca.

126. "The Judges Are Building an Internet Roadblock," *Globe and Mail*, October 8, 2005.

127. See "Policy for Access to Supreme Court of Canada Court Records," February 9, 2009, available online at http://www.scc-csc.gc.ca/case-dossier/rec-doc/pol-eng.asp.

128. Dean Jobb, "Courts Struggle To Balance Privacy and Openness in Giving Access to Court Files over the Internet," *The Lawyers Weekly*, July 18, 2008. Available online at http://www.lawyersweekly.ca/index.php?section=article&articleid=726.

129. *Courts of Justice Act*, RSO 1990, c. C.43, s. 137(2); *Court of Queen's Bench Act*, CCSM c. C280, s. 77(1); *Supreme Court Act*, RSPEI 1988, c. S-10, s. 58(2).

130. *Federal Court Rules*, 1998, SOR/98-106, rules 151(1) and (2).

131. *Sierra Club of Canada v. Canada (Minister of Finance)*, [2002] 2 SCR 522, at paragraphs 53–57.

132. *Potash Corp. of Saskatchewan v. Barton*, [2002] SJ no. 484 (QL) (QB). See also John Jaffey, "Nine Years Later, Saskatchewan Court Vacates Sealing Order," *The Lawyers Weekly*, October 11, 2002.

133. Cristin Schmitz, "Superior Court Releases Judgment, Then Declares It Sealed," *The Lawyers Weekly*, May 9, 2003.

134. *Toronto Star Newspapers Ltd. v. Ontario*, [2003] OJ no. 4006; aff'd. by the Supreme Court, *R v. Toronto Star Newspapers Ltd., et al.*, 2005 SCC 41. See also Cristin

Schmitz, "Appeal Court Lays Down Rules on Sealing of Search Warrants," *The Lawyers Weekly*, October 31, 2003.

135. *R v. Eurocopter Canada Ltd.*, 2003 CanLII 32308 (Ont. SC). See also Shannon Kari, "Openness of Courts Cited as Eurocopter Documents Unsealed," *The Lawyers Weekly*, November 23, 2003, 24.

136. *R v. Ottawa Citizen Group Inc.*, 2005 CanLII 18835 (Ont. CA).

137. Don Butler, "Judge's Decision to Lift Publication Ban Hailed as Important Victory in Fight for Open Justice," *Ottawa Citizen*, October 12, 2007.

138. Ben Gelinas, "Journal Denied Access to Twitchell Search Warrants," *Edmonton Journal*, September 18, 2009.

139. See Fred Kozak and Matthew Woodley, "Right of Access to Search Warrants Restricted by Administrative Impediments," *The Lawyers Weekly*, May 12, 2006, 17, and Karen Calland, Lindsay Kines, and Kim Westad, "Ten Courthouses, No Consistent Policy," *Times-Colonist* (Victoria), February 4, 2010.

140. *Goodman v. Rossi* (1995), 24 OR (3d) 359 (CA); *Orfus Reality v. D.G. Jewellery of Canada Ltd.* (1995), 24 OR (3d) 1995 (CA).

141. *Kyuquot Logging Ltd. v. British Columbia Forest Products Ltd.* (1986), 30 DLR (4th) 65 (BCCA).

142. *Lac d'Amiante du Québec Ltée v. 2858-0702 Québec Inc.*, 2001 SCC 51.

143. The media's right to publish the contents of discovery transcripts filed with the courts was confirmed in *Moore v. Bertuzzi*, 2007 CanLII 57934 (Ont. SC).

144. *Human Rights Act*, RSNS 1989, c. 214, s. 34(1).

145. *Human Rights Code*, CCSM c. H175, s. 39(3).

146. *Canadian Human Rights Act*, RSC 1985, c. H-6, s. 52.

147. See s. 41 of British Columbia's *Adoption Act*, RSBC 1996, c. 5, and Alberta's *Adult Adoption Act*, RSA 2000, c. A-1, s. 8, which give judges the power to hold private hearings. In Prince Edward Island, s. 32 of the *Adoption Act*, c. A-4.1, states that adoption hearings and files are private unless a judge is satisfied that providing access would not be contrary to the best interests of the child.

148. See, for example, *Civil Code of Quebec*, SQ 1991, c. 64, s. 582, and Saskatchewan's *Adoption Act*, 1998, SS 1998, c. A-5.2, s. 20(1).

149. *Fatalities Inquiries Act*, RSA 2000, c. F-9, ss. 41 and 42; *Fatality Investigations Act*, SNS 2001, c. 31, s. 32.

150. *Fatalities Inquiries Act*, CCSM c. F5-2, s. 31.

151. *Canadian Broadcasting Corp. v. Manitoba (Attorney General) et al.*, 2008 MBCA 94.

152. *Coroners Act*, RSNB 1973, c. C-23, s. 21.

153. *Coroners Act*, SPEI, c. C-25, s. 11.

154. *Coroners Act*, RSO 1990, c. C.37, s. 32; *Coroners Act*, RSBC 1996, c. 72, s. 28.

155. *Coroners Act*, RSNWT 1988, c. C-20, s. 36.

156. *National Defence Act*, RSC 1985, c. N-5, ss. 180(1), 180(2), and 236(2).

157. *Extradition Act*, SC 1999, c. 18, s. 27.

158. *Immigration and Refugee Protection Act*, SC 2001, c. 27, s. 166.

159. *Judges Act*, RSC 1985, c. J-1, s. 63(6).

160. Richard Blackwell, "Judges Complain of Poisoned Atmosphere: Unsealed Documents Reveal Messy Feud in Ontario Courthouse Just Outside Toronto," *Globe and Mail*, February 11, 2006.

161. *Courts of Justice Act*, RSO 1990, c. C.43, ss. 51.6(7) and (8).

162. *Provincial Court Act*, RSNS 1989, c. 238, s. 17J.

163. *Provincial Court Act*, RSBC 1996, c. 379, s. 27(2).

164. *Judicature Act*, RSA 2000, c. J-2, ss. 36(1) and 37(4).

165. *Corrections and Conditional Release Act*, SC 1992, c. 20, ss. 140(4) and (5).

166. Ibid., ss. 144(1) and (2).

167. Ontario *Rules of Practice*, SOR/92-270; *New Brunswick Rules of Practice*, SOR/93-262; *Prince Edward Island Supreme Court Rules*, rule 79.28(2).

168. *Statutory Powers Procedure Act*, RSO 1980, c. 484, s. 9(1).

169. *Re Ottawa Police Force v. Lalande* (1986), 57 OR (2d) 509 (Dist. Ct.).

170. *Canadian Broadcasting Corp. v. Summerside (City)* (1999), 170 DLR (4th) 731.

171. In 2009 the Law Society of New Brunswick became the last to open its discipline hearings. See Donalee Moulton, "NB Law Society Last To Have Public Disciplinary Hearings," *The Lawyers Weekly*, December 11, 2009, 1, 8.

172. *Legal Profession Act*, CCSM c. L107, ss. 71(9) and 78(1).

173. *Regulated Health Professions Act*, 1991, SO 1991, c. 18, ss. 45(1), (2), and (3).

174. See, for example, British Columbia's *Inquiry Act*, RSBC 1996, c. 224, and Saskatchewan's *Public Inquiries Act*, RSS 1978, c. P-38.

175. *Public Inquiries Act*, RSO 1990, c. P.41, s. 4.

176. Henry, supra note 74.

PART FOUR
Doing the Right Thing

CHAPTER 12

Ethics and Professional Responsibility

Hollywood has hailed journalists as heroes—think of Bob Woodward and Carl Bernstein, whose dogged efforts unravelled the Watergate scandal, as depicted in the book and movie *All the President's Men*. But reporters are just as likely to be portrayed as shady characters, people who are willing to bend the rules—even break a few laws, if necessary—to get the story. So it may come as a surprise to learn that an American study released in 2004 found journalists to be more ethical than most people think. A standardized test of moral development was administered to a random sample of 249 print and broadcast journalists in the United States. The journalists scored higher than nurses, university students, business professionals, and the average adult. Only philosophers, physicians, and medical students have rated higher in terms of their moral and ethical reasoning. "Thinking like a journalist," the study concluded, "involves moral reflection, done at a level that in most instances equals or exceeds members of other learned professions."[1]

Journalists make tough calls every day: If a politician denigrates his opponent in an off-the-record conversation, should a journalist report his words or let them pass? When is it proper for a journalist to mislead a source or use a hidden camera? Do graphic images and profanity have a place on the evening newscast? Can a journalist join the parent–teacher association at her child's school, or a political party for that matter? Most news organizations have developed an in-house code of ethics to deal with these and other dilemmas.[2] Press councils have been established in all provinces except Saskatchewan to review complaints about media coverage, and these serve as forums to review and sometimes criticize the methods that journalists use to gather the news. At times, the line between law and ethics becomes blurred. A court-ordered publication ban may prohibit the media from identifying the victim of a crime, but what should the media do when no ban is imposed? The decision is no longer a legal one—it is now an ethical issue, and the question becomes whether disclosing the victim's name is the fair and proper thing to do. And the libel defence of responsible communication on matters of public interest, created in 2009 and discussed in Chapter

4, means Canada's courts will be putting journalists' conduct and methods under the microscope in the years to come. Adhering to high ethical standards is not only the right thing to do—professionalism in reporting and presenting the news could be the difference between winning and losing a libel action.

This chapter examines the dilemmas and restrictions—some of them legal, most of them ethical—that journalists routinely face as they do their jobs.

Dealing with Sources

Using Anonymous Sources

When to quote an unnamed source is perhaps the most common ethical dilemma to face a journalist. A politician's press aide has a juicy tidbit to share about an opposition critic. A former member of a bike gang offers to reveal the inner workings of the gang's narcotics operations. These sources come from different worlds but they have one thing in common—both will provide the information to a journalist only if their names are not used.

The argument for identifying sources in such situations is strong. The media deal with facts, and the source of those facts may be as important as the facts themselves. The press aide's leak may be less important than his attempt to use the media to discredit a rival. The former gang member's inside knowledge boosts the credibility of his information, as does putting a name and a face to his allegations. And sources can abuse their anonymity: they can manipulate the media and spread false information, using the journalist's ethical duty to protect them from retribution and accountability. Unnamed officials leaked damaging allegations to the press about Maher Arar, the Canadian engineer jailed and tortured in Syria in 2003, as part of a campaign to smear him as a terrorist. An inquiry exonerated Arar, condemned the police and intelligence officials responsible for the leaks, and exposed the dangers of giving unnamed sources a platform to promote their agendas or distort the news.[3]

The Canadian Association of Journalists (CAJ) has developed ethical guidelines for investigative reporting that advise journalists to use named sources whenever possible. "We should strive to fully identify the sources in our stories—for credibility and accountability," the guidelines state. "When sources are secret, the reader or audience has less information on which to judge the reliability of the source's comments. Also, anonymity might encourage the source to make irresponsible statements."[4] *The Canadian Press Stylebook* warns that overuse of anonymous sources tends to weaken and undermine news reports. "The public interest is best served when someone with facts or opinions to make public is identified by the press by name and qualifications," it opines. "Readers need to see named sources to help them decide on the credibility and importance of the information."[5] And the Radio-Television News Directors Association of Canada (RTNDA), in its code of ethics for the broadcast media, urges journalists to "make every effort to attribute news on the record. Confidential sources should be used only when it is clearly in the public interest to gather or convey important information or when a person providing information might be harmed."[6] An American reporting textbook puts the case bluntly: "the public has a right to know where we're getting the stuff we put into the papers and on the air."[7]

Yet unnamed sources still have a role to play in uncovering and bolstering news stories. In 2005 Edward Greenspon, then editor-in-chief of the *Globe and Mail*, described them as "integral to good journalism."[8] The CAJ guidelines describe unnamed sources as "a vital tool in the free flow of information" and acknowledge that there may be "clear and pressing reasons" to withhold the identity of a source. The person's job or safety could be at stake if he is identified as the source of the information. It may be impossible to find someone willing to be quoted by name. Or, the source's identity and motives may be of little consequence. If a tip about government waste or corruption comes from a low-level bureaucrat, for example, the information is more important than the identity of its source. For some stories, unnamed sources are not quoted but provide information that points journalists in the right direction. To uncover the Watergate scandal—a web of political espionage and a high-level coverup that forced Richard Nixon to resign as president in 1974—*Washington Post* reporters Woodward and Bernstein followed leads offered by an insider dubbed "Deep Throat." The identity of their key source remained a secret for three decades, until former FBI assistant director W. Mark Felt came forward in 2005 to acknowledge his role in assisting the *Post*'s investigation.[9]

Most major news organizations have developed policies that govern when and how unnamed sources should be used. The *Globe and Mail*'s code of conduct calls on writers to minimize the use of unnamed sources and notes that "quotes with names attached carry more weight."[10] The *New York Times* requires its reporters to consider two questions before using an anonymous source: How much direct knowledge does the source possess, and what motives might the person have to mislead or exaggerate, or to hide important information?[11] *The Canadian Press Stylebook* urges journalists to seek out documentation and at least one other source—even a second unnamed one—to confirm information obtained from an unnamed source. It offers additional guidelines. Efforts must be made to seek out the other side of the story if someone is being criticized or the comments reflect only one side of a controversy. The information must be in the public interest and it must be clear that the source is not trying to manipulate the news.[12] Supervisors must be consulted before a story based on unnamed sources can be distributed on the Canadian Press news service. Some newsrooms have instituted similar policies, as has the CAJ. Its guidelines emphasize that such policies ensure "editorial control, verification, and honesty."

When unnamed sources are used, the public must be able to judge the source's credibility and whether anonymity was necessary. "We will explain the need for anonymity to our readers and audiences," the CAJ guidelines declare, adding that "confidential sources should be identified as accurately as possible by affiliation or status." The terms "informed sources" and "a source close to the investigation" are meaningless; it is better to provide specific descriptions such as "a senior police investigator" or "a civil servant who has worked on the file." Descriptions must not be misleading. Information from a single unnamed source must not be reported as "sources say." A senior police investigator must be a high-ranking member of the force, not a junior officer or a civilian employee of the police.

Despite guidelines such as these—and the pitfalls of using unnamed sources—journalists continue to pepper news stories and columns with the views of unidentified and unaccountable insiders. The trend is most pronounced in political reporting: a 2007 study of more than 180 articles on federal politics published in the *Globe and Mail* found that journalists relied heavily on unnamed sources, at times basing front-page stories almost entirely on anonymous comments. The study's author, journalism professor Denise Rudnicki, said the findings suggest journalists "rarely say no to a source's request for anonymity" and "may even too quickly offer it up in exchange for information, no matter how bland." More than half the stories examined relied on unnamed sources "to provide background colour on the game and strategy of politics"—the mood in closed-door meetings or attacks on an opponent's character or motives—rather than important information about events and policies. Such reporting allows politicians, party insiders, and bureaucrats "to smuggle information of questionable value into the media," she concluded, and "undermines meaningful public discourse by inviting readers to judge how well the game of politics is played, and not the merits of public policy."[13] Media critic Robert Fulford has suggested that journalists sometimes use unnamed sources to make their stories seem more important than they are. "A fact is just a fact," he noted, "but a fact delivered by a nameless 'official' smells of intrigue."[14] The message is clear: journalists should resist any temptation to misuse—or overuse—unnamed sources.

A final note on using unnamed sources: never use information obtained directly from sources who will not identify themselves. Reporters must know who is providing the information they use and why they are providing it. Anonymous tips and documents leaked in plain brown envelopes must be verified with credible, known sources before the information is published or broadcast.

Handling "Off-the-Record" Stipulations and Other Restrictions on Interviews

A source may agree to provide information on the condition that her name not be used. Another may be adamant that his tip is "off the record." A third may insist that he is speaking on "background" and the information cannot be attributed to anyone. Sources ask journalists to make these kinds of deals on a daily basis. But terms like "background" and "off the record" do not have precise definitions. A politician who is adept at dealing with the media may understand when she is being quoted; a father who is still in shock after learning that his child has died in a car accident may not. Not even journalists agree on what these terms mean. Can background information be used to pursue the information from other sources? Does "off the record" mean that the person can be quoted verbatim but the information must be attributed to an unnamed official? There are no clear-cut answers, so it is essential that the reporter and the source agree on how quotations and information can be used. "Be sure everyone is operating under the same meanings," advises *The Canadian Press Stylebook*.[15]

The CAJ's guidelines for investigative reporting offer a starting point when negotiating with sources. They define three levels of confidentiality:

Not for attribution We may quote statements directly but the source may not be named, although a general description of his or her position may be given ("a government official," or "a party insider"). In TV and radio, the identity may be shielded by changing the voice or appearance.

On background We may use the thrust of statements and generally describe the source, but we may not use direct quotes.

Off the record We may not report the information, which can be used solely to help our own understanding or perspective. There is not much point in knowing something if it can't be reported, so this undertaking should be used sparingly, if at all.

Although these definitions reflect the consensus of veteran Canadian investigative journalists, there are other interpretations. Some journalists use the terms "off the record" and "not for attribution" interchangeably, and publish quotations obtained off the record without naming the source. In the United States, political reporters and their sources apply another term, "deep background," to information that can be published or broadcast but must not be attributed to anyone, even an unnamed government official.[16] Regardless of the term used or the agreement made, journalists must ensure they are on the same page as their sources.

At times, it may not be clear whether certain comments have been made on or off the record. A source may indicate in the midst of an interview that she wants to say something off the record or not for attribution. If the condition is accepted, a journalist must ensure that there is no confusion over when the on-the-record or for-attribution portion of the interview resumes. Once the information has been provided, ask the source to confirm that the interview is back on the record or that the source can again be quoted by name. Confusion can also arise if a source provides information without conditions but later claims that the information was provided off the record. In handling such cases, a journalist must take into account whether the person made a genuine mistake or is simply trying to manipulate the media. Someone who has never spoken to a journalist before deserves more sympathetic treatment than a veteran politician or press aide who has dealt with journalists for years.

The communications director of former prime minister Jean Chrétien garnered little sympathy in 2002 when she described US President George Bush as "a moron"—a remark promptly reported by Robert Fife, a former *National Post* reporter. Françoise Ducros made the comment while speaking to reporters after the close of an official press briefing. The incident led to soul-searching within the media, with some journalists criticizing Fife for eavesdropping on what was essentially a private conversation between Ducros and other reporters. But the former dean of journalism at the University of Western Ontario, Peter Desbarats, considered the comment fair game. "In terms of media ethics the Ducros affair isn't even borderline," he wrote in the *Globe and Mail*. "This was the most powerful spin doctor in the country, on the job in an official setting, making injudicious comments about the most powerful head of government in the world [with]in the hearing of at least one journalist."[17]

Keeping Promises

Journalists must proceed with caution when a source asks for protection or demands that certain conditions be met before granting an interview. A promise is a verbal contract that the journalist and the journalist's employer are legally bound to honour. "A promise by your reporter," media lawyer Stuart Robertson cautions newsroom managers, "is a promise by your news organization."[18] If a journalist agrees that an interview is off the record and then decides to identify the source in the story anyway,

Dealing with Young Persons

Journalists must be cautious when interviewing or filming children and teenagers. A minor—anyone under the age of majority—is too young to make a legally binding contract, and can do so only with the permission of a parent or legal guardian. "This creates an especially tricky problem for the media who come into contact with kids in the course of researching and presenting news stories," notes media lawyer Stuart Robertson.

If a child agrees to be interviewed, for instance, the law does not recognize this as a valid agreement. Should the child's parent object to the interview being used, the journalist would have no legal right to print or broadcast it. The same problem would arise if a 16-year-old provided documents or photographs to be used in a story—the law would not recognize the teen's consent to their use; if the youth's parents objected to the material being made public and sued for invasion of privacy, the journalist could not use the teenager's consent as a defence.

As noted in Chapter 5, permission should be obtained before photographing or filming a young person, and the same is true of interviews. Often consent is implied, as when a parent or guardian invites a journalist to speak to their child or is present during the interview. It would be prudent, though, to get the consent in writing or as an audio or video recording. "Working through the parents of the child," Robertson advises, "is usually one sure way of dealing with a party who can at least be held to a contract." Teachers and school officials who are used to dealing with media requests for interviews or images of young people may have signed releases from parents and guardians on file, to speed up the process.

The legal risk for a journalist depends on the age of the child and the nature of the story being reported. The older the teenager, the less likely this will be a problem. The parents of a first-year university student, for instance, are unlikely to object to their child being interviewed about the impact of high tuition fees. If the student revealed confidential or embarrassing information about the family's financial woes, however, the parents would likely view the matter differently and could seek damages for violation of their privacy. Likewise, using young persons as sources for a story on pregnancy or drug use among teens would be fraught with far more risk than interviews with kids taking part in a soccer game or chess tournament.

Dealing with young persons raises ethical issues as well as legal ones. No reporter or camera operator wants to be accused of taking advantage of a child or teenager for the sake of a story. Taking the time to obtain the consent of a parent or guardian before dealing with a minor should prevent any misunderstandings or legal headaches after an interview or image is published.

(Source: Stuart M. Robertson, *The Law & Kids!* (Dunedin, ON: Hallion Press, 1993), 28–30.)

the promise has been broken. This would be a serious violation of ethical standards, and, at best, the journalist's credibility and reputation for trustworthiness would suffer. At worst, a court could hold the journalist and news organization legally responsible for any injury that the source suffered as a result of the verbal contract being breached. If a source lost her job as a result of being identified, for example, the journalist and news organization could be sued and ordered to pay damages as compensation.

Legal actions over agreements between writers and sources are rare, but there is one high-profile example. Brian Mulroney sued author Peter Newman in 2005 over publication of Newman's book *The Secret Mulroney Tapes: Unguarded Confessions of a Prime Minister*. The tapes were no secret to Mulroney—he knew Newman was researching a biography when they spoke on the phone dozens of times during his time in office, from 1984 to 1993. But his lawsuit claimed there was a written agreement that Newman would use the material to produce a "scholarly and serious" biography, not a "scandalous" book based on the raw tapes, in which Mulroney made disparaging comments about former political colleagues and opponents. Mulroney sued Newman for "breach of confidence"—the two had been friends for decades—and sought an injunction preventing Newman from publishing or broadcasting the tapes, which were also the basis for a CBC documentary. He also wanted Newman's profits from using the tapes to be turned over to charity and the tapes deposited in the national archives. The suit was settled out of court within a year, so the incident did not set a legal precedent. The settlement terms were not disclosed but Newman was able to continue to sell the book.[19]

The courts have also intervened to prevent information from being published or broadcast if conditions have been placed on its use. The CBC's investigative program *the fifth estate* has been barred from broadcasting interviews with a convicted murderer and with accountants who investigated corruption in Romania. The CBC had agreed to allow the murderer to see its story, which included the interview, before it aired.[20] The accountants were promised that their information would not be used without their consent.[21] The courts ruled in both cases that the promises were binding on the CBC. Journalists should never give a source the right to veto or make changes to a story, except in instances when an editor or producer has approved this approach and the news organization is prepared to honour the request. The CBC's guidelines impose a blanket prohibition, declaring that "participants in programs will not be granted the right to veto any portion of a program."[22]

A promise of confidentiality to a source can also come back to haunt a news organization. While the courts may recognize a journalist's right to protect a source (as discussed under the heading "Protecting Sources" in Chapter 5), a news organization may be obliged to fight a costly—and ultimately unsuccessful—battle to honour such a pledge. Journalists should never make a promise of confidentiality without verifying, in advance, how far their employer is willing to go to protect a source. The CAJ's guidelines for investigative reporting offer this advice:

> We should not make any commitments to anonymous sources without consultation with senior management. Journalists should be wary about entering into arrangements that they cannot fulfill. Sometimes sources request additional protection. For example, they may ask for legal assistance or protection if they are revealed or endangered. If you and your employer agree this is reasonable, spell out the terms.

Paying for Information

In rare instances, a source will request money or expenses in exchange for sharing information with a journalist or agreeing to be interviewed. The source could be the key figure in a major political scandal or a janitor who's trying to make a few bucks by flogging a confidential report discovered while emptying the trash. Whatever the circumstances, paying for information raises serious ethical concerns for journalists. The CBC's ethical guidelines state that the broadcaster, as a rule, does not pay its sources for news, adding: "The journalist's task is to gather information freely given."[23] Author and *Globe and Mail* columnist Ian Brown has pointed out three pitfalls of paying sources to tell their story: sources "might make stuff up to justify the payment"; journalists may not subject sources to the same rigorous questioning as other interview subjects; and "payment always makes a media outlet look shifty."[24]

"Chequebook journalism," as this practice is known, is not common in Canada. The leading Canadian textbook on journalism ethics cites only a half-dozen instances. They include a purported Mafia enforcer who was paid $3,700 to provide insights into organized crime and the *Toronto Sun*'s payment of $10,000 in a bidding war for the wedding photos of Paul Bernardo and Karla Homolka after the couple was charged with murdering two Ontario teenagers.[25] Such deals should not be entered into without careful consideration. Will the public view the payment as dishonest or unethical? Will money induce the source to lie or tailor the information to fit the story that the media are pursuing? The damage is compounded if the source is a criminal and the media are seen as helping someone profit from crime.

When payment is requested, alternative sources of information should be explored and efforts should be made to persuade the source to provide information free of charge. Nick Russell, an expert in media ethics, acknowledges that there may be times when paying for information is the only way to get the story. In such cases, "journalists have to balance the need for the story against the possible loss of public trust."[26] CBC guidelines provide a framework for all journalists to follow. They require a senior producer to approve any payment to a source and they stipulate that the payment must be revealed when the story is broadcast, so members of the audience can judge whether the payment has influenced the news. The CBC's guidelines forbid payments of fees or expenses to members of Parliament and other politicians, as such payments could place the politician in a conflict of interest or be seen as a bribe.[27]

Telling the Truth

Misleading Sources

Journalists are not spies. They gather their information openly, and their notebooks, audio recorders, or cameras are held in plain view of the people being quoted or filmed. Bill Kovach and Tom Rosenstiel, two veteran American journalists who are leading a campaign for greater transparency in media reports, insist that honesty is the best policy. "Journalists," they write, "should not lie to or mislead their sources in the process of trying to tell the truth to their audiences."[28] If journalists fail to tell the truth up front, the thinking goes, such tactics can create doubts about their commitment to telling the truth in their stories. Yet journalists may be tempted to mislead sources. Writers for the *National Post* once contacted the agents for five Hollywood stars and posed as film school students trying to flog a script. The paper published transcripts of the calls as a feature, even though none of the agents realized they were speaking to a journalist or that their words would appear in print.[29]

Journalists should identify themselves and their news organization each time they speak to a source. The benefits of this practice are clear—it prevents misunderstandings, promotes trust, and confirms that the reporter is straightforward and honest. Journalists should not strike up a conversation with someone by pretending to be a bystander or an interested citizen. Never assume that, if you identify yourself as a reporter, people will refuse to speak to you. Most people are willing to help, either by providing information or by referring the journalist to other sources.

There is an exception: if a secretary or receptionist is screening a source's calls, it is not unethical to ask to speak to the source without revealing you are a journalist. If a secretary asks who is calling, however, you should be honest and identify yourself. And, of course, once the call is put through, you should identify yourself to the source you hope to quote.

Misleading the Public

Re-enactments and Dramatizations

Television news reports—particularly investigative pieces and feature stories—often re-create the sound and images of key events. A car crash may be staged or actors may be hired to re-create a meeting or a crime. Music, lighting, slow-motion, and other special effects may be used to add drama to the scene. Whatever production methods are used, it is essential that the re-creation does not distort reality. "Re-enactments, reconstructions and dramatizations can be used as effective tools in the full and accurate reporting of a significant story," the CAJ's guidelines note, "but they should reflect the event they portray as closely as possible." Dramatizations should not be mixed with real footage or sounds, the guidelines advise. The CBC's journalistic policy also warns against mixing fact and fiction and requires that "any reconstruction or simulation must coincide as closely as possible with the event that it purports to portray."[30] The CBC and CAJ guidelines state that re-creations and dramatizations must be flagged with an on-screen label or referred to in the script, to ensure that the audience is not misled. Under the *RTNDA Code of Ethics*, broadcast journalists should not present news that is "rehearsed or re-enacted without informing the audience."[31]

Doctored Photos

Computer programs make it easy for a photographer or editor to alter a digital image. Photographs are routinely lightened or darkened to improve contrast and the picture's appearance once it is published. But this technology must not be used to alter the reality captured in a photograph. A *Los Angeles Times* photographer was fired in 2003 after he combined two photos to create a more dramatic image of a US soldier standing guard over a group of Iraqi civilians. The doctored photo ran on the paper's front page before the editing was discovered. Gary Hershorn, a photo editor for the Reuters news agency, called the incident "a black mark on photojournalism."[32] The *RTNDA Code of Ethics* also cautions broadcasters to verify that amateur video and audio recordings are genuine before airing them.[33]

The Canadian Press Stylebook reminds photographers and editors that the content of a photo must not be altered. Retouching should be limited to the removal of dust spots and scratches that are not part of the image itself. Photos can be cropped, and contrast and colour balance can be altered as required, but "exaggerated use of these features to add, remove or give prominence to details in the photo is not acceptable."[34]

Going Undercover

There are times when journalists resort to clandestine methods in order to gather the news. If restaurant reviewers announced their presence when they dined out, owners and chefs would no doubt ensure that the meal would be far better than any other patron could expect. It is also common for reporters investigating complaints about poor service or shoddy goods to pose as consumers to find out whether the complaints are valid.

Some media outlets have undertaken more elaborate undercover operations. To collect evidence that health inspectors were taking bribes and kickbacks, the *Chicago Sun-Times* once opened a tavern called the Mirage, installed hidden cameras, and operated it for six months with reporters posing as the staff.[35] In 1992, two ABC News reporters posing as employees used hidden cameras to investigate allegations of unsanitary conditions at Food Lion supermarkets in the Carolinas.[36] More recently, a writer for London's *Daily Mirror* used his own name and a fake reference to secure a job as a footman at Buckingham Palace—and to expose the lax security measures in place to protect the Queen and visiting US President George Bush.[37] The Canadian media have also employed clandestine methods to uncover wrongdoing. *Toronto Star* reporters posed as telemarketers to expose a cross-border fraud scam and used hidden cameras to document filthy conditions inside an illegal slaughterhouse.[38]

Working undercover raises serious ethical issues and the possibility of legal consequences for journalists. The *Sun-Times'* Mirage stories had an immense impact and led to the firing or prosecution of many corrupt city officials, but the paper was denied a Pulitzer Prize because of concerns that its targets were the victims of entrapment.[39] Clandestine methods may also expose journalists and their employers to criminal prosecution or lawsuits. Two *Toronto Star* reporters who tried to bribe a liquor inspector while posing as bar owners were arrested after the police swooped down on their sting operation. They were detained for four hours but released without charges being laid.[40] ABC News was sued for fraud and trespass over its Food Lion stories but a jury's award of $5.5 million was wiped out on appeal.[41] And, as discussed in the privacy law section of Chapter 5, lying to get a job or to gain access to someone's home could bring a lawsuit claiming damages for invasion of privacy or the harm caused by the journalist's deceit.

The CAJ's investigative guidelines advise journalists to conduct undercover research "with a strong moral compass, with sensitivity to those being investigated and with openness to readers and audiences." Lying, clandestine methods, and using hidden cameras and microphones are justified

> only in cases where illegal or fraudulent activity is strongly suspected to have taken place, the public trust is abused or public safety is at risk. Documentary evidence of

problems may not exist and officials may fail to respond to inquiries. Sources may not exist, or refuse to speak for fear of retribution.

In short, the story must be of sufficient importance to the public interest to justify the use of subterfuge. And deception should be a last resort. Journalists must ensure "all traditional, socially acceptable methods of investigation have been exhausted before resorting to the clandestine," Nick Russell argues.[42] The CBC's *Journalistic Standards and Practices* guide states that "as a general rule, journalism should be conducted in the open"; clandestine methods should only be used after considering "whether the information to be obtained is of such significance as to warrant being made public but is unavailable by other means." Finally, a senior CBC producer must approve the use of hidden microphones or cameras.[43] Under the RTNDA's ethical code, the use of hidden recording devices is justified only when "necessary to the credibility or accuracy of a story in the public interest."[44]

Many journalists have posed as beggars or homeless persons in order to write a first-hand account of what it is like to be down and out in our society.[45] But do their methods pass the test for going undercover? It is clearly in the public interest to expose such conditions and to report what steps community agencies and the government are taking to help the poor and the homeless. But there are other ways to tell this story. Interviewing homeless persons and accompanying them from soup kitchen to shelter will capture the gritty reality of life on the streets; the experiences of a journalist who poses as a homeless person, in contrast, conveys what it is like to pretend to be homeless for a short time. There are other considerations. Is it proper for a reporter who poses as a beggar to take money from members of the public under false pretenses? Should a journalist eat free meals and take a bed in a shelter, denying these comforts to those who need them most? Journalists, editors, and producers must consider these questions and the impact of their methods before embarking on an undercover assignment.

When deception is used to gather information, the public must not be deceived. The story must include a description of the clandestine methods used and an explanation of why they were seen as necessary, so that the audience can decide whether the ends have justified the means.

Playing Loose with the Facts

Jayson Blair sullied the image of the august *New York Times* when it was revealed in 2003 that he had invented quotes and descriptions in numerous stories about the snipers who terrorized Washington, DC and the families of soldiers killed or wounded in Iraq. Stephen Glass was a prolific writer for *The New Republic*, *The Atlantic Monthly*, and other US magazines until it was discovered he was systematically fabricating people and events. Here in Canada, an award-winning medical reporter, Brad Evenson, left the *National Post* in 2004 after false information was discovered in nine of his articles. The stories contained quotes that were "either the result of other conversations, Internet exchanges or readings but they were not made by the people cited," the *Post* explained.

Taking liberties with the truth can be just as devastating to a journalist's career—and to the media's reputation—as inventing facts and people. The *New York Times* fired journalist Michael Finkel in 2001 for creating a composite character—a 15-year-old African slave—as the focus of a cover story in the newspaper's weekend magazine. In 2003, two weeks after the discovery of Jayson Blair's fabrications, the *Times* suspended Pulitzer Prize–winning writer Rick Bragg for failing to give credit to freelance writers who had contributed to his stories.

All of these cases underscore the pitfalls of blurring the line between fact and fiction. Journalists must resist any temptation to embellish, invent, or distort as they document the people and events they encounter. "Journalism's first obligation is to the truth," Bill Kovach and Tom Rosenstiel state in their book *The Elements of Journalism*. It is a credo that all journalists should adopt.

(Sources: Simon Houpt, "Plagiarism Scandal Rocks New York Times," *Globe and Mail*, May 12, 2003; Simon Houpt, "The Consequences of Truth," *Globe and Mail*, June 22, 2005; Gloria Galloway, "Writer Fabricated Names, Quotes, National Post Says," *Globe and Mail*, July 3, 2004; Matthew Rose, Douglas A. Blackmon, and Brian Steinberg, "New York Times Suspension Exposes Issue over Bylines," *Wall Street Journal*, May 27, 2003; Bill Kovach and Tom Rosenstiel, *The Elements of Journalism: What Newspeople Should Know and the Public Should Expect* (New York: Crown Publishers, 2001), chapter 2.)

To Make Public or Withhold?

Graphic Images

The Associated Press photo that ran on the front page of Halifax's *Sunday Herald* newspaper was a close-up of the wizened hand of one of the more than 200,000 victims of the December 2004 Asian tsunamis. "It is impossible to convey the breadth of destruction caused by this disaster in mere words," the paper's editor, Paul O'Connell, would later explain. "Only a photograph as striking as this one can truly bring it home." *Sunday Herald* readers thought otherwise. The paper was deluged with angry calls and letters from readers who objected to the photo as shocking and tasteless. The outcry forced O'Connell to print a front-page item the following week in which he defended his decision to run the photo and promised readers that their views had been heard.[46]

It is one of the toughest calls that an editor has to make—deciding whether a disturbing photo or video clip captures the grim reality of the news, or simply exploits the suffering of others. Editors were divided on whether to publish photos showing people jumping to their deaths from the World Trade Center towers during the 9/11 terrorist attacks on New York City; some newspapers used the images but many chose to rely on less-disturbing images to illustrate the story. When the infamous photos of Iraqi prisoners being abused and humiliated at the Abu Ghraib prison appeared in newspapers and on television programs around the world, the *Globe and Mail*'s then-editor-in-chief, Edward Greenspon, was surprised at the muted response. "I think readers understand … that these pictures form a critical part of the public record, as uncomfortable as that might be," he noted.[47] Newsrooms faced a tough judgment call in 2010 when the courts released photographs of Russell Williams, a military colonel who pleaded guilty to murder and sexual assault, modelling lingerie he stole during burglaries. The *Toronto Star* ran one of the images on its front page, arguing it was important to present evidence of Williams's "depraved double life." The *Globe and Mail* opted for a front-page close-up of Williams, with a menacing look on his face, and published a selection of the lingerie photos on its website "for readers who decide they want to see some of that evidence." Both newspapers published items explaining their decisions and the ethical issues involved.[48]

Editors should ask themselves a series of questions when deciding whether images are too graphic to use in print or on television. Do the pictures inform or merely shock? Are they newsworthy or do they demand attention simply because they are riveting or unusual? Do they help tell the story, or do they deflect attention from the point that the journalist is trying to make? Perhaps most importantly, do they capture the essence of the story in a way that words alone do not? Images of corpses and grief flashed around the world shatter the privacy of those caught up in accidents or disasters, and can compound their suffering. An American text on media ethics acknowledges this but says the test must be newsworthiness:

> The broken-hearted father whose child was just run over, a shocked eight-year-old boy watching his teenage brother gunned down by police, the would-be suicide on a bridge—all [are] pitiful scenes that communicate something of human tragedy and are therefore to be considered news.

The text adds a moral guideline for editors, photographers, and camera operators: "suffering individuals are entitled to dignity and respect, despite the fact that events may have made them part of the news."[49] The *Canadian Press Stylebook* offers similar advice, noting that "an individual's grief is personal and private" and should not be exploited to enhance the news.[50] The *Globe and Mail* requires that senior editors review any photo that depicts nudity, a dead body, people holding vulgar signs, or abused animals before such images are published.[51]

Bruce Wark, a former CBC journalist who taught ethics at the University of King's College School of Journalism in Halifax, concluded that editors are more likely to run a graphic photo from a foreign land than one that depicts a similar incident in their own communities. Journalists and their audiences "identify more readily with people like us ... people closer to home seem more human," he notes. "We worry about turning them into objects as we portray their suffering."[52] The bottom line, Nick Russell says, is that editors—as well as their readers and viewers—must be convinced that the motivation for using the image will stand up to scrutiny. Russell suggests a checklist of blunt questions that editors should ask themselves about the rationale for running a graphic or disturbing image:

- Is it to provide audience thrills?
- To boost circulation?
- To communicate some social message?
- To show off an outstanding picture?
- Or is it simply because the picture has indisputable, intrinsic news value?[53]

Television is a powerful medium and footage showing incidents of violence, grieving, and death can be far more disturbing than photos that appear in print. The CBC's production guidelines state that scenes depicting private grief, human suffering, nudity, and explicit sex should be broadcast only when they are vital to promoting understanding of the information being presented to the audience. A feature story on the proliferation of pornography, for example, calls for the use of images that would not normally be broadcast. Likewise, violent scenes must not be exploited and should be broadcast "where its depiction is an essential fact of the reality being portrayed." The guidelines add that when scenes depicting violent acts or grieving are used, they should not be aired for prolonged periods.[54]

Profanity and Graphic Descriptions

The titles of two books published in the summer of 2005 created a dilemma for some media outlets. One was *On Bullshit*; the other was *Your Call Is Important to Us: The Truth About Bullshit*. But on a few review pages and bestseller lists, the titles were changed to *On Bull----* and *Your Call Is Important to Us: The Truth About Bull----*. These examples suggest prissiness on the part of the editors who made the changes but in other cases, discretion is called for. Profanity and vulgarities may be common in books and movies, but using them in media reports disseminated to a wide audience requires careful deliberation. Is it necessary to use a quotation containing vulgar language, or can the speaker's words be paraphrased to remove the offending terms? Does the strong language add meaning, or does it detract from what is being said?

As is the case with explicit images, it is a matter of striking a balance between the news value of the words and language the audience considers acceptable. "The fact that an obscenity is spoken in public does not constitute justification for including it in a story," notes *The Globe and Mail Style Book*. "Few stories lose by the deletion of such expressions." The precise words used can be left to the reader's imagination, with a newspaper reporting instead that "a crowd shouted obscenities, or that a speech featured salty, ribald or coarse language, sexual jokes, [or] references to bodily functions."[55] *The Canadian Press Stylebook* offers similar advice, but notes that an exception should be made if a politician or other prominent person uses such language in public. Using coarse language may also be appropriate if deleting it would create an inaccurate impression of the speaker, or if it is the best way to convey the emotion or seriousness that underlies what is being said.[56] CBC policy states, as a general rule, that profanity and offensive expressions are not to be used and "shock value is not a permissible criterion" for using them. Exceptions are made if the words are essential to the story or if editing them out would undermine the information being presented. If the words are broadcast, listeners and viewers should be cautioned in advance that a program or segment contains coarse language.[57]

Reports on violent crimes or deadly accidents and disasters may call for similar discretion when deciding whether certain details should be withheld or the audience should be warned of gruesome descriptions. Media outlets faced this dilemma in 2007 when graphic testimony was heard at Robert Pickton's trial on charges of murdering six Vancouver-area women; a search of his farm had uncovered the severed heads, hands, feet, and other body parts of the victims. The *National Post's* approach was to insert a warning to readers at the beginning of stories on the trial that contained disturbing material. "We urge you to exercise discretion and keep the stories that concern you out of the hands of your children," Editor-in-Chief Douglas Kelly advised readers at the outset of the trial. As well, the paper withheld material it did not consider suitable for publication in print while posting the full reports on its website. "The rationale is that reading on the Web involves a conscious decision to read the story because of the need to first click on the headline," Kelly explained.[58] While this seems to be an odd strategy—taking material deemed too disturbing to print and offering it to a far wider audience, as well as making it easily accessible to Internet-savvy young people—it shows the difficulty of drawing a line between informing and offending.

Getting It Right in the Age of Instant News

Using Social Media as a Reporting and Publishing Tool

Canadian music icon Gordon Lightfoot reportedly was on his way to the dentist in February 2010 when he heard the news on his car radio: He had just died.

The news was greatly exaggerated, of course, but it gained enough credence and repetition through Twitter, the online social-networking tool, that the Canwest News Service distributed a story confirming Lightfoot's death at age 71. What began as a crank phone call to Lightfoot's American managers snowballed—at the speed of the Internet and via a flurry of "tweets" of less than 140 characters—into a textbook example of the perils of instant news.

It was not the first time social media played a role in giving false news a life of its own. In October 2008 Matthew Ingram, then an editor with the *Globe and Mail*, retweeted a citizen posting to a CNN website that said Apple Computer CEO Steve Jobs had suffered a heart attack. Ingram distributed the post without verifying it was true and soon Apple shareholders were the ones having heart attacks—the company's stock price temporarily plummeted until the report was refuted. And when a soldier went on a shooting rampage at the Fort Hood military base in Texas in late 2009, some news outlets relied on Twitter messages to report, erroneously, that multiple gunmen were involved.

But Twitter has emerged as a legitimate reporting tool and a real-time source of facts and images. When an airliner made an emergency landing in New York City in January 2009, a bystander's tweeted photo of the plane floating on the Hudson River reached thousands of people within minutes. Later that year, after the Iranian government shut down media coverage of post-election demonstrations, protesters used Twitter to provide a steady stream of information to the outside world. Researchers at George Washington University surveyed close to 400 American reporters and editors in 2009 and found that the majority used Twitter, Facebook, and other social media tools to gather information for their stories.

The torrent of information readily available through social media presents new challenges for journalists. Internet and social-networking tools "have the detrimental effect of potentially speeding up the spread of rumours or wrong information," warned a 2010 report on the future of the news business prepared for the Organisation for Economic Co-operation and Development. "Journalism deals in facts, not rumour and innuendo," the *Toronto Star*'s public editor, Kathy English, noted in a pair of June 2010 columns that explored the ethics of using social media to report and disseminate the news. "Does this new means of communicating information online in real time compromise standards of accuracy? Should journalists tweet rumours or should all tweets be verified?"

The answer, of course, is journalists should verify first, then report. "Authentication is essential," states a *Los Angeles Times* policy on using social media. "When transmitting information online—as in re-Tweeting material from other sources—apply the same standards and level of caution you would in more formal publication." The Associated Press issued guidelines urging its journalists to exercise caution: "Don't report things or break news that we haven't published, no matter the format, and that includes retweeting unconfirmed information not fit for AP's wires."

The Ethics Advisory Committee of the Canadian Association of Journalists, in a discussion paper on social media reporting released in mid-2010, advised journalists to carefully weigh the value of reporting information quickly against the harm it could create, even if accurate. One example of potentially harmful information is the name of an accident victim, which might be tweeted by journalists before relatives have been notified; another is the panic that could ensue if rumours of a bomb scare were communicated to occupants of an office building. Journalists, the discussion paper said, should use "extreme caution" when faced with "surprising information tweeted by third parties—especially when it reflects negatively on a person or an organization." The key questions to ask are: Who is the source? Is the person in a position to know this? Has the source provided solid information in the past?

These are questions journalists have always asked when assessing the credibility of sources and the accuracy of information. "Tight deadlines, crowd sourcing, receiving rumours that are disguised as facts ... these are all a part of traditional newsgathering. Social media has simply sped up the process significantly," Ivor Shapiro, chair of the CAJ's Ethics Advisory Committee and a Ryerson University journalism professor, has noted. "Journalism just has to figure out how to keep up without sacrificing the truth."

As for Gordon Lightfoot, the singer-songwriter took the news of his death in stride. As he joked in a radio interview that finally put the Internet rumours to rest, "I haven't had so much airplay on my music ... for weeks."

(Sources: James Adams, "Gordon Lightfoot Very Much Alive," *Globe and Mail*, February 18, 2010; Rebecca Fleming, "I Didn't Kill Gordon Lightfoot," ibid., February 25, 2010; "National Survey Finds Majority of Journalists Now Depend on Social Media for Story Research," press release available online at http://ca.cision.com/news_room/press_releases/press_releases_overview.asp; Kathy English, "Will Twitter Transform Journalism?" *Toronto Star*, June 12, 2010; English, "Is Twitter a Threat to Journalistic Credibility?" ibid., June 19, 2010; *The Evolution of News and the Internet*, a report of the Organisation for Economic Co-operation and Development's Directorate for Science, Technology and Industry, June 11, 2010, available online at http://www.oecd.org/dataoecd/30/24/45559596.pdf; "Guidelines for Re-Tweeting or Re-Posting Information Found in Social Media," draft guidelines prepared by the Ethics Advisory Committee of the Canadian Association of Journalists, May 26, 2010, available online at http://www.j-source.ca/english_new/detail.php?id=5164.)

Naming Names

Telling the truth means naming names. Journalists' sources and the people they cover should be identified by name wherever possible. The leader of a citizen's group lobbying the city to reject a new housing project loses any claim to personal privacy. The identity of the woman accused of second-degree murder should not be a secret known only to the police and the courts. The politician espousing a controversial policy or point of view should not be allowed to take anonymous potshots at the government.

But there may be legal and ethical restrictions on when journalists can identify the people involved in a story. As noted in Chapter 9, a statute or court-imposed publication ban may shield the identity of a witness or victim of crime, and the *Youth Criminal Justice Act* bans disclosure of the identities of children and teenagers when young persons are prosecuted for criminal offences. People facing criminal charges, however, have no legal right to have their names banned from publication. This practice is consistent with the concept of an open, accountable justice system; the public has a right to know who is being punished and for what crime. As well, naming names "silences the rumour mill," notes Nick Russell. "It may be better that one specific teacher, charged with assault, be embarrassed than having all male teachers in the community under suspicion."[59]

Journalists and media organizations must strive to be fair and consistent when they name names. If a community newspaper covers every impaired-driving case, no exception should be made for the elderly woman who pleads with a reporter or editor to keep her name out of the paper. The same approach should be taken if the mayor tries to squelch a story about his son being convicted of vandalism. The media should not subject some people to public scrutiny and spare others from such embarrassment. At the same time, news organizations should develop policies to determine whether minor offences such as vandalism should be covered at all, with exceptions made when a public figure is involved or the case has the potential to lead to changes in the law. To ensure consistency, if a newspaper or broadcaster reports that someone has been charged with an offence, the outcome of the case must also be reported. Police forces often release public alerts that reveal the names and photographs of convicted sex offenders who have been released after serving a prison sentence but are considered dangerous and likely to reoffend. Media outlets should have policies to determine when these alerts should be run and how they should be reported.

In some cases, the identity of the person involved in a news story may be less important than what happened and what it means. A court ruling that changes the divorce law for everyone, for example, is more important than the identity of the divorcing couple who brought the issue before the courts. The ruling and its implications could be covered without naming and singling out the people involved.

The media should take special care when dealing with allegations of sexual assault. The stigma associated with the crime is so strong that some persons, after being accused of the offence, have committed suicide. In one case, a former Nova Scotia youth worker killed himself in 1998 after a news story revealed he had confessed to sexually abusing children years earlier. The disclosure was made in court documents filed in a related civil case and the man had not been charged with an offence.[60] If the police have already charged someone, there are compelling grounds to identify the person in media reports, but discretion should be exercised when dealing with unproven allegations that may never lead to criminal charges.

Respecting Diversity

Media reports should respect minorities and Canada's multicultural society. The *Criminal Code* outlaws hate propaganda, and CRTC regulations forbid the broadcast of words and images that denigrate minority groups, but, as discussed in Chapter 5, these restrictions focus on clearly abusive and overtly racist comments. With these points in mind, journalists should refer to a person's race, sexual orientation, or ethnic background only when this information is relevant to the story. The *Globe and Mail* advises its reporters to restrict such references to stories about cultural events, biographical sketches, and police searches for fugitives and missing persons. Race, the paper says, should be referred to in stories only when it is an important factor, "as when an assault was the result of racial taunts."[61] *The Canadian Press Stylebook* advises journalists to use "fairness, sensitivity and good taste" when identifying people by age, gender, race, colour, nationality, religion, sexual orientation, or personal appearance. "Race is pertinent when it motivates an incident or when it helps to explain the emotions of those in confrontation," such as in stories on racial controversy, immigration issues, and debates over language rights. The style book offers examples of when it is appropriate to mention race and ethnicity, such as identifying a woman facing deportation as a Pole or a recipient of hate mail as being Jewish.[62]

Care should be taken as well in stories that deal with people with disabilities. "Disabilities should be mentioned only if they are germane to the story," says *The Globe and Mail Style Book*. When making reference is appropriate, the paper prefers the word "disabled" to "handicapped." There is an exception—"mentally handicapped" should be used instead of the term "mentally retarded" or the politically correct term "mentally challenged." Referring to someone as having a mental illness is appropriate; describing the person as crazy or insane is not. Older terms like "crippled" and "deaf and dumb" have outlived their usefulness, and can be replaced with phrases such as "uses a wheelchair" or "uses sign language." Specific references to a person's abilities or limitations are recommended—descriptions such as "walks with a cane" or "functions at a Grade 4 level" are inoffensive as well as informative.[63]

Media Watchdogs

Journalism is perhaps the most public and accountable of professions: in the words of Ian Hargreaves, a prominent British journalist, it "strides out into the world and demands a response." The work of journalists is presented to a wide audience, where it generates debate, condemnation, and, occasionally, praise. The facts, as reported, may be disputed; questions may be raised about the journalist's thoroughness or objectivity; a columnist's conclusions may be attacked as unfair or off-base. Complaints and criticisms such as these may surface in a letter to the editor, as a comment posted at the end of an online report, or via an angry phone call to the newsroom. Or they may lead to a formal complaint to one of three watchdogs that monitor the ethical standards of the Canadian media.

Press councils, the Canadian Broadcast Standards Council, and in-house ombudspersons investigate complaints of questionable or unethical conduct. They have no power to punish offenders but provide a mechanism to review and resolve complaints about how the news is reported and presented. They give members of the public a better understanding of the media's role and how it operates, and offer journalists guidance on where to draw the line when gathering and reporting the news. "While they don't by any means solve all problems," media ethics expert Nick Russell has noted, "they provide yet another opportunity for news consumers to hold the media's feet to the fire."

Press Councils

As noted at the beginning of this chapter, all provinces except Saskatchewan have press councils to review readers' complaints about newspaper coverage. Membership is voluntary and there are a few holdouts, notably the *National Post*. Newspaper owners created and fund the councils, in part to stave off persistent calls for government to create bodies to oversee the press—despite the obvious impact such official oversight would have on press freedom. Ontario has the largest council with 228 members—including 37 dailies—as of 2009, with a combined circulation of 4.7 million copies. British Columbia, Alberta, Manitoba, and Quebec each have a council, while newspapers in the four Atlantic provinces have banded together to form a single body.

Councils have two roles. They promote good journalistic practices: British Columbia's council, for instance, has developed a detailed code of practice and Ontario's offers advice on everything from the proper way to deal with quotations from sources to the duties of editorial writers. Second, councils convene panels of journalists and laypersons to investigate and resolve complaints filed against member papers. The Ontario council adjudicated 524 complaints between its inception in 1972 and 2007, and upheld about one out of two as justified. Exactly 100 complaints were filed in 2007, and of this number 9 were adjudicated and 6 were upheld. Opinion pieces tend to attract more complaints than news stories—editorials, columns, editorial cartoons, and letters to the editor accounted for three-quarters of all complaints lodged against Ontario papers in 2007.

Press councils have no power to punish those who are found to have treated a complainant unfairly or violated ethical standards and practices. Member papers, however, undertake to publish the findings of adjudication hearings, helping to make the press accountable to the people it serves. A press council's "very existence," Ontario council chair Robert Elgie argued in 2005, "sends a message to the press that they should have appropriate procedures in place" to resolve public concerns about coverage and practices "before they get to the complaint stage."

Canadian Broadcast Standards Council

More than 730 private sector radio and television broadcasters belong to this industry body, which investigates complaints from viewers and listeners about newscasts and entertainment programs. Established in 1990, it convenes panels of industry and public representatives to determine whether a program or segment conforms to codes of conduct developed by the

Radio-Television News Directors Association of Canada (RTNDA) and the Canadian Association of Broadcasters. The council has investigated an array of complaints: lack of fairness and
balance; sexist and biased reporting; misquoting of sources; invasion of privacy; sensational,
inaccurate, and incomplete reporting; and the use of graphic and violent images or intrusive
footage of people grieving the loss of loved ones.

There are no penalties for violating the codes of conduct, but the council's rulings are
made public and broadcasters must air a statement acknowledging any ethical lapses. A
controversial television interview with then-Liberal leader Stéphane Dion during the 2008
federal election campaign is an example of how the process works. Halifax-based CTV Atlantic
taped an interview in which Dion appeared to have difficulty understanding the opening
question; the interview was aborted three times before continuing and the network, despite
initially agreeing to edit the false starts, aired the entire segment. The interview was a severe
blow to Dion's credibility just days before voters went to the polls and re-elected a Conserva-
tive minority government. Almost 40 complaints were lodged with the council, including
allegations that CTV had shown political bias or was trying to embarrass, demean, and belittle
Dion; one complainant called it "a low-brow attack on a person who was struggling to understand a poorly phrased question in (his) second language." An adjudicative panel reviewed
the segment and the applicable sections of the broadcast ethics codes and sought an explanation from the broadcaster. It eventually ruled that CTV Atlantic had violated the RTNDA
code, which requires journalists to treat interview subjects and sources with courtesy and
decency. The station was required to announce the findings twice during its prime-time
programming.

A searchable online database of the council's decisions—offering insights into how broadcast codes of ethics are interpreted—is available at http://www.cbsc.ca/english/index.php.

Ombudspersons

Two major Canadian media organizations—the CBC and *Toronto Star*—have in-house ombudspersons to field and investigate complaints about coverage.

As a public broadcaster, the CBC is not a member of the Broadcast Standards Council.
Instead, it has created an independent office within the corporation to review complaints
about news and current affairs programs broadcast on radio, on television, and online by its
English- and French-language services. His or her mandate is to ensure the "accuracy, integrity
and fairness" of the material aired and to identify violations of the CBC's journalistic standards
and practices. Findings are communicated to the complainant, CBC management, and the
journalists involved, and the ombudsperson makes public an annual report that reviews some
complaints and assesses the overall quality of CBC news programming. In the 2008–09 reporting year, the office fielded 2,666 complaints, comments, or concerns about CBC news programs
or the broadcaster's policies and general programming.

In the mid-1990s, five Canadian newspapers employed an ombudsperson—sometimes
known as a "public editor" or "readers' advocate." As of 2010 the *Toronto Star* was the only
major paper with an in-house official to respond to reader complaints and concerns. The role

of the *Star*'s public editor, according to the newspaper's website, is to act as a "reader advocate and guarantor of accuracy" and a liaison between the paper and its print and online readers. The public editor is the contact person when someone spots an error or seeks a correction, and writes a column on media trends and issues arising from the *Star*'s coverage. Some of the criticism can be biting: in a 2010 column, public editor Kathy English explained to readers how "a complete breakdown in newsroom communication and the journalistic practice of careful verification" caused the paper to identify the wrong person as the victim of a murder. The error, she added, was "the most egregious" she had handled in three years as public editor.

(Sources: Ian Hargreaves, *Journalism: A Very Short Introduction* (Oxford: Oxford University Press, 2005), 18; Nick Russell, *Morals and the Media: Ethics in Canadian Journalism*, 2nd ed. (Vancouver: UBC Press, 2006), 228–32; *Ontario Press Council 2005 Annual Report*, 5; Ontario Press Council website, http://www.ontpress.com; British Columbia Press Council website, http://www.bcpresscouncil.org; CJCH-TV (CTV Atlantic) re *CTV News at 6* (Stéphane Dion interview) CBSC Decision 08/09-0196+ (January 12, 2009), available online at http://www.ccnr.ca/english/decisions/index.php; CBC Office of the Ombudsman website, http://www.cbc.ca/ombudsman; *Toronto Star* Public Editor columns, http://www.thestar.com/comment/columnists/94572.)

Drawing the Line

Conflicts of Interest

Journalists cannot afford to have divided loyalties. They are paid to report the truth as they see it. They must have the freedom to cover events and controversies without being hamstrung by connections to the people and institutions they report on. And the public—the people who rely on the reporter's initiative and insight—must have confidence that journalists are not suppressing stories or pulling punches to protect their friends.

Common sense dictates that a reporter should beg off any story that involves family or friends. If a reporter's spouse works for a company, he must avoid covering stories that involve the company and its competitors. But journalists at most news outlets are allowed to write for other newspapers and magazines, as long as the publication is not a direct competitor and the work is conducted on the journalist's own time. Even so, the optics of a journalist writing speeches or press releases for companies or politicians are so poor that no journalist should take on such work, even one who does not cover business or politics. Nor can writers be seen to be favouring or supporting groups or organizations to which they belong; to avoid such conflicts, they should resist joining in the first place. The possibility of a conflict may appear remote, but the news business casts a broad net. A city hall reporter who volunteers as a Girl Guide leader may be dismayed to discover that the Girl Guides have petitioned city hall to exempt them from a bylaw that forbids the sale of cookies outside stores. Freelance columnists are in a different position, and are often hired to write about certain issues precisely because of their community involvement and outside interests. Most news organizations have established rules to ensure that their employees do not find themselves in a conflict-of-interest position. The *Globe and Mail*'s code of conduct, for example, requires journalists to seek approval to serve on the board of directors of a company, a charity, or a community or advocacy group. Such posts are off-limits to journalists who routinely cover issues involving the group; and writers or columnists involved in such organizations must disclose their involvement in their stories.[64]

The CBC has strict rules to prevent conflicts of interest from colouring the news, and backs them with the threat of disciplinary action, including dismissal. Staff and contract employees must disclose possible conflicts and are forbidden to use their position at the CBC to further their private interests.[65]

Most media codes of conduct restrict the political activities of their journalists. The *Globe and Mail* acknowledges that its employees have the right to be politically active but at the same time emphasizes that the newspaper "must be and must seem to be impartial." The level of permissible political activity depends on the journalist's job: reporters and columnists who routinely write about politics, and the editors who handle their copy, "are barred from most political activity other than voting." Prohibited activities include joining or giving money to a political party, taking part in marches or demonstrations, working on a campaign, and erecting lawn signs or wearing campaign buttons. Journalists on other beats "are free to engage in political activity in a private capacity, taking care not to appear to represent *The Globe*." For example, the code of conduct permits a sports reporter to run a friend's campaign for a position on the school board. But *Globe* journalists are advised to avoid positions for themselves, even a low-level post such as riding association president.[66] Any journalist who runs for a school board or city council, or seeks a party's nomination to run in an upcoming federal or provincial election, would likely be required to take a leave of absence or resign.

Junkets and Freebies

Newsroom policies on junkets and freebies have become more strict in recent decades. When Peter Desbarats was a rookie reporter on the police beat for the *Montreal Gazette* in the 1950s, journalists routinely accepted gifts and money:

> [J]ournalistic ethics meant, more or less, whatever a journalist could get away with. I recall one of my editors assuring me that it was permissible to accept anything that one could eat or drink, but that cash payments should be avoided. This was considered to be unusually high-minded at the time.[67]

Today, the pendulum has swung in the opposite direction, and with good reason. Accepting gifts and favours undermines a journalist's reputation for independence and credibility. Even the appearance of being influenced may erode the public's confidence in the journalist's objectivity.

Gifts are permitted in certain cases. Most newsroom codes of ethics outline the kinds of freebies the media organization considers appropriate. The *Globe and Mail*'s code of conduct states that newsroom staffers "may accept no benefit of more than token value offered to them because they work for the newspaper."[68] Similarly, CBC journalists must refuse any gift, benefit, or money that is offered to influence—or that would appear to influence—a CBC decision. Exceptions are made for gifts "of modest value distributed as advertising or goodwill gestures, or modest hospitality offered as a general courtesy."[69] Eating a complimentary meal while waiting to cover an after-dinner speech is considered appropriate at most media outlets.

Media outlets also have policies governing items sent to their newsrooms. Newsrooms are deluged with review copies of books and the latest music and movie releases, not to mention consumer goods that range from inexpensive household products to pricey computer and high-tech gadgets. Reviewers usually keep copies of the books and music CDs they write about, but shy away from taking home more expensive items. Some media organizations solve the problem by collecting the free stuff that flows into the newsroom and holding raffles or sales for their staff, with the proceeds donated to charity.

What about the source who offers to pick up the tab for lunch? "It would be foolish to ban every gift of every nature and to let rule-obedience ruin friendships and the natural flow of relationships," says Nick Russell. The answer, he concludes, is to return the favour. "If the source buys lunch today, the reporter needs to ensure it is understood that he buys lunch tomorrow."[70]

Free trips are another matter. Travel writers often use free airline tickets to reach the far-flung destinations they write about, and stay in complimentary hotel rooms when they arrive. This practice continues to be accepted because few news organizations have the resources to send writers on expensive trips. Free travel for journalists covering election campaigns and for sports writers who are on the road with the home team, however, is no longer tolerated.[71] Many journalism award competitions require applicants to disclose whether travel or other costs were subsidized as a story was being researched. Accepting free trips from government agencies is perhaps the most serious threat to the media's independence. In 1999 the Department of Foreign Affairs paid $27,000 to send the editors of eight community newspapers in the Atlantic provinces to Boston for a briefing with consular officials. The result was a spate of positive stories about business prospects in New England. An editor who turned down the offer argued that those who went became "pawns" in "a PR exercise for Foreign Affairs."[72] Sometimes, though, accepting free travel may be unavoidable. A military flight may be the only means to reach Canadian troops serving overseas, for example. The CBC bans all junkets and will consider accepting free travel for its journalists "only when no commercial transport is available."[73] Such situations are rare and, when a news organization accepts free travel, the resulting story should reveal who paid the bill.

Assisting Police and Other Investigators

Reporters investigating wrongdoing and journalists on the police beat may feel pressured—or tempted—to help the police. A detective may call with a request for archived news stories about a person or event. A police source may mention over coffee that he would like a copy of a public document that the reporter used in a recent story. Maybe an investigator simply wants to pick the journalist's brain for information that could help with an ongoing investigation. *The Canadian Press Stylebook* draws the line at providing notes, unpublished information or images, recordings, research files, and "anything of a private or confidential nature" unless the police have a search warrant authorizing the seizure of such material. "There is normally no objection," it adds,

CANADIAN ASSOCIATION OF JOURNALISTS
STATEMENT OF PRINCIPLES AND ETHICS GUIDELINES—INVESTIGATIVE JOURNALISM

APPROVED AT 2004 ANNUAL GENERAL MEETING

Preamble

Our privilege and duty as investigative journalists is to defend free speech, inform self-governing citizens, encourage deliberation on public policy and serve the public interest.

These duties sometimes require that journalists reveal criminal activity, investigate abuses of power, expose wrong-doing, protect the public's health and safety and support the open administration of justice and government.

Investigative journalism employs special methods that raise ethical and legal issues. The stories of investigative journalism have serious consequences for individuals, organizations and society. Investigative journalism, therefore, has distinct responsibilities.

Truthfulness

Our primary duty is to seek and report the truth as completely and independently as possible. We will make every effort to ensure the accuracy of our reports.

We will act as an independent voice for the public at large. We will not be intimidated by power or influenced by special interests, advertisers or news sources. We will not allow the independence of our journalism to be compromised by conflicts of interest.

We will use confidential sources who are in a position to know and whose evidence is verified by other independent sources. We will be wary of sources who may be motivated by malice or bias.

Transparency

We will be transparent in our actions, especially where our stories are controversial, have far-reaching impact, or require special techniques.

Special investigative methods [such as deception and hidden cameras] will be used only if:

- The information is important for the public
- There is no other way to obtain the information
- Any harm to individuals or organizations is out-weighed by the benefits of making the information public
- We are able to plan the investigation carefully

Accountability

We will be accountable for our actions. We will explain to the public the nature and reasons for our investigations. We will explain why we used confidential sources, or hidden recording devices, or why we misrepresented ourselves.

We will respond promptly and openly to complaints from the public. We will be ready to explain how a story was investigated and what editorial standards were used. We will correct quickly any errors in our stories.

Fairness

We will give individuals or organizations that are publicly criticized an opportunity to respond. We will make a genuine and exhaustive effort to contact them. Where possible, we will give them an opportunity to respond before the story is published or broadcast.

Privacy

Canadians have a right to privacy, yet they also have a right to know about their public institutions and the people who are elected or hired to serve their interests. They have a right to know the social impact of private organizations and corporations. We will not infringe upon someone's privacy unless it is in the public interest. Where privacy is infringed, we will seek to minimize any harm done to people, especially the vulnerable, the traumatized and the young. Each situation should be judged in the light of common sense, humanity and the public's right to know.

(Source: Canadian Association of Journalists website, http://www.caj.ca/?p=155.)

"to providing police with copies of stories or photographs that have already been published, or other routine material of a non-confidential nature, as a matter of courtesy."[74] After all, journalists are constantly asking the police for information. Is there any harm in returning the favour?

Yes, there may well be, because helping the police—even when the information or material requested is innocuous or already publicly available—can compromise a journalist's independence and create the *appearance* of taking sides. "Journalists do not exist to make the work of the police easier," Nick Russell notes, and the media should not be seen "as an arm of the law" or "ready accomplices of authority."[75] Ask investigative reporter Stevie Cameron, author of *On the Take* and other exposés of political scandals. She was publicly branded a confidential informant after providing her research file on the controversial Airbus passenger jets contract to RCMP investigators, who were looking into allegations of kickbacks. Cameron agreed to meet with the RCMP in hopes of finding out more about the investigation. "I wanted a scoop," she later explained to a journalists' forum in Halifax.[76] The 1995 meeting and the fact that the police designated Cameron a confidential informant—without her knowledge—came to light in 2003, igniting a controversy over whether journalists should trade information with the police. Cameron insisted that all the information she provided was available to the police on the public record, but even the appearance of cooperating with the authorities can undermine the media's independence. Journalists must keep in mind that such favours are likely to be exposed if an investigation leads to criminal charges. The rules of disclosure entitle defendants facing charges to review all the information that the police have gathered in the course of an investigation—including the details of any contact with journalists and any information that the journalists have provided.[77]

Cameron has offered blunt advice to other journalists who find themselves in her position: "Never talk to the police."[78] Reporters, of course, should continue to work with their police sources in search of stories. But the information flow should not be a two-way street. Journalists must avoid the appearance of taking sides and helping the police. The CAJ's guidelines for investigative reporting address the issue head-on. "The public should not perceive journalists to be agents of the police. When that happens we undermine our credibility and stifle the flow of future information from sensitive sources." There are exceptions: a journalist who learns that a crime is about to be committed or that someone's life is at risk has a duty, as a citizen, to notify the authorities. "But in the vast majority of circumstances," the guidelines add, "we serve the public interest by maintaining strict independence from police, the justice system and government institutions."

A journalist must not be seen to be assisting any other official investigation. CBC Television reporter Krista Erickson was reassigned from covering federal politics in 2008 after she was accused of providing information that a Liberal MP used to question former prime minister Brian Mulroney at a parliamentary committee hearing. After an internal review, the CBC concluded she had used "inappropriate tactics as a result of journalistic zeal, rather than partisan interest" but her actions were "inconsistent" with the network's policies and procedures. "Any situation which could cause reasonable apprehension that a journalist or the organization is biased or under the influence of any pressure group, whether ideological, political, financial, social or cultural," the CBC announced at the conclusion of its review, "must be avoided."[79]

Ethics and Professional Responsibility: A Summary

Reporting and writing the news can be an ethical minefield. Journalists choose the right course by striving to be fair. They use their common sense. They treat sources and the subjects of stories with respect. They think about how the public will judge their methods. They tell the truth and avoid becoming entangled in conflicts of interest. They are fiercely independent. Most importantly, they realize that their conduct will reflect on the image of all journalists.

NOTES

1. Renita Coleman and Lee Wilkins, "The Moral Development of Journalists: A Comparison with Other Professions and a Model for Predicting High Quality Ethical Reasoning" (2004), vol. 81, no. 3 *Journalism and Mass Communications Quarterly* 511–27, at 521.

2. See, for example, the detailed code of conduct developed by senior editors and writers at the *Globe and Mail*, reproduced in J.A. Mcfarlane and Warren Clements, *The Globe and Mail Style Book: A Guide to Language and Usage* (Toronto: McClelland & Stewart, 1998), 425–34.

3. For a thorough analysis of how the media failed Arar and the risks of using unnamed sources, see Andrew Mitrovica, "Hear No Evil, Write No Lies," *The Walrus*, December 2006/January 2007, 37–42.

4. Canadian Association of Journalists, *Statement of Principles and Ethics Guidelines— Investigative Journalism*, available online at http://www.caj.ca/?p=155.

5. Patti Tasko, ed., *The Canadian Press Stylebook*, 15th ed. (Toronto: Canadian Press, 2008), 24.

6. *RTNDA Code of Ethics: The Standard for Canadian Broadcasting Excellence*, available online at http://www.rtndacanada.com/ethics/codeofethics.asp.

7. John Chancellor and Walter R. Mears, *The New News Business: A Guide to Writing and Reporting* (New York: HarperCollins Publishers, 1995), 117.

8. Edward Greenspon, "The Question of Anonymous Sources and the Big Lesson of Deep Throat," *Globe and Mail*, June 4, 2005.

9. For more on Felt's role in uncovering the Watergate scandal, see Evan Thomas, "A Long Shadow: Understanding Deep Throat," *Newsweek*, June 12, 2005, 22–32, and Bob Woodward, *The Secret Man: The Story of Watergate's Deep Throat* (New York: Simon and Schuster, 2005).

10. Greenspon, supra note 8.

11. Bill Kovach and Tom Rosenstiel, *The Elements of Journalism: What Newspeople Should Know and the Public Should Expect* (New York: Crown Publishers, 2001), 90.

12. Tasko, supra note 5, at 25.

13. Denise Rudnicki, "'Insiders Say': The Use of Unnamed Sources in the Globe and Mail," *Canadian Journal of Media Studies*, vol. 2, no. 1 (April 2007), 41–75, at 63–64 and 66.

14. Quoted in ibid., at 59.

15. Tasko, supra note 5, at 27.

16. According to definitions set out in James Q. Wilson, *American Government*, Brief Version, 5th ed. (Boston: Houghton Mifflin Company, 2000), 84.

17. Peter Desbarats, "Guess What: You're on the Record," *Globe and Mail*, November 30, 2002; Edward Greenspon, "Walking the Ethics Tightrope," ibid.

18. Stuart M. Robertson, *Newsroom Legal Crisis Management: What To Do When a Crisis Hits* (Dunedin, ON: Hallion Press, 1991), 47.

19. "Former PM Mulroney Suing Author over Tapes," CBC News Online, November 24, 2005; Jane Taber, "Mulroney, Author Settle Lawsuit," *Globe and Mail*, June 13, 2006.

20. This Alberta ruling is discussed in Michael G. Crawford, *The Journalist's Legal Guide*, 4th ed. (Toronto: Carswell, 2002), 274–75.

21. *Peat Marwick Thorne v. Canadian Broadcasting Corp.* (1991), 84 DLR (4th) 656 (Ont. Gen. Div.).

22. *Journalistic Standards and Practices* (Toronto: Canadian Broadcasting Corporation, 2001), 111.

23. Ibid., at 75.

24. Ian Brown, "Talk Isn't Cheap These Days, but Our Heroes Are Getting Cheaper," *Globe and Mail*, January 2, 2010.

25. Nick Russell, *Morals and the Media: Ethics in Canadian Journalism*, 2nd ed. (Vancouver: UBC Press, 2006), 57–58.

26. Ibid., at 59.

27. *Journalistic Standards and Practices*, supra note 22, at 75–77.

28. Kovach and Rosenstiel, supra note 11, at 82.

29. "Don't Call Us—We'll Call You," *National Post*, January 30, 1999.

30. *Journalistic Standards and Practices*, supra note 22, at 101–102.

31. *RTNDA Code of Ethics*, supra note 6.

32. Phill Snel, "Seeing Is Not Believing" (Spring 2003), *Media* 17.

33. *RTNDA Code of Ethics*, supra note 6.

34. Tasko, supra note 5, at 101.

35. Curtis D. MacDougall and Robert D. Reid, *Interpretive Reporting*, 9th ed. (New York: Macmillan Publishing Company, 1987), 215.

36. Sandra Davidson, "Food Lyin' and Other Buttafuocos" (November-December 1998), *IRE Journal* 6–8.

37. Jill Lawless, Associated Press, "Reporter Shreds Palace Security, Serves Chocolates to Bush Entourage," *Chronicle-Herald* (Halifax), November 20, 2003.

38. Rob Cribb and Christian Cotroneo, "Toronto a Hotbed for Phone Fraud—Telemarketers Sell Phony Credit Cards to U.S., Europe," *Toronto Star*, November 2, 2002; Rob Cribb and Dale Brazao, "On the Killing Floor in Vaughan's Illegal Farm Slaughterhouse," *Toronto Star*, December 16, 2000.

39. Russell, supra note 25, at 130.

40. Kevin Donovan and Phillip Mascoll, "Liquor Official Questioned Amid Allegations of Bribes," *Toronto Star*, August 18, 1992; Jack Lakey, "2 Star Reporters Held 4 Hours," ibid.

41. "ABC Wins Appeal in Food Lion Case," Reuters news service report, October 20, 1999.

42. Russell, supra note 25, at 133.

43. *Journalistic Standards and Practices*, supra note 22, at 83, 85.

44. *RTNDA Code of Ethics*, supra note 6.

45. See, for example, Brendan Elliott, "A Day of Begging," *Daily News* (Halifax), April 4, 1999.

46. Paul O'Connell, "Why We Ran the Photo," *Sunday Herald* (Halifax), January 16, 2005. The photo was published in the paper's January 9, 2005 edition.

47. Edward Greenspon, "Seeking To Put Painful Events and Images in Perspective," *Globe and Mail*, May 15, 2004.

48. Kathy English, "English: Why the Star Ran Russell Williams Photo," *Toronto Star*, October 22, 2010; Sylvia Stead, "Why Tuesday's Front Page Did Not Include a Photo of Russell Williams in Women's Lingerie," *Globe and Mail*, October 19, 2010.

49. Clifford C. Christians, Mark Fackler, Kim B. Rotzoll, and Kathy Brittain McKee, *Media Ethics: Cases and Moral Reasoning* (New York: Longman, 2001), 124–25.

50. Tasko, supra note 5, at 31.

51. Mcfarlane and Clements, supra note 2, at 251.

52. Bruce Wark, "Journalism as a Morality Play" (Fall 2001), *Media* 18–19, at 19.

53. Russell, supra note 25, at 164.

54. *Journalistic Standards and Practices*, supra note 22, at 104–105.

55. Mcfarlane and Clements, supra note 2, at 250–51.

56. Tasko, supra note 5, at 17.

57. *Journalistic Standards and Practices*, supra note 22, at 104, 106.

58. Douglas Kelly, "Note to Readers," *National Post*, January 23, 2007.

59. Russell, supra note 25, at 100–101.

60. "Abuser's Death Was Avoidable—Lawyer," *Chronicle-Herald* (Halifax), January 17, 1998.

61. Mcfarlane and Clements, supra note 2, at 307.

62. Tasko, supra note 5, at 18, 20–21, 23.

63. Mcfarlane and Clements, supra note 2, at 92–94.

64. Ibid., at 429.

65. *Journalistic Standards and Practices*, supra note 22, at 136–44.

66. Ibid., at 431.

67. Peter Desbarats, *Guide to Canadian News Media* (Toronto: Harcourt Brace Jovanovich Canada, 1990), 175.

68. Mcfarlane and Clements, supra note 2, at 429.

69. *Journalistic Standards and Practices*, supra note 22, at 144–45.

70. Russell, supra note 25, at 66.

71. For a discussion of these issues, see ibid., 62–64.

72. Mike Trickey, "Foreign Affairs Gave Trips, Cash to Journalists," *National Post*, September 8, 1999.

73. *Journalistic Standards and Practices*, supra note 22, at 148.

74. Tasko, supra note 5, at 236.

75. Nick Russell, *Morals and the Media: Ethics in Canadian Journalism* (Vancouver: UBC Press, 1994), 88.

76. Mike and Linda Whitehouse, "Fighting for Free Expression" (Spring 2004), *Media* 30–31, at 31. For more information on Cameron's dealings with the police and the debate it sparked, see Elysse Zarek, "The Wrong Arm of the Law" (Summer 2005), *Ryerson Review of Journalism* 48–53.

77. For a detailed discussion of this issue, see Dean Jobb, "Be Wise with Your Words" (Fall 2004), *Media* 34.

78. Whitehouse, supra note 76, at 31.

79. "CBC Ottawa Reporter Reassigned After Probe," *Globe and Mail*, January 22, 2008.

Glossary of Terms

abet   the act of encouraging, inducing, counselling, or inciting another to do a certain thing, usually a crime

absolute privilege   this immunity from being sued exists when there is a legal or moral obligation on a person to provide information, and the person to whom the information is given has a corresponding duty or interest to receive it

access coordinators   officials of a government agency or other public body who process freedom-of-information requests for access to records

accessory   someone who contributes to, or aids in, the commission of a crime

acts   bills that have passed through the required legislative steps and have become law; synonymous with statute and legislation

actus reus   Latin for "guilty act"; the essential element of a crime that must be proved to secure a conviction; almost always an act, but it can also be an omission to act

adjournment   the suspension of a trial, either for a fixed period of time or indefinitely

administration of justice   the court process of doing justice to parties and upholding legal rights

affidavits   written statements of facts, sworn to and signed by witnesses before a notary public or another person authorized to witness an oath

aggravated damages   damages awarded in civil cases where a defendant has been subjected to humiliation, distress, or embarrassment

appellant   the party appealing a case from a lower court to a higher court

arraignment   an accused person's first appearance in court to answer to criminal charges

assistance order   an order requiring a person in control of a premises to help the police locate and seize items sought under a search warrant

bail   in criminal law, a court's release of a person being held in custody on criminal charges; also known as judicial interim release

battery   intentional, wrongful physical contact with a person without his consent; battery is a tort

bill   a draft of a proposed statute or law

bylaw   see **ordinance**

case name   the name of a case, usually drawn from the identities of the parties to an action

case reports   the published rulings and precedents of a single court, or the rulings of various courts on specific areas of the law

chambers   a court session held in a civil case to hear evidence and argument on an application or to resolve pre-trial issues

charge to the jury   the final address by the judge to a jury before a verdict is delivered; the judge sums up the case and instructs the jury as to the rules of law applicable to the various issues

circumstantial evidence   indirect evidence that links a person to the scene of a crime or creates an inference that the person was involved

closing argument   a speech analyzing the evidence and suggesting how it supports the accused person's guilt or innocence

committal   a judge's referral of a case to trial following a preliminary hearing

common law   judge-made law, embodying legal precedents that the courts have developed over hundreds of years, as opposed to written statutes

concurring judgment   a separate opinion delivered by one or more judges of an appeal court that agrees with the court's majority decision, but offers its own reasons for reaching that decision

conditional sentences   sentences served in the community that are subject to conditions (often referred to as house arrest); if the conditions are not met, the offender may be jailed

confidential informant   a person who provides information in confidence to the police and whose identity is not to be revealed without the person's permission

contract   a legally binding agreement between parties obliging each party to do or not to do a certain thing

conventions   in constitutional law, an unwritten practice or custom that has become enshrined as a form of law

costs   a court can order legal costs to be paid by the loser to the winner after a civil trial is concluded; the court has the final say on costs and may decide not to award costs

counsel   in a criminal context, the offence of a person who procures a criminal act performed by someone else—that is, counsels someone to commit a crime

counterclaim   a defendant's claim against a plaintiff, served at the same time as the defendant's statement of defence; the counterclaim, however, asserts an independent cause of action, and doesn't act as a defence against the original claim

crime   an offence against the public good; a violation of the law that is prosecuted by the state and can be punished by a fine, imprisonment, or other form of punishment

Crown attorneys   public prosecutors in Canada who perform the majority of criminal prosecutions

Dagenais **test**   developed by the Supreme Court of Canada in its ruling in *Dagenais v. Canadian Broadcasting Corp.*, this test states that a publication ban should only be imposed when no other measures could prevent a serious risk to interests at stake; if a ban is imposed, it should only be to the extent necessary to prevent a real and substantial risk to the fairness of the proceedings in question

damages   compensation ordered by a court to someone injured or suffering a loss due to another's fault or negligence

defamation   a tort arising from a false or malicious attack on the reputation of a person; an intentional false communication, either published (libel) or publicly spoken (slander)

default judgment   judgment entered against a party who fails to defend against a claim brought by another party—for example, a defendant who fails to submit a statement of defence

defendant   the person, company, or organization that defends a civil action taken by a plaintiff; also, a person facing criminal charges

demand for particulars   a formal request from counsel for further and better details of an allegation of fact made in a pleading

direct evidence   evidence in the form of testimony from a witness who relates what that person personally saw, heard, or experienced

directed verdict   situation in which a judge instructs a jury as to what its verdict must be; usually arises when the party with the burden of proof failed to present a *prima facie* case

discharge   a court order ending a prosecution at the preliminary hearing stage if there is not enough evidence to warrant a trial; also, a form of sentence that leaves an offender without a criminal record

dissenting judgment   the minority opinion of a judge that runs contrary to the conclusions of the majority

distinguish   to point out an essential difference between cases to prove that a case introduced to the court as a precedent is, in fact, inapplicable

diversion programs   a form of sentencing under which first-time offenders who plead guilty are dealt with and punished outside the normal court process

docket   the official list of cases before the court

due process   the normal course of events in the administration of justice, in which the legal rights of litigants and persons accused of crimes are upheld and respected

election   for certain offences, an accused person's choice to be tried by a judge and jury or by a judge

ex parte   proceedings where one of the parties has not received notice and, therefore, is neither present nor represented

examinations for discovery   pre-trial examination of witnesses to obtain facts and information about the plaintiff's or defendant's case, to assist in preparation for trial

exclusion order   a court order excluding members of the public and journalists from the courtroom for all or part of a hearing

factum   a document outlining the arguments to be raised in court, combined with citations to leading cases on each point

fair comment   a defence to a defamation action, in which the defendant argues that the comment made was based on fact; for the defence to succeed, the facts upon which the comment is based must be true, and the comment must be fair

fair dealing   use of another person's creative work in a manner that does not infringe upon copyright, usually for research, teaching, or private study

finding   the result of a court's or jury's deliberations

finding the facts   a conclusion reached by a court after due consideration; a determination of the truth after considering statements from opposing parties at trial

general damages   damages awarded for losses that the law presumes to be the natural and probable consequence of a wrong; general damages consider such things as pain and suffering or loss of reputation

hearsay   evidence of what someone else heard or witnessed, and generally not admissible in court; also known as second-hand evidence

hybrid offences   crimes that can be treated as either summary conviction offences or indictable offences; the Crown attorney decides how to treat these crimes

in camera   a court proceeding is said to be held *in camera* when the public and the media are barred from the courtroom

indictable offences   more serious offences than those that can proceed by summary conviction, and often tried by a jury

indictment   a formal document, drafted after the preliminary hearing stage of a criminal case, outlining the indictable offence(s) an accused person will face at trial

information   the document that sets out the allegations in a criminal case

inherent jurisdiction   a broad doctrine allowing a court to control its own process and the procedures before it; the powers that the court may draw upon as necessary whenever it is just or equitable to do so

injunction   a court order prohibiting a party from doing something (restrictive injunction) or compelling them to do something (mandatory injunction)

innuendo   an indirect method of stating or writing defamatory material, in which seemingly innocent words take on a libellous meaning from their arrangement or context

interlocutory application   an interim proceeding heard in chambers during the course of a civil case, to deal with legal issues

intra vires   within the power of a level of government or a corporation

investigative hearing   as an anti-terrorism measure, judges have been empowered to compel a person to answer questions outside a formal trial, even if the person does not face charges

judicial activism   when judges veer from strict adherence to judicial precedent, usually in favour of progressive and new social policies; such decisions from the bench usually intrude into legislative and executive matters

judicial interim release   see **bail**

libel   a defamatory statement made in permanent form via print, writing, pictures, or signs

libel chill   the practice of using a threat to sue for libel to silence critics or to squelch media coverage

majority judgment   the opinion of an appellate court in which the majority of its members join; the majority judgment decides the outcome of the case

manslaughter   a homicide committed without the intent to kill

mens rea   Latin for "guilty mind"; another element for criminal responsibility; many serious crimes require the proof of *mens rea* before a person can be convicted

mistrial   an order ending a trial when the accused person's right to a fair trial has been compromised; the Crown has the right to put the accused person on trial before a new judge or jury

negligence   the tort of neglecting to do something that a reasonable and prudent person would do, or doing something that a reasonable and prudent person would *not* do

non-statutory ban   publication ban imposed at the discretion of a judge; usually in place to protect the fairness and integrity of a trial, or the privacy or safety of a victim or witness

nuisance   excessive or unlawful use of one's property that causes inconvenience to neighbours or the general public; nuisance is a tort

open justice   a presumption in both civil and common law jurisdictions that court hearings are open to the public and the media

orders in council   government (Cabinet) orders of a legislative nature that create regulations, make appointments to public office, or implement government policies

ordinance   a local law passed and enforced by a municipal government; another term for bylaw

party   a person whose name is designated on record as plaintiff or defendant; also, a person who has taken part in a transaction such as an agreement or a contract

peace officer   police officers, sheriffs, and others whose duties involve the keeping of the peace through the enforcement of laws and ordinances

plagiarism   the act of stealing ideas, words, or language of another, and passing them off as the product of one's own mind

plaintiff   the person who brings a lawsuit against a defendant or respondent; also known as a claimant, petitioner, or applicant

plea   the formal response of an accused person (guilty or not guilty), or one made on behalf of the accused, in a criminal prosecution

plea bargaining   see **plea negotiation**

plea negotiation   agreement between the Crown and defence on a charge to which the accused will plead guilty, or on the sentence to be recommended to the judge; also known as plea bargaining

pleadings   the part of a civil case in which the parties set out, in writing, the facts and legal arguments that support their position

precedents   court decisions that set out legal principles or serve as examples or authorities for future cases that deal with similar legal issues; precedents allow people to have a reasonable expectation of the legal solutions that apply to a given situation

preferred indictment   a procedure that enables Crown prosecutors to bypass the preliminary inquiry and take a case directly to trial, or to reinstate the prosecution of an accused person who was discharged at a preliminary hearing

preliminary hearing   the hearing before a provincial court judge to determine whether there is enough evidence to send an accused person to trial

presumptive offence   under the *Youth Criminal Justice Act*, a specified offence that could draw a sentence similar to that imposed on an adult; subsequent convictions for serious violent crimes *may* bring an adult sentence

pre-trial motions   legal motions made in court before a trial begins; they can be made in the court where the accused first appears, or in the court where the trial will be held

prima facie **case**   a case supported by evidence sufficient, on its face, for it to be taken as proved in the absence of defence evidence to the contrary

principles of equity   applied when justice is administered according to fairness, as opposed to the common law

probation   a form of punishment in which a judge orders a person to report regularly to a probation officer and to observe conditions, such as abstaining from alcohol

publication ban   a court order prohibiting the media and members of the public from disclosing the identity of crime victims or witnesses, or from publicizing the evidence heard in a criminal or civil case

publication contempt   a form of contempt committed outside the courtroom, in which a media report containing banned or prejudicial information threatens an accused person's right to a fair trial

punitive damages   damages awarded in civil cases to punish a defendant whose actions have been found to be malicious or high-handed; also known as exemplary damages

qualified privilege   this privilege shields media coverage of legislative debates, court hearings, public meetings, and other official proceedings from defamation actions; the privilege is qualified in that it is conditional on news reports being fair, accurate, and published without malice

regulations   detailed laws created by Cabinet under the authority of a statute

respondent   the party responding to a plaintiff's claim filed in court (usually referred to as a "defendant"); also, the party who wins at the first court level but has to respond to an appeal launched by the appellant

restitution   the act of restoring something to its owner, or the act of making good

restorative justice programs   programs that enable the victim of a crime, the offender, and members of the community to discuss the appropriate sentence for the offender; commonly used for young offenders

return   a peace officer's report to a judge or justice of the peace after a search warrant has been executed

scandalizing the courts   a form of contempt that can be used to punish those who make unwarranted and sensational attacks on the conduct of the courts or the integrity of individual judges

special damages   civil damages that cannot be presumed from a wrongful act but are quantifiable—for example, out-of-pocket expenses or lost earnings

specific performance   a court order to fulfill contractual obligations

standard of proof   the burden of proof required in a particular type of case: in criminal cases, the standard is proof beyond a reasonable doubt; in civil cases, the standard is proof on a balance of probabilities

stare decisis   to abide by, or adhere to, decided cases. It is a basic principle of the common law that, once a precedent has been set, the courts will apply it in similar cases

statement of claim   the plaintiff's pleading in an action; the statement of claim outlines the plaintiff's allegations against the defendant, as well as the relief the plaintiff seeks

statement of defence   the defendant's pleading in an action, in response to the plaintiff's statement of claim

statutes   written laws passed by the legislative branch of government; also known as legislation

statutory ban   publication bans required by statutes such as the *Criminal Code* or the *Youth Criminal Justice Act*

stay of proceedings   a court order permanently halting a criminal prosecution as a result of an abuse of the legal process; Crown attorneys also have the power to issue a stay to temporarily halt a prosecution for up to one year

***sub judice* rule**   Latin for "under or before a court," this rule pertains to the restrictions on publicity that apply once a case is before the courts

subsequent rights   rights granted to permit the reuse of copyrighted material

summary conviction offences   less serious criminal offences; both the procedure and the punishment for summary conviction offences tend to be less onerous than for indictable offences

surety   security in the form of money or property that supports someone's release on bail; it is forfeited to the Crown if the accused person fails to appear in court

suspended sentence   a sentence that is not imposed; instead, the offender is placed on probation; failure to abide by the conditions of probation may lead to the sentence being imposed

third-party action   an action by a defendant against a person who is not already a party to the action

tort   a wrong committed by one person against another, for which damages can be obtained in a civil court; also, that body of the law allowing an injured person to obtain compensation from the person who caused the injury

trespassing   illegal entry onto another person's property

trier of fact   the party or parties obliged to make findings of fact; a jury, or the judge in a non-jury trial

ultra vires   beyond the power of a level of government or a corporation

undertaking   a promise or stipulation in legal proceedings that creates an obligation

***voir dire* hearing**   a trial within a trial, usually on the admissibility of contested evidence; in jury trials, juries are excused during a *voir dire*

Wigmore test   a test consisting of four criteria to determine, on a case-by-case basis, whether a communication is privileged: (1) the communication must originate in a confidence that it will not be disclosed; (2) this confidentiality must be essential to maintain the relation between the parties; (3) the relation between the parties must be one that, in the opinion of the community, ought to be painstakingly fostered; and (4) the benefits of disclosing the communication must outweigh the damage caused to the parties who exchanged the confidential information

Table of Cases

*See also **www.emp.ca/medialaw** for summaries, links, and commentary on recent key cases.*

Index

C